PLAYFAIR
FOOTBALL
ANNUAL 1996-97

EDITOR: GLENDA ROLLIN
EXECUTIVE EDITOR: JACK ROLLIN

HEADLINE

First published in 1996
by HEADLINE BOOK PUBLISHING

10 9 8 7 6 5 4 3 2 1

Cover photograph Left: Dwight Yorke (Aston Villa); right: Matthew Jackson
(Everton) (*Action Images*)

ISBN 0 7472 5340 4

Typeset by Wearset, Boldon, Tyne and Wear

Printed and bound in Great Britain by
BPC Paperbacks Ltd
A member of
The British Printing Company Ltd

HEADLINE BOOK PUBLISHING
A division of Hodder Headline PLC
338 Euston Road
London NW1 3BH

CONTENTS

Other Football

Information and Records

EDITORIAL

In reaching the semi-final of Euro 96, England gave themselves a launch pad towards the 1998 World Cup Finals in France. In two years' time, there may well be far more foreign players appearing in English football than even last season, which saw more than 100 full internationals born outside the United Kingdom playing here.

Inevitably, the tournament in England during the summer of 1996 put the spotlight on many other players and the close season has seen the arrival of familiar names and others less so from various European countries.

One of the most expensive arrivals was Fabrizio Ravanelli, the Italian international forward, who cost Middlesbrough £7,000,000, a figure which equals the transfer of Colombian-born Faustino Asprilla from Parma to Newcastle last season. There are obvious problems with signing players from abroad. They often have difficulty settling down and critics claim that the endless stream of players from abroad does nothing to promote the development of home-grown talent. Others have made only brief appearances and moved on without making any significant impression.

Even so, the impact made by some foreign players in English football has been extremely significant. After one season with Chelsea, Ruud Gullit established himself to the extent that when manager Glenn Hoddle moved on to become manager of the England team in succession to Terry Venables, Gullit took over his role at Chelsea. Then again, the experience of Eric Cantona who showed remarkable discipline compared with his previous outbursts which cost him a lengthy suspension is worth noting. He captained Manchester United in the latter stages of the season and showed he had lost none of his exceptional ability. He was elected Football Writers' Association Player of the Season, but was surprisingly left out of the French team in Euro 96.

But, the actual experience of Manchester United in 1995-96 was perhaps surprisingly quite different. During the season, they signed only three players from outside the club, two of them reserve goalkeepers and only one other played in the first team and he was a trialist from France.

Six of United's regular first team squad – David Beckham, Nicky Butt, the Neville brothers Gary and Phil, Ryan Giggs and Paul Scholes were all products of the club's successful trainee system. In addition to winning the Premier League, the reserves won the Pontin's League and the 'A' team the Lancashire League.

But the average for the Premier League was distinctly higher at 27,550 compared with 24,270 in the previous season. But because there were 82 games fewer played in it, the total was down. The Football League crowds were also slightly up overall with a one percent increase.

Goalscoring remains at a very modest level and the introduction of three points for a win back in 1981–82 appears to have had no marked improvement in the reduction of drawn games.

In 1994–95 the Premier League managed an average number of goals a game at 2.59. Last season there was a marginal increase of 0.01 to 2.60.

However, in terms of the number of players used by clubs in the four divisions, the introduction of a third substitute regardless of whether he was a goalkeeper or not, helped to produce much higher totals of players. Indeed, Birmingham City established a record by fielding 46 different players while Torquay also beat the previous record by using 43.

On a wider scale, the experiment of using a so-called 'golden goal' to decide drawn cup matches proved to be a failure in Euro 96. Two of the quarter-finals and both semi-finals had to be decided by penalty kicks and though the final itself in which Germany beat the Czech Republic 2-1 was decided by sudden death, teams seem to be quite content to trust to the lottery of taking penalties rather than risk conceding a goal.

ARSENAL

Adams, Tony A.
Black, Michael J.
Crowe, Jason W. R.
Harper, Lee C. P.
Hillier, David
Kiwomya, Christopher M.
Marshall, Scott R.
Merson, Paul C.
Platt, David A.
Rose, Matthew
Shaw, Paul
Winterburn, Nigel

Bartram, Vincent L.
Bould, Stephen A.
Dickov, Paul
Hartson, John
Hughes, Stephen J.
Linighan, Andrew
McGoldrick, Eddie J. P.
Morrow, Stephen J.
Rankin, Isaiah
Seaman, David A.
Taylor, Ross E.
Wright, Ian E.

Bergkamp, Dennis N.
Clarke, Adrian J.
Dixon, Lee M.
Helder, Glenn
Keown, Martin R.
Macdonald, James
McGowan, Gavin G.
Parlour, Raymond
Read, Paul
Selley, Ian
Wicks, Matthew

League Appearances: Adams, T. 21; Bergkamp, D. 33; Bould, S. 19; Clarke, A. 4(2); Dickov, P. 1(6); Dixon, L. 38; Hartson, J. 15(4); Helder, G. 15(9); Hillier, D. 3(2); Hughes, S. (1); Jensen, J. 13(2); Keown, M. 34; Linighan, A. 17(1); Marshall, S. 10(1); McGoldrick, E. (1); McGowan, G. 1; Merson, P. 38; Morrow, S. 3(1); Parlour, R. 20(2); Platt, D. 27(2); Rose, M. 1(3); Seaman, D. 38; Shaw, P. (3); Winterburn, N. 36; Wright, I. 31
League (49): Wright 15 (3 pens), Bergkamp 11, Platt 6, Merson 5, Hartson 4, Dixon 2, Winterburn 2, Adams 1, Dickov 1, Helder 1, Marshall 1.
Coca-Cola Cup (17): Wright 7 (1 pen), Bergkamp 5, Adams 2, Bould 1, Hartson 1, Keown 1.
FA Cup (1): Wright 1.
Ground: Arsenal Stadium, Highbury, London N5 1BU. Telephone (0171) 704 4000.
Record attendance: 73,295 v Sunderland, Div 1, 9 March 1935. **Capacity:** 38,500.
Manager: Bruce Rioch.
Secretary: K. J. Friar.
Honours – Football League: Division 1 Champions – 1930–31, 1932–33, 1933–34, 1934–35, 1937–38, 1947–48, 1952–53, 1970–71, 1988–89, 1990–91. **FA Cup winners** 1929–30, 1935–36, 1949–50, 1970–71, 1978–79, 1992–93. **Football League Cup winners** 1986–87, 1992–93. **European Competitions: European Cup-Winners' Cup winners:** 1993–94. **Fairs Cup winners:** 1969–70.
Colours: Red shirts with white sleeves, white shorts, red and white stockings.

ASTON VILLA

Bosnich, Mark J.
Burchell, Lee A.
Charles, Gary A.
Ehiogu, Ugochuku
Hines, Leslie D.
King, Philip G.
McGrath, Paul
Murray, Scott G.
Rachel, Adam
Staunton, Stephen
Townsend, Andrew D.
Yorke, Dwight

Brock, Stuart A.
Byfield, Darren
Davis, Neil
Farrelly, Gareth
Joachim, Julian K.
Kirby, Alan
Middleton, Darren
Oakes, Michael C.
Scimeca, Riccardo
Taylor, Ian K.
Walker, Richard M.

Browne, Paul
Carr, Franz A.
Draper, Mark A.
Hendrie, Lee A.
Johnson, Thomas
Lee, Alan D.
Milosevic, Savo
Petty, Ben J.
Southgate, Gareth
Tiler, Carl
Wright, Alan

League Appearances: Bosnich, M. 38; Browne, P. 2; Carr, F. 1; Charles, G. 34; Davis, N. (2); Draper, M. 36; Ehiogu, U. 36; Farrelly, G. 1(4); Fenton, G. (3); Hendrie, L. 2(1); Joachim, J. 4(7); Johnson, T. 17(6); McGrath, P. 29(1); Milosevic, S. 36(1); Murray, S. 3; Scimeca, R. 7(10); Southgate, G. 31; Spink, N. (2); Staunton, S. 11(2); Taylor, I. 24(1); Tiler, C. 1; Townsend, A. 32(1); Wright, A. 38; Yorke, D. 35
League (52): Yorke 17 (2 pens), Milosevic 12, Johnson 5, Taylor 3, Draper 2, McGrath 2, Townsend 2, Wright 2, Charles 1, Ehiogu 1, Joachim 1, Southgate 1, own goals 3.
Coca-Cola Cup (16): Yorke 6 (2 pens), Johnson 2, Draper 1, Ehiogu 1, Milosevic 1, Southgate 1, Staunton 1, Taylor 1, Townsend 1, own goal 1.
FA Cup (8): Draper 2, Yorke 2 (1 pen), Carr 1, Johnson 1, Milosevic 1, Taylor 1.
Ground: Villa Park, Trinity Rd, Birmingham B6 6HE. Telephone (0121) 327 2299.
Record attendance: 76,588 v Derby Co, FA Cup 6th rd, 2 March 1946.
Capacity: 39,339.
Manager: Brian Little.
Secretary: Steven Stride.
Honours – Football League: Division 1 Champions – 1893–94, 1895–96, 1896–97, 1898–99, 1899–1900, 1909–10, 1980–81. Division 2 Champions – 1937–38, 1959–60. Division 3 Champions – 1971–72. **FA Cup:** Winners 1887, 1895, 1897, 1905, 1913, 1920, 1957. **Football League Cup:** Winners 1961, 1975, 1977, 1994, 1996. **European Competitions: European Cup winners:** 1981–82. **European Super Cup winners:** 1982–83.
Colours: Claret shirts, sky blue trim, white shorts, claret and sky blue trim, claret stockings, sky blue trim.

BARNET   DIV. 3

Campbell, Jamie
Dunwell, Richard K.
Hodges, Lee L.
Mills, Daniel R.
Simpson, Philip M.
Wilson, Paul R.

Codner, Robert A. G.
Gale, Shaun M.
Howarth, Lee
Pardew, Alan S.
Taylor, Maik S.

Devine, Sean T.
Gallagher, Kieran
Macdonald, David H.
Primus, Linvoy S.
Tomlinson, Michael L.

League Appearances: Adams, K. 1; Brady, M. 1(1); Campbell, J. 14(10); Charles, L. 2(3); Codner, R. 8; Cooper, M. 26(7); Devine, S. 35; Dunwell, R. 3(10); Dyer, A. 30(5); Freedman, D. 5; Gale, S. 44; Hodges, L. 34(6); Howarth, L. 19; McDonald, D. 30(2); Mills, D. 5(14); Newell, P. 1; Pardew, A. 41; Primus, L. 42; Robbins, T. 9(6); Scott, P. 19(1); Simpson, P. 24; Smith, G. (1); Stimson, M. 5; Taylor, M. 45; Thomas, G. 16; Thompson, N. 1(1); Tomlinson, M. 17(8); Wilson, P. 29(4)
League (65): Devine 19 (1 pen), Hodges 17, Cooper 8, Primus 4, Wilson 4, Freedman 3, Dyer 2, Tomlinson 2, Campbell 1, Dunwell 1, Gale 1, Robbins 1, Simpson 1, own goal 1.
Coca-Cola Cup (0).
FA Cup (3): Devine 1, Hodges 1, Primus 1.
Ground: Underhill Stadium, Barnet Lane, Barnet, Herts EN5 2BE. Telephone (0181) 441 6932.
Record attendance: 11,026 v Wycombe Wanderers. FA Amateur Cup 4th Round 1951–52. **Capacity:** 3887.
Manager: Ray Clemence MBE.
Secretary: Alison Ashworth.
Honours – FA Amateur Cup winners 1945–46. **GM Vauxhall Conference winners** 1990–91.
Colours: Amber and black striped shirts, black shorts, black stockings.

BARNSLEY   DIV. 1

Archdeacon, Owen D.
Bishop, Darren C.
Clyde, Darran E. J.
Eaden, Nicholas J.
Gregory, Andrew
Jones, Scott
O'Connell, Brendan
Redfern, Neil D.
Sheridan, Darren S.
Ten Heuvel, Laurens
Wilson, Daniel J.

Beckett, Luke J.
Bochenski, Simon
Davis, Steven P.
Fearon, Dean A.
Hurst, Glynn
Liddell, Andrew M.
Payton, Andrew P.
Regis, David
Shirtliff, Peter A.
Van Der Velden, Carel J.

Bennett, Troy
Bullock, Martin J.
De Zeeuw, Adrianus J.
Fleming, James G.
Jackson, Christopher D.
Moses, Adrian P.
Perry, Jonathan M.
Rose, Karl B.
Sollitt, Adam J.
Watson, David N.

League Appearances: Archdeacon, O. 36(2); Bishop, C. 12(1); Bochenski, S. (1); Bullock, M. 25(16); Butler, L. 1(2); Davis, S. 27; De Zeeuw, A. 31; Eaden, N. 46; Fleming, G. 2(1); Hurst, G. (5); Jackson, C. 6(2); Jones, S. 4; Kane, P. 4; Liddell, A. 43; Molby, J. 5; Moses, A. 21(3); O'Connell, B. 20(5); Payton, A. 37(3); Rammell, A. 11(9); Redfearn, N. 45; Regis, D. 4(8); Sheridan, D. 38(3); Shirtliff, P. 32; Shotton, M. 2; Ten-Heuvel, L. 1(2); Van der Velden, C. 6(1); Viveash, A. 2; Watson, D. 45
League (60): Payton 17, Redfearn 14 (3 pens), Liddell 9, Davis 5, Rammell 4, Archdeacon 3, Eaden 2, Bullock 1, De Zeeuw 1, Moses 1, O'Connell 1, Regis 1, Viveash 1.
Coca-Cola Cup (4): Payton 3, Rammell 1.
FA Cup (1): Redfearn 1.
Ground: Oakwell Ground, Grove St, Barnsley S71 1ET. Telephone (01226) 211211.
Record attendance: 40,255 v Stoke C, FA Cup 5th rd, 15 February 1936. **Capacity:** 19,101.
Manager: Danny Wilson.
Secretary: Michael Spinks.
Honours – Football League: Division 3 (N) Champions – 1933–34, 1938–39, 1954–55. **FA Cup:** Winners 1912.
Colours: Red shirts, white shorts, red stockings.

BIRMINGHAM CITY   DIV. 1

Barnes, Paul L.
Bass, Jonathan D. M.
Breen, Gary
Devlin, Paul J.
Edwards, Andrew D.
Frain, John W.
Griemink, Bart
Legg, Andrew
Otto, Ricky
Rea, Simon
Webb, Matthew L.

Barnes, Steven L.
Bennett, Ian M.
Castle, Stephen C.
Doherty, Neil
Finnan, Stephen
Francis, Kevin D. M.
Hunt, Jonathan R.
Martin, Jae A.
Peschisolido, Paolo P.
Robinson, Steven E.

Barnett, David
Bowen, Jason P.
Cornforth, John M.
Donowa, Brian L.
Forsyth, Richard M.
Grainger, Martin R.
Johnson, Michael O.
Muir, Ian J.
Poole, Gary J.
Tait, Paul R.

League Appearances: Barber, F. 1; Barnes, P. 15; Barnes, S. (3); Bass, J. 5; Bennett, I. 24; Bowen, J. 16(7); Breen, G. 17(1); Bull, G. 3(5); Castle, S. 12(3); Charlery, K. 8(9); Claridge, S. 28; Cooper, G. 16(2); Cornforth, J. 8; Daish, L. 16(1); Devlin, P. 16; Doherty, N. (2); Donowa, L. 5(8); Edwards, A. 36(1); Finnan, S. 6(6); Forsyth, R. 12(14); Frain, J. 22(1); Francis, K. 11(8); Grainger, M. 8; Griemink, B. 20; Hiley, S. 5; Hill, D. 5; Hunt, J. 43(2); Johnson, M. 31(2); Legg, A. 9(3); Lowe, K. (2); Martin, J. 1(6); Muir, I. 1; Otto, R. 6(12); Peschisolido, P. 7(2); Poole, G. 27(1); Preece, D. 6; Rea, S. (1); Richardson, I. 3(4); Rushfeldt, S. 3(4); Sahlin, D. (1); Samways, V. 12; Sansome, P. 1; Sheridan, J. 1(1); Tait, P. 23(4); Ward, M. 13; Whyte, C. 4
League (61): Hunt 11 (4 pens), Claridge 8, Barnes P 7, Devlin 7 (3 pens), Bowen 4, Charlery 4, Francis 3, Tait 3, Ward 3 (1 pen), Forsyth 2, Otto 2, Breen 1, Castle 1, Doherty 1, Edwards 1, Finnan 1, Legg 1, Peschisolido 1.
Coca-Cola Cup (17): Francis 4, Bowen 2, Charlery 2, Daish 2, Hunt 2, Claridge 1, Cooper 1, Edwards 1, Rushfeldt 1, own goal 1.
FA Cup (2): Hunt 1, Poole 1.
Ground: St Andrews, Birmingham B9 4NH. Telephone (0121) 772 0101.
Record attendance: 66,844 v Everton, FA Cup 5th rd,11 February 1939. **Capacity:** 25,936.
Manager: Trevor Francis.
Secretary: Alan Jones BA, MBA
Honours – Football League: Division 2 Champions – 1892–93, 1920–21, 1947–48, 1954–55, 1994–95. **Football League Cup:** Winners 1963. **Leyland Daf Cup:** Winners 1991. **Auto Windscreens Shield:** Winners 1995.
Colours: Blue shirts, white shorts, blue/white stockings.

BLACKBURN ROVERS   FA PREMIERSHIP

Beattie, James S.	Benson, Mark T.	Berg, Henning
Bohinen, Lars	Broomes, Marlon C.	Cassin, Graham J.
Chisholm, Craig	Coleman, Christopher	Coughlan, Graham
Croft, Gary	Duff, Damien A.	Fenton, Graham A.
Flitcroft, Garry W.	Flowers, Timothy D.	Gallacher, Kevin W.
Gill, Wayne J.	Given, Seamus J. J.	Gudmundsson, Niklas
Harford, Paul	Hendry, Edward C. J.	Hitchen, Steven J.
Holmes, Matthew J. E.	Hope, Richard P.	Johnson, Damien M.
Kenna, Jeffrey J.	Le Saux, Graeme P.	Malone, Christopher J.
Marker, Nicholas R. T.	McCrone, Christian P.	McKinlay, William
Morgan, Thomas P.	Newell, Michael C.	Pearce, Ian A.
Reed, Adam M.	Ripley, Stuart E.	Shearer, Alan
Sherwood, Tim A.	Staton, Luke R.	Sutton, Christopher R.
Warhurst, Paul	Whealing, Anthony J.	Wilcox, Jason M.
Worrell, David		

League Appearances: Atkins, M. (4); Batty, D. 23; Berg, H. 38; Bohinen, L. 17(2); Coleman, C. 19(1); Fenton, G. 4(10); Flitcroft, G. 3; Flowers, T. 37; Gallacher, K. 14(2); Gudmundsson, N. 1(3); Hendry, C. 33; Holmes, M. 8(1); Kenna, J. 32; Le Saux, G. 13(1); Makel, L. (3); Marker, N. 8(1); McKinlay, B. 13(6); Mimms, B. 1(1); Newell, M. 26(4); Pearce, I. 12; Ripley, S. 28; Shearer, A. 35; Sherwood, T. 33; Sutton, C. 9(4); Warhurst, P. 1(9); Wilcox, J. 10
League (61): Shearer 31 (3 pens), Fenton 6, Bohinen 4, Newell 3, Sherwood 3, Wilcox 3, Gallacher 2, McKinlay 2, Batty 1, Hendry 1, Holmes 1, Le Saux 1, Marker 1, Pearce 1, own goal 1.
Coca-Cola Cup (8): Shearer 5, Newell 1, Sutton 1, own goal 1.
FA Cup (0).

Ground: Ewood Park, Blackburn BB2 4JF. Telephone (01254) 698888.
Record attendance: 61,783 v Bolton W, FA Cup 6th rd, 2 March, 1929. **Capacity:** 31,367.
Manager: Ray Harford.
Secretary: John W. Howarth FAAI.
Honours – FA Premier League: Champions – 1994–95. Football League: Division 1 Champions – 1911–12, 1913–14. Division 2 Champions – 1938–39. Division 3 Champions – 1974–75. **FA Cup:** Winners 1884, 1885, 1886, 1890, 1891, 1928. **Full Members' Cup:** Winners 1986–87.
Colours: Blue and white halved shirts, white shorts, white stockings, blue trim.

BLACKPOOL   DIV. 2

Allardyce, Craig S.	Banks, Steven	Barlow, Andrew J.
Beech, Christopher S.	Bonner, Mark	Bradshaw, Darren S.
Bryan, Marvin L.	Darton, Scott R.	Ellis, Anthony J.
Gouck, Andrew S.	Hooks, John R.	Linighan, David
Lydiate, Jason L.	Martin, Lee B.	Mellon, Michael J.
Mitchell, Neil N.	Morrison, Andrew C.	Pascoe, Colin J.
Philpott, Lee	Preece, Andrew P.	Quinn, Stephen J.
Symons, Paul	Thorpe, Lee A.	Watson, Andrew A.

League Appearances: Allardyce, C. (1); Banks, S. 24; Barber, F. 1; Barlow, A. 34; Beech, C. 3(15); Bonner, M. 41(1); Bradshaw, D. 25; Brown, P. 5(8); Brown, R. 2(1); Bryan, M. 44(2); Capleton, M. 1; Charnock, P. (4); Darton, S. 5(4); Ellis, T. 41(2); Gouck, A. 8(8); Holden, R. 19(3); Linighan, D. 29; Lydiate, J. 30(2); Mellon, M. 45; Morrison, A. 29; Nixon, E. 20; Pascoe, C. (1); Philpott, L. 4(6); Preece, A. 37(4); Quinn, J. 42(2); Thorpe, L. (1); Watson, A. 14(13); Yallop, F. 3
League (67): Ellis 14, Preece 14 (3 pens), Quinn 9 (4 pens), Mellon 6, Watson 6, Linighan 4, Bonner 3, Morrison 3, Holden 2, Barlow 1, Bryan 1, Gouck 1, Lydiate 1, own goals 2.
Coca-Cola Cup (3): Ellis 2, Mellon 1.
FA Cup (5): Quinn 2, Lydiate 1, Preece 1, Quinn 1.
Ground: Bloomfield Rd Ground, Blackpool FY1 6JJ. Telephone (01253) 404331.
Record attendance: 38,098 v Wolverhampton W, Division 1, 17 September 1955.
Capacity: 9701.
Manager: Gary Megson.
Secretary: Carol Banks.
Honours – Football League: Division 2 Champions – 1929–30. **FA Cup:** Winners 1953. **Anglo-Italian Cup:** Winners 1971.
Colours: Tangerine shirts with navy and white trim, white shorts, tangerine stockings with navy blue tops.

BOLTON WANDERERS   DIV. 1

Bergsson, Gudni	Blake, Nathan A.	Branagan, Keith G.
Burnett, Wayne	Coleman, Simon	Curcic, Sasa
Davison, Aidan J.	De Freitas, Fabian	Fairclough, Courtney H.
Feeney, Gareth T.	Green, Scott P.	Lee, David M.
McAnespie, Stephen	McGinlay, John	Paatelainen, Mika
Phillips, James N.	Sellars, Scott	Small, Bryan
Spooner, Nicholas	Strong, Greg	Stubbs, Alan

Taggart, Gerald P.   Taylor, Scott J.   Thompson, Alan
Todd, Andrew   Ward, Gavin J.   Whitehead, Stuart D.
Whittaker, Stuart

League Appearances: Bergsson, G. 34; Blake, N. 14(4); Branagan, K. 31; Burnett, W. (1); Coleman, S. 12; Coyle, O. 2(3); Curcic, S. 28; Davison, A. 2; De Freitas, F. 17(10); Fairclough, C. 33; Green. S. 26(5); Lee, D. 9(9); McAnespie, S. 7(2); McAteer, J. 4; McGinlay, J. 29(3); Paatelainen, M. 12(3); Patterson, M. 12(4); Phillips, J. 37; Sellars, S. 27; Small, B. 1; Sneekes, R. 14(3); Strong, G. (1); Stubbs, A. 24(1); Taggart, G. 11; Taylor, S. (1); Thompson, A. 23(3); Todd, A. 9(3); Ward, G. 5
League (39): McGinlay 6 (1 pen), De Freitas 5, Bergsson 4, Curcic 4, Stubbs 4, Green 3, Sellars 3, Todd 2, Blake 1, Coleman 1, Lee 1, Paatelainen 1, Patterson 1 (pen), Sneekes 1, Taggart 1, Thompson 1 (pen).
Coca-Cola Cup (7): McGinlay 2, Sneekes 2, Curcic 1, Patterson 1, Thompson 1.
FA Cup (3): Curcic 2, McGinlay 1.
Ground: Burnden Park, Bolton BL3 2QR. Telephone Bolton (01204) 389200.
Record attendance: 69,912 v Manchester C, FA Cup 5th rd, 18 February 1933.
Capacity: 20,500.
Manager: Colin Todd.
Secretary: Des McBain.
Honours – Football League: Division 2 Champions – 1908–09, 1977–78. Division 3 Champions – 1972–73. **FA Cup winners** 1923, 1926, 1929, 1958. **Sherpa Van Trophy:** Winners 1989.
Colours: White shirts, navy blue shorts, blue stockings.

AFC BOURNEMOUTH   DIV. 2

Andrews, Ian E.   Bailey, John A.   Beardsmore, Russell P.
Brissett, Jason C.   Coll, Owen O.   Cox, Ian G.
Fletcher, Steven M.   Glass, James R.   Holland, Matthew R.
McElhatton, Michael T. Mean, Scott   Morris, Mark J.
Murray, Robert J.   O'Neill, John J.   Oldbury, Marcus J.
Pennock, Adrian B.   Rawlinson, Mark D.   Robinson, Stephen
Town, David E.   Watson, Mark L.   Young, Neil A.

League Appearances: Andrews, I. 26; Bailey, J. 36(8); Beardsmore, R. 44; Brissett, J. 43; Casper, C. 16; Coll, O. 8; Cox, I. 8; Cureton, J. (5); Dean, M. 4(1); Duberry, M. 7; Fletcher, S. 3(4); Glass, J. 13; Holland, M. 43; Howe, E. 4(1); Jones, S. 44; McElhatton, M. 2(2); Mean, S. 13(1); Mitchell, P. 2(2); Morris, M. 28(3); Moss, N. 7; Murray, R. 30(5); Ndah, G. 12; O'Neill, J. 2(4); Oldbury, M. 2(11); Pennock, A. 16(1); Rawlinson, M. 3(16); Robinson, S. 36(5); Santos, Y. (3); Scott, K. 8; Strong, S. (1); Town, D. 1(6); Victory, J. 5(11); Young, N. 40(1)
League (51): Jones 17, Holland 10, Robinson 7 (2 pens), Bailey 4, Brissett 3, Murray 2, Ndah 2, Casper 1, Fletcher 1, Mean 1, Morris 1, Scott 1, Victory 1.
Coca-Cola Cup (5): Jones 3, Morris 1, Oldbury 1.
FA Cup (1): Robinson 1.
Ground: Dean Court Ground, Bournemouth BH7 7AF. Telephone (01202) 395381.
Record attendance: 28,799 v Manchester U, FA Cup 6th rd, 2 March 1957.
Capacity: 11,000.
Manager: Mel Machin.
Secretary: K. R. J. MacAlister.
Honours – Football League: Division 3 Champions – 1986–87 **Associate Members' Cup:** Winners 1984.
Colours: Red shirts with black stripe, white shorts, white stockings.

11

BRADFORD CITY   DIV. 1

Brightwell, David J.   Bullimore, Wayne A.   Duxbury, Lee E.
Ford, Jonathan S.   Hamilton, Derrik V.   Hansen, Glenn A.
Huxford, Richard J.   Jacobs, Wayne G.   Jewell, Paul
Kiwomya, Andrew D.   Liburd, Richard J.   Midgley, Craig S.
Mitchell, Graham L.   Mohan, Nicholas   Murray, Shaun
Ormondroyd, Ian   Showler, Paul   Shutt, Carl S.
Stallard, Mark   Tolson, Neil   Wright, Thomas E.
Youds, Edward P.

League Appearances: Brightwell, D. 21(1); Bullimore, W. 1(1); Duxbury, L. 30;
Foley, S. (1); Ford, J. 18(1); Gould, J. 9; Grayston, N. 2; Hamilton, D. 18(6);
Harper, S. 1; Huxford, R. 21(5); Jacobs, W. 28; Jewell, P. 7(11); Kernaghan, A. 5;
Kiwomya, A. 7(9); Liburd, R. 33; Midgley, C. (5); Mitchell, G. 32(1); Mohan, N. 39;
Murray, S. 25(9); Ormondroyd, I. 28(9); Robson, G. 4(2); Showler, P. 29(4); Shutt,
C. 22(12); Stallard, M. 20(1); Tolson, N. 12(19); Ward, G. 36; Wright, T. 28(6);
Youds, E. 30
League (71): Stallard 9, Showler 8 (1 pen), Shutt 8, Tolson 8, Ormondroyd 6,
Duxbury 4, Mohan 4, Wright 4 (2 pens), Youds 4, Hamilton 3, Jewell 3, Kiwomya
2, Murray 2, Huxford 1, Liburd 1, Midgley 1, Mitchell 1, own goals 2.
Coca-Cola Cup (13): Showler 4, Ormondroyd 3, Wright 2, Youds 2, Hamilton 1,
Tolson 1.
FA Cup (6): Jacobs 2, Showler 2, Ormondroyd 1, Robson 1.
Ground: The Pulse Stadium, Bradford BD8 7DY. Telephone (01274) 773355.
Record attendance: 39,146 v Burnley, FA Cup 4th rd, 11 March 1911. **Capacity:**
18,100.
Manager: Chris Kamara.
Secretary: Shaun A. Harvey.
Honours – Football League: Division 2 Champions – 1907–08. Division 3
Champions – 1984–85. Division 3 (N) Champions – 1928–29. **FA Cup:** Winners
1911.
Colours: Claret and amber striped shirts, black shorts, black stockings.

BRENTFORD   DIV. 2

Abrahams, Paul   Anderson, Ijah M.   Asaba, Carl E.
Ashby, Barry J.   Bates, Jamie   Bent, Marcus N.
Davis, Paul V.   Dearden, Kevin C.   Fernandes, Tamer H.
Forster, Nicholas M.   Harvey, Lee D.   Hurdle, Agustus A. J.
Hutchings, Carl E.   McGhee, David   Omigie, Joseph I.
Smith, Paul W.   Statham, Brian   Taylor, Robert A.

League Appearances: Abrahams, P. 14(3); Anderson, I. 25; Annon, D. (1); Ansah,
A. 6; Asaba, C. 5(5); Ashby, B. 31(2); Bates, J. 36; Bent, M. 8(4); Canham, S. 14;
Davis, P. 5; Dearden, K. 41; Fernandes, T. 5; Forster, N. 37(1); Grainger, M. 33;
Greene, D. 11; Harvey, L. 38(2); Hooker, J. 4; Hurdle, G. 11(3); Hutchings, C.
20(3); Martin, D. 14(5); McGhee, D. 31(5); Mundee, D. 5(1); Omigie, J. 3(7);
Ravenscroft, C. 1; Smith, P. 46; Statham, B. 17; Sussex, A. 3; Taylor, R. 42
League (43): Taylor 11, Forster 5, McGhee 5, Bates 4, Smith 4, Abrahams 3,
Grainger 3 (1 pen), Anderson 2, Asaba 2, Ansah 1, Ashby 1, Bent 1, Martin 1.
Coca-Cola Cup (7): Forster 2, Anderson 1, Grainger 1 (pen), Harvey 1, McGhee 1,
Taylor 1.

FA Cup (10): Bent 3, Taylor 3, Smith 2, Ashby 1, own goal 1.
Ground: Griffin Park, Braemar Rd, Brentford, Middlesex TW8 0NT. Telephone (0181) 847 2511.
Record attendance: 39,626 v Preston NE, FA Cup 6th rd, 5 March 1938. **Capacity:** 13,870.
Manager: David Webb.
Secretary: Polly Kates.
Honours – Football League: Division 2 Champions – 1934–35. Division 3 Champions – 1991–92. Division 3 (S) Champions – 1932–33. Division 4 Champions – 1962–63.
Colours: Red and white vertical striped shirts, red shorts, red stockings.

BRIGHTON & HOVE ALBION   DIV. 3

Andrews, Phillip D.	Fox, Mark S.	Fox, Simon M.
Hobson, Gary	Maskell, Craig D.	McCarthy, Paul J.
McDonald, Thomas P.	McDougald, David E. J.	McGarrigle, Kevin
Mundee, Denny W. J.	Ormerod, Mark I.	Parris, George
Rust, Nicholas C. I.	Smith, Peter J.	Storer, Stuart J.
Thompson-Minton, Jeffrey S.	Tuck, Stuart G.	Virgo, James R.
Yorke-Johnson, Ross		

League Appearances: Allan, D. 8; Andrews, P. (8); Berry, G. 6; Bull, G. 10; Byrne, J. 15(10); Case, J. (2); Chapman, I. 36; Coughlan, D. 1; Foster, S. 8; Fox, M. (2); Fox, S. (6); Hobson, G. 9; Johnson, R. 19(1); Maskell, C. 15; McCarthy, P. 33; McDonald, P. 5; McDougald, J. 34(3); McGarrigle, K. 8(6); Minton, J. 37(2); Munday, S. 6(3); Mundee, D. 31(1); Myall, S. 27(6); Osman, R. 11(1); Parris, G. 38; Rowe, Z. 9; Rust, N. 46; Smith, P. 28(3); Storer, S. 28(10); Tuck, S. 7(1); Wilkins, D. 31(4)
League (46): Minton 8, McDougald 4, Maskell 4, Chapman 3, Mundee 3 (2 pens), Rowe 3, Wilkins 3, Berry 2, Bull 2, Byrne 2, Myall 2, Parris 2, Storer 2, Foster 1, McCarthy 1, McGarrigle 1, Smith 1, own goals 2.
Coca-Cola Cup (0).
FA Cup (6): McDougald 3, Byrne 2, Smith 1.
Ground: Goldstone Ground, Old Shoreham Rd, Hove, Sussex BN3 7DE. Telephone (01273) 778855.
Record attendance: 36,747 v Fulham, Division 2, 27 December 1958. **Capacity:** 13,600.
Manager: Jimmy Case.
Secretary: Derek Allan.
Honours – Football League: Division 3 (S) Champions – 1957–58. Division 4 Champions – 1964–65.
Colours: Blue and white striped shirts, blue shorts, white stockings.

BRISTOL CITY   DIV. 2

Agostino, Paul	Barclay, Dominic A.	Barnard, Darren S.
Bent, Junior A.	Brennan, James G.	Bryant, Matthew

13

Carey, Louis A.
Fowler, Jason K. G.
Huggins, Dean S.
Nugent, Kevin P.
Paterson, Scott
Shail, Mark E. D.

Dryden, Richard A.
Hansen, Vegard
Kuhl, Martin
Owers, Gary
Plummer, Dwayne J.
Tinnion, Brian

Edwards, Robert W.
Hewlett, Paul M.
McLeary, Alan T.
Partridge, Scott M.
Seal, David
Welch, Keith J.

League Appearances: Agostino, P. 29(11); Armstrong, G. 6; Baird, I. 1; Barber, P. 3; Barclay, D. (2); Barnard, D. 33(1); Bent, J. 33(7); Bryant, M. 31(1); Carey, L. 22(1); Dryden, R. 17(1); Dykstra, S. 8; Edwards, R. 18(1); Fowler, J. 6(4); Hansen, V. 7(1); Hewlett, M. 27; Kite, P. 3(1); Kuhl, M. 46; Maskell, C. 5; McLeary, A. 30(1); Munro, S. 3; Nugent, K. 29(5); Owers, G. 34(3); Partridge, S. 3(6); Paterson, S. 16(2); Plummer, D. 1(10); Seal, D. 19(11); Shail, M. 9(3); Starbuck, P. 5; Tinnion, B. 27(3); Welch, K. 35
League (55): Agostino 10, Seal 10, Nugent 8, Kuhl 6 (1 pen), Barnard 4, Tinnion 3, Bent 2, Hewlett 2, Owers 2, Dryden 1, Maskell 1, Partridge 1, Paterson 1, Starbuck 1, own goals 3.
Coca-Cola Cup (4): Seal 3, Agostino 1.
FA Cup (0).
Ground: Ashton Gate, Bristol BS3 2EJ. Telephone (0117) 9632812.
Record attendance: 43,335 v Preston NE, FA Cup 5th rd, 16 February 1935.
Capacity: 17,888.
Manager: Joe Jordan.
Secretary: Ian Wilson.
Honours – Football League: Division 2 Champions – 1905–06. Division 3 (S) Champions – 1922–23, 1926–27, 1954–55. **Welsh Cup winners** 1934. **Anglo-Scottish Cup:** Winners 1977–78. **Freight Rover Trophy winners** 1985–86.
Colours: Red shirts, white shorts, red and white stockings.

BRISTOL ROVERS   DIV. 2

Archer, Lee
Browning, Marcus T.
Collett, Andrew A.
Hayfield, Matthew A.
Pritchard, David M.
Tillson, Andrew

Beadle, Peter C.
Channing, Justin A.
French, Jonathan C.
Higgs, Shane P.
Skinner, Justin
White, Thomas M.

Bowey, Steven
Clark, William R.
Gurney, Andrew R.
Miller, Paul A.
Stewart, Marcus P.

League Appearances: Archer, L. 13(6); Armstrong, C. 13(1); Beadle, P. 26(1); Browning, M. 45; Channing, J. 35(1); Clark, B. 38(1); Collett, A. 26; Davis, M. 1(3); French, J. 3(7); Gurney, A. 42(1); Hayfield, M. 3(3); Low, J. (1); Matthew, D. 8; McLean, I. 4(3); Miller, P. 37(1); Morgan, S. 5; Parkin, B. 20; Paul, M. 9(4); Pritchard, D. 12; Skinner, J. 23(5); Sterling, W. 28(2); Stewart, M. 44; Taylor, G. 7; Tillson, A. 38; Tovey, P. 8; White, T. (2); Wright, I. 15(3); Wyatt, M. 3(1)
League (57): Stewart 21 (3 pens), Beadle 12, Gurney 6, Browning 4, Miller 4, Taylor 4, Clark 2, Archer 1, French 1, Paul 1, Tillson 1.
Coca-Cola Cup (5): Stewart 4, Miller 1.
FA Cup (1): Archer 1.
Ground: Twerton Park, Twerton, Bath BA2 1DB. Telephone: (0117) 861743.
Record attendance: 9464 v Liverpool, FA Cup 4th rd, 8 February 1992 (Twerton Park). 38,472 v Preston NE, FA Cup 4th rd, 30 January 1960 (Eastville). **Capacity:** 8943.
Manager: Ian Holloway.

Honours – **Football League:** Division 3 (S) Champions – 1952–53. Division 3 Champions – 1989–90.
Colours: Blue and white quartered shirts, white shorts, blue stockings.

BURNLEY   DIV. 2

Adams, Derek W.
Brass, Christopher P.
Eyres, David
Hoyland, Jamie W.
Parkinson, Gary
Smith, Ian P.
Vinnicombe, Christopher

Beresford, Marlon
Cooke, Andrew R.
Harrison, Gerald R.
Joyce, Warren G.
Robinson, Spencer L.
Swan, Peter H.
Weller, Paul

Borland, John R.
Dowell, Wayne A.
Helliwell, Ian
Nogan, Kurt
Russell, Wayne L.
Thompson, Stephen J.
Winstanley, Mark A.

League Appearances: Adams, D. (2); Beresford, M. 36; Bishop, C. 9; Borland, J. 1; Brass, C. 7(2); Cooke, A. 10(13); Dowell, W. 1; Eyres, D. 39(3); Francis, J. 4(18); Harper, A. 3(1); Harrison, G. 35; Heath, A. 5(2); Helliwell, I. 3(1); Hoyland, J. 21(2); Joyce, W. 42(1); Mahorn, P. 3(5); McDonald, P. 8(1); McMinn, T. 7(3); Nogan, K. 46; Parkinson, G. 29; Pender, J. 1; Philliskirk, T. 7(1); Randall, A. 12(3); Robinson, L. 11(5); Russell, W. 10; Smith, P. 3(7); Swan, P. 31(1); Thompson, S. 18; Vinnicombe, C. 35; Weller, P. 24(1); Winstanley, M. 45
League (56): Nogan 20, Eyres 6 (3 pens), Cooke 5, Joyce 5, Swan 5, Winstanley 3, Francis 2, Robinson 2, Vinnicombe 2, Harrison 1, McDonald 1, Mahorn 1, Philliskirk 1, Weller 1, own goal 1.
Coca-Cola Cup (4): Nogan 3, Randall 1.
FA Cup (1): Eyres 1.
Ground: Turf Moor, Burnley BB10 4BX. Telephone (01282) 700000.
Record attendance: 54,775 v Huddersfield T, FA Cup 3rd rd, 23 February 1924.
Capacity: 22,966.
Manager: Adrian Heath.
Secretary:
Honours – **Football League:** Division 1 Champions – 1920–21, 1959–60. Division 2 Champions – 1897–98, 1972–73. Division 3 Champions – 1981–82. Division 4 Champions – 1991–92. **FA Cup winners** 1913–14. **Anglo-Scottish Cup:** Winners 1978–79.
Colours: Claret and blue shirts, white shorts and stockings.

BURY   DIV. 2

Bimson, Stuart J.
Carter, Mark C.
Jackson, Michael J.
Kelly, Gary A.
Matthews, Robert D.
Reid, Shaun
Stant, Philip
West, Dean

Brabin, Gary
Daws, Nicholas J.
Johnrose, Leonard
Lancaster, David
Pugh, David
Rigby, Antony A.
Steele, Winfield
Woodward, Andrew S.

Bracey, Lee M. I.
Hughes, Ian
Johnson, David A.
Lucketti, Christopher J.
Reid, Nicholas S.
Shuttleworth, Barry
Thomson, Peter D.

League Appearances: Bimson, S. 16; Brabin, G. 5; Bracey, L. 21; Carter, M. 28(4); Cross, R. 13; Daws, N. 33(4); Edwards, P. 4; Harle, M. (1); Hughes, I. 30(2); Hulme, K. (1); Jackson, M. 31; Johnrose, L. 34; Johnson, D. 21(15); Kelly, G. 25; Lancaster, D. 1(4); Lucketti, C. 42; Matthews, R. 11(5); Matthewson, T. 16; Mulligan, J. (2);

15

Paskin, J. (12); Pugh, D. 42; Reid, N. 13(5); Reid, S. 20(1); Richardson, N. 3(2); Rigby, T. 33(8); Sertori, M. 4(7); Stant, P. 27(7); West, D. 32(5); Woodward, A. 1
League (66): Carter 16 (5 pens), Pugh 10, Stant 9, Rigby 7, Johnrose 6, Johnson 5, Jackson 4, Matthews 4, Daws 1, Lucketti 1, Sertori 1, West 1, own goal 1.
Coca-Cola Cup (9): Stant 4, Carter 2 (1 pen), Daws 1, Johnson 1, Rigby 1.
FA Cup (0)
Ground: Gigg Lane, Bury BL9 9HR. Telephone (0161) 764 4881.
Record attendance: 35,000 v Bolton W, FA Cup 3rd rd, 9 January 1960. **Capacity:** 11,936
Manager: Stan Ternent.
Assistant Secretary: J. Neville.
Honours – Football League: Division 2 Champions – 1894–95. Division 3 Champions – 1960–61. **FA Cup winners** 1900, 1903.
Colours: White shirts, royal blue shorts, royal blue stockings.

CAMBRIDGE UNITED   DIV. 3

Barnwell-Edinboro, Jamie Barrett, Scott   Beall, Matthew J.
Craddock, Jody D.   Davies, Martin L.   Granville, Daniel P.
Hyde, Micah   Joseph, Marc E.   Joseph, Matthew N. A.
Kyd, Michael R.   Pack, Lenny J.   Palmer, Lee J.
Raynor, Paul J.   Richards, Tony S.   Thompson, David G.
Turner, Robert P.   Vowden, Colin D.

League Appearances: Adekola, D. 1(4); Barnwell-Edinboro, J. 7; Barrett, S. 31; Barrick, D. 2(1); Beall, M. 15; Benjamin, T. (5); Butler, S. 16; Clark, P. 2; Corazzin, C. 31; Craddock, J. 44(2); Davies, M. 15; Fowler, J. (2); Granville, D. 31(4); Gutzmore, L. (2); Hayes, A. 1; Howes, S. (1); Hyde, M. 20(4); Illman, N. 1(4); Jeffrey, A. 20(7); Joseph, Marc 10(2); Joseph, Matthew 42; Kyd, M. 3(6); Middleton, C. 38(2); Middleton, L. 1(2); Pack, L. 2(9); Palmer, L. 30; Perkins, D. 1(1); Pick, G. 2(2); Rattle, J. 7(2); Raynor, P. 35; Richards, T. 15(4); Robinson, D. 4(13); Stock, R. 15(2); Thompson, D. 14(1); Turner, R. 10; Vowden, C. 22(2); Wanless, P. 14; Watson, M. 1(3); Westley, S. 3; Wosahlo, B. (4)
League (61): Butler 10 (1 pen), Corazzin 10 (1 pen), Middleton C 8, Beall 4, Hyde 4 (2 pens), Craddock 3, Raynor 3, Turner 3, Barnwell-Edinboro 2, Matthew Joseph 2, Adekola 1, Barrick 1, Kyd 1, Palmer 1, Perkins 1, Richards 1, Robinson 1, Stock 1, Wanless 1, Watson 1, own goals 2.
Coca-Cola Cup (2): Corazzin 2 (1 pen).
FA Cup (1): Butler 1.
Ground: Abbey Stadium, Newmarket Rd, Cambridge CB5 8LN. Telephone (01223) 566500. **Capacity:** 9667
Record attendance: 14,000 v Chelsea, Friendly, 1 May 1970.
Manager: Tommy Taylor.
Secretary: Steve Greenall.
Honours – Football League: Division 3 Champions – 1990–91. Division 4 Champions – 1976–77.
Colours: Amber & black shirts, black shorts, black & amber stockings.

CARDIFF CITY   DIV. 3

Adams, Darren S.   Baddeley, Lee M.   Dale, Carl
Flack, Steven R.   Gardner, James   Harding, Paul
Haworth, Simon O.   Jarman, Lee   Johnson, Glenn P.

Perry, Jason Philliskirk, Anthony Rodgerson, Ian
Scott, Andrew M. Wigg, Nathan M. Williams, Stephen D.
Young, Scott

League Appearances: Adams, D. 8(6); Baddeley, L. 27(3); Bird, A. 9(3); Bolesan, M. (1); Brazil, D. 19(1); Dale, C. 44; Dobbs, G. 3; Downing, K. 3(1); Evans, A. 1(1); Evans, T. 1(1); Flack, S. 5(5); Fleming, H. 20(2); Gardner, J. 32(3); Harding, P. 36; Harper, A. 5; Haworth, S. 7(6); Ingram, C. 4(4); Jarman, L. 31(1); Johnson, G. 1(4); Jones, I. 1; McGorry, B. 7; Oatway, C. 2; Osman, R. 14(1); Perry, J. 13(1); Philliskirk, T. 28; Rodgerson, I. 28(6); Scott, A. (1); Scully, T. 13(1); Searle, D. 41; Shaw, P. 6; Vick, L. (2); Wigg, N. 14(6); Williams, D. 42; Williams, S. 4; Young, S. 37(4)
League (41): Dale 21 (4 pens), Gardner 4, Philliskirk 4, Adams 3, Bird 3, Flack 1, Ingram 1, Rodgerson 1, Searle 1, own goals 2.
Coca-Cola Cup (4): Dale 2, Bird 1, Rodgerson 1.
FA Cup (3): Dale 2, Jarman 1.
Ground: Ninian Park, Cardiff CF1 8SX. Telephone Cardiff (01222) 398636.
Record attendance: 61,566, Wales v England, 14 October 1961. **Capacity:** 20,284.
Manager: Phil Neal.
Secretary: Barry Doughty.
Honours – Football League: Division 3 (S) Champions – 1946–47. **FA Cup winners** 1926–27 (only occasion the Cup has been won by a club outside England). **Welsh Cup winners** 21 times.
Colours: Blue shirts, blue shorts, blue stockings.

CARLISLE UNITED   DIV. 3

Aspinall, Warren Caig, Antony Currie, David N.
Day, Mervyn R. Delap, Rory J. Edmondson, Darren S.
Hayward, Steve L. Hopper, Tony Jansen, Matthew B.
Joyce, Joseph P. McAlindon, Gareth E. Peacock, Lee A.
Prokas, Richard Reeves, David Robinson, Jamie
Thomas, Roderick C. Thorpe, Jeffrey R. Varty, John W.
Walling, Dean A.

League Appearances: Allen, C. 3; Aspinall, W. 36(6); Atkinson, B. 2; Bennett, G. 26; Caig, T. 33; Conway, P. 13(9); Currie, D. 41(1); Delap, R. 5(14); Donachie, D. (1); Dowell, W. 2(5); Edmondson, D. 40(2); Elliott, T. 13; Gallimore, T. 36; Hayward, S. 36(2); Hopper, T. 1(4); McAlindon, G. (3); Moore, N. 13; Murray, P. 23(5); Peacock, L. 12(10); Philliskirk, T. 3; Prokas, R. 17(3); Reeves, D. 43; Robinson, J. 18(2); Smart, A. 3(1); Thomas, R. 28(8); Thorpe, J. 16(18); Walling, D. 43
League (57): Reeves 13, Currie 9, Aspinall 6, Bennett 5, Hayward 4 (1 pen), Conway 3, Delap 3, Gallimore 2 (2 pens), Peacock 2, Robinson 2, Walling 2, Edmondson 1, Murray 1, Philliskirk 1, Thomas 1, Thorpe 1, own goal 1.
Coca-Cola Cup (4): Reeves 2, Aspinall 1, Walling 1.
FA Cup (1): Reeves 1.
Ground: Brunton Park, Carlisle CA1 1LL. Telephone (01228) 26237.
Record attendance: 27,500 v Birmingham C, FA Cup 3rd rd, 5 January 1957 and v Middlesbrough, FA Cup 5th rd, 7 February 1970. **Capacity:** 16,651.
Manager: Mervyn Day.
Acting Secretary: A. Ritchie.
Honours – Football League: Division 3 Champions – 1964–65, 1994–95.
Colours: Blue shirts, white shorts, blue stockings.

CHARLTON ATHLETIC   DIV. 1

Allen, Bradley J.
Brown, Steven B.
Curbishley, Llewellyn
Linger, Paul H.
Nicholls, Kevin J. R.
Robson, Mark A.
Stuart, Jamie C.
Wright, Robert A.

Balmer, Stuart M.
Chandler, Dean A. R.
Jones, Keith A.
Mortimer, Paul H.
Petterson, Andrew K.
Rufus, Richard R.
Sturgess, Paul C.

Bowyer, Lee D.
Chapple, Philip R.
Leaburn, Carl W.
Newton, Shaun O.
Robinson, John R. C.
Salmon, Michael B.
Whyte, David A.

League Appearances: Allen, B. 10; Ammann, M. 10(1); Balmer, S. 30(2); Bowyer, L. 41; Brown, S. 17(2); Chandler, D. (1); Chapple, P. 13(3); Garland, P. 3; Grant, K. 20(10); Humphrey, J. 28; Jackson, M. 8; Jones, K. 24(1); Leaburn, C. 38(2); Linger, P. 2(6); Mortimer, P. 13(6); Nelson, G. 12(18); Newton, S. 39(2); Petterson, A. 9; Robinson, J. 43(1); Robson, M. 11(16); Rufus, R. 40(1); Salmon, M. 27; Stuart, J. 27; Sturgess, P. 13; Walsh, C. 5(1); Whyte, C. 10(1); Whyte, D. 11(14); Williams, P. 2(7)
League (57): Leaburn 9 (1 pen), Bowyer 8, Grant 7, Robinson 6, Mortimer 5 (4 pens), Newton 5, Allen 3 (1 pen), Nelson 3, Chapple 2, Stuart 2, Whyte D 2 (1 pen), Balmer 1, Linger 1, Robson 1 (pen), own goals 2.
Coca-Cola Cup (11): Bowyer 5, Robinson 2, Garland 1, Grant 1, Leaburn 1, Newton 1.
FA Cup (6): Grant 2, Bowyer 1, Mortimer 1 (pen), Robinson 1, Whyte D 1.
Ground: The Valley, Floyd Road, Charlton, London SE7 8BL. Telephone (0181) 293 4567.
Record attendance: 75,031 v Aston Villa, FA Cup 5th rd, 12 February 1938 (at The Valley). **Capacity:** 15,000.
Manager: Alan Curbishley.
Secretary: Chris Parkes.
Honours – Football League: Division 3 (S) Champions – 1928–29, 1934–35.
FA Cup winners 1947.
Colours: Red shirts, white shorts, red stockings.

CHELSEA   FA PREMIERSHIP

Barness, Anthony
Clement, Neil
Furlong, Paul A.
Hughes, John P.
Johnsen, Erland
Lee, David J.
Morris, Jody
Nicholls, Mark
Phelan, Terrence M.
Spencer, John

Burley, Craig W.
Colgan, Nicholas V.
Gullit (Dil) Ruud
Hughes, Leslie M.
Kharine, Dmitri V.
McCann, Christian
Myers, Andrew
Peacock, Gavin K.
Rocastle, David C.
Stein, Mark E. S.

Clarke, Stephen
Duberry, Michael W.
Hitchcock, Kevin
Izzet, Mustafa K.
Kjeldbjerg, Jakob
Minto, Scott C.
Newton, Edward J. I.
Petrescu, Dan V.
Sinclair, Frank M.
Wise, Dennis F.

League Appearances: Burley, C. 16(6); Clarke, S. 21(1); Dow, A. 1; Duberry, M. 22; Furlong, P. 14(14); Gullit, R. 31; Hall, G. 5; Hitchcock, K. 12; Hughes, M. 31; Johnsen, E. 18(4); Kharine, D. 26; Lee, D. 29(2); Minto, S. 10; Morris, J. (1); Myers, A. 20; Newton, E. 21(3); Peacock, G. 17(11); Petrescu, D. 22(2); Phelan, T. 12; Rocastle, D. 1; Sinclair, F. 12(1); Spackman, N. 13(3); Spencer, J. 23(5); Stein, M. 7(1); Wise, D. 34(1)

18

League (46): Spencer 13, Hughes 8 (1 pen), Wise 7 (2 pens), Peacock 5, Furlong 3, Gullit 3, Petrescu 2, Hall 1, Lee 1, Newton 1, Sinclair 1, own goal 1.
Coca-Cola Cup (0)
FA Cup (15): Hughes 4, Gullit 3, Duberry 2, Peacock 2, Furlong 1, Petrescu 1, Spencer 1, Wise 1 (pen).
Ground: Stamford Bridge, London SW6 1HS. Telephone (0171) 385 5545.
Record attendance: 82,905 v Arsenal, Division 1, 12 October 1935.
Capacity: 31,791 (up to 41,000).
Manager: Ruud Gullit.
Secretary: Yvonne Todd.
Honours – Football League: Division 1 Champions – 1954–55. **FA Cup winners** 1970. **Football League Cup winners** 1964–65. **Full Members' Cup winners** 1985–86. **Zenith Data Systems Cup winners** 1989–90. **European Cup-Winners' Cup winners** 1970–71.
Colours: Royal blue with white and amber shirts, royal blue and white shorts, white stockings.

CHESTER CITY   DIV. 3

Alsford, Julian	Davidson, Ross J.	Fisher, Neil J.
Flitcroft, David J.	Jackson, Peter A.	Jenkins, Iain
Milner, Andrew J.	Murphy, John J.	Noteman, Kevin S.
Preece, Roger	Priest, Christopher	Ratcliffe, Kevin
Regis, Cyrille	Richardson, Nicholas J.	Rimmer, Stuart A.
Rogers, David R.	Shelton, Gary	Whelan, Spencer R.

League Appearances: Alsford, J. 22(2); Bishop, E. 7(2); Brien, T. 8; Brown, G. 1(2); Burnham, J. 40; Chambers, L. 2(6); Cutler, N. 1; Davidson, R. 19; Fisher, N. 43(1); Flitcroft, D. 7(2); Jackson, P. 36; Jenkins, I. 12(1); Kenworthy, J. 5(2); Milner, A. 35(7); Murphy, J. 1(17); Noteman, K. 27(6); Preece, R. 1; Priest, C. 38(1); Regis, C. 29; Richardson, N. 36(1); Rimmer, S. 30(11); Rogers, D. 14(6); Ryan, D. 2(2); Shelton, G. 10(1); Stewart, B. 45; Whelan, S. 35(4)
League (72): Priest 13 (3 pens), Rimmer 13, Noteman 9 (1 pen), Regis 7, Bishop 5, Milner 4, Richardson 4, Murphy 3, Fisher 2, Whelan 2, Burnham 1, Chambers 1, Davidson 1, Flitcroft 1, Jackson 1, Kenworthy 1, Rogers 1 (pen), Ryan 1 (pen), Shelton 1, own goal 1.
Coca-Cola Cup (8): Milner 3, Bishop 2, Chambers 1, Murphy 1, Whelan 1.
FA Cup (1): Milner 1.
Ground: The Deva Stadium, Bumpers Lane, Chester CH1 4LT. Telephone (01244) 371376, 371809.
Record attendance: 20,500 v Chelsea, FA Cup 3rd rd (replay), 16 January, 1952 (at Sealand Road). **Capacity:** 6000.
Manager: Kevin Ratcliffe.
Secretary: Derek Barber JP, AMITD.
Honours – Welsh Cup winners 1908, 1933, 1947. **Debenhams Cup:** Winners 1977.
Colours: Blue and white striped shirts, blue shorts, blue stockings.

CHESTERFIELD   DIV. 2

Beasley, Andrew	Carr, Darren	Curtis, Thomas
Davies, Kevin C.	Dyche, Sean M.	Hewitt, James R.
Holland, Paul	Howard, Jonathan	Jules, Mark A.
Law, Nicholas	Lormor, Anthony	Lund, Gary J.

Mercer, William   Morris, Andrew D.   Perkins, Christopher P.
Robinson, Philip J.   Rogers, Lee J.   Williams, Mark S.

League Appearances: Beasley, A. 11; Carr, D. 1; Curtis, T. 46; Davies, K. 28(2); Dyche, S. 39(2); Fairclough, W. (2); Hazel, D. 16(5); Hewitt, J. 23(5); Holland, P. 16(1); Howard, J. 16(14); Jules, M. 28(4); Law, N. 38; Lormor, T. 38(3); Lund, G. 6(2); Madden, L. 1; McDougall, J. 9; Mercer, B. 34; Morris, A. 14(2); Moss, D. 6(7); Narbett, J. 11(6); Perkins, C. 18(4); Pierce, D. 1; Roberts, D. 6(8); Robinson, P. 38(1); Rogers, L. 20(1); Williams, M. 42
League (56): Lormor 13, Robinson 9, Law 7 (6 pens), Morris 5, Davies 4, McDougald 3, Williams 3, Hewitt 2, Holland 2, Howard 2, Jules 2, Lund 1, Narbett 1, own goals 2.
Coca-Cola Cup (1): Roberts 1.
FA Cup (4): Davies 2, Lormor 2.
Ground: Recreation Ground, Chesterfield S40 4SX. Telephone (01246) 209765.
Record attendance: 30,968 v Newcastle U, Division 2, 7 April 1939. **Capacity:** 8880.
Manager: John Duncan.
Secretary: Mick Horton.
Honours – Football League: Division 3 (N) Champions – 1930–31, 1935–36. Division 4 Champions – 1969–70, 1984–85. **Anglo-Scottish Cup winners** 1980–81.
Colours: Blue shirts, white shorts, blue stockings.

COLCHESTER UNITED   DIV. 3

Adcock, Anthony C.   Betts, Simon R.   Burley, George E.
Caldwell, Garrett E. J.   Cawley, Peter   Dunne, Joseph J.
Emberson, Carl W.   English, Anthony K.   Fry, Christopher D.
Gibbs, Paul   Gregory, David S.   Haydon, Nicholas
Kinsella, Mark A.   Lewis, Ben   Lock, Anthony C.
Locke, Adam S.   McCarthy, Anthony P.   Reinelt, Robert S.
Whitton, Stephen P.

League Appearances: Abrahams, P. 8; Adcock, T. 41; Ball, S. 6(2); Betts, S. 45; Boyce, R. (2); Caesar, G. 23; Cawley, P. 42; Cheetham, M. 25(3); Dennis, T. 24(8); Duguid, K. 7(9); Dunne, J. 2(3); Emberson, C. 41; English, T. 20(1); Fry, C. 35(3); Gibbs, P. 13(11); Greene, D. 14; Gregory, D. 7(3); Kinsella, M. 45; Lewis, B. 1(1); Locke, A. 22(3); Mardenborough, S. 4(8); McCarthy, T. 44; McGleish, S. 10(5); Petterson, A. 5; Reinelt, R. 12(10); Whitton, S. 10(2)
League (61): Adcock 12 (2 pens), Reinelt 7, McGleish 6, Betts 5 (2 pens), Kinsella 5, Dennis 3, Gibbs 3, Locke 3, Abrahams 2, Caesar 2, Cheetham 2, Fry 2, Mardenborough 2, Whitton 2, Ball 1, Cawley 1, Duguid 1, Dunne 1, Greene 1.
Coca-Cola Cup (3): Adcock 1, Cheetham 1, Kinsella 1.
FA Cup (0).
Ground: Layer Rd Ground, Colchester CO2 7JJ. Telephone (01206) 574042.
Record attendance: 19,072 v Reading, FA Cup 1st rd, 27 Nov, 1948. **Capacity:** 7190.
Manager: Steve Wignall.
Secretary: Mrs Marie Partner.
Honours – GM Vauxhall Conference winners 1991–92. **FA Trophy winners** 1991–92.
Colours: Blue and white striped shirts, white shorts, white stockings.

COVENTRY CITY   FA PREMIERSHIP

Batista, Carlos A.
Borrows, Brian
Christie, Iyseden
Dublin, Dion
Gillespie, Gary T.
Hawkins, Colin J.
Lamptey, Nii O.
O'Toole, Gavin F.
Prenderville, Barry J. R.
Shaw, Richard E.
Strachan, Gordon D.
Williams, James D.

Blake, Timothy A.
Burrows, David
Costello, Lorcan M.
Ducros, Andrew J.
Goodwin, Scott
Healy, Brett W.
Mitten, Paul J.
Ogrizovic, Steven
Richardson, Kevin
Shilton, Samuel
Telfer, Paul N.
Williams, Paul D.

Boland, Willie J.
Busst, David J.
Daish, Liam S.
Filan, John R.
Hall, Marcus T. J.
Jess, Eoin
Ndlovu, Peter
Pickering, Albert G.
Salako, John A.
Soares, Isaias M.
Whelan, Noel D.
Willis, Adam P.

League Appearances: Barnwell-Edinboro, J. (1); Boland, W. 2(1); Borrows, B. 21; Burrows, D. 11; Busst, D. 16(1); Christie, I. (1); Cook, P. 2(1); Daish, L. 11; Dublin, D. 34; Filan, J. 13; Hall, M. 24(1); Isaias , 9(2); Jess, E. 9(3); Lamptey, N. 3(3); Ndlovu, P. 27(5); Ogrizovic, S. 25; Pickering, A. 26(4); Rennie, D. 9(2); Richardson, K. 33; Salako, J. 34(3); Shaw, R. 21; Strachan, G. 5(7); Telfer, P. 31; Whelan, N. 21; Whyte, C. 1; Williams, P. 30(2)
League (42): Dublin 14, Whelan 8, Ndlovu 5, Salako 3 (1 pen), Busst 2, Isaias 2, Rennie 2, Williams 2, Daish 1, Jess 1, Telfer 1, own goal 1.
Coca-Cola Cup (7): Lamptey 2, Busst 1, Ndlovu 1 (pen), Richardson 1, Salako 1, Williams P 1.
FA Cup (6): Dublin 2, Pickering 1, Salako 1, Telfer 1, Whelan 1.
Ground: Highfield Road Stadium, King Richard Street, Coventry CV2 4FW. Telephone (01203) 234000.
Record attendance: 51,455 v Wolverhampton W, Division 2, 29 April 1967
Capacity: 23,500.
Manager: Ron Atkinson.
Secretary: Graham Hover.
Honours – Football League: Division 2 Champions – 1966–67. Division 3 Champions – 1963–64. Division 3 (S) Champions 1935–36. **FA Cup winners** 1986–87.
Colours: Sky blue and navy striped shirts, navy shorts and stockings.

CREWE ALEXANDRA   DIV. 2

Adebola, Bamberdele
Garvey, Stephen H.
Little, Colin C.
Pope, Steven A.
Smith, Gareth S.
Unsworth, Lee P.

Barr, William J.
Gayle, Mark S. R.
Macauley, Steven R.
Rivers, Mark A.
Tierney, Francis
Westwood, Ashley M.

Collins, Wayne A.
Lightfoot, Christopher I.
Murphy, Daniel B.
Savage, Robert W.
Turpin, Simon A.
Whalley, Gareth

League Appearances: Adebola, D. 20(9); Barr, B. 15(2); Blissett, G. 10; Booty, M. 21; Clarkson, P. 1(4); Collier, D. 2(4); Collins, W. 37(5); Edwards, R. 29(3); Ellison, L. (1); Garvey, S. 18(11); Gayle, M. 46; Lennon, N. 25; Lightfoot, C. 5(1); Little, C. 7(5); Macauley, S. 27(2); McAllister, B. 13; Murphy, D. 41(1); Ridings, D. 1; Rivers, M. 24(9); Savage, R. 28(2); Smith, S. 24(5); Tierney, F. 21(1); Unsworth, L. 16(13); Westwood, A. 31(2); Whalley, G. 44

League (77): Edwards 15, Murphy 10, Rivers 10, Adebola 8, Macauley 7, Savage 7 (2 pens), Westwood 4, Booty 2, Garvey 2, Lennon 2, Tierney 2, Whalley 2, Blissett 1, Collins 1, Little 1, McAllister 1, Smith 1 (pen), own goal 1.
Coca-Cola Cup (9): Edwards 4, Adebola 1, Collins 1, Lennon 1, Unsworth 1, Whalley 1.
FA Cup (11): Rivers 3, Adebola 2, Edwards 2, Booty 1, Murphy 1, Unsworth 1, Westwood 1.
Ground: Football Ground, Gresty Rd, Crewe CW2 6EB. Telephone (01270) 213014.
Record attendance: 20,000 v Tottenham H, FA Cup 4th rd, 30 January 1960.
Capacity: 6000.
Manager: Dario Gradi.
Secretary: Mrs Gill Palin.
Honours – Welsh Cup: Winners 1936, 1937.
Colours: Red shirts, white shorts, red stockings.

CRYSTAL PALACE   DIV. 1

Andersen, Leif E.	Boxall, Daniel J.	Burton-Godwin, Osagyefo L. E.
Cyrus, Andrew	Davies, Gareth M.	Dyer, Bruce A.
Edworthy, Marc	Enquist, Bjorn	Folan, Anthony S.
Freedman, Douglas A.	Ginty, Rory V.	Gordon, Dean D.
Harris, Jason A. S.	Hopkin, David	Houghton, Raymond J.
Martyn, Antony N.	Matthew, Damian	McKenzie, Leon M.
Ndah, George E.	Parry, David M.	Pitcher, Darren E. J.
Quinn, Robert J.	Roberts, Andrew J.	Rodger, Simon L.
Scully, Anthony D. T.	Thomson, Steven	Tuttle, David P.
Veart, Thomas C.	Vincent, Jamie R.	Wales, Danny P.

League Appearances: Andersen, L. 12(4); Boere, J. (8); Boxall, D. 1; Brown, K. 5(1); Coleman, C. 17; Cox, I. 1(3); Cundy, J. 4; Davies, G. 17(3); Dowie, I. 4; Dyer, B. 21(14); Edworthy, M. 44; Freedman, D. 37(2); Gale, T. 2; Gordon, D. 34; Hopkin, D. 41(1); Houghton, R. 41; Launders, B. (2); Martyn, N. 46; Matthew, D. 4(4); McKenzie, L. 4(8); Ndah, G. 17(6); Pitcher, D. 36; Quinn, R. 1; Roberts, A. 36(2); Rodger, S. 14(10); Scully, T. (2); Shaw, R. 15; Sparrow, P. 1; Taylor, G. 18(2); Tuttle, D. 9(1); Veart, C. 5(7); Vincent, J. 19(6)
League (67): Freedman 20, Dyer 13, Gordon 8 (3 pens), Hopkin 8, Houghton 4, Ndah 4, Brown 2, Davies 2, Dowie 2, Boere 1, Taylor 1, Tuttle 1, own goal 1.
Coca-Cola Cup (6): Hopkin 4, McKenzie 1, Vincent 1.
FA Cup (3): Cox 1, Dyer 1, Taylor 1.
Ground: Selhurst Park, London SE25 6PU. Telephone (0181) 768 6000.
Record attendance: 51,482 v Burnley, Division 2, 11 May 1979. **Capacity:** 26,400.
Manager: Dave Bassett.
Club Secretary: Mike Hurst.
Honours – Football League: Division 1 – Champions 1993–94. Division 2 Champions – 1978–79. Division 3 (S) 1920–21. **Zenith Data Systems Cup winners 1991.**
Colours: Red and blue shirts, white shorts, white stockings.

DARLINGTON   DIV. 3

Appleby, Matthew W.   Bannister, Gary   Barnard, Mark
Blake, Robert J.   Brumwell, Phillip   Carmichael, Matthew
Carss, Anthony J.   Crosby, Andrew K.   Gaughan, Steven E.
Gregan, Sean M.   Johnson, Frank J.   Olsson, Paul
Painter, Peter R.   Shaw, Simon R.   Twynham, Gary S.

League Appearances: Appleby, M. 42(1); Bannister, G. 39(2); Barnard, M. 37; Blake, R. 23(6); Brumwell, P. 16(12); Burridge, J. 3; Carmichael, M. ; Carss, A. 13(15); Crosby, A. 45; Gaughan, S. 34(7); Gregan, S. 38; Guinan, S. 3; Himsworth, G. 26(2); Lucas, D. 6; Mattison, P. 1(6); McMahon, S. 6(4); Muir, I. 4; Naylor, G. 3(1); Neves, R. 3(2); Newell, P. 21; Olsson, P. 34; Painter, R. 33(2); Paulo, P. 4(2); Pollitt, M. 15; Quitongo, J. 1; Robinson, P. (4); Shaw, S. 36(5); Stephenson, A. 1; Twynham, G. 11(2); Worboys, G. 6(8)
League (60): Blake 11, Bannister 10, Painter 8, Appleby 6 (2 pens), Olsson 4, Barnard 3, Gaughan 3, Himsworth 3, Carmichael 2, Carss 2, Worboys 2, Crosby 1, Guinan 1, McMahon 1, Muir 1, Naylor 1, Shaw 1.
Coca-Cola Cup (1): Carss 1.
FA Cup (6): Bannister 1, Brumwell 1, Gaughan 1, Olsson 1, Painter 1, Shaw 1.
Ground: Feethams Ground, Darlington DL1 5JB. Telephone (01325) 465097.
Record attendance: 21,023 v Bolton W, League Cup 3rd rd, 14 November 1960.
Capacity: 7046.
Manager: Jim Platt.
Secretary: S. Morgon.
Honours – Football League: Division 3 (N) Champions – 1924–25. Division 4 Champions – 1990–91.
Colours: Black and white.

DERBY COUNTY   FA PREMIERSHIP

Ashbee, Ian   Boden, Christopher D.   Carbon, Matthew P.
Carsley, Lee K.   Cooper, Kevin L.   Davies, William
Flynn, Sean M.   Gabbiadini, Marco   Hoult, Russell
Kavanagh, Jason C.   Kozluk, Robert   Powell, Christopher G. R.
Powell, Darryl A.   Preece, David W.   Quy, Andrew J.
Radzki, Lee M.   Rowett, Gary   Simpson, Paul D.
Smith, Craig   Stimac, Igor   Sturridge, Dean C.
Sutton, Stephen J.   Sutton, Wayne F.   Taylor, Martin J.
Tretton, Andrew D.   Trollope, Paul J.   Van Der Laan, Robertus P.
Ward, Ashley S.   Wassall, Darren P.   Willems, Ron
Wrack, Darren   Wright, Nicholas J.   Yates, Dean R.

League Appearances: Boden, D. 4; Carbon, M. 2(4); Carsley, L. 31(4); Cooper, K. (1); Flynn, S. 29(13); Gabbiadini, M. 33(6); Harkes, J. 7(1); Hodges, G. 1(8); Hoult, R. 40(1); Kavanagh, J. 8(1); Nicholson, S. 19(1); Powell, C. 19; Powell, D. 37; Preece, D. 10(3); Rowett, G. 34(1); Simpson, P. 21(18); Stallard, M. 3; Stimac, I. 27; Sturridge, D. 33(6); Sutton, S. 6; Sutton, W. 1; Trollope, P. 7(10); Van der Laan, R. 39; Ward, A. 5(2); Wassall, D. 16(1); Webster, S. 3; Willems, R. 31(2); Wrack, D. 2(8); Yates, D. 38

23

League (71): Sturridge 20 (1 pen), Gabbiadini 11, Willems 11 (3 pens), Simpson 10 (2 pens), Van der Laan 6, Powell D 5, Flynn 2, Yates 2, Carsley 1, Preece 1, Stimac 1, Ward 1.
Coca-Cola Cup (4): Gabbiadini 1, Simpson 1, Stallard 1, Willems 1.
FA Cup (2): Gabbiadini 1, Simpson 1.
Ground: Baseball Ground, Shaftesbury Crescent, Derby DE23 8NB. Telephone (01332) 340105.
Record attendance: 41,826 v Tottenham H, Division 1, 20 September 1969.
Capacity: 18,000.
Manager: Jim Smith.
Secretary: Keith Pearson.
Honours – Football League: Division 1 Champions – 1971–72, 1974–75. Division 2 Champions – 1911–12, 1914–15, 1968–69, 1986–87. Division 3 (N) 1956–57. **FA Cup winners** 1945–46.
Colours: White shirts, black shorts, white stockings.

DONCASTER ROVERS   DIV. 3

Byng, David G.
Cramb, Colin
Hayrettin, Hakan
Moore, Darren M.
Parrish, Sean
Smith, Michael
Wheeler, Adam

Clark, Ian D.
Doling, Stuart J.
Jones, Graeme A.
Murphy, James A.
Robertson, Paul
Utley, Darren
Williams, Dean P.

Colcombe, Scott
Gore, Ian G.
Marquis, Paul R.
O'Connor, Gary
Schofield, John D.
Warren, Lee A.

League Appearances: Ashley, K. 3; Barker, R. 5(1); Brabin, G. 31; Brodie, S. 5; Carmichael, M. 19(8); Clark, I. 14(9); Colcombe, S. 21(9); Cramb, C. 20(1); Darby, D. 8(9); Doling, S. (1); Gore, I. 5; Hackett, W. 7; Harper, S. (1); Jones, G. 31(1); Kirby, R. 32(4); Knight, J. 1(3); Marquis, P. 15; Maxfield, S. 12(7); Meara, J. (1); Measham, I. 7(3); Moore, D. 35; Murphy, J. 17(6); Norbury, M. 2(3); Noteman, K. 4; O'Connor, G. 8; Parrish, S. 39(2); Peel, N. 2; Robertson, P. 12(4); Schofield, J. 40(1); Smith, M. 12(1); Speight, M. 1; Suckling, P. 21; Utley, D. 1; Warren, L. 40(2); Wilcox, R. 4; Williams, D. 17; Williams, P. 2(1); Wright, J. 13
League (49): Jones 10 (1 pen), Cramb 7 (1 pen), Parrish 5, Carmichael 4, Darby 4, Schofield 4 (2 pens), Brabin 3, Colcombe 3, Moore 2, Brodie 1, Clark 1, Marquis 1, Maxfield 1, Noteman 1, Williams PA 1, own goal 1.
Coca-Cola Cup (1): Wilcox 1.
FA Cup (2): Carmichael 1, Jones 1 (pen).
Ground: Belle Vue Ground, Doncaster DN4 5HT. Telephone (01302) 539441.
Record attendance: 37,149 v Hull C, Division 3 (N), 2 October 1948. **Capacity:** 8608.
Manager: Sammy Chung.
Secretary: Mrs K. J. Oldale.
Honours – Football League: Division 3 (N) Champions – 1934–35, 1946–47, 1949–50. Division 4 Champions – 1965–66, 1968–69.
Colours: All red.

EVERTON   FA PREMIERSHIP

Ablett, Gary I.
Barrett, Earl D.
Ferguson, Duncan

Allen, Graham
Branch, Paul M.
Grant, Anthony J.

Amokachi, Daniel O.
Ebbrell, John K.
Grugel, Mark A.

Hills, John D.
Horne, Barry
Kanchelskis, Andrei
McCann, Gavin P.
O'Connor, Jonathan
Quayle, Mark
Short, Craig J.
Stuart, Graham C.

Hinchcliffe, Andrew G.
Hottiger, Marc
Kearton, Jason B.
Moore, Neil
Parkinson, Joseph S.
Rideout, Paul D.
Southall, Neville
Unsworth, David G.

Holcroft, Peter I.
Jackson, Matthew A.
Limpar, Anders
Moore, Richard
Price, Christopher
Samways, Vincent
Speare, James
Watson, David

League Appearances: Ablett, G. 13; Amokachi, D. 17(8); Barlow, S. (3); Barrett, E. 8; Branch, M. 1(2); Ebbrell, J. 24(1); Ferguson, D. 16(2); Grant, T. 11(2); Hinchcliffe, A. 23(5); Holmes, P. 1; Horne, B. 25(1); Hottiger, M. 9; Jackson, M. 14; Kanchelskis, A. 32; Limpar, A. 22(6); O'Connor, J. 3(1); Parkinson, J. 28; Rideout, P. 19(6); Samways, V. 3(1); Short, C. 22(1); Southall, N. 38; Stuart, G. 27(2); Unsworth, D. 28(3); Watson, D. 34
League (64): Kanchelskis 16, Stuart 9, Amokachi 6, Rideout 6, Ferguson 5, Ebbrell 4, Limpar 3, Parkinson 3, Hinchcliffe 2 (2 pens), Short 2, Unsworth 2 (2 pens), Grant 1, Horne 1, Hottiger 1, Samways 1, Watson 1, own goal 1.
Coca-Cola Cup (2): Hinchcliffe 1 (pen), Stuart 1.
FA Cup (8): Stuart 3, Ferguson 2, Ablett 1, Amokachi 1, Ebbrell 1.
Ground: Goodison Park, Liverpool L4 4EL. Telephone (0151) 330 2200.
Record attendance: 78,299 v Liverpool, Division 1, 18 September 1948. **Capacity:** 40,200.
Manager: Joe Royle.
Secretary: Michael J. Dunford.
Honours – Football League: Division 1 Champions – 1890–91, 1914–15, 1927–28, 1931–32, 1938–39, 1962–63, 1969–70, 1984–85, 1986–87. Division 2 Champions – 1930–31. **FA Cup:** Winners 1906, 1933, 1966, 1984, 1995. **European Competitions:** European Cup-Winners' Cup winners: 1984–85.
Colours: Blue shirts, white shorts, black/blue stockings.

EXETER CITY   DIV. 3

Bailey, Danny S.
Buckle, Paul J.
Hare, Matthew
Parsley, Neil
Richardson, Jonathan D. P.

Blake, Noel L.
Came, Mark R.
McConnell, Barry
Pears, Richard J.

Braithwaite, Leon J.
Fox, Peter D.
Medlin, Nicholas R. M.
Rice, Gary J.

League Appearances: Anderson, C. 5(8); Bailey, D. 41(1); Blake, N. 44; Bradbury, L. 14; Braithwaite, L. 14(9); Buckle, P. 22; Came, M. 38; Cecere, M. 5(8); Chamberlain, M. 29(4); Cooper, M. 26(1); Coughlin, R. 6(2); Foster, A. 4(3); Fox, P. 46; Gavin, M. 24(4); Hare, M. 10(3); Hughes, D. 25(1); McConnell, B. 1(7); Medlin, N. 2(4); Morgan, J. 2(4); Myers, C. 7(1); Parsley, N. 29(3); Pears, R. 19(3); Phillips, M. 11(2); Rice, G. 17(2); Richardson, J. 43; Ross, M. 7; Sharpe, J. 9(5); Thirlby, A. (2); Turner, R. 6(6)
League (46): Cooper 6 (2 pens), Bradbury 5, Pears 5, Came 4, Braithwaite 3, Phillips 3, Turner 3, Blake 2, Buckle 2, Gavin 2, Ross 2, Bailey 1, Cecere 1, Chamberlain 1, Richardson 1, Sharpe 1, own goals 4.
Coca-Cola Cup (1): Richardson 1.
FA Cup (0).
Ground: St James Park, Exeter EX4 6PX. Telephone (01392) 54073.
Record attendance: 20,984 v Sunderland, FA Cup 6th rd (replay), 4 March 1931.
Capacity: 10,570.

Manager: Peter Fox.
Secretary: Margaret Bond.
Honours – Football League: Division 4 Champions – 1989–90. **Division 3 (S) Cup:** Winners 1934.
Colours: Red and white striped shirts, black shorts, red stockings.

FULHAM   DIV. 3

Adams, Michael R.	Angus, Terence N.	Barkus, Lea P.
Blake, Mark C.	Brooker, Paul	Conroy, Michael K.
Cusack, Nicholas J.	Hamill, Rory	Herrera, Roberto
Jupp, Duncan A.	Lange, Anthony S.	McAree, Rodney J.
Mison, Michael	Morgan, Simon C.	Scott, Robert
Thomas, Martin R.		

League Appearances: Adams, M. 5; Angus, T. 30(1); Barber, P. 13; Barkus, L. 3(6); Blake, M. 35(3); Bolt, D. 7(4); Bower, D. 4; Brazil, G. 17(1); Brooker, P. 9(11); Conroy, M. 38(2); Cusack, N. 38(4); Finnigan, T. 1(1); Gray, M. 6; Hamill, R. 6(19); Hamsher, J. (3); Harrison, L. 5; Herrera, R. 42(1); Jupp, D. 35(1); Lange, T. 41; Marshall, J. 14(2); McAree, R. 16(1); Mison, M. 16(7); Moore, K. 17(3); Morgan, S. 41; Scott, R. 21; Simpson, G. 5(2); Taylor, M. 7; Thomas, M. 32(5); Williams, C. 2(11)
League (57): Conroy 9, Morgan 6, Blake 5 (2 pens) Cusack 5, Scott 5, Thomas 5, Mison 4, Adams 2, Angus 2, Bolt 2 (2 pens), Brooker 2, Hamill 2, McAree 2, Barber 1, Barkus 1, Brazil 1, Moore 1, own goals 2.
Coca-Cola Cup (6): Conroy 2, Barkus 1, Brazil 1, Cusack 1, Mison 1.
FA Cup (9): Conroy 3, Angus 1, Brooker 1, Cusack 1, Hamill 1, Jupp 1, Thomas 1.
Ground: Craven Cottage, Stevenage Rd, Fulham, London SW6 6HH. Telephone (0171) 736 6561.
Record attendance: 49,335 v Millwall, Division 2, 8 October 1938. **Capacity:** 14,969.
Manager: Micky Adams.
Secretary: Mrs Janice O'Doherty.
Honours – Football League: Division 2 Champions – 1948–49. Division 3 (S) Champions – 1931–32.
Colours: White shirts, red and black trim, black shorts, white stockings red and black trim.

GILLINGHAM   DIV. 2

Bailey, Dennis L.	Butler, Philip A.	Butler, Stephen
Carpenter, Richard	Fortune-West, Leopold O.	Freeman, Darren B. A.
Green, Richard E.	Harris, Mark A.	Martin, David
Naylor, Dominic J.	O'Connor, Mark A.	Puttnam, David P.
Ratcliffe, Simon	Rattray, Kevin W.	Smith, Neil J.
Stannard, James	Thomas, Glen A.	Watson, Paul D.

League Appearances: Ansah, A. (2); Arnott, A. (1); Bailey, D. 40(5); Brown, S. (1); Butler, S. 14(6); Butler, T. 34(2); Carpenter, R. 7(5); Castle, S. 5(1); Dunne, J. 1(1); Fortune-West, L. 36(4); Foster, A. 1(10); Freeman, D. 4(6); Gayle, J. 9; Green, R. 35; Harris, M. 44; Manuel, B. 6(4); Martin, D. 27(4); Micklewhite, G. 17(14); Naylor, D. 30(1); O'Connor, M. 18; Puttnam, D. 10(16); Ratcliffe, S. 41; Rattray, K. 18(8); Smith, N. 36(1); Stannard, J. 46; Thomas, G. 14(1); Watson, A. 10; Watson, P. 3(5)

League (49): Fortune-West 12, Bailey 8 (1 pen), Butler S 5 (1 pen), Gayle 3, Ratcliffe 3, Rattray 3, Butler T 2, Green 2, Harris 2, Castle 1, Foster 1, Martin 1, Naylor 1, O'Connor 1, Puttnam 1, Smith 1, Watson A 1, own goal 1.
Coca-Cola Cup (3): Bailey 1, Fortune-West 1, Naylor 1.
FA Cup (6): Fortune-West 2, Bailey 1, Martin 1, Ratcliffe 1, own goal 1.
Ground: Priestfield Stadium, Gillingham ME7 4DD. Telephone (0134) 851854, 576828.
Record attendance: 23,002 v QPR, FA Cup 3rd rd 10 January 1948. **Capacity:** 10,600.
Manager: Tony Pulis.
Acting Secretary: Mrs G. E. Poynter.
Honours – Football League: Division 4 Champions – 1963–64.
Colours: Blue shirts, white shorts, white stockings.

GRIMSBY TOWN   DIV. 1

Childs, Gary P. C.	Clare, Daryl A.	Crichton, Paul A.
Fickling, Ashley	Forrester, Jamie M.	Gallimore, Anthony M.
Gowshall, Joby	Groves, Paul	Handyside, Peter D.
Jobling, Kevin A.	Lester, Jack W.	Lever, Mark
Livingstone, Stephen	McDermott, John	Mendonca, Clive P.
Neil, James D.	Pearcey, Jason K.	Rodger, Graham
Shakespeare, Craig R.	Smith, Richard G.	Southall, Leslie N.
Walker, John	Woods, Neil S.	

League Appearances: Bonetti, I. 19; Butler, P. 3; Childs, G. 33(2); Clare, D. (1); Crichton, P. 44; Croft, G. 36; Dobbin, J. 21(5); Fickling, A. 5(6); Flatts, M. 4(1); Forrester, J. 23(5); Gallimore, T. 10; Gambaro, E. (1); Groves, P. 46; Handyside, P. 30; Jewell, P. 2(3); Jobling, K. 3; Laws, B. 21(6); Lester, J. (5); Lever, M. 23(1); Livingstone, S. 33(5); McDermott, J. 27(1); Mendonca, C. 8; Neil, J. 1; Pearcey, J. 2; Rodger, G. 14(2); Shakespeare, C. 24(4); Smith, R. 18; Southall, N. 28(5); Walker, J. 1(1); Warner, V. 3; Watson, T. (2); Woods, N. 24(9).
League (55): Livingstone 11, Groves 10, Forrester 5, Mendonca 4 (1 pen), Bonetti 3, Childs 3, Dobbin 3, Woods 3, Shakespeare 2 (1 pen), Southall 2, Croft 1, Gallimore 1, Jewell 1, Laws 1, Lever 1, McDermott 1, Walker 1, own goals 2.
Coca-Cola Cup (2): Southall 1, Woods 1.
FA Cup (12): Forrester 3, Livingstone 2, Woods 2, Bonetti 1, Childs 1, Groves 1, Laws 1, Southall 1.
Ground: Blundell Park, Cleethorpes, South Humberside DN35 7PY. Telephone (01472) 697111.
Record attendance: 31,651 v Wolverhampton W, FA Cup 5th rd, 20 February 1937.
Capacity: 8686.
Manager: Brian Laws.
Secretary: Ian Fleming.
Honours – Football League: Division 2 Champions – 1900–01, 1933–34. Division 3 (N) Champions – 1925–26, 1955–56. Division 3 Champions – 1979–80. Division 4 Champions – 1971-72. **League Group Cup:** Winners 1981–82.
Colours: Black and white striped shirts, black shorts, white stockings.

HARTLEPOOL UNITED   DIV. 3

Allon, Joseph B.   Halliday, Stephen W.   Homer, Christopher
Houchen, Keith M.   Howard, Steven J.   Ingram, Stuart D.
McAuley, Sean   McGuckin, Thomas I.   Tait, Michael P.

League Appearances: Allinson, J. 3(1); Allon, J. 22; Billing, P. 35(1); Canham, T. 25(4); Conlon, P. 11(4); Debont, A. 1; Dixon, A. 3; Ford, G. 2(1); Foster, L. (1); Gallagher, I. 1; Halliday, S. 36(3); Henderson, D. 33(3); Homer, C. 1(4); Horne, B. 32; Houchen, K. 36(2); Howard, S. 32(7); Hutt, S. (1); Ingram, D. 32(1); Jones, S. 7(2); Key, L. 1; Lee, G. 3(3); Lowe, K. 13; Lynch, C. 13(6); McAuley, S. 46; McGuckin, I. 40; O'Connor, P. 1; Oliver, K. 7(6); Reddish, S. 18(2); Roberts, B. 4; Slater, D. (1); Sloan, S. 1(5); Stokoe, G. 8; Tait, M. 38(1); Walton, P. 1(5).
League (47): Allon 8, Halliday 7, Howard 7, Houchen 6, Conlon 4, Henderson 3, Lowe 3, Ingram 2, McGuckin 2, Tait 2, Canham 1, Lynch 1, own goal 1.
Coca-Cola Cup (1): McGuckin 1.
FA Cup (2): Halliday 1, Sloan 1.
Ground: The Victoria Ground, Clarence Road, Hartlepool TS24 8B2. Telephone (01429) 272584.
Record attendance: 17,426 v Manchester U, FA Cup 3rd rd, 5 January 1957.
Capacity: 7229.
Manager: Keith Houchen.
Secretary: Stuart Bagnall.
Honours – Nil.
Colours: Blue and white stripes.

HEREFORD UNITED   DIV. 3

Brough, John R.   Downing, Keith G.   Fishlock, Murray E.
James, Anthony C.   Mackenzie, Christopher N. Pitman, Jamie R.
Preedy, Phillip   Smith, Dean   Stoker, Gareth
Warner, Robert M.   White, Stephen J.   Wilkins, Richard J.

League Appearances: Blatherwick, S. 10; Brough, J. 22; Clarke, D. 5; Cross, N. 32(5); Debont, A. 8; Downing, K. 29; Evans, D. 24; Fishlock, M. 26(1); Hall, L. (1); Hargreaves, C. 15(2); James, T. 17; Lloyd, K. 25(2); Lyne, N. 22(10); MacKenzie, C. 38; Pick, G. 10(4); Pitman, J. 12(1); Pounder, T. 31(3); Preedy, P. 5(8); Reece, A. 6; Smith, D. 39(1); Steele, T. (7); Stoker, G. 30(3); Watkiss, S. 19; White, S. 39(1); Wilkins, R. 42
League (65): White 29 (2 pens), Cross 8, Smith 8 (3 pens), Fishlock 3, Stoker 3, Wilkins 3, Hargreaves 2, James 2, Pounder 2, Blatherwick 1, Brough 1, Lyne 1, Mackenzie 1, Preedy 1.
Coca-Cola Cup (2): Reece 1, Smith 1.
FA Cup (6): White 3, Brough 1, Cross 1, Stoker 1.
Ground: Edgar Street, Hereford HR4 9JU. Telephone (01432) 276666.
Record attendance: 18,114 v Sheffield W, FA Cup 3rd rd, 4 January 1958.
Capacity: 8843.
Manager: Graham Turner.
Secretary: J. Fennessy.
Honours – Football League: Division 3 Champions – 1975–76. **Welsh Cup winners:** 1990.
Colours: White & black striped shirts, black shorts, white stockings.

HUDDERSFIELD TOWN

DIV. 1

Baldry, Simon	Booth, Andrew D.	Bullock, Darren J.
Collins, Sam J.	Collins, Simon	Cowan, Thomas
Crosby, Gary	Dalton, Paul	Dunn, Iain G. W.
Dyson, Jonathan P.	Edwards, Robert	Francis, Stephen S.
Gray, Kevin J.	Heary, Thomas M.	Illingworth, Jeremy M.
Jenkins, Stephen R.	Jepson, Ronald F.	Kelly, Mark A.
Lawson, Ian J.	Makel, Lee R.	Murphy, Stephen
Norman, Anthony J.	O'Connor, Derek P.	Reid, Paul R.
Rowe, Rodney C.	Ryan, Robert P.	Scully, Patrick J.
Sinnott, Lee		

League Appearances: Baldry, S. 3(11); Booth, A. 43; Brown, K. 5; Bullock, D. 42; Collins, S. 18(12); Cowan, T. 43; Crosby, G. (1); Dalton, P. 29; Dunn, I. 3(11); Duxbury, L. 3; Dyson, J. 15(2); Edwards, R. 13; Francis, S. 43; Gray, K. 38; Jenkins, S. 31; Jepson, R. 40(3); Logan, R. 2; Makel, L. 33; Norman, T. 3; Reid, P. 8(5); Rowe, R. 6(8); Scully, P. 25; Sinnott, L. 32; Thornley, B. 12; Trevitt, S. 4; Turner, A. 2(3); Ward, M. 7(1); Whitney, J. 3(1)
League (61): Booth 16, Jepson 12 (4 pens), Edwards 7, Bullock 6, Dalton 5, Collins 3, Cowan 2, Makel 2, Thornley 2, Jenkins 1, Rowe 1, Scully 1, Turner 1, own goals 2.
Coca-Cola Cup (6): Booth 3, Bullock 1, Collins 1, Dalton 1.
FA Cup (7): Booth 2, Jepson 2 (1 pen), Bullock 1, Cowan 1, Rowe 1.
Ground: The Alfred McAlpine Stadium, Huddersfield HD1 6PX. Telephone (01484) 420335/6.
Record attendance: 67,037 v Arsenal, FA Cup 6th rd, 27 February 1932. **Capacity:** 19,500.
Manager: Brian Horton.
Secretary: Alan D. Sykes.
Honours – Football League: Division 1 Champions – 1923–24, 1924–25, 1925–26. Division 2 Champions – 1969–70. Division 4 Champions – 1969–70. **FA Cup winners** 1922.
Colours: Blue and white striped shirts, white shorts, white stockings.

HULL CITY

DIV. 3

Allison, Neil J.	Brown, Andrew S.	Carroll, Roy E.
Darby, Duane A.	Dewhurst, Robert M.	Fewings, Paul J.
Gilbert, Kenneth R.	Lowthorpe, Adam	Mann, Neil
Marks, Jamie H.	Mason, Andrew J.	Maxfield, Scott
Peacock, Richard J.	Quigley, Michael A.	Trevitt, Simon
Wharton, Paul W.	Wilson, Stephen L.	

League Appearances: Abbott, G. 31; Allison, N. 33(2); Brown, L. 21(2); Carroll, R. 23; Dakin, S. 2(4); Darby, D. 8; Davison, B. 11; Dewhurst, R. 16; Fettis, A. 4(3); Fewings, P. 16(9); Fidler, R. (1); Gilbert, K. 6(7); Gordon, G. 3(10); Graham, J. 24; Hobson, G. 28(1); Humphries, G. 9(3); Lawford, C. 20(11); Lee, C. 25(3); Lowthorpe, A. 15(4); Mann, N. 34(4); Marks, J. 4(1); Mason, A. 10(10); Maxfield, S. 3(1); Peacock, R. 39(6); Quigley, M. 9(4); Trevitt, S. 25; Watson, T. 4; Wharton, P. 7(2); Wilkinson, I. 8; Williams, A. 33(1); Wilson, S. 19; Windass, D. 16

29

League (36): Peacock 7, Abbott 6, Davison 4 (1 pen), Windass 4 (1 pen), Gordon 3, Allison 2, Fewings 2, Brown 1, Darby 1, Graham 1, Lee 1, Mann 1, Mason 1, Quigley 1, Wilkinson 1.
Coca-Cola Cup (5): Windass 3, Allison 1, Fewings 1.
FA Cup (0).
Ground: Boothferry Park, Hull HU4 6EU. Telephone (01482) 351119.
Record attendance: 55,019 v Manchester U, FA Cup 6th rd, 26 February 1949.
Capacity: 16,564.
Manager: Terry Dolan.
Secretary: M.W. Fish.
Honours – Football League: Division 3 (N) Champions – 1932–33, 1948–49. Division 3 Champions – 1965–66.
Colours: Black and amber striped shirts, black shorts, amber stockings.

IPSWICH TOWN   DIV. 1

Ellis, Kevin E.	Forrest, Craig L.	Gaughan, Kevin
Gregory, Neil R.	Marshall, Ian P.	Mason, Paul D.
Mathie, Alexander M.	Milton, Simon C.	Mowbray, Anthony M.
Naylor, Richard A.	Norfolk, Lee R.	Scowcroft, James B.
Sedgley, Stephen P.	Slater, Stuart I.	Stockwell, Michael T.
Swailes, Christopher W.	Tanner, Adam D.	Taricco, Mauricio R.
Thomsen, Claus	Uhlenbeek, Gustaaf R.	Vaughan, Anthony J.
Wark, John	Williams, David G.	Wright, Richard I.

League Appearances: Appleby, R. (3); Barber, F. 1; Chapman, L. 2(4); Forrest, C. 21; Gregory, N. 5(12); Linighan, D. 2; Marshall, I. 35; Mason, P. 24(2); Mathie, A. 39; Milton, S. 34(3); Mowbray, T. 19; Palmer, S. 5; Petterson, A. 1; Scowcroft, J. 13(10); Sedgley, S. 40; Slater, S. 11(6); Stockwell, M. 33(4); Swailes, C. 4(1); Tanner, A. 3(7); Taricco, M. 36(3); Thompson, N. 5; Thomsen, C. 36(1); Uhlenbeek, G. 37(3); Vaughan, T. 19(6); Wark, J. 13(1); Williams, G. 42; Wright, R. 23; Yallop, F. 3(4)
League (79): Marshall 19, Mathie 18, Milton 9, Mason 7, Sedgley 4 (2 pens), Uhlenbeek 4, Gregory 2, Mowbray 2, Scowcroft 2, Slater 2, Thomsen 2, Wark 2 (1 pen), Stockwell 1, Thompson 1, Vaughan 1, Williams 1, own goals 2.
Coca-Cola Cup (2): Sedgley 1, Thomsen 1.
FA Cup (3): Mason 3.
Ground: Portman Road, Ipswich, Suffolk IP1 2DA. Telephone (01473) 219211.
Record attendance: 38,010 v Leeds U, FA Cup 6th rd, 8 March 1975. **Capacity:** 22,600.
Manager: George Burley.
Secretary: David C. Rose.
Honours – Football League: Division 1 Champions – 1961–62. Division 2 Champions – 1960–61, 1967–68, 1991–92. Division 3 (S) Champions – 1953–54, 1956–57. FA Cup: Winners 1977–78. **European Competitions:** UEFA Cup winners: 1980–81, 1982–83.
Colours: Blue shirts, white shorts, blue stockings.

LEEDS UNITED — FA PREMIERSHIP

Beeney, Mark R.
Bowman, Robert A.
Byrne, Nicky
Dorigo, Anthony R.
Foster, Martin
Jackson, Mark G.
Kewell, Harry
Maybury, Alan
Pemberton, John M.
Speed, Gary A.
Wetherall, David

Beesley, Paul
Boyle, Wesley S.
Couzens, Andrew J.
Evans, Paul A.
Gray, Andrew D.
Jobson, Richard I.
Masinga, Philemon R.
McAllister, Gary
Radebe, Lucas
Tinkler, Mark
Wright, Andrew J.

Blunt, Jason
Brolin, Tomas
Deane, Brian C.
Ford, Mark
Harte, Ian P.
Kelly, Garry
Matthews, Lee J.
Palmer, Carlton L.
Shepherd, Paul
Wallace, Rodney S.
Yeboah, Anthony

League Appearances: Beeney, M. 10; Beesley, P. 8(2); Blunt, J. 2(1); Bowman, R. 1(2); Brolin, T. 17(2); Chapman, L. 2; Couzens, A. 8(6); Deane, B. 30(4); Dorigo, T. 17; Ford, M. 12; Gray, A. 12(3); Harte, I. 22(3); Jackson, M. 1(1); Jobson, R. 12; Kelly, G. 34; Kewell, H. 2; Lukic, J. 28; Masinga, P. 5(4); Maybury, A. 1; McAllister, G. 36; Palmer, C. 35; Pemberton, J. 16(1); Radebe, L. 10(3); Sharp, K. (1); Speed, G. 29; Tinkler, M. 5(4); Wallace, R. 12(12); Wetherall, D. 34; Whelan, N. 3(5); White, D. 1(3); Worthington, N. 12(4); Yeboah, T. 22
League (40): Yeboah 12, Deane 7, McAllister 5 (2 pens), Brolin 4, Wetherall 4, Palmer 2, Speed 2, Dorigo 1, Jobson 1, Wallace 1, White 1.
Coca-Cola Cup (13): Speed 3, Yeboah 3, Deane 2, Masinga 2, Couzens 1, McAllister 1, own goal 1.
FA Cup (7): McAllister 3, Deane 1, Speed 1, Wallace 1, Yeboah 1.
Ground: Elland Road, Leeds LS11 0ES. Telephone (0113) 2716037.
Record attendance: 57,892 v Sunderland, FA Cup 5th rd (replay), 15 March 1967.
Capacity: 40,000.
Manager: Howard Wilkinson.
Company Secretary: Nigel Pleasants.
Honours – Football League: Division 1 Champions – 1968–69, 1973–74, 1991–92. Division 2 Champions – 1923–24, 1963–64, 1989–90. **FA Cup:** Winners 1972. **Football League Cup:** Winners 1967–68. **European Competitions: European Fairs Cup winners:** 1967–68, 1970–71.
Colours: All white, yellow and blue trim.

LEICESTER CITY — FA PREMIERSHIP

Carey, Brian P.
Hallam, Craig D.
Kaamark, Pontus S.
Lennon, Neil F.
Parker, Garry S.
Robins, Mark G.
Walsh, Steven
Willis, James A.

Claridge, Stephen E.
Heskey, Emile W. I.
Kalac, Zeljko
Lewis, Neil A.
Poole, Kevin
Rolling, Franck J.
Watts, Julian

Grayson, Simon N.
Hill, Colin F.
Lawrence, James H.
McMahon, Sam K.
Roberts, Iwan W.
Taylor, Scott D.
Whitlow, Michael

League Appearances: Blake, M. 6(2); Carey, B. 16(3); Claridge, S. 14; Corica, S. 16; Gee, P. 1(1); Grayson, S. 39(2); Heskey, E. 20(10); Hill, C. 24(3); Izzet, M. 8(1); Joachim, J. 14(8); Kalac, Z. 1; Kamark, P. 1; Lawrence, N. 10(5); Lennon, N. 14(1); Lewis, N. 10(4); Lowe, D. 21(7); McMahon, S. 12(1); Parker, G. 36(4); Philpott, L. 1(5); Poole, K. 45; Roberts, I. 34(3); Robins, M. 19(12); Rolling, F. 17; Smith, R. 1; Taylor, S. 39; Walsh, S. 37; Watts, J. 9; Whitlow, M. 41(1); Willis, J. 11(1)

League (66): Roberts 19, Heskey 7, Robins 6, Taylor 6, Claridge 5, Walsh 4, Lowe 3, Parker 3 (1 pen), Whitlow 3, Corica 2, Grayson 2, Carey 1, Izzet 1, Joachim 1, Lennon 1, Lewis 1, McMahon 1.
Coca-Cola Cup (6): Robins 4, Joachim 1, Roberts 1.
FA Cup (0).
Ground: City Stadium, Filbert St, Leicester LE2 7FL. Telephone (0116) 2555000.
Record attendance: 47,298 v Tottenham H, FA Cup 5th rd, 18 February 1928.
Capacity: 22,517.
Manager: Martin O'Neill.
Football Secretary: Ian Silvester.
Honours – Football League: Division 2 Champions – 1924–25, 1936–37, 1953–54, 1956–57, 1970–71, 1979–80. **Football League Cup:** Winners 1964.
Colours: Royal blue and white.

LEYTON ORIENT   DIV. 3

Arnott, Andrew J.	Austin, Kevin	Ayorinde, Samuel T.
Baker, Joseph P. J.	Caldwell, Peter J.	Chapman, Daniel G.
Hanson, David P.	Hendon, Ian M.	Inglethorpe, Alex M.
Kelly, Anthony O. N.	McCarthy, Alan J.	Purse, Darren J.
Shearer, Lee S.	Warren, Mark W.	West, Colin

League Appearances: Arnott, A. 19; Austin, K. 32(8); Ayorinde, S. 1; Baker, J. 4(16); Bellamy, G. 32; Berry, G. 4(3); Brooks, S. 34(7); Caldwell, P. 28; Chapman, D. 38; Cockerill, G. 38; Currie, D. 9(1); Fearon, R. 18; Gray, A. 3(4); Hanson, D. 7(4); Hendon, I. 38; Inglethorpe, A. 30; Kelly, R. 5(1); Kelly, T. 32(2); Lakin, B. 5(3); McCarthy, A. 40(3); Purse, D. 9(3); Shearer, L. 5(3); Stanislaus, R. 20(1); Warren, M. 15(7); Watson, M. 1(1); West, C. 39; Williams, L. 1(2)
League (44): West 16 (1 pen), Inglethorpe 9, Arnott 3, Kelly T 3, Brooks 2, Chapman 2, Hendon 2, Austin 1, Bellamy 1, Cockerill 1, Hanson 1, Shearer 1, Warren 1, Watson 1.
Coca-Cola Cup (2): Austin 1, West 1 (pen).
FA Cup (0).
Ground: Leyton Stadium, Brisbane Road, Leyton, London E10 5NE. Telephone (0181) 539 2223/4.
Record attendance: 34,345 v West Ham U, FA Cup 4th rd, 25 January 1964.
Capacity: 12,573.
Manager: Pat Holland.
Secretary: David Burton.
Honours – Football League: Division 3 Champions – 1969–70. Division 3 (S) Champions – 1955–56.
Colours: Red shirts with white pinstripe, white shorts, red stockings.

LINCOLN CITY   DIV. 3

Ainsworth, Gareth	Alcide, Colin J.	Barnett, Jason V.
Bos, Gijsbert	Brown, Grant A.	Brown, Stephen R.
Davies, Neil	Dixon, Ben	Fleming, Terry M.
Holmes, Steven P.	Minett, Jason	Richardson, Barry
Robertson, John N.	Wanless, Paul S.	Westley, Shane L. M.
Whitney, Jonathan D.		

League Appearances: Ainsworth, G. 31; Alcide, C. 22(5); Allon, J. 3(1); Appleton, M. 4; Barnett, J. 27(5); Bos, G. 10(1); Bound, M. 3(1); Brightwell, D. 5; Brown, G. 34; Brown, S. 22(4); Carbon, M. 26; Daley, P. 6(6); Davis, D. 3; Daws, T. 8(3); Dixon, B. 10(2); Dyer, A. 1; Fleming, T. 17(5); Greenall, C. 4; Holmes, S. 23; Huckerby, D. 16; Hulme, K. 4(1); Johnson, A. 17(5); Johnson, D. 14(10); Key, L. 5; Leaning, A. 7; Megson, G. 2; Minett, J. 39(3); Mudd, P. 2(2); Onwere, U. 33(2); Platnauer, N. (1); Puttnam, D. 4(1); Richardson, B. 34; Robertson, J. 21(1); Storey, B. (2); Wanless, P. 7(1); West, D. 7(1); Westley, S. 9; Whitney, J. 25(1); Williams, S. 1(2)

League (57): Ainsworth 12, Alcide 6, Bos 5, Minett 5 (3 pens), Onwere 4 (3 pens), Brown S 3, Carbon 3, Daws 3, Barnett 2 (1 pen), Holmes 2, Huckerby 2, Whitney 2, Daley 1, Johnson D 1, Puttnam 1, Storey 1, West 1, Westley 1, own goals 2.

Coca-Cola Cup (0).

FA Cup (0).

Ground: Sincil Bank, Lincoln LN5 8LD. Telephone (01522) 522224.

Record attendance: 23,196 v Derby Co, League Cup 4th rd, 15 November 1967.

Capacity: 10,918.

Manager: John Beck.

Secretary: G.R. Davey.

Honours – Football League: Division 3 (N) Champions – 1931–32, 1947–48, 1951–52. Division 4 Champions – 1975–76.

Colours: Red and white striped shirts, black shorts, red stockings with white trim.

LIVERPOOL   FA PREMIERSHIP

Babb, Philip A.
Carragher, James L.
Collymore, Stanley V.
Harkness, Steven
Jones, Phillip L.
Matteo, Dominic
Neal, Ashley J.
Scales, John R.
Warner, Anthony R.

Barnes, John C. B.
Cassidy, Jamie
Culshaw, Thomas A.
James, David B.
Jones, Robert M.
McAteer, Jason W.
Redknapp, Jamie F.
Thomas, Michael L.
Whitehead, Russell

Bjornebye, Stig I.
Charnock, Philip A.
Fowler, Robert B.
Jensen, Michael S.
Kennedy, Mark
McManaman, Steven
Ruddock, Neil
Thompson, David A.
Wright, Mark

League Appearances: Babb, P. 28; Barnes, J. 36; Bjornebye, S. 2; Clough, N. 1(1); Collymore, S. 30(1); Fowler, R. 36(2); Harkness, S. 23(1); James, D. 38; Jones, R. 33; Kennedy, M. 1(3); Matteo, D. 5; McAteer, J. 27(2); McManaman, S. 38; Redknapp, J. 19(4); Ruddock, N. 18(2); Rush, I. 10(10); Scales, J. 27; Thomas, M. 18(9); Wright, M. 28

League (70): Fowler 28 (1 pen), Collymore 14, McManaman 6, Ruddock 5, Rush 5, Barnes 3, Redknapp 3, Wright 2, Harkness 1, Thomas 1, own goals 2.

Coca-Cola Cup (7): Fowler 2, Harkness 1, McManaman 1, Rush 1, Scales 1, Thomas 1.

FA Cup (19): Fowler 6, Collymore 5, McAteer 3, McManaman 2, Rush 1, own goals 2.

Ground: Anfield Road, Liverpool L4 0TH. Telephone (0151) 263 2361.

Record attendance: 61,905 v Wolverhampton W, FA Cup 4th rd, 2 February 1952.

Capacity: 41,000.

Manager: Roy Evans.

Chief Executive/General Secretary: Peter Robinson.

Honours – Football League: Division 1 – Champions 1900–01, 1905–06, 1921–22, 1922–23, 1946–47, 1963–64, 1965–66, 1972–73, 1975–76, 1976–77, 1978–79, 1979–80, 1981–82, 1982–83, 1983–84, 1985–86, 1987–88, 1989–90 (Liverpool have a record number of 18 League Championship wins). Division 2 Champions – 1893–94,

33

1895–96, 1904–05, 1961–62. FA Cup: Winners 1965, 1974, 1986, 1989, 1992. **League Cup:** Winners 1981, 1982, 1983, 1984, 1995. Super Cup: Winners 1985–86. **European Competitions: European Cup winners:** 1976–77, 1977–78, 1980–81, 1983–84. **UEFA Cup winners:** 1972–73, 1975–76. **Super Cup winners:** 1977. **Colours:** All red.

LUTON TOWN   DIV. 2

Abbey, Nathanael	Alexander, Graham	Chenery, Ben R.
Davis, Kelvin G.	Davis, Stephen M.	Evers, Sean A.
Feuer, Anthony I.	Grant, Kim T.	Greene, David M.
Guentchev, Bontcho L.	Harvey, Richard G.	Hughes, Ceri M.
James, Julian C.	Johnson, Marvin A.	Kean, Robert S.
Linton, Desmond M.	Marshall, Dwight W.	McLaren, Paul A.
Oakes, Scott J.	Oldfield, David C.	Patterson, Darren J.
Peake, Trevor	Pedersen, Johnny V.	Riseth, Vidar
Simpson, Gary J.	Skelton, Aaron M.	Taylor, John P.
Thomas, Mitchell A.	Thorpe, Anthony	Upson, Matthew J.
Waddock, Gary P.	Willmott, Christopher A.	Woodsford, Jamie M.

League Appearances: Alexander, G. 35(2); Chenery, B. 2; Davis, K. 6; Davis, S. 36; Douglas, S. 3(5); Evers, S. 1; Feuer, T. 38; Grant, K. 10; Guentchev, B. 25(10); Harvey, R. 28(8); Hughes, C. 21(2); James, J. 23(4); Johnson, G. 4(1); Johnson, M. 34(2); Linton, D. 6(4); Marshall, D. 23(3); McLaren, P. 9(3); Oakes, S. 26(3); Oldfield, D. 23(11); Patterson, D. 21(2); Peake, T. 15(3); Riseth, V. 6(5); Sommer, J. 2; Taylor, J. 18(10); Thomas, M. 25(2); Thorpe, T. 23(10); Tomlinson, G. 1(6); Vilstrup, J. 6(1); Waddock, G. 32(4); Wilkinson, P. 3; Woodsford, J. 1(2)
League (40): Guentchev 9 (4 pens), Marshall 9, Thorpe 7 (1 pen), Grant 3, Oakes 3, Davis S 2, Oldfield 2, Alexander 1, Douglas 1, Harvey 1, Hughes 1, McLaren 1.
Coca-Cola Cup (2): Johnson 1, Marshall 1.
FA Cup (1): Marshall 1.
Ground: Kenilworth Road Stadium, 1 Maple Rd, Luton, Beds. LU4 8AW. Telephone (01582) 411622.
Record attendance: 30,069 v Blackpool, FA Cup 6th rd replay, 4 March 1959.
Capacity: 9975.
Manager: Lennie Lawrence.
Secretary: Cherry Newbery.
Honours – Football League: Division 2 Champions – 1981–82. Division 4 Champions – 1967–68. Division 3 (S) Champions – 1936–37. **Football League Cup winners** 1987–88.
Colours: White shirts with blue and orange trim, blue shorts with white and orange trim, blue stockings, with white, orange trim.

MANCHESTER CITY   DIV. 1

Beagrie, Peter S.	Beech, Christopher	Bentley, James G.
Brightwell, Ian R.	Brown, Michael R.	Callaghan, Anthony S.
Clough, Nigel H.	Creaney, Gerard	Crooks, Lee R.
Curle, Keith	Dibble, Andrew	Edghill, Richard A.
Foster, John C.	Freeman, Nathan	Frontzeck, Michael
Greenacre, Christopher M.	Harris, Samuel R.	Hiley, Scott
Immel, Eike	Ingram, Rae	Kavelashvili, Mikhail

Kelly, Raymond   Kernaghan, Alan N.   Kerr, David W.
Kinkladze, Georgi   Lomas, Stephen M.   Margetson, Martyn W.
McGlinchey, Brian K.   Morley, David T.   Phillips, Martin J.
Quinn, Niall J.   Rosler, Uwe   Rowlands, Aled J. R.
Summerbee, Nicholas J.   Symons, Christopher J.   Tarpey, Gerard E.
Thomas, Scott L.   Whitley, James   Whitley, Jeffrey

League Appearances: Beagrie, P. 4(1); Brightwell, I. 26(3); Brown, M. 16(5); Clough, N. 15; Creaney, G. 6(9); Curle, K. 32; Edghill, R. 13; Ekelund, R. 2(2); Flitcroft, G. 25; Foster, J. 4; Frontzeck, M. 11(1); Hiley, S. 2(4); Immel, E. 38; Ingram, R. 5; Kavelashvili, M. 3(1); Kernaghan, A. 4(2); Kerr, D. (1); Kinkladze, G. 37; Lomas, S. 32(1); Mazzarelli, G. 2; Phelan, T. 9; Phillips, M. 2(9); Quinn, N. 24(8); Rosler, U. 34(2); Summerbee, N. 33(4); Symons, K. 38; Walsh, P. 3
League (33): Rosler 9 (1 pen), Quinn 8, Kinkladze 4, Creaney 3, Lomas 3, Clough 2, Symons 2, Kavelashvili 1, Summerbee 1.
Coca-Cola Cup (4): Rosler 2, Curle 1 (pen), Quinn 1.
FA Cup (10): Quinn 2, Rosler 2, Clough 1, Creaney 1, Flitcroft 1, Kinkladze 1, Lomas 1, own goal 1.
Ground: Maine Road, Moss Side, Manchester M14 7WN. Telephone (0161) 224 5000.
Record attendance: 84,569 v Stoke C, FA Cup 6th rd, 3 March 1934 (British record for any game outside London or Glasgow). **Capacity:** 31,257.
Manager: Alan Ball.
General Secretary: J. B. Halford.
Honours – Football League: Division 1 Champions – 1936–37, 1967–68. Division 2 Champions – 1898–99, 1902–03, 1909–10, 1927–28, 1946–47, 1965–66. **FA Cup winners** 1904, 1934, 1956, 1969. **Football League Cup winners** 1970, 1976.
European Competitions: European Cup-Winners' Cup winners: 1969–70.
Colours: Sky blue shirts, white shorts, white stockings.

MANCHESTER UNITED   FA PREMIERSHIP

Appleton, Michael A.   Beckham, David R. J.   Brebner, Grant I.
Brightwell, Stuart   Brown, David A.   Bruce, Stephen R.
Butt, Nicholas   Cantona, Eric   Casper, Christopher M.
Clegg, Michael J.   Cole, Andrew   Cooke, Terence J.
Coton, Anthony P.   Culkin, Nicholas J.   Curtis, John C. K.
Davies, Simon I.   Gibson, Paul R.   Giggs, Ryan J.
Hilton, David   Irwin, Joseph D.   Keane, Roy M.
May, David   McClair, Brian J.   McGibbon, Patrick C. G.
Mulryne, Philip P.   Murdock, Colin J.   Mustoe, Neil J.
Neville, Gary A.   Neville, Philip J.   O'Kane, John A.
Pallister, Garry A.   Pilkington, Kevin W.   Schmeichel, Peter B.
Scholes, Paul   Sharpe, Lee S.   Smith, Thomas E.
Teather, Paul   Thornley, Benjamin L.   Tomlinson, Graham
Wallwork, Ronald   Wilson, Mark A.

League Appearances: Beckham, D. 26(7); Bruce, S. 30; Butt, N. 31(1); Cantona, E. 30; Cole, A. 32(2); Cooke, T. 1(3); Davies, S. 1(5); Giggs, R. 30(3); Irwin, D. 31; Keane, R. 29; May, D. 11(5); McClair, B. 12(10); Neville, G. 30(1); Neville, P. 21(3); O'Kane, J. (1); Pallister, G. 21; Parker, P. 5(1); Pilkington, K. 2(1); Prunier, W. 2; Schmeichel, P. 36; Scholes, P. 16(10); Sharpe, L. 21(10); Thornley, B. (1)
League (73): Cantona 14 (4 pens), Cole 11, Giggs 11, Scholes 10, Beckham 7, Keane 6, Sharpe 4, McClair 3, Butt 2, Bruce 1, Irwin 1, May 1, Pallister 1, own goal 1.

Coca-Cola Cup (3): Scholes 2, Cooke 1.
FA Cup (14): Cantona 5 (1 pen), Cole 2, Sharpe 2, Beckham 1, Butt 1, Giggs 1, Parker 1, Scholes 1.
Ground: Old Trafford, Manchester M16 0RA. Telephone (0161) 872 1661.
Record attendance: 76,962 Wolverhampton W v Grimsby T, FA Cup semi-final. 25 March 1939. **Capacity:** 54,000
Manager: Alex Ferguson CBE.
Secretary: Kenneth Merrett.
Honours – FA Premier League: Champions – 1992–93, 1993–94, 1995–96. **Football League:** Division 1 Champions – 1907–8, 1910–11, 1951–52, 1955–56, 1956–57, 1964–65, 1966–67. Division 2 Champions – 1935–36, 1974–75. **FA Cup winners** 1909, 1948, 1963, 1977, 1983, 1985, 1990, 1994, 1996. **Football League Cup winners** 1991–92. **European Competitions: European Cup winners:** 1967–68. **European Cup-Winners' Cup winners:** 1990–91. **European Fairs Cup winners:** 1964–65. **Super Cup winners:** 1991.
Colours: Red shirts, white shorts, black stockings.

MANSFIELD TOWN   DIV. 3

Bowling, Ian	Doolan, John	Eustace, Scott D.
Hackett, Warren J.	Hadley, Stewart A.	Harper, Steven J.
Ireland, Simon P.	Kilcline, Brian	Onuora, Ifem
Parkin, Stephen J.	Peters, Mark	Sale, Mark D.
Sherlock, Paul G.	Wood, Simon	

League Appearances: Alexander, K. (1); Baraclough, I. 11; Barber, P. 4; Boothroyd, A. 42(1); Bowling, I. 44; Brien, T. 4; Carmichael, M. 1; Clarke, D. 12(3); Doolan, J. 42; Eustace, S. 25(2); Hackett, W. 32; Hadley, S. 27(6); Harper, S. 29; Howarth, L. 17; Ireland, S. 38(1); Kerr, D. 4(1); Kilcline, B. 18(1); Lampkin, K. 2(4); Onuora, I. 7(7); Parkin, S. 25(1); Peel, N. 2; Peters, M. 21; Robinson, I. 4(5); Sale, M. 24(3); Sedgemore, B. 4(5); Sherlock, P. 14(4); Slawson, S. 21(8); Timons, C. 16(1); Todd, M. 10(2); Trinder, J. 1; Varadi, I. 1; Weaver, N. 1; Williams, R. 5(5); Wood, S. 9(1)
League (54): Hadley 8, Sale 7, Harper 5, Ireland 5, Slawson 5, Hackett 3, Williams 3, Baraclough 2, Boothroyd 2 (2 pens), Doolan 2, Peters 2, Sherlock 2, Barber 1, Carmichael 1, Eustace 1, Onuora 1, Parkin 1, Robinson 1, Timons 1, Wood 1.
Coca-Cola Cup (1): Sale 1.
FA Cup (4): Doolan 1, Harper 1, Parkin 1, Sherlock 1.
Ground: Field Mill Ground, Quarry Lane, Mansfield NG18 5DA. Telephone (01623) 23567.
Record attendance: 24,467 v Nottingham F, FA Cup 3rd rd, 10 January 1953.
Capacity: 7033.
Manager: Andy King.
Secretary: Christine Reynolds.
Honours – Football League: Division 3 Champions – 1976–77. Division 4 Champions – 1974–75. **Freight Rover Trophy winners** 1986–87.
Colours: Amber & blue striped shirts, amber shorts, blue stockings.

MIDDLESBROUGH   FA PREMIERSHIP

Anderson, Vivian A.	Bagayoke, Salif	Barmby, Nicholas J.
Barron, Michael J.	Blackmore, Clayton G.	Cox, Neil J.
Cummins, Michael	Fjortoft, Jan A.	Fleming, Curtis

Freestone, Christopher M.
Junior (Juninho), Oswaldo G.
Lee, Patrick M.
Miller, Alan J.
Morris, Christopher B.
Ormerod, Anthony
Richardson, Paul
Stamp, Phillip L.
Vickers, Stephen
White, Alan
Wilkinson, Paul

Hendrie, John G.
Kavanagh, Graham A.
Liddle, Craig G.
Moore, Alan
Mustoe, Robbie
Pearson, Nigel D.
Roberts, Ben J.
Summerbell, Mark
Walsh, Gary
White, Darren

Hignett, Craig J.
Leal (Branco), Claudio I. V.
McCargle, Stephen
Moreno, Jaime M.
O'Halloran, Keith J.
Pollock, Jamie
Robson, Bryan
Swalwell, Andrew D.
Whelan, Philip J.
Whyte, Derek

League Appearances: Barmby, N. 32; Barron, M. 1; Blackmore, C. 4(1); Branco, 5(2); Campbell, A. 1(1); Cox, N. 35; Fjortoft, J. 27(1); Fleming, C. 13; Freestone, C. 2(1); Hendrie, J. 7(6); Hignett, C. 17(5); Juninho, 20(1); Kavanagh, G. 6(1); Liddle, C. 12(1); Miller, A. 6; Moore, A. 5(7); Moreno, J. 2(5); Morris, C. 22(1); Mustoe, R. 21; O'Halloran, K. 2(1); Pearson, N. 36; Pollock, J. 31; Robson, B. 1(1); Stamp, P. 11(1); Summerbell, M. (1); Vickers, S. 32; Walsh, G. 32; Whelan, P. 9(4); Whyte, D. 24(1); Wilkinson, P. 2(1).
League (35): Barmby 7, Fjortoft 6, Hignett 5 (2 pens), Cox 2, Juninho 2, Morris 2, Stamp 2, Fleming 1, Freestone 1, Hendrie 1, Kavanagh 1 (pen), Mustoe 1, Pollock 1, Vickers 1, Whelan 1, own goal 1.
Coca-Cola Cup (7): Fjortoft 2, Hignett 2, Barmby 1, Mustoe 1, Vickers 1.
FA Cup (2): Barmby 1, Pollock 1.
Ground: Cellnet Riverside Stadium, Middlesbrough, Cleveland TS3 6RS. Telephone (01642) 227227.
Record attendance: 53,596 v Newcastle U, Division 1, 27 December 1949.
Capacity: 30,500.
Manager: Bryan Robson.
Secretary: Karen Nelson.
Honours — Football League: Division 1 Champions 1994–95. Division 2 Champions 1926–27, 1928–29, 1973–74. **Amateur Cup winners** 1895, 1898, **Anglo-Scottish Cup:** Winners 1975–76.
Colours: Red shirts, white shorts, red stockings.

MILLWALL   DIV. 2

Aris, Steven
Cadette, Richard R.
Connor, James R.
Forbes, Steven D.
Iga, Andrew
Lavin, Gerard
McRobert, Lee
Nightingale, Lewis
Rogan, Anthony G. P.
Thatcher, Ben D.
Witter, Anthony J.

Berry, Greg J.
Canoville, Dean
Dolby, Tony C.
Fuchs, Uwe
Keller, Kasey
Malkin, Christopher G.
Neill, Lucas E.
Rae, Alex
Savage, David P. T.
Van Blerk, Jason C.

Bowry, Robert
Carter, Timothy D.
Doyle, Maurice
Harle, Michael J. L.
Keown, Darren P.
Markey, Brendon
Newman, Richard A.
Roche, Stephen M.
Stevens, Keith H.
Webber, Damian J.

League Appearances: Bennett, M. 1(1); Berry, G. 1; Black, K. 1(2); Bowry, B. 33(5); Cadette, R. (1); Carter, T. 4; Connor, J. 7(1); Dixon, K. 15(7); Dolby, T. 6(4); Doyle, M. 15(3); Forbes, S. (4); Fuchs, U. 21(11); Gordon, D. 6; Keller, K. 42; Kulkov, V. 6; Lavin, G. 18(2); Malkin, C. 39(4); McRobert, L. 1(6); Neill, L. 5(8); Newman, R. 34(2); Rae, A. 37; Rogan, A. 4(4); Savage, D. 17(10); Stevens, K. 39;

37

Taylor, S. 12(10); Thatcher, B. 41(1); Van Blerk, J. 42; Webber, D. 8(8); Weir, M. 8; Witter, T. 30(1); Yuran, S. 13
League (43): Rae 13 (5 pens), Malkin 11, Dixon 5 (1 pen), Fuchs 5, Bowry 2, Stevens 2, Black 1, Newman 1, Van Blerk 1, Witter 1, Yuran 1.
Coca-Cola Cup (4): Taylor 2, Rae 1 (pen), Savage 1.
FA Cup (3): Rae 2, Malkin 1.
Ground: The Den, Zampa Road, Bermondsey SE16 3LN. Telephone (0171) 232 1222.
Record attendance: 20,093 v Arsenal, FA Cup 3rd rd, 10 January 1994. **Capacity:** 20,146.
Manager: Jimmy Nicholl.
Chief Executive/Secretary: Graham Hortop.
Honours – Football League: Division 2 Champions – 1987–88. Division 3 (S) Champions – 1927–28, 1937–38. Division 4 Champions – 1961–62. **Football League Trophy winners** 1982–83.
Colours: Blue shirts, white shorts, blue stockings.

NEWCASTLE UNITED   FA PREMIERSHIP

Albert, Philippe
Asprilla Hinestroza, Faustino H.
Brayson, Paul
Eatock, David
Ferdinand, Leslie
Harper, Stephen
Howey, Stephen N.
Kitson, Paul
Srnicek, Pavel

Allen, Malcolm
Barton, Warren D.
Beardsley, Peter A.
Clark, Lee
Elliott, Robert J.
Gillespie, Keith R.
Hislop, Neil S.
Huckerby, Darren
Lee, Robert M.
Watson, Stephen C.

Arnison, Paul S.
Batty, David
Beresford, John
Crawford, James
Elliott, Stuart T.
Ginola, David
Holland, Christopher J.
Keen, Peter
Peacock, Darren

League Appearances: Albert, P. 19(4); Asprilla, F. 11(3); Barton, W. 30(1); Batty, D. 11; Beardsley, P. 35; Beresford, J. 32(1); Clark, L. 22(6); Elliott, R. 5(1); Ferdinand, L. 37; Fox, R. 2(2); Gillespie, K. 26(2); Ginola, D. 34; Hislop, S. 24; Hottiger, M. (1); Howey, S. 28; Huckerby, D. (1); Kitson, P. 2(5); Lee, R. 36; Peacock, D. 33(1); Sellars, S. 2(4); Srnicek, P. 14(1); Watson, S. 15(8)
League (66): Ferdinand 25, Lee 8 (1 pen), Beardsley 8 (2 pens), Ginola 5, Albert 4, Gillespie 4, Asprilla 3, Watson 3, Clark 2, Kitson 2, Batty 1, Howey 1.
Coca-Cola Cup (13): Ferdinand 3, Beardsley 2, Peacock 2, Albert 1, Barton 1, Gillespie 1, Lee 1, Sellars 1, Watson 1.
FA Cup (3): Albert 1, Beardsley 1 (pen), Ferdinand 1.
Ground: St James' Park, Newcastle-upon-Tyne NE1 4ST. Telephone (0191) 201 8400.
Record attendance: 68,386 v Chelsea, Division 1, 3 Sept 1930. **Capacity:** 36,610.
Manager: Kevin Keegan.
General Manager/Secretary: R. Cushing.
Honours – Football League: Division 1 – Champions 1904–05, 1906–07, 1908–09, 1926–27, 1992–93. Division 2 Champions – 1964–65. **FA Cup winners** 1910, 1924, 1932, 1951, 1952, 1955. **Texaco Cup winners** 1973–74, 1974–75. **European Competitions: European Fairs Cup winners:** 1968–69. **Anglo-Italian Cup winners:** Winners 1973.
Colours: Black and white striped shirts, black shorts, black stockings.

NORTHAMPTON TOWN
DIV. 3

Burns, Christopher
Gibb, Alistair S.
Lee, Christian
Peer, Dean
Turley, William L.
White, Jason G.

Cahill, Oliver F.
Grayson, Neil
Maddison, Lee R.
Sampson, Ian
Warburton, Raymond
Woodman, Andrew J.

Colkin, Lee
Hunter, Roy I.
O'Shea, Daniel E.
Thompson, Garry L.
Warner, Michael J.

League Appearances: Armstrong, G. 4; Beckford, J. (1); Burns, C. 40(3); Cahill, O. 2(1); Colkin, L. 14(10); Doherty, N. 3(6); Gibb, A. 12(11); Grayson, N. 37(5); Hughes, D. 7(1); Hunter, R. 26(8); Lee, C.1(4); Maddison, L. 21; Mountfield, D. 4; Norton, D. 42(2); O'Shea, D. 37(1); Peer, D. 37(5); Sampson, I. 30(3); Scott, R. 5; Smith, T. 2; Taylor, M. 1; Taylor, S. 1(1); Thompson, G. 21(13); Turley, B. 2; Warburton, R. 44; White, J. 40(5); Williams, G. 25(10); Woodman, A. 44; Worboys, G. 4(9)
League (51): White 16 (1 pen), Grayson 11, Burns 7 (2 pens), Sampson 4, Warburton 3, Gibb 2, Thompson 2, Armstrong 1, Colkin 1, Doherty 1, Peer 1, Williams 1, Worboys 1.
Coca-Cola Cup (3): Burns 1 (pen), Colkin 1, Peer 1.
FA Cup (1): Warburton 1.
Ground: Sixfields, Upton Way, Northampton NN5 4EG. Telephone (01604) 757773.
Record attendance: 24,523 v Fulham, Division 1, 23 April 1966. **Capacity:** 7653.
Manager: Ian Atkins.
Secretary: Barry Collins.
Honours – Football League: Division 3 Champions – 1962–63. Division 4 Champions – 1986–87.
Colours: Claret with white shirts, yellow panel, white shorts, claret stockings.

NORWICH CITY
DIV. 1

Adams, Neil J.
Brownrigg, Andrew D.
Eadie, Darren M.
Johnson, Andrew J.
Mills, Daniel J.
Polston, John D.
Scott, Keith
Sutch, Daryl

Akinbiyi, Adeola P.
Carey, Shaun P.
Fleck, Robert
Marshall, Andrew J.
Newman, Robert N.
Prior, Spencer J.
Shore, James A.
Ullathorne, Robert

Bradshaw, Carl
Cureton, Jamie
Gunn, Bryan J.
Milligan, Michael J.
O'Neill, Keith P.
Rush, Matthew J.
Simpson, Karl E.
Wright, Jonathan

League Appearances: Adams, N. 40(2); Akinbiyi, A. 13(9); Bowen, M. 30(1); Bradshaw, C. 18(3); Carey, S. 6(3); Crook, I. 27(1); Cureton, J. 4(8); Eadie, D. 29(2); Fleck, R. 37(4); Goss, J. 9(7); Gunn, B. 43; Johnson, A. 23(3); Marshall, A. 3; Milligan, M. 21(7); Mills, D. 8(6); Molby, J. 3; Newman, R. 15(8); Newsome, J. 26(1); O'Neill, K. 12(7); Polston, J. 27(3); Prior, S. 42(2); Rush, M. 1(1); Scott, K. 5(7); Sheron, M. 2(5); Simpson, K. 1; Sutch, D. 7(6); Ullathorne, R. 26(3); Ward, A. 28; Wright, J. 1
League (59): Fleck 10, Ward 10, Johnson 7, Eadie 6, Newsome 4, Akinbiyi 3, Adams 2, Bowen 2, Crook 2, Cureton 2, Milligan 2, Scott 2, Bradshaw 1, Goss 1, Newman 1, O'Neill 1, Prior 1, Sheron 1, own goal 1.
Coca-Cola Cup (16): Ward 3, Akinbiyi 2, Fleck 2, Sheron 2, Crook 1, Eadie 1, Johnson 1, Mills 1, Molby 1, Ullathorne 1, own goal 1.

FA Cup (1): Newsome 1.
Ground: Carrow Road, Norwich NR1 1JE. Telephone (01603) 760760.
Record attendance: 43,984 v Leicester C, FA Cup 6th rd, 30 March 1963. **Capacity:** 21,994.
Manager: Mike Walker.
Secretary: A. R. W. Neville.
Honours – Football League: Division 2 Champions – 1971–72, 1985–86. Division 3 (S) Champions – 1933–34. **Football League Cup:** Winners 1962, 1985.
Colours: Yellow shirts, green shorts, yellow stockings.

NOTTINGHAM FOREST   FA PREMIERSHIP

Archer, Paul	Armstrong, Steven C.	Atkinson, Craig
Barber, Andrew J.	Bart-Williams, Christopher G.	Black, Kingsley
Blatherwick, Steven S.	Bough, Gareth G.	Burns, John C.
Campbell, Kevin J.	Chettle, Stephen	Clark, Richard
Cooper, Colin T.	Cowling, Lee	Crossley, Mark G.
Dawson, Andrew	Fettis, Alan	Finnigan, John
Fitchett, Scott	Gemmill, Scot	George, Daniel S.
Grim, Robert J.	Guinan, Stephen	Haaland, Alf I. R.
Henry, David	Howe, Stephen R.	Irving, Richard J.
Lee, Jason	Lyttle, Desmond	McGregor, Paul A.
Melton, Stephen	Morgan, Ian	O'Neill, Shane
Orr, Stephen	Pearce, Stuart	Phillips, David O.
Rigby, Malcom R.	Roy, Bryan E. S.	Silenzi, Andrea
Smith, Paul A.	Stone, Steven B.	Stratford, Lee
Thom, Stuart	Todd, Andrew J.	Turner, Barry
Walker, Justin	Walley, Mark	Warner, Vance
Whitney, Scott	Woan, Ian S.	Wright, Thomas J.

League Appearances: Allen, C. 1(2); Bart-Williams, C. 33; Black, K. 1(1); Bohinen, L. 7; Campbell, K. 21; Chettle, S. 37; Cooper, C. 37; Crossley, M. 38; Gemmill, S. 26(5); Guinan, S. 1(1); Haaland, A. 12(5); Howe, S. 4(5); Irving, R. (1); Lee, J. 21(7); Lyttle, D. 32(1); McGregor, P. 7(7); Pearce, S. 31; Phillips, D. 14(4); Roy, B. 25(3); Silenzi, A. 3(7); Stone, S. 34; Woan, I. 33
League (50): Lee 8, Roy 8 (1 pen) Woan 8, Stone 7, Cooper 5, Campbell 3, Pearce 3 (2 pens), Howe 2, McGregor 2, Allen 1, Gemmill 1, Lyttle 1, own goal 1.
Coca-Cola Cup (4): Bohinen 2, Pearce 1, Silenzi 1.
FA Cup (10): Campbell 3, Woan 3 (1 pen) Pearce 2 (1 pen), Roy 1, Silenzi 1.
Ground: City Ground, Nottingham NG2 5FJ. Telephone (0115) 9526000.
Record attendance: 49,945 v Manchester U, Division 1, 28 October 1967. **Capacity:** 30,602.
Manager: Frank Clark.
Secretary: Paul White.
Honours – Football League: Division 1 – Champions 1977–78. Division 2 Champions – 1906–07, 1921–22. Division 3 (S) Champions – 1950–51. **FA Cup:** Winners 1898, 1959. **Football League Cup:** Winners 1977–78, 1978–79, 1988–89, 1989–90. **Anglo-Scottish Cup:** Winners 1976–77. **Simod Cup:** Winners 1989. **Zenith Data Systems Cup:** Winners 1991–92. **European Competitions: European Cup winners:** 1978–79, 1979–80, 1980–81. **Super Cup winners:** 1979–80.
Colours: Red shirts, black shoulders, white shorts, red stockings.

NOTTS COUNTY   DIV. 2

Agana, Patrick A. O.   Arkins, Vincent   Baraclough, Ian R.
Battersby, Tony   Butler, Peter J.   Derry, Shaun P.
Forsyth, Michael E.   Gallagher, Thomas D.   Galloway, Michael A.
Hogg, Graeme J.   Hunt, James M.   Jemson, Nigel B.
Jones, Gary   Martindale, Gary   Murphy, Shaun P.
Pollitt, Michael F.   Redmile, Matthew I.   Richardson, Ian G.
Ridgway, Ian D.   Rogers, Paul A.   Simpson, Michael
Strodder, Gary J.   Turner, Philip   Walker, Richard N.
Ward, Darren   Wilder, Christopher J.

League Appearances: Agana, T. 20(9); Arkins, V. 17(6); Ashcroft, L. 4(2);
Baraclough, I. 35; Battersby, T. 14(7); Derry, S. 12; Devlin, P. 26; Finnan, S. 14(3);
Gallagher, T. 21(1); Galloway, M. 7(2); Hogg, G. 10; Hoyle, C. 2; Hunt, J. 10;
Jemson, N. 2(1); Jones, G. 16(2); Legg, A. 24(1); Marsden, C. 3; Martindale, G.
13(3); McSwegan, G. (3); Mills, G. 11(2); Murphy, S. 39; Nicol, S. 13; Richardson, I.
15; Rogers, P. 21; Short, C. (2); Simpson, M. 18(5); Strodder, G. 43; Turner, P. 12;
Walker, R. 11; Ward, D. 46; White, D. 18(2); Wilder, C. 9
League (63): White 8 (1 pen), Arkins 7, Battersby 7, Devlin 6 (1 pen), Martindale
6, Jones 5, Legg 4, Murphy 3, Strodder 3, Agana 2, Baraclough 2, Finnan 2,
Gallagher 2, Nicol 2, Rogers 2, Hunt 1, Turner 1.
Coca-Cola Cup (6): White 6 (1 pen).
FA Cup (4): Legg 2, Gallagher 1, Rogers 1.
Ground: County Ground, Meadow Lane, Nottingham NG2 3HJ. Telephone (0115)
952 9000.
Record attendance: 47,310 v York C, FA Cup 6th rd, 12 March 1955. **Capacity:** 20,300.
Manager: Steve Thompson.
Secretary: Ian Moat.
Honours – Football League: Division 2 Champions – 1896–97, 1913–14, 1922–23.
Division 3 (S) Champions – 1930–31, 1949–50. Division 4 Champions – 1970–71.
FA Cup: Winners 1893–94. **Anglo-Italian Cup:** Winners 1995.
Colours: Black and white striped shirts, white shorts, black stockings.

OLDHAM ATHLETIC   DIV. 1

Allott, Mark S.   Banger, Nicholas L.   Barlow, Stuart
Beckford, Darren R.   Beresford, David   Darnbrough, Lee
Fleming, Craig   Gannon, John S.   Gerrard, Paul W.
Graham, Richard E.   Halle, Gunnar   Hallworth, Jonathan G.
Henry, Nicholas I.   Holden, Andrew I.   Hughes, Andrew J.
Innes, Mark   Lonergan, Darren   Makin, Christopher
McCarthy, Sean C.   McNiven, David J.   McNiven, Scott A.
Orlygsson, Thorvaldur   Pemberton, Martin C.   Redmond, Stephen
Richardson, Lee J.   Richardson, Lloyd M.   Rickers, Paul S.
Serrant, Carl   Sharp, Graeme M.   Snodin, Ian

League Appearances: Banger, N. 8(5); Barlow, S. 21(5); Beckford, D. 12(8);
Beresford, D. 8(20); Bernard, P. 7; Brennan, M. 23(2); Creaney, G. 8(1); Fleming,
C. 21(1); Gannon, J. 5; Gerrard, P. 36; Graham, R. 31(1); Halle, G. 37; Hallworth,
J. 10(1); Henry, N. 14; Hughes, A. 10(5); Jobson, R. 12; Lonergan, D. 1(1); Makin,
C. 39; McCarthy, S. 30(5); McNiven, S. 14(1); Olney, I. 1; Orlygsson, T. 15(1);

41

Pemberton, M. (2); Pointon, N. 3(1); Redmond, S. 37(3); Richardson, L. 27;
Rickers, P. 23; Serrant, C. 20; Snodin, I. 24(2); Vonk, M. 5; Wilkinson, P. 4
League (54): Richardson 11 (7 pens), McCarthy 10, Barlow 7, Brennan 3, Halle 3,
Banger 2, Beckford 2, Beresford 2, Creaney 2, Makin 2, Bernard 1, Graham 1,
Hughes 1, Redmond 1, Serrant 1, Vonk 1, Wilkinson 1, own goals 3.
Coca-Cola Cup (1): Halle 1.
FA Cup (2): Beckford 2 (1 pen).
Ground: Boundary Park, Oldham OL1 2PA. Telephone (0161) 624 4972.
Record attendance: 47,671 v Sheffield W, FA Cup 4th rd. 25 January 1930.
Capacity: 13,700.
Manager: Graeme Sharp.
Secretary: Terry Cale.
Honours – Football League: Division 2 Champions – 1990–91, Division 3 (N)
Champions – 1952–53. Division 3 Champions – 1973–74.
Colours: All blue with red and white trim.

OXFORD UNITED   DIV. 1

Aldridge, Martin J.	Allen, Christopher A.	Angel, Mark
Beauchamp, Joseph D.	Druce, Mark A.	Elliott, Matthew S.
Ford, Michael P.	Ford, Robert J.	Gilchrist, Philip A.
Gray, Martin D.	Lewis, Michael	Marsh, Simon T.
Massey, Stuart A.	Moody, Paul	Murphy, Matthew S.
Reeves, Stephen T.	Robinson, Leslie	Rush, David
Smith, David C.	Whitehead, Philip M.	

League Appearances: Aldridge, M. 15(3); Allen, C. 13(11); Angel, M. 16(11);
Beauchamp, J. 25(7); Biggins, W. 8(2); Carter, T. 12; Druce, M. 1(7); Elliott, M. 45;
Ford, B. 26(2); Ford, M. 43(1); Gilchrist, P. 42; Gray, M. 6(1); Lewis, M. 5(14);
Marsh, S. 2(3); Massey, S. 33(2); Moody, P. 30(12); Murphy, M. 13(21); Powell, P.
1(2); Robinson, L. 40(1); Rush, D. 41(2); Smith, D. 45; Whitehead, P. 34; Wood, S.
10(1)
League (76): Moody 17 (2 pens), Rush 11, Aldridge 9, Elliott 8, Beauchamp 7,
Murphy 5, Massey 4, Allen 3, Ford B 3, Gilchrist 3, Ford M 2, Angel 1, Biggins 1
(pen), Smith 1, own goal 1.
Coca-Cola Cup (7): Allen 2, Biggins 1 (pen), Moody 1, Murphy 1, Robinson 1,
Smith 1.
FA Cup (16): Moody 5, Massey 4, Ford B 2, Wood 2, Beauchamp 1, Ford M 1,
Rush 1.
Ground: Manor Ground, Headington, Oxford OX3 7RS. Telephone (01865)
61503.
Record attendance: 22,750 v Preston NE, FA Cup 6th rd, 29 February 1964.
Capacity: 9572.
Manager: Denis Smith.
Secretary: Mick Brown.
Honours – Football League: Division 2 Champions – 1984–85. Division 3
Champions – 1967–68, 1983–84. **Football League Cup:** Winners 1985–86.
Colours: Gold shirts with blue sleeves, blue shorts, blue stockings.

PETERBOROUGH UNITED   DIV. 2

Basham, Michael   Carter, Darren S.   Charlery, Kenneth
Clark, Simon   Ebdon, Marcus   Farrell, Sean P.
Foran, Mark J.   Grazioli, Guiliano S. L. Griffiths, Carl B.
Heald, Gregory J.   Le Bihan, Neil E. R.   McGleish, Scott
Morrison, David E.   Power, Lee M.   Sedgemore, Benjamin R.
Sheffield, Jonathan   Spearing, Anthony   Tyler, Mark R.

League Appearances: Ansah, A. (2); Ashley, K. 9; Basham, M. 13(1); Blount, M.
4(1); Breen, G. 25; Carter, D. 30(7); Charlery, K. 19; Clark, S. 39(1); Codner, R.
1(1); Dobson, T. 4; Drury, A. (1); Ebdon, M. 39; Farrell, S. 20(6); Foran, M. 17;
Furnell, A. (1); Grazioli, G. 2(1); Gregory, D. (3); Griffiths, C. 4; Heald, G. 40;
Hooper, D. 4; Inman, N. 1; Le Bihan, N. 16(9); Manuel, B. 13; Martindale, G.
26(5); McGleish, S. 3(9); Meredith, T. 1(1); Morrison, D. 21(3); Power, L. 25(13);
Rioch, G. 13(5); Robinson, S. 5; Sedgemore, B. 13(4); Shaw, P. 12; Sheffield, J. 46;
Spearing, T. 9; Williams, L. 32(1); Williams, S. (3)
League (59): Martindale 15 (1 pen), Farrell 9, Charlery 7, Power 6 (1 pen), Shaw 5,
Heald 4, Ebdon 2 (1 pen), Morrison 2, Ansah 1, Basham 1, Carter 1, Clark 1,
Foran 1, Grazioli 1, Griffiths 1, Manuel 1, Spearing 1.
Coca-Cola Cup (5): Manuel 3, Le Bihan 1, Martindale 1.
FA Cup (6): Farrell 3, Le Bihan 2, Ebdon 1.
Ground: London Road Ground, Peterborough PE2 8AL. Telephone (01733)
63947.
Record attendance: 30,096 v Swansea T, FA Cup 5th rd, 20 February 1965.
Capacity: 15,500.
Manager: Barry Fry.
Company Secretary: Miss Caroline Hand.
Honours – Football League: Division 4 Champions – 1960–61, 1973–74.
Colours: Royal blue shirts, white shorts, white stockings.

PLYMOUTH ARGYLE   DIV. 2

Baird, Ian J.   Barlow, Martin D.   Billy, Christopher A.
Blackwell, Kevin P.   Clayton, Gary   Corazzin, Giancarlo M.
Curran, Christopher   Dungey, James A.   Evans, Michael J.
Heathcote, Michael   Illman, Neil D.   Leadbitter, Christopher J.
Littlejohn, Adrian S.   Logan, Richard A.   Mauge, Ronald C.
O'Hagan, Daniel A. N.   Patterson, Mark   Saunders, Mark
Williams, Paul R. C.   Wotton, Paul A.

League Appearances: Baird, I. 24(3); Barlow, M. 25(3); Billy, C. 22(10); Blackwell,
K. 20; Burnett, W. 6; Cherry, S. 16; Clayton, G. 32(4); Corazzin, C. 1(5); Curran, C.
6(2); Evans, M. 41(4); Hammond, N. 4; Heathcote, M. 44; Hill, K. 21(3); Hodgson,
D. 3(2); Leadbitter, C. 29(4); Littlejohn, A. 40(2); Logan, R. 25(6); Magee, K. (4);
Mauge, R. 36(1); McCall, S. 2(2); Nugent, K. 4(2); O'Hagan, D. (6); Partridge, S.
6(1); Patterson, M. 42(1); Petterson, A. 6; Saunders, M. 4(6); Shilton, S. (1);
Twiddy, C. 1(1); Williams, P. 46; Wotton, P. (1)
League (68): Littlejohn 17, Evans 12 (2 pens), Mauge 7, Baird 5, Barlow 5, Billy 4,
Heathcote 4, Logan 4, Clayton 4, Partridge 2, Williams 2, Corazzin 1 (pen),
Leadbitter 1, Saunders 1, own goal 1.
Coca-Cola Cup (1): Heathcote 1.
FA Cup (5): Baird 1, Heathcote 1, Leadbitter 1, Littlejohn 1, own goal 1.

Ground: Home Park, Plymouth, Devon PL2 3DQ. Telephone (01752) 562561.
Record attendance: 43,596 v Aston Villa, Division 2, 10 October 1936.
Capacity: 19,630.
Manager: Neil Warnock.
Secretary: Michael Holladay.
Honours – Football League: Division 3 (S) Champions – 1929–30, 1951–52.
Division 3 Champions – 1958–59.
Colours: Green and black striped shirts, black shorts, black stockings.

PORTSMOUTH   DIV. 1

Allen, Martin J.	Awford, Andrew T.	Bradbury, Lee M.
Burton, Deon J.	Butters, Guy	Carter, James W. C.
Dobson, Anthony J.	Durnin, John	Flahavan, Aaron A.
Hall, Paul A.	Hinshelwood, Danny M.	Igoe, Samuel G.
Knight, Alan E.	McGrath, Lloyd A.	McLoughlin, Alan F.
Perrett, Russell	Pethick, Robert J.	Rees, Jason M.
Russell, Lee	Simpson, Fitzroy	Thomson, Andrew J.
Tilley, Anthony J.	Walsh, Paul A.	Waterman, David G.
Wood, Paul A.		

League Appearances: Allen, M. 27; Awford, A. 17(1); Bradbury, L. 3(9); Burton, D. 24(8); Butters, G. 37; Carter, J. 31(4); Creaney, G. 3; Dobson, T. 7(2); Durnin, J. 30(11); Gittens, J. 14(1); Griffiths, C. 2(12); Hall, P. 44(2); Hinshelwood, D. 5; Igoe, S. 4(18); Knight, A. 42; McLoughlin, A. 38(2); Perrett, R. 8(1); Pethick, R. 30(8); Poom, M. 4; Rees, J. 15(6); Russell, L. 17(2); Simpson, F. 27(3); Stimson, M. 14; Symons, K. 1; Thomson, A. 15(1); Walsh, P. 21; Whitbread, A. 13; Wood, P. 13(2)
League (61): Hall 10, McLoughlin 10 (6 pens), Burton 7, Simpson 5 (1 pen), Walsh 5, Allen 4, Carter 4, Creaney 3 (1 pen), Durnin 3, Butters 2, Griffiths 2 (1 pen), Awford 1, Gittens 1, Rees 1, Stimson 1, Wood 1, own goal 1.
Coca-Cola Cup (0).
FA Cup (0).
Ground: Fratton Park, Frogmore Rd, Portsmouth PO4 8RA. Telephone (01705) 731204.
Record attendance: 51,385 v Derby Co, FA Cup 6th rd, 26 February 1949.
Capacity: 26,452.
Manager: Terry Fenwick.
Secretary: Paul Weld.
Honours – Football League: Division 1 Champions – 1948–49, 1949–50. Division 3 (S) Champions – 1923–24. Division 3 Champions – 1961–62, 1982–83. **FA Cup:** Winners 1939.
Colours: Blue shirts, white shorts, red stockings.

PORT VALE   DIV. 1

Aspin, Neil	Bogie, Ian	Corden, Simon W.
Cunningham, Dean	Eyre, Richard P.	Foyle, Martin J.
Glover, Dean V.	Glover, Edward L.	Griffiths, Gareth J.
Guppy, Stephen A.	Hill, Andrew R.	Holwyn, Jermaine T.
McCarthy, Jonathan D.	Mills, Rowan L.	Musselwhite, Paul S.
Naylor, Anthony J.	O'Reilly, Justin M.	Porter, Andrew M.
Stokes, Dean A.	Talbot, Stuart	Tankard, Allen J.
Van Heusden, Arjan	Walker, Raymond	

League Appearances: Aspin, N. 22; Bogie, I. 27(6); Corden, W. 2; Foyle, M. 24(1); Glover, D. 27(2); Glover, L. 17(7); Griffiths, G. 40(1); Guppy, S. 43(1); Hill, A. 35; Kent, K. (1); Lawton, C. 2; McCarthy, J. 44(1); Mills, L. 20(12); Musselwhite, P. 39; Naylor, T. 30(9); Porter, A. 44(1); Samuel, R. 9; Sandeman, B. 1; Stokes, D. 16(2); Talbot, S. 8(12); Tankard, A. 28(1); Van Heusden, A. 7; Walker, R. 21(13)
League (59): Naylor 11, Porter 10 (4 pens), Foyle 8, Mills 8, McCarthy 7, Guppy 4, Bogie 3 (1 pen), Glover L 3, Griffiths 2, Aspin 1, Samuel 1, own goal 1.
Coca-Cola Cup (3): Glover D 1, Glover L 1, Mills 1.
FA Cup (9): Bogie 2, Foyle 2, Walker 2, McCarthy 1, Naylor 1, Porter 1 (pen).
Ground: Vale Park, Burslem, Stoke-on-Trent ST6 1AW. Telephone (01782) 814134.
Record attendance: 50,000 v Aston Villa, FA Cup 5th rd, 20 February 1960.
Capacity: 22,356
Manager: John Rudge.
Secretary: R. A. Allan.
Honours – Football League: Division 3 (N) Champions – 1929–30, 1953–54. Division 4 Champions – 1958–59.
Colours: White shirts, black shorts, black and white stockings.

PRESTON NORTH END   DIV. 2

Atkinson, Graeme
Brown, Michael A.
Davey, Simon
Kidd, Ryan A.
McDonald, Neil R.
Moyes, David W.
Smart, Allan A. C.
Wilcox, Russell

Barrick, Dean
Bryson, James I. C.
Gage, Kevin W.
Kilbane, Kevin D.
McKenna, Paul S.
Saville, Andrew V.
Sparrow, Paul
Wilkinson, Stephen J.

Bennett, Gary M.
Cartwright, Lee
Grant, Anthony J.
Lucas, David A.
Moilanen, Teuvo J.
Sharp, Raymond
Squires, James A.

League Appearances: Ainsworth, G. (2); Atkinson, G. 42(2); Barrick, D. 39(1); Bennett, G. 5(3); Birch, P. 11; Bishop, C. 4; Brown, M. 6(4); Bryson, I. 44; Cartwright, L. 22(4); Davey, S. 37(1); Fensome, A. 20; Fleming, T. 5; Gage, K. 4(3); Grant, T. (1); Holmes, S. 8; Johnson, A. 2; Kidd, R. 23(7); Kilbane, K. 7(4); Lancashire, G. 2(4); Lucas, D. 1; Magee, K. 4(1); McDonald, N. 8(3); Moilanen, T. 2; Moyes, D. 41; Raynor, P. 2(1); Richardson, B. 3; Saville, A. 44; Sharp, R. 1; Smart, A. (2); Sparrow, P. 13; Squires, J. 3(4); Vaughan, J. 40; Wilcox, R. 27; Wilkinson, S. 36(6)
League (78): Saville 29 (1 pen), Davey 10, Wilkinson 10, Bryson 9 (1 pen), Atkinson 5, Cartwright 3, Moyes 3, Birch 2, Lancashire 2, Bennett 1, Brown 1, Kilbane 1, Wilcox 1, own goal 1.
Coca-Cola Cup (3): Bryson 1, Cartwright 1, Kidd 1.
FA Cup (3): Cartwright 1, Wilcox 1, Wilkinson 1.
Ground: Deepdale, Preston PR1 6RU. Telephone (01772) 902020.
Record attendance: 42,684 v Arsenal, Division 1, 23 April 1938. **Capacity:** 18,700.
Manager: Gary Peters.
Secretary: Mrs Audrey Shaw.
Honours – Football League: Division 1 Champions – 1888–89 (first champions), 1889–90. Division 2 Champions – 1903–04, 1912–13, 1950–51. Division 3 Champions – 1970–71, 1995–96. **FA Cup winners** 1889, 1938.
Colours: White and navy shirts, navy shorts, navy stockings.

QUEENS PARK RANGERS   DIV. 1

Bardsley, David J.

Barker, Simon

Brazier, Matthew R.

Brevett, Rufus E.

Challis, Trevor M.

Charles, Lee

Dichio, Daniele S. E.

Dykstra, Sieb

Gallen, Kevin A.

Goodridge, Gregory R.

Graham, Mark R.

Hateley, Mark W.

Hurst, Richard A.

Impey, Andrew R.

Maddix, Daniel S.

Mahoney-Johnson, Michael A.

McDermott, Andrew

McDonald, Alan

Murray, Paul

Perry, Mark J.

Plummer, Christopher S.

Quashie, Nigel F.

Ready, Karl

Roberts, Anthony M.

Sharp, Lee

Sinclair, Trevor

Sommer, Juergen P.

Yates, Stephen

League Appearances: Allen, B. 5(3); Bardsley, D. 28(1); Barker, S. 33; Brazier, M. 6(5); Brevett, R. 27; Challis, T. 10(1); Charles, L. (4); Dichio, D. 21(8); Gallen, K. 26(4); Goodridge, G. (7); Hateley, M. 10(4); Holloway, I. 26(1); Impey, A. 28(1); Maddix, D. 20(2); McDonald, A. 25(1); Murray, P. 1; Osborn, S. 6(3); Penrice, G. (3); Plummer, C. (1); Quashie, N. 11; Ready, K. 16(6); Roberts, T. 5; Sinclair, T. 37; Sommer, J. 33; Wilkins, R. 11(4); Yates, S. 30; Zelic, N. 3(1)
League (38): Dichio 10, Gallen 8, Barker 5, Impey 3, Hateley 2, Sinclair 2, Allen 1, Brevett 1, Goodridge 1, Holloway 1, McDonald 1, Osborn 1, Ready 1, own goal 1.
Coca-Cola Cup (6): Dichio 1, Gallen 1, Impey 1, Ready 1, Sinclair 1, own goal 1.
FA Cup (3): Quashie 2, Sinclair 1.
Ground: South Africa Road, W12 7PA. Telephone (0181) 743 0262.
Record attendance: 35,353 v Leeds U, Division 1, 27 April 1974. **Capacity:** 19,148.
Manager: Ray Wilkins.
Secretary: Miss S. F. Marson.
Honours – Football League: Division 2 Champions – 1982–83. Division 3 (S) Champions – 1947–48. Division 3 Champions – 1966–67. **Football League Cup winners** 1966–67.
Colours: Blue and white hooped shirts, white shorts, white stockings.

READING   DIV. 1

Bass, David

Bernal, Andrew

Booty, Martyn J.

Carey, Alan W.

Caskey, Darren M.

Gilkes, Earl G. M.

Gooding, Michael C.

Hammond, Nicholas D.

Holsgrove, Paul

Hopkins, Jeffrey

Kerr, Dylan

Lambert, Christopher J. P.

Lovell, Stuart A.

McPherson, Keith A.

Meaker, Michael J.

Mihailov, Borislav B.

Morley, Trevor W.

Nogan, Lee M.

Parkinson, Philip J.

Quinn, James M.

Simpson, Derek F.

Swales, Stephen C.

Thorp, Michael S.

Wdowczyk, Dariusz J.

Williams, Adrian

Williams, Martin K.

League Appearances: Bernal, A. 34; Booty, M. 17; Brown, K. 12; Caskey, D. 15; Codner, R. 3(1); Freeman, A. (1); Gilkes, M. 36(8); Gooding, M. 37(3); Gordon, N. (1); Hammond, N. 5; Holsgrove, P. 27(3); Hopkins, J. 14; Jones, T. 13(8); Kerr, D. 4(4); Lambert, J. 10(5); Lovell, S. 28(7); McPherson, K. 16; Meaker, M. 15(6); Mihailov, B. 16; Morley, T. 14(3); Nogan, L. 32(7); Parkinson, P. 36(6); Quinn, J. 20(15); Sheppard, S. 18; Sutton, S. 2; Swales, S. 4(5); Thorp, M. 2; Wdowczyk, D. 29(1); Williams, A. 31; Williams, M. 11(4); Woods, C. 5
League (54): Quinn 11 (2 pens), Nogan 10, Lovell 7 (2 pens), Lambert 4, Morley 4, Gooding 3, Williams A 3, Bernal 2, Caskey 2, Kerr 2, Booty 1, Brown 1, Holsgrove 1, Williams M 1, own goals 2.

Coca-Cola Cup (10): Quinn 4 (1 pen), Lovell 2, Lambert 1, Morley 1, Nogan 1, own goal 1.
FA Cup (3): Quinn 2, Morley 1.
Ground: Elm Park, Norfolk Road, Reading RG30 2EF. Telephone (01189) 507878.
Record attendance: 33,042 v Brentford, FA Cup 5th rd, 19 February 1927.
Capacity: 15,000.
Joint Managers: Jimmy Quinn, Mick Gooding.
Secretary: Ms Andrea Barker.
Honours – Football League: Division 2 Champions – 1993–94. Division 3 Champions – 1985–86. Division 3 (S) Champions – 1925–26. Division 4 Champions – 1978–79. **Simod Cup winners** 1987–88.
Colours: Royal blue and white hooped shirts, white shorts, white stockings.

ROCHDALE   DIV. 3

Bayliss, David A.	Butler, Paul J.	Deary, John S.
Formby, Kevin	Gray, Ian J.	Lyons, Paul
Martin, Dean S.	Peake, Jason W.	Russell, Alexander J.
Stuart, Mark R.	Taylor, Jamie L.	Thackeray, Andrew J.
Thompson, David S.	Whitehall, Steven C.	

League Appearances: Barlow, N. 1(1); Bayliss, D. 25(3); Butler, P. 38; Clarke, C. 6; Deary, J. 36; Formby, K. 18; Gray, I. 20; Hall, D. 9(5); Hardy, J. 5(2); Key, L. 14; Lancaster, D. 13(1); Lyons, P. 1(2); Martin, D. 33(4); Mitchell, N. 3(1); Moulden, P. 6(10); Peake, J. 45(1); Pilkington, K. 6; Powell, F. (2); Price, J. 3; Proctor, J. 1(2); Russell, A. 20(5); Ryan, D. 4(3); Shaw, G. 9(9); Stuart, M. 32(2); Taylor, J. 8(8); Thackeray, A. 27(2); Thompson, D. 43; Thompstone, I. 11(14); Valentine, P. 22(1); Whitehall, S. 46; Williams, P. 1(11)
League (57): Whitehall 20 (8 pens), Stuart 13, Deary 4, Peake 4, Thompson 4, Butler 3, Taylor 3, Lancaster 2, Hall 1, Moulden 1, Thompstone 1, own goal 1.
Coca-Cola Cup (3): Shaw 1, Thompstone 1, own goal 1.
FA Cup (8): Deary 2, Moulden 2, Peake 2, Martin 1, Whitehall 1 (pen).
Ground: Spotland, Sandy Lane, Rochdale OL11 5DS. Telephone (01706) 44648.
Record attendance: 24,231 v Notts Co, FA Cup 2nd rd, 10 December 1949.
Capacity: 6448.
Manager: Graham Barrow.
Secretary: Miss Karen Smyth.
Honours – Nil.
Colours: Blue with red and white chevrons.

ROTHERHAM UNITED   DIV. 2

Berry, Trevor J.	Blades, Paul A.	Bowyer, Gary D.
Breckin, Ian	Clarke, Matthew J.	Farrelly, Stephen
Garner, Darren J.	Goater, Leonardo S.	Goodwin, Shaun L.
Hayward, Andrew W.	Hurst, Paul M.	McGlashan, John
Monington, Mark D.	Richardson, Neil T.	Roscoe, Andrew R.
Smith, Scott D.	Viljoen, Nik	

League Appearances: Berry, T. 33(3); Blades, P. 34; Bowyer, G. 23(4); Breckin, I. 37(2); Clarke, M. 40; Davison, B. 1; Garner, D. 31; Goater, S. 44; Goodwin, S. 25(1); Hayward, A. 22(14); Hurst, P. 32(8); James, M. (1); Jeffrey, M. 22; Jemson,

47

N. 16; McGlashan, J. 13(3); McLean, I. 9; Monington, M. 7(4); Moore, N. 10(1); Muggleton, C. 6; Pettinger, P. (1); Pike, M. (2); Richardson, N. 23(2); Roscoe, A. 44(1); Smith, S. 11(3); Viljoen, N. 5(3); Wilder, C. 18

League (54): Goater 18 (4 pens), Berry 7, Jeffrey 5, Jemson 5 (1 pen), Goodwin 4, Hayward 2, McGlashan 2, Richardson 2 (1 pen), Roscoe 2, Viljoen 2, Blades 1, Breckin 1, Garner 1, Hurst 1, own goal 1.

Coca-Cola Cup (7): Goater 3, Hayward 2, Jeffrey 1, McGlashan 1.

FA Cup (3): Goater 2 (1 pen), McGlashan 1.

Ground: Millmoor Ground, Rotherham S60 1HR. Telephone (01709) 512434.

Record attendance: 25,000 v Sheffield U, Division 2, 13 December 1952 and v Sheffield W, Division 2, 26 January 1952. **Capacity:** 11,514

Joint Managers: Archie Gemmill, John McGovern.

Secretary: N. Darnill.

Honours – Football League: Division 3 Champions – 1980–81. Division 3 (N) Champions – 1950–51. Division 4 Champions – 1988–89. **Auto Windscreens Shield:** Winners 1996

Colours: Red shirts, white shorts, red stockings.

SCARBOROUGH   DIV. 3

Hicks, Stuart J.   Ironside, Ian   Knowles, Darren T.
Lucas, Richard   Martin, Kevin   Ritchie, Andrew T.
Rockett, Jason   Sunderland, Jonathan P.   Willgrass, Alexandre P.

League Appearances: Anthony, G. 2; Boardman, C. 6(3); Charles, S. 41; Cook, M. 2; Curtis, A. 3(2); D'Auria, D. 18; Fairclough, W. 7; Foreman, M. 1(3); Gardner, J. 5(1); Heald, O. 1(8); Hicks, S. 39(2); Ironside, I. 40; Kelly, G. 6; Kinnaird, P. 3; Knowles, D. 46; Lucas, R. 44; Magee, K. 26(2); Midgley, C. 14(2); Myers, C. 8(1); O'Riordan, D. 1; Page, D. 26(11); Partridge, S. 5(2); Ritchie, A. 33(4); Robinson, R. 1; Rockett, J. 39; Sansam, C. 5(1); Sunderland, J. 3(3); Thew, L. 9(5); Todd, M. 23; Toman, A. 12(4); Trebble, N. 25(7); Wells, M. 10(4); Willgrass, A. 2(5)

League (39): Ritchie 8 (2 pens), Charles 5, Page 5, Trebble 5, Rockett 4, Toman 2, D'Auria 1, Gardner 1, Heald 1, Hicks 1, Knowles 1, Magee 1, Midgley 1, Todd 1, Wells 1, own goal 1.

Coca-Cola Cup (1): D'Auria 1.

FA Cup (0).

Ground: The McCain Stadium, Seamer Road, Scarborough YO12 4HF. Telephone (01723) 735094.

Record attendance: 11,130 v Luton T, FA Cup 3rd rd, 8 January 1938. **Capacity:** 6899.

Manager: Mick Wadsworth.

Secretary: Mrs Gillian Russell.

Honours – FA Trophy: Winners 1973, 1976, 1977. **GM Vauxhall Conference:** Winners 1987.

Colours: Red shirts, white shorts, red stockings.

SCUNTHORPE UNITED   DIV. 3

Bradley, Russell   Clarkson, Philip I.   D'Auria, David A.
Eyre, John R.   Hope, Christopher J.   Housham, Steven J.
Knill, Alan R.   McFarlane, Andrew A.   Paterson, James
Samways, Mark   Turnbull, Lee M.   Walsh, Michael S.
Wilson, Paul A.

League Appearances: Bradley, R. 36(2); Bullimore, W. 11(3); Butler, L. 2; Clarkson, P. 21(3); D'Auria, D. 27; Eyre, J. 36(3); Ford, T. 35(3); Germaine, G. 11; Graham, D. 1(2); Hope, C. 38(2); Housham, S. 21(7); Jones, R. 11; Knill, A. 38; McFarlane, A. 41(5); Murfin, A. 1; Nicholson, M. 13(23); O'Halloran, K. 6(1); Paterson, J. 23(3); Samways, M. 33; Sansam, C. 2(3); Thornber, S. 14(2); Turnbull, L. 16(7); Varadi, I. (2); Walsh, M. 22(3); Wilson, P. 40; Young, S. 7(7)
League (67): McFarlane 16, Eyre 10, Ford 7, Clarkson 6, D'Auria 5 (1 pen), Hope 3, Jones 3, Knill 3, Turnbull 3, Bullimore 2 (2 pens), Paterson 2, Bradley 1, Graham 1, Nicholson 1, Sansam 1, Wilson 1 (pen), Young 1, own goal 1.
Coca-Cola Cup (4): Eyre 2, Ford 1, McFarlane 1.
FA Cup (5): McFarlane 2, Eyre 1, Ford 1, Paterson 1.
Ground: Glanford Park, Scunthorpe, South Humberside DN15 8TD. Telephone (01724) 848077.
Record attendance: Old Showground: 23,935 v Portsmouth, FA Cup 4th rd, 30 January 1954. Glanford Park: 8775 v Rotherham U, Division 4, 1 May 1989.
Capacity: 9183.
Team Manager: Mick Buxton.
Secretary: A. D. Rowing.
Honours – Division 3 (N) Champions – 1957–58.
Colours: Sky blue with claret shirts, sky blue shorts, claret and white trim, sky blue stockings, claret and white trim.

SHEFFIELD UNITED   DIV. 1

Anthony, Graham J.	Beard, Mark	Bettney, Christopher J.
Dyer, Liam D.	Hartfield, Charles J.	Hawes, Steven R.
Hocking, Matthew J.	Hodgson, Douglas J. H.	Hutchison, Donald
Kelly, Alan T.	Nilsen, Roger	Patterson, Mark A.
Quinn, Wayne R.	Reed, John P.	Scott, Andrew
Short, Christian M.	Starbuck, Philip M.	Taylor, Gareth K.
Tracey, Simon P.	Vonk, Michel C.	Walker, Andrew F.
Ward, Mitchum D.	White, David	Whitehouse, Dane L.
Wood, Paul J.		

League Appearances: Ablett, G. 12; Angell, B. 6; Battersby, T. 3(7); Beard, M. 13(7); Blake, N. 20(2); Blount, M. 7(1); Cowans, G. 18(2); Davidson, R. 1; Fitzgerald, S. 6; Flo, J. 17(2); Foran, M. 6(1); Gage, K. 2; Gannon, J. 12; Gayle, B. 3(2); Hawes, S. 1(1); Heath, A. (4); Hodges, G. 15(7); Hodgson, D. 12(4); Holland, P. 11(7); Hutchison, D. 18(1); Kelly, A. 34(1); Mercer, B. 1; Muggleton, C. (1); Nilsen, R. 39; Patterson, M. 21; Reed, J. (2); Rogers, P. 13(3); Scott, A. 3(4); Scott, R. 2(3); Short, C. 13(2); Starbuck, P. 5(6); Taylor, G. 10; Tracey, S. 11; Tuttle, D. 26; Veart, C. 17(10); Vonk, M. 17; Walker, A. 12(2); Ward, M. 39(3); White, D. 24(4); Whitehouse, D. 36(2)
League (57): Blake 12, Walker 8, White 7, Veart 5, Flo 4, Whitehouse 4 (2 pens), Hodges 3, Angell 2, Hutchison 2, Patterson 2, Taylor 2, Battersby 1, Holland 1, Scott R 1, Starbuck 1, Ward 1 (pen).
Coca-Cola Cup (4): Flo 1, Holland 1, Veart 1, Whitehouse 1 (pen).
FA Cup (2): Veart 1, Whitehouse 1.
Ground: Bramall Lane Ground, Sheffield S2 4SU. Telephone (0114) 2738955.
Record attendance: 68,287 v Leeds U, FA Cup 5th rd, 15 February 1936.
Capacity: 23,459 (up to 30,200).

Team Manager: Howard Kendall.
Secretary: D. Capper AFA.
Honours – Football League: Division 1 Champions – 1897–98. Division 2 Champions – 1952–53. Division 4 Champions – 1981–82. **FA Cup:** Winners 1899, 1902, 1915, 1925.
Colours: Red and white striped shirts, black shorts, black stockings.

SHEFFIELD WEDNESDAY   FA PREMIERSHIP

Atherton, Peter	Barker, Richard I.	Batty, Mark P.
Blinker, Reginald W.	Bright, Mark A.	Briscoe, Lee S.
Daly, Matthew	Degryse, Marc	Donaldson, O'Neil M.
Hirst, David E.	Humphreys, Richie J.	Hyde, Graham
Jones, Ryan A.	Kovacevic, Darko	Linighan, Brian
Newsome, Jon	Nicol, Stephen	Nolan, Ian R.
Pembridge, Mark	Poric, Adem	Pressman, Kevin P.
Scargill, Jonathan M.	Sheridan, John J.	Smith, Gavin D.
Stefanovic, Dejan	Waddle, Christopher R.	Walker, Desmond S.
Whittingham, Guy	Williams, Michael A.	

League Appearances: Atherton, P. 36; Blinker, R. 9; Bright, M. 15(10); Briscoe, L. 22(4); Degryse, M. 30(4); Donaldson, O. 1(2); Hirst, D. 29(1); Humphreys, R. 1(4); Hyde, G. 14(12); Ingesson, K. 3(2); Kovacevic, D. 8(8); Newsome, J. 8; Nicol, S. 18(1); Nolan, I. 29; Pearce, A. 3; Pembridge, M. 24(1); Petrescu, D. 8; Platts, M. (2); Pressman, K. 30; Sheridan, J. 13(4); Sinton, A. 7(3); Stefanovic, D. 5(1); Waddle, C. 23(9); Walker, D. 36; Watts, J. 9(2); Whittingham, G. 27(2); Williams, M. 2(3); Woods, C. 8
League (48): Hirst 13 (4 pens), Degryse 8, Bright 7, Whittingham 6, Kovacevic 4, Blinker 2, Waddle 2, Donaldson 1, Hyde 1, Newsome 1, Pembridge 1, Watts 1, own goal 1.
Coca-Cola Cup (10): Degryse 4, Bright 3, Hirst 1, Pembridge 1, Whittingham 1.
FA Cup (0).
Ground: Hillsborough, Sheffield, S6 1SW. Telephone (0114) 2343122.
Record attendance: 72,841 v Manchester C, FA Cup 5th rd, 17 February 1934.
Capacity: 39,814
Manager: David Pleat.
Secretary: Graham Mackrell FCCA.
Honours – Football League: Division 1 Champions – 1902–03, 1903–04, 1928–29, 1929–30. Division 2 Champions – 1899–1900, 1925–26, 1951–52, 1955–56, 1958–59. **FA Cup winners** 1896, 1907, 1935. **Football League Cup winners** 1990–91.
Colours: Blue and white striped shirts, blue shorts, blue stockings.

SHREWSBURY TOWN   DIV. 2

Anthrobus, Stephen A.	Berkley, Austin J.	Currie, Darren P.
Dempsey, Mark A.	Edwards, Paul A.	Evans, Paul S.
Lynch, Thomas M.	Reed, Ian P.	Rowbotham, Darren
Scott, Richard P.	Seabury, Kevin	Simkin, Darren S.
Spink, Dean P.	Stevens, Ian D.	Taylor, Robert M.
Walton, David L.	Whiston, Peter	Wray, Shaun W.

League Appearances: Anthrobus, S. 27(12); Berkley, A. 36(2); Boden, C. 5; Clarke, T. 15; Cope, J. (1); Currie, D. 11(2); Dempsey, M. 17(11); Edwards, P. 31; Evans, P. 25(9); Hughes, M. 2; Jackson, D. (1); Kay, J. 7; Lynch, T. 22(3); Megson, G. 2; Reed, I. 9(2); Robinson, C. 2(2); Rowbotham, D. 20(6); Scott, R. 36; Seabury, K. 26(8); Spink, D. 32(2); Stevens, I. 27(5); Stewart, S. 4; Summerfield, K. (1); Taylor, M. 38; Walton, D. 35; Watson, M. 1; Whiston, P. 28; Withe, C. 30(2); Woods, R. 18(5); Wray, S. (3)

League (58): Stevens 12 (1 pen), Anthrobus 10, Rowbotham 8 (2 pens), Scott 6, Spink 6, Evans 3 (1 pen), Lynch 3 (3 pens), Currie 2, Dempsey 2, Reed 2, Whiston 2, Berkley 1, Taylor 1.

Coca-Cola Cup (3): Lynch 1 (pen), Rowbotham 1 (pen), Seabury 1.

FA Cup (17): Scott 3, Spink 3, Dempsey 2, Evans 2, Whiston 2, Anthrobus 1, Rowbotham 1 (pen), Stevens 1, Withe 1, own goal 1.

Ground: Gay Meadow, Shrewsbury SY2 6AB. Telephone (01743) 360111.

Record attendance: 18,917 v Walsall, Division 3, 26 April 1961. **Capacity:** 8000.

Manager: Fred Davies.

Secretary: M. J. Starkey.

Honours – Football League: Division 3 Champions – 1978–79, 1993–94. **Welsh Cup winners** 1891, 1938, 1977, 1979, 1984, 1985.

Colours: Blue shirts, white trim, blue shorts, blue stockings, white trim.

SOUTHAMPTON   FA PREMIERSHIP

Beasant, David	Benali, Francis V.	Bennett, Frank
Blamey, Nathan	Charlton, Simon T.	Dodd, Jason R.
Hall, Richard A.	Heaney, Neil	Hughes, David R.
Le Tissier, Matthew P.	Maddison, Neil S.	Magilton, James
Monkou, Kenneth J.	Moss, Neil G.	Neilson, Alan B.
Oakley, Matthew	Robinson, Matthew R.	Sheerin, Paul
Shipperley, Neil J.	Tisdale, Paul R.	Venison, Barry
Warren, Christer	Watson, Gordon W. G.	Widdrington, Thomas

League Appearances: Beasant, D. 36; Benali, F. 28(1); Bennett, F. 5(6); Charlton, S. 24(2); Dodd, J. 37; Grobbelaar, B. 2; Hall, R. 30; Heaney, N. 15(2); Hughes, D. 6(5); Le Tissier, M. 34; Maddison, N. 13(2); Magilton, J. 31; Maskell, C. (1); McDonald, P. (1); Monkou, K. 31(1); Neilson, A. 15(3); Oakley, M. 5(5); Robinson, M. (5); Shipperley, N. 37; Tisdale, P. 5(4); Venison, B. 21(1); Walters, M. 4(1); Warren, C. 1(6); Watson, G. 18(7); Widdrington, T. 20(1)

League (34): Le Tissier 7 (3 pens), Shipperley 7, Magilton 3 (1 pen), Watson 3, Dodd 2, Heaney 2, Monkou 2, Widdrington 2, Hall 1, Hughes 1, Maddison 1, Tisdale 1, own goals 2.

Coca-Cola Cup (8): Le Tissier 2, Shipperley 2, Watson 2, Hall 1, Monkou 1.

FA Cup (10): Shipperley 3, Magilton 2, Dodd 1, Hall 1, Le Tissier 1, Oakley 1, Watson 1.

Ground: The Dell, Milton Road, Southampton SO15 2XH. Telephone (01703) 220505.

Record attendance: 31,044 v Manchester U, Division 1, 8 October 1969. **Capacity:** 15,000.

Manager: Graeme Souness.

Secretary: Brian Truscott.

Honours – Football League: Division 3 (S) Champions – 1921–22. Division 3 Champions – 1959–60. **FA Cup:** Winners 1975–76.

Colours: Red and white striped shirts, black shorts, red and white hooped stockings.

SOUTHEND UNITED   DIV. 1

Bodley, Michael J.   Boere, Jeroen W. J.   Byrne, Paul P.
Dublin, Keith B. L.   Gridelet, Phillp R.   Hails, Julian
Lapper, Michael S.   Marsh, Michael A.   McNally, Mark
Rammell, Andrew V.   Roche, David   Roget, Leo T. E.
Royce, Simon   Sansome, Paul E.   Stimson, Mark
Sussex, Andrew R.   Thomson, Andrew   Tilson, Stephen B.
Whelan, Ronald A.

League Appearances: Ansah, A. (4); Barness, A. 5; Belsvik, P. 3; Bodley, M. 38(1);
Boere, J. 6; Brown, K. 6; Byrne, P. 38(3); Charlery, K. 2(1); Dublin, K. 42(1);
Gridelet, P. 37(3); Hails, J. 39(3); Hone, M. 11(5); Iorfa, D. 1(1); Jones, G. 14(9);
Lapper, M. 23(1); Marsh, M. 40; McNally, M. 20; Powell, C. 27; Rammell, A. 6(1);
Read, P. 3(1); Regis, D. 25(4); Roget, L. 4(4); Royce, S. 46; Stimson, M. 10; Sussex,
A. 1(1); Thomson, A. 22(11); Tilson, S. 23(5); Turner, A. 4(2); Whelan, R. 1; Willis,
R. 9(1)
League (52): Regis 8, Thomson 6, Byrne 5, Marsh 5 (2 pens), Hails 4, Dublin 3,
Tilson 3, Willis 3, Boere 2, Gridelet 2, Jones 2, McNally 2, Rammell 2, Belsvik 1,
Bodley 1, Read 1, Roget 1, own goal 1.
Coca-Cola Cup (2): Byrne 1, Jones 1.
FA Cup (0).
Ground: Roots Hall Football Ground, Victoria Avenue, Southend-on-Sea
SS2 6NQ. Telephone (01702) 304050
Record attendance: 31,090 v Liverpool FA Cup 3rd rd, 10 January 1979. **Capacity:**
12,485
Manager: Ronnie Whelan.
Secretary: J. W. Adams.
Honours – Football League: Division 4 Champions – 1980–81.
Colours: All royal blue.

STOCKPORT COUNTY   DIV. 2

Armstrong, Alun   Beaumont, Christopher P. Bennett, Thomas M.
Bound, Matthew T.   Connelly, Sean P.   Dinning, Tony
Durkan, Kieron J.   Eckhardt, Jeffrey E.   Edwards, Neil R.
Flynn, Michael A.   Gannon, James P.   Jeffers, John J.
Landon, Richard J.   Marsden, Christopher   Mike, Adrian R.
Mutch, Andrew T.   Todd, Lee   Ware, Paul D.

League Appearances: Armstrong, A. 44(2); Beaumont, C. 38(5); Bennett, T. 24;
Bound, M. 26; Chalk, M. 5(5); Connelly, S. 42(1); Croft, B. (3); Dickins, M. 1;
Dinning, T. 1(9); Durkan, K. 11(5); Eckhardt, J. 30(5); Edwards, N. 45; Flynn, M.
46; Gannon, J. 22(1); Helliwell, I. 18(4); Jeffers, J. 21(2); Landon, R. 7(4);
Marsden, C. 19(1); Mike, A. 4(4); Mutch, A. 11; Oliver, M. 7(2); Thornley, B. 8(2);
Todd, L. 42; Ware, P. 22(5); Williams, M. 12(5)
League (61): Armstrong 13, Helliwell 9, Eckhardt 6, Flynn 6, Bound 5 (2 pens),
Landon 5, Mutch 4, Jeffers 3, Ware 3, Bennett 1 (pen), Dinning 1, Gannon 1,
Marsden 1, Oliver 1, Thornley 1, Williams 1.
Coca-Cola Cup (6): Armstrong 2, Chalk 1, Eckhardt 1, Gannon 1, Helliwell 1.
FA Cup (11): Eckhardt 4, Armstrong 3, Bound 1, Helliwell 1, own goals 2.
Ground: Edgeley Park, Hardcastle Road, Stockport, Cheshire SK3 9DD.
Telephone (0161) 286 8888.

Record attendance: 27,833 v Liverpool, FA Cup 5th rd, 11 February 1950.
Capacity: 12,500.
Manager: Dave Jones.
Secretary: Gary Glendenning BA ACA.
Honours – Football League: Division 3 (N) Champions – 1921–22, 1936–37. Division 4 Champions – 1966–67.
Colours: White shirts, with double royal pinstripe, white shorts, white stockings.

STOKE CITY   DIV. 1

Beeston, Carl F.	Birch, Mark	Callan, Aidan J.
Carruthers, Martin G.	Clarkson, Ian S.	Cranson, Ian
Devlin, Mark A.	Dreyer, John B.	Gayle, John
Gleghorn, Nigel W.	Keen, Kevin I.	Macari, Michael
Macari, Paul	Morgan, Philip J.	Muggleton, Carl D.
Overson, Vincent D.	Potter, Graham S.	Prudhoe, Mark
Sandford, Lee R.	Sheron, Michael N.	Sigurdsson, Larus O.
Stokoe, Graham L.	Sturridge, Simon A.	Wallace, Raymond G.
Whittle, Justin P.	Woods, Stephen J.	

League Appearances: Beeston, C. 13(3); Brightwell, D. (1); Carruthers, M. 10(14); Clarkson, I. 43; Cranson, I. 23(1); Devlin, M. 5(5); Dreyer, J. 4(15); Gayle, J. 5(5); Gleghorn, N. 46; Keen, K. 27(6); Muggleton, C. 6; Orlygsson, T. 6(1); Overson, V. 18; Peschisolido, P. 20(6); Potter, G. 38(3); Prudhoe, M. 39; Sandford, L. 46; Scott, K. 6(1); Sheron, M. 23(5); Sigurdsson, L. 46; Sinclair, R. 1; Sturridge, S. 30(11); Wallace, R. 44; Whittle, J. 7(1)
League (60): Sheron 15, Sturridge 13 (1 pen), Gleghorn 9, Peschisolido 6, Wallace 6, Carruthers 3, Gayle 3, Keen 3, Cranson 1, Potter 1.
Coca-Cola Cup (1): Peschisolido 1.
FA Cup (1): Sturridge 1.
Ground: Victoria Ground, Stoke-on-Trent ST4 4EG. Telephone (01782) 413511.
Record attendance: 51,380 v Arsenal, Division 1, 29 March 1937. **Capacity:** 24,054.
Manager: Lou Macari.
Secretary: M. J. Potts.
Honours – Football League: Division 2 Champions – 1932–33, 1962–63, 1992–93. Division 3 (N) Champions – 1926–27. **Football League Cup:** Winners 1971–72. **Autoglass Trophy winners** 1992.
Colours: Red and white striped shirts, white shorts, white stockings.

SUNDERLAND   FA PREMIERSHIP

Agnew, Stephen M.	Aiston, Sam J.	Angell, Brett
Armstrong, Gordon I.	Atkinson, Brian	Ball, Kevin A.
Bracewell, Paul W.	Bridges, Michael	Brodie, Stephen E.
Chamberlain, Alec F. R.	Grant, Stephen H.	Gray, Michael
Gray, Philip	Hall, Gareth D.	Heckingbottom, Paul
Holloway, Darren	Howey, Lee M.	Kelly, David T.
Kubicki, Dariusz	Mawson, David	Melville, Andrew R.
Mullin, John	Ord, Richard J.	Pickering, Steven
Preece, David	Russell, Craig S.	Scott, Martin
Smith, Martin	Stewart, Paul A.	

League Appearances: Agnew, S. 26(3); Aiston, S. 4(10); Angell, B. 2; Armstrong, G. (1); Atkinson, B. 5(2); Ball, K. 35(1); Bracewell, P. 38; Bridges, M. 2(13); Chamberlain, A. 29; Cooke, T. 6; Given, S. 17; Gray, Martin 4(3); Gray, Michael 46; Gray, P. 28(4); Hall, G. 8(6); Howey, L. 17(10); Kelly, D. 9(1); Kubicki, D. 46; Melville, A. 40; Mullin, J. 5(5); Ord, R. 41(1); Russell, C. 35(6); Scott, M. 43; Smith, M. 9(11); Stewart, P. 11(1)

League (59): Russell 13, Gray P 8, Scott 6 (4 pens), Agnew 5, Ball 4, Bridges 4, Michael Gray 4, Melville 4, Howey 3, Kelly 2, Smith 2, Mullin 1, Ord 1, Stewart 1, own goal 1.

Coca-Cola Cup (4): Howey 2, Angell 1, own goal 1.

FA Cup (3): Agnew 1, Gray P 1, Russell 1.

Ground: Roker Park Ground, Sunderland SR6 9SW. Telephone (0191) 514 0332.

Record attendance: 75,118 v Derby Co, FA Cup 6th rd replay, 8 March 1933.

Capacity: 22,657.

Manager: Peter Reid.

Secretary: Mark Blackbourne.

Honours – Football League: Division 1 Champions – 1891–92, 1892–93, 1894–95, 1901–02, 1912–13, 1935–36, 1995–96. Division 2 Champions – 1975–76. Division 3 Champions – 1987–88. **FA Cup:** Winners 1937, 1973.

Colours: Red and white striped shirts, black shorts, red stockings, white turnover.

SWANSEA CITY   DIV. 3

Ampadu, Patrick K.   Brown, Linton   Chapple, Shaun R.
Clode, Mark J.   Coates, Jonathan S.   Cook, Andrew C.
Edwards, Christian N. H. Freestone, Roger   Garnett, Shaun M.
Heggs, Carl S.   Hodge, John   Jones, Lee
Jones, Stephen R.   McDonald, Colin   Molby, Jan
Penney, David M.   Price, Jason J.   Thomas, David J.
Torpey, Stephen D. J.   Walker, Keith C.

League Appearances: Ampadu, K. 40(3); Barnhouse, D. 12(3); Barnwell-Edinboro, J. 2(2); Basham, M. 9(2); Beresford, D. 4(2); Brown, L. 3(1); Chapman, L. 7; Chapple, S. 15(7); Clode, M. 25(5); Coates, J. 7(11); Cook, A. 30(3); Cornforth, J. 17; Dennison, R. 9; Edwards, C. 36(2); Freestone, R. 45; Garnett, S. 9; Heggs, C. 28(4); Hodge, J. 34(7); Hurst, G. 2; Jenkins, S. 15; Jones, L. 1; Jones, S. 16(1); Lampard, F. 8(1); Mardenborough, S. 1; McDonald, C. 3; Molby, J. 12; O'Leary, K. 1; Pascoe, C. 9(4); Penney, D. 28(1); Perrett, D. 2(2); Thomas, D. 3(13); Torpey, S. 41(1); Walker, K. 32(1)

League (43): Torpey 15, Heggs 5, Chapman 4, Ampadu 2, Chapple 2, Cornforth 2, Edwards 2, Freestone 2 (2 pens), Molby 2 (1 pen), Basham 1, Hodge 1, Hurst 1, Lampard 1, Pascoe 1, Thomas 1, own goal 1.

Coca-Cola Cup (4): Hodge 2, Ampadu 1, Torpey 1.

FA Cup (0).

Ground: Vetch Field, Swansea SA1 3SU. Telephone (01792) 474114.

Record attendance: 32,796 v Arsenal, FA Cup 4th rd, 17 February 1968. **Capacity:** 16,540.

Team Manager: Jan Molby.

Secretary: George Taylor.

Honours – Football League: Division 3 (S) Champions – 1924–25, 1948–49. **Autoglass Trophy:** Winners 1994. **Welsh Cup:** Winners 9 times.

Colours: White shirts with black trim, white shorts, black stockings.

SWINDON TOWN   DIV. 1

Allen, Paul K.   Allison, Wayne   Collins, Lee
Cowe, Steven M.   Culverhouse, Ian B.   Digby, Fraser C.
Drysdale, Jason   Finney, Stephen K.   Gooden, Ty M.
Hooper, Dean R.   Horlock, Kevin   McLaren, Ross
McMahon, Stephen   Murray, Edwin J.   O'Sullivan, Wayne S. J.
Robinson, Mark J.   Seagraves, Mark   Smith, Alex P.
Talia, Francesco   Taylor, Shaun   Thorne, Peter L.

League Appearances: Allen, P. 25(2); Allison, W. 43(1); Beauchamp, J. 1(2); Bodin, P. 32(1); Collins, L. 2(3); Cowe, S. 4(7); Culverhouse, I. 46; Digby, F. 25; Drysdale, J. 10(3); Finney, S. 22(8); Given, S. 5; Gooden, T. 14(12); Grant, T. 3; Horlock, K. 44(1); Leitch, D. 7; Ling, M. 12(4); McMahon, S. 20(1); Murray, E. 3(2); O'Sullivan, W. 27(7); Preece, D. 7; Robinson, M. 46; Seagraves, M. 25(3); Smith, A. 2(6); Talia, F. 16; Taylor, S. 43; Thorne, P. 22(4)
League (71): Allison 17, Finney 12 (1 pen), Horlock 12 (1 pen), Thorne 10, Taylor 7, Gooden 3 (1 pen), O'Sullivan 3, Bodin 2 (1 pen), Cowe 1, Grant 1, Murray 1, Preece 1, Robinson 1.
Coca-Cola Cup (5): Allison 1, Beauchamp 1, Finney 1, Gooden 1, Horlock 1.
FA Cup (10): Horlock 3, Allison 2, Finney 2, Allen 1, Bodin 1, Ling 1.
Ground: County Ground, Swindon, Wiltshire SN1 2ED. Telephone (01793) 430430.
Record attendance: 32,000 v Arsenal, FA Cup 3rd rd, 15 January 1972. **Capacity:** 15,760.
Manager: Steve McMahon.
Secretary: Steve Jones.
Honours – Football League: Division 2 Champions – 1995–96. Division 4 Champions – 1985–86. **Football League Cup:** Winners 1968–69. **Anglo-Italian Cup:** Winners 1970.
Colours: All red.

TORQUAY UNITED   DIV. 3

Baker, David P.   Barrow, Lee A.   Hancox, Richard C.
Hathaway, Ian A.   Jack, Rodney   Ndah, James J. O.
Newland, Raymond J.   Oatway, Anthony P. D.   Stamps, Scott
Watson, Alexander F.   Winter, Steven D.

League Appearances: Baker, P. 17; Barnes, B. 36; Barrow, L. 35(6); Bayes, A. 28; Bedeau, A. (1); Buckle, P. 11; Byng, D. 4(10); Canham, S. 4(1); Cooke, J. 5; Coughlin, R. 5(5); Croft, B. ; Curran, C. 17(2); Garner, S. 20; Gore, I. 25; Gregg, M. 3; Haddaoui, R. 9; Hall, M. 16; Hancox, R. 15(10); Hathaway, I. 22(4); Hawthorne, M. 17(5); Hodges, K. 1; Jack, R. 22(3); Kelly, T. 26(5); Laight, E. 8(12); Mateu, J. 1; Monk, G. 1(1); Moors, C. 3; Ndah, J. 4(4); Newhouse, A. 29; Newland, R. 24; O'Riordan, D. 22(7); Oatway, C. 4; Partridge, S. 12(2); Povey, N. 1(3); Preston, M. 10(1); Ramsey, P. (1); Stamps, S. 20(3); Thomas, W. 4(4); Travis, S. (1); Watson, A. 18; Williams, P. 1(5); Winter, S. 6(2)
League (30): Baker 4 (1 pen), Buckle 4 (4 pens), Ndah 3, Gore 2, Jack 2, Laight 2, Newhouse 2, Partridge 2, Watson 2, Curran 1, Garner 1, Hancox 1, Hathaway 1, Mateu 1, Stamps 1, own goal 1.
Coca-Cola Cup (4): Barrow 2 Hathaway 1, Hawthorne 1.
FA Cup (6): Barrow 1, Byng 1, Gore 1, Hathaway 1, Hawthorne 1, Mateu 1.

Ground: Plainmoor Ground, Torquay, Devon TQ1 3PS. Telephone (01803) 328666.
Record attendance: 21,908 v Huddersfield T, FA Cup 4th rd, 29 January 1955.
Capacity: 6000.
Player-Manager: Kevin Hodges.
Secretary/General Manager: D. F. Turner.
Honours – Nil
Colours: Yellow and navy striped shirts, navy shorts, yellow stockings.

TOTTENHAM HOTSPUR   FA PREMIERSHIP

Allen, Rory W.	Anderton, Darren R.	Arber, Mark A.
Armstrong, Christopher	Austin, Dean B.	Brady, Gary
Brown, Simon J.	Calderwood, Colin	Campbell, Sulzeer
Carr, Stephen	Clapham, James R.	Clemence, Stephen N.
Cundy, Jason V.	D'Arcy, Ross	Day, Christopher N.
Dozzell, Jason A. W.	Edinburgh, Justin C.	Fenn, Neale M. C.
Fox, Ruel A.	Gain, Peter	Hill, Daniel R. L.
Howells, David	Kerslake, David	Mabbutt, Gary V.
Maher, Kevin	Mahorn, Paul G.	Mannix, Alan
McMahon, Gerard J.	Nethercott, Stuart	Rosenthal, Ronny
Scott, Kevin W.	Sheringham, Edward P.	Sinton, Andrew
Slade, Steven A.	Spencer, Simon	Townley, Leon
Turner, Andrew P.	Walker, Ian M.	Webb, Simon
Wilson, Clive	Wormull, Simon J.	

League Appearances: Anderton, D. 6(2); Armstrong, C. 36; Austin, D. 28; Calderwood, C. 26(3); Campbell, S. 31; Caskey, D. 3; Cundy, J. (1); Dozzell, J. 24(4); Dumitrescu, I. 5; Edinburgh, J. 15(7); Fox, R. 26; Howells, D. 29; Kerslake, D. 2; Mabbutt, G. 32; McMahon, G. 7(7); Nethercott, S. 9(4); Rosenthal, R. 26(7); Scott, K. (2); Sheringham, T. 38; Sinton, A. 8(1); Slade, S. 1(4); Walker, I. 38; Wilson, C. 28
League (50): Sheringham 16 (2 pens), Armstrong 15, Fox 6, Dozzell 3, Howells 3, Anderton 2, Campbell 1, Rosenthal 1, own goals 3.
Coca-Cola Cup (9): Armstrong 3, Sheringham 3, Howells 1, Rosenthal 1, own goal 1.
FA Cup (12): Sheringham 5, Armstrong 4, Rosenthal 2, Wilson 1.
Ground: 748 High Rd, Tottenham, London N17 0AP. Telephone (0181) 365 5000.
Record attendance: 75,038 v Sunderland, FA Cup 6th rd, 5 March 1938. **Capacity:** 33,083.
Manager: Gerry Francis.
Secretary: Peter Barnes.
Honours – Football League: Division 1 Champions – 1950–51, 1960–61. Division 2 Champions – 1919–20, 1949–50. **FA Cup:** Winners 1901 (as non-League club), 1921, 1961, 1962, 1967, 1981, 1982, 1991 (8 wins stands as the record). **Football League Cup:** Winners 1970–71, 1972–73. **European Competitions: European Cup-Winners' Cup winners:** 1962–63. **UEFA Cup winners:** 1971–72, 1983–84.
Colours: White shirts, navy blue shorts, navy stockings.

TRANMERE ROVERS   DIV. 1

Aldridge, John W.   Branch, Graham   Brannon, Gerald D.
Challinor, David P.   Cook, Paul A.   Coyne, Daniel
Crawford, Keith T.   Higgins, David A.   Irons, Kenneth
Jardine, Jamie   Jones, Gary S.   Jones, Martin W.
Jones, Paul N.   Kenworthy, Jonathan R.   Mahon, Alan J.
McGreal, John   Moore, Ian   Morgan, Alan M.
Morrissey, John J.   Mungall, Steven H.   Nevin, Patrick K. F.
Nixon, Eric W.   O'Brien, Liam F.   Rogers, Alan
Scott, Gary C.   Stevens, Michael G.   Teale, Shaun
Thomas, Tony   Woods, Billy

League Appearances: Aldridge, J. 45; Bennett. G. 26(3); Branch, G. 11(9);
Brannan, G. 44; Cook, P. 15; Coyne, D. 46; Garnett, S. 17(1); Higgins, D. 16(1);
Irons, K. 25(7); Jones, G. 17(7); Kenworthy, J. (4); Mahon, A. (2); McGreal, J. 32;
Moore, I. 27(9); Morgan, A. (4); Morrissey, J. 8(8); Mungall, S. 2(4); Nevin, P. 39(1);
O'Brien, L. 18(4); Rogers, A. 25(1); Stevens, G. 33(1); Teale, S. 29; Thomas, T. 31
League (64): Aldridge 27 (3 pens), Bennett 9, Moore 9, O'Brien 4, Irons 3, Nevin
3, Branch 2, Rogers 2, Cook 1, Jones 1, Morgan 1, own goals 2.
Coca-Cola Cup (6): Aldridge 2, Jones 2, Brannan 1, Moore 1.
FA Cup (0).
Ground: Prenton Park, Prenton Road West, Birkenhead L42 9PN. Telephone
(0151) 608 3677.
Record attendance: 24,424 v Stoke C, FA Cup 4th rd, 5 February 1972.
Capacity: 16,789.
Manager: John Aldridge.
Secretary: Norman Wilson FAAI.
Honours – Football League Division 3 (N) Champions – 1937–38. **Welsh Cup:**
Winners 1935. **Leyland Daf Cup:** Winners 1990.
Colours: All white.

WALSALL   DIV. 2

Bradley, Darren M.   Butler, Martin N.   Daniel, Raymond C.
Evans, Duncan W.   Houghton, Scott A.   Keister, John E. S.
Lightbourne, Kyle L.   Marsh, Christopher J.   Mountfield, Derek N.
Ntamark, Charles B.   O'Connor, Martin J.   Rogers, Darren J.
Roper, Ian R.   Ryder, Stuart H.   Viveash, Adrian L.
Walker, James B.   Wilson, Kevin J.   Wood, Trevor J.

League Appearances: Bradley, D. 45; Butler, M. 13(15); Daniel, R. 23(2); Evans,
W. 20(4); Houghton, S. 38(2); Keister, J. 9(12); Kerr, J. (1); Lightbourne, K. 37(6);
Marsh, C. 39(2); Mountfield, D. 28; Ntamark, C. 34(8); O'Connor, M. 41; Palmer,
C. 15; Platt, C. (4); Ricketts, M. (1); Rogers, D. 23(2); Roper, I. 3(2); Ryder, S.
1(2); Smith, C. (1); Viveash, A. 31; Walker, J. 26; Watkiss, S. 14(1); Wilson, K. 46;
Wood, T. 20
League (60): Lightbourne 15, Wilson 15, O'Connor 9 (3 pens), Houghton 6, Butler
4, Marsh 2, Platt 2, Bradley 1, Mountfield 1, Ricketts 1, own goals 4.
Coca-Cola Cup (4): Evans 1, Houghton 1, O'Connor 1, Wilson 1.

FA Cup (13): Lightbourne 3, Bradley 2, Houghton 2, Marsh 2, Wilson 2, O'Connor 1, own goal 1.
Ground: Bescot Stadium, Bescot Cresent, Walsall WS1 4SA. Telephone (01922) 22791.
Record attendance: 10,628 B International, England v Switzerland, 20 May 1991.
Capacity: 9000.
Manager: Chris Nicholl.
Secretary/Commercial Manager: Roy Whalley.
Honours – Football League: Division 4 Champions – 1959–60.
Colours: Red shirts, black shorts, white stockings.

WATFORD   DIV. 2

Bazeley, Darren S.	Connolly, David J.	Dixon, Kerry M.
Foster, Colin J.	Hessenthaler, Andrew	Holdsworth, David G.
Johnson, Richard M.	Lowndes, Nathan P.	Ludden, Dominic J. R.
Millen, Keith D.	Miller, Kevin	Mooney, Thomas J.
Page, Robert J.	Palmer, Stephen L.	Penrice, Gary K.
Phillips, Kevin	Porter, Gary	Ramage, Craig D.
Simpson, Colin R.	White, Devon W.	

League Appearances: Andrews, W. (1); Barnes, D. 10; Bazeley, D. 35(6); Beadle, P. 3; Caskey, D. 6; Cherry, S. 4; Connolly, D. 7(4); Dixon, K. 8(3); Foster, C. 26; Gibbs, N. 8(1); Hessenthaler, A. 30; Hill, D. 1; Hodge, S. 2; Holdsworth, D. 26(1); Johnson, R. 17(3); Lavin, G. 16; Ludden, D. 9(3); Millen, K. 32(1); Miller, K. 42; Mooney, T. 38(4); Moralee, J. 17(8); Neill, W. 1; Page, R. 16(3); Palmer, S. 35; Payne, D. 9(3); Penrice, G. 4(3); Phillips, K. 26(1); Pitcher, G. 2(7); Porter, G. 28(1); Ramage, C. 34(2); Simpson, C. ; Ward, D. (1); White, D. 9(7); Wilkinson, P. 4
League (62): Ramage 15, Phillips 11 (2 pens), Connolly 8 (2 pens), Mooney 6 (1 pen), Foster 5, White 5, Moralee 3, Bazeley 1, Caskey 1, Holdsworth 1, Johnson 1, Palmer 1, Payne 1, Penrice 1, Pitcher 1, Porter 1.
Coca-Cola Cup (3): Bazeley 1, Johnson 1, Phillips 1.
FA Cup (1): Mooney 1.
Ground: Vicarage Road Stadium, Watford WD1 8ER. Telephone (01923) 496000.
Record attendance: 34,099 v Manchester U, FA Cup 4th rd (replay), 3 February 1969. **Capacity:** 22,000.
Team Manager: Kenny Jackett.
Secretary: John Alexander.
Honours – Football League: Division 3 Division 1 – 1968–69. Division 4 Champions – 1977–78.
Colours: Yellow shirts, black shorts, black stockings.

WEST BROMWICH ALBION   DIV. 1

Agnew, Paul	Ashcroft, Lee	Brien, Anthony J.
Buckley, Simon J.	Burgess, Daryl	Coldicott, Stacy
Cunnington, Shaun G.	Cutler, Neil A.	Darby, Julian T.
Donovan, Kevin	Germaine, Gary	Gilbert, David J.
Hamilton, Ian R.	Hargreaves, Christian	Herbert, Craig J.

Holmes, Paul
Nicholson, Shane M.
Rodosthenous, Michael
Spink, Nigel P.

Hunt, Andrew
Raven, Paul D.
Smith, David
Taylor, Robert

Mardon, Paul J.
Reece, Paul J.
Sneekes, Richard

League Appearances: Agnew, P. 3; Angell, B. (3); Ashcroft, L. 11(15); Brien, T. 2; Burgess, D. 45; Butler, P. 9; Coldicott, S. 21(12); Comyn, A. 3; Cunnington, S. 8(1); Darby, J. 19(3); Donovan, K. 28(6); Edwards, P. 13(3); Fettis, A. 3; Gilbert, D. 35(5); Hamilton, I. 39(2); Hargreaves, C. (1); Holmes, P. 18; Hunt, A. 44(1); King, P. 4; Mardon, P. 35(4); Naylor, S. 27; Nicholson, S. 18; Phelan, M. 1; Raven, P. 40; Reece, P. 1; Rees, T. 3(6); Smith, D. 9(7); Sneekes, R. 13; Spink, N. 15; Taylor, B. 39(3)
League (60): Taylor 17, Hunt 14 (3 pens) Sneekes 10, Gilbert 5, Ashcroft 4 (1 pen), Raven 4, Hamilton 3, Burgess 2, Darby 1.
Coca-Cola Cup (8): Taylor 3, Burgess 2, Donovan 2, Hunt 1.
FA Cup (3): Coldicott 1, Hunt 1, Raven 1.
Ground: The Hawthorns, West Bromwich B71 4LF. Telephone (0121) 525 8888.
Record attendance: 64,815 v Arsenal, FA Cup 6th rd, 6 March 1937. **Capacity:** 25,296.
Manager: Alan Buckley.
Secretary: Dr. John J. Evans BA, PHD. (Wales).
Honours – Football League: Division 1 Champions – 1919–20. Division 2 Champions – 1901–02, 1910–11. **FA Cup:** Winners 1888, 1892, 1931, 1954, 1968.
Football League Cup: Winners 1965–66.
Colours: Navy blue and white striped shirts, white shorts, blue and white stockings.

WEST HAM UNITED   FA PREMIERSHIP

Bilic, Slaven
Boogers, Marco
Canham, Scott W.
Da Cruz Carvalho, Daniel
  (on loan from Sporting
  Lisbon)
Jones, Stephen G.
Lazaridis, Stan
Miklosko, Ludek
Omoyinmi, Emmanuel
Rieper, Marc
Shipp, Daniel A.
Williamson, Daniel A.

Bishop, Ian W.
Breacker, Timothy S.
Cottee, Antony R.
Dicks, Julian A.
Dumitrescu, Ilie
Hodges, Lee L.
Lampard, Frank J.
Mautone, Steve
Moncur, John F.
Philson, Graeme
Rowland, Keith
Slater, Robert D.

Blaney, Steven D.
Brown, Kenneth J.
Coyne, Christopher
Dowie, Iain
Ferdinand, Rio G.
Hughes, Michael E.
  (on loan from
  Strasbourg)
Moore, Jason M.
Potts, Steven J.
Sealey, Leslie J.
Whitbread, Adrian R.

League Appearances: Allen, M. 3; Bilic, S. 13; Bishop, I. 35; Boere, J. (1); Boogers, M. (4); Breacker, T. 19(3); Brown, K. 3; Cottee, T. 30(3); Dani, . 3(6); Dicks, J. 34; Dowie, I. 33; Dumitrescu, I. 2(1); Ferdinand, R. (1); Finn, N. 1; Gordon, D. (1); Harkes, J. 6(5); Hughes, M. 28; Hutchison, D. 8(4); Lampard, F. 2; Lazaridis, S. 2(2); Martin, A. 10(4); Miklosko, L. 36; Moncur, J. 19(1); Potts, S. 34; Rieper, M. 35(1); Rowland, K. 19(4); Sealey, L. 1(1); Slater, R. 16(6); Watson, M. (1); Whitbread, A. (2); Williamson, D. 28(1)
League (43): Cottee 10, Dicks 10 (5 pens), Dowie 8, Williamson 4, Dani 2, Hutchison 2, Rieper 2, Slater 2, Allen 1, Bishop 1, own goal 1.
Coca-Cola Cup (5): Cottee 2, Bishop 1, Dicks 1 (pen), Moncur 1.

FA Cup (3): Dowie 1, Hughes 1, Moncur 1.
Ground: Boleyn Ground, Green Street, Upton Park, London E13 9AZ. Telephone (0181) 548 2748.
Record attendance: 42,322 v Tottenham H, Division 1, 17 October 1970. **Capacity:** 25,985.
Manager: Harry Redknapp.
Secretary: Richard Skirrow.
Honours – Football League: Division 2 Champions – 1957–58, 1980–81. **FA Cup: Winners** 1964, 1975, 1980. **European Competitions: European Cup-Winners' Cup winners:** 1964–65.
Colours: Claret shirts, white shorts, light blue and claret stockings.

WIGAN ATHLETIC   DIV. 3

Biggins, Wayne	Black, Anthony P.	Butler, John E.
Carragher, Mathew	Diaz, Isidro	Farnworth, Simon
Greenall, Colin A.	Johnson, Gavin	Kilford, Ian A.
Lancashire, Graham	Love, Michael J.	Lowe, David A.
Martinez, Roberto	Pender, John P.	Seba, Jesus
Sharp, Kevin P.		

League Appearances: Barnwell-Edinboro, J. 2(8); Benjamin, I. 1(2); Biggins, W. 15(3); Black, T. 8(13); Butler, J. 33; Carragher, M. 22(6); Diaz, I. 31(6); Doolan, J. 2(1); Farnworth, S. 43; Farrell, A. 21(2); Felgate, D. 3; Greenall, C. 37; Johnson, G. 27; Kelly, T. 2; Kilford, I. 18(7); Lancashire, G. 5; Leonard, M. 32(3); Lightfoot, C. 11(3); Lowe, D. 7; Lyons, A. 14(8); Martinez, R. 42; Miller, D. 4(3); Mutch, A. 7; Ogden, N. 10; Pender, J. 40(1); Rimmer, N. 27(3); Robertson, J. 14; Seba, J. 8(12); Sharp, K. 20
League (62): Diaz 10, Martinez 9 (1 pen), Leonard 7, Sharp 6 (1 pen), Johnson 3, Kilford 3, Lancashire 3, Lowe 3, Seba 3, Biggins 2 (1 pen), Black 2, Greenall 2, Barnwell-Edinboro 1, Butler 1, Farrell 1, Lightfoot 1, Lyons 1, Mutch 1, Pender 1, Robertson 1, own goal 1.
Coca-Cola Cup (2): Lyons 1 (pen), Martinez 1.
FA Cup (9): Martinez 3, Black 2, Diaz 2, Leonard 1, own goal 1.
Ground: Springfield Park, Wigan WN6 7BA. Telephone (01942) 244433.
Capacity: 6901.
Record attendance: 27,500 v Hereford U, FA Cup 2nd rd, 12 December 1953.
Manager: John Deehan.
Secretary: Mrs Brenda Spencer.
Honours – Freight Rover Trophy: Winners 1984–85.
Colours: Blue and white striped shirts, black shorts, blue stockings.

WIMBLEDON   FA PREMIERSHIP

Ardley, Neal C.	Blackwell, Dean R.	Blissett, Gary P.
Castledine, Stewart M.	Clarke, Andrew W.	Cunningham, Kenneth
Earle, Robert G.	Ekoku, Efangwu	Elkins, Gary
Euell, Jason J.	Fear, Peter	Fitzgerald, Scott B.
Futcher, Andrew R.	Gayle, Marcus A.	Goodman, Jonathan
Harford, Michael G.	Heald, Paul A.	Hodges, Daniel W.

Holdsworth, Dean C.
Laidlaw, Iain L.
Murphy, Brendan F.
Pearce, Andrew J.
Reeves, Alan

Jones, Vincent P.
Leonhardsen, Oyvind
Newhouse, Aidan R.
Perry, Christopher J.
Sullivan, Neil

Kimble, Alan F.
McAllister, Brian
Payne, Grant
Piper, Leonard H.
Thorn, Andrew C.

League Appearances: Ardley, N. 4(2); Blackwell, D. 8; Blissett, G. (4); Castledine, S. 2(2); Clarke, A. 9(9); Cunningham, K. 32(1); Earle, R. 37; Ekoku, E. 28(3); Elkins, G. 7(3); Euell, J. 4(5); Fear, P. 4; Fitzgerald, S. 2(2); Gayle, M. 21(13); Goodman, J. 9(18); Harford, M. 17(4); Heald, P. 18; Holdsworth, D. 31(2); Jones, V. 27(4); Kimble, A. 31; Leonhardsen, O. 28(1); McAllister, B. 2; Pearce, A. 6(1); Perry, C. 35(2); Reeves, A. 21(3); Segers, H. 3(1); Skinner, J. 1; Sullivan, N. 16; Talboys, S. 3(2); Thorn, A. 11(3); Tracey, S. 1
League (55): Earle 11, Holdsworth 10 (1 pen), Ekoku 7, Goodman 6, Gayle 5, Leonhardsen 4, Jones 3 (1 pen), Clarke 2, Euell 2, Harford 2, Castledine 1, Reeves 1, own goal 1.
Coca-Cola Cup (7): Holdsworth 4 (1 pen), Earle 2, Clarke 1.
FA Cup (11): Ekoku 3, Goodman 3, Holdsworth 2, Clarke 1, Earle 1, Leonhardsen 1.
Ground: Selhurst Park, South Norwood, London SE25 6PY. Telephone (0181) 771 2233.
Record attendance: 30,115 v Manchester U, FA Premier League, 9 May 1993.
Capacity: 26,309.
Manager: Joe Kinnear.
Secretary: Steve Rooke.
Honours – Football League: Division 4 Champions – 1982–83. **FA Cup:** Winners 1987–88.
Colours: All navy blue with yellow trim.

WOLVERHAMPTON WANDERERS   DIV. 1

Atkins, Mark N.
Corica, Stephen C.
De Jong, Davy
Emblen, Neil R.
Froggatt, Stephen J.
Law, Brian J.
Pearce, Dennis A.
Robinson, Carl P.
Thomas, Geoffrey R.
Westwood, Christopher J.
Young, Eric

Birch, Paul
Daley, Anthony M.
De Wolf, Johannes H.
Ferguson, Darren
Goodman, Donald R.
Masters, Neil B.
Rankine, Simon M.
Smith, James J. A.
Thompson, Andrew R.
Williams, Mark F.

Bull, Stephen G.
De Bont, Andrew C.
Dennison, Robert
Foley, Dominic J.
Jones, Paul S.
Osborn, Simon E.
Richards, Dean I.
Stowell, Michael
Venus, Mark
Wright, Jermaine M.

League Appearances: Atkins, M. 26(6); Birch, P. 5(2); Bull, S. 42(2); Corica, S. 17; Cowans, G. 10(6); Crowe, G. 1(1); Daley, T. 16(2); De Wolf, J. 14(1); Emblen, N. 30(3); Ferguson, D. 26(7); Foley, D. 1(4); Froggatt, S. 13(5); Goodman, D. 43(1); Jones, P. 8; Kelly, D. 3(2); Law, B. 5(2); Masters, N. 3; Osborn, S. 21; Pearce, D. 3(2); Rankine, M. 27(5); Richards, D. 36(1); Samways, V. 3; Shirtliff, P. 2; Smith, J. 10(3); Stowell, M. 38; Thomas, G. (2); Thompson, A. 45; Venus, M. 19(3); Williams, M. 5(7); Wright, J. 4(3); Young, E. 30
League (56): Goodman 16, Bull 15, Thompson 6 (5 pens), Atkins 3, Daley 3, Emblen 2, Osborn 2, Young 2, Crowe 1, De Wolf 1, Ferguson 1 (pen), Froggatt 1, Law 1, Richards 1, own goal 1.

Coca-Cola Cup (11): Goodman 3, Atkins 2, Daley 1, Emblen 1, Ferguson 1, Venus 1, Williams 1, Wright 1.
FA Cup (4): Bull 2, Ferguson 1, Goodman 1.
Ground: Molineux Grounds, Wolverhampton WV1 4QR. Telephone (01902) 655000.
Record attendance: 61,315 v Liverpool, FA Cup 5th rd, 11 February 1939.
Capacity: 28,525.
Team Manager: Mark McGhee.
Secretary: Tom Finn.
Honours – Football League: Division 1 Champions – 1953–54, 1957–58, 1958–59. Division 2 Champions – 1931–32, 1976–77. Division 3 (N) Champions – 1923–24. Division 3 Champions – 1988–89. Division 4 Champions – 1987–88. **FA Cup:** Winners 1893, 1908, 1949, 1960. **Football League Cup:** Winners 1973–74, 1979–80. **Sherpa Van Trophy winners** 1988.
Colours: Gold shirts, black shorts, gold stockings.

WREXHAM   DIV. 2

Brace, Deryn P. J.	Brammer, David	Cartwright, Mark N.
Chalk, Martyn P. G.	Coady, Lewis	Connolly, Karl
Cross, Jonathan N.	Futcher, Stephen A.	Hardy, Philip
Hughes, Bryan	Humes, Anthony	Hunter, Barry V.
Jones, Barry	Marriot, Andrew	McGregor, Mark D. T.
Morris, Stephen	Owen, Gareth	Phillips, Wayne
Russell, Kevin J.	Skinner, Craig R.	Ward, Peter
Watkin, Stephen	Williams, Scott J.	

League Appearances: Brace, D. 16; Brammer, D. 11; Chalk, M. 19; Connolly, K. 45(1); Cross, J. 4(3); Durkan, K. 6(2); Hardy, P. 41(1); Hughes, B. 11(11); Humes, T. 26(1); Hunter, B. 30(1); Jones, B. 39(1); Jones, L. 20; Marriott, A. 46; McGregor, M. 27(5); Morris, S. 4(9); Owen, G. 11(8); Phillips, W. 43(1); Russell, K. 37(3); Skinner, C. 21(2); Ward, P. 33(1); Watkin, S. 16(13)
League (76): Connolly 18 (4 pens), Jones L 9, Russell 7, Watkin 7 (1 pen), Phillips 5, Ward 5, Chalk 4, Humes 3, Hunter 3, Morris 3, Skinner 3, Brammer 2, Owen 2, Brace 1, McGregor 1, own goals 3.
Coca-Cola Cup (2): Russell 1, Watkin 1.
FA Cup (3): Connolly 1 (pen), Hunter 1, Watkin 1.
Ground: Racecourse Ground, Mold Road, Wrexham LL11 2AN. Telephone (01978) 262129.
Record attendance: 34,445 v Manchester U, FA Cup 4th rd, 26 January 1957.
Capacity: 9200.
Manager: Brian Flynn.
Secretary: D. L. Rhodes.
Honours – Football League: Division 3 Champions – 1977–78. **Welsh Cup:** Winners 22 times.
Colours: Red shirts, white shorts, red stockings.

WYCOMBE WANDERERS   DIV. 2

Bell, Michael   Brown, Stephen   Carroll, David F.
Clark, Anthony J.   Cousins, Jason M.   Crossley, Matthew J. W.
Desouza, Juan M. I.   Evans, Terence W.   Farrell, David
Lawrence, Matthew   McGavin, Steven J.   McGorry, Brian P.
Patterson, Gary   Rowbotham, Jason   Ryan, Keith J.
Skiverton, Terence J.   Williams, John

League Appearances: Bell, M. 40(1); Blissett, G. 4; Brown, S. 38; Carroll, D. 46;
Castledine, S. 7; Clark, A. 1(2); Cousins, J. 28(2); Crossley, M. 12; De Souza, M.
38(5); Dykstra, S. 13; Evans, T. 26(2); Farrell, D. 27(6); Foran, M. 5; Garner, S.
8(5); Hardyman, P. 12(3); Hemmings, T. (3); Howard, T. 36(3); Hyde, P. 17;
Lawrence, M. 1(2); Markman, D. (2); McGavin, S. 22(9); McGorry, B. (4);
Moussaddik, C. 1; Patterson, G. 31(6); Roberts, B. 15; Rowbotham, J. 27; Ryan, K.
18(5); Skiverton, T. 3(1); Soloman, J. 6(1); Stapleton, S. 1; Williams, J. 23(6)
League (63): De Souza 18 (1 pen), Carroll 8 (2 pens), Williams 8, Farrell 7 (1 pen),
Ryan 4, Castledine 3, Evans 3, Blissett 2, Garner 2, Howard 2, McGavin 2 (2 pens),
Bell 1, Crossley 1, Patterson 1, Skiverton 1.
Coca-Cola Cup (3): De Souza 2, Crossley 1.
FA Cup (1): Patterson 1.
Ground: Adams Park, Hillbottom Road, Sands, High Wycombe HP12   4HJ.
Telephone (01494) 472100.
Record attendance: 9002 v West Ham U, FA Cup 3rd rd, 7 January 1995. **Capacity:**
9650.
Manager: Alan Smith.
Secretary: John Reardon.
Honours – GM Vauxhall Conference winners: 1993. **FA Trophy winners:** 1991,
1993.
Colours: Light & dark blue striped shirts, light blue shorts, light blue stockings.

YORK CITY   DIV. 2

Atkin, Paul A.   Atkinson, Patrick   Barras, Anthony
Bull, Gary W.   Bushell, Stephen   Campbell, Neil A.
Cresswell, Richard P. W.   Hall, Wayne   Himsworth, Gary P.
Jordan, Scott D.   Kiely, Dean L.   McMillan, Lyndon A.
Murty, Graeme S.   Naylor, Glenn   Osborne, Wayne
Oxley, Scott   Pepper, Colin N.   Pouton, Alan
Randall, Adrian J.   Sharples, John B.   Stephenson, Paul
Tutill, Stephen A.   Warrington, Andrew C.   Williams, Darren

League Appearances: Atkin, P. 25(4); Atkinson, P. 20(2); Baker, P. 11(7); Barnes,
P. 30; Barras, T. 32; Bull, G. 15; Bushell, S. 17(6); Cresswell, R. 9(7); Curtis, A. (1);
Hall, W. 21(2); Himsworth, G. 7(1); Jordan, S. 18(8); Kiely, D. 40; Matthews, R.
14(3); McMillan, A. 46; Murty, G. 31(4); Naylor, G. 20(5); Osborne, W. 5(1);
Oxley, S. 1(1); Pepper, N. 39(1); Peverell, N. 11(9); Randall, A. 13(3); Scaife, N.
(1); Sharples, J. 10; Stephenson, P. 24(3); Tutill, S. 25; Warrington, A. 6; Williams,
D. 16(2)

League (58): Barnes 15 (2 pens), Bull 8 (1 pen), Pepper 8 (2 pens), Naylor 7, Baker 5, Barras 3, Murty 2, Stephenson 2, Cresswell 1, Himsworth 1, Jordan 1, McMillan 1, Matthews 1, Peverell 1, own goals 2.
Coca-Cola Cup (11): Barnes 5, Baker 2, Barras 1, Jordan 1, Pepper 1, Peverell 1.
FA Cup (0).
Ground: Bootham Crescent, York YO3 7AQ. Telephone (01904) 624447.
Record attendance: 28,123 v Huddersfield T, FA Cup 6th rd, 5 March 1938.
Capacity: 9534.
Manager: Alan Little.
Secretary: Keith Usher.
Honours – Football League: Division 4 Champions – 1983–84.
Colours: Red shirts, blue shorts, red stockings.

LEAGUE REVIEW

Manchester United achieved their third FA Carling Premiership title in four years and also completed their second League and Cup double in three years.

Their prospects of winning the championship appeared to be remote in January as Newcastle held a 12-point lead over them at this stage. But Newcastle experienced problems from February onwards. During this period they were only able to take four points from a possible 18. This unhappy spell ended for them in a 4-3 defeat at Liverpool which was easily the match of the season if not one of the most outstanding in League history.

Then it was Manchester United who took control for the rest of the season apart from a slip up at Southampton where they were 3-0 down at half-time but decided to change their grey shirts during the interval and retrieved one goal at least. This was United's only defeat in their last sixteen matches.

Liverpool, who still had a remote chance of catching the top two, were unable to sustain this type of performance and it was a disappointing season for Blackburn, the champions, who also failed to make any impression in Europe. However, they did manage to beat Nottingham Forest 7-0, thus ending Forest's record-breaking run of 25 Premier League games without defeat.

Arsenal disappointed after a promising start and were just pipped for fourth place by Aston Villa. Everton improved noticeably during the season and finished sixth.

Tottenham, who were as high in the table as third in January following a convincing 4-1 win over Manchester United were unable to sustain this effort and both West Ham and Chelsea found results not in keeping with their performances and a lack of scoring kept them in mid-table.

Middlesbrough had a disastrous run of 13 games without a win, Leeds won only three league games in the second half of the season, but Wimbledon's ability to escape relegation was again well to the fore.

Both Queens Park Rangers and Bolton had appeared to be doomed to relegation towards the end of the season but there was a scramble on the last day involving the other relegation place. Coventry, Southampton and Manchester City were all involved and there was a chance that Sheffield Wednesday were about to be drawn into it. In the event it was Manchester City who failed having scored only 33 goals during the season. They will play next season in the newly-sponsored Nationwide Football League First Division.

Joining the Premier League next season will be Sunderland, Derby County and Leicester City who emerged successfully from the play-offs.

Down from the First Division went Watford, Luton and Millwall who amazingly were top in December. Up from the Second Division are Swindon, Oxford and Bradford from the play-offs. Into Division Three go Carlisle, Swansea and Brighton. York, who had beaten Manchester United in the Coca-Cola Cup earlier in the season, had to wait until the final match to survive. Preston won Division Three and achieved automatic promotion with Gillingham and Bury. They were joined from the play-offs by Plymouth. At the bottom of the division, Torquay survived the indignity of relegation to the Vauxhall Conference because Stevenage's ground did not meet the required criteria specified by the Football League.

Rangers again dominated the scene in the Scottish League, though the margin was for them a mere four points over Celtic. They, too, achieved a League and Cup double, beating Hearts 5-1 in the Scottish Cup.

Earlier in the season, Aberdeen had won the Scottish Coca-Cola Cup Final, beating Dundee 2-0.

Dunfermline Athletic won automatic promotion to the Premier Division and were joined by Dundee United who beat Partick Thistle in the play-offs.

HOME TEAM	Arsenal	Aston Villa	Blackburn R	Bolton W	Chelsea	Coventry C	Everton	Leeds U	Liverpool	Manchester C
Arsenal	—	2-0	0-0	2-1	1-1	1-1	1-2	2-1	0-0	3-1
Aston Villa	1-1	—	2-0	1-0	0-1	4-1	1-0	3-0	0-2	0-1
Blackburn R	1-1	1-1	—	3-1	3-0	5-1	0-3	1-0	2-3	2-0
Bolton W	1-0	0-2	2-1	—	2-1	1-2	1-1	0-2	0-1	1-1
Chelsea	1-0	1-2	2-3	3-2	—	2-2	0-0	4-1	2-2	1-1
Coventry C	0-0	0-3	5-0	0-2	1-0	—	2-1	0-0	1-0	2-1
Everton	0-2	1-0	1-0	3-0	1-1	2-2	—	2-0	1-1	2-0
Leeds U	0-3	2-0	0-0	0-1	3-1	3-1	2-2	—	1-0	0-1
Liverpool	3-1	3-0	3-0	5-2	2-0	0-0	1-2	5-0	—	6-0
Manchester C	0-1	1-0	1-1	1-0	0-1	1-1	0-2	0-0	2-2	—
Manchester U	1-0	0-0	1-0	3-0	1-1	1-0	2-0	1-0	2-2	1-0
Middlesbrough	2-3	0-2	2-0	1-4	2-0	2-1	0-2	1-1	2-1	4-1
Newcastle U	2-0	1-0	1-0	2-1	3-0	3-0	1-0	2-1	2-1	3-1
Nottingham F	0-1	1-1	1-5	3-2	0-0	0-0	3-2	2-1	1-0	3-0
QPR	1-1	1-0	0-1	2-1	1-2	1-1	3-1	1-2	1-2	1-0
Sheffield W	1-0	2-0	2-1	4-2	0-0	4-3	2-5	6-2	1-1	1-1
Southampton	0-0	0-1	1-0	1-0	2-3	1-0	2-2	1-1	1-3	1-1
Tottenham H	2-1	0-1	2-3	2-2	1-1	3-1	0-0	2-1	1-3	1-0
West Ham U	0-1	1-4	1-1	1-0	1-3	3-2	2-1	1-2	0-0	4-2
Wimbledon	0-3	3-3	1-1	3-2	1-1	0-2	2-3	2-4	1-0	3-0

Manchester U	Middlesbrough	Newcastle U	Nottingham F	QPR	Sheffield W	Southampton	Tottenham H	West Ham U	Wimbledon
1-0	1-1	2-0	1-1	3-0	4-2	4-2	0-0	1-0	1-3
3-1	0-0	1-1	1-1	4-2	3-2	3-0	2-1	1-1	2-0
1-2	1-0	2-1	7-0	1-0	3-0	2-1	2-1	4-2	3-2
0-6	1-1	1-3	1-1	0-1	2-1	0-1	2-3	0-3	1-0
1-4	5-0	1-0	1-0	1-1	0-0	3-0	0-0	1-2	1-2
0-4	0-0	0-1	1-1	1-0	0-1	1-1	2-3	2-2	3-3
2-3	4-0	1-3	3-0	2-0	2-2	2-0	1-1	3-0	2-4
3-1	0-1	0-1	1-3	1-3	2-0	1-0	1-3	2-0	1-1
2-0	1-0	4-3	4-2	1-0	1-1	1-1	0-0	2-0	2-2
2-3	0-1	3-3	1-1	2-0	1-0	2-1	1-1	2-1	1-0
—	2-0	2-0	5-0	2-1	2-2	4-1	1-0	2-1	3-1
0-3	—	1-2	1-1	1-0	3-1	0-0	0-1	4-2	1-1
0-1	1-0	—	3-1	2-1	2-0	1-0	1-1	3-0	6-1
1-1	1-0	1-1	—	3-0	1-0	1-0	2-1	1-1	4-1
1-1	1-1	2-3	1-1	—	0-3	3-0	2-3	3-0	0-3
0-0	0-1	0-2	1-3	1-3	—	2-2	1-3	0-1	2-1
3-1	2-1	1-0	3-4	2-0	0-1	—	0-0	0-0	0-0
4-1	1-1	1-1	0-1	1-0	1-0	1-0	—	0-1	3-1
0-1	2-0	2-0	1-0	1-0	1-1	2-1	1-1	—	1-1
2-4	0-0	3-3	1-0	2-1	2-2	1-2	0-1	0-1	—

ENDSLEIGH INSURANCE LEAGUE

HOME TEAM	Barnsley	Birmingham C	Charlton Ath	C Palace	Derby Co	Grimsby T	Huddersfield T	Ipswich T	Leicester C	Luton T
Barnsley	—	0-5	1-2	1-1	2-0	1-1	3-0	3-3	2-2	1-0
Birmingham C	0-0	—	3-4	0-0	1-4	3-1	2-0	3-1	2-2	4-0
Charlton Ath	1-1	3-1	—	0-0	0-0	0-1	2-1	0-2	0-1	1-1
C Palace	4-3	3-2	1-1	—	0-0	5-0	0-0	1-1	0-1	2-0
Derby Co	4-1	1-1	2-0	2-1	—	1-1	3-2	1-1	0-1	1-1
Grimsby T	3-1	2-1	1-2	0-2	1-1	—	1-1	3-1	2-2	0-0
Huddersfield T	3-0	4-2	2-2	3-0	0-1	1-3	—	2-1	3-1	1-0
Ipswich T	2-2	2-0	1-5	1-0	1-0	2-2	2-1	—	4-2	0-1
Leicester C	2-2	3-0	1-1	2-3	0-0	2-1	2-1	0-2	—	1-1
Luton T	1-3	0-0	0-1	0-0	1-2	3-2	2-2	1-2	1-1	—
Millwall	0-1	2-0	0-2	1-4	0-1	2-1	0-0	2-1	1-1	1-0
Norwich C	3-1	1-1	0-1	1-0	1-0	2-2	2-0	2-1	0-1	1-0
Oldham Ath	0-1	4-0	1-1	3-1	0-1	1-0	3-0	1-1	3-1	1-0
Portsmouth	0-0	0-1	2-1	2-3	2-2	3-1	1-1	0-1	2-1	4-0
Port Vale	3-0	1-2	1-3	1-2	1-1	1-0	1-0	2-1	0-2	1-0
Reading	0-0	0-1	0-0	0-2	3-2	0-2	3-1	1-4	1-1	3-1
Sheffield U	1-0	1-1	2-0	2-3	0-2	1-2	0-2	2-2	1-3	1-0
Southend U	0-0	3-1	1-1	1-1	1-2	1-0	0-0	2-1	2-1	0-1
Stoke C	2-0	1-0	1-0	1-2	1-1	1-2	1-1	3-1	1-0	5-0
Sunderland	2-1	3-0	0-0	1-0	3-0	1-0	3-2	1-0	1-2	1-0
Tranmere R	1-3	2-2	0-0	2-3	5-1	0-1	3-1	5-2	1-1	1-0
Watford	2-1	1-1	1-2	0-0	0-0	6-3	0-1	2-3	0-1	1-1
WBA	2-1	1-0	1-0	2-3	3-2	3-1	1-2	0-0	2-3	0-2
Wolverhampton W	2-2	3-2	0-0	0-2	3-0	4-1	0-0	2-2	2-3	0-0

DIVISION 1 1995–96 RESULTS

	Millwall	Norwich C	Oldham Ath	Portsmouth	Port Vale	Reading	Sheffield U	Southend U	Stoke C	Sunderland	Tranmere R	Watford	WBA	Wolverhampton W
	3-1	2-2	2-1	0-0	1-1	0-1	2-2	1-1	3-1	0-1	2-1	2-1	1-1	1-0
	2-2	3-1	0-0	2-0	3-1	1-2	0-1	2-0	1-1	0-2	1-0	1-0	1-1	2-0
	2-0	1-1	1-1	2-1	2-2	2-1	1-1	0-3	2-1	1-1	0-0	2-1	4-1	1-1
	1-2	0-1	2-2	0-0	2-2	0-2	0-0	2-0	1-1	0-1	2-1	4-0	1-0	3-2
	2-2	2-1	2-1	3-2	0-0	3-0	4-2	1-0	3-1	3-1	6-2	1-1	3-0	0-0
	1-2	2-2	1-1	2-1	1-0	0-0	0-2	1-1	1-0	0-4	1-1	0-0	1-0	3-0
	3-0	3-2	0-0	0-1	0-2	3-1	1-2	3-1	1-1	1-1	1-0	1-0	4-1	2-1
	0-0	2-1	2-1	3-2	5-1	1-2	1-1	1-1	4-1	3-0	1-2	4-2	2-1	1-2
	2-1	3-2	2-0	4-2	1-1	1-1	0-2	1-3	2-3	0-0	0-1	1-0	1-2	1-0
	1-0	1-3	1-1	3-1	3-2	1-2	1-0	3-1	1-2	0-2	3-2	0-0	1-2	2-3
	—	2-1	0-1	1-1	1-2	1-1	1-0	0-0	2-3	1-2	2-2	1-2	2-1	0-1
	0-0	—	2-1	1-1	2-1	3-3	0-0	0-1	0-1	0-0	1-1	1-2	2-2	2-3
	2-2	2-0	—	1-1	2-2	2-1	2-1	0-1	2-0	1-2	1-2	0-0	1-2	0-0
	0-1	1-0	2-1	—	1-2	0-0	1-2	4-2	3-3	2-2	0-2	4-2	0-2	0-2
	0-1	1-0	1-3	0-2	—	3-2	2-3	2-1	1-0	1-1	1-1	1-1	3-1	2-2
	1-2	0-3	2-0	0-1	2-2	—	0-3	3-3	1-0	1-1	1-0	0-0	3-1	3-0
	2-0	2-1	2-1	4-1	1-1	0-0	—	3-0	0-0	0-0	0-2	1-1	1-2	2-1
	2-0	1-1	1-1	2-1	2-1	0-0	2-1	—	2-4	0-2	2-0	1-1	2-1	2-1
	1-0	1-1	0-1	2-1	0-1	1-1	2-2	1-0	—	1-0	0-0	2-0	2-1	2-0
	6-0	0-1	1-0	1-1	0-0	2-2	2-0	1-0	0-0	—	0-0	1-1	0-0	2-0
	2-2	1-1	2-0	1-2	2-1	2-1	1-1	3-0	0-0	2-0	—	2-3	2-2	2-2
	0-1	0-2	2-1	1-2	5-2	4-2	2-1	2-2	3-0	3-3	3-0	—	1-1	1-1
	1-0	1-4	1-0	2-1	1-1	2-0	3-1	3-1	0-1	0-1	1-1	4-4	—	0-0
	1-1	0-2	1-3	2-2	0-1	1-1	1-0	2-0	1-4	3-0	2-1	3-0	1-1	—

HOME TEAM	Blackpool	AFC Bournemouth	Bradford C	Brentford	Brighton & HA	Bristol C	Bristol R	Burnley	Carlisle U	Chesterfield
Blackpool	—	2-1	4-1	1-0	2-1	3-0	3-0	3-1	3-1	0-0
AFC Bournemouth	1-0	—	3-1	1-0	3-1	1-1	2-1	0-2	2-0	2-0
Bradford C	2-1	1-0	—	2-1	1-3	3-0	2-3	2-2	3-1	2-1
Brentford	1-2	2-0	2-1	—	0-1	2-2	0-0	1-0	1-1	1-2
Brighton & HA	1-2	2-0	0-0	0-0	—	0-2	2-0	1-0	1-0	0-2
Bristol C	1-1	3-0	2-1	0-0	0-1	—	0-2	0-1	1-1	2-1
Bristol R	1-1	0-2	1-0	2-0	1-0	2-4	—	1-0	1-1	1-0
Burnley	0-1	0-0	2-3	1-0	3-0	0-0	0-1	—	2-0	2-2
Carlisle U	1-2	4-0	2-2	2-1	1-0	2-1	1-2	2-0	—	1-1
Chesterfield	1-0	3-0	2-1	2-2	1-0	1-1	2-1	4-2	3-0	—
Crewe Alex	1-2	2-0	1-2	3-1	3-1	4-2	1-2	3-1	2-1	3-0
Hull C	2-1	1-1	2-3	0-1	0-0	2-3	1-3	3-0	2-5	0-0
Notts Co	1-1	2-0	0-2	4-0	2-1	2-2	4-2	1-1	3-1	4-1
Oxford U	1-0	2-0	0-0	2-1	1-1	2-0	1-2	5-0	4-0	1-0
Peterborough U	0-0	4-5	3-1	0-1	3-1	1-1	0-0	0-2	6-1	0-1
Rotherham U	2-1	1-0	2-0	1-0	1-0	2-3	1-0	1-0	2-2	0-1
Shrewsbury T	0-2	1-2	1-1	2-1	2-1	4-1	1-1	3-0	1-1	0-0
Stockport Co	1-1	3-1	1-2	1-1	3-1	0-0	2-0	0-0	2-0	0-1
Swansea C	0-2	1-1	2-0	2-1	2-1	2-1	2-2	2-4	1-1	3-2
Swindon T	1-1	2-2	4-1	2-2	0-0	2-0	2-1	0-0	2-1	1-1
Walsall	1-1	0-0	2-1	0-1	2-1	2-1	1-1	3-1	2-1	3-0
Wrexham	1-1	5-0	1-2	2-2	1-1	0-0	3-2	0-2	3-2	3-0
Wycombe W	0-1	1-2	5-2	2-1	0-2	1-1	1-1	4-1	4-0	1-0
York C	0-2	3-1	0-3	2-2	3-1	0-1	0-1	1-1	1-1	0-1

DIVISION 2 1995–96 RESULTS

Crewe Alex	Hull C	Notts Co	Oxford U	Peterborough U	Rotherham U	Shrewsbury T	Stockport Co	Swansea C	Swindon T	Walsall	Wrexham	Wycombe W	York C
2-1	1-1	1-0	1-1	2-1	1-2	2-1	0-1	4-0	1-1	1-2	2-0	1-1	1-3
0-4	2-0	0-2	0-1	3-0	2-1	0-2	3-2	3-1	0-0	0-0	1-1	2-3	2-2
2-1	1-1	1-0	1-0	2-1	2-0	3-1	0-1	5-1	1-1	1-0	2-0	0-4	2-2
2-1	1-0	0-0	1-0	3-0	1-1	0-2	1-0	0-0	0-2	1-0	1-0	1-0	2-0
2-2	4-0	1-0	1-2	1-2	1-1	2-2	1-1	0-2	1-3	0-3	2-2	1-2	1-3
3-2	4-0	0-2	0-2	0-1	4-3	2-0	1-0	1-0	0-0	0-2	3-1	0-0	1-1
1-2	2-1	0-3	2-0	1-1	1-0	2-1	1-3	2-2	1-4	2-0	1-2	2-1	1-0
0-1	2-1	3-4	0-2	2-1	2-1	2-1	4-3	3-0	0-0	1-1	2-2	1-1	3-3
1-0	2-0	0-0	1-2	1-1	2-0	1-1	0-1	3-0	0-1	1-1	1-2	4-2	2-0
1-2	0-0	1-0	1-0	1-1	3-0	1-0	1-2	3-2	1-3	1-1	1-1	3-1	2-1
—	1-0	2-2	1-2	2-1	0-2	3-0	0-1	4-1	0-2	1-0	0-0	2-0	1-1
1-2	—	0-0	0-0	2-3	1-4	2-3	1-1	0-0	0-1	1-0	1-1	4-2	0-3
0-1	1-0	—	1-1	1-0	2-1	1-1	1-0	4-0	1-3	2-1	1-0	2-0	2-2
1-0	2-0	1-1	—	4-0	1-1	6-0	2-1	5-1	3-0	3-2	1-1	1-4	2-0
3-1	3-1	0-1	1-1	—	1-0	2-2	0-1	1-1	0-2	2-3	1-1	3-0	6-1
2-2	1-1	2-0	1-0	5-1	—	2-2	2-0	1-1	0-2	0-1	0-1	0-0	2-2
2-3	1-1	0-1	2-0	1-1	3-1	—	1-2	1-2	1-2	0-2	2-2	1-1	2-1
1-1	0-0	2-0	4-2	0-1	1-1	0-2	—	2-0	1-1	0-1	2-3	1-1	3-0
2-1	0-0	0-0	1-1	0-0	0-0	3-1	0-3	—	0-1	2-1	1-3	1-2	0-1
2-1	3-0	1-0	1-1	2-0	1-0	0-1	0-0	3-0	—	1-1	1-1	0-0	3-0
3-2	3-0	0-0	2-2	1-1	3-1	3-0	0-2	4-1	0-0	—	1-2	0-1	2-0
2-3	5-0	1-1	2-1	1-0	7-0	1-1	2-3	1-0	4-3	3-0	—	1-0	2-3
1-1	2-2	1-1	0-3	1-1	1-1	2-0	4-1	0-1	1-2	1-0	1-1	—	2-1
2-3	0-1	1-3	1-0	3-1	2-2	1-2	2-2	0-0	2-0	1-0	1-0	2-1	—

ENDSLEIGH INSURANCE LEAGUE

HOME TEAM	Barnet	Bury	Cambridge U	Cardiff C	Chester C	Colchester U	Darlington	Doncaster R	Exeter C	Fulham
Barnet	—	0-0	2-0	1-0	1-1	1-1	1-1	1-1	3-2	3-0
Bury	0-0	—	1-2	3-0	1-1	0-0	0-0	4-1	2-0	3-0
Cambridge U	1-1	2-4	—	4-2	1-1	3-1	0-1	2-2	1-1	0-0
Cardiff C	1-1	0-1	1-1	—	0-0	1-2	0-2	3-2	0-1	1-4
Chester C	0-2	1-1	1-1	4-0	—	1-1	4-1	0-3	2-2	1-1
Colchester U	3-2	1-0	2-1	1-0	1-2	—	1-1	1-0	1-1	2-2
Darlington	1-1	4-0	0-0	0-1	3-1	2-2	—	1-2	1-0	1-1
Doncaster R	1-0	0-1	2-1	0-0	1-2	3-2	1-1	—	2-0	0-2
Exeter C	1-0	1-1	1-0	0-1	2-2	2-2	0-1	1-0	—	2-1
Fulham	1-1	0-0	0-2	4-2	2-0	1-1	2-2	3-1	2-1	—
Gillingham	1-0	3-0	3-0	1-0	3-1	0-1	0-0	4-0	1-0	1-0
Hartlepool U	0-0	1-2	1-2	2-1	2-1	2-1	1-1	0-1	0-0	1-0
Hereford U	4-1	3-4	5-2	1-3	1-0	1-1	1-0	1-0	2-2	1-0
Leyton Orient	3-3	0-2	3-1	4-1	0-2	0-1	1-1	3-1	0-3	1-0
Lincoln C	1-2	2-2	1-3	0-1	0-0	0-0	0-2	4-0	0-1	4-0
Mansfield T	2-1	1-5	2-1	1-1	3-4	1-2	2-2	0-0	1-1	1-0
Northampton T	0-2	4-1	3-0	1-0	1-0	2-1	1-1	3-3	0-0	2-0
Plymouth Arg	1-1	1-0	1-0	0-0	4-2	1-1	0-1	3-1	2-2	3-0
Preston NE	0-1	0-0	3-3	5-0	2-0	2-0	1-1	1-0	2-0	1-1
Rochdale	0-4	1-1	3-1	3-3	1-3	1-1	1-2	1-0	4-2	1-1
Scarborough	1-1	0-2	2-0	1-0	0-0	0-0	1-2	0-2	0-0	2-2
Scunthorpe U	2-0	1-2	1-2	1-1	0-2	1-0	3-3	2-2	4-0	3-1
Torquay U	1-1	0-2	0-3	0-0	1-1	2-3	0-1	1-2	0-2	2-1
Wigan Ath	1-0	1-2	3-1	3-1	2-1	2-0	1-1	2-0	1-0	1-1

DIVISION 3 1994–95 RESULTS

Gillingham	Hartlepool U	Hereford U	Leyton Orient	Lincoln C	Mansfield T	Northampton T	Plymouth Arg	Preston NE	Rochdale	Scarborough	Scunthorpe U	Torquay U	Wigan Ath
0-2	5-1	1-3	3-0	3-1	0-0	2-0	1-2	1-0	0-4	1-0	1-0	4-0	5-0
1-0	0-3	2-0	2-1	7-1	0-2	0-1	0-5	0-0	1-1	0-2	3-0	1-0	2-1
0-0	0-1	2-2	2-0	2-1	0-2	0-1	2-3	2-1	2-1	4-1	1-2	1-1	2-1
2-0	2-0	3-2	0-0	1-1	3-0	0-1	0-1	0-1	1-0	2-1	0-1	0-0	3-0
1-1	2-0	2-1	1-1	5-1	2-1	1-0	3-1	1-1	1-2	5-0	3-0	4-1	0-0
1-1	4-1	2-0	0-0	3-0	1-3	1-0	2-1	2-2	1-0	1-1	2-1	3-1	1-2
1-0	1-0	1-0	2-0	3-2	1-1	1-2	2-0	1-2	0-1	1-2	0-0	1-2	2-1
0-1	1-0	0-0	4-1	1-1	0-0	1-0	0-0	2-2	0-3	1-0	2-0	1-0	2-1
0-0	1-0	0-2	2-2	1-1	2-2	1-2	1-1	1-1	2-0	2-0	1-0	0-0	0-4
0-0	2-2	0-0	2-1	1-2	4-2	1-3	4-0	2-2	1-1	1-0	1-3	4-0	1-0
—	2-0	1-1	1-1	2-0	2-0	0-0	1-0	1-1	1-0	1-0	0-0	2-0	2-1
1-1	—	0-1	4-1	3-0	1-1	2-1	2-2	0-2	1-1	1-1	2-0	2-2	1-2
0-0	4-1	—	3-2	1-0	0-1	1-0	3-0	0-1	2-0	0-0	3-0	2-1	2-2
0-1	4-1	0-1	—	2-0	1-0	2-0	0-1	0-2	2-0	1-0	0-0	1-0	1-1
0-3	1-1	2-1	1-0	—	2-1	1-0	0-0	0-0	1-2	3-1	2-2	5-0	2-4
0-1	0-3	1-2	0-0	1-2	—	0-0	1-1	0-0	2-2	2-0	1-1	2-0	1-0
1-1	0-0	1-1	1-2	1-1	3-3	—	1-0	1-2	2-1	2-0	1-2	1-1	0-0
1-0	3-0	0-1	1-1	3-0	1-0	1-0	—	0-2	2-0	5-1	1-3	4-3	3-1
0-0	3-0	2-2	4-0	1-2	6-0	0-3	3-2	—	1-2	3-2	2-2	1-0	1-1
2-0	4-0	0-0	1-0	3-3	1-1	1-2	0-1	0-3	—	0-2	1-1	3-0	0-2
0-2	1-2	2-2	2-1	0-0	1-1	2-1	2-2	1-2	1-1	—	1-4	2-1	0-0
1-1	2-1	0-1	2-0	2-3	1-1	0-0	1-1	1-2	1-3	3-3	—	1-0	3-1
0-0	0-0	1-1	1-0	0-2	1-1	3-0	0-2	0-4	1-0	0-0	1-8	—	1-1
2-1	1-0	2-1	1-0	1-1	2-6	1-2	0-1	0-1	2-0	2-0	2-1	3-0	—

FA Carling Premiership

			Home		Goals		Away		Goals			
		P	W	D	L	F	A	W	D	L	F	A	GD	Pts

		P	W	D	L	F	A	W	D	L	F	A	GD	Pts
1	Manchester U	38	15	4	0	36	9	10	3	6	37	26	+38	82
2	Newcastle U	38	17	1	1	38	9	7	5	7	28	28	+29	78
3	Liverpool	38	14	4	1	46	13	6	7	6	24	21	+36	71
4	Aston Villa	38	11	5	3	32	15	7	4	8	20	20	+17	63
5	Arsenal	38	10	7	2	30	16	7	5	7	19	16	+17	63
6	Everton	38	10	5	4	35	19	7	5	7	29	25	+20	61
7	Blackburn R	38	14	2	3	44	19	4	5	10	17	28	+14	61
8	Tottenham H	38	9	5	5	26	19	7	8	4	24	19	+12	61
9	Nottingham F	38	11	6	2	29	17	4	7	8	21	37	-4	58
10	West Ham U	38	9	5	5	25	21	5	4	10	18	31	-9	51
11	Chelsea	38	7	7	5	30	22	5	7	7	16	22	+2	50
12	Middlesbrough	38	8	3	8	27	27	3	7	9	8	23	-15	43
13	Leeds U	38	8	3	8	21	21	4	4	11	19	36	-17	43
14	Wimbledon	38	5	6	8	27	33	5	5	9	28	37	-15	41
15	Sheffield W	38	5	7	7	30	31	5	3	11	18	30	-13	40
16	Coventry C	38	6	7	6	21	23	2	7	10	21	37	-18	38
17	Southampton	38	7	7	5	21	18	2	4	13	13	34	-18	38
18	Manchester C	38	7	7	5	21	19	2	4	13	12	39	-25	38
19	QPR	38	6	5	8	25	26	3	1	15	13	31	-19	33
20	Bolton W	38	5	4	10	16	31	3	1	15	23	40	-32	29

LEADING GOALSCORERS 1995-96

	League	FA Cup	Coca-Cola Cup	Other Cups	Total
FA CARLING PREMIERSHIP					
Alan Shearer (*Blackburn R*)	31	0	5	1	37
Robbie Fowler (*Liverpool*)	28	6	2	0	36
Les Ferdinand (*Newcastle U*)	25	1	3	0	29
Dwight Yorke (*Aston Villa*)	17	2	6	0	25
Teddy Sheringham (*Tottenham H*)	16	5	3	0	24
Andrei Kanchelskis (*Everton*)	16	0	0	0	16
Ian Wright (*Arsenal*)	15	1	7	0	23
Chris Armstrong (*Tottenham H*)	15	4	3	0	22
Eric Cantona (*Manchester U*)	14	5	0	0	19
Stan Collymore (*Liverpool*)	14	5	0	0	19
Dion Dublin (*Coventry C*)	14	2	0	0	16
David Hirst (*Sheffield W*)	13	0	1	0	14
John Spencer (*Chelsea*)	13	1	0	0	14
Tony Yeboah (*Leeds U*)	12	1	3	3	19
Savo Milosevic (*Aston Villa*)	12	1	1	0	14

Endsleigh Insurance League Division 1

			Home				Away				Goals		
		P	W	D	L	F	A	W	D	L	F	A	GD	Pts
1	Sunderland	46	13	8	2	32	10	9	9	5	27	23	+26	83
2	Derby Co	46	14	8	1	48	22	7	8	8	23	29	+20	79
3	Crystal Palace	46	9	9	5	34	22	11	6	6	33	26	+19	75
4	Stoke C	46	13	6	4	32	15	7	7	9	28	34	+11	73
5	Leicester C	46	9	7	7	32	29	10	7	6	34	31	+6	71
6	Charlton Ath	46	8	11	4	28	23	9	5	9	29	22	+12	71
7	Ipswich T	46	13	5	5	45	30	6	7	10	34	39	+10	69
8	Huddersfield T	46	14	4	5	42	23	3	8	12	19	35	+3	63
9	Sheffield U	46	9	7	7	29	25	7	7	9	28	29	+3	62
10	Barnsley	46	9	10	4	34	28	5	8	10	26	38	-6	60
11	WBA	46	11	5	7	34	29	5	7	11	26	39	-8	60
12	Port Vale	46	10	5	8	30	29	5	10	8	29	37	-7	60
13	Tranmere R	46	9	9	5	42	29	5	8	10	22	31	+4	59
14	Southend U	46	11	4	8	30	22	4	6	13	22	39	-9	59
15	Birmingham C	46	11	7	5	37	23	4	6	13	24	41	-3	58
16	Norwich C	46	7	9	7	26	24	7	6	10	33	31	+4	57
17	Grimsby T	46	8	10	5	27	25	6	4	13	28	44	-14	56
18	Oldham Ath	46	10	7	6	33	20	4	7	12	21	30	+4	56
19	Reading	46	8	7	8	28	30	5	10	8	26	33	-9	56
20	Wolverhampton W	46	8	9	6	34	28	5	7	11	22	34	-6	55
21	Portsmouth	46	8	6	9	34	32	5	7	11	27	37	-8	52
22	Millwall	46	7	6	10	23	28	6	7	10	20	35	-20	52
23	Watford	46	7	8	8	40	33	3	10	10	22	37	-8	48
24	Luton T	46	7	6	10	30	34	4	6	13	10	30	-24	45

ENDSLEIGH INSURANCE DIVISION 1

	League	FA Cup	Coca-Cola Cup	Other Cups	Total
John Aldridge (Tranmere R)	27	0	2	0	29
Dougie Freedman (Crystal Palace)	23	0	0	0	23
(Includes three League goals for Barnet)					
Paul Barnes (Birmingham C)	22	0	5	2	29
(All except seven League goals for York C)					
Rob Edwards (Huddersfield T)	22	2	4	0	28
(All except seven League goals for Crewe Alex)					
Dean Sturridge (Derby Co)	20	0	0	0	20
Iwan Roberts (Leicester C)	19	0	1	0	20
Ian Marshall (Ipswich T)	19	0	0	0	19
Alex Mathie (Ipswich T)	18	0	0	1	19
Bob Taylor (WBA)	17	0	3	3	23
Andy Payton (Barnsley)	17	0	3	0	20
Andy Booth (Huddersfield T)	16	2	3	0	21
Don Goodman (Wolverhampton W)	16	1	3	0	20
Mike Sheron (Stoke C)	16	0	2	0	18
(Includes one League, two Coca-Cola Cup goals for Norwich C)					
Steve Bull (Wolverhampton W)	15	0	2	0	17
Craig Ramage (Watford)	15	0	0	0	15

Endsleigh Insurance League Division 2

			Home		Goals		Away			Goals			
		P	W	D	L	F	A	W	D	L	F	A	GD	Pts
1	Swindon T	46	12	10	1	37	16	13	7	3	34	18	+37	92
2	Oxford U	46	17	4	2	52	14	7	7	9	24	25	+37	83
3	Blackpool	46	14	5	4	41	20	9	8	6	26	20	+27	82
4	Notts Co	46	14	4	5	42	21	7	9	7	21	18	+24	78
5	Crewe Alex	46	13	3	7	40	24	9	4	10	37	36	+17	73
6	Bradford C	46	15	4	4	41	25	7	3	13	30	44	+2	73
7	Chesterfield	46	14	6	3	39	21	6	11	17	30	+5		72
8	Wrexham	46	12	6	5	51	27	6	10	7	25	28	+21	70
9	Stockport Co	46	8	9	6	30	20	11	4	8	31	27	+14	70
10	Bristol R	46	12	4	7	29	28	8	6	9	28	32	-3	70
11	Walsall	46	12	7	4	38	20	7	5	11	22	25	+15	69
12	Wycombe W	46	9	8	6	36	26	7	10	27	33	+4		60
13	Bristol C	46	10	6	7	28	22	5	9	9	27	38	-5	60
14	AFC Bournemouth	46	12	5	6	33	25	4	5	14	18	45	-19	58
15	Brentford	46	12	6	5	24	15	3	7	13	19	34	-6	58
16	Rotherham U	46	11	7	5	31	20	3	7	13	23	42	-8	56
17	Burnley	46	9	8	6	35	28	5	5	13	21	40	-12	55
18	Shrewsbury T	46	7	8	8	32	29	6	6	11	26	41	-12	53
19	Peterborough U	46	9	6	8	40	27	4	7	12	19	39	-7	52
20	York C	46	8	6	9	28	29	5	7	11	30	44	-15	52
21	Carlisle U	46	11	6	6	35	20	1	7	15	22	52	-15	49
22	Swansea C	46	8	8	7	27	29	3	6	14	16	50	-36	47
23	Brighton & HA	46	6	7	10	25	31	4	3	16	21	38	-23	40
24	Hull C	46	4	8	11	26	37	1	8	14	10	41	-42	31

DIVISION 2

	League	FA Cup	Coca-Cola Cup	Other Cups	Total
Marcus Stewart (*Bristol R*)	21	0	4	5	30
Gary Martindale (*Notts Co*)	21	0	1	4	26
(*All except six League goals for Peterborough U*)					
Kurt Nogan (*Burnley*)	20	0	3	3	26
Shaun Goater (*Rotherham U*)	18	2	3	1	24
Karl Connolly (*Wrexham*)	18	1	0	2	21
Miguel De Souza (*Wycombe W*)	18	0	2	0	20
Paul Moody (*Oxford U*)	17	5	1	1	24
Wayne Allison (*Swindon T*)	17	2	1	0	20
Steve Jones (*Bournemouth*)	17	0	3	0	20
Kyle Lightbourne (*Walsall*)	15	3	0	6	24
Kevin Wilson (*Walsall*)	15	2	1	1	19
Steve Torpey (*Swansea C*)	15	0	1	1	17
Tony Ellis (*Blackpool*)	14	0	2	1	17

Endsleigh Insurance League Division 3

				Home					Away					
					Goals						Goals			
		P	W	D	L	F	A	W	D	L	F	A	GD	Pts
1	Preston NE	46	11	8	4	44	22	12	9	2	34	16	+40	86
2	Gillingham	46	16	6	1	33	6	6	11	6	16	14	+29	83
3	Bury	46	11	8	6	33	21	11	7	5	33	27	+18	79
4	Plymouth Arg	46	14	5	4	41	20	8	7	8	27	29	+19	78
5	Darlington	46	10	6	7	30	21	10	12	1	30	21	+18	78
6	Hereford U	46	13	5	5	40	22	7	9	7	25	25	+18	74
7	Colchester U	46	13	7	3	37	22	5	11	7	24	29	+10	72
8	Chester C	46	11	9	3	45	22	7	7	9	27	31	+19	70
9	Barnet	46	13	6	4	40	19	5	10	8	25	26	+20	70
10	Wigan Ath	46	15	3	5	36	21	5	7	11	26	35	+6	70
11	Northampton	46	9	10	4	32	22	9	3	11	19	22	+7	67
12	Scunthorpe U	46	8	8	7	36	30	7	7	9	31	31	+6	60
13	Doncaster R	46	11	6	6	25	19	5	5	13	24	41	-11	59
14	Exeter C	46	9	9	5	25	22	4	9	10	21	31	-7	57
15	Rochdale	46	7	8	8	32	33	7	5	11	25	28	-4	55
16	Cambridge U	46	8	8	7	34	30	6	4	13	27	41	-10	54
17	Fulham	46	10	9	4	39	26	2	8	13	18	37	-6	53
18	Lincoln C	46	8	7	8	32	26	5	7	11	25	47	-16	53
19	Mansfield T	46	6	10	7	25	29	5	10	8	29	35	-10	53
20	Hartlepool U	46	8	9	6	30	24	4	4	15	17	43	-20	49
21	Leyton Orient	46	11	4	8	29	22	1	7	15	15	41	-19	47
22	Cardiff C	46	8	6	9	24	22	3	6	14	17	42	-23	45
23	Scarborough	46	5	11	7	22	28	5	5	15	17	41	-30	40
24	Torquay U	46	4	9	10	17	36	1	5	17	13	48	-54	29

DIVISION 3

	League	FA Cup	Coca-Cola Cup	Other Cups	Total
Steve White (Hereford U)	29	3	0	1	33
Andy Saville (Preston NE)	29	0	0	1	30
Carl Dale (Cardiff C)	21	2	3	5	31
Steve Whitehall (Rochdale)	20	1	0	3	24
Sean Devine (Barnet)	19	1	0	0	20
Lee Hodges (Barnet)	17	1	0	0	18
Adrian Littlejohn (Plymouth Arg)	17	1	0	0	18
Andy McFarlane (Scunthorpe U)	16	2	1	2	21
Mark Carter (Bury)	16	0	2	0	18
Colin West (Leyton Orient)	16	0	1	0	17
Jason White (Northampton T)	16	0	0	0	16

LEAGUE POSITIONS: FA PREMIER FROM 1992–93 AND DIVISION 1 1970–71 TO 1991–92

	1994-95	1993-94	1992-93	1991-92	1990-91	1989-90	1988-89	1987-88	1986-87	1985-86	1984-85	1983-84	1982-83
Arsenal	12	4	10	4	1	4	1	6	4	7	7	6	10
Aston Villa	18	10	2	7	17	2	17	–	22	16	10	10	6
Birmingham C	–	–	–	–	–	–	–	–	–	21	–	20	17
Blackburn R	1	2	4	–	–	–	–	–	–	–	–	–	–
Blackpool	–	–	–	–	–	–	–	–	–	–	–	–	–
Bolton W	–	–	–	–	–	–	–	–	–	–	–	–	–
Brighton & HA	–	–	–	–	–	–	–	–	–	–	–	–	22
Bristol C	–	–	–	–	–	–	–	–	–	–	–	–	–
Burnley	–	–	–	–	–	–	–	–	–	–	–	–	–
Carlisle U	–	–	–	–	–	–	–	–	–	–	–	–	–
Charlton Ath	–	–	–	–	–	19	14	17	19	–	–	–	–
Chelsea	11	14	11	14	11	5	–	18	14	6	6	–	–
Coventry C	16	11	15	19	16	12	7	10	10	17	18	19	19
Crystal Palace	19	–	20	10	3	15	–	–	–	–	–	–	–
Derby Co	–	–	–	–	20	16	5	15	–	–	–	–	–
Everton	15	17	13	12	9	6	8	4	1	2	1	7	7
Huddersfield T	–	–	–	–	–	–	–	–	–	–	–	–	–
Ipswich T	22	19	16	–	–	–	–	–	–	20	17	12	9
Leeds U	5	5	17	1	4	–	–	–	–	–	–	–	–
Leicester C	21	–	–	–	–	–	–	–	20	19	15	15	–
Liverpool	4	8	6	6	2	1	2	1	2	1	2	1	1
Luton T	–	–	–	20	18	17	16	9	7	9	13	16	18
Manchester C	17	16	9	5	5	14	–	–	21	15	–	–	20
Manchester U	2	1	1	2	6	13	11	2	11	4	4	4	3
Middlesbrough	–	–	21	–	–	–	18	–	–	–	–	–	–
Millwall	–	–	–	–	–	20	10	–	–	–	–	–	–
Newcastle U	6	3	–	–	–	–	20	8	17	11	14	–	–
Norwich C	20	12	3	18	15	10	4	14	5	–	20	14	14
Nottingham F	3	–	22	8	8	9	3	3	8	8	9	3	5
Notts Co	–	–	–	21	–	–	–	–	–	–	–	21	15
Oldham Ath	–	21	19	17	–	–	–	–	–	–	–	–	–
Oxford U	–	–	–	–	–	–	21	18	18	–	–	–	–
Portsmouth	–	–	–	–	–	–	–	19	–	–	–	–	–
QPR	8	9	5	11	12	11	9	5	16	13	19	5	–
Sheffield U	–	20	14	9	13	–	–	–	–	–	–	–	–
Sheffield W	13	7	7	3	–	18	15	11	13	5	8	–	–
Southampton	10	18	18	16	14	7	13	12	12	14	5	2	12
Stoke C	–	–	–	–	–	–	–	–	–	22	18	18	13
Sunderland	–	–	–	19	–	–	–	–	–	21	13	–	–
Swansea C	–	–	–	–	–	–	–	–	–	–	–	–	21
Swindon T	–	22	–	–	–	–	–	–	–	–	–	–	–
Tottenham H	7	15	8	15	10	3	6	13	3	10	3	8	4
Watford	–	–	–	–	–	–	–	20	9	12	11	11	2
WBA	–	–	–	–	–	–	–	–	–	22	12	17	11
West Ham U	14	13	–	22	–	–	19	16	15	3	16	9	8
Wimbledon	9	6	12	13	7	8	12	7	6	–	–	–	–
Wolv'hampton W	–	–	–	–	–	–	–	–	–	–	–	22	–

1981-82	1980-81	1979-80	1978-79	1977-78	1976-77	1975-76	1974-75	1973-74	1972-73	1971-72	1970-71	
5	3	4	7	5	8	17	16	10	2	5	1	Arsenal
11	1	7	8	8	4	16	–	–	–	–	–	Aston Villa
16	13	–	21	11	13	19	17	19	10	–	–	Birmingham C
–	–	–	–	–	–	–	–	–	–	–	–	Blackburn R
–	–	–	–	–	–	–	–	–	–	22	–	Blackpool
–	22	17	–	–	–	–	–	–	–	–	–	Bolton W
13	19	16	–	–	–	–	–	–	–	–	–	Brighton & HA
–	–	20	13	17	18	–	–	–	–	–	–	Bristol C
–	–	–	–	–	21	10	6	–	–	–	21	Burnley
–	–	–	–	–	–	22	–	–	–	–	–	Carlisle U
–	–	–	–	–	–	–	–	–	–	–	–	Charlton Ath
–	–	–	22	16	–	–	21	17	12	7	6	Chelsea
14	16	15	10	7	19	14	14	16	19	18	10	Coventry C
–	22	13	–	–	–	–	–	–	21	20	18	Crystal Palace
–	–	21	19	12	15	4	1	3	7	1	9	Derby Co
8	15	19	4	3	9	11	4	7	17	15	14	Everton
–	–	–	–	–	–	–	–	–	–	22	15	Huddersfield T
2	2	3	6	1	3	6	3	4	4	13	19	Ipswich T
20	9	11	5	9	10	5	9	1	3	2	2	Leeds U
–	21	–	–	22	11	7	18	9	16	12	–	Leicester C
1	5	1	1	2	1	1	2	2	1	3	5	Liverpool
–	–	–	–	–	–	–	20	–	–	–	–	Luton T
10	12	17	15	4	2	8	8	14	11	4	11	Manchester C
3	8	2	9	10	6	3	–	21	18	8	8	Manchester U
22	14	9	12	14	12	13	7	–	–	–	–	Middlesbrough
–	–	–	–	–	–	–	–	–	–	–	–	Millwall
–	–	–	21	5	15	15	15	9	11	12	–	Newcastle U
–	20	12	16	13	16	10	–	22	20	–	–	Norwich C
12	7	5	2	1	–	–	–	–	–	21	16	Nottingham F
15	–	–	–	–	–	–	–	–	–	–	–	Notts Co
–	–	–	–	–	–	–	–	–	–	–	–	Oldham Ath
–	–	–	–	–	–	–	–	–	–	–	–	Oxford U
–	–	–	–	–	–	–	–	–	–	–	–	Portsmouth
–	–	20	19	14	2	11	8	–	–	–	–	QPR
–	–	–	–	–	22	6	13	14	10	–	–	Sheffield U
–	–	–	–	–	–	–	–	–	–	–	–	Sheffield W
7	6	8	14	–	–	–	–	20	13	19	7	Southampton
18	11	18	–	–	21	12	5	15	17	13	–	Stoke C
19	17	–	–	20	–	–	–	–	–	–	–	Sunderland
6	–	–	–	–	–	–	–	–	–	–	–	Swansea C
–	–	–	–	–	–	–	–	–	–	–	–	Swindon T
4	10	14	11	–	22	9	19	11	8	6	3	Tottenham H
–	–	–	–	–	–	–	–	–	–	–	–	Watford
17	4	10	3	6	7	–	–	22	16	17	–	WBA
9	–	–	20	17	18	13	18	6	14	20	–	West Ham U
–	–	–	–	–	–	–	–	–	–	–	–	Wimbledon
21	18	6	18	15	–	20	12	12	5	9	4	Wolv'hampton W

LEAGUE POSITIONS: DIVISION 1 FROM 1992–93 AND DIVISION 2 1970–71 TO 1991–92

	1994-95	1993-94	1992-93	1991-92	1990-91	1989-90	1988-89	1987-88	1986-87	1985-86	1984-85	1983-84	1982-83
Aston Villa	–	–	–	–	–	–	–	2	–	–	–	–	–
Barnsley	6	18	13	16	8	19	7	14	11	12	11	14	10
Birmingham C	–	22	19	–	–	–	23	19	19	–	2	–	–
Blackburn R	–	–	6	19	5	5	5	5	12	19	5	6	11
Blackpool	–	–	–	–	–	–	–	–	–	–	–	–	–
Bolton W	3	14	–	–	–	–	–	–	–	–	–	–	22
Bournemouth	–	–	–	–	–	–	22	12	17	–	–	–	–
Bradford C	–	–	–	–	–	23	14	4	10	13	–	–	–
Brentford	–	–	22	–	–	–	–	–	–	–	–	–	–
Brighton & HA	–	–	–	23	6	18	19	–	22	11	6	9	–
Bristol C	23	13	15	17	9	–	–	–	–	–	–	–	–
Bristol R	–	–	24	13	13	–	–	–	–	–	–	–	–
Burnley	22	–	–	–	–	–	–	–	–	–	–	–	21
Bury	–	–	–	–	–	–	–	–	–	–	–	–	–
Cambridge U	–	–	23	5	–	–	–	–	–	–	–	–	–
Cardiff C	–	–	–	–	–	–	–	–	–	–	21	15	–
Carlisle U	–	–	–	–	–	–	–	–	–	20	16	7	14
Charlton Ath	15	11	12	7	16	–	–	–	–	2	17	13	17
Chelsea	–	–	–	–	–	–	1	–	–	–	–	1	18
Crystal Palace	–	1	–	–	–	3	6	6	5	15	18	15	–
Derby Co	9	6	8	3	–	–	–	1	–	–	–	20	13
Fulham	–	–	–	–	–	–	–	–	–	22	9	11	4
Grimsby T	10	16	9	19	–	–	–	–	21	15	10	5	19
Hereford U	–	–	–	–	–	–	–	–	–	–	–	–	–
Huddersfield T	–	–	–	–	–	–	–	23	17	16	13	12	–
Hull C	–	–	–	–	24	14	21	15	14	6	–	–	–
Ipswich T	–	–	–	1	14	9	8	8	5	–	–	–	–
Leeds U	–	–	–	–	–	1	10	7	4	14	7	10	8
Leicester C	–	4	6	4	22	13	15	13	–	–	–	–	3
Leyton Orient	–	–	–	–	–	–	–	–	–	–	–	–	–
Luton T	16	20	20	–	–	–	–	–	–	–	–	–	–
Manchester C	–	–	–	–	–	–	2	9	–	–	3	4	–
Manchester U	–	–	–	–	–	–	–	–	–	–	–	–	–
Mansfield T	–	–	–	–	–	–	–	–	–	–	–	–	–
Middlesbrough	1	9	–	2	7	21	–	3	–	21	19	17	16
Millwall	12	3	7	15	5	–	1	16	9	–	–	–	–
Newcastle U	–	–	1	20	11	3	–	–	–	–	–	3	5
Norwich C	–	–	–	–	–	–	–	–	–	–	–	–	–
Nottingham F	–	2	–	–	–	–	–	–	–	–	–	–	–
Notts Co	24	7	17	–	4	–	–	–	–	–	20	–	–
Oldham Ath	14	–	–	–	1	8	16	10	3	8	14	19	7
Oxford U	–	23	14	21	10	17	17	–	–	–	1	–	–
Peterborough U	–	24	10	–	–	–	–	–	–	–	–	–	–
Plymouth Arg	–	–	–	22	18	16	18	16	7	–	–	–	–
Port Vale	17	–	–	24	15	11	–	–	–	–	–	–	–
Portsmouth	18	17	3	9	17	12	20	–	2	4	4	16	–
Preston NE	–	–	–	–	–	–	–	–	–	–	–	–	–
QPR	–	–	–	–	–	–	–	–	–	–	–	–	1

1981-82	1980-81	1979-80	1978-79	1977-78	1976-77	1975-76	1974-75	1973-74	1972-73	1971-72	1970-71	
–	–	–	–	–	–	–	2	14	3	–	–	Aston Villa
6	–	–	–	–	–	–	–	–	–	–	–	Barnsley
–	–	3	–	–	–	–	–	–	–	2	9	Birmingham C
10	4	–	22	5	12	15	–	–	–	–	21	Blackburn R
–	–	–	–	20	5	10	7	5	7	6	–	Blackpool
19	18	–	–	1	4	4	10	11	–	–	22	Bolton W
–	–	–	–	–	–	–	–	–	–	–	–	Bournemouth
–	–	–	–	–	–	–	–	–	–	–	–	Bradford C
–	–	–	–	–	–	–	–	–	–	–	–	Brentford
–	–	–	2	4	–	–	–	–	22	–	–	Brighton & HA
–	21	–	–	–	–	2	5	16	5	8	19	Bristol C
–	22	19	16	18	15	18	19	–	–	–	–	Bristol R
–	–	21	13	11	16	–	–	–	1	7	–	Burnley
–	–	–	–	–	–	–	–	–	–	–	–	Bury
14	13	8	12	–	–	–	–	–	–	–	–	Cambridge U
20	19	15	9	19	18	–	21	17	20	19	3	Cardiff C
–	–	–	–	–	20	19	–	3	18	10	4	Carlisle U
13	–	22	19	17	7	9	–	–	–	21	20	Charlton Ath
12	12	4	–	–	2	11	–	–	–	–	–	Chelsea
15	–	–	1	9	–	–	–	20	–	–	–	Crystal Palace
16	6	–	–	–	–	–	–	–	–	–	–	Derby Co
–	–	20	10	10	17	12	9	13	9	20	–	Fulham
17	7	–	–	–	–	–	–	–	–	–	–	Grimsby T
–	–	–	–	–	22	–	–	–	–	–	–	Hereford U
–	–	–	–	–	–	–	–	–	21	–	–	Huddersfield T
–	–	–	–	22	14	14	8	9	13	12	5	Hull C
–	–	–	–	–	–	–	–	–	–	–	–	Ipswich T
–	–	–	–	–	–	–	–	–	–	–	–	Leeds U
8	–	1	17	–	–	–	–	–	–	–	1	Leicester C
22	17	14	11	14	19	13	12	4	15	17	17	Leyton Orient
1	5	6	18	13	6	7	–	2	12	13	6	Luton T
–	–	–	–	–	–	–	–	–	–	–	–	Manchester C
–	–	–	–	–	–	–	1	–	–	–	–	Manchester U
–	–	–	21	–	–	–	–	–	–	–	–	Mansfield T
–	–	–	–	–	–	–	–	1	4	9	7	Middlesbrough
–	–	–	21	16	10	–	20	12	11	3	8	Millwall
9	11	9	8	–	–	–	–	–	–	–	–	Newcastle U
3	–	–	–	–	–	–	3	–	–	1	10	Norwich C
–	–	–	–	–	3	8	16	7	14	–	–	Nottingham F
–	2	17	6	15	8	5	14	10	–	–	–	Notts Co
11	15	11	14	8	13	17	18	–	–	–	–	Oldham Ath
–	–	–	–	–	–	20	11	18	8	15	14	Oxford U
–	–	–	–	–	–	–	–	–	–	–	–	Peterborough U
–	–	–	–	–	21	16	–	–	–	–	–	Plymouth Arg
–	–	–	–	–	–	–	–	–	–	–	–	Port Vale
–	–	–	–	–	–	22	17	15	17	16	16	Portsmouth
–	20	10	7	–	–	–	–	21	19	18	–	Preston NE
5	8	5	–	–	–	–	–	–	2	4	11	QPR

LEAGUE POSITIONS: DIVISION 1 FROM 1992–93 AND DIVISION 2 1970–71 TO 1991–92 (cont.)

	1994-95	1993-94	1992-93	1991-92	1990-91	1989-90	1988-89	1987-88	1986-87	1985-86	1984-85	1983-84	1982-83
Reading	2	–	–	–	–	–	–	–	22	13	–	–	–
Rotherham U	–	–	–	–	–	–	–	–	–	–	–	–	20
Sheffield U	8	–	–	–	–	–	2	–	21	9	7	18	–
Sheffield W	–	–	–	–	–	–	–	–	–	–	–	2	6
Shrewsbury T	–	–	–	–	–	–	22	18	18	17	8	8	9
Southampton	–	–	–	–	–	–	–	–	–	–	–	–	–
Southend U	13	15	18	12	–	–	–	–	–	–	–	–	–
Stoke C	11	10	–	–	–	24	13	11	8	10	–	–	–
Sunderland	20	12	21	18	–	6	11	–	20	18	–	–	–
Swansea C	–	–	–	–	–	–	–	–	–	–	–	21	–
Swindon T	21	–	5	8	21	4	6	12	–	–	–	–	–
Tottenham H	–	–	–	–	–	–	–	–	–	–	–	–	–
Tranmere R	5	5	4	14	–	–	–	–	–	–	–	–	–
Walsall	–	–	–	–	–	–	24	–	–	–	–	–	–
Watford	7	19	16	10	20	15	4	–	–	–	–	–	–
WBA	19	21	–	–	23	20	9	20	15	–	–	–	–
West Ham U	–	–	2	–	2	7	–	–	–	–	–	–	–
Wimbledon	–	–	–	–	–	–	–	–	–	3	12	–	–
Wolv'hampton W	4	8	11	11	12	10	–	–	–	–	–	22	2
Wrexham	–	–	–	–	–	–	–	–	–	–	–	–	–
York C	–	–	–	–	–	–	–	–	–	–	–	–	–

LEAGUE POSITIONS: DIVISION 2 FROM 1992–93 AND DIVISION 3 1970–71 TO 1991–92

	1994-95	1993-94	1992-93	1991-92	1990-91	1989-90	1988-89	1987-88	1986-87	1985-86	1984-85	1983-84	1982-83
Aldershot	–	–	–	–	–	–	24	20	–	–	–	–	–
Aston Villa	–	–	–	–	–	–	–	–	–	–	–	–	–
Barnet	–	24	–	–	–	–	–	–	–	–	–	–	–
Barnsley	–	–	–	–	–	–	–	–	–	–	–	–	–
Barrow	–	–	–	–	–	–	–	–	–	–	–	–	–
Birmingham C	1	–	–	2	12	7	–	–	–	–	–	–	–
Blackburn R	–	–	–	–	–	–	–	–	–	–	–	–	–
Blackpool	12	20	18	–	–	23	19	10	9	12	–	–	–
Bolton W	–	–	2	13	4	6	10	–	21	18	17	10	–
Bournemouth	19	17	17	8	9	–	–	–	1	15	10	17	14
Bradford C	14	7	10	16	8	–	–	–	–	1	7	12	–
Brentford	2	16	–	1	6	13	7	12	11	10	13	20	9
Brighton & HA	16	14	9	–	–	–	–	2	–	–	–	–	–
Bristol C	–	–	–	–	–	2	11	5	6	9	5	–	–
Bristol R	4	8	–	–	–	1	5	8	19	16	6	5	7

	1981-82	1980-81	1979-80	1978-79	1977-78	1976-77	1975-76	1974-75	1973-74	1972-73	1971-72	1970-71
Reading	–	–	–	–	–	–	–	–	–	–	–	–
Rotherham U	7	–	–	–	–	–	–	–	–	–	–	–
Sheffield U	–	–	20	12	11	–	–	–	–	–	–	2
Sheffield W	4	10	–	–	–	–	–	22	19	10	14	15
Shrewsbury T	18	14	13	–	–	–	–	–	–	–	–	–
Southampton	–	–	–	–	2	9	6	13	–	–	–	–
Southend U	–	–	–	–	–	–	–	–	–	–	–	–
Stoke C	–	–	–	3	7	–	–	–	–	–	–	–
Sunderland	–	–	2	4	6	–	1	4	6	6	5	13
Swansea C	–	3	12	–	–	–	–	–	–	–	–	–
Swindon T	–	–	–	–	–	–	–	–	22	16	11	12
Tottenham H	–	–	–	–	3	–	–	–	–	–	–	–
Tranmere R	–	–	–	–	–	–	–	–	–	–	–	–
Walsall	–	–	–	–	–	–	–	–	–	–	–	–
Watford	2	9	18	–	–	–	–	–	–	–	22	18
WBA	–	–	–	–	–	–	3	6	8	–	–	–
West Ham U	–	1	7	5	–	–	–	–	–	–	–	–
Wimbledon	–	–	–	–	–	–	–	–	–	–	–	–
Wolv'hampton W	–	–	–	–	–	1	–	–	–	–	–	–
Wrexham	21	16	16	15	–	–	–	–	–	–	–	–
York C	–	–	–	–	–	–	21	15	–	–	–	–

	1981-82	1980-81	1979-80	1978-79	1977-78	1976-77	1975-76	1974-75	1973-74	1972-73	1971-72	1970-71
Aldershot	–	–	–	–	–	–	21	20	8	–	–	–
Aston Villa	–	–	–	–	–	–	–	–	–	–	1	4
Barnet	–	–	–	–	–	–	–	–	–	–	–	–
Barnsley	–	2	11	–	–	–	–	–	–	–	–	–
Barrow	–	–	–	–	–	–	–	–	–	–	–	–
Birmingham C	–	–	–	–	–	–	–	–	–	–	–	–
Blackburn R	–	–	–	–	–	–	–	1	13	3	10	–
Blackpool	–	23	18	12	–	–	–	–	–	–	–	–
Bolton W	–	–	–	–	–	–	–	–	–	1	–	–
Bournemouth	–	–	–	–	–	–	–	21	11	7	3	–
Bradford C	–	–	–	–	–	–	–	–	–	–	24	19
Brentford	8	9	19	10	–	–	–	–	–	–	–	–
Brighton & HA	–	–	–	–	–	2	4	19	19	–	2	14
Bristol C	23	–	–	–	–	–	–	–	–	–	–	–
Bristol R	15	–	–	–	–	–	–	–	2	5	6	6

LEAGUE POSITIONS: DIVISION 2 FROM 1992–93 AND DIVISION 3 1970–71 TO 1991–92 (cont.)

	1994–95	1993–94	1992–93	1991–92	1990–91	1989–90	1988–89	1987–88	1986–87	1985–86	1984–85	1983–84	1982–83
Burnley	–	6	13	–	–	–	–	–	–	–	21	12	–
Bury	–	–	–	21	7	5	13	14	16	20	–	–	–
Cambridge U	20	10	–	–	1	–	–	–	–	–	24	–	–
Cardiff C	22	19	–	–	–	21	16	–	–	22	–	–	2
Carlisle U	–	–	–	–	–	–	–	–	22	–	–	–	–
Charlton Ath	–	–	–	–	–	–	–	–	–	–	–	–	–
Chester C	23	–	24	18	19	16	8	15	15	–	–	–	–
Chesterfield	–	–	–	–	–	–	22	18	17	17	–	–	24
Colchester U	–	–	–	–	–	–	–	–	–	–	–	–	–
Crewe Alex	3	–	–	–	–	–	–	–	–	–	–	–	–
Crystal Palace	–	–	–	–	–	–	–	–	–	–	–	–	–
Darlington	–	–	–	24	–	–	–	–	22	13	–	–	–
Derby Co	–	–	–	–	–	–	–	–	–	3	7	–	–
Doncaster R	–	–	–	–	–	–	24	13	11	14	–	–	23
Exeter C	–	22	19	20	16	–	–	–	–	–	–	24	19
Fulham	–	21	12	9	21	20	4	9	18	–	–	–	–
Gillingham	–	–	–	–	–	–	23	13	5	5	4	8	13
Grimsby T	–	–	–	3	–	–	22	–	–	–	–	–	–
Halifax T	–	–	–	–	–	–	–	–	–	–	–	–	–
Hartlepool U	–	23	16	11	–	–	–	–	–	–	–	–	–
Hereford U	–	–	–	–	–	–	–	–	–	–	–	–	3
Huddersfield T	5	11	15	3	11	8	14	–	–	–	–	–	–
Hull C	8	9	20	14	–	–	–	–	–	–	3	4	–
Leyton Orient	24	18	7	10	13	14	–	–	–	–	22	11	20
Lincoln C	–	–	–	–	–	–	–	–	–	21	19	14	6
Luton T	–	–	–	–	–	–	–	–	–	–	–	–	–
Mansfield T	–	–	22	–	24	15	15	19	10	–	–	–	–
Middlesbrough	–	–	–	–	–	–	–	–	2	–	–	–	–
Millwall	–	–	–	–	–	–	–	–	–	–	2	9	17
Newport Co	–	–	–	–	–	–	–	–	23	19	18	13	4
Northampton T	–	–	–	–	–	22	20	6	–	–	–	–	–
Notts Co	–	–	–	–	–	3	9	4	7	8	–	–	–
Oldham Ath	–	–	–	–	–	–	–	–	–	–	–	–	–
Oxford U	7	–	–	–	–	–	–	–	–	–	–	1	5
Peterborough U	15	–	6	–	–	–	–	–	–	–	–	–	–
Plymouth Arg	21	3	14	–	–	–	–	–	–	2	15	19	8
Portsmouth	–	–	–	–	–	–	–	–	–	–	–	–	1
Port Vale	–	2	3	–	–	–	3	11	12	–	–	23	–
Preston NE	–	–	21	17	17	19	6	16	–	–	23	16	16
Reading	–	1	8	12	15	10	18	–	–	1	9	–	21
Rochdale	–	–	–	–	–	–	–	–	–	–	–	–	–
Rotherham U	17	15	11	–	23	9	–	21	14	14	12	18	–
Scunthorpe U	–	–	–	–	–	–	–	–	–	–	21	–	–
Sheffield U	–	–	–	–	–	–	2	–	–	–	–	3	11
Sheffield W	–	–	–	–	–	–	–	–	–	–	–	–	–
Shrewsbury T	18	–	–	22	18	11	–	–	–	–	–	–	–
Southend U	–	–	–	–	2	–	21	17	–	–	–	22	15
Southport	–	–	–	–	–	–	–	–	–	–	–	–	–

1981-82	1980-81	1979-80	1978-79	1977-78	1976-77	1975-76	1974-75	1973-74	1972-73	1971-72	1970-71	
1	8	–	–	–	–	–	–	–	–	–	–	Burnley
–	–	21	19	15	7	13	14	–	–	–	22	Bury
–	–	–	–	2	–	–	–	21	–	–	–	Cambridge U
–	–	–	–	–	–	2	–	–	–	–	–	Cardiff C
2	19	6	6	13	–	–	–	–	–	–	–	Carlisle U
–	3	–	–	–	–	–	3	14	11	–	–	Charlton Ath
24	18	9	16	5	13	17	–	–	–	–	–	Chester C
11	5	4	20	9	18	15	15	5	16	13	5	Chesterfield
–	22	5	7	8	–	22	11	–	–	–	–	Colchester U
–	–	–	–	–	–	–	–	–	–	–	–	Crewe Alex
–	–	–	–	–	3	5	5	–	–	–	–	Crystal Palace
–	–	–	–	–	–	–	–	–	–	–	–	Darlington
–	–	–	–	–	–	–	–	–	–	–	–	Derby C
19	–	–	–	–	–	–	–	–	–	–	23	Doncaster R
18	11	8	9	17	–	–	–	–	–	–	–	Exeter C
3	13	–	–	–	–	–	–	–	–	–	2	Fulham
6	15	16	4	7	12	14	10	–	–	–	24	Gillingham
–	–	1	–	–	23	18	16	6	9	–	–	Grimsby T
–	–	–	–	–	–	24	17	9	20	17	3	Halifax T
–	–	–	–	–	–	–	–	–	–	–	–	Hartlepool U
–	–	–	23	–	1	12	18	–	–	–	–	Hereford U
17	4	–	–	–	–	24	10	–	–	–	–	Huddersfield T
–	24	20	8	–	–	–	–	–	–	–	–	Hull C
–	–	–	–	–	–	–	–	–	–	–	–	Leyton Orient
4	–	–	24	16	9	–	–	–	–	–	–	Lincoln C
–	–	–	–	–	–	–	–	–	–	–	–	Luton T
–	–	23	18	–	1	11	–	–	–	21	7	Mansfield T
–	–	–	–	–	–	–	–	–	–	–	–	Middlesbrough
9	16	14	–	–	–	3	–	–	–	–	–	Millwall
16	12	–	–	–	–	–	–	–	–	–	–	Newport Co
–	–	–	–	–	22	–	–	–	–	–	–	Northampton T
–	–	–	–	–	–	–	–	2	4	–	–	Notts Co
–	–	–	–	–	–	–	1	4	11	–	–	Oldham Ath
5	14	17	11	18	17	–	–	–	–	–	–	Oxford U
–	–	21	4	16	10	7	–	–	–	–	–	Peterborough U
10	7	15	15	19	–	–	2	17	8	8	15	Plymouth Arg
13	6	–	24	20	–	–	–	–	–	–	–	Portsmouth
–	–	–	21	19	12	6	20	6	15	17	–	Port Vale
14	–	–	3	6	8	9	–	–	–	–	1	Preston NE
12	10	7	–	21	–	–	–	–	–	–	21	Reading
–	–	–	–	–	–	–	24	13	18	16	–	Rochdale
–	1	13	17	20	4	16	–	21	5	8	–	Rotherham U
–	–	–	–	–	–	–	–	24	–	–	–	Scunthorpe U
–	21	12	–	–	–	–	–	–	–	–	–	Sheffield U
–	–	3	14	14	8	20	–	–	–	–	–	Sheffield W
–	–	1	11	10	9	–	22	15	12	13	–	Shrewsbury T
7	–	22	13	–	–	23	18	12	14	–	–	Southend U
–	–	–	–	–	–	–	–	23	–	–	–	Southport

	1994-95	1993-94	1992-93	1991-92	1990-91	1989-90	1988-89	1987-88	1986-87	1985-86	1984-85	1983-84	1982-83
Stockport Co	11	4	6	5	–	–	–	–	–	–	–	–	–
Stoke C	–	–	1	4	14	–	–	–	–	–	–	–	–
Sunderland	–	–	–	–	–	–	–	1	–	–	–	–	–
Swansea C	10	13	5	19	20	17	12	–	–	24	20	–	–
Swindon T	–	–	–	–	–	–	–	–	3	–	–	–	–
Torquay U	–	–	–	23	–	–	–	–	–	–	–	–	–
Tranmere R	–	–	–	–	5	4	–	–	–	–	–	–	–
Walsall	–	–	5	–	–	24	–	3	8	6	11	6	10
Watford	–	–	–	–	–	–	–	–	–	–	–	–	–
WBA	–	–	4	7	–	–	–	–	–	–	–	–	–
Wigan Ath	–	–	23	15	10	18	17	7	4	4	16	15	18
Wimbledon	–	–	–	–	–	–	–	–	–	–	–	2	–
Wolv'hampton W	–	–	–	–	–	–	1	–	–	23	–	–	–
Wrexham	13	12	–	–	–	–	–	–	–	–	–	–	22
Wycombe W	6	–	–	–	–	–	–	–	–	–	–	–	–
York C	9	5	–	–	–	–	23	20	7	8	–	–	–

LEAGUE POSITIONS: DIVISION 3 FROM 1992–93 AND DIVISION 4 1970–71 TO 1991–92

	1994-95	1993-94	1992-93	1991-92	1990-91	1989-90	1988-89	1987-88	1986-87	1985-86	1984-85	1983-84	1982-83
Aldershot	–	–	–	*	23	22	–	–	6	16	13	5	18
Barnet	11	–	3	7	–	–	–	–	–	–	–	–	–
Barnsley	–	–	–	–	–	–	–	–	–	–	–	–	–
Barrow	–	–	–	–	–	–	–	–	–	–	–	–	–
Blackpool	–	–	4	5	–	–	–	–	–	–	2	6	21
Bolton W	–	–	–	–	–	–	3	–	–	–	–	–	–
Bournemouth	–	–	–	–	–	–	–	–	–	–	–	–	–
Bradford C	–	–	–	–	–	–	–	–	–	–	–	–	–
Bradford PA	–	–	–	–	–	–	–	–	–	–	–	–	–
Brentford	–	–	–	–	–	–	–	–	–	–	–	–	–
Bristol C	–	–	–	–	–	–	–	–	–	–	–	4	14
Burnley	–	–	–	1	6	16	16	10	22	14	–	–	–
Bury	4	13	7	–	–	–	–	–	–	–	4	15	5
Cambridge U	–	–	–	–	–	6	8	15	11	22	–	–	–
Cardiff C	–	–	1	9	13	–	–	2	13	–	–	–	–
Carlisle U	1	7	18	22	20	8	12	23	–	–	–	–	–
Chester C	–	2	–	–	–	–	–	–	–	2	16	24	13
Chesterfield	3	8	12	13	18	7	–	–	–	–	1	13	–

*Record expunged

1981-82	1980-81	1979-80	1978-79	1977-78	1976-77	1975-76	1974-75	1973-74	1972-73	1971-72	1970-71	
-	-	-	-	-	-	-	-	-	-	-	-	Stockport Co
-	-	-	-	-	-	-	-	-	-	-	-	Stoke C
-	-	3	-	-	-	-	-	-	23	14	11	Sunderland
22	17	10	5	10	11	19	4	-	-	-	-	Swansea C
-	-	-	-	-	-	-	-	-	-	23	10	Swindon T
-	-	-	23	12	14	-	22	16	10	20	18	Torquay U
20	20	-	22	6	15	7	8	15	17	9	20	Tranmere R
-	-	-	2	-	-	-	23	7	19	-	-	Walsall
-	-	-	-	-	-	-	-	-	-	-	-	Watford
-	-	-	-	-	-	-	-	-	-	-	-	WBA
21	-	24	-	-	-	-	-	-	-	-	-	Wigan Ath
-	-	-	-	-	-	-	-	-	-	-	-	Wimbledon
-	-	-	-	-	-	-	-	-	-	-	-	Wolv'hampton W
-	-	-	-	1	5	6	13	4	12	16	9	Wrexham
-	-	-	-	-	-	-	-	-	-	-	-	Wycombe W
-	-	-	-	-	24	-	-	3	18	19	-	York C

1981-82	1980-81	1979-80	1978-79	1977-78	1976-77	1975-76	1974-75	1973-74	1972-73	1971-72	1970-71	
16	6	10	5	5	17	-	-	-	4	17	13	Aldershot
-	-	-	-	-	-	-	-	-	-	-	-	Barnet
-	-	4	7	6	12	15	13	14	-	-	-	Barnsley
-	-	-	-	-	-	-	-	-	-	22	24	Barrow
12	-	-	-	-	-	-	-	-	-	-	-	Blackpool
4	13	11	18	17	13	6	-	-	-	-	2	Bolton W
2	14	5	15	-	4	17	10	8	16	-	-	Bournemouth
-	-	-	-	4	15	18	8	19	-	3	14	Bradford C
-	-	-	-	-	-	-	-	-	-	-	-	Bradford PA
-	-	-	-	-	-	-	-	-	-	-	-	Brentford
-	-	-	-	-	-	-	-	-	-	-	-	Bristol C
-	-	-	-	-	-	-	-	-	-	-	-	Burnley
9	12	-	-	-	-	-	4	12	9	-	-	Bury
-	-	-	-	-	1	13	6	-	3	10	20	Cambridge U
-	-	-	-	-	-	-	-	-	-	-	-	Cardiff C
-	-	-	-	-	-	-	-	-	-	-	-	Carlisle U
-	-	-	-	-	-	-	4	7	15	20	5	Chester C
-	-	-	-	-	-	-	-	-	-	-	-	Chesterfield

LEAGUE POSITIONS: DIVISION 3 FROM 1992–93 AND DIVISION 4 1970–71 TO 1991–92 (cont.)

	1994-95	1993-94	1992-93	1991-92	1990-91	1989-90	1988-89	1987-88	1986-87	1985-86	1984-85	1983-84	1982-83
Colchester U	10	17	10	–	–	24	22	9	5	6	7	8	6
Crewe Alex	–	3	6	6	–	–	3	17	17	12	10	16	23
Darlington	20	21	15	–	1	–	24	13	–	–	3	14	17
Doncaster R	9	15	16	21	11	20	23	–	–	–	–	2	–
Exeter C	22	–	–	–	–	1	13	22	14	21	18	–	–
Fulham	8	–	–	–	–	–	–	–	–	–	–	–	–
Gillingham	19	16	21	11	15	14	–	–	–	–	–	–	–
Grimsby T	–	–	–	–	–	2	9	–	–	–	–	–	–
Halifax T	–	–	22	20	22	23	21	18	15	20	21	21	11
Hartlepool U	18	–	–	3	19	19	16	18	7	19	23	22	–
Hereford U	16	20	17	17	17	17	15	19	16	10	5	11	24
Huddersfield T	–	–	–	–	–	–	–	–	–	–	–	–	–
Hull C	–	–	–	–	–	–	–	–	–	–	–	–	2
Leyton Orient	–	–	–	–	–	–	6	8	7	5	–	–	–
Lincoln C	12	18	8	10	14	10	10	–	24	–	–	–	–
Maidstone U	–	–	–	18	19	5	–	–	–	–	–	–	–
Mansfield T	6	12	–	3	–	–	–	–	–	3	14	19	10
Newport Co	–	–	–	–	–	–	–	24	–	–	–	–	–
Northampton T	17	22	20	16	10	–	–	–	1	8	23	18	15
Notts Co	–	–	–	–	–	–	–	–	–	–	–	–	–
Oldham Ath	–	–	–	–	–	–	–	–	–	–	–	–	–
Peterborough U	–	–	–	4	9	17	7	10	17	11	7	9	–
Portsmouth	–	–	–	–	–	–	–	–	–	–	–	–	–
Port Vale	–	–	–	–	–	–	–	–	–	4	12	–	3
Preston NE	5	5	–	–	–	–	–	–	2	23	–	–	–
Reading	–	–	–	–	–	–	–	–	–	–	–	3	–
Rochdale	15	9	11	8	12	12	18	21	21	18	17	22	20
Rotherham U	–	–	–	2	–	–	1	–	–	–	–	–	–
Scarborough	21	14	13	12	9	18	5	12	–	–	–	–	–
Scunthorpe U	7	11	14	5	8	11	4	4	8	15	9	–	4
Sheffield U	–	–	–	–	–	–	–	–	–	–	–	–	–
Shrewsbury T	–	1	9	–	–	–	–	–	–	–	–	–	–
Southend U	–	–	–	–	–	3	–	–	3	9	20	–	–
Southport	–	–	–	–	–	–	–	–	–	–	–	–	–
Stockport Co	–	–	–	2	4	20	20	19	11	22	12	16	–
Swansea C	–	–	–	–	–	–	–	6	12	–	–	–	–
Swindon T	–	–	–	–	–	–	–	–	–	1	8	17	8
Torquay U	13	6	19	–	7	15	14	5	23	24	24	9	12
Tranmere R	–	–	–	–	–	2	14	20	19	6	10	19	–
Walsall	2	10	5	15	16	–	–	–	–	–	–	–	–
Watford	–	–	–	–	–	–	–	–	–	–	–	–	–
Wigan Ath	14	19	–	–	–	–	–	–	–	–	–	–	–
Wimbledon	–	–	–	–	–	–	–	–	–	–	–	–	1
Wolv'hampton W	–	–	–	–	–	–	1	4	–	–	–	–	–
Workington	–	–	–	–	–	–	–	–	–	–	–	–	–
Wrexham	–	–	2	14	24	21	7	11	9	13	15	20	–
Wycombe W	–	4	–	–	–	–	–	–	–	–	–	–	–
York C	–	–	4	19	21	13	11	–	–	–	–	1	7

1981-82	1980-81	1979-80	1978-79	1977-78	1976-77	1975-76	1974-75	1973-74	1972-73	1971-72	1970-71	
6	–	–	–	–	3	–	–	3	22	11	6	Colchester U
24	18	23	24	15	12	16	18	21	21	24	15	Crewe Alex
13	8	22	21	19	11	20	21	20	24	19	12	Darlington
–	3	12	22	12	8	10	17	22	17	12	–	Doncaster R
–	–	–	–	–	2	7	9	10	8	15	9	Exeter C
–	–	–	–	–	–	–	–	–	–	–	–	Fulham
–	–	–	–	–	–	–	–	2	9	13	–	Gillingham
–	–	–	2	6	–	–	–	–	–	1	19	Grimsby T
19	23	18	23	20	21	–	–	–	–	–	–	Halifax T
14	9	19	13	21	22	14	13	11	20	18	23	Hartlepool U
10	22	21	14	–	–	–	–	–	2	–	–	Hereford U
–	–	1	9	11	9	5	–	–	–	–	–	Huddersfield T
8	–	–	–	–	–	–	–	–	–	–	–	Hull C
–	–	–	–	–	–	–	–	–	–	–	–	Leyton Orient
–	2	7	–	–	–	1	5	12	10	5	21	Lincoln C
–	–	–	–	–	–	–	–	–	–	–	–	Maidstone U
20	7	–	–	–	–	–	1	17	6	–	–	Mansfield T
–	–	3	8	16	19	22	12	9	5	14	22	Newport C
22	10	13	19	10	–	2	16	5	23	21	7	Northampton T
–	–	–	–	–	–	–	–	–	–	–	1	Notts Co
–	–	–	–	–	–	–	–	–	–	–	3	Oldham Ath
5	5	8	–	–	–	–	–	1	19	8	16	Peterborough U
–	4	7	–	–	–	–	–	–	–	–	–	Portsmouth
7	19	20	16	–	–	–	–	–	–	–	–	Port Vale
–	–	–	–	–	–	–	–	–	–	–	–	Preston NE
–	–	–	1	8	–	3	7	6	7	16	–	Reading
21	15	24	20	24	18	15	19	–	–	–	–	Rochdale
–	–	–	–	–	–	–	3	15	–	–	–	Rotherham U
–	–	–	–	–	–	–	–	–	–	–	–	Scarborough
23	16	14	12	14	20	9	24	18	–	4	17	Scunthorpe U
1	–	–	–	–	–	–	–	–	–	–	–	Sheffield U
–	–	–	–	–	–	2	–	–	–	–	–	Shrewsbury T
–	1	–	–	2	10	–	–	–	–	2	18	Southend U
–	–	–	–	23	23	23	11	–	1	7	8	Southport
18	20	16	17	18	14	21	20	24	11	23	11	Stockport Co
–	–	–	–	3	5	11	22	14	–	–	–	Swansea C
–	–	–	–	–	–	–	–	–	–	–	–	Swindon T
15	17	9	11	9	6	9	14	16	18	–	–	Torquay U
11	21	15	–	–	–	4	–	–	–	–	–	Tranmere R
–	–	2	–	–	–	–	–	–	–	–	–	Walsall
–	–	–	1	7	8	–	–	–	–	–	–	Watford
3	11	6	6	–	–	–	–	–	–	–	–	Wigan Ath
–	4	–	3	13	–	–	–	–	–	–	–	Wimbledon
–	–	–	–	–	–	–	–	–	–	–	–	Wolv'hampton W
–	–	–	–	–	24	24	23	23	13	6	10	Workington
–	–	–	–	–	–	–	–	–	–	–	–	Wrexham
–	–	–	–	–	–	–	–	–	–	–	–	Wycombe W
17	24	17	10	22	–	–	–	–	–	–	4	York C

LEAGUE CHAMPIONSHIP HONOURS

FA PREMIER LEAGUE
Maximum points: 126

	First	Pts	Second	Pts	Third	Pts
1992–93	Manchester U	84	Aston Villa	74	Norwich C	72
1993–94	Manchester U	92	Blackburn R	84	Newcastle U	77
1994–95	Blackburn R	89	Manchester U	88	Nottingham F	77

Maximum points: 114

1995–96	Manchester U	82	Newcastle U	78	Liverpool	71

DIVISION 1
Maximum points: 138

1992–93	Newcastle U	96	West Ham U*	88	Portsmouth††	88
1993–94	Crystal Palace	90	Nottingham F	83	Millwall††	74
1994–95	Middlesbrough	82	Reading††	79	Bolton W	77
1995–96	Sunderland	83	Derby Co	79	Crystal Palace††	75

DIVISION 2
Maximum points: 138

1992–93	Stoke C	93	Bolton W	90	Port Vale††	89
1993–94	Reading	89	Port Vale	88	Plymouth Arg††	85
1994–95	Birmingham C	89	Brentford††	85	Crewe Alex††	83
1995–96	Swindon T	92	Oxford U	83	Blackpool††	82

DIVISION 3
Maximum points: 126

1992–93	Cardiff C	83	Wrexham	80	Barnet	79
1993–94	Shrewsbury T	79	Chester C	74	Crewe Alex	73
1994–95	Carlisle U	91	Walsall	83	Chesterfield	81

Maximum points: 138

1995–96	Preston NE	86	Gillingham	83	Bury	79

†† *Not promoted after play-offs.*

FOOTBALL LEAGUE
Maximum points: a 44; b 60

	First	Pts	Second	Pts	Third	Pts
1888–89a	Preston NE	40	Aston Villa	29	Wolverhampton W	28
1889–90a	Preston NE	33	Everton	31	Blackburn R	27
1890–91a	Everton	29	Preston NE	27	Notts Co	26
1891–92b	Sunderland	42	Preston NE	37	Bolton W	36

DIVISION 1 to 1991–92
Maximum points: a 44; b 52; c 60; d 68; e 76; f 84; g 126; h 120; k 114.

	First	Pts	Second	Pts	Third	Pts
1892–93c	Sunderland	48	Preston NE	37	Everton	36
1893–94c	Aston Villa	44	Sunderland	38	Derby Co	36
1894–95c	Sunderland	47	Everton	42	Aston Villa	39
1895–96c	Aston Villa	45	Derby Co	41	Everton	39
1896–97c	Aston Villa	47	Sheffield U*	36	Derby Co	36
1897–98c	Sheffield U	42	Sunderland	37	Wolverhampton W*	35
1898–99d	Aston Villa	45	Liverpool	43	Burnley	39
1899–1900d	Aston Villa	50	Sheffield U	48	Sunderland	41
1900–01d	Liverpool	45	Sunderland	43	Notts Co	40
1901–02d	Sunderland	44	Everton	41	Newcastle U	37

	First	Pts	Second	Pts	Third	Pts
1902–03d	The Wednesday	42	Aston Villa*	41	Sunderland	41
1903–04d	The Wednesday	47	Manchester C	44	Everton	43
1904–05d	Newcastle U	48	Everton	47	Manchester C	46
1905–06e	Liverpool	51	Preston NE	47	The Wednesday	44
1906–07e	Newcastle U	51	Bristol C	48	Everton*	45
1907–08e	Manchester U	52	Aston Villa	43	Manchester C	43
1908–09e	Newcastle U	53	Everton	46	Sunderland	44
1909–10e	Aston Villa	53	Liverpool	48	Blackburn R*	45
1910–11e	Manchester U	52	Aston Villa	51	Sunderland*	45
1911–12e	Blackburn R	49	Everton	46	Newcastle U	44
1912–13e	Sunderland	54	Aston Villa	50	Sheffield W	49
1913–14e	Blackburn R	51	Aston Villa	44	Middlesbrough*	43
1914–15e	Everton	46	Oldham Ath	45	Blackburn R*	43
1919–20f	WBA	60	Burnley	51	Chelsea	49
1920–21f	Burnley	59	Manchester C	54	Bolton W	52
1921–22f	Liverpool	57	Tottenham H	51	Burnley	49
1922–23f	Liverpool	60	Sunderland	54	Huddersfield T	53
1923–24f	Huddersfield T*	57	Cardiff C	57	Sunderland	53
1924–25f	Huddersfield T	58	WBA	56	Bolton W	55
1925–26f	Huddersfield T	57	Arsenal	52	Sunderland	48
1926–27f	Newcastle U	56	Huddersfield T	51	Sunderland	49
1927–28f	Everton	53	Huddersfield T	51	Leicester C	48
1928–29f	Sheffield W	52	Leicester C	51	Aston Villa	50
1929–30f	Sheffield W	60	Derby Co	50	Manchester C*	47
1930–31f	Arsenal	66	Aston Villa	59	Sheffield W	52
1931–32f	Everton	56	Arsenal	54	Sheffield W	50
1932–33f	Arsenal	58	Aston Villa	54	Sheffield W	51
1933–34f	Arsenal	59	Huddersfield T	56	Tottenham H	49
1934–35f	Arsenal	58	Sunderland	54	Sheffield W	49
1935–36f	Sunderland	56	Derby Co*	48	Huddersfield T	48
1936–37f	Manchester C	57	Charlton Ath	54	Arsenal	52
1937–38f	Arsenal	52	Wolverhampton W	51	Preston NE	49
1938–39f	Everton	59	Wolverhampton W	55	Charlton Ath	50
1946–47f	Liverpool	57	Manchester U*	56	Wolverhampton W	56
1947–48f	Arsenal	59	Manchester U*	52	Burnley	52
1948–49f	Portsmouth	58	Manchester U*	53	Derby Co	53
1949–50f	Portsmouth*	53	Wolverhampton W	53	Sunderland	52
1950–51f	Tottenham H	60	Manchester U	56	Blackpool	50
1951–52f	Manchester U	57	Tottenham H*	53	Arsenal	53
1952–53f	Arsenal*	54	Preston NE	54	Wolverhampton W	51
1953–54f	Wolverhampton W	57	WBA	53	Huddersfield T	51
1954–55f	Chelsea	52	Wolverhampton W*	48	Portsmouth*	48
1955–56f	Manchester U	60	Blackpool*	49	Wolverhampton W	49
1956–57f	Manchester U	64	Tottenham H*	56	Preston NE	56
1957–58f	Wolverhampton W	64	Preston NE	59	Tottenham H	51
1958–59f	Wolverhampton W	61	Manchester U	55	Arsenal*	50
1959–60f	Burnley	55	Wolverhampton W	54	Tottenham H	53
1960–61f	Tottenham H	66	Sheffield W	58	Wolverhampton W	57
1961–62f	Ipswich T	56	Burnley	53	Tottenham H	52
1962–63f	Everton	61	Tottenham H	55	Burnley	54
1963–64f	Liverpool	57	Manchester U	53	Everton	52
1964–65f	Manchester U*	61	Leeds U	61	Chelsea	56
1965–66f	Liverpool	61	Leeds U*	55	Burnley	55
1966–67f	Manchester U	60	Nottingham F*	56	Tottenham H	56
1967–68f	Manchester C	58	Manchester U	56	Liverpool	55
1968–69f	Leeds U	67	Liverpool	61	Everton	57

* Won or placed on goal average.

	First	Pts	Second	Pts	Third	Pts
1969–70f	Everton	66	Leeds U	57	Chelsea	55
1970–71f	Arsenal	65	Leeds U	64	Tottenham H*	52
1971–72f	Derby Co	58	Leeds U*	57	Liverpool*	57
1972–73f	Liverpool	60	Arsenal	57	Leeds U	53
1973–74f	Leeds U	62	Liverpool	57	Derby Co	48
1974–75f	Derby Co	53	Liverpool*	51	Ipswich T	51
1975–76f	Liverpool	60	QPR	59	Manchester U	56
1976–77f	Liverpool	57	Manchester C	56	Ipswich T	52
1977–78f	Nottingham F	64	Liverpool	57	Everton	55
1978–79f	Liverpool	68	Nottingham F	60	WBA	59
1979–80f	Liverpool	60	Manchester U	58	Ipswich T	53
1980–81f	Aston Villa	60	Ipswich T	56	Arsenal	53
1981–82g	Liverpool	87	Ipswich T	83	Manchester U	78
1982–83g	Liverpool	82	Watford	71	Manchester U	70
1983–84g	Liverpool	80	Southampton	77	Nottingham F*	74
1984–85g	Everton	90	Liverpool*	77	Tottenham H	77
1985–86g	Liverpool	88	Everton	86	West Ham U	84
1986–87g	Everton	86	Liverpool	77	Tottenham H	71
1987–88h	Liverpool	90	Manchester U	81	Nottingham F	73
1988–89k	Arsenal*	76	Liverpool	76	Nottingham F	64
1989–90k	Liverpool	79	Aston Villa	70	Tottenham H	63
1990–91k	Arsenal†	83	Liverpool	76	Crystal Palace	69
1991–92g	Leeds U	82	Manchester U	78	Sheffield W	75

No official competition during 1915–19 and 1939–46.
† 2 pts deducted

DIVISION 2 to 1991–92

Maximum points: a 44; b 56; c 60; d 68; e 76; f 84; g 126; h 132; k 138.

	First	Pts	Second	Pts	Third	Pts
1892–93a	Small Heath	36	Sheffield U	35	Darwen	30
1893–94b	Liverpool	50	Small Heath	42	Notts Co	39
1894–95c	Bury	48	Notts Co	39	Newton Heath*	38
1895–96c	Liverpool*	46	Manchester C	46	Grimsby T*	42
1896–97c	Notts Co	42	Newton Heath	39	Grimsby T	38
1897–98c	Burnley	48	Newcastle U	45	Manchester C	39
1898–99d	Manchester C	52	Glossop NE	46	Leicester Fosse	45
1899–1900d	The Wednesday	54	Bolton W	52	Small Heath	46
1900–01d	Grimsby T	49	Small Heath	48	Burnley	44
1901–02d	WBA	55	Middlesbrough	51	Preston NE*	42
1902–03d	Manchester C	54	Small Heath	51	Woolwich A	48
1903–04d	Preston NE	50	Woolwich A	49	Manchester U	48
1904–05d	Liverpool	58	Bolton W	56	Manchester U	53
1905–06e	Bristol C	66	Manchester U	62	Chelsea	53
1906–07e	Nottingham F	60	Chelsea	57	Leicester Fosse	48
1907–08e	Bradford C	54	Leicester Fosse	52	Oldham Ath	50
1908–09e	Bolton W	52	Tottenham H*	51	WBA	51
1909–10e	Manchester C	54	Oldham Ath*	53	Hull C*	53
1910–11e	WBA	53	Bolton W	51	Chelsea	49
1911–12e	Derby Co*	54	Chelsea	54	Burnley	52
1912–13e	Preston NE	53	Burnley	50	Birmingham	46
1913–14e	Notts Co	53	Bradford PA*	49	Woolwich A	49
1914–15e	Derby Co	53	Preston NE	50	Barnsley	47
1919–20f	Tottenham H	70	Huddersfield T	64	Birmingham	56
1920–21f	Birmingham*	58	Cardiff C	58	Bristol C	51
1921–22f	Nottingham F	56	Stoke C*	52	Barnsley	52

	First	Pts	Second	Pts	Third	Pts
1922–23f	Notts Co	53	West Ham U*	51	Leicester C	51
1923–24f	Leeds U	54	Bury*	51	Derby Co	51
1924–25f	Leicester C	59	Manchester U	57	Derby Co	55
1925–26f	Sheffield W	60	Derby Co	57	Chelsea	52
1926–27f	Middlesbrough	62	Portsmouth*	54	Manchester C	54
1927–28f	Manchester C	59	Leeds U	57	Chelsea	54
1928–29f	Middlesbrough	55	Grimsby T	53	Bradford PA*	48
1929–30f	Blackpool	58	Chelsea	55	Oldham Ath	53
1930–31f	Everton	61	WBA	54	Tottenham H	51
1931–32f	Wolverhampton W	56	Leeds U	54	Stoke C	52
1932–33f	Stoke C	56	Tottenham H	55	Fulham	50
1933–34f	Grimsby T	59	Preston NE	52	Bolton W*	51
1934–35f	Brentford	61	Bolton W*	56	West Ham U	56
1935–36f	Manchester U	56	Charlton Ath	55	Sheffield U*	52
1936–37f	Leicester C	56	Blackpool	55	Bury	52
1937–38f	Aston Villa	57	Manchester U*	53	Sheffield U	53
1938–39f	Blackburn R	55	Sheffield U	54	Sheffield W	53
1946–47f	Manchester C	62	Burnley	58	Birmingham C	55
1947–48f	Birmingham C	59	Newcastle U	56	Southampton	52
1948–49f	Fulham	57	WBA	56	Southampton	55
1949–50f	Tottenham H	61	Sheffield W*	52	Sheffield U*	52
1950–51f	Preston NE	57	Manchester C	52	Cardiff C	50
1951–52f	Sheffield W	53	Cardiff C*	51	Birmingham C	51
1952–53f	Sheffield U	60	Huddersfield T	58	Luton T	52
1953–54f	Leicester C*	56	Everton	56	Blackburn R	55
1954–55f	Birmingham C*	54	Luton T*	54	Rotherham U	54
1955–56f	Sheffield W	55	Leeds U	52	Liverpool*	48
1956–57f	Leicester C	61	Nottingham F	54	Liverpool	53
1957–58f	West Ham U	57	Blackburn R	56	Charlton Ath	55
1958–59f	Sheffield W	62	Fulham	60	Sheffield U*	53
1959–60f	Aston Villa	59	Cardiff C	58	Liverpool*	50
1960–61f	Ipswich T	59	Sheffield U	58	Liverpool	52
1961–62f	Liverpool	62	Leyton Orient	54	Sunderland	53
1962–63f	Stoke C	53	Chelsea*	52	Sunderland	52
1963–64f	Leeds U	63	Sunderland	61	Preston NE	56
1964–65f	Newcastle U	57	Northampton T	56	Bolton W	50
1965–66f	Manchester C	59	Southampton	54	Coventry C	53
1966–67f	Coventry C	59	Wolverhampton W	58	Carlisle U	52
1967–68f	Ipswich T	59	QPR*	58	Blackpool	58
1968–69f	Derby Co	63	Crystal Palace	56	Charlton Ath	50
1969–70f	Huddersfield T	60	Blackpool	53	Leicester C	51
1970–71f	Leicester C	59	Sheffield U	56	Cardiff C*	53
1971–72f	Norwich C	57	Birmingham C	56	Millwall	55
1972–73f	Burnley	62	QPR	61	Aston Villa	50
1973–74f	Middlesbrough	65	Luton T	50	Carlisle U	49
1974–75f	Manchester U	61	Aston Villa	58	Norwich C	53
1975–76f	Sunderland	56	Bristol C*	53	WBA	53
1976–77f	Wolverhampton W	57	Chelsea	55	Nottingham F	52
1977–78f	Bolton W	58	Southampton	57	Tottenham H*	56
1978–79f	Crystal Palace	57	Brighton & HA*	56	Stoke C	56
1979–80f	Leicester C	55	Sunderland	54	Birmingham C*	53
1980–81f	West Ham U	66	Notts Co	53	Swansea C*	50
1981–82g	Luton T	88	Watford	80	Norwich C	71
1982–83g	QPR	85	Wolverhampton W	75	Leicester C	70
1983–84g	Chelsea*	88	Sheffield W	88	Newcastle U	80

* Won or placed on goal average/goal difference.
†† Not promoted after play-offs.

93

	First	Pts	Second	Pts	Third	Pts
1984–85g	Oxford U	84	Birmingham C	82	Manchester C	74
1985–86g	Norwich C	84	Charlton Ath	77	Wimbledon	76
1986–87g	Derby Co	84	Portsmouth	78	Oldham Ath††	75
1987–88h	Millwall	82	Aston Villa*	78	Middlesbrough	78
1988–89k	Chelsea	99	Manchester C	82	Crystal Palace	81
1989–90k	Leeds U*	85	Sheffield U	85	Newcastle U††	80
1990–91k	Oldham Ath	88	West Ham U	87	Sheffield W	82
1991–92k	Ipswich T	84	Middlesbrough	80	Derby Co	78

No competition during 1915–19 and 1939–46.

DIVISION 3 to 1991–92
Maximum points: 92; 138 from 1981–82.

	First	Pts	Second	Pts	Third	Pts
1958–59	Plymouth Arg	62	Hull C	61	Brentford*	57
1959–60	Southampton	61	Norwich C	59	Shrewsbury T*	52
1960–61	Bury	68	Walsall	62	QPR	60
1961–62	Portsmouth	65	Grimsby T	62	Bournemouth*	59
1962–63	Northampton T	62	Swindon T	58	Port Vale	54
1963–64	Coventry C*	60	Crystal Palace	60	Watford	58
1964–65	Carlisle U	60	Bristol C*	59	Mansfield T	59
1965–66	Hull C	69	Millwall	65	QPR	57
1966–67	QPR	67	Middlesbrough	55	Watford	54
1967–68	Oxford U	57	Bury	56	Shrewsbury T	55
1968–69	Watford*	64	Swindon T	64	Luton T	61
1969–70	Orient	62	Luton T	60	Bristol R	56
1970–71	Preston NE	61	Fulham	60	Halifax T	56
1971–72	Aston Villa	70	Brighton & HA	65	Bournemouth*	62
1972–73	Bolton W	61	Notts Co	57	Blackburn R	55
1973–74	Oldham Ath	62	Bristol R*	61	York C	61
1974–75	Blackburn R	60	Plymouth Arg	59	Charlton Ath	55
1975–76	Hereford U	63	Cardiff C	57	Millwall	56
1976–77	Mansfield T	64	Brighton & HA	61	Crystal Palace*	59
1977–78	Wrexham	61	Cambridge U	58	Preston NE*	56
1978–79	Shrewsbury T	61	Watford†	60	Swansea C	60
1979–80	Grimsby T	62	Blackburn R	59	Sheffield W	58
1980–81	Rotherham U	61	Barnsley*	59	Charlton Ath	59
1981–82	Burnley*	80	Carlisle U	80	Fulham	78
1982–83	Portsmouth	91	Cardiff C	86	Huddersfield T	82
1983–84	Oxford U	95	Wimbledon	87	Sheffield U*	83
1984–85	Bradford C	94	Millwall	90	Hull C	87
1985–86	Reading	94	Plymouth Arg	87	Derby Co	84
1986–87	Bournemouth	97	Middlesbrough	94	Swindon T	87
1987–88	Sunderland	93	Brighton & HA	84	Walsall	82
1988–89	Wolverhampton W	92	Sheffield U*	84	Port Vale	84
1989–90	Bristol R	93	Bristol C	91	Notts Co	87
1990–91	Cambridge U	86	Southend U	85	Grimsby T*	83
1991–92	Brentford	82	Birmingham C	81	Huddersfield T	78

* Won or placed on goal average/goal difference.

DIVISION 4 (1958–1992)
Maximum points: 92; 138 from 1981–82.

	First	Pts	Second	Pts	Third	Pts
1958–59	Port Vale	64	Coventry C*	60	York C	60
1959–60	Walsall	65	Notts Co*	60	Torquay U	60
1960–61	Peterborough U	66	Crystal Palace	64	Northampton T*	60

	First	Pts	Second	Pts	Third	Pts
1961–62†	Millwall	56	Colchester U	55	Wrexham	53
1962–63	Brentford	62	Oldham Ath*	59	Crewe Alex	59
1963–64	Gillingham*	60	Carlisle U	60	Workington	59
1964–65	Brighton & HA	63	Millwall*	62	York C	62
1965–66	Doncaster R*	59	Darlington	59	Torquay U	58
1966–67	Stockport Co	64	Southport*	59	Barrow	59
1967–68	Luton T	66	Barnsley	61	Hartlepools U	60
1968–69	Doncaster R	59	Halifax T	57	Rochdale*	56
1969–70	Chesterfield	64	Wrexham	61	Swansea C	60
1970–71	Notts Co	69	Bournemouth	60	Oldham Ath	59
1971–72	Grimsby T	63	Southend U	60	Brentford	59
1972–73	Southport	62	Hereford U	58	Cambridge U	57
1973–74	Peterborough U	65	Gillingham	62	Colchester U	60
1974–75	Mansfield T	68	Shrewsbury T	62	Rotherham U	59
1975–76	Lincoln C	74	Northampton T	68	Reading	60
1976–77	Cambridge U	65	Exeter C	62	Colchester U*	59
1977–78	Watford	71	Southend U	60	Swansea C*	56
1978–79	Reading	65	Grimsby T*	61	Wimbledon*	61
1979–80	Huddersfield T	66	Walsall	64	Newport Co	61
1980–81	Southend U	67	Lincoln C	65	Doncaster R	56
1981–82	Sheffield U	96	Bradford C*	91	Wigan Ath	91
1982–83	Wimbledon	98	Hull C	90	Port Vale	88
1983–84	York C	101	Doncaster R	85	Reading*	82
1984–85	Chesterfield	91	Blackpool	86	Darlington	85
1985–86	Swindon T	102	Chester C	84	Mansfield T	81
1986–87	Northampton T	99	Preston NE	90	Southend U	80
1987–88	Wolverhampton W	90	Cardiff C	85	Bolton W	78
1988–89	Rotherham U	82	Tranmere R	80	Crewe Alex	78
1989–90	Exeter C	89	Grimsby T	79	Southend U	75
1990–91	Darlington	83	Stockport Co*	82	Hartlepool U	82
1991–92†*	Burnley	83	Rotherham U*	77	Mansfield T	77

‡ *Maximum points:* 88 owing to Accrington Stanley's resignation. †† *Not promoted after play-offs.*
†* *Maximum points:* 126 owing to Aldershot being expelled.

DIVISION 3—SOUTH (1920–1958)

Maximum points: a 84; b 92.

	First	Pts	Second	Pts	Third	Pts
1920–21a	Crystal Palace	59	Southampton	54	QPR	53
1921–22a	Southampton*	61	Plymouth Arg	61	Portsmouth	53
1922–23a	Bristol C	59	Plymouth Arg*	53	Swansea T	53
1923–24a	Portsmouth	59	Plymouth Arg	55	Millwall	54
1924–25a	Swansea T	57	Plymouth Arg	56	Bristol C	53
1925–26a	Reading	57	Plymouth Arg	56	Millwall	53
1926–27a	Bristol C	62	Plymouth Arg	60	Millwall	56
1927–28a	Millwall	65	Northampton T	55	Plymouth Arg	53
1928–29a	Charlton Ath*	54	Crystal Palace	54	Northampton T*	52
1929–30a	Plymouth Arg	68	Brentford	61	QPR	51
1930–31a	Notts Co	59	Crystal Palace	51	Brentford	50
1931–32a	Fulham	57	Reading	55	Southend U	53
1932–33a	Brentford	62	Exeter C	58	Norwich C	57
1933–34a	Norwich C	61	Coventry C*	54	Reading*	54
1934–35a	Charlton Ath	61	Reading	53	Coventry C	51
1935–36a	Coventry C	57	Luton T	56	Reading	54
1936–37a	Luton T	58	Notts Co	56	Brighton & HA	53
1937–38a	Millwall	56	Bristol C	55	QPR*	53

	First	Pts	Second	Pts	Third	Pts
1938–39a	Newport Co	55	Crystal Palace	52	Brighton & HA	49
1939–46	Competition cancelled owing to war.					
1946–47a	Cardiff C	66	QPR	57	Bristol C	51
1947–48a	QPR	61	Bournemouth	57	Walsall	51
1948–49a	Swansea T	62	Reading	55	Bournemouth	52
1949–50a	Notts Co	58	Northampton T*	51	Southend U	51
1950–51b	Nottingham F	70	Norwich C	64	Reading*	57
1951–52b	Plymouth Arg	66	Reading*	61	Norwich C	61
1952–53b	Bristol R	64	Millwall*	62	Northampton T	62
1953–54b	Ipswich T	64	Brighton & HA	61	Bristol C	56
1954–55b	Bristol C	70	Leyton Orient	61	Southampton	59
1955–56b	Leyton Orient	66	Brighton & HA	65	Ipswich T	64
1956–57b	Ipswich T*	59	Torquay U	59	Colchester U	58
1957–58b	Brighton & HA	60	Brentford*	58	Plymouth Arg	58

* Won or placed on goal average.

DIVISION 3—NORTH (1921–1958)
Maximum points: a 76; b 84; c 80; d 92.

	First	Pts	Second	Pts	Third	Pts
1921–22a	Stockport Co	56	Darlington*	50	Grimsby T	50
1922–23a	Nelson	51	Bradford PA	47	Walsall	46
1923–24b	Wolverhampton W	63	Rochdale	62	Chesterfield	54
1924–25b	Darlington	58	Nelson*	53	New Brighton	53
1925–26b	Grimsby T	61	Bradford PA	60	Rochdale	59
1926–27b	Stoke C	63	Rochdale	58	Bradford PA	55
1927–28b	Bradford PA	63	Lincoln C	55	Stockport Co	54
1928–29g	Bradford C	63	Stockport Co	62	Wrexham	52
1929–30b	Port Vale	67	Stockport Co	63	Darlington*	50
1930–31b	Chesterfield	58	Lincoln C	57	Wrexham*	54
1931–32c	Lincoln C*	57	Gateshead	57	Chester	50
1932–33b	Hull C	59	Wrexham	57	Stockport Co	54
1933–34b	Barnsley	62	Chesterfield	61	Stockport Co	59
1934–35b	Doncaster R	57	Halifax T	55	Chester	54
1935–36b	Chesterfield	60	Chester*	55	Tranmere R	55
1936–37b	Stockport Co	60	Lincoln C	57	Chester	53
1937–38b	Tranmere R	56	Doncaster R	54	Hull C	53
1938–39b	Barnsley	67	Doncaster R	56	Bradford C	52
1939–46	Competition cancelled owing to war.					
1946–47b	Doncaster R	72	Rotherham U	60	Chester	56
1947–48b	Lincoln C	60	Rotherham U	59	Wrexham	50
1948–49b	Hull C	65	Rotherham U	62	Doncaster R	50
1949–50b	Doncaster R	55	Gateshead	53	Rochdale*	51
1950–51d	Rotherham U	71	Mansfield T	64	Carlisle U	62
1951–52d	Lincoln C	69	Grimsby T	66	Stockport Co	59
1952–53d	Oldham Ath	59	Port Vale	58	Wrexham	56
1953–54d	Port Vale	69	Barnsley	58	Scunthorpe U	57
1954–55d	Barnsley	65	Accrington S	61	Scunthorpe U*	58
1955–56d	Grimsby T	68	Derby Co	63	Accrington S	59
1956–57d	Derby Co	63	Hartlepools U	59	Accrington S*	58
1957–58d	Scunthorpe U	66	Accrington S	59	Bradford C	57

* Won or placed on goal average.

PROMOTED AFTER PLAY-OFFS
(Not accounted for in previous section)
1986–87   Aldershot to Division 3.
1987–88   Swansea C to Divison 3.
1988–89   Leyton Orient to Division 3.
1989–90   Cambridge U to Division 3; Notts Co to Division 2; Sunderland to
           Division 1.
1990–91   Notts Co to Division 1; Tranmere R to Division 2; Torquay U to
           Division 3.
1991–92   Blackburn R to Premier League; Peterborough U to Division 1.
1992–93   Swindon T to Premier League; WBA to Division 1; York C to Division 2.
1993–94   Leicester C to Premier League; Burnley to Division 1; Wycombe W to
           Division 2.
1994–95   Huddersfield T to Division 1.
1995–96   Leicester C to Premier League; Bradford C to Division 1; Plymouth Arg
           to Division 2

RELEGATED CLUBS

FA PREMIER LEAGUE TO DIVISION 1

1992–93 Crystal Palace, Middlesbrough, Nottingham F
1993–94 Sheffield U, Oldham Ath, Swindon T
1994–95 Crystal Palace, Norwich C, Leicester C, Ipswich T
1995–96 Manchester C, QPR, Bolton W

DIVISION 1 TO DIVISION 2

1898–99 Bolton W and Sheffield W	1926–27 Leeds U and WBA
1899–1900 Burnley and Glossop	1927–28 Tottenham H and
1900–01 Preston NE and WBA	Middlesbrough
1901–02 Small Heath and Manchester C	1928–29 Bury and Cardiff C
1902–03 Grimsby T and Bolton W	1929–30 Burnley and Everton
1903–04 Liverpool and WBA	1930–31 Leeds U and Manchester U
1904–05 League extended. Bury and	1931–32 Grimsby T and West Ham U
Notts Co, two bottom clubs in	1932–33 Bolton W and Blackpool
First Division, re-elected.	1933–34 Newcastle U and Sheffield U
1905–06 Nottingham F and	1934–35 Leicester C and Tottenham H
Wolverhampton W	1935–36 Aston Villa and Blackburn R
1906–07 Derby Co and Stoke C	1936–37 Manchester U and Sheffield W
1907–08 Bolton W and Birmingham C	1937–38 Manchester C and WBA
1908–09 Manchester C and Leicester	1938–39 Birmingham C and Leicester C
Fosse	1946–47 Brentford and Leeds U
1909–10 Bolton W and Chelsea	1947–48 Blackburn R and Grimsby T
1910–11 Bristol C and Nottingham F	1948–49 Preston NE and Sheffield U
1911–12 Preston NE and Bury	1949–50 Manchester C and
1912–13 Notts Co and Woolwich	Birmingham C
Arsenal	1950–51 Sheffield W and Everton
1913–14 Preston NE and Derby Co	1951–52 Huddersfield T and Fulham
1914–15 Tottenham H and Chelsea*	1952–53 Stoke C and Derby Co
1919–20 Notts Co and Sheffield W	1953–54 Middlesbrough and Liverpool
1920–21 Derby Co and Bradford PA	1954–55 Leicester C and Sheffield W
1921–22 Bradford C and Manchester U	1955–56 Huddersfield T and Sheffield U
1922–23 Stoke C and Oldham Ath	1956–57 Charlton Ath and Cardiff C
1923–24 Chelsea and Middlesbrough	1957–58 Sheffield W and Sunderland
1924–25 Preston NE and Nottingham F	1958–59 Portsmouth and Aston Villa
1925–26 Manchester C and Notts Co	1959–60 Luton T and Leeds U

1960–61 Preston NE and Newcastle U	1981–82 Leeds U, Wolverhampton W, Middlesbrough
1961–62 Chelsea and Cardiff C	
1962–63 Manchester C and Leyton Orient	1982–83 Manchester C, Swansea C, Brighton & HA
1963–64 Bolton W and Ipswich T	
1964–65 Wolverhampton W and Birmingham C	1983–84 Birmingham C, Notts Co, Wolverhampton W
1965–66 Northampton T and Blackburn R	1984–85 Norwich C, Sunderland, Stoke C
1966–67 Aston Villa and Blackpool	1985–86 Ipswich T, Birmingham C, WBA
1967–68 Fulham and Sheffield U	
1968–69 Leicester C and QPR	1986–87 Leicester C, Manchester C, Aston Villa
1969–70 Sunderland and Sheffield W	
1970–71 Burnley and Blackpool	1987–88 Chelsea**, Portsmouth, Watford, Oxford U
1971–72 Huddersfield T and Nottingham F	
1972–73 Crystal Palace and WBA	1988–89 Middlesbrough, West Ham U, Newcastle U
1973–74 Southampton, Manchester U, Norwich C	1989–90 Sheffield W, Charlton Ath, Millwall
1974–75 Luton T, Chelsea, Carlisle U	1990–91 Sunderland and Derby Co
1975–76 Wolverhampton W, Burnley, Sheffield U	1991–92 Luton T, Notts Co, West Ham U
1976–77 Sunderland, Stoke C, Tottenham H	1992–93 Brentford, Cambridge U, Bristol R
1977–78 West Ham U, Newcastle U, Leicester C	1993–94 Birmingham C, Oxford U, Peterborough U
1978–79 QPR, Birmingham C, Chelsea	1994–95 Swindon T, Burnley, Bristol C, Notts Co
1979–80 Bristol C, Derby Co, Bolton W	
1980–81 Norwich C, Leicester C, Crystal Palace	1995–96 Millwall, Watford, Luton T

**Relegated after play-offs.
*Subsequently re-elected to Division 1 when League was extended after the War.

DIVISION 2 TO DIVISION 3

1920–21 Stockport Co	1949–50 Plymouth Arg and Bradford PA
1921–22 Bradford PA and Bristol C	1950–51 Grimsby T and Chesterfield
1922–23 Rotherham Co and Wolverhampton W	1951–52 Coventry C and QPR
1923–24 Nelson and Bristol C	1952–53 Southampton and Barnsley
1924–25 Crystal Palace and Coventry C	1953–54 Brentford and Oldham Ath
1925–26 Stoke C and Stockport Co	1954–55 Ipswich T and Derby Co
1926–27 Darlington and Bradford C	1955–56 Plymouth Arg and Hull C
1927–28 Fulham and South Shields	1956–57 Port Vale and Bury
1928–29 Port Vale and Clapton Orient	1957–58 Doncaster R and Notts Co
1929–30 Hull C and Notts Co	1958–59 Barnsley and Grimsby T
1930–31 Reading and Cardiff C	1959–60 Bristol C and Hull C
1931–32 Barnsley and Bristol C	1960–61 Lincoln C and Portsmouth
1932–33 Chesterfield and Charlton Ath	1961–62 Brighton & HA and Bristol R
1933–34 Millwall and Lincoln C	1962–63 Walsall and Luton T
1934–35 Oldham Ath and Notts Co	1963–64 Grimsby T and Scunthorpe U
1935–36 Port Vale and Hull C	1964–65 Swindon T and Swansea T
1936–37 Doncaster R and Bradford C	1965–66 Middlesbrough and Leyton Orient
1937–38 Barnsley and Stockport Co	
1938–39 Norwich C and Tranmere R	1966–67 Northampton T and Bury
1946–47 Swansea T and Newport Co	1967–68 Plymouth Arg and Rotherham U
1947–48 Doncaster R and Millwall	1968–69 Fulham and Bury
1948–49 Nottingham F and Lincoln C	1969–70 Preston NE and Aston Villa
	1970–71 Blackburn R and Bolton W

1971–72 Charlton Ath and Watford
1972–73 Huddersfield T and Brighton & HA
1973–74 Crystal Palace, Preston NE, Swindon T
1974–75 Millwall, Cardiff C, Sheffield W
1975–76 Oxford U, York C, Portsmouth
1976–77 Carlisle U, Plymouth Arg, Hereford U
1977–78 Blackpool, Mansfield T, Hull C
1978–79 Sheffield U, Millwall, Blackburn R
1979–80 Fulham, Burnley, Charlton Ath
1980–81 Preston NE, Bristol C, Bristol R
1981–82 Cardiff C, Wrexham, Orient
1982–83 Rotherham U, Burnley, Bolton W
1983–84 Derby Co, Swansea C, Cambridge U
1984–85 Notts Co, Cardiff C, Wolverhampton W

1985–86 Carlisle U, Middlesbrough, Fulham
1986–87 Sunderland**, Grimsby T, Brighton & HA
1987–88 Huddersfield T, Reading, Sheffield U**
1988–89 Shrewsbury T, Birmingham C, Walsall
1989–90 Bournemouth, Bradford C, Stoke C
1990–91 WBA and Hull C
1991–92 Plymouth Arg, Brighton & HA, Port Vale
1992–93 Preston NE, Mansfield T, Wigan Ath, Chester C
1993–94 Fulham, Exeter C, Hartlepool U, Barnet
1994–95 Cambridge U, Plymouth Arg, Cardiff C, Chester C, Leyton Orient
1995–96 Carlisle U, Swansea C, Brighton & HA, Hull C

DIVISION 3 TO DIVISION 4

1958–59 Rochdale, Notts Co, Doncaster R, Stockport Co
1959–60 Accrington S, Wrexham, Mansfield T, York C
1960–61 Chesterfield, Colchester U, Bradford C, Tranmere R
1961–62 Newport Co, Brentford, Lincoln C, Torquay U
1962–63 Bradford PA, Brighton & HA, Carlisle U, Halifax T
1963–64 Millwall, Crewe Alex, Wrexham, Notts Co
1964–65 Luton T, Port Vale, Colchester U, Barnsley
1965–66 Southend U, Exeter C, Brentford, York C
1966–67 Doncaster R, Workington, Darlington, Swansea T
1967–68 Scunthorpe U, Colchester U, Grimsby T, Peterborough U (demoted)
1968–69 Oldham Ath, Crewe Alex, Hartlepool, Northampton T
1969–70 Bournemouth, Southport, Barrow, Stockport Co
1970–71 Reading, Bury, Doncaster R, Gillingham
1971–72 Mansfield T, Barnsley, Torquay U, Bradford C
1972–73 Rotherham U, Brentford, Swansea C, Scunthorpe U

1973–74 Cambridge U, Shrewsbury T, Southport, Rochdale
1974–75 Bournemouth, Tranmere R, Watford, Huddersfield T
1975–76 Aldershot, Colchester U, Southend U, Halifax T
1976–77 Reading, Northampton T, Grimsby T, York C
1977–78 Port Vale, Bradford C, Hereford U, Portsmouth
1978–79 Peterborough U, Walsall, Tranmere R, Lincoln C
1979–80 Bury, Southend U, Mansfield T, Wimbledon
1980–81 Sheffield U, Colchester U, Blackpool, Hull C
1981–82 Wimbledon, Swindon T, Bristol C, Chester
1982–83 Reading, Wrexham, Doncaster R, Chesterfield
1983–84 Scunthorpe U, Southend U, Port Vale, Exeter C
1984–85 Burnley, Orient, Preston NE, Cambridge U
1985–86 Lincoln C, Cardiff C, Wolverhampton W, Swansea C
1986–87 Bolton W**, Carlisle U, Darlington, Newport Co
1987–88 Doncaster R, York C, Grimsby T, Rotherham U**
1988–89 Southend U, Chesterfield, Gillingham, Aldershot

**Relegated after play-offs.

99

1989–90 Cardiff C, Northampton T,
        Blackpool, Walsall
1990–91 Crewe Alex, Rotherham U,
        Mansfield T

1991–92 Bury, Shrewsbury T,
        Torquay U, Darlington

LEAGUE TITLE WINS

FA PREMIER LEAGUE – Manchester U 3, Blackburn R 1.

LEAGUE DIVISION 1 – Liverpool 18, Arsenal 10, Everton 9, Manchester U 7, Aston Villa 7, Sunderland 7, Newcastle U 5, Sheffield W 4, Huddersfield T 3, Leeds U 3, Wolverhampton W 3, Blackburn R 2, Portsmouth 2, Preston NE 2, Burnley 2, Manchester C 2, Tottenham H 2, Derby Co 2, Chelsea 1, Sheffield U 1, WBA 1, Ipswich T 1, Nottingham F 1, Crystal Palace 1, Middlesbrough 1.

LEAGUE DIVISION 2 – Leicester C 6, Manchester C 6, Sheffield W 5, Birmingham C (one as Small Heath) 5, Derby Co 4, Liverpool 4, Ipswich T 3, Leeds U 3, Notts Co 3, Preston NE 3, Middlesbrough 3, Stoke C 3, Grimsby T 2, Norwich C 2, Nottingham F 2, Tottenham H 2, WBA 2, Aston Villa 2, Burnley 2, Chelsea 2, Manchester U 2, West Ham U 2, Wolverhampton W 2, Bolton W 2, Swindon T, Huddersfield T, Bristol C, Brentford, Bury, Bradford C, Everton, Fulham, Sheffield U, Newcastle U, Coventry C, Blackpool, Blackburn R, Sunderland, Crystal Palace, Luton T, QPR, Oxford U, Millwall, Oldham Ath, Reading 1 each.

LEAGUE DIVISION 3 – Portsmouth 2, Oxford U 2, Carlisle U 2, Preston NE 2, Shrewsbury T 2, Plymouth Arg, Southampton, Bury, Northampton T, Coventry C, Hull C, QPR, Watford, Leyton Orient, Aston Villa, Bolton W, Oldham Ath, Blackburn R, Hereford U, Mansfield T, Wrexham, Grimsby T, Rotherham U, Burnley, Bradford C, Bournemouth, Reading, Sunderland, Wolverhampton W, Bristol R, Cambridge U, Brentford, Cardiff C 1 each.

LEAGUE DIVISION 4 – Chesterfield 2, Doncaster R 2, Peterborough U 2, Port Vale, Walsall, Millwall, Brentford, Gillingham, Brighton, Stockport Co, Luton T, Notts Co, Grimsby T, Southport, Mansfield T, Lincoln C, Cambridge U, Watford, Reading, Huddersfield T, Southend U, Sheffield U, Wimbledon, York C, Swindon T, Northampton T, Wolverhampton W, Rotherham U, Exeter C, Darlington, Burnley 1 each.

To 1957–58

DIVISION 3 (South) – Bristol C 3; Charlton Ath, Ipswich T, Millwall, Notts Co, Plymouth Arg, Swansea T 2 each; Brentford, Bristol R, Cardiff C, Crystal Palace, Coventry C, Fulham, Leyton Orient, Luton T, Newport Co, Nottingham F, Norwich C, Portsmouth, QPR, Reading, Southampton, Brighton & HA 1 each.

DIVISION 3 (North) – Barnsley, Doncaster R, Lincoln C 3 each; Chesterfield, Grimsby T, Hull C, Port Vale, Stockport Co 2 each; Bradford PA, Bradford C, Darlington, Derby Co, Nelson, Oldham Ath, Rotherham U, Stoke C, Tranmere R, Wolverhampton W, Scunthorpe U 1 each.

TRANSFERS 1995–96

June 1995

	From	To
30 Armstrong, Christopher P.	Crystal Palace	Tottenham Hotspur
7 Barton, Warren D.	Wimbledon	Newcastle United
7 Bennett, Thomas M.	Wolverhampton Wanderers	Stockport County
19 Butler, John E.	Stoke City	Wigan Athletic
21 Carter, Darren S.	Leyton Orient	Peterborough United
29 Clarke, Matthew L.	Halesowen Harriers	Halesowen Town
30 Cuggy, Michael S.	Margate	Hastings Town
15 Edworthy, Marc	Plymouth Argyle	Crystal Palace
12 Eustace, Scott D.	Leicester City	Mansfield Town
9 Ferdinand, Leslie	Queens Park Rangers	Newcastle United
12 Finnan, Stephen J.	Welling United	Birmingham City
18 Finney, Stephen K.	Manchester City	Swindon Town
5 Fisher, Neil J.	Bolton Wanderers	Chester City
26 Garner, Darren	Dorchester Town	Rotherham United
19 Griffiths, Bryan K.	Telford United	Southport
20 Holland, Paul	Mansfield Town	Sheffield United
22 Jeffrey, Michael R.	Newcastle United	Rotherham United
23 Muir, Ian J.	Tranmere Rovers	Birmingham City
1 Neilson, Alan B.	Newcastle United	Southampton
15 Payne, Stephen R.	Crawley Town	Sutton United
23 Rattray, Kevin	Woking	Gillingham
2 Richards, Dean I.	Bradford City	Wolverhampton Wanderers
6 Seagraves, Mark	Bolton Wanderers	Swindon Town
24 Taylor, Stephen C.	Bromsgrove Rovers	Crystal Palace
7 Turnbull, Lee M.	Wycombe Wanderers	Scunthorpe United
15 Vansittart, Jonathan	Crawley Town	Sutton United
15 White, Jason G.	Scarborough	Northampton Town
16 Wilkinson, Stephen J.	Mansfield Town	Preston North End
12 Wilson, Clive	Queens Park Rangers	Tottenham Hotspur
12 Yates, Jason	Bridgnorth Town	Clevedon Town

TEMPORARY TRANSFERS

19 Appleton, Michael A.	Manchester United	Wimbledon
10 O'Kane, John A.	Manchester United	Wimbledon
22 O'Shea, Daniel E.	Northampton Town	Wimbledon
22 Sampson, Ian	Northampton Town	Tottenham Hotspur
19 Tomlinson, Graham	Manchester United	Wimbledon

JULY 1995

10 Alexander, Graham	Scunthorpe United	Luton Town
25 Allison, Wayne	Bristol City	Swindon Town
24 Allon, Joseph B.	Port Vale	Lincoln City
31 Anderson, Ijah M.	Southend United	Brentford
10 Aspinall, Warren	AFC Bournemouth	Carlisle United
5 Bailey, John A.	Enfield	AFC Bournemouth
15 Barber, Philip A.	Millwall	Bristol City
3 Barkus, Lea F.	Reading	Fulham
1 Bart-Williams, Chris	Sheffield Wednesday	Nottingham Forest
14 Bennett, Gary M.	Wrexham	Tranmere Rovers
18 Blades, Paul A.	Wolverhampton Wanderers	Rotherham United
21 Bowen, Jason P.	Swansea City	Birmingham City
4 Bowry, Robert	Crystal Palace	Millwall
1 Caldwell, Peter J.	Queens Park Rangers	Leyton Orient
1 Campbell, Kevin J.	Arsenal	Nottingham Forest
24 Castle, Stephen C.	Plymouth Argyle	Birmingham City
3 Charlery, Kenneth	Peterborough United	Birmingham City
3 Collymore, Stanley V.	Nottingham Forest	Liverpool
19 Darby, Duane A.	Torquay United	Doncaster Rovers
5 Davies, Gareth M.	Hereford United	Crystal Palace
13 Davis, Stephen M.	Burnley	Luton Town
3 Dempsey, Mark A.	Leyton Orient	Shrewsbury Town
5 Draper, Mark A.	Leicester City	Aston Villa
10 Edwards, Andrew D.	Southend United	Birmingham City
5 Eyre, John R.	Oldham Athletic	Scunthorpe United
4 Fairclough, Courtney H.	Leeds United	Bolton Wanderers
13 Farrelly, Stephen	Macclesfield Town	Rotherham United
7 Felgate, David W.	Chester City	Wigan Athletic
25 Ford, Jonathan S.	Swansea City	Bradford City
13 Forsyth, Richard	Kidderminster Harriers	Birmingham City

17 Gray, Ian J.	Oldham Athletic	Rochdale
20 Hannigan, Al J.	Enfield	Rushden & Diamonds
28 Heald, Paul A.	Leyton Orient	Wimbledon
27 Heathcote, Michael	Cambridge United	Plymouth Argyle
28 Heggs, Carl S.	West Bromwich Albion	Swansea City
21 Hopkin, David	Chelsea	Crystal Palace
13 Hoult, Russell	Leicester City	Derby County
12 Hyatt, Frederick	Wokingham Town	Hayes
19 Irving, Richard J.	Manchester United	Nottingham Forest
13 Kelly, Anthony G.	Peterborough United	Wigan Athletic
6 Kelly, Anthony O. N.	Bury	Leyton Orient
13 Landon, Richard J.	Plymouth Argyle	Stockport County
7 Lightfoot, Christopher I.	Chester City	Wigan Athletic
13 Malkin, Christopher G.	Tranmere Rovers	Millwall
31 Mauge, Ronald C.	Bury	Plymouth Argyle
13 Meaker, Michael J.	Queens Park Rangers	Reading
18 Mohan, Nicholas	Leicester City	Bradford City
19 Moore, Darren M.	Torquay United	Doncaster Rovers
21 Newman, Richard A.	Crystal Palace	Millwall
18 Oldfield, David C.	Leicester City	Luton Town
21 Ormonroyd, Ian	Leicester City	Bradford City
11 Osborn, Simon E.	Reading	Queens Park Rangers
20 Pembridge, Mark A.	Derby County	Sheffield Wednesday
28 Powell, Darryl A.	Portsmouth	Derby County
27 Power, Lee M.	Bradford City	Peterborough United
5 Preece, Andrew P.	Crystal Palace	Blackpool
13 Reid, Shaun	Rochdale	Bury
21 Roberts, Andrew J.	Millwall	Crystal Palace
21 Rowett, Gary	Everton	Derby County
13 Russell, Kevin J.	Notts County	Wrexham
26 Sale, Mark D.	Preston North End	Mansfield Town
29 Saville, Andrew V.	Birmingham City	Preston North End
24 Sheffield, Jonathan	Cambridge United	Peterborough United
21 Short, Craig J.	Derby County	Everton
21 Skinner, Craig R.	Plymouth Argyle	Wrexham
13 Southall, Leslie N.	Hartlepool United	Grimsby Town
1 Southgate, Gareth	Crystal Palace	Aston Villa
20 Stanislaus, Roger E. P.	Bury	Leyton Orient
13 Strodder, Gary J.	West Bromwich Albion	Notts County
26 Sugrue, James S.	Kingstonian	Aldershot Town
13 Swales, Stephen C.	Scarborough	Reading
13 Taylor, Scott D.	Reading	Leicester City
11 Telfer, Paul N.	Luton Town	Coventry City
13 Ward, Darren	Mansfield Town	Notts County
18 Ward, Gavin J.	Leicester City	Bradford City
19 Ward, Peter	Stockport County	Wrexham
27 Westwood, Ashley M.	Manchester United	Crewe Alexandra

TEMPORARY TRANSFERS

| 21 Galloway, Michael | Celtic | Leicester City |

AUGUST 1995

9 Allon, Andrew	Margate	Ashford Town
9 Anthrobus, Stephen A.	Wimbledon	Shrewsbury Town
15 Bailey, Dennis L.	Queens Park Rangers	Gillingham
18 Banks, Steven	Gillingham	Blackpool
8 Barber, Philip A.	Millwall	Bristol City
8 Barmby, Nicholas J.	Tottenham Hotspur	Middlesbrough
8 Beard, Mark	Millwall	Sheffield United
4 Beesley, Paul	Sheffield United	Leeds United
11 Billy, Christopher A.	Huddersfield Town	Plymouth Argyle
19 Birch, Troy J.	Hayes	Wealdstone
22 Bradford, Lee T.	Dorchester Town	Weymouth
11 Bryan, Marvin L.	Queens Park Rangers	Blackpool
25 Byrne, Paul P.	Celtic	Southend United
11 Clayton, Gary	Huddersfield Town	Plymouth Argyle
11 Conroy, Michael K.	Preston North End	Fulham
14 Cunnington, Shaun G.	Sunderland	West Bromwich Albion
11 Dalton, Paul	Plymouth Argyle	Huddersfield Town
11 Flynn, Sean M.	Coventry City	Derby County
10 Gilbert, David J.	Grimsby Town	West Bromwich Albion
16 Goodridge, Gregory R.S.	Torquay United	Queens Park Rangers

18 Griffiths, Carl B.	Manchester City	Portsmouth
16 Grocutt, Darren	Burton Albion	Bromsgrove Rovers
10 Hammond, Nicholas D.	Swindon Town	Plymouth Argyle
25 Hill, Andrew R.	Manchester City	Port Vale
11 Hislop, Neil S.	Reading	Newcastle United
18 Hodgson, Philip	Morecambe	Netherfield
15 Holmes, Matthew J.	West Ham United	Blackburn Rovers
25 Kanchelskis, Andrei	Manchester United	Everton
5 McCarthy, Alan J.	Queens Park Rangers	Leyton Orient
1 McCarthy, Jonathan D.	York City	Port Vale
7 McFarlane, Andrew A.	Swansea City	Scunthorpe United
16 McGorry, Brian P.	Peterborough United	Wycombe Wanderers
1 MacKenzie, Stuart M.	Yeading	Farnborough Town
3 Marshall, Shaun	Hitchin Town	Stevenage Borough
18 May, Leroy A.	Stafford Rangers	Kidderminster Harriers
23 Mike, Adrian R.	Manchester City	Stockport County
3 Mills, Rowan L.	Derby County	Port Vale
17 Morton, Neil	Altrincham	Barrow
14 Mullin, John	Burnley	Sunderland
21 Ndah, Jamie	Kingstonian	Torquay United
21 Patterson, Darren J.	Crystal Palace	Luton Town
18 Pender, John P.	Burnley	Wigan Athletic
15 Reed, Adam M.	Darlington	Blackburn Rovers
7 Richardson, Nicholas J.	Cardiff City	Bury
2 Ross, Brian J.	Marine	Chorley
18 Rush, Matthew J.	West Ham United	Norwich City
7 Salako, John A.	Crystal Palace	Coventry City
21 Salmon, Marc R.	Harlow Town	Charlton Athletic
22 Saunders, Mark P.	Tiverton Town	Plymouth Argyle
25 Shirtliff, Peter A.	Wolverhampton Wanderers	Barnsley
18 Simpson, Fitzroy	Manchester City	Portsmouth
15 Slater, Robert D.	Blackburn Rovers	West Ham United
10 Smith, Malcolm A.	Ashford Town	Margate
5 Smith, Neil	Cheltenham Town	Rushden & Diamonds
29 Sommer, Jurgen P.	Luton Town	Queens Park Rangers
9 Sperry, Gary	Bognor Regis Town	Ryde
8 Stephenson, Paul	Brentford	York City
14 Strong, Greg	Wigan Athletic	Bolton Wanderers
11 Swan, Peter H.	Plymouth Argyle	Burnley
18 Symons, Christopher J.	Portsmouth	Manchester City
2 Taggart, Gerald P.	Barnsley	Bolton Wanderers
11 Teal, Shaun	Aston Villa	Tranmere Rovers
15 Todd, Andrew	Middlesbrough	Bolton Wanderers
11 Ullathorne, Simon	Gloucester City	Hastings Town
25 Van der Laan, Robertus P.	Port Vale	Derby County
11 Walsh, Gary	Manchester United	Middlesbrough
11 Williams, Karl I.	Warrington Town	Macclesfield Town
11 Williams, Mark S.	Shrewsbury Town	Chesterfield
11 Williams, Paul D.	Derby County	Coventry City
2 Williams, Paul R.C.	Coventry City	Plymouth Argyle
10 Wilson, Paul A.	York City	Scunthorpe United
8 Woods, Billy	Cork City	Tranmere Rovers

TEMPORARY TRANSFERS

25 Armstrong, Gordon I.	Sunderland	Bristol City
11 Beresford, David	Oldham Athletic	Swansea City
24 Berry, Greg J.	Millwall	Brighton & Hove Albion
11 Brightwell, David J.	Manchester City	Lincoln City
31 Brodie, Stephen E.	Sunderland	Doncaster Rovers
8 Bull, Gary W.	Nottingham Forest	Brighton & Hove Albion
25 Castledine, Stewart M.	Wimbledon	Wycombe Wanderers
26 Fleck, Robert	Chelsea	Norwich City
11 Foran, Mark J.	Sheffield United	Wycombe Wanderers
7 Given, Seamus J.J.	Blackburn Rovers	Swindon Town
11 Harmon, Darren J.	Northampton Town	Cambridge United
11 Harris, Mark A.	Swansea City	Gillingham
21 Heywood, David I.	Hailsowen Town	Bilston Town
10 Hodgson, Douglas J.H.	Sheffield United	Plymouth Argyle
21 Jardine, Jamie	Tranmere Rovers	Chorley
16 Jewell, Paul	Bradford City	Grimsby Town
3 Kane, Paul	Aberdeen	Barnsley
11 Key, Lance	Sheffield Wednesday	Lincoln City

29 Lowe, Kenneth	Birmingham City	Hartlepool United
26 Martin, Eliot J.	Gillingham	Margate
19 Monk, Ian L.	Macclesfield Town	Leigh RMI
25 Moore, Neil	Everton	Carlisle United
28 Morah, Olisa H.	Cambridge United	Braintree Town
24 Mutch, Andrew T.	Swindon Town	Wigan Athletic
11 Oatway, Anthony	Cardiff City	Coleraine
11 Pettinger, Paul A.	Leeds United	Rotherham United
26 Reilly, James L.	Sudbury Town	Purfleet
25 Sedgemore, Benjamin R.	Birmingham City	Mansfield Town
3 Shaw, Paul	Arsenal	Cardiff City
11 Shipp, Daniel A.	West Ham United	Dagenham & Redbridge
1 Simpson, Gary	Luton Town	Aylesbury United
29 Stewart, Paul A.	Liverpool	Sunderland
11 Stewart, Simon A.	Sheffield Wednesday	Shrewsbury Town
2 Stuart, Mark R.	Rochdale	Chesterfield
4 Swan, Peter H.	Plymouth Argyle	Burnley
19 Timons, Christopher	Mansfield Town	Halifax Town
10 Tracey, Simon P.	Sheffield United	Nottingham Forest
10 Viveash, Adrian L.	Swindon Town	Barnsley
29 Webster, Simon P.	West Ham United	Derby County

SEPTEMBER 1995

30 Arkins, Vincent	Shelbourne	Notts County
21 Atkins, Mark N.	Blackburn Rovers	Wolverhampton Wanderers
11 Barrick, Dean	Cambridge United	Preston North End
19 Beard, Simon A.	Sittingbourne	Hastings Town
7 Bernard, Paul R.J.	Oldham Athletic	Aberdeen
2 Boere, Jeroen W.J.	West Ham United	Crystal Palace
29 Carruthers, Matthew J.	Dover Athletic	Ashford Town
14 Creaney, Gerard	Portsmouth	Manchester City
8 Dowie, Iain	Crystal Palace	West Ham United
11 Farrell, David	Aston Villa	Wycombe Wanderers
7 Ferguson, Derek	Sunderland	Falkirk
29 Fleck, Robert	Chelsea	Norwich City
7 Foley, Dominic	St James Gate	Wolverhampton Wanderers
8 Freedman, Douglas A.	Barnet	Crystal Palace
2 Greenall, Colin A.	Lincoln City	Wigan Athletic
29 Hackett, Brendan	Hednesford Town	Rushden & Diamonds
1 Harper, Steven J.	Doncaster Rovers	Mansfield Town
14 Harris, Mark A.	Swansea City	Gillingham
29 Hume, Kevin	Bury	Lincoln City
12 Humphreys, Delwyn J.	Kidderminster Harriers	Northwich Victoria
1 Johnson, Michael O.	Notts County	Birmingham City
14 Keast, Douglas W.	Rushden & Diamonds	Burton Albion
20 Kelly, David T.	Wolverhampton Wanderers	Sunderland
26 Masters, Paul J.	Havant Town	Salisbury City
8 Matthews, Robert D.	Luton Town	York City
6 McAteer, Jason W.	Bolton Wanderers	Liverpool
14 Murphy, James A.	Blackpool	Doncaster Rovers
7 Newbery, Richard J.	Woking	Wokingham Town
29 Nugent, Kevin P.	Plymouth Argyle	Bristol City
25 O'Neill, Steven A.	Altrincham	Bamber Bridge
8 Palmer, Stephen L.	Ipswich Town	Watford
11 Raynor, Paul J.	Preston North End	Cambridge United
7 Richardson, Nicholas J.	Bury	Chester City
11 Rowbotham, Jason	Raith Rovers	Crystal Palace
29 Taylor, Gareth K.	Bristol Rovers	Portsmouth
14 Walsh, Paul A.	Manchester City	VS Rugby
21 Warner, Ashley S.	Gloucester City	Witton Albion
3 Watson, Liam	Marine	Bury
29 West, Dean	Lincoln City	Preston North End
22 Wilcox, Russell	Doncaster Rovers	Wycombe Wanderers
14 Williams, John	Coventry City	

TEMPORARY TRANSFERS

11 Allen, Martin J.	West Ham United	Portsmouth
15 Appleton, Michael A.	Manchester United	Lincoln City
11 Arkins, Vincent	Shelbourne	Notts County
29 Barker, Richard I.	Sheffield Wednesday	Doncaster Rovers
29 Barton, Stuart A.	Bamber Bridge	Atherton LR
8 Berry, Trevor J.	Aston Villa	Rotherham United
29 Black, Kingsley	Nottingham Forest	Millwall

11 Blatherwick, Steven S.	Nottingham Forest	Hereford United
11 Bound, Matthew T.	Stockport County	Lincoln City
11 Brightwell, David J.	Manchester City	Stoke City
7 Brown, Kenneth J.	West Ham United	Huddersfield Town
15 Browne, Corey	Dover Athletic	Stevenage Borough
17 Bull, Gary W.	Nottingham Forest	Brighton & Hove Albion
22 Charles, Lee	Queens Park Rangers	Barnet
22 Cole, Peter	Ashton United	Netherfield
29 Colgan, Nicholas V.	Chelsea	Millwall
11 Collier, Daniel J.	Crewe Alexandra	York City
8 Cureton, Jamie	Norwich City	AFC Bournemouth
3 Dobbs, Gerald F.	Wimbledon	Cardiff City
29 Dewberry, Michael W.	Chelsea	AFC Bournemouth
23 Dykstra, Sieb	Queens Park Rangers	Bristol City
29 Edwards, Matthew D.	Kettering Town	Walton & Hersham
11 Evans, Richard J.	Marlow	Yeading
11 Feuer, Antony I.	West Ham United	Luton Town
27 Foot, Daniel F.	Southend United	Dover Athletic
14 Freeman, Mark W.	Hednesford Town	Gloucester City
22 Gibb, Alistair S.	Norwich City	Northampton Town
12 Goodacre, Samuel D.	Stalybridge Celtic	Gainsborough Town
26 Hague, Paul	Leyton Orient	Dagenham & Redbridge
18 Harper, Stephen A.	Newcastle United	Bradford City
22 Jardine, Jamie	Tranmere Rovers	Chorley
18 Jewell, Paul	Bradford City	Grimsby Town
17 Johnson, Alan K.	Lincoln City	Preston North End
4 Jones, Martin	Tranmere Rovers	Altrincham
15 Joseph, Marc E.	Cambridge United	Cambridge City
22 Kerr, David W.	Manchester City	Mansfield Town
18 Ludlow, Lee	Halifax Town	Spennymoor United
12 Maddison, Lee R.	Bristol Rovers	Northampton Town
15 Marquis, Paul R.	Doncaster Rovers	Gateshead
14 McDonald, Paul	Southampton	Burnley
15 Mercer, William	Sheffield United	Chesterfield
22 Molby, Jan	Liverpool	Barnsley
18 Monk, Ian L.	Macclesfield Town	Leigh RMI
26 Moore, Neil	Everton	Carlisle United
7 Morah, Olisa	Cambridge United	Braintree Town
29 Morah, Olisa	Cambridge United	Welling United
8 Muir, Ian J.	Birmingham City	Darlington
1 Omigie, Joseph	Brentford	Woking
15 Parker, Adam	Stevenage Borough	Hitchin Town
15 Parsons, Mark C.	Kettering Town	Aylesbury United
12 Penman, Jon D.	Southport	Marine
22 Perkins, Declan O.	Southend United	Cambridge United
26 Petterson, Andrew K.	Charlton Athletic	Ipswich Town
22 Quy, Andrew	Derby County	Stalybridge Celtic
1 Ridout, John	Enfield	Purfleet
4 Rolling, Frank	Ayr United	Leicester City
19 Savage, Robert T.	Bashley	Fareham Town
24 Sedgemore, Benjamin R.	Birmingham City	Mansfield Town
9 Simpson, Gary	Luton Town	Aylesbury United
8 Smith, Richard G.	Leicester City	Grimsby Town
15 Starbuck, Philip M.	Sheffield United	Bristol City
21 Stimson, Mark	Portsmouth	Barnet
8 Talia, Francesco	Blackburn Rovers	Swindon Town
17 Thorpe, Lee A.	Blackpool	Bangor
11 Watson, Alexander F.	AFC Bournemouth	Gillingham
4 Watson, Mark L.	West Ham United	Leyton Orient
25 Wells, Mark	Scarborough	Dagenham & Redbridge
21 Whiston, Peter	Southampton	Shrewsbury Town

OCTOBER 1995

9 Allon, Joseph B.	Lincoln City	Hartlepool United
27 Arnold, Ian	Kettering Town	Stalybridge Celtic
13 Baraclough, Ian R.	Mansfield Town	Notts County
9 Barnard, Darren S.	Chelsea	Bristol City
13 Barnes, Steven L.	Welling United	Birmingham City
27 Barnett, Jason V.	Wolverhampton Wanderers	Lincoln City
12 Beauchamp, Joseph D.	Swindon Town	Oxford United
13 Berry, Trevor J.	Aston Villa	Rotherham United
14 Bohinen, Lars	Nottingham Forest	Blackburn Rovers

6 Brown, Steven R.	Gillingham	Lincoln City
13 Coughlin, Russell J.	Exeter City	Torquay United
30 Doling, Stuart J.	Lymington AFC	Doncaster Rovers
8 Edey, Cecil	Witton Albion	Macclesfield Town
6 Fox, Ruel A.	Newcastle United	Tottenham Hotspur
20 Hackett, Warren J.	Doncaster Rovers	Mansfield Town
4 Hanson, David	Hednesford Town	Leyton Orient
27 Hoddle, Carl	Woking	Enfield
25 Jobson, Richard I.	Oldham Athletic	Leeds United
27 Lay, David A.	Slough Town	Chesham United
26 Logan, Richard A.	Huddersfield Town	Plymouth Argyle
5 Lowndes, Nathan P.	Leeds United	Watford
6 McSwegan, Gary J.	Notts County	Dundee United
27 Maddison, Lee R.	Bristol Rovers	Northampton Town
13 Makel, Lee R.	Blackburn Rovers	Huddersfield Town
6 Mowbray, Anthony	Celtic	Ipswich Town
20 Munro, Stuart	Bristol City	Falkirk
2 Perrett, Russell	Lymington AFC	Portsmouth
9 Pointon, Neil G.	Oldham Athletic	Heart of Midlothian
7 Puttnam, David P.	Lincoln City	Gillingham
20 Richardson, Barry	Preston North End	Lincoln City
21 Simpson, Philip M.	Stevenage Borough	Barnet
3 Smart, Stephen J.	Sutton United	Aylesbury United
17 Thompson, Steven	Wycombe Wanderers	Woking
19 Tierling, Lee A.	Woking	Welling United
28 Tiler, Carl	Nottingham Forest	Aston Villa
6 Walker, David J.	Dover Athletic	Gravesend & Northfleet
6 Westley, Shane L.M.	Cambridge United	Lincoln City
24 Whiston, Peter	Southampton	Shrewsbury Town
31 Whitney, John D.	Huddersfield Town	Lincoln City

TEMPORARY TRANSFERS

4 Beauchamp, Joseph D.	Swindon Town	Oxford United
13 Blake, Robert J.	Darlington	Waterford United
9 Brown, Dereck	Walton & Hersham	St Albans City
27 Brown, Kenneth J.	West Ham United	Reading
13 Buckle, Paul J.	Torquay United	Exeter City
12 Burnett, Wayne	Plymouth Argyle	Bolton Wanderers
30 Capleton, Melvin D.R.	Blackpool	Cork City
27 Caskey, Darren M.	Tottenham Hotspur	Watford
30 Clarkson, Phillip I.	Crewe Alexandra	Scunthorpe United
17 Cobb, Paul M.	Enfield	Purfleet
20 Collinson, David	Ashford Town	Margate
5 Cullip, Daniel	Oxford United	Kettering Town
28 Cutler, Neil A.	West Bromwich Albion	Coventry City
13 Debont, Andrew	Wolverhampton Wanderers	Hartlepool United
5 Dennison, Robert	Wolverhampton Wanderers	Swansea City
30 Dunphy, Nicholas	Peterborough United	Cheltenham Town
20 Fowler, John A.	Cambridge United	Cambridge City
28 Gorman, Paul M.	Welling United	Fisher 93
20 Gray, Martin D.	Sunderland	Fulham
21 Greene, Dennis B.	Dagenham & Redbridge	Chelmsford City
5 Higgs, Shane P.	Bristol Rovers	York City
20 Holmes, Steven P.	Preston North End	Lincoln City
31 Hooper, Michael D.	Newcastle United	Sunderland
27 Horner, Phillip M.	Blackpool	Southport
5 Jones, Lee	Swansea City	Crewe Alexandra
24 Keys, Martin	Bilston Town	Solihull Borough
20 King, Nathan P.	Shrewsbury Town	Stafford Rangers
30 King, Phillip G.	Aston Villa	West Bromwich Albion
13 Kirkham, Peter J.	Darlington	Waterford United
6 Lampard, Frank J.	West Ham United	Swansea City
7 Lawrence, Stephen P.	Dover Athletic	Margate
6 Lomas, Andrew J.	Rushden & Diamonds	Slough Town
20 Martin, Lee C.	Shrewsbury Town	Stafford Rangers
13 Mattison, Paul A.	Darlington	Cork City
16 McDonald, Paul	Southampton	Burnley
6 Morgan, Philip J.	Stoke City	Macclesfield Town
13 Naylor, Glenn	York City	Darlington
13 Ndah, George E.	Crystal Palace	AFC Bournemouth
1 Oghani, George W.	Northwich Victoria	Guiseley
13 Partridge, Scott M.	Bristol City	Torquay United

12 Paterson, James	Falkirk	Scunthorpe United
27 Peel, Nathan J.	Burnley	Mansfield Town
27 Perifimou, Christopher	Barnet	Hendon
26 Petterson, Andrew K.	Charlton Athletic	Ipswich Town
26 Philiskirk, Anthony	Burnley	Carlisle United
6 Read, Paul C.	Arsenal	Sheffield United
23 Rhodes, Andrew C.	St Johnstone	Preston North End
19 Roberts, Ben J.	Middlesbrough	Hartlepool United
24 Sharp, Lee	Queens Park Rangers	Lincoln United
20 Shaw, Paul	Arsenal	Peterborough United
13 Simkin, Darren S.	Shrewsbury Town	Telford United
27 Sunderland, Jonathan	Blackpool	Northwich Victoria
27 Taylor, Stephen C.	Crystal Palace	Northampton Town
21 Tobin, Steven R.	Macclesfield Town	Hyde United
26 Tovey, Paul	Bristol Rovers	Sligo Rovers
27 Watson, Mark L.	West Ham United	Cambridge United
13 Watson, Thomas R.	Grimsby Town	Hull City
26 Wilkinson, Paul	Middlesbrough	Oldham Athletic
26 Williams, Karl I.	Macclesfield Town	Ashton United
27 Woods, Christopher C.	Sheffield Wednesday	Reading
17 Wood, Simon O.	Coventry City	VS Rugby

NOVEMBER 1995

1 Ainsworth, Gareth	Preston North End	Lincoln City
21 Barlow, Stuart	Everton	Oldham Athletic
17 Bartlett, Richard	Newport (IW)	Weymouth
17 Beadle, Peter C.	Watford	Bristol Rovers
11 Bennett, Gary E.	Sunderland	Carlisle United
11 Brown, Dereck	Waltham & Hersham	Welling United
3 Buckle, Paul J.	Torquay United	Exeter City
4 Bywater, Paul R.	Bridgnorth Town	Stafford Rangers
17 Chenoweth, Paul	Bath City	Cheltenham Town
16 Collins, Lee	Albion Rovers	Swindon Town
24 Darby, Julian T.	Coventry City	West Bromwich Albion
16 Duxbury, Lee E.	Huddersfield Town	Bradford City
8 Fenton, Graham A.	Aston Villa	Blackburn Rovers
14 Grant, Anthony	Leeds United	Preston North End
30 Hercules, Cliff N.	Aylesbury United	Slough Town
3 Hills, John D.	Blackpool	Everton
10 Huckerby, Darren C.	Lincoln City	Newcastle United
3 Jenkins, Stephen R.	Swansea City	Huddersfield Town
24 Lavin, Gerard	Watford	Millwall
6 McDonald, Neil R.	Bolton Wanderers	Preston North End
7 Mayers, Kenneth	Bamber Bridge	Chorley
24 Nicol, Stephen	Notts County	Sheffield Wednesday
3 Paterson, James	Falkirk	Scunthorpe United
22 Pearce, Andrew J.	Sheffield Wednesday	Wimbledon
18 Penrice, Gary K.	Queens Park Rangers	Watford
15 Petrescu, Dan V.	Sheffield Wednesday	Chelsea
3 Phelan, Terrence M.	Manchester City	Chelsea
24 Phillips, Martin J.	Exeter City	Manchester City
17 Pollitt, Michael F.	Darlington	Notts County
3 Price, Ryan	Birmingham City	Macclesfield Town
3 Rolling, Frank	Ayr United	Leicester City
15 Scott, Keith	Stoke City	Norwich City
30 Sharp, Kevin P.	Leeds United	Wigan Athletic
15 Shaw, Richard E.	Crystal Palace	Coventry City
15 Sheron, Michael N.	Norwich City	Stoke City
21 Talia, Francesco	Blackburn Rovers	Swindon Town
6 Trundle, Lee C.	Burscough	Chorley
24 Watson, Alexander F.	AFC Bournemouth	Torquay United
24 Williams, Nicholas B.	Yeovil Town	Newport (IW)
7 Wood, Jeffrey J.	Barking	Aldershot Town

TEMPORARY TRANSFERS

15 Ansah, Andrew	Southend United	Brentford
10 Barber, Frederick	Luton Town	Ipswich Town
3 Barber, Philip A.	Bristol City	Mansfield Town
1 Barker, Richard I.	Sheffield Wednesday	Doncaster Rovers
11 Bensted, David T.	Harrow Borough	Aylesbury United
17 Biggins, Wayne	Oxford United	Wigan Athletic
11 Blatherwick, Steven S.	Nottingham Forest	Hereford United
27 Brown, Kenneth J.	West Ham United	Reading

3 Burnett, Wayne	Plymouth Argyle	Bolton Wanderers
3 Canham, Scott W.	West Ham United	Torquay United
25 Cartwright, Mike N.	Wrexham	Runcorn
17 Cobb, Paul M.	Enfield	Purfleet
30 Colgan, Nicholas V.	Chelsea	Millwall
16 Currie, Darren P.	West Ham United	Leyton Orient
20 Davis, Michael	Bristol Rovers	Bangor
24 Davison, Robert	Rotherham United	Hull City
20 Fettis, Alan	Hull City	West Bromwich Albion
24 Fitzgerald, Scott B.	Wimbledon	Sheffield United
13 Gentle, Dominic	Boreham Wood	Purfleet
20 Gray, Martin	Sunderland	Fulham
1 Grazioli, Giuliano	Peterborough United	Yeovil Town
24 Greene, David M.	Luton Town	Colchester United
11 Hague, Paul	Leyton Orient	Dagenham & Redbridge
11 Haines, Danny	Cheltenham Town	Evesham United
24 Harper, Alan	Burnley	Cardiff City
24 Hill, Daniel R.L.	Tottenham Hotspur	Birmingham City
22 Holmes, Steven P.	Preston North End	Lincoln City
27 Horner, Philip M.	Blackpool	Southport
17 Keys, Martin	Bilston Town	Solihull Borough
17 Kyd, Michael R.	Cambridge United	Bishops Stortford
6 Lawrence, Stephen P.	Dover Athletic	Margate
17 Linighan, David	Ipswich Town	Blackpool
24 Martin, Kevin	Scarborough	Guiseley
30 Morah, Olisa H.	Cambridge United	Welling United
8 Morgan, Philip J.	Stoke City	Macclesfield Town
1 Muggleton, Carl D.	Stoke City	Rotherham United
14 Noah, George E.	Crystal Palace	AFC Bournemouth
17 Norbury, Michael S.	Doncaster Rovers	Linfield
10 Powell, Jay	Kidderminster Harriers	Bridgnorth Town
24 Preece, David W.	Derby County	Birmingham City
7 Read, Paul	Arsenal	Southend United
13 Rea, Simon	Birmingham City	Kettering Town
9 Richards, Tony S.	Cambridge United	Sligo Rovers
11 Ross, Michael P.	Plymouth Argyle	Exeter City
3 Russell, Alexander J.	Rochdale	Glenavon
24 Scott, Robert	Sheffield United	Northampton Town
20 Shaw, Paul	Arsenal	Peterborough United
10 Simkin, Darren S.	Shrewsbury Town	Telford United
24 Smart, Allan A.C.	Preston North End	Carlisle United
20 Theodosiou, Andrew	Dover Athletic	Chesham United
6 Thornley, Benjamin L.	Manchester United	Stockport County
18 Tobin, Steven R.	Macclesfield Town	Hyde United
1 Tracey, Simon P.	Sheffield United	Wimbledon
24 Trevitt, Simon	Huddersfield Town	Hull City
28 Turner, Andrew P.	Tottenham Hotspur	Huddersfield Town
17 Vonk, Michel C.	Manchester City	Oldham Athletic
24 Wardley, Stuart	Bishop Stortford	Saffron Walden Town
18 Washington, Darren T.	Leek Town	Ashton United
9 Whitbread, Adrian R.	West Ham United	Portsmouth
17 White, David	Leeds United	Sheffield United
3 Yallop, Frank W.	Ipswich Town	Blackpool

DECEMBER 1]1995

5 Alcide, Colin J.	Emley	Lincoln City
22 Aldridge, Martin J.	Northampton Town	Oxford United
18 Basham, Michael	Swansea City	Peterborough United
18 Biggins, Wayne	Oxford United	Wigan Athletic
24 Birkby, Dean	Bath City	Yeovil Town
23 Blake, Nathan A.	Sheffield United	Bolton Wanderers
29 Brightwell, David J.	Manchester City	Bradford City
29 Bull, Gary W.	Nottingham Forest	Birmingham City
15 Bullimore, Wayne A.	Scunthorpe United	Bradford City
15 Butler, Stephen	Cambridge United	Gillingham
16 Coleman, Christopher	Crystal Palace	Blackburn Rovers
29 Cowans, Gordon S.	Wolverhampton Wanderers	Sheffield United
16 Cramb, Colin	Heart of Midlothian	Doncaster Rovers
22 Curran, Christopher	Torquay United	Plymouth Argyle
6 D'Auria, David A.	Scarborough	Scunthorpe United
8 Dawber, Mark	Chertsey Town	Hendon
14 Feuer, Anthony I.	West Ham United	Luton Town

7 Fleming, Terry M.	Preston North End	Lincoln City
22 Green, Andrew J.	Altrincham	Barrow
15 Heath, Adrian P.	Burnley	Sheffield United
22 Heritage, Peter M.	Stamco	Margate
21 McDonald, Tony	Chorley	Witton Albion
8 McNally, Mark	Celtic	Southend United
12 Mercer, William	Sheffield United	Chesterfield
15 Monk, Ian L.	Macclesfield Town	Morecambe
20 Moss, Neil G.	AFC Bournemouth	Southampton
28 Oatway, Anthony P.D.	Cardiff City	Torquay United
22 Orlygsson, Thorvaldur	Stoke City	Oldham Athletic
22 Osborn, Simon E.	Queens Park Rangers	Wolverhampton Wanderers
22 Patterson, Mark A.	Bolton Wanderers	Sheffield United
7 Philliskirk, Anthony	Burnley	Cardiff City
22 Pritchard, Dean B.	Witton Albion	Altrincham
28 Randall, Adrian J.	Burnley	York City
5 Robertson, John N.	Wigan Athletic	Lincoln City
9 Rogers, Paul A.	Sheffield United	Notts County
7 Sellars, Scott	Newcastle United	Bolton Wanderers
29 Short, Christian M.	Notts County	Sheffield United
14 Stott, Steve T.W.	Kettering Town	Rushden & Diamonds
29 Thomson, Andrew	Swindon Town	Portsmouth
21 Trevitt, Simon	Huddersfield Town	Hull City
21 Vonk, Michel C.	Manchester City	Sheffield United
22 Whalley, David N.	Altrincham	Witton Albion
16 Whelan, Noel D.	Leeds United	Coventry City
29 White, David	Leeds United	Sheffield United
8 Williams, Dean A.	Aylesbury United	Hayes
1 Windass, Dean	Hull City	Aberdeen
20 Wingfield, Philip	Kingstonian	Farnborough Town

TEMPORARY TRANSFERS

29 Abrahams, Paul	Brentford	Colchester United
9 Aldridge, Martin J.	Northampton Town	Dagenham & Redbridge
15 Barber, Frederick	Luton Town	Blackpool
3 Barber, Philip A.	Bristol City	Mansfield Town
15 Barnwell-Edinboro, Jamie	Coventry City	Swansea City
8 Bateman, Robert S.	Slough Town	Berkhamsted Town
7 Blissett, Gary P.	Wimbledon	Wycombe Wanderers
1 Bradbury, Lee	Portsmouth	Exeter City
22 Brightwell, David J.	Manchester City	Bradford City
28 Brown, Kenneth J.	West Ham United	Reading
1 Brownrigg, Andrew D.	Norwich City	Kettering Town
5 Burnett, Wayne	Plymouth Argyle	Bolton Wanderers
15 Coates, Daniel	Hednesford Town	Halesowen Town
22 Cobb, Paul M.	Enfield	Purfleet
14 Cundy, Jason V.	Tottenham Hotspur	Crystal Palace
8 Cunningham, Carl M.	Derby County	Buxton
16 Currie, Darren	West Ham United	Leyton Orient
3 Cutler, Neil	West Bromwich Albion	Tamworth
1 Davies, William	Derby County	Buxton
29 Davison, Robert	Rotherham United	Hull City
2 Edwards, Michael	Tranmere Rovers	Northwich Victoria
1 Evans, David A.	Cardiff City	Pontypridd Town
8 Evans, Terry	Cardiff City	Barry Town
26 Fleming, David	Enfield	Bromley
13 Flory, Andrew	Yeovil Town	Weymouth
13 Fowler, John A.	Cambridge United	Cambridge City
19 Freeman, Darren B.A.	Gillingham	Glenavon
15 Fuff, Glen B.	Rushden & Diamonds	Rothwell Town
4 Furnell, Andrew P.	Peterborough United	VS Rugby
22 Gentle, Dominic	Boreham Wood	Grays Athletic
9 Germaine, Gary	West Bromwich Albion	Telford United
21 Glass, James R.	Crystal Palace	Gillingham
1 Grazioli, Giuliano	Peterborough United	Yeovil Town
24 Greene, David M.	Luton Town	Colchester United
14 Guinan, Stephen	Nottingham Forest	Darlington
11 Haines, Danny	Cheltenham Town	Evesham United
15 Hall, Derek R.	Rochdale	Altrincham
20 Hall, Gareth D.	Chelsea	Sunderland
13 Hammond, Nicholas D.	Plymouth Argyle	Reading
8 Harle, Michael J.L.	Millwall	Bury

24	Hill, Daniel R.L.	Tottenham Hotspur	Birmingham City
23	Holmes, Steven P.	Preston North End	Lincoln City
15	Hooper, Dean R.	Swindon Town	Peterborough United
1	Hooper, Michael D.	Newcastle United	Sunderland
27	Horner, Philip M.	Blackpool	Southport
15	Hurst, Glynn	Barnsley	Swansea City
15	Johnson, Gavin	Luton Town	Wigan Athletic
22	Kellman, David	Hayes	Molesey
8	Kenworthy, Jonathan R.	Tranmere Rovers	Chester City
15	Key, Lance W.	Sheffield Wednesday	Hartlepool United
17	Linighan, David	Ipswich Town	Blackpool
14	Lucas, David A.	Preston North End	Darlington
28	Maskell, Craig D.	Southampton	Bristol City
7	Midgley, Craig S.	Bradford City	Scarborough
8	Mitchell, Neil N.	Blackpool	Rochdale
29	Molby, Jan	Liverpool	Norwich City
5	Muggleton, Carl D.	Stoke City	Rotherham United
14	Ndah, George E.	Crystal Palace	AFC Bournemouth
7	Newhouse, Aidan R.	Wimbledon	Torquay United
15	Nicholls, Mark	Chelsea	Chertsey Town
22	Petterson, Andrew K.	Charlton Athletic	Bradford City
21	Pickett, Ross	Slough Town	Chesham United
12	Powell, Jay	Kidderminster Harriers	Bridgnorth Town
22	Preece, David W.	Derby County	Birmingham City
8	Roberts, Ben J.	Middlesbrough	Wycombe Wanderers
15	Robinson, Steven	Birmingham City	Kidderminster Harriers
29	Rogers, Paul A.	Sheffield United	Notts County
1	Roget, Leo T.E.	Sheffield United	Dover Athletic
20	Ross, Michael P.	Plymouth Argyle	Exeter City
21	Samways, Vincent	Everton	Wolverhampton Wanderers
1	Scott, Andrew M.	Cardiff City	Pontypridd Town
24	Scott, Robert	Sheffield United	Northampton Town
8	Senior, Trevor J.	Farnborough Town	Newport (IW)
20	Shaw, Paul	Arsenal	Peterborough United
8	Simkin, Darren S.	Shrewsbury Town	Telford United
22	Simpson, Derek	Reading	Bangor
7	Smart, Erskine	St Albans City	Hendon
12	Sussex, Andrew R.	Southend United	Brentford
6	Thornley, Benjamin L.	Manchester United	Stockport County
14	Titterton, David S.	Hednesford Town	Burton Albion
16	Tobin, Steven R.	Macclesfield Town	Hyde United
19	Turner, Robert P.	Exeter City	Cambridge United
30	Twigg, Darren	Leek Town	Stafford Rangers
25	Wardley, Stuart	Bishops Stortford	Saffron Walden Town
7	Warren, Matthew T.	Derby County	VS Rugby
24	Whitbread, Adrian R.	West Ham United	Portsmouth
11	White, David	Leeds United	Sheffield United
9	Whyte, Christopher A.	Birmingham City	Coventry City
1	Wilkinson, Paul	Middlesbrough	Watford
22	Williams, Martin	Reading	Bangor
1	Williams, Richard J.	Hednesford Town	Atherstone United
9	Wollen, Andrew J.	Gloucester Town	Whitney Town

JANUARY 1996

26	Arnott, Andrew J.	Gillingham	Leyton Orient
19	Baker, David P.	York City	Torquay United
16	Barber, Frederick	Luton Town	Birmingham City
8	Battersby, Anthony	Sheffield United	Notts County
19	Biggins, Wayne	Oxford United	Wigan Athletic
19	Booty, Martyn J.	Crewe Alexandra	Reading
3	Burnett, Wayne	Plymouth Argyle	Bolton Wanderers
24	Clough, Nigel H.	Liverpool	Manchester City
23	Coton, Anthony P.	Manchester City	Manchester United
12	Dixon, Kerry M.	Millwall	Watford
12	Fettis, Alan	Hull City	Nottingham Forest
13	Hall, Gareth D.	Chelsea	Sunderland
10	Hammond, Nicholas D.	Plymouth Argyle	Reading
8	Hobbs, Paul	Aylesbury United	Hendon
8	Holland, Paul	Sheffield United	Chesterfield
11	Hutchison, Donald	West Ham United	Sheffield United
26	Linighan, David	Ipswich Town	Blackpool
12	Matthews, Robert D.	York City	Bury

2 McBean, Peter	Bridgnorth Town	Hinckley Town
29 Newell, Paul C.	Barnet	Darlington
12 Newland, Raymond J.	Chester City	Torquay United
18 O'Connor, Gary	Heart of Midlothian	Doncaster Rovers
31 Powell, Christopher G.	Southend United	Derby County
10 Scott, Robert	Sheffield United	Fulham
10 Sedgemore, Benjamin R.	Birmingham City	Peterborough United
23 Sinton, Andrew	Sheffield Wednesday	Tottenham Hotspur
12 Smith, Alex P.	Everton	Swindon Town
31 Spink, Nigel P.	Aston Villa	West Bromwich Albion
31 Stallard, Mark	Derby County	Bradford City
15 Thomas, Glen A.	Barnet	Gillingham
3 Thomson, Andrew J.	Swindon Town	Portsmouth
11 Titterton, David S.	Hednesford Town	Burton Albion
18 Walters, Mark E.	Liverpool	Southampton
10 Weaver, Steven A.	Salisbury City	Clevedon Town
3 Wilder, Christopher J.	Rotherham United	Notts County
18 Worboys, Gavin A.	Darlington	Northampton Town

TEMPORARY TRANSFERS

30 Angell, Brett	Sunderland	Sheffield United
5 Armstrong, Craig	Nottingham Forest	Bristol Rovers
5 Armstrong, Gordon I.	Sunderland	Northampton Town
19 Atkinson, Brian	Sunderland	Carlisle United
19 Barber, Philip A.	Bristol City	Fulham
11 Barclay, Dominic	Bristol City	Bangor
23 Barton, Stuart A.	Bamber Bridge	Netherfield
12 Bishop, Darren C.	Barnsley	Preston North End
12 Boden, Christopher D.	Derby County	Shrewsbury Town
25 Bolton, James L.	Kingstonian	Hendon
4 Brownrigg, Andrew D.	Norwich City	Kettering Town
13 Butler, Peter J.	Notts County	Grimsby Town
31 Canham, Scott W.	West Ham United	Brentford
11 Casper, Christopher M.	Manchester United	AFC Bournemouth
10 Chapman, Lee R.	Ipswich Town	Leeds United
12 Charlery, Kenneth	Birmingham City	Southend United
19 Clark, Anthony J.	Wycombe Wanderers	Hitchin Town
22 Cooke, Terence J.	Manchester United	Sunderland
27 Cooper, Simon	Cheltenham Town	Dorchester Town
9 Cutler, Neil	West Bromwich Albion	Tamworth
26 Davidson, Ross J.	Sheffield United	Chester City
1 Davies, William	Derby County	Buxton
30 Davison, Robert	Rotherham United	Hull City
29 Dobson, Anthony J.	Portsmouth	Peterborough United
12 Forbes, Scott	Bishops Stortford	Saffron Walden Town
4 Furnell, Andrew P.	Peterborough United	VS Rugby
19 Garner, Simon	Wycombe Wanderers	Torquay United
7 Germaine, Gary	West Bromwich Albion	Telford United
5 German, David	Macclesfield Town	Ashton United
12 Gilbert, Kenneth	Aberdeen	Hull City
19 Given, Seamus J.J.	Blackburn Rovers	Sunderland
31 Glass, James R.	Crystal Palace	Burnley
18 Grant, Anthony J.	Everton	Swindon Town
1 Grazioli, Giuliano	Peterborough United	Yeovil Town
6 Haines, Danny	Cheltenham Town	Evesham United
12 Holmes, Paul	Everton	West Bromwich Albion
26 Howarth, Lee	Mansfield Town	Barnet
16 Johnson, Gavin	Luton Town	Wigan Athletic
26 Jones, Philip L.	Liverpool	Wrexham
12 Jones, Ryan A.	Sheffield Wednesday	Scunthorpe United
12 Lancashire, Graham	Preston North End	Wigan Athletic
17 Linighan, David	Ipswich Town	Blackpool
5 Marginson, Karl K.	Macclesfield Town	Ashton United
12 Marsden, Christopher	Notts County	Stockport County
5 Martin, Kevin	Scarborough	Guiseley
26 Martin, Lee B.	Blackpool	Bradford City
21 Matthew, Damian	Crystal Palace	Bristol Rovers
19 McLean, Ian	Bristol Rovers	Rotherham United
9 Nixon, Eric W.	Tranmere Rovers	Reading
22 Partridge, Scott M.	Bristol City	Plymouth Argyle
19 Petterson, Andrew K.	Charlton Athletic	Plymouth Argyle
9 Powell, Jay	Kidderminster Harriers	Bridgnorth Town

26 Richards, David S.	Walsall	Leicester United
19 Richardson, Ian G.	Birmingham City	Notts County
5 Roberts, Ben J.	Middlesbrough	Wycombe Wanderers
26 Samuels, Dean	Boreham Wood	Bromley
9 Sansome, Paul E.	Southend United	Birmingham City
22 Scargill, Jonathan M.	Sheffield Wednesday	Matlock Town
5 Scully, Anthony D.T.	Crystal Palace	Cardiff City
8 Smithard, Matthew P.	Leeds United	Northampton Town
12 Stallard, Mark	Derby County	Bradford City
19 Sutton, Stephen J.	Derby County	Reading
12 Thomas, Mark L.	Wimbledon	Dulwich Hamlet
25 Tyler, Mark R.	Peterborough United	Billericay Town
26 Wanless, Paul S.	Lincoln City	Woking
7 Warren, Matthew T.	Derby County	VS Rugby
12 Whyte, Christopher A.	Birmingham City	West Ham United
1 Williams, Richard J.	Hednesford Town	Atherstone United
6 Wollen, Andrew J.	Gloucester City	Newport (IW)

FEBRUARY 1996

22 Allen, Martin J.	West Ham United	Portsmouth
9 Breen, Gary	Peterborough United	Birmingham City
9 Burton, Nicholas J.	Yeovil Town	Aldershot Town
6 Byng, David G.	Torquay United	Doncaster Rovers
28 Caskey, Darren M.	Tottenham Hotspur	Reading
20 Chalk, Martyn P.G.	Stockport County	Wrexham
9 Charlery, Kenneth	Birmingham City	Peterborough United
16 Corica, Stephen C.	Leicester City	Wolverhampton Wanderers
8 Currie, Darren P.	West Ham United	Shrewsbury Town
24 Daish, Liam S.	Birmingham City	Coventry City
5 Daly, Stephen	Wembley	Boreham Wood
16 Durkan, Kieron J.	Wrexham	Stockport County
2 Erieno, Soloman	Aldershot Town	Carshalton Athletic
2 Foran, Mark J.	Sheffield United	Peterborough United
5 Gibb, Alistair S.	Norwich City	Northampton Town
16 Gilbert, Kenneth R.	Aberdeen	Hull City
16 Haines, Danny	Cheltenham Town	Evesham United
9 Helliwell, Ian	Stockport County	Burnley
16 Himsworth, Gary P.	Darlington	York City
29 Hinshelwood, Danny M.	Nottingham Forest	Portsmouth
15 Hodges, Glyn P.	Sheffield United	Derby County
15 Holmes, Paul	Everton	West Bromwich Albion
29 Howarth, Lee	Mansfield Town	Barnet
1 Iorfa, Dominic	Southend United	Falkirk
2 Joachim, Julian K.	Leicester City	Aston Villa
16 Johnson, Gavin	Luton Town	Wigan Athletic
23 Lennon, Neil F.	Crewe Alexandra	Leicester City
16 Marsden, Christopher	Notts County	Stockport County
2 McCue, James G.	West Bromwich Albion	Partick Thistle
16 McDonald, Paul	Southampton	Brighton & Hove Albion
16 Mintram, Spencer	Worthing	Farnborough Town
22 Molby, Jan	Liverpool	Swansea City
22 Pitman, Jamie R.	Swindon Town	Hereford United
22 Rammell, Andrew V.	Barnsley	Southend United
22 Regis, David	Southend United	Barnsley
29 Russell, Keith D.	Atherstone United	Hednesford Town
2 Stanborough, Nicholas	Gresley Rovers	Hinckley Athletic
14 Tinson, Darren L.	Northwich Victoria	Macclesfield Town
23 Walker, Andrew F.	Celtic	Sheffield United
16 Watkiss, Stuart P.	Walsall	Hereford United
23 White, Devon W.	Notts County	Watford
26 Williams, Steven R.	Lincoln City	Peterborough United

TEMPORARY TRANSFERS

24 Allen, Christopher	Oxford United	Nottingham Forest
19 Barber, Philip A.	Bristol City	Fulham
2 Barness, Anthony	Chelsea	Southend United
2 Barnwell-Edinboro, Jamie	Coventry City	Wigan Athletic
23 Black, Simon A.	Birmingham City	Ilkeston Town
2 Boden, Christopher D.	Derby County	Shrewsbury Town
6 Bradbury, Lee	Portsmouth	Exeter City
16 Braybrook, Kevin P.	Portsmouth	Yeovil Town
16 Brien, Anthony J.	West Bromwich Albion	Mansfield Town
23 Brown, Wayne L.	Bristol City	Salisbury City

112

5 Butler, Lee S.	Barnsley	Scunthorpe United
25 Canham, Scott W.	West Ham United	Brentford
11 Casper, Christopher M.	Manchester United	AFC Bournemouth
15 Castle, Stephen	Birmingham City	Gillingham
9 Charlery, Kenneth L.	Birmingham City	Peterborough United
9 Charnock, Philip A.	Liverpool	Blackpool
7 Cherry, Steven R.	Watford	Plymouth Argyle
17 Clark, Anthony J.	Wycombe Wanderers	Hitchin Town
29 Cook, Paul A.	Coventry City	Tranmere Rovers
22 Cottrill, Ian T.	Worcester City	Moor Green
8 Cutler, Neil	West Bromwich Albion	Tamworth
26 Davidson, Ross	Sheffield United	Chester City
2 Davies, William	Derby County	Bangor
29 Dobson, Anthony J.	Portsmouth	Peterborough United
16 Doherty, Neil	Birmingham City	Northampton Town
5 Edwards, Paul R.	West Bromwich Albion	Bury
9 Ellison, Anthony L.	Crewe Alexandra	Stalybridge Celtic
16 Forbes, Scott	Bishops Stortford	Saffron Walden Town
23 Furnell, Andrew P.	Peterborough United	Chertsey Town
20 Garner, Simon	Wycombe Wanderers	Torquay United
6 Germaine, Gary	West Bromwich Albion	Telford United
15 German, David	Macclesfield Town	Winsford United
20 Given, Seamus J.J.	Blackburn Rovers	Sunderland
1 Glass, James R.	Crystal Palace	Burnley
2 Glenister, Andrew A.	Alfreton Town	Matlock Town
16 Goodwin, Nicholas J.	Telford United	Cheltenham Town
2 Gordon, Neville	Reading	Woking
23 Gray, Andrew	Leyton Orient	Enfield
10 Grazioli, Giuliano	Peterborough United	Enfield
11 Green, Matthew R.	Derby County	Bangor
2 Hannigan, Al J.	Rushden & Diamonds	Yeovil Town
16 Hanson, David	Leyton Orient	Welling United
19 Hargreaves, Christian	West Bromwich Albion	Hereford United
23 Hiley, Scott	Birmingham City	Manchester City
15 Hill, Daniel R.L.	Tottenham Hotspur	Watford
16 Jemson, Nigel B.	Notts County	Rotherham United
10 Jennings, Gareth J.	Hednesford Town	Stafford Rangers
14 Jones, Ryan A.	Sheffield Wednesday	Scunthorpe United
3 Kellman, David	Hayes	Waltham & Hersham
2 Kernaghan, Alan N.	Manchester City	Bradford City
19 Lancaster, David	Bury	Rochdale
7 Lemoine, Adrian D.	Ashford Town	Tonbridge
16 Lemoine, Matthew B.	Ashford Town	Tonbridge
9 Marginson, Karl K.	Macclesfield Town	Ashton United
12 Marsden, Christopher	Notts County	Stockport County
14 Martin, Lee A.	Celtic	Coventry City
25 Martin, Lee B.	Blackpool	Bradford City
12 Matthew, Damien	Crystal Palace	Bristol Rovers
23 McGleish, Scott	Peterborough United	Colchester United
17 McLean, Ian	Bristol Rovers	Rotherham United
7 Midgley, Craig S.	Bradford City	Scarborough
25 Miles, Benjamin D.	Swansea City	Slough Town
8 Morgan, Philip J.	Stoke City	Macclesfield Town
9 Nicholson, Shane M.	Derby County	West Bromwich Albion
9 Nixon, Eric W.	Tranmere Rovers	Blackpool
2 Osgood, David R.	Aldershot Town	Bracknell Town
23 Peel, Nathan J.	Burnley	Doncaster Rovers
2 Pilkington, Kevin W.	Manchester United	Rochdale
2 Procopi, Carl	Hendon	Leighton Town
19 Restarick, Stephen L.	Dover Athletic	Crawley Town
29 Richards, David S.	Walsall	Leicester United
17 Richardson, Ian G.	Birmingham City	Notts County
14 Samways, Vincent	Everton	Birmingham City
16 Scargill, Jonathan M.	Sheffield Wednesday	Matlock Town
16 Scott, Keith	Norwich City	AFC Bournemouth
1 Sharpe, John J.	Manchester City	Exeter City
23 Shepherd, George J.	Macclesfield Town	Droylsden
8 Sheridan, John J.	Sheffield Wednesday	Birmingham City
23 Stokoe, Graham	Stoke City	Hartlepool United
22 Taylor, Stephen C.E.	Crystal Palace	Rushden & Diamonds
7 Theodosiou, Andrew	Dover Athletic	Crawley Town
22 Thornley, Benjamin L.	Manchester United	Huddersfield Town

16 Tobin, Steven R.	Macclesfield Town	Droylsden
25 Tyler, Mark R.	Peterborough United	Billericay Town
16 Warner, Michael	Northampton Town	Telford United
2 Warner, Vance	Nottingham Forest	Grimsby Town
6 Warren, Matthew T	Derby County	VS Rugby
26 Waters, Jamie S.	Cheltenham Town	Witney Town
2 Watson, Mark L.	West Ham United	Shrewsbury Town

MARCH 1996

28 Alford, Carl P.	Kettering Town	Rushden & Diamonds
28 Allen, Bradley J.	Queens Park Rangers	Charlton Athletic
4 Barnes, Paul L.	York City	Birmingham City
29 Barnwell-Edinboro, Jamie	Coventry City	Cambridge United
2 Batty, David	Blackburn Rovers	Newcastle United
27 Bennett, Gary M.	Tranmere Rovers	Preston North End
21 Bennett, Ian	Leicester United	Tamworth
1 Boere, Jeroen W.J.	Crystal Palace	Southend United
29 Brabin, Gary	Doncaster Rovers	Bury
22 Brown, Linton	Hull City	Swansea City
22 Campbell, David A.	Leicester United	Tamworth
8 Carbon, Matthew P.	Lincoln City	Derby County
28 Chapman, Lee R.	Ipswich Town	Swansea City
1 Claridge, Stephen E.	Birmingham City	Leicester City
28 Coll, Owen O.	Tottenham Hotspur	AFC Bournemouth
29 Cook, Paul A.	Coventry City	Tranmere Rovers
1 Cooper, Simon	Cheltenham Town	Gloucester City
26 Corazzin, Giancarlo M.	Cambridge United	Plymouth Argyle
26 Cornforth, John M.	Swansea City	Birmingham City
28 Cowe, Steven M.	Aston Villa	Swindon Town
28 Cox, Ian G.	Crystal Palace	AFC Bournemouth
29 Croft, Gary	Grimsby Town	Blackburn Rovers
22 Darby, Duane A.	Doncaster Rovers	Hull City
26 Davidson, Ross J.	Sheffield United	Chester City
1 Devlin, Paul J.	Notts County	Birmingham City
15 Dudley, Derek A.	Halesowen Town	Telford United
9 Dumitrescu, Ilie	Tottenham Hotspur	West Ham United
8 Edwards, Robert	Crewe Alexandra	Huddersfield Town
26 Flitcroft, Garry	Manchester City	Blackburn Rovers
28 Gallimore, Anthony M.	Carlisle United	Grimsby Town
8 Gannon, John S.	Sheffield United	Oldham Athletic
11 Garnett, Shaun M.	Tranmere Rovers	Swansea City
8 Glass, James R.	Crystal Palace	AFC Bournemouth
22 Gore, Ian G.	Torquay United	Doncaster Rovers
26 Grainger, Martin R.	Brentford	Birmingham City
28 Grant, Kim T.	Charlton Athletic	Luton Town
22 Gray, Andrew	Leyton Orient	Slough Town
28 Gray, Martin D.	Sunderland	Oxford United
29 Griffiths, Carl B.	Portsmouth	Peterborough United
7 Hobson, Gary	Hull City	Brighton & Hove Albion
15 Holmes, Steven P.	Preston North End	Lincoln City
9 Hottiger, Marc	Newcastle United	Everton
27 Illman, Neil D.	Eastwood Town	Plymouth Argyle
25 Johnson, David D.	Rushden & Diamonds	Gloucester City
1 Jones, Gary	Southend United	Notts County
8 Lancashire, Graham	Preston North End	Wigan Athletic
23 Lee, Justin D.	Abingdon Town	Oxford City
1 Legg, Andrew	Notts County	Birmingham City
22 Lightfoot, Christopher I.	Wigan Athletic	Crewe Alexandra
2 Lowe, David A.	Leicester City	Wigan Athletic
9 Lynch, Anthony J.	Stevenage Borough	Yeovil Town
1 Lyons, Andrew	Wigan Athletic	Partick Thistle
7 Martindale, Gary	Peterborough United	Notts County
1 Maskell, Craig D.	Southampton	Brighton & Hove Albion
27 Maxfield, Scott	Doncaster Rovers	Hull City
22 McDonald, Colin	Falkirk	AFC Bournemouth
8 Mitchell, Paul R.	West Ham United	Gravesend & Northfleet
13 Newbery, Richard J.	Wokingham Town	Sheffield Wednesday
15 Newsome, Jon	Norwich City	West Bromwich Albion
1 Nicholson, Shane M.	Derby County	Stafford Rangers
28 Norbury, Michael S.	Guiseley	AFC Bournemouth
28 O'Neill, Jon J.	Celtic	Stafford Rangers
28 O'Reilly, Justin	Gresley Rovers	Port Vale

28 Paris, Alan	Slough Town	Stevenage Borough
29 Peschisolido, Paolo	Stoke City	Birmingham City
22 Phillips, Leslie M.	Marlow	Oxford City
22 Philpott, Lee	Leicester City	Blackpool
25 Pick, Gary	Hereford United	Cambridge United
21 Powell, Darren K.	Bashley	Weymouth
22 Richardson, Ian G.	Birmingham City	Notts County
28 Sharples, John	Ayr United	York City
11 Smith, Richard G.	Leicester City	Grimsby Town
12 Sneekes, Richard	Bolton Wanderers	West Bromwich Albion
8 Sparrow, Paul	Crystal Palace	Preston North End
6 Stewart, Paul A.	Liverpool	Sunderland
15 Stimson, Mark	Portsmouth	Southend United
12 Sugure, James S.	Aldershot Town	Hayes
24 Sunderland, Jonathan P.	Blackpool	Scarborough
8 Taylor, Gareth K.	Crystal Palace	Sheffield United
29 Taylor, Scott J.	Millwall	Bolton Wanderers
16 Tompkins, Mark	Tooting & Mitcham United	Bromley
27 Trebble, Neil D.	Scarborough	Stevenage Borough
8 Tuttle, David P.	Sheffield United	Crystal Palace
6 Veart, Thomas C.	Sheffield United	Crystal Palace
21 Ward, Ashley S.	Norwich City	Derby County
29 Ward, Gavin J.	Bradford City	Bolton Wanderers
22 Ward, Mark W.	Birmingham City	Huddersfield Town
29 Watts, Julian	Sheffield Wednesday	Leicester City
2 Williams, Richard J.	Hednesford Town	Atherstone Town
18 Wood, Simon O.	Coventry City	Mansfield Town

TEMPORARY TRANSFERS

1 Ablett, Gary I.	Everton	Sheffield United
31 Acteson, Robert	Hendon	Berkhamsted Town
29 Adams, Darren S.	Cardiff City	Woking
8 Allan, Derek T.	Southampton	Brighton & Hove Albion
28 Angell, Brett A.M.	Sunderland	West Bromwich Albion
1 Anthony, Graham J.	Sheffield United	Scarborough
28 Armstrong, Craig	Nottingham Forest	Bristol Rovers
28 Ashcroft, Lee	West Bromwich Albion	Notts County
29 Ashenden, Scott	Boreham Wood	Grays Athletic
8 Bailey, Gavin J.	Sheffield Wednesday	Matlock Town
4 Barnwell-Edinboro, Jamie	Coventry City	Wigan Athletic
30 Bellingham, Mark	Chelmsford City	Halesowen Town
22 Berry, Greg J.	Millwall	Leyton Orient
7 Birch, Paul	Wolverhampton Wanderers	Preston North End
28 Bishop, Charles D.	Barnsley	Burnley
30 Black, Simon A.	Birmingham City	Gloucester City
11 Blissett, Gary P.	Wimbledon	Crewe Alexandra
22 Brien, Anthony J.	West Bromwich Albion	Chester City
1 Brown, Kenneth J.	West Ham United	Southend United
28 Brown, Kenneth J.	West Ham United	Crystal Palace
28 Butler, Peter J.F.	Notts County	West Bromwich Albion
26 Casper, Christopher M.	Manchester United	AFC Bournemouth
16 Cherry, Steve R.	Watford	Plymouth Argyle
21 Clark, Anthony J.	Wycombe Wanderers	Hitchin Town
1 Cooper, Simon	Cheltenham Town	Dorchester Town
22 Cottrill, Ian T.	Worcester City	Moor Green
22 Cowe, Steven M.	Aston Villa	Swindon Town
22 Creaney, Gerard	Manchester City	Oldham Athletic
1 Cross, Jonathan N.	Wrexham	Cliftonville
27 Cutler, Neil A.	West Bromwich Albion	Chester City
13 Daws, Anthony	Lincoln City	Halifax Town
21 De Bont, Andrew C.	Wolverhampton Wanderers	Hereford United
16 Doherty, Neil P.	Birmingham City	Northampton Town
29 Dowell, Wayne A.	Burnley	Carlisle United
7 Dykstra, Sieb	Queens Park Rangers	Wycombe Wanderers
29 Eflitts, Justin S.	Telford United	Stafford Rangers
28 Evans, Paul A.	Leeds United	Crystal Palace
28 Fairclough, Wayne R.	Chesterfield	Scarborough
5 Finnan, Stephen	Birmingham City	Notts County
28 Flatts, Mark	Arsenal	Grimsby Town
24 Foreman, Darren	Hednesford Town	Barrow
22 Foster, Adrian M.	Gillingham	Exeter City
14 Gayle, John	Stoke City	Gillingham

8 Germaine, Gary	West Bromwich Albion	Scunthorpe United
15 German, David	Macclesfield Town	Winsford United
22 Given, Shamus J.J.	Blackburn Rovers	Sunderland
17 Goodwin, Nicholas J.	Telford United	Cheltenham Town
21 Gordon, Dale A.	West Ham United	Millwall
29 Gould, Jonathan A.	Coventry City	Bradford City
1 Greene, David M.	Luton Town	Brentford
1 Grime, Nicholas	Stevenage Borough	Berkhamsted Town
22 Hanson, David	Leyton Orient	Welling United
20 Hargreaves, Christian	West Bromwich Albion	Hereford United
1 Harris, Jason A.	Crystal Palace	Dover Athletic
28 Hathaway, Ian A.	Torquay United	Chesterfield
30 Hawtin, Dale C.	Crewe Alexandra	Hyde United
29 Hollamby, Ian	Bishops Stortford	Saffron Walden Town
25 Holmes, David J.	Gloucester City	Rushden & Diamonds
18 Howell, Ian R.	Cheltenham Town	Gloucester City
28 Illman, Neil D.	Plymouth Argyle	Cambridge United
28 Izzet, Mustafa K.	Chelsea	Leicester City
27 Jackson, Matthew A.	Everton	Charlton Athletic
26 Jemson, Nigel B.	Notts County	Rotherham United
11 Jennings, Gareth J.	Hednesford Town	Stafford Rangers
30 Jones, Alexander	Stalybridge Celtic	Chorley
29 Joseph, Marc E.	Cambridge United	Shrewsbury Town
28 Kay, John	Sunderland	Preston North End
21 Kearton, Jason B.	Everton	Leyton Orient
28 Kelly, Russell	Chelsea	Rochdale
1 Key, Lance W.	Sheffield Wednesday	Rochdale
30 Knight, Keith	Gloucester City	Cheltenham Town
24 Lancaster, David	Bury	Rochdale
28 Launders, Brian T.	Crystal Palace	Oldham Athletic
28 Leitch, Donald S.	Heart of Midlothian	Swindon Town
5 Lemoine, Adrian D.	Ashford Town	Tonbridge
15 Lemoine, Matthew B.	Ashford Town	Tonbridge
15 Lock, Anthony	Colchester United	Chelmsford City
22 Mahorn, Paul G.	Tottenham Hotspur	Burnley
8 Martin, Lee C.	Shrewsbury Town	Bridgnorth Town
2 Mason, Richard M.	Sheffield Wednesday	Boston United
8 McAllister, Brian	Wimbledon	Crewe Alexandra
28 McDougald, David E.J.	Brighton & Hove Albion	Chesterfield
28 McGleish, Scott	Peterborough United	Colchester United
22 McGorry, Brian P.	Wycombe Wanderers	Cardiff City
8 Mean, Scott	AFC Bournemouth	West Ham United
28 Mitchell, Neil N.	Blackpool	Southport
28 Moore, Neil	Everton	Rotherham United
1 Morgan, Stephen A.	Coventry City	Bristol Rovers
15 Mudd, Paul	Lincoln City	Halifax Town
28 Muggleton, Carl D.	Stoke City	Sheffield United
8 Murray, Paul	Carlisle United	Queens Park Rangers
5 Nixon, Eric W.	Tranmere Rovers	Blackpool
25 O'Halloran, Keith J.	Middlesbrough	Scunthorpe United
28 Osgood, David R.	Aldershot Town	Bracknell Town
8 Partridge, Scott	Bristol City	Scarborough
28 Petterson, Andrew K.	Charlton Athletic	Colchester United
1 Phillips, Mark	Stevenage Borough	Berkhamsted Town
28 Pearce, Stephen	Wolverhampton Wanderers	Hednesford Town
8 Powell, Jay	Kidderminster Harriers	Bedworth United
30 Preddie, Delroy E.	Slough Town	Walton & Hersham
21 Preece, David W.	Derby County	Swindon Town
31 Procopi, Carl	Hendon	Molesey
1 Reece, Paul J.	West Bromwich Albion	Ilkeston Town
1 Restarick, Stephen L.	Dover Athletic	Crawley Town
28 Ridings, David J.	Crewe Alexandra	Hednesford Town
28 Robinson, Carl P.	Wolverhampton Wanderers	Shrewsbury Town
8 Robinson, Steven E.	Birmingham City	Peterborough United
28 Rowe, Ezekiel B.	Chelsea	Brighton & Hove Albion
15 Scargill, Jonathan M.	Sheffield Wednesday	Matlock Town
29 Scott, Andrew M.	Cardiff City	Bath City
1 Setori, Mark A.	Bury	Whitton Albion
1 Sharpe, John J.	Manchester City	Exeter City
29 Simpkins, John P.	Newport (IW)	Salisbury City
28 Simpson, Gary	Luton Town	Fulham
8 Sparrow, Paul	Crystal Palace	Preston North End

29 Spencer, Michael	Bath City	Salisbury City
20 Theodosiou, Andrew	Dover Athletic	Crawley Town
25 Thornley, Benjamin L.	Manchester United	Huddersfield Town
22 Tomlinson, Graeme M.	Manchester United	Luton Town
1 Tucker, Andrew L.	Cheltenham Town	Gloucester City
28 Turner, Andrew P.	Tottenham Hotspur	Southend United
19 Tiler, Mark R.	Peterborough United	Billericay Town
8 Wanless, Paul S.	Lincoln City	Cambridge United
16 Warner, Michael	Northampton Town	Telford United
27 Waters, Jamie S.	Cheltenham Town	Whitney Town
28 Weir, Michael	Hibernian	Millwall
28 Wilkinson, Paul	Middlesbrough	Luton Town
2 Williams, Dean A.	Hayes	Chesham United
29 Williams, Dean A.	Hayes	Hitchin Town
28 Williams, Paul A.	Rochdale	Doncaster Rovers
28 Williams, Paul A.	Charlton Athletic	Torquay United
29 Williams, Steven R.	Peterborough United	Cambridge City
1 Woodsford, Jamie	Luton Town	Portadown
1 Wright, Jermaine M.	Wolverhampton Wanderers	Doncaster Rovers

APRIL 1996

3 Barnwell-Edinboro, Jamie	Coventry City	Cambridge United
1 Hiley, Scott P.	Birmingham City	Manchester City

TEMPORARY TRANSFERS

3 Abblet, Gary I.	Everton	Sheffield United
4 Bibbo, Salvatore	Sheffield United	Ards
1 Black, Simon A.	Birmingham City	Gloucester City
11 Blissett, Gary P.	Wimbledon	Crewe Alexandra
27 Cutler, Neil	West Bromwich Albion	Chester City
7 Dean, Craig	Tamworth	Hinckley Town
22 Debont, Andrew	Wolverhampton Wanderers	Hereford United
2 Evans, Paul A.	Leeds United	Crystal Palace
2 Finnan, Stephen J.	Birmingham City	Notts County
9 Germaine, Gary	West Bromwich Albion	Scunthorpe United
23 Gordon, Dale A.	West Ham United	Millwall
1 Greene, David M.	Luton Town	Brentford
1 Grime, Nicholas	Stevenage Borough	Berkhamsted Town
21 Hargreaves, Christian	West Bromwich Albion	Hereford United
1 Harris, Jason A.	Crystal Palace	Dover Athletic
2 Hathaway, Ian A.	Torquay United	Chesterfield
30 Hawtin, Dale	Crewe Alexandra	Hyde United
30 Izzet, Mustafa K.	Chelsea	Leicester City
28 Jackson, Matthew A.	Everton	Charlton Athletic
11 Jennings, Gareth J.	Hednesford Town	Stafford Rangers
1 Key, Lance W.	Sheffield Wednesday	Rochdale
16 Lemoine, Adrian D.	Ashford Town	Tonbridge
24 Mason, Richard M.	Sheffield Wednesday	Boston United
11 McAllister, Brian	Wimbledon	Crewe Alexandra
12 McDougald, David E.	Brighton & Hove Albion	Chesterfield
22 Moore, Neil	Everton	Rotherham United
5 Nixon, Eric W.	Tranmere Rovers	Blackpool
17 Osgood, David R.	Aldershot Town	Bracknell Town
1 Reece, Paul J.	West Bromwich Albion	Ilkeston Town
1 Sharpe, John J.	Manchester City	Exeter City
22 Tomlinson, Graeme	Manchester United	Luton Town
1 Wanless, Paul S.	Lincoln City	Cambridge United
2 Wright, Jermaine M.	Wolverhampton Wanderers	Doncaster Rovers

MAY 1996

19 Cherry, Steve R.	Watford	Plymouth Argyle
16 Jones, Stephen G.	AFC Bournemouth	West Ham United
2 Murray, Paul	Carlisle United	Queens Park Rangers
24 Rush, Ian J.	Liverpool	Leeds United
13 Smart, Stephen J.	Aylesbury United	Hendon
31 Tucker, Mark J.	Woking	Rushden & Diamonds
16 Watson, Mark L.	West Ham United	AFC Bournemouth

TEMPORARY TRANSFERS

7 Allan, Derek T.	Southampton	Brighton & Hove Albion
9 Brown, Kenneth J.	West Ham United	Crystal Palace
5 Gould, Jonathan A.	Coventry City	Bradford City

FA CUP REVIEW 1996

Although the occasion was always likely to overshadow the proceedings, the 1996 final was one of the poorest seen at Wembley. As a milestone in the history of the game itself, Manchester United's achievement of a second League and Cup double will be the only interesting statistic to survive a hugely disappointing affair.

Liverpool weaved some pretty patterns at times but showed little penetration and no punch, while United's efforts were the more determined and direct. Just when it appeared that the game was boringly drifting into the possibility of extra time, the United captain Eric Cantona - the first player born outside the British Isles to captain a Cup Final team - scored the only goal, reacting quickly to a punch-out by David James the Liverpool goalkeeper. There were just four minutes remaining.

Giant-killing acts were few and far between. Of the non-League fraternity, only Gravesend & Northfleet and Woking survived to the third round and both were despatched, respectively losing 3-0 to Aston Villa and 2-0 to Swindon Town. Premier League teams who stumbled at the first hurdle against lesser opposition were Sheffield Wednesday, beaten 2-0 at Charlton Athletic, Blackburn Rovers after a replay against Ipswich Town and Arsenal similarly against Sheffield United.

Manchester United had a scare against Sunderland but won the replay 2-1 at Roker Park. Highest scorers at this stage were Liverpool, who beat Rochdale 7-0 and Grimsby Town who accounted for Luton Town 7-1. However, in a second round replay, Walsall had won a bizarre replay against Torquay United 8-4 in extra time after the teams had finished 3-3 after 90 minutes.

Port Vale provided the first shock in the fourth round beating Everton 2-1 in a replay, while Grimsby Town took three goals off West Ham United without reply at the second attempt.

Postponements due to bad weather had their usual disrupting effects and the fourth round had not been completed when the fifth round was due to begin. Manchester United edged out their City neighbours 2-1 and both Wimbledon and Southampton escaped after replays.

Nottingham Forest defeated Tottenham Hotspur on penalties as again the fifth round encroached upon the quarter-finals. By this stage, only Premier League sides had prevailed. It was the first time in 100 years that the last eight had come from the top division. Here, Chelsea and Wimbledon needed a replay as did Leeds United and Liverpool. Manchester United were fortunate to defeat Southampton 2-0 but Aston Villa ended Nottingham Forest's run 1-0. Chelsea and Liverpool emerged from their replays to reach the semi-finals. Liverpool scored twice in the last four minutes to beat Aston Villa 4-0 and two goals in three minutes enabled Manchester United to come back from being a goal down to Chelsea to win 2-1.

In the final itself, few players enhanced their reputation. High-priced strikers Stan Collymore (Liverpool) and Andy Cole (Manchester United) failed to make any impact and were both replaced. Only Steve McManaman on the Liverpool side appeared to be capable of breaking down United's defence and they were never able to threaten from the flanks.

Footballer of the Year Cantona, had an impressive first half but appeared to have drifted out of the match until his late, telling strike. The improving David Beckham showed his potential in the United midfield and Roy Keane was his usual combative self. Goal chances were scarce and Liverpool were frequently forced to shoot ineffectively from long range.

There were only two bookings; Jamie Redknapp for an innocuous challenge and Phil Babb for a slightly more serious offence. Indeed there was very little for the 79,007 crowd to enthuse over, apart from the obvious partizan loyalties.

FA CUP 1995-96 – sponsored by Littlewood Pools

FIRST ROUND

Burnley	(1) 1	Walsall	(1) 3
Barnet	(2) 2	Woking	(2) 2
Barrow	(2) 2	Nuneaton	(1) 1
Blackpool	(0) 2	Chester C	(0) 1
Bognor Regis	(0) 1	Ashford T	(1) 1
Bournemouth	(0) 0	Bristol C	(0) 0
Bradford C	(3) 4	Burton Alb	(3) 3
Brentford	(1) 1	Farnborough	(0) 1
Bury	(0) 0	Blyth Spartans	(1) 2
Carlisle U	(1) 1	Preston NE	(0) 2
Cinderford T	(1) 2	Bromsgrove R	(0) 1
Exeter C	(0) 0	Peterborough U	(1) 1
Fulham	(3) 7	Swansea C	(0) 0
Gravesend & N	(1) 2	Colchester U	(0) 0
Hartlepool U	(1) 2	Darlington	(2) 4
Hereford U	(0) 1	Stevenage B	(1) 1
Hitchin	(2) 2	Bristol R	(1) 1
Hull C	(0) 0	Wrexham	(0) 0
Kidderminster H	(1) 2	Sutton U	(0) 2
Kingstonian	(0) 5	Wisbech	(1) 1
Mansfield T	(3) 4	Doncaster R	(0) 2
Newport (IW)	(1) 1	Enfield	(1) 1
Northampton T	(0) 1	Hayes	(0) 0
Northwich Vic	(0) 1	Scunthorpe U	(0) 3
Oxford U	(2) 9	Dorchester	(0) 1
Rochdale	(3) 5	Rotherham U	(0) 3
Runcorn	(0) 1	Wigan Ath	(1) 1
Rushden & D	(0) 1	Cardiff C	(2) 3
Scarborough	(0) 0	Chesterfield	(0) 2
Shrewsbury T	(4) 11	Marine	(0) 2
Slough	(0) 0	Plymouth Arg	(0) 2
Spennymoor U	(0) 0	Colwyn Bay	(0) 1
Stockport Co	(3) 5	Lincoln C	(0) 0
Swindon T	(2) 4	Cambridge U	(0) 1
Telford U	(1) 2	Witton Alb	(1) 1
Torquay U	(0) 1	Leyton Orient	(0) 0
Canvey Island	(1) 2	Brighton & HA	(2) 2
York C	(0) 0	Notts Co	(1) 1
Wycombe W	(0) 1	Gillingham	(0) 1

FIRST ROUND REPLAYS

Ashford	(0) 0	Bognor Regis	(0) 1
Brighton & HA	(1) 4	Canvey Island	(0) 1
Bristol C	(0) 0	Bournemouth	(1) 1
Enfield	(1) 2	Newport (IW)	(0) 1
Gillingham	(1) 1	Wycombe W	(0) 0
Sutton U	(0) 1	Kidderminster H	(1) 1
(aet; Sutton U won 3-2 on penalties)			
Wigan Ath	(2) 4	Runcorn	(2) 2
Woking	*(1) 2	Barnet	(1) 1
Wrexham	(0) 0	Hull C	(0) 0
(aet; Wrexham won 3-1 on penalties)			
Altrincham	(0) 0	Crewe Alex	(0) 2
Farnborough T	(0) 0	Brentford	(1) 4

119

SECOND ROUND

Barrow	(0) 0	Wigan Ath	(0) 4
Blackpool	(0) 2	Colwyn Bay	(0) 0
Bournemouth	(0) 0	Brentford	(1) 1
Bradford C	(1) 2	Preston NE	(0) 1
Cinderford T	(0) 1	Gravesend & N	(0) 1
Crewe Alex	(1) 2	Mansfield T	(0) 0
Enfield	(1) 1	Woking	(0) 1
Fulham	(0) 0	Brighton & HA	(0) 0
Gillingham	(0) 3	Hitchin	(0) 0
Hereford U	(1) 2	Sutton U	(0) 0
Oxford U	(1) 2	Northampton T	(0) 0
Peterborough U	(3) 4	Bognor Regis	(0) 0
Rochdale	(0) 2	Darlington	(1) 2
Scunthorpe U	(0) 1	Shrewsbury T	(0) 1
Stockport Co	(2) 2	Blyth Spartans	(0) 0
Swindon T	(0) 2	Cardiff C	(0) 0
Telford U	(0) 0	Notts Co	(1) 2
Torquay U	(1) 1	Walsall	(1) 1
Wrexham	(2) 3	Chesterfield	(0) 2
Kingstonian	(1) 1	Plymouth Arg	(1) 2

SECOND ROUND REPLAYS

Darlington	(0) 0	Rochdale	(0) 1
Shrewsbury T	(2) 2	Scunthorpe U	(0) 1
Walsall	*(1) 8	Torquay U	(1) 4
Woking	(0) 2	Enfield	(0) 1
Brighton & HA	(0) 0	Fulham	(0) 0
(aet; Fulham won 4-1 on penalties)			
Gravesend & N	(1) 3	Cinderford T	(0) 0

THIRD ROUND

Arsenal	(0) 1	Sheffield U	(0) 1
Barnsley	(0) 0	Oldham Ath	(0) 0
Birmingham C	(0) 1	Wolverhampton W	(1) 1
Bradford C	(0) 0	Bolton W	(1) 3
Charlton Ath	(2) 2	Sheffield W	(0) 0
Crewe Alex	(3) 4	WBA	(1) 3
Crystal Palace	(0) 0	Port Vale	(0) 0
Fulham	(0) 1	Shrewsbury T	(0) 3
Gravesend & N	(0) 0	Aston Villa	(1) 3
Grimsby T	(4) 7	Luton T	(0) 1
Hereford U	(0) 1	Tottenham H	(1) 1
Huddersfield T	(1) 2	Blackpool	(1) 1
Ipswich T	(0) 0	Blackburn R	(0) 0
Leicester C	(0) 0	Manchester C	(0) 0
Liverpool	(3) 7	Rochdale	(0) 0
Manchester U	(1) 2	Sunderland	(0) 2
Millwall	(0) 3	Oxford U	(1) 3
Norwich C	(0) 1	Brentford	(1) 2
Notts Co	(0) 1	Middlesbrough	(0) 2
Peterborough U	(0) 0	Wrexham	(0) 0
Plymouth Arg	(1) 1	Coventry C	(0) 3
Reading	(0) 3	Gillingham	(1) 1
Stoke C	(1) 1	Nottingham F	(0) 1
Swindon T	(1) 2	Woking	(0) 0
Tranmere R	(0) 0	QPR	(0) 2
Walsall	(0) 1	Wigan Ath	(0) 0

Watford	(1) 1	Wimbledon	(1) 1
West Ham U	(0) 2	Southend U	(0) 0
Chelsea	(1) 1	Newcastle U	(0) 1
Derby Co	(0) 2	Leeds U	(0) 4
Everton	(2) 2	Stockport Co	(1) 2
Southampton	(1) 3	Portsmouth	(0) 0

THIRD ROUND REPLAYS

Blackburn R	*(0) 0	Ipswich T	(0) 1
Oxford U	(0) 1	Millwall	(0) 0
Port Vale	*(2) 4	Crystal Palace	(1) 3
Shrewsbury T	(0) 2	Fulham	(1) 1
Sunderland	(1) 1	Manchester U	(0) 2
Manchester C	(2) 5	Leicester C	(0) 0
Newcastle U	(1) 2	Chelsea	(0) 2
(aet; Chelsea won 4-2 on penalties)			
Nottingham F	(1) 2	Stoke C	(0) 0
Sheffield U	(0) 1	Arsenal	(0) 0
Stockport Co	(1) 2	Everton	(0) 3
Tottenham H	(2) 5	Hereford U	(0) 1
Wimbledon	(0) 1	Watford	(0) 0
Wolverhampton W	(1) 2	Birmingham C	(0) 1
Oldham Ath	(1) 2	Barnsley	(0) 1

FOURTH ROUND

Everton	(1) 2	Port Vale	(0) 2
Reading	(0) 0	Manchester U	(1) 3
Tottenham H	(1) 1	Wolverhampton W	(0) 0
Sheffield U	(0) 0	Aston Villa	(0) 0
QPR	(0) 1	Chelsea	(2) 2
Huddersfield T	(0) 2	Peterborough U	(0) 0
Charlton Ath	(2) 3	Brentford	(1) 2
Coventry C	(1) 2	Manchester C	(1) 2
Middlesbrough	(0) 0	Wimbledon	(0) 0
Nottingham F	(0) 1	Oxford U	(0) 1
Southampton	(0) 1	Crewe Alex	(1) 1
West Ham U	(1) 1	Grimsby T	(1) 1
Swindon T	(0) 1	Oldham Ath	(0) 0
Ipswich T	(1) 1	Walsall	(0) 0
Bolton W	(0) 0	Leeds U	(1) 1
Shrewsbury T	(0) 0	Liverpool	(1) 4

FOURTH ROUND REPLAYS

Wolverhampton W	(0) 0	Tottenham H	(2) 2
Crewe Alex	(0) 2	Southampton	(3) 3
Oxford U	(0) 0	Nottingham F	(1) 3
Wimbledon	(0) 1	Middlesbrough	(0) 0
Grimsby T	(1) 3	West Ham U	(0) 0
Manchester C	(1) 2	Coventry C	(0) 1
Port Vale	(1) 2	Everton	(1) 1

FIFTH ROUND

Huddersfield T	(1) 2	Wimbledon	(0) 2
Ipswich T	(0) 1	Aston Villa	(2) 3
Swindon T	(1) 1	Southampton	(1) 1
Manchester U	(1) 2	Manchester C	(1) 1
Nottingham F	(0)	Tottenham H	(0)
(Abandoned after 15 minutes; snow)			

Grimsby T	(0) 0	Chelsea	(0) 0
Leeds U	(0) 0	Port Vale	(0) 0
Liverpool	(1) 2	Charlton Ath	(0) 1
Nottingham F	(1) 2	Tottenham H	(2) 2

FIFTH ROUND REPLAYS

Port Vale	(1) 1	Leeds U	(0) 2
Chelsea	(1) 4	Grimsby T	(0) 1
Southampton	(0) 2	Swindon T	(0) 0
Wimbledon	(2) 3	Huddersfield T	(1) 1
Tottenham H	(1) 1	Nottingham F	(1) 1

(aet; Nottingham F won 3-1 on penalties)

SIXTH ROUND

Chelsea	(0) 2	Wimbledon	(0) 2
Leeds U	(0) 0	Liverpool	(0) 0
Manchester U	(0) 2	Southampton	(0) 0
Nottingham F	(0) 0	Aston Villa	(1) 1

SIXTH ROUND REPLAYS

| Liverpool | (0) 3 | Leeds U | (0) 0 |
| Wimbledon | (1) 1 | Chelsea | (1) 3 |

SEMI-FINALS

| Aston Villa | (0) 0 | Liverpool | (1) 3 |
| Chelsea | (1) 1 | Manchester U | (0) 2 |

FINAL at Wembley
11 May

Liverpool (0) 0

Manchester U (0) 1 *(Cantona)*   79,007

Liverpool: James; McAteer, Jones (Thomas), Scales, Wright, Babb, McManaman, Redknapp, Collymore (Rush), Barnes, Fowler.
Manchester U: Schmeichel; Irwin, Neville P, May, Keane, Pallister, Cantona, Beckham (Neville G), Cole (Scholes), Butt, Giggs.
Referee: D. Gallagher (Banbury)

* after extra time

PAST FA CUP FINALS

Details of one goalscorer is not available in 1878.

1872	The Wanderers ......1 *Betts*	Royal Engineers 0	
1873	The Wanderers ......2 *Kinnaird, Wollaston*	Oxford University 0	
1874	Oxford University ......2 *Mackarness, Patton*	Royal Engineers 0	
1875	Royal Engineers ......1 *Renny-Tailyour*	Old Etonians ......1* *Bonsor*	
Replay	Royal Engineers ......2 *Renny-Tailyour, Stafford*	Old Etonians 0	
1876	The Wanderers ......1 *Edwards*	Old Etonians ......1* *Bonsor*	
Replay	The Wanderers ......3 *Wollaston, Hughes 2*	Old Etonians 0	
1877	The Wanderers ......2 *Kenrick, Heron*	Oxford University ......1* *Kinnaird (og)*	
1878	The Wanderers ......3 *Kenrick 2, Kinnaird*	Royal Engineers ......1 *Unknown*	
1879	Old Etonians ......1 *Clerke*	Clapham Rovers 0	
1880	Clapham Rovers ......1 *Lloyd-Jones*	Oxford University 0	
1881	Old Carthusians ......3 *Wyngard, Parry, Todd*	Old Etonians 0	
1882	Old Etonians ......1 *Anderson*	Blackburn Rovers 0	
1883	Blackburn Olympic ......2 *Costley, Matthews*	Old Etonians ......1* *Goodhart*	
1884	Blackburn Rovers ......2 *Brown, Forrest*	Queen's Park, Glasgow ......1 *Christie*	
1885	Blackburn Rovers ......2 *Forrest, Brown*	Queen's Park, Glasgow 0	
1886	Blackburn Rovers 0	West Bromwich Albion 0	
Replay	Blackburn Rovers ......2 *Brown, Sowerbutts*	West Bromwich Albion 0	
1887	Aston Villa ......2 *Hunter, Hodgetts*	West Bromwich Albion 0	
1888	West Bromwich Albion ......2 *Woodhall, Bayliss*	Preston NE ......1 *Goodall*	
1889	Preston NE ......3 *Dewhurst, Ross, Thompson*	Wolverhampton W 0	
1890	Blackburn Rovers ......6 *Dewar, John Southworth,* *Lofthouse, Townley 3*	Sheffield W ......1 *Bennett*	

1891	Blackburn Rovers................3	Notts Co.................................1
	Dewar, John Southworth,	*Oswald*
	Townley	
1892	West Browmwich Albion 3	Aston Villa 0
	Geddes, Nicholdes, Reynolds	
1893	Wolverhampton W 1	Everton 0
	Allen	
1894	Notts Co..............................4	Bolton W 1
	Watson, Logan 3	*Cassidy*
1895	Aston Villa 1	West Bromwich Albion 0
	Devey	
1896	Sheffield W 2	Wolverhampton W................1
	Spiksley 2	*Black*
1897	Aston Villa 3	Everton 2
	Campbell, Wheldon,	*Boyle, Bell*
	Crabtree	
1898	Nottingham F 3	Derby Co 1
	Cape 2, McPherson	*Bloomer*
1899	Sheffield U...........................4	Derby Co 1
	Bennett, Beers, Almond,	*Boag*
	Priest	
1900	Bury......................................4	Southampton 0
	McLuckie 2, Wood, Plant	
1901	Tottenham H.........................2	Sheffield U............................2
	Brown 2	*Bennett, Priest*
Replay	Tottenham H.........................3	Sheffield U............................1
	Cameron, Smith, Brown	*Priest*
1902	Sheffield U...........................1	Southampton 1
	Common	*Wood*
Replay	Sheffield U...........................2	Southampton 1
	Hedley, Barnes	*Brown*
1903	Bury......................................6	Derby Co 0
	Ross, Sagar, Leeming 2,	
	Wood, Plant	
1904	Manchester C 1	Bolton W 0
	Meredith	
1905	Aston Villa 2	Newcastle U 0
	Hampton 2	
1906	Everton 1	Newcastle U 0
	Young	
1907	Sheffield W 2	Everton 1
	Stewart, Simpson	*Sharp*
1908	Wolverhampton W 3	Newcastle U 1
	Hunt, Hedley, Harrison	*Howie*
1909	Manchester U........................1	Bristol C 0
	A. Turnbull	
1910	Newcastle U 1	Barnsley................................1
	Rutherford	*Tuffnell*
Replay	Newcastle U 2	Barnsley................................0
	Shepherd 2 (1 pen)	

1911	Bradford C 0	Newcastle U 0
Replay	Bradford C 1	Newcastle U 0
	Spiers	
1912	Barnsley 0	West Bromwich Albion 0
Replay	Barnsley 1	West Bromwich Albion 0*
	Tuffnell	
1913	Aston Villa 1	Sunderland 0
	Barber	
1914	Burnley 1	Liverpool 0
	Freeman	
1915	Sheffield U 3	Chelsea 0
	Simmons, Fazackerley, Kitchen	
1920	Aston Villa 1	Huddersfield T 0*
	Kirton	
1921	Tottenham H 1	Wolverhampton W 0
	Dimmock	
1922	Huddersfield T 1	Preston NE 0
	Smith (pen)	
1923	Bolton W 2	West Ham U 0
	Jack, J.R. Smith	
1924	Newcastle U 2	Aston Villa 0
	Harris, Seymour	
1925	Sheffield U 1	Cardiff C 0
	Tunstall	
1926	Bolton W 1	Manchester C 0
	Jack	
1927	Cardiff C 1	Arsenal 0
	Ferguson	
1928	Blackburn Rovers 3	Huddersfield T 1
	Roscamp 2, McLean	*A. Jackson*
1929	Bolton W 2	Portsmouth 0
	Butler, Blackmore	
1930	Arsenal............................2	Huddersfield T 0
	James, Lambert	
1931	West Bromwich Albion 2	Birmingham 1
	W.G. Richardson 2	*Bradford*
1932	Newcastle U 2	Arsenal 1
	Allen 2	*John*
1933	Everton 3	Manchester C 0
	Stein, Dean, Dunn	
1934	Manchester C 2	Portsmouth 1
	Tilson 2	*Rutherford*
1935	Sheffield W 4	West Bromwich Albion 2
	Rimmer 2, Palethorpe, Hooper	*Boyes, Sandford*
1936	Arsenal............................1	Sheffield U 0
	Drake	
1937	Sunderland 3	Preston NE 1
	Gurney, Carter, Burbanks	*F. O'Donnell*

1938	Preston NE 1	Huddersfield T 0*
	Mutch (pen)	
1939	Portsmouth 4	Wolverhampton W 1
	Parker 2, Barlow, Anderson	*Dorsett*
1946	Derby Co 4	Charlton Ath...................................1*
	H. Turner (og), Doherty, Stamps 2	*H. Turner*
1947	Charlton Ath 1	Burnley 0*
	Duffy	
1948	Manchester U 4	Blackpool 2
	Rowley 2, Pearson, Anderson	*Shimwell (pen), Mortensen*
1949	Wolverhampton W 3	Leicester C 1
	Pye 2, Smyth,	*Griffiths*
1950	Arsenal 2	Liverpool 2
	Lewis 2	
1951	Newcastle U 2	Blackpool 0
	Milburn 2	
1952	Newcastle U 1	Arsenal 0
	G. Robledo	
1953	Blackpool.............................4	Bolton W 3
	Mortensen 3, Perry	*Lofthouse, Moir, Bell*
1954	West Bromwich Albion 3	Preston NE 2
	Allen 2 (1 pen), Griffin	*Morrison, Wayman*
1955	Newcastle U 3	Manchester C....................................1
	Milburn, Mitchell, Hannah	*Johnstone*
1956	Manchester C.......................3	Birmingham C...................................1
	Hayes, Dyson, Johnstone	*Kinsey*
1957	Aston Villa 2	Manchester U 1
	McParland 2	*T. Taylor*
1958	Bolton W 2	Manchester U 0
	Lofthouse 2	
1959	Nottingham F.......................2	Luton T 1
	Dwight, Wilson	*Pacey*
1960	Wolverhampton W 3	Blackburn Rovers.............................0
	McGrath (og), Deeley 2	
1961	Tottenham H.........................2	Leicester C 0
	Smith, Dyson	
1962	Tottenham H.........................3	Burnley 1
	Greaves, Smith, Blanchflower (pen)	*Robson*
1963	Manchester U 3	Leicester C 1
	Herd 2, Law	*Keyworth*
1964	West Ham U 3	Preston NE 2
	Sissons, Hurst, Boyce	*Holden, Dawson*
1965	Liverpool 2	Leeds U 1*
	Hunt, St John	*Bremner*

1966	Everton 3	Sheffield W 2	
	Trebilcock 2, Temple	*McCalliog, Ford*	
1967	Tottenham H............................2	Chelsea 1	
	Robertson, Saul	*Tambling*	
1968	West Browmwich Albion 1	Everton 0*	
	Astle		
1969	Manchester C...........................1	Leicester C 0	
	Young		
1970	Chelsea.....................................2	Leeds U 2*	
	Houseman, Hutchinson	*Charlton, Jones*	
Replay	Chelsea.....................................2	Leeds U 1*	
	Osgood, Webb	*Jones*	
1971	Arsenal......................................2	Liverpool 1*	
	Kelly, George	*Heighway*	
1972	Leeds U 1	Arsenal......................................0	
	Clarke		
1973	Sunderland 1	Leeds U 0	
	Porterfield		
1974	Liverpool 3	Newcastle 0	
	Keegan 2, Heighway		
1975	West Ham U..............................2	Fulham 0	
	A. Taylor 2		
1976	Southampton 1	Manchester U 0	
	Stokes		
1977	Manchester U............................2	Liverpool 1	
	Pearson, J. Greenhoff	*Case*	
1978	Ipswich T 1	Arsenal......................................0	
	Osborne		
1979	Arsenal......................................3	Manchester U 2	
	Talbot, Stapleton, Sunderland	*McQueen, McIlroy*	
1980	West Ham U..............................1	Arsenal......................................0	
	Brooking		
1981	Tottenham H............................1	Manchester C............................1*	
	Hutchison (og)	*Hutchison*	
Replay	Totteham H...............................3	Manchester C............................2	
	Villa 2, Crooks	*Mackenzie, Reeves (pen)*	
1982	Tottenham H............................1	QPR...1*	
	Hoddle	*Fenwick*	
Replay	Tottenham H............................1	QPR...0	
	Hoddle (pen)		
1983	Manchester U............................2	Brighton & HA..........................2*	
	Stapleton, Wilkins	*Smith, Stevens*	
Replay	Manchester U............................4	Brighton & HA..........................0	
	Robson 2, Whiteside, Muhren (pen)		
1984	Everton 2	Watford......................................0	
	Sharp, Gray		
1985	Manchester U............................1	Everton 0*	
	Whiteside		

1986	Liverpool 3	Everton 1
	Rush 2, Johnston	*Lineker*
1987	Coventry C 3	Tottenham H................2*
	Bennett, Houchen,	*C. Allen, Kilcline (og)*
	Mabbutt (og)	
1988	Wimbledon.................1	Liverpool 0
	Sanchez	
1989	Liverpool 3	Everton 2*
	Aldridge, Rush 2	*McCall 2*
1990	Manchester U..............3	Crystal Palace 3*
	Robson, Hughes 2	*O'Reilly, Wright 2*
Replay	Manchester U..............1	Crystal Palace 0
	Martin	
1991	Tottenham H...............2	Nottingham F...............1*
	Stewart, Walker (og)	*Pearce*
1992	Liverpool 2	Sunderland 0
	Thomas, Rush	
1993	Arsenal......................1	Sheffield W..................1*
	Wright	*Hirst*
Replay	Arsenal......................2	Sheffield W..................1*
	Wright, Linighan	*Waddle*
1994	Manchester U..............4	Chelsea 0
	Cantona 2 (2 pens),	
	Kanchelskis, McClair	
1995	Everton 1	Manchester U 0
	Rideout	

*After extra time

SUMMARY OF FA CUP WINNERS SINCE 1871

Manchester United	9
Tottenham Hotspur	8
Aston Villa	7
Blackburn Rovers	6
Newcastle United	6
Arsenal	6
Everton	5
Liverpool	5
The Wanderers	5
West Bromwich Albion	5
Bolton Wanderers	4
Manchester City	4
Sheffield United	4
Wolverhampton Wanderers	4
Sheffield Wednesday	3
West Ham United	3
Bury	2
Nottingham Forest	2
Old Etonians	2
Preston North End	2
Sunderland	2
Barnsley	1
Blackburn Olympic	1
Blackpool	1
Bradford City	1
Burnley	1
Cardiff City	1
Charlton Athletic	1
Chelsea	1
Clapham Rovers	1
Coventry City	1
Derby County	1
Huddersfield Town	1
Ipswich Town	1
Leeds United	1
Notts County	1
Old Carthusians	1
Oxford University	1
Portsmouth	1
Royal Engineers	1
Southampton	1
Wimbledon	1

APPEARANCES IN FA CUP FINAL

Manchester United	14
Arsenal	12
Everton	12
Newcastle United	11
Liverpool	11
West Bromwich Albion	10
Aston Villa	9
Tottenham Hotspur	9
Blackburn Rovers	8
Manchester City	8
Wolverhampton Wanderers	8
Bolton Wanderers	7
Preston North End	7
Old Etonians	6
Sheffield United	6
Sheffield Wednesday	6
Huddersfield Town	5
The Wanderers	5
Chelsea	4
Derby County	4
Leeds United	4
Leicester City	4
Oxford University	4
Royal Engineers	4
Sunderland	4
West Ham United	4
Blackpool	3
Burnley	3
Nottingham Forest	3
Portsmouth	3
Southampton	3
Barnsley	2
Birmingham City	2
Bury	2
Cardiff City	2
Charlton Athletic	2
Clapham Rovers	2
Notts County	2
Queen's Park (Glasgow)	2
Blackburn Olympic	1
Bradford City	1
Brighton & Hove Albion	1
Bristol City	1
Coventry City	1
Crystal Palace	1
Fulham	1
Ipswich Town	1
Luton Town	1
Old Carthusians	1
Queen's Park Rangers	1
Watford	1
Wimbledon	1

COCA-COLA CUP REVIEW 1996

Aston Villa equalled Liverpool's record of five League Cup wins when they easily overcame a disappointing Leeds United 3-0 in one of the most one-sided finals seen in the competition.

Villa's League form had been encouraging for several months, but the reverse situation had affected Leeds, who only managed to threaten early in the second half before Villa scored their second goal.

The opening score came in the 21st minute when Savo Milosevic beat John Lukic in the Leeds goal with a left-foot shot from fully 30 yards. After that flurry of activity from the Leeds left flank, Villa scored the second goal ten minutes into the second half which their domination had always predicted. A left-wing cross from Alan Wright was only cleared by Lucas Radebe straight to Ian Taylor who volleyed in from just outside the penalty area.

Both Milosevic and Dwight Yorke caused plenty of problems for the Leeds defence and Andy Townsend in midfield was easily the outstanding player on the field. However, it was not until the last minute that Villa added to their score when Milosevic found Yorke inside the penalty area and he scored with a right-foot shot from about 15 yards.

Villa had started their campaign with a convincing 6-0 win over Peterborough United, but were held 1-1 in the return game. They were fortunate to be drawn at home in the next three rounds, beating Stockport County 2-0, Queens Park Rangers 1-0 and Wolverhampton Wanderers 1-0 to reach the semi-final. They shared four goals with Arsenal at Highbury and came through on the away goals rule when the second leg at Villa Park finished without a goal.

Leeds also only played one Premier League team before the semi-final, after beginning their run by being held to a goalless draw at home by Second Division Notts County. Leeds won 3-2 at Meadow Lane and then won 1-0 at Derby County. Blackburn Rovers provided their only Premier opposition in the fourth round, but Leeds came through to win 2-1 and accounted for Reading in the fifth round by the same score.

In the semi-final against Birmingham, they looked decidedly ill at ease after going a goal down, but won 2-1 and completed the tie with a 3-0 win at Elland Road.

The holders, Liverpool, were beaten in the fourth round at Anfield by Newcastle United, who in turn lost 2-0 at Arsenal in the next round.

One of the early Premier League casualties were Wimbledon, who lost a high-scoring tie against Charlton Athletic 8-7 on aggregate. Charlton had won 5-4 away with Lee Bowyer scoring a hat-trick and the second leg ended 3-3. But the biggest shock was Manchester United's failure to account for Second Division York City. Fielding a weakened team, but still possessing sufficient quality to have dealt with their opponents, they lost 3-0 at Old Trafford with Paul Barnes scoring twice including one penalty. Though United won 3-1 at York in the second leg, they went out on aggregate scores. Chelsea were edged out 1-0 by Stoke and Millwall beat Everton 4-2 after extra time in the second leg.

Premier teams were not having the competition to themselves as Bradford City beat Nottingham Forest 5-4 on aggregate. Moreover, four more Premier heads rolled in the fourth round, Southampton losing 2-1 at Reading, Coventry similarly at Wolverhampton, while Birmingham beat Middlesbrough 2-0 in a replay and Norwich defeated Bolton in a penalty shoot-out. Yet just Birmingham survived the quarter-finals.

Attendances revealed an increase of more than 200,000 over the previous season.

PAST LEAGUE CUP FINALS

Played as two legs up to 1966

1961	Rotherham U 2	Aston Villa 0	
	Webster, Kirkman		
	Aston Villa 3	Rotherham U 0*	
	O'Neill, Burrows, McParland		
1962	Rochdale 0	Norwich C 3	
		Lythgoe 2, Punton	
	Norwich C 1	Rochdale 0	
	Hill		
1963	Birmingham C 3	Aston Villa 1	
	Leek 2, Bloomfield	*Thomson*	
	Aston Villa 0	Birmingham C 0	
1964	Stoke C 1	Leicester C 1	
	Bebbington	*Gibson*	
	Leicester C 3	Stoke C 2	
	Stringfellow, Gibson, Riley	*Viollet, Kinnell*	
1965	Chelsea 3	Leicester C 2	
	Tambling, Venables (pen), McCreadie	*Appleton, Goodfellow*	
	Leicester C 0	Chelsea 0	
1966	West Ham U 2	WBA 1	
	Moore, Byrne	*Astle*	
	WBA 4	West Ham U 1	
	Kaye, Brown, Clark, Williams	*Peters*	
1967	QPR 3	WBA 2	
	Morgan R, Marsh, Lazarus	*Clark C 2*	
1968	Leeds U 1	Arsenal 0	
	Cooper		
1969	Swindon T 3	Arsenal 1*	
	Smart, Rogers 2	*Gould*	
1970	Manchester C 2	WBA 1*	
	Doyle, Pardoe	*Astle*	
1971	Tottenham H 2	Aston Villa 0	
	Chivers 2		
1972	Chelsea 1	Stoke C 2	
	Osgood	*Conroy, Eastham*	
1973	Tottenham H 1	Norwich C 0	
	Coates		
1974	Wolverhampton W 2	Manchester C 1	
	Hibbitt, Richards	*Bell*	
1975	Aston Villa 1	Norwich C 0	
	Graydon		
1976	Manchester C 2	Newcastle U 1	
	Barnes, Tueart	*Gowling*	
1977	Aston Villa 0	Everton 0	
Replay	Aston Villa 1	Everton 1*	
	Kenyon (og)	*Latchford*	

Replay	Aston Villa	3	Everton	2*
	Little 2, Nicholl		Latchford, Lyons	
1978	Nottingham F	0	Liverpool	0*
Replay	Nottingham F	1	Liverpool	0
	Robertson (pen)			
1979	Nottingham F	3	Southampton	2
	Birtles 2, Woodcock		Peach, Holmes	
1980	Wolverhampton W	1	Nottingham F	0
	Gray			
1981	Liverpool	1	West Ham U	1*
	Kennedy A		Stewart (pen)	
Replay	Liverpool	2	West Ham U	1
	Dalglish, Hansen		Goddard	
1982	Liverpool	3	Tottenham H	1*
	Whelan 2, Rush		Archibald	
1983	Liverpool	2	Manchester U	1*
	Kennedy, Whelan		Whiteside	
1984	Liverpool	0	Everton	0*
Replay	Liverpool	1	Everton	0
	Souness			
1985	Norwich C	1	Sunderland	0
	Chisholm (og)			
1986	Oxford U	3	QPR	0
	Hebberd, Houghton, Charles			
1987	Arsenal	2	Liverpool	1
	Nicholas 2		Rush	
1988	Luton T	3	Arsenal	2
	Stein B 2, Wilson		Hayes, Smith	
1989	Nottingham F	3	Luton T	1
	Clough 2, Webb		Harford	
1990	Nottingham F	1	Oldham Ath	0
	Jemson			
1991	Sheffield W	1	Manchester U	0
	Sheridan			
1992	Manchester U	1	Nottingham F	0
	McClair			
1993	Arsenal	2	Sheffield W	1
	Merson, Morrow		Harkes	
1994	Aston Villa	3	Manchester U	1
	Atkinson, Saunders 2 (1 pen)		Hughes	
1995	Liverpool	2	Bolton W	1
	McManaman		Thompson	

*After extra time

COCA COLA CUP 1995-96

FIRST ROUND FIRST LEG

Doncaster R	(0) 1	Shrewsbury T	(1) 1
Barnet	(0) 0	Charlton Ath	(0) 0
Birmingham C	(1) 1	Plymouth Arg	(0) 0
Bradford C	(2) 2	Blackpool	(0) 1
Cambridge U	(1) 2	Swindon T	(1) 1
Chester C	(2) 4	Wigan Ath	(0) 1
Chesterfield	(0) 0	Bury	(0) 1
Colchester U	(2) 2	Bristol C	(1) 1
Fulham	(1) 3	Brighton & HA	(0) 0
Gillingham	(0) 1	Bristol R	(0) 1
Hereford U	(0) 0	Oxford U	(1) 2
Huddersfield T	(1) 1	Port Vale	(1) 2
Hull C	(0) 1	Carlisle U	(0) 2
Luton T	(0) 1	Bournemouth	(1) 1
Mansfield T	(0) 0	Burnley	(1) 1
Notts Co	(2) 2	Lincoln C	(0) 0
Preston NE	(0) 1	Sunderland	(0) 1
Rochdale	(1) 2	York C	(0) 1
Scarborough	(0) 1	Hartlepool U	(0) 0
Scunthorpe U	(1) 4	Rotherham U	(1) 1
Stockport Co	(1) 1	Wrexham	(0) 0
Swansea C	(2) 4	Peterborough U	(0) 1
Torquay U	(0) 0	Exeter C	(0) 1
Walsall	(2) 2	Brentford	(1) 2
WBA	(1) 1	Northampton T	(0) 1
Wycombe W	(2) 3	Leyton Orient	(0) 0
Portsmouth	(0) 0	Cardiff C	(1) 2
Crewe Alex	(0) 4	Darlington	(0) 0

FIRST ROUND SECOND LEG

Blackpool	(0) 2	Bradford C	(0) 3
Bournemouth	*(1) 2	Luton T	(1) 1
Brentford	(2) 3	Walsall	(1) 1
Brighton & HA	(0) 0	Fulham	(0) 2
Bristol C	(1) 2	Colchester U	(0) 1
(aet; Bristol C won 5-3 on penalties)			
Burnley	(1) 3	Mansfield T	(0) 1
Cardiff C	(0) 1	Portsmouth	(0) 0
Carlisle U	(0) 2	Hull C	(2) 4
Charlton Ath	(1) 2	Barnet	(0) 0
Hartlepool U	(1) 1	Scarborough	(0) 0
(aet; Hartlepool U won 7-6 on penalties)			
Leyton Orient	(1) 2	Wycombe W	(0) 0
Lincoln C	(0) 0	Notts Co	(0) 2
Northampton T	(0) 2	WBA	(1) 4
Oxford U	(3) 3	Hereford U	(0) 2
Peterborough U	(1) 3	Swansea C	(0) 0
(aet; Peterborough U won on away goals)			
Plymouth Arg	(1) 1	Birmingham C	(0) 2
Port Vale	(0) 1	Huddersfield T	(2) 3
Rotherham U	(1) 5	Scunthorpe U	(0) 0
Shrewsbury T	(0) 0	Doncaster R	(0) 0
(aet; Shrewsbury T won on away goals)			
Wigan Ath	(0) 1	Chester C	(2) 3

133

York C	(1) 5	Rochdale	(0) 1
Bristol R	(1) 4	Gillingham	(1) 2
Exeter C	(1) 1	Torquay U	(1) 1
(aet; Torquay U won on away goals)			
Sunderland	(0) 3	Preston NE	(2) 2
Swindon T	(0) 2	Cambridge U	(0) 0
Bury	(0) 2	Chesterfield	(1) 1
Darlington	(0) 1	Crewe Alex	(0) 1
Wrexham	(1) 2	Stockport Co	(0) 2

SECOND ROUND FIRST LEG

Bolton W	(0) 1	Brentford	(0) 0
Bradford C	(1) 3	Nottingham F	(1) 2
Bristol C	(0) 0	Newcastle U	(3) 5
Cardiff C	(0) 0	Southampton	(1) 3
Crewe Alex	(1) 2	Sheffield W	(2) 2
Hartlepool U	(0) 0	Arsenal	(2) 3
Huddersfield T	(1) 2	Barnsley	(0) 0
Leeds U	(0) 0	Notts Co	(1) 1
Oxford U	(0) 1	QPR	(1) 1
Shrewsbury T	(1) 1	Derby Co	(2) 3
Southend U	(1) 2	Crystal Palace	(0) 2
Stockport Co	(1) 1	Ipswich T	(1) 1
Tranmere R	(0) 1	Oldham Ath	(0) 0
Watford	(0) 1	Bournemouth	(1) 1
Wimbledon	(1) 4	Charlton Ath	(2) 5
Wycombe W	(0) 0	Manchester C	(0) 0
Aston Villa	(3) 6	Peterborough U	(0) 0
Birmingham C	(2) 3	Grimsby T	(1) 1
Bristol R	(0) 0	West Ham U	(1) 1
Coventry C	(2) 2	Hull C	(0) 0
Leicester C	(1) 2	Burnley	(0) 0
Liverpool	(1) 2	Sunderland	(0) 0
Manchester U	(0) 0	York C	(1) 3
Middlesbrough	(2) 2	Rotherham U	(1) 1
Millwall	(0) 0	Everton	(0) 0
Norwich C	(3) 6	Torquay U	(0) 1
Reading	(0) 1	WBA	(0) 1
Sheffield U	(1) 2	Bury	(0) 1
Stoke C	(0) 0	Chelsea	(0) 0
Swindon T	(2) 2	Blackburn R	(2) 3
Tottenham H	(3) 4	Chester C	(0) 0
Wolverhampton W	(1) 2	Fulham	(0) 0

SECOND ROUND SECOND LEG

Arsenal	(2) 5	Hartlepool U	(0) 0
Barnsley	(1) 4	Huddersfield T	(0) 0
Bournemouth	(0) 1	Watford	(0) 1
(aet; Watford won 6-5 on penalties)			
Brentford	(1) 2	Bolton W	(0) 3
Burnley	(0) 0	Leicester C	(0) 2
Bury	(2) 4	Sheffield U	(0) 2
Charlton Ath	(1) 3	Wimbledon	(1) 3
(aet; Charlton won 8-7 on penalties)			
Crystal Palace	(1) 2	Southend U	// (0) 0
Fulham	(0) 1	Wolverhampton W	(1) 5
Grimsby T	(0) 1	Birmingham C	(0) 1
Ipswich T	(1) 1	Stockport Co	*(0) 2

134

Notts Co	(1) 2	Leeds U	(1) 3
Peterborough U	(1) 1	Aston Villa	(0) 1
QPR	*(0) 2	Oxford U	(1) 1
Rotherham U	(0) 0	Middlesbrough	(0) 1
WBA	(1) 2	Reading	(1) 4
York C	(1) 1	Manchester U	(2) 3
Blackburn R	(1) 2	Swindon T	(0) 0
Chelsea	(0) 0	Stoke C	(0) 1
Chester C	(1) 1	Tottenham H	(2) 3
Derby Co	(1) 1	Shrewsbury T	(0) 1
Everton	(0) 2	Millwall	*(0) 4
Hull C	(0) 0	Coventry C	(1) 1
Manchester C	(2) 4	Wycombe W	(0) 0
Newcastle U	(0) 3	Bristol C	(1) 1
Nottingham F	(1) 2	Bradford C	(0) 2
Oldham Ath	(1) 1	Tranmere R	(1) 3
Sheffield W	(3) 5	Crewe Alex	(2) 2
Southampton	(0) 2	Cardiff C	(1) 1
Sunderland	(0) 0	Liverpool	(1) 1
Torquay U	(0) 2	Norwich C	(0) 3
West Ham U	(0) 3	Bristol R	(0) 0

THIRD ROUND

Barnsley	(0) 0	Arsenal	(2) 3
Birmingham C	(1) 1	Tranmere R	(0) 1
Bolton W	(0) 0	Leicester C	(0) 0
Reading	(0)	Bury	(2)
(Abandoned 29 minutes, pitch waterlogged)			
Watford	(1) 1	Blackburn R	(0) 2
Aston Villa	(0) 2	Stockport Co	(0) 0
Coventry C	(0) 3	Tottenham H	(2) 2
Crystal Palace	(2) 2	Middlesbrough	(2) 2
Derby Co	(0) 0	Leeds U	(0) 1
Liverpool	(1) 4	Manchester C	(0) 0
Millwall	(0) 0	Sheffield W	(1) 2
Norwich C	(0) 0	Bradford C	(0) 0
QPR	(1) 3	York C	(1) 1
Southampton	(1) 2	West Ham U	(1) 1
Stoke C	(0) 0	Newcastle U	(2) 4
Wolverhampton W	(0) 0	Charlton Ath	(0) 0
Reading	(0) 2	Bury	(0) 1

THIRD ROUND REPLAYS

Bradford C	(1) 3	Norwich C	*(2) 5
Charlton Ath	(0) 1	Wolverhampton W	*(1) 2
Leicester C	(0) 2	Bolton W	(1) 3
Middlesbrough	(1) 2	Crystal Palace	(0) 0
Tranmere R	(0) 1	Birmingham C	*(0) 3

FOURTH ROUND

Reading	(1) 2	Southampton	(1) 1
Arsenal	(1) 2	Sheffield W	(1) 1
Aston Villa	(0) 1	QPR	(0) 0
Leeds U	(2) 2	Blackburn R	(0) 1
Liverpool	(0) 0	Newcastle U	(0) 1
Middlesbrough	(0) 0	Birmingham C	(0) 0
Norwich C	(0) 0	Bolton W	(0) 0
Wolverhampton W	(2) 2	Coventry C	(0) 1

135

FOURTH ROUND REPLAYS

Birmingham C	(2) 2	Middlesbrough	(0) 0
Bolton W	(0) 0	Norwich C	(0) 0

(aet; Norwich C won 3-2 on penalties)

FIFTH ROUND

Arsenal	(1) 2	Newcastle U	(0) 0
Aston Villa	(0) 1	Wolverhampton W	(0) 0
Leeds U	(2) 2	Reading	(1) 1
Norwich C	(0) 1	Birmingham C	(0) 1

FIFTH ROUND REPLAY

Birmingham C	(0) 2	Norwich C	(0) 1

SEMI-FINAL FIRST LEG

Birmingham C	(1) 1	Leeds U	(0) 2
Arsenal	(2) 2	Aston Villa	(1) 2

SEMI-FINAL SECOND LEG

Aston Villa	(0) 0	Arsenal	(0) 0

(aet; Aston Villa won on away goals)

Leeds U	(0) 3	Birmingham C	(0) 0

FINAL at Wembley
24 MARCH

Aston Villa (1) 3 *(Milosevic, Taylor, Yorke)*

Leeds U (0) 0   77,056

Aston Villa: Bosnich; Charles, Wright, Southgate, McGrath, Ehiogu, Taylor, Draper, Milosevic, Townsend, Yorke.
Leeds U: Lukic; Kelly, Radebe (Brolin), Palmer, Wetherall, Pemberton, Gray, Ford (Deane), Yeboah, McAllister, Speed.
Referee: R. Hart (Darlington).

* after extra time

ANGLO ITALIAN CUP 1994-95

INTERNATIONAL STAGE

Ancona	(0) 1	Oldham Ath	(0) 0
Birmingham C	(2) 2	Genoa	(2) 3
Cesena	(1) 2	Port Vale	(0) 2
Luton T	(1) 1	Perugia	(2) 4
Foggia	(0) 1	Stoke C	(0) 1
Ipswich T	(0) 2	Reggiana	(1) 1
Salernitana	(0) 0	WBA	(0) 0
Southend U	(0) 0	Brescia	(0) 0
Oldham Ath	(0) 0	Cesena	(0) 0
Port Vale	(0) 2	Ancona	(0) 0
Genoa	(3) 4	Luton T	(0) 0
Perugia	(0) 0	Birmingham C	(0) 1
Brescia	(1) 2	Ipswich T	(0) 2
Reggiana	(0) 1	Southend U	(0) 1
Stoke C	(1) 2	Salernitana	(1) 2
WBA	(1) 1	Foggia	(1) 2
Cesena	(0) 2	Luton T	(0) 0
Oldham Ath	(2) 2	Perugia	(0) 0
Port Vale	(0) 0	Genoa	(0) 0
Foggia	(0) 0	Ipswich T	(1) 1
Salernitana	(1) 2	Southend U	(0) 1
Stoke C	(0) 1	Brescia	(0) 1
WBA	(0) 2	Reggiana	(1) 1
Ancona	(0) 1	Birmingham C	(2) 2
Birmingham C	(1) 3	Cesena	(0) 1
Genoa	(0) 0	Oldham Ath	(0) 0
Luton T	(1) 5	Ancona	(0) 0
Perugia	(1) 3	Port Vale	(3) 5
Brescia	(0) 0	WBA	(0) 1
Ipswich T	(2) 2	Salernitana	(0) 0
Southend U	(1) 1	Foggia	(0) 2

SEMI-FINALS

Foggia	(0) 0	Cesena	(0) 0
Genoa	(0) 0	Salernitana	(0) 0
Ipswich T	(1) 2	Port Vale	(2) 4
Birmingham C	(0) 2	WBA	(1) 2

ITALIAN FINAL, FIRST LEG

Cesena	(0) 0	Genoa	(2) 4

ITALIAN FINAL, SECOND LEG

Genoa	(0) 1	Cesena	(0) 0

ANGLO-FINAL, FIRST LEG

WBA	(0) 0	Port Vale	(0) 0

ANGLO-FINAL, SECOND LEG

Port Vale	(1) 3	WBA	(0) 1

FINAL at Wembley
17 MARCH

Genoa	(3) 5	Port Vale	(0) 2

137

AUTO WINDSCREENS SHIELD 1995-96

FIRST ROUND

Doncaster R	(1) 1	Bradford C	(1) 1
Blackpool	(1) 1	Crewe Alex	(0) 0
Chester C	(0) 0	Rotherham U	(0) 1
Lincoln C	(1) 4	Rochdale	(1) 3
Mansfield T	(1) 2	Wrexham	(1) 2
Scarborough	(0) 0	Hull C	(1) 2
Stockport Co	(0) 1	Chesterfield	(0) 1
Wigan Ath	(0) 1	Scunthorpe U	(0) 1
Cambridge U	(0) 1	Brighton & HA	(1) 4
Colchester U	(2) 5	Torquay U	(0) 2
Hereford U	(0) 3	Cardiff C	(1) 3
Oxford U	(3) 3	Bristol C	(0) 0
Plymouth Arg	(0) 0	Peterborough U	(1) 3
Shrewsbury T	(0) 1	Swansea C	(0) 1
Bournemouth	(0) 0	Brentford	(1) 1
Wycombe W	(1) 1	Fulham	(1) 1
Peterborough U	(0) 0	Northampton T	(0) 0
Swansea C	(0) 0	Leyton Orient	(0) 0
Cardiff C	(1) 3	Gillingham	(1) 2
Fulham	(1) 2	Walsall	(2) 5
Brentford	(1) 1	Exeter C	(0) 0
Brighton & HA	(0) 0	Bristol R	(0) 2
Bristol C	(1) 2	Barnet	(0) 0
Torquay U	(1) 1	Swindon T	(1) 1
Crewe Alex	(4) 8	Hartlepool U	(0) 0
Rotherham U	(0) 1	Burnley	(1) 1
Chesterfield	(2) 2	Notts Co	(0) 1
Scunthorpe U	(1) 4	Bury	(0) 0
Wrexham	(0) 1	York C	(0) 0
Hull C	(0) 1	Preston NE	(0) 0
Bradford C	(1) 1	Carlisle U	(0) 1
Rochdale	(2) 5	Darlington	(1) 2
Leyton Orient	(0) 1	Shrewsbury T	(2) 3
Gillingham	(2) 2	Hereford U	(0) 2
Northampton T	(1) 1	Plymouth Arg	(0) 0
Walsall	(4) 5	Wycombe W	(0) 0
Exeter C	(0) 0	Bournemouth	(0) 2
Bristol R	(1) 3	Cambridge U	(0) 0
Barnet	(0) 2	Oxford U	(0) 3
Hartlepool U	(2) 3	Blackpool	(2) 2
Burnley	(1) 1	Chester C	(0) 1
Notts Co	(1) 1	Stockport Co	(0) 0
Darlington	(0) 0	Lincoln	(0) 1
York C	(0) 1	Mansfield T	(0) 0
Preston NE	(1) 2	Scarborough	(0) 1
Carlisle U	(0) 1	Doncaster R	(1) 1
Swindon T	(0) 2	Colchester U	(0) 0
Bury	(0) 0	Wigan Ath	(0) 0

SECOND ROUND

Doncaster R	(0) 1	Notts Co	(0) 3
Chesterfield	(0) 2	Rochdale	(1) 1
Hull C	(0) 1	Blackpool	(0) 2

138

| Lincoln C | (0) 2 | Preston NE | (0) 1 |
| Rotherham U | (0) 0 | Wigan Ath | (0) 0 |

(aet; Rotherham U won 4-1 on penalties)

Scunthorpe U	(0) 0	York C	(2) 3
Wrexham	(1) 1	Carlisle U	(1) 2
Brentford	(0) 0	Fulham	(0) 1
Bristol R	(1) 2	Bournemouth	(0) 1
Cardiff C	(0) 1	Northampton T	(1) 2
Oxford U	(1) 1	Colchester U	(1) 2
Peterborough U	(0) 1	Swansea C	(0) 0

(aet; Peterborough U won in sudden death)

| Shrewsbury T | (0) 0 | Bristol C | (0) 0 |

(aet; Shrewsbury T won 7-6 on penalties)

Walsall	(1) 1	Brighton & HA	(1) 2
Swindon T	(0) 0	Hereford U	(1) 1
Crewe Alex	(0) 0	Burnley	(0) 1

(aet; Burnley won in sudden death)

NORTHERN SECTION QUARTER-FINALS

Carlisle U	(3) 5	Burnley	(0) 0
Blackpool	(0) 0	Chesterfield	(0) 1
Rotherham U	(2) 3	Lincoln C	(0) 1
York C	(0) 1	Notts Co	(0) 0

SOUTHERN SECTION QUARTER-FINALS

| Fulham | (1) 1 | Bristol R | (1) 2 |

(aet; Bristol R won in sudden death)

Hereford U	(1) 1	Northampton T	(0) 0
Peterborough U	(1) 3	Colchester U	(0) 2
Shrewsbury T	(1) 4	Brighton & HA	(1) 2

NORTHERN SECTION SEMI-FINALS

| Carlisle U | (1) 1 | Chesterfield | (0) 0 |
| Rotherham U | (2) 4 | York C | (1) 1 |

SOUTHERN SECTION SEMI-FINALS

| Shrewsbury T | (0) 4 | Hereford U | (0) 1 |
| Peterborough U | (0) 0 | Bristol R | (0) 1 |

NORTHERN SECTION FINAL, FIRST LEG

| Rotherham U | (0) 2 | Carlisle U | (0) 0 |

SOUTHERN SECTION FINAL, FIRST LEG

| Shrewsbury T | | Bristol R | (0) 1 |

NORTHERN SECTION FINAL, SECOND LEG

| Carlisle U | (0) 0 | Rotherham U | (2) 2 |

SOUTHERN SECTION FINAL, SECOND LEG

| Bristol R | (0) 0 | Shrewsbury T | (0) 1 |

FINAL(at Wembley)
14 APRIL

| Rotherham U | (1) 2 | Shrewsbury T | (0) 1 |

FA CHARITY SHIELD WINNERS 1908–95

1908	Manchester U v QPR	
	4-0 after 1-1 draw	
1909	Newcastle U v Northampton T	2-0
1910	Brighton v Aston Villa	1-0
1911	Manchester U v Swindon T	8-4
1912	Blackburn R v QPR	2-1
1913	Professionals v Amateurs	7-2
1920	Tottenham H v Burnley	2-0
1921	Huddersfield T v Liverpool	1-0
1922	Not played	
1923	Professionals v Amateurs	2-0
1924	Professionals v Amateurs	3-1
1925	Amateurs v Professionals	6-1
1926	Amateurs v Professionals	6-3
1927	Cardiff C v Corinthians	2-1
1928	Everton v Blackburn R	2-1
1929	Professionals v Amateurs	3-0
1930	Arsenal v Sheffield W	2-1
1931	Arsenal v WBA	1-0
1932	Everton v Newcastle U	5-3
1933	Arsenal v Everton	3-0
1934	Arsenal v Manchester C	4-0
1935	Sheffield W v Arsenal	1-0
1936	Sunderland v Arsenal	2-1
1937	Manchester C v Sunderland	2-0
1938	Arsenal v Preston NE	2-1
1948	Arsenal v Manchester U	4-3
1949	Portsmouth v Wolverhampton W	1-1*
1950	World Cup Team v Canadian Touring Team	4-2
1951	Tottenham H v Newcastle U	2-1
1952	Manchester U v Newcastle U	4-2
1953	Arsenal v Blackpool	3-1
1954	Wolverhampton W v WBA	4-4*
1955	Chelsea v Newcastle U	3-0
1956	Manchester U v Manchester C	1-0
1957	Manchester U v Aston Villa	4-0
1958	Bolton W v Wolverhampton W	4-1
1959	Wolverhampton W v Nottingham F	3-1
1960	Burnley v Wolverhampton W	2-2*
1961	Tottenham H v FA XI	3-2
1962	Tottenham H v Ipswich T	5-1
1963	Everton v Manchester U	4-0
1964	Liverpool v West Ham U	2-2*
1965	Manchester U v Liverpool	2-2*
1966	Liverpool v Everton	1-0
1967	Manchester U v Tottenham H	3-3*
1968	Manchester C v WBA	6-1
1969	Leeds U v Manchester C	2-1
1970	Everton v Chelsea	2-1
1971	Leicester C v Liverpool	1-0
1972	Manchester C v Aston Villa	1-0
1973	Burnley v Manchester C	1-0
1974	Liverpool v Leeds U	1-1
1975	Derby Co v West Ham U	2-0
1976	Liverpool v Southampton	1-0
1977	Liverpool v Manchester U	0-0*
1978	Nottingham F v Ipswich T	5-0
1979	Liverpool v Arsenal	3-1
1980	Liverpool v West Ham U	1-0
1981	Aston Villa v Tottenham H	2-2*
1982	Liverpool v Tottenham H	1-0
1983	Manchester U v Liverpool	2-0
1984	Everton v Liverpool	1-0
1985	Everton v Manchester U	2-0
1986	Everton v Liverpool	1-1*
1987	Everton v Coventry C	1-0
1988	Liverpool v Wimbledon	2-1
1989	Liverpool v Arsenal	1-0
1990	Liverpool v Manchester U	1-1*
1991	Arsenal v Tottenham H	0-0*
1992	Leeds U v Liverpool	4-3
1993	Manchester U† v Arsenal	1-1

*Each club retained shield for six months. †Won on penalties.

FA CHARITY SHIELD 1995

Everton (0) 1, Blackburn R (0) 0

At Wembley, 12 August 1995, attendance 40,149

Everton: Southall; Barrett, Hinchliffe, Parkinson, Unsworth, Ablett, Samways, Horne, Grant (Watson), Rideout, Limpar.

Scorer: Samways.

Blackburn R: Flowers; Kenna (Atkins), Le Saux, Batty, Pearce, Sutton, Ripley (Makel), Sherwood, Shearer, Newell, Gallacher (Marker).

ABERDEEN PREM. DIV.

Ground: Pittodrie Stadium, Aberdeen AB2 1QH (01224) 632328
Ground capacity: 21,634. **Colours:** All red with white trim.
Manager: Roy Aitken.
League Appearances: Bernard P 27(4); Booth S 20(4); Buchan J 1(3); Christie K (2); Craig M (1); Dodds W 28(3); Glass S 32; Grant B 22(3); Hetherston P 9(2); Inglis J 24; Irvine B 17(1); Jess E 25; Kpedekpo M 1(4); McKimmie S 29; McKinnon R (1); Miller J 31; Robertson H 5(6); Rowson D 7(2); Shearer D 15(15); Smith G 33; Snelders T 6(1); Thomson S (4); Watt M 30; Windass D 19(1); Woodthorpe C 15
Goals–League (52): Booth 9, Miller 9, Dodds 7, Windass 6, Glass 3, Irvine 3, Jess 3, Shearer 3, Bernard 1, Buchan 1, Inglis 1, Woodthorpe 1, own goals 5.
Scottish Cup (7): Shearer 3, Windass 3, Bernard 1.
Coca-Cola Cup (13): Dodds 5, Booth 3, Inglis 1, Miller 1, Shearer 1, Woodthorpe 1, own goal 1.

AIRDRIEONIANS DIV. 1

Ground: Broadwood Stadium, Cumbernauld G68 9NE (01236) 762067
Ground capacity: 6300. **Colours:** White shirts with red diamond, white shorts.
Manager: Alex MacDonald.
League Appearances: Black K 33; Bonar P 9(3); Boyle J 36; Connelly G (8); Connolly P 6; Cooper S 24; Davies J 33(2); Duffield P 19(5); Harvey A 27(7); Hetherston P 7(1); Jack P 9(5); Martin J 20; McClelland J 1(2); McIntyre J 22(7); McIntyre T 12(5); McPeak A (1); Rhodes A 16; Sandison J 30; Smith A 28(3); Stewart A 30; Sweeney S 24; Tait S 2(2); Wilson M 8(5)
Goals–League (43): McIntyre J 9, Duffield 6, Cooper 4, Hetherston 4, Connolly P 3, Davies 3, Smith 3, Black 2 (1 pen), Boyle 2, Harvey 2, McIntyre T 2, Sandison 1, own goals 2.
Scottish Cup (6): Duffield 3, Bonar 1, Cooper 1, Smith 1.
Coca-Cola Cup (7): Boyle 2, Duffield 2, Cooper 1, McIntyre J 1, own goal 1.
League Challenge Cup (2): Boyle 1, McIntyre J 1.

ALBION ROVERS DIV. 3

Ground: Cliftonhill Stadium, Main Street, Coatbridge ML5 3RB (01236) 606334
Ground capacity: 1238. **Colours:** Yellow shirts with black trim, black shorts.
Manager: Vinnie Moore.
League Appearances: Bell D 17(4); Brown M 7; Byrne D 17; Clark M 11; Collins L 8; Crawford P 11(13); Deeley B 15(5); Duncan M 1(2); Friar P 5; Gallagher J 33; Henderson B 3(4); Lavery J 4; MacFarlane C 16; McBride J 12(1); McConville R 1; McDonald D 24(1); McEwan A 5(2); McNally A 6; Miller D 2; Moffat J 21; Moonie D 4; Moore V 8; Morrison A 1; Osborne M 9; Percy A 1; Pickering M 8(1); Quinn K (1); Reilly J 7(3); Reilly R 3; Richardson J 1; Riley D 1; Robertson S 1; Russell R 5(7); Ryan M 20(3); Scott M 3; Seggie D 2(4); Shanks C 17(2); Smith B 3(1); Speirs C 9; Strain B 20(6); Thompson D 7; Watson B 1; Willock A 12(5); Wright A 1; Young G 32; Yule R 1(1)
Goals–League (37): Young 12, McBride 5, Crawford 2, MacFarlane 2, Moore 2,

Strain 2, Willock 2, Byrne 1, Collins 1, McDonald 1, McEwan 1, McNally 1, Reilly J 1, Reilly R 1, Scott 1, Speirs 1, Watson 1.
Scottish Cup (0).
Coca-Cola Cup (0).
League Challenge Cup (3): Crawford 1, McBride 1, Scott 1.

ALLOA   DIV. 3

Ground: Recreation Park, Alloa FK10 1RR (01259) 722695
Ground capacity: 4100. **Colours:** Gold shirts with black trim, black shorts.
Manager: Tom Hendrie.
League Appearances: Balfour R 26; Bennett N 25; Cadden S 13(3); Conway V 7(1); Cully D 4(4); Cummings P 1; Diver D 11(1); Gilmour J 20(5); Graham P 9; Hannah K 6(4); Johnston N 9(7); Kane K 4; Kirkham D 2(1); Lamont W 1; Lawrie D 5; Little T 8(6); Mackay S 16(1); McAneny P 29; McAvoy N 17; McCardle R 1; McCormack J 15(4); McCulloch K 12(1); McKenzie C 3(2); Moffat B 33(2); Morrison S 21(5); Nelson M 16(5); Newbigging W 15(1); Rixon S 17(9); Smith G 14(2); Stewart W 1; Watters W 3(1); Whyte M 18(7); Wylie R 14(5)
Goals–League (26): Moffat 5, Rixon 5, Gilmour 2, Mackay 2, Morrison 2, Whyte 2, Bennett 1, Cadden 1, Hannah 1, Johnston 1, McAnenay 1, McCulloch 1, Newbigging 1, Watters 1.
Scottish Cup (1): Rixon.
Coca-Cola Cup (2): Moffat 1, Rixon 1.
League Challenge Cup (4): Moffat 3, Diver 1.

ARBROATH   DIV. 3

Ground: Gayfield Park, Arbroath DD11 1QB (01241) 872157
Ground capacity: 6488. **Colours:** Maroon shirts with sky blue trim, white shorts.
Manager: John Brogan.
League Appearances: Clark P 13(1); Crawford J 19(2); Dunn G 25(1); Elder S 29(1); Elliot D 13(11); Florence S 8(3); Fowler J 5(9); Gardner L 15(2); Hinchcliffe C 11; Kerr J 4(4); Kerr R 1; Lindsay J 7(3); McAulay J 33(2); McCabe G 12(7); McCormick S 28(3); McLean C 1; McMillan T 5(2); McVicar D 8; Middleton A 15(1); Peters S 31(2); Pew D 32(4); Phinn J 5; Porteous I 10(6); Roberts P 4(7); Scott S 1; Sexton B 2(5); Ward J 18; Waters M 14(3); Watters W 20(3); Welsh B 2(4)
Goals–League (41): McCormick 8, Pew 8, Elliot 5, Porteous 4, Gardner 3, Watters W 3, Elder 2, Kennedy 2, Roberts 2, Waters M 2, Sexton 2, Ward 1.
Scottish Cup (2): McCormick 1, Pew 1.
Coca-Cola Cup (3): McCormick 2, Lindsay 1.
League Challenge Cup (0).

AYR UNITED   DIV. 2

Ground: Somerset Park, Ayr KA8 9NB (01292) 263435
Ground capacity: 12,128. **Colours:** White shirts with black sleeves, black shorts.
Manager: Gordon Dalziel.

League Appearances: Agnew S 2(1); Balfour E 12(2); Barnstaple K 2(3); Bell R 4(1); Biggart K 9(16); Bilsland B 15(6); Boyce D 4; Burns G (1); Byrne D 8(2); Chalmers P 5; Clarke J 7(2); Connelly S 1(1); Connie C 10(3); Coyle R 4; Dalziel G 16(7); Diver D 9; Duncan C 21; English I 8; George D 24(1); Henderson D 11; Hood G 19(1); Jamieson W 20; Kinnaird P 16(2); Lamont W 4; Law R 6; MacFarlane C 3(2); McKilligan N 7(3); Mooney S 1; Moore V 11; Napier C 10; Nolan J 1; Paavola T 3; Rolling F 2; Scott M 7; Sharples J 26; Shepherd A 10(1); Smith H 9; Smith M 8(2); Stainrod S 2; Steele T 10(5); Tannock R 12(2); Traynor J 20(4); Wilson S 7(1); Wilson W 9(1); Yule R 1(1)

Goals–League (40): Bilsland 5, English 5, Dalziel 4, Diver 4, Sharples 4, Henderson 3, Hood 2, Kinnaird 2, Moore 2, Paavola 2, Balfour 1, Chalmers 1, George 1, Jamieson 1, Smith M 1, Steele 1, Wilson W 1.

Scottish Cup (0).

Coca-Cola Cup (0).

Goals–League Challenge Cup (1): Bilsland 1.

BERWICK RANGERS   DIV. 2

Ground: Shielfield Park, Berwick-on-Tweed TD15 2EF (01289) 307424
Ground capacity: 4131. **Colours:** Gold with black seams and trim, black shorts.
Manager: Ian Ross.
League Appearances: Banks A 26(4); Chivers D (1); Clarke J 3(2); Clegg N (6); Cole A 8; Coughlin J 3; Cowan M 25(1); Forrester P 25(10); Fraser G 36; Gallacher J 4; Govan M (1); Graham T 33; Irvine W 35; Kane K 22(6); McGlynn D 15(2); McQueen J 5(1); Neil M 33(2); Reid A 23(1); Rutherford P 6(3); Thomson M 1; Thomson M 1; Valentine C 31; Walton K 13(10); Wilson M 17(8); Young N 31

Goals–League (64): Irvine 13 (1 pen), Forrester 10, Fraser 7, McGlynn 6, Banks 5 (2 pens), Neil 5, Walton 5, Cowan 3, Graham 3, Reid 2, Rutherford 2, Cole 1, Kane 1, Wilson 1.

Scottish Cup (6): Kane 2, Fraser 1, Irvine 1, Reid 1, own goal 1.

Coca-Cola Cup (1): Clegg.

League Challenge Cup (1): Cole 1.

BRECHIN CITY   DIV. 2

Ground: Glebe Park, Brechin DD9 6BJ (01356) 622856
Ground capacity: 3980. **Colours:** Red with white trim.
Manager: John Young.
League Appearances: Allan R 33; Baillie R 2(6); Balfour D 1; Brand R 9(5); Brown B 1; Brown R 36; Buick G 12; Cairney H 33; Christie G 25(2); Conway F 30; Farnan C 35; Ferguson S 20(1); Garden S 1(1); Graham R 1(1); Heddle I 7(1); Kerrigan S 2(4); Marr S 1; McKellar J 18(4); McNeill W 28(3); Mearns G 8; Mitchell B 36; Price G 1; Reid S (1); Ross A 23(3); Scott D 21; Smith R 9(5); Sorbie S 3

Goals–League (41): Ross 8, McNeill 7, Brand 6, McKellar 3, Brown 2, Buick 2, Cairney 2, Christie 2, Farnan 2, Mitchell 2, Price 2, Ferguson 1, Smith 1, Sorbie 1.

Scottish Cup (3): Cairney 1 (pen), Christie 1, Mitchell 1.

Coca-Cola Cup (2): Brand 2.

League Challenge Cup (4): Brand 2, Brown 1, Mearns 1.

143

CELTIC   PREM. DIV.

Ground: Celtic Park, Glasgow G40 3RE (0141) 556 2611
Ground capacity: 47,500. **Colours:** Green and white hooped shirts, white shorts.
Manager: Tommy Burns.
League Appearances: Boyd T 34; Cadete J 2(4); Collins J 26(3); Donnelly S 35; Falconer W (2); Grant P 30; Gray S 3(2); Hay C 1(3); Hughes J 26; Mackay M 9(2); Marshall G 36; McKinlay T 32; McLaughlin B 11(15); McNamara J 26; McQuilken J 3(1); McStay P 29(1); O'Donnell P 14(1); O'Neil B 3(2); Thom A 31(1); Van Hooijdonk P 34; Vata R 5(1); Walker A 4(12); Wieghorst M 2(9)
Goals–League (74): Van Hooijdonk 26 (4 pens), Collins 11 (2 pens), Donnelly 6, Cadete 5, Thom 5, McLaughlin 4, Grant 3, O'Donnell 3, Walker 3, Hughes 2, McStay 2, Gray 1, Mackay 1, McNamara 1, Wieghorst 1.
Scottish Cup (8): Van Hooijdonk 4, Donnelly 2, McLaughlin 1, Thom 1.
Coca-Cola Cup (5): Van Hooijdonk 2, Collins 1 (pen), Donnelly 1, Thom 1.

CLYDE   DIV. 2

Ground: Broadwood Stadium, Cumbernauld G68 9NE (01236) 451511
Ground capacity: 8200. **Colours:** White shirts with red and black trim, black shorts.
Manager: Alex Smith.
League Appearances: Angus I 33; Annand E 35; Brown J 9; Brownlie P 2(2); Campbell P (2); Coleman S (1); Dawson R 8; Dickson J 5(8); Falconer M 2(7); Ferguson G 26(1); Gillies K 30; Harrison T 21(6); Hillcoat J 25; Knox K 28(1); McCarron J 1(1); McCheyne G 11(10); McCluskey G 5(11); McConnell I 15(5); McEwan C 1; McLay J 9(2); McQueen J 11; Muir J (1); Nicholas C 31; Nisbet I 4(12); O'Neill M 19(4); Parks G 1; Patterson P 4(9); Prunty J 11(8); Thomson J 24; Watson G 25
Goals–League (47): Annand 21 (3 pens), Nicholas 5, Harrison 4, McCluskey 3, Angus 2, McConnell 2, O'Neill 2, Thomson 2, Falconer 1, Knox 1, McCarron 1, McCheyne 1, Nisbet 1, Patterson 1.
Scottish Cup (9): Annand 3, Nicholas 2, Angus 1, Harrison 1, McCheyne 1, McConnell 1.
Coca-Cola Cup (1): Annand 1.
League Challenge Cup (0).

CLYDEBANK   DIV. 1

Ground: Home matches at Boghead Park, Dumbarton (0141) 955 9048
Ground capacity: 5503. **Colours:** White, black and red trim, white shorts.
Coach: Brian Wright.
League Appearances: Agnew P 4(3); Bowman G 33; Brannigan K 5; Connell G 34; Connelly D 3(4); Crawford D (1); Currie T 27(1); Dunn R 3(2); Eadie K 26(2); Flannigan C 8(17); Grady J 35(1); Hardie D (1); Irons D 8; Jack S 14(4); Keane G (1); Kerrigan S (1); Lansdowne A 10(4); Lovering P 11(10); Matthews G 36; McLaughlin I 1; Melvin W (1); Miller S 3(4); Murdoch S 27(1); Nicholls D 35; Robertson J 25(6); Sutherland C 25(1); Teale G 9(7); Tomlinson C 14
Goals–League (39): Grady 11, Eadie 9, Robertson 5, Nicholls 3, Bowman 2, Connell 2, Flannigan 2, Sutherland 2, Irons 1, Lovering 1, Teale 1.

144

Scottish Cup (0).
Coca-Cola Cup (1): Robertson 1.
League Challenge Cup (5): Grady 2, Kerrigan 2, Nicholls.

COWDENBEATH   DIV. 3

Ground: Central Park, Cowdenbeath KY4 9EY (01383) 610166
Ground capacity: 5268. **Colours:** Royal blue stripes with red trim, white shorts.
Manager: Thomas Steven.
League Appearances: Bowmaker K 16(5); Brock J 4(6); Brough G 3(4); Buckley G 6(9); Chapman G (1); Conn S 16(2); Demelo A 1(5); Hamilton A 12(3); Humphreys M 35; Hutchison K 1(1); Mackenzie A 8; Malloy B 18; Maratea D 13(2); McGregor S 2; McMahon B 28; Meldrum G 35; Millar G 6(7); O'Neill H 16(2); Oliver S 4(1); Petrie E 3(2); Russell N 32(1); Scott D 26(2); Smith C 2(4); Soutar G 3(5); Spence J (3); Steven S 36; Stewart W 3(9); Wardell S 1; Winter C 32; Wood G 30(1); Yardley M 4
Goals–League (45): Scott 11, Wood 7, Buckley 3, Conn 3, Mackenzie 3, Steven 3, Bowmaker 2, Humphreys 2, Meldrum 2, O'Neill 2, Winter 2, Yardley 2, McMahon 1, Malloy 1, Soutar 1.
Scottish Cup (1): Maratea 1.
Coca-Cola Cup (1): Scott 1.
League Challenge Cup (0).

DUMBARTON   DIV. 2

Ground: Boghead Park, Dumbarton G82 2JA (01389) 62569, 67864
Ground capacity: 5503. **Colours:** All gold.
Manager: Jim Fallon.
League Appearances: Burns H 10(1); Charnley J 16(2); Dallas S 8(14); Dennison P 2; Fabiani R 19(1); Foster A 10(2); Gibson C 23(6); Glancy M 1; Goldie J 1(1); Gow S 20(1); Granger A 20(11); Hamilton J 3; King T 27(1); MacFarlane I 22; Marsland J 18; Martin P 12; McGarvey M 14(10); McGivern S 9(2); McKinnon S 31(2); Meechan J 31(1); Meechan K 12(1); Melvin M 32(1); Mooney M 31(5); Sharpe L 14(1); Ward H 10(4)
Goals–League (23): Mooney M 5 (1 pen), Granger 3 (1 pen), Dallas 2, Gibson 2, McGarvey 2, Ward 2, Burns 1, Charnley 1, Foster 1, McKinnon 1, Martin 1, Sharpe 1, own goal 1.
Scottish Cup (1): Mooney M 1.
Coca-Cola Cup (0).
League Challenge Cup (0).

DUNDEE   DIV. 1

Ground: Dens Park, Dundee DD3 7JY (01382) 826104
Ground capacity: 14,177. **Colours:** Dark blue shirts with red and white trim, white shorts.
Manager: Jim Duffy.
League Appearances: Adamczuk D 8(5); Anderson I 9(8); Bain K 7(3); Britton G

15(10); Cargill A 11(7); Charnley J 12; Duffy C 31; Duffy J 19; Farningham R 13(5); Hamilton J 30(3); Hutchison M (1); Magee D (1); Manley R 17; Mathers P 1; McBain R 3(3); McCann N 22; McKeown G 13(4); McQueen T 21; O'Driscoll J 1(4); Pageaud M 35; Rae G 4(2); Shaw G 33(3); Smith B 20; Teasdale M 1; Tosh P 29(1); Tully C 2; Vrto D 25(2); Wieghorst M 14

Goals–League (53): Hamilton 14, Tosh 9, Shaw 7, Wieghorst 4, Charnley 3, Duffy C 3, Farningham 3, Britton 2, McCann 2, Bain 1, Cargill 1, McKeown 1, O'Driscoll 1, own goals 2.

Scottish Cup (1): Duffy C 1.

Coca-Cola Cup (15): McCann 5, Shaw 3, Wieghorst 3, Hamilton 2, Tosh 2.

League Challenge Cup (8): Hamilton 3, Anderson 2, Cargill 2, Shaw 1.

DUNDEE UNITED   PREM. DIV.

Ground: Tannadice Park, Dundee DD3 7JW (01382) 833166
Ground capacity: 12,616. **Colours:** Tangerine shirts with black trim, black shorts.
Manager: Billy Kirkwood.
League Appearances: Bett J 23; Bowman D 16(1); Brewster C 23(7); Caldwell N 2; Connolly P 3(3); Coyle O 20(8); Crabbe S 1(1); Dailly C 20(9); Hannah D 4(3); Honeyman B (1); Johnson G 25(3); Keith M (4); Malpas M 30; Maxwell A 35; McKinlay W 5; McKinnon R 5(4); McLaren A 23(7); McQuilken J 6(3); McSwegan G 19(6); O'Hanlon K 1; Perry M 18(2); Pressley S 35; Robertson A 1(3); Shannon R 26; Walker P (2); Welsh B 21(2); Winters R 34(1)
Goals–League (73): Brewster 17, McSwegan 17, Winters 7, Coyle 5, Johnson 4, McKinlay 4, McLaren 3, Bett 2, Malpas 2, Perry 2, Pressley 2, Connolly 1, Dailly 1, Hannah 1, Shannon 1, Welsh 1, own goals 3.
Scottish Cup (4): Coyle 3, Brewster 1.
Coca-Cola Cup (5): Connolly 2, Caldwell 1, McKinlay 1, Winters 1.
League Challenge Cup (4): Brewster 1, Dailly 1, Honeyman 1, McKinlay 1.

DUNFERMLINE ATHLETIC   PREM. DIV.

Ground: East End Park, Dunfermline KY12 7RB (01383) 724295
Ground capacity: 18,328. **Colours:** Black and white striped shirts, black shorts.
Manager: Bert Paton.
League Appearances: Bingham D 12(3); Callaghan T (3); Clark J 11; Cooper N 2(2); Den Bieman I 16(10); Farrell G 4(2); Fenwick P (1); Ferguson S (1); Fleming D 25(8); French H 21(2); Hegarty R 3(6); Ireland C 10; Kinnaird P 6(3); McCathie N 18; McCulloch M 4(6); McNamara J 7; Millar M 24; Miller C 25; Moore A 28; Petrie S 31(3); Rice B 5(1); Rissanen K 1(1); Robertson C 27(1); Shaw G 17(11); Smith A 17(2); Smith P 10(1); Tod A 36; Van De Kamp G 26; Westwater I 10(1)
Goals–League (73): Petrie 13, Shaw 12, Smith A 9, Millar M 5 (1 pen), Moore 5, Robertson 5, Tod 5, French 4, Bingham 3, Fleming 3, McCathie 3, Clark 1, Den Bieman 1, Hegarty 1, McNamara 1, own goals 2.
Scottish Cup (3): Bingham 1, Petrie 1, Smith A 1.
Coca-Cola Cup (4): Den Bieman 1, McCathie 1, Moore 1, Petrie 1.
League Challenge Cup (6): Shaw 2, McNamara 1, Millar M 1, Petrie 1, Tod 1.

EAST FIFE   DIV. 1

Ground: Bayview Park, Methil, Fife KY8 3AG (moving 1996–97) (01333) 426323
Ground capacity: 5385. **Colours:** Amber shirts with black trim, amber shorts.
Manager: Steve Archibald.
League Appearances: Allan G 36; Andrew B 10(6); Archibald S 29(2); Balmain K 1; Beaton D 32(1); Broddle J 6; Chalmers P 6(2); Cusick J 33; Demmin C 3; Dixon A 17(3); Donaghy M 32; Dwarika A 12(10); Ferguson P 5(1); Gartshore P 6(4); Gibb R 24; Hamill A 12(3); Hamilton L 35; Hildersley R 5; Hope D 18(7); Hunter P (3); Hutcheon S 7(18); McStay J 34; Robertson D 1; Scott R 32(2); Sneddon A (3); Struthers D (2); Winiarski S (1)
Goals–League (50): Scott 11, Dwarika 8, Archibald 6, Allan 4, Beaton 4 (1 pen), Chalmers 4, Hutcheon 4, Donaghy 3, Cusick 2, Gartshore 2, Gibb 1, McStay 1.
Scottish Cup (4): Allan 1, Dwarika 1, Gibb 1, Scott 1.
Coca-Cola Cup (5): Scott 3, Allan 1, Hutcheon 1.
League Challenge Cup (2): Scott 2.

EAST STIRLINGSHIRE   DIV. 3

Ground: Firs Park, Falkirk FK2 7AY (01324) 623583
Ground capacity: 1880. **Colours:** Black and white hoops, black shorts.
Manager: Billy Little.
League Appearances: Abercromby M 17(5); Cameron D (6); Cuthbert L (2); Docherty R 4(2); Dodds J (1); Dwyer P 31; Farquhar A 5(3); Frater A 1(2); Geraghty M 11; Hunter M 12(7); Lamont P 6(7); Lawrie D 1; Lee I 31(2); Lee R 34; MacLean S 18(8); McBride M 28(3); McDougall G 28; McKenna T 3(1); Millar G 3(1); Moffat J 8; Murray N 3(2); Neill A 31(2); Orr J 6(1); Ross B 20(1); Russell G 30; Scott C 3; Sneddon S 23; Stirling D 11(15); Watt D 28(2)
Goals–League (58): Dwyer 21, McBride 8, MacLean 5, Hunter 4, Lee I 4, Geraghty 3, Watt 3, Abercromby 2, Lamont 2, Neill 2, Sneddon 2, own goals 2.
Scottish Cup (0).
Coca-Cola Cup (2): Abercromby 2 (1 pen).
League Challenge Cup (0).

FALKIRK   DIV. 1

Ground: Brockville Park, Falkirk FK1 5AX (01324) 624121, 632487
Ground capacity: 13,401. **Colours:** Dark blue shirts with white trim, white shorts.
Manager: Eamonn Bannon.
League Appearances: Abbott G (1); Clark J 14(3); Craig A 14; Elliot D 31(1); Ferguson D 26; Finnigan A 8(1); Fulton S 4(1); Graham A 8; Gray A 16; Hagen D 21(4); Hamilton G (1); Henderson N (9); Inglis N 1; Iorfa D 3(1); James K 10(3); Johnston F 3(3); Johnston M 31; Kirk S 16(4); Lamont W 7; Lawrie A 1; MacKenzie S 27(3); McDonald C 4(5); McGowan J 27(2); McGraw M 2(7); McGrillen P 24(6); McLaughlin J 15(1); Munro S 13; Napier C 3(1); Oliver N 3; Parks A 28; Rice B 1(4); Seaton A (1); Weir D 34; Whiteside G (2); Wright G 1(1)
Goals–League (31): McGrillen 6, Johnston M 5, Kirk 4, Craig 3, Weir 3, Clark 2 (1 pen), James 2, Finnigan 1, Iorfa 1, McDonald 1, McGowan 1, Mackenzie 1, McLaughlin 1.
Scottish Cup (0).
Coca-Cola Cup (3): Johnston M 2, Henderson 1.

FORFAR ATHLETIC   DIV. 3

Ground: Station Park, Forfar, Angus (01307) 463576, 462259
Ground capacity: 8732. **Colours:** Sky blue and navy shorts, navy shorts.
Manager: Tommy Campbell.
League Appearances: Allison J 22(4); Archibald E 9; Arthur G 33; Bingham D 5;
Bowes M 27(2); Christie S (2); Craig D 27(1); Donegan J 3(4); Glennie S 24(1);
Hamilton J 19; Hannigan P 21(12); Heddle I 6(2); Henderson D 5; Higgins G
24(2); Inglis G 18(5); Irvine N 16(3); Loney J 2(3); Mann R 25(1); McKillop A 22;
McPhee I 19; McVicar D 23; Morgan A 34; O'Neill H 4(2); Paterson A 2(6);
Sexton B 5(2); Strain J 1(2)
Goals–League (37): Higgins 12, Hannigan 6, Morgan 6, Bingham 3, Mann 3,
Bowes 2, Craig 2, Inglis 2, Allison 1.
Scottish Cup (8): Bowes 3, Inglis 2, Morgan 2, Mann 1.
Coca-Cola Cup (1): Loney 1.
League Challenge Cup (2): Bingham 1, Mann 1.

GREENOCK MORTON   DIV. 1

Ground: Cappielow Park, Greenock (01475) 723571
Ground capacity: 14,267. **Colours:** Royal blue tartan shirts, royal blue shorts.
Manager: Allan McGraw.
League Appearances: Anderson J 29(1); Blaikie A (3); Blair P 3(15); Boe A 3;
Collins D 36; Cormack P 23(2); Hawke W 34(1); Hunter J (1); Johnstone D 27(2);
Laing D 3(23); Lilley D 35; Lindberg J 26; Mahood A 31; McArthur S 17(6);
McCahill S 24; McInnes D 12; McPherson C 17(7); Rajamaki M 34(2); Reid B 9;
Wylie D 33
Goals–League (57): Lilley 14, Hawke 13, Rajamaki 11, Anderson 4, Mahood 4,
Johnstone 3, Cormack 2, Lindberg 2, Collins 1, Laing 1, McCahill 1, McInnes 1.
Scottish Cup (3): Cormack 1, Lilley 1, Rajamaki 1.
Coca-Cola Cup (0).
Goals–League Challenge Cup (0).

HAMILTON ACADEMICAL   DIV. 2

Ground: Cliftonhill Stadium, Main Street, Coatbridge ML5 9XX (01236) 606334
(match days)
Ground capacity: 1238. **Colours:** Red and white hooped shirts, white shorts.
Manager: Iain Munro.
League Appearances: Baptie C 31; Chalmers P 1; Clark G 14(3); Cormack D 10(1);
Craig D 17; Diver D 1(3); Ferguson A 26; Geraghty M 17(3); Hartley P 29(2);
Hillcoat C 31; Lorimer D 5(10); Macfarlane D (1); McCarrison D (3); McCloy S
1(4); McCormick S 5(4); McCulloch S 4(6); McEntegart S 28(1); McIntosh C 23;
McInulty S 17(2); McKenzie P 11(12); McParland I (1); McQuade J 9(4); McStay R
16(4); Paterson C 9; Quitongo J 18(4); Renicks S 29(1); Sherry J 24(1); Thomson S
19(2); Tighe M 1
Goals–League (40): Hartley 11, Geraghty 6, McEntegart 4, McStay 4, Quitongo 4,
Clark 3, Baptie 1, Craig 1, McCulloch 1, McIntosh 1 (pen), McQuade 1, Renicks 1,
Sherry 1, own goal 1.

Scottish Cup (0).
Coca-Cola Cup (0).
League Challenge Cup (2): Clark 2.

HEART OF MIDLOTHIAN   PREM. DIV.

Ground: Tynecastle Park, Gorgie Road, Edinburgh EH11 2NL (0131) 337 6132
Ground capacity: 16,613. **Colours:** Maroon shirts, white shorts.
Manager: Jim Jefferies.
League Appearances: Berry N 16(3); Bruno P 22; Callaghan S (1); Cameron C 4;
Colquhoun J 20(11); Eskilson H 9(2); Fulton S 26; Hagen D 5(2); Hamilton B 8(4);
Hogarth M 1; Jamieson W 2(3); Johnston A 30(3); Lawrence A 17(9); Leitch S
4(2); Levein C 1; Locke G 29; Mackay G 21(5); McManus A 16(1); McPherson D
22(4); Millar J 16(4); Miller C 2(1); Naysmith G (1); Nelson C 4; O'Connor G 3;
Pointon N 21(1); Ritchie P 28; Robertson J 28(5); Rousset G 25; Smith H 3; Smith
P 4(5); Thomas K (3); Winnie D 6; Wishart F 1; Wright G 2
Goals–League (55): Robertson 11 (1 pen), Johnston 9 (1 pen), Lawrence 5,
Colquhoun 4, Locke 4, Millar J 4, Pointon 3, Cameron 2, Eskilsson 2, Fulton 2,
Mackay 2, McManus 2, Bruno 1, Hagen 1, McPherson 1, Ritchie 1, own goal 1.
Scottish Cup (8): Ritchie 2, Berry 1, Colquhoun 1, Johnston 1, Lawrence 1,
McPherson 1, Robertson 1.
Coca-Cola Cup (9): McPherson 3, Colquhoun 1, Hagen 1, Hamilton 1, Lawrence 1,
Leitch 1, Robertson 1 (pen).

HIBERNIAN   PREM. DIV.

Ground: Easter Road Stadium, Edinburgh EH7 5QG (0131) 661 2159
Ground capacity: 16,218. **Colours:** Green shirts with white sleeves and collar, white
shorts.
Manager: Alex Miller.
League Appearances: Dods D 14(1); Donald G 2(11); Dow A 8; Evans G 12(11);
Farrell D 7(1); Harper K 14(2); Hunter G 22; Jackson C 19(4); Jackson D 36;
Leighton J 36; Love G 10(4); McAllister K 29(2); McGinlay P 30(1); McLaughlin J
9; Millen A 25; Miller G 1(3); Miller W 13; Mitchell G 6; O'Neill M 26(2); Renwick
M 1(1); Tortolano J 15(1); Tweed S 31; Weir M 5(4); Wright K 25(3)
Goals–League (43): Jackson D 9 (3 pens), Wright 9, O'Neill 6, McGinlay 5,
McAllister 4, Harper 3, Evans 2, Jackson C 2, Donald 1, Dow 1, Weir 1.
Scottish Cup (0).
Coca-Cola Cup (3): Jackson D 2 (1 pen), McGinlay 1.

INVERNESS CALEDONIAN THISTLE   DIV. 3

Ground: Telford Street Park, Inverness (01463) 230274 (moving 1996–97)
Ground capacity: 5498. **Colours:** Blue shirts with white trim, white shorts.
Manager: S.W.Paterson.
League Appearances: Bennett G 30(3); Benson R 3; Brennan D 11(3); Calder J 34;
Christie C 24(5); Green D 4(7); Hastings R 28; Hercher A 30(4); Lisle M 7(5);
MacArthur I 24; MacMillan N 3(5); McAllister M 15(5); McGinlay D 9(13);

149

McKenzie P (4); McRitchie M 2; Mitchell C 12(9); Noble M 36; Ross D 28(4); Scott J 28(2); Stewart I 33(3); Teasdale M 19; Thomson B 16(4)

Goals–League (64): Stewart 23 (2 pens), Christie 12, Hercher 10, Ross 4, Mitchell 3, Hastings 2, Scott 2, Teasdale 2, Thomson 2, Brennan 1, Green 1, McAllister 1, own goal 1.

Scottish Cup (6): Hercher 2, Ross 1, Stewart 1, Teasdale 1, Thomson 1.

Coca-Cola Cup (1): own goal 1.

League Challenge Cup (1): MacMillan

KILMARNOCK   PREM. DIV.

Ground: Rugby Park, Kilmarnock KA1 2DP (01563) 525184

Ground capacity: 18,128. **Colours:** Blue and white striped shirts, blue shorts.

Manager: Alex Totten.

League Appearances: Anderson D 28; Black T 30; Brown T 19(5); Connor R 22(1); Findlay W 2(1); Geddes R 2; Henry J 22(6); Holt G 16(8); Lauchlan J 5; Lekovic D 33; MacPherson A 35; Maskrey S 14(8); McIntyre J 7; McKee C 19(9); Meldrum C 1; Mitchell A 29; Montgomerie R 12(2); Reilly M 22(6); Roberts M 2(9); Skilling M 13(1); Whitworth N 28; Wright P 35(1)

Goals–League (39): Wright 13, Brown 6, Black 4, McKee 4, Henry 3, Mitchell 3, McIntyre 2, MacPherson 2, Maskrey 1, Skilling 1, own goal 1.

Scottish Cup (3): Wright 2, Anderson 1.

Coca-Cola Cup (2): Roberts 1, Wright 1.

LIVINGSTON   DIV. 2

Ground: Almondvale Stadium, Livingston EH54 7DN (01506) 417 000

Ground capacity: 16,500. **Colours:** Amber with black trim, black shorts.

Manager: Jim Leishman.

League Appearances: Alleyne D 19(1); Bailey L 20(7); Callaghan W 6(17); Campbell S 19; Coulston D (1); Davidson G 32; Douglas R 24; Duthie M 25(4); Graham T 15; Harvey G 6(12); Hislop K 4; Laidlaw S 1; Martin C 1(1); McBride J (2); McCartney C 4; McLeod G 34; McMartin M 36; Sinclair C 17(4); Smart C 31; Sorbie S 5(6); Stoute H 12; Thorburn S 3(3); Tierney G 16; Williamson S 23(3); Wright G 7(3); Young J 36

Goals–League (51): Young 18, Bailey 5, McLeod 4, Duthie 3, Harvey 3, McMartin 3, Sinclair 3, Alleyne 2, Campbell 2 (1 pen), Laidlaw 2, Tierney 2, Williamson 2, Hislop 1, Smart 1.

Scottish Cup (5): Harvey 3, Duthie 2.

Coca-Cola Cup (4): Young 2, Bailey 1, McMartin 1.

League Challenge Cup (4): Callaghan 1, McLeod 1, Sinclair 1, Young 1.

MONTROSE   DIV. 3

Ground: Links Park, Montrose DD10 8QD (01674) 673200

Ground capacity: 4338. **Colours:** Royal blue with white sleeves, white shorts.

Manager: Dave Smith.

League Appearances: Brown M (1); Cooper C 19(3); Craib M 26(1); Ferrie A

8(14); Garden M 1; Grant D 24(1); Haro M 19; Kennedy A 14(2); Kydd S 4(7); Larter D 33; MacDonald I 34; MacRonald C 3(1); Mailer C 32(1); Massie R 3; Masson C 8(1); Masson P 19(2); McAvoy N 12(1); McGlashan C 33; Robertson I 11; Smith S 25(3); Stephen L 22(3); Taylor S 11(16); Tindal K 17(3); Tosh J 18(1)

Goals–League (33): McGlashan 16, Taylor 5, Kennedy 4, MacDonald 2, Smith 2, Grant 1, McAvoy 1, Mailer 1, Masson P 1.

Scottish Cup (6): McGlashan 3, Kennedy 2, Masson P 1.

Coca-Cola Cup (0).

League Challenge Cup (3): Grant 1, McGlashan 1, Masson P 1.

MOTHERWELL   PREM DIV

Ground: Fir Park, Motherwell ML1 2QN (01698) 333333
Ground capacity: 13,742. **Colours:** Amber shirts with claret trim, claret shorts.
Manager: Alex McLeish.
League Appearances: Arnott D 23(4); Burns A 14(14); Coyne T 9(5); Davies M 26(7); Denham G 11(2); Dolan J 24(3); Essandoh R (4); Falconer W 15; Ferguson P 1; Hendry J 8(8); Howie S 36; Krivokapic M 13; Lambert P 35; Martin B 33; May E 28; McCart C 20; McCulloch L (1); McKinnon R 27; McLeish A 1; McMillan S 10(2); McSkimming S 13(2); Philliben J 19(5); Ritchie I 5(5); Roddie A 12(12); Ross I 1; Van Der Gaag M 12
Goals–League (28): Falconer 5, Coyne 4 (1 pen), Arnott 3, Burns 3, Davies 2, Hendry 2, Lambert 2 (1 pen), Martin 2, McSkimming 1, May 1, Van Der Gaag 1, own goals 2.
Scottish Cup (0).
Coca-Cola Cup (4): Arnott 3, Lambert 1.

PARTICK THISTLE   DIV. 1

Ground: Firhill Park, Glasgow G20 7BA (0141) 945 4811
Ground capacity: 21,776. **Colours:** Red and yellow striped shirts, black shorts.
Manager: Murdo MacLeod.
League Appearances: Adams C 1(4); Ayton S 1(4); Cairns M 3; Cameron I 32(3); Craig A 9; Curran H 3(4); Dinnie A 31; Docherty S 19(5); Foster W 19; Gibson A 8(13); Henderson N 12(4); Lyons A 9; MacLeod M 1; Macdonald W 11(6); McCue J 2(1); McDonald R 12(4); McKee K 10(1); McMahon S (1); McWilliams D 25(2); Milne C 19(3); Pittman S 14; Shepherd A (1); Slavin J 8; Smith T 24(1); Stirling J 2; Tierney G 1; Turner T 20(2); Walker N 33; Watson G 32; Welsh S 35
Goals–League (29): Lyons 5, McDonald R 5, Docherty 3, McWilliams 3, Turner 3, Craig 2, Smith 2, Cameron 1, Foster 1, Gibson 1, Henderson 1, Macdonald W 1, Watson 1.
Scottish Cup (0).
Coca-Cola Cup (10): Craig 4, McWilliams 2, Curran 1, Foster 1, McDonald R 1, Pittman 1.

QUEEN OF THE SOUTH   DIV. 2

Ground: Palmerston Park, Dumfries DG2 9BA (01387) 254853
Ground capacity: 8352. **Colours:** Royal blue shirts, white shorts.
Co-Managers: Rowan Alexander and Mark Shanks.
League Appearances: Alexander R (1); Allen C 1; Brown J 9(6); Bryce T 35(1); Burridge J 6; Butter J 26; Campbell C 15(1); Campbell D 11(6); Cody S 13(3); Dobie M 17(1); Graham C (3); Harris C 25(8); Hetherington K 6; Jackson D 4(1); Kennedy D 34(1); Leslie S 10(3); Lilley D 23; Mallan S 27(5); McAllister J 2; McColm R 4; McFarlane A 23(2); McKeown B 30(1); McKeown D 30(3); McLaren J 10(13); Millar J (1); Pettit S (1); Ramsay S 16(10); Telfer G (2); Wilson S 19(5)
Goals–League (54): Mallan 12, Bryce 10, Harris 9 (1 pen), Dobie 6, McLaren 6, Campbell D 3 (1 pen), Wilson 2, Cody 1, Jackson 1, McFarlane 1, Telfer 1, own goals 2.
Scottish Cup (2): Bryce 1 (pen), Mallan 1.
Coca-Cola Cup (3): Campbell D 1, Harris 1, Mallan 1 (pen).
League Challenge Cup (0).

QUEEN'S PARK   DIV. 3

Ground: Hampden Park, Glasgow G42 9BA (0141) 632 1275
Ground capacity: 38,335. **Colours:** Black and white hooped shirts, white shorts.
Coach: Hugh McCann.
League Appearances: Arbuckle J 35; Brodie D 7(11); Bruce G 8; Callan D 23(7); Caven R 31; Chalmers J 28; Edgar S 28(5); Elder G 26; Ferguson P 23; Ferry D 9(8); Fraser R 13(3); Graham D 32(1); Kennedy K (7); Kerr G 4(4); Matchett J 3(2); Maxwell I 29; McCusker J 3(4); McGinlay M (1); McGoldrick K 36; McGrath D 5(1); McInally A 4(4); McPhee B 20(12); Orr G 11(1); Porter C 6(10); Smith M 1; Ward J 1(1); Wilson D 10(3)
Goals–League (40): Edgar 6, McGoldrick 6, Ferry 5, McPhee 5, Caven 4, Fraser 2, Graham 2, McCusker 2, Maxwell 2, Orr 2, Arbuckle 1, Callan 1, Porter 1, own goal 1.
Scottish Cup (4): Edgar 3, McGoldrick 1.
Coca-Cola Cup (1): McPhee 1.
League Challenge Cup (0).

RAITH ROVERS   PREM. DIV.

Ground: Stark's Park, Pratt Street, Kirkcaldy KY1 1SA (01592) 263514
Ground capacity: 9300. **Colours:** Navy blue shirts, white shorts.
Manager: Jimmy Thomson.
League Appearances: Bonar P 4(1); Broddle J 23(4); Buist M 2; Cameron C 30; Coyle R 22(2); Crawford S 21(7); Dair J 18(1); Dargo C (1); Dennis S 25; Duffield P 9; Forrest G (1); Fridge L 1; Geddes R 9; Graham A 18(7); Humphries M 9; Kirk S 6(1); Kirkwood D 25(3); Krivokapic M 5; Landells G (1); Lennon D 31(3); McAnespie S 2(1); McCulloch G 7; McInally J 23(2); McKilligan N 1(2); McMillan I 4(4); Millar J 3; Nicholl J (1); Raeside R 6(2); Rougier A 17(5); Sellars N (1); Sinclair D 31(1); Taylor A 1(9); Thomson SM 9; Thomson SY 26; Wilson B 8(5)

Goals–League (41): Cameron 9, Duffield 5, Graham 5, Lennon 5, Crawford 3, Dair 3, Sinclair 3, Kirkwood 2, Kirk 1, McCulloch 1 (pen), Millar 1, Raeside 1, Rougier 1, Thomson SM 1.
Scottish Cup (3): Crawford 2, Lennon 1.
Coca-Cola Cup (3): Kirkwood 2, Rougier 1.

RANGERS   PREM. DIV.

Ground: Ibrox Stadium, Glasgow G51 2XD (0141) 427 8500
Ground capacity: 50,500. **Colours:** Royal blue shirts, red and white trim, white shorts.
Manager: Walter Smith.
League Appearances: Andersen E 6; Bollan G 4; Brown J 8(6); Cleland A 21(4); Durie D 21(6); Durrant I 6(9); Ferguson I 16(2); Gascoigne P 27(1); Goram A 30; Gough R 29; Laudrup B 22; McCall S 19(2); McCoist A 18(7); McGinty B 2; McInnes D 5(1); McLaren A 36; Mikhailichenko A 6(5); Miller C 17(6); Moore C 9(2); Murray N 2(3); Petric G 32(1); Robertson D 25; Salenko O 14(2); Scott C 3; Shields G 1; Snelders T 2; Steven T 5(1); Thomson W 1; Van Vossen P 3(4); Wright S 6
Goals–League (85): Durie 17 (2 pens), McCoist 16 (3 pens), Gascoigne 14 (2 pens), Salenko 7, Andersen 6, Gough 3, McCall 3, McLaren 3, Miller 3, Robertson 3, Ferguson 2, Laudrup 2 (1 pen), Cleland 1, Moore 1, Petric 1, own goals 3.
Scottish Cup (24): Durie 4 (1 pen), Cleland 3, Ferguson 3, Gascoigne 3, Laudrup 3, Miller 3, McCoist 1, Mikhailichenko 1, Robertson 1, Van Vossen 1, own goal 1.
Coca-Cola Cup (8): McCoist 3, Hateley 2, Gascoigne 1, McCall 1, Salenko 1.

ROSS COUNTY   DIV. 3

Ground: Victoria Park, Dingwall IV15 9QW (01349) 862253
Ground capacity: 5400. **Colours:** Dark blue shirts, white shorts.
Manager: Neale Cooper.
League Appearances: Bellshaw J 35; Bradshaw P 4(4); Connelly G 27(4); Crainie D 5; Ferries K 31(5); Furphy W 28(3); Golabek S 22; Grant B 16(18); Herd W 36; Hutchison S 32; MacLeod A 15(10); MacPherson J 19(5); Mackay D 36; McFee R (13); McMillan D 4; Milne C 31(3); Robertson C 11(6); Ruickbie R 1(4); Somerville C 23(1); Stewart R (1); Watt W 2(3); Williamson R 18(3)
Goals–League (56): Milne 15 (3 pens), MacPherson 12, Grant 11, Connelly 3, MacLeod 3, Bellshaw 2, Ferries 2, Golabek 2, Somerville 2, Williamson 2, Bradshaw 1, Furphy 1.
Scottish Cup (2): Robertson 1, own goal 1.
Coca-Cola Cup (0).
League Challenge Cup (2): Connelly 1, Milne 1.

ST JOHNSTONE   DIV. 1

Ground: McDiarmid Park, Crieff Road, Perth PH1 2SJ (01738) 626961
Ground capacity: 10,721. **Colours:** Royal blue shirts with white trim, white shorts.
Manager: Paul Sturrock.
League Appearances: Cherry P 13(2); Davidson C 1; Donaldson E 15; English I

(1); Farquhar G 10(5); Ferguson I 3(7); Grant R 19(8); Griffin D 22(9); Irons D 9(8); Jenkinson L 18; Main A 34; McCluskey S 2; McGowne K 23; McLean S 1(5); McQuillan J 25; O'Boyle G 35; O'Neil J 34; Preston A 25(2); Proctor M 2(4); Robertson S 2; Scott P 28; Sekerlioglu A 17; Tosh S 8(1); Twaddle K 17(9); Weir J 29; Whiteford A 3(1); Young S 1(3)

Goals–League (60): O'Boyle 21, Scott 8, O'Neil 6, Grant 5, Twaddle 4, Jenkinson 2, McGowne 2, McQuillan 2, Preston 2, Sekerlioglu 2, Farquhar 1, Ferguson 1, Griffin 1, Tosh 1, own goals 2.
Scottish Cup (5): Scott 3, Grant 1, O'Boyle 1.
Coca-Cola Cup (1): O'Boyle 1.
League Challenge Cup (2): O'Neil 1, Scott 1.

ST MIRREN   DIV. 1

Ground: St Mirren Park, Paisley PA3 2EJ (0141) 889 2558, 840 1337
Ground capacity: 15,410. **Colours:** Black and white striped shirts, black shorts.
Manager: Jimmy Bone.
League Appearances: Archdeacon P 16(4); Baker M 26; Bone A 3(2); Boyd J 12(2); Combe A 20; Dawson R 8; Dick J 24(2); Fenwick P 26; Fullarton J 19(3); Galloway G 1; Gillies R 28(5); Hetherston B 16(7); Hringsson H (1); Inglis G (1); Iwelumo C 2(3); Lavety B 27(2); Law R 14(5); Love F (1); Makele J 1; McGrotty G 3(7); McIntyre P 20(6); McLaughlin B 29(1); McMillan J (8); McWhirter N 17; Milne D 1(4); Money C 13; Prentice A (2); Scrimgour D 3; Smith B 6(6); Taylor S 14(10); Watson S 18(12); Yardley M 29

Goals–League (46): Lavety 11, Yardley 8 (1 pen), Boyd 3, Fenwick 3, Gillies 3, Taylor 3, Archdeacon 2, Dick 2, Fullarton 2, Hetherston 2, McLaughlin 2, Bone 1, Iwelumo 1, McMillan 1, Watson 1, own goal 1.
Scottish Cup (0).
Coca-Cola Cup (1): McLaughlin 1.
League Challenge Cup (3): Lavety 2, Dawson 1 (pen).

STENHOUSEMUIR   DIV. 2

Ground: Ochilview Park, Stenhousemuir FK5 5QL (01324) 562992
Ground capacity: 3520. **Colours:** Maroon shirts with silver trim, white shorts.
Manager: Terry Christie.
League Appearances: Aitken N 7(14); Armstrong G 34; Bannon E 29; Brannigan K 11; Christie M 18(1); Clarke J (1); Fisher J 33; Haddow L 24(2); Henderson J 6(5); Hunter P 25(3); Hutchison G 35(1); Little G 2(5); Little I 33; Logan P 8(6); Mathieson M 30(1); McGeachie G 21(1); McKenzie R 36; Roseburgh D 6(4); Scott C 6(2); Sprott A 30(1); Steel T 1(2); Swanson D 1(3)

Goals–League (51): Mathieson 10, Hutchison 9, Little I 9, Hunter 8, Sprott 8, Fisher 2, Aitken 1, Bannon 1, Henderson 1, Logan 1, own goal 1.
Scottish Cup (6): Little I 2, Hutchison 1, McGeachie 1, Mathieson 1, own goal 1.
Coca-Cola Cup (1): Hutchison.
League Challenge Cup (8): Hutchison 4, Little I 1, Logan 1, Mathieson 1, own goal 1.

STIRLING ALBION   DIV. 1

Ground: Forthbank Stadium, Springkerse Industrial Estate, Stirling FK7 7UJ (01786) 450399
Ground capacity: 3808. Colours: Red shirts with white sleeves, white shorts.
Manager: Kevin Drinkell.
League Appearances: Bennett N 1(7); Bone A 27; Deas P 35; Farquhar A (3); Gibson J 18(11); Kirkham D (2); McCormick S 33; McGeown M 26; McGrotty G 2(4); McInnes I 15(1); McKechnie M 3; McLeod J 23(3); McQuilter R 35; Mitchell C 32(4); Monaghan M 10; Paterson A 33; Paterson G 26; Roberts P (3); Taggart C 33(2); Tait T 28; Watson P 5(3); Watters W (2); Wood D 11(3)
Goals–League (83): McCormick 25, Bone 18, Taggart 8, Tait 7, Gibson 6, McInnes 4, Paterson G 4, McQuilter 3, McLeod 2, Mitchell 2, Wood 2, Watson 1, own goal 1.
Scottish Cup (4): McCormick 3, Mitchell 1.
Coca-Cola Cup (4): McCormick 1, McLeod 1, Taggart 1, Tait 1.
Goals–League Challenge Cup (9): McCormick 3, McLeod 2, Tait 2, Gibson 1, Taggart 1.

STRANRAER   DIV. 2

Ground: Stair Park, Stranraer DG9 8BS (01776) 703271
Ground capacity: 6100. Colours: Royal blue shirts with geometrical design, white shorts.
Manager: Campbell Money.
League Appearances: Bilsland B 4(6); Callaghan T 2(7); Connelly D 3(2); Crawford D 12(2); Duffy B 9; Duncan G 29(4); Ferguson W 1(10); Gallagher A 18(1); Grant A 18(4); Henderson D 20; Howard N 28(2); Hughes J 32; Kerrigan S 19(2); McAulay I 23(2); McCaffrey J 7; McGowan N 1(3); McGuire D 5(10); McLean P 1(3); McMillan J 4(2); Millar G 19(2); Pickering M (1); Reilly R 14(9); Robertson J 33(1); Ross G 27; Shepherd A 2; Skippen R (1); Sloan T 36; Walker T 29(3)**Goals–League** (38): Grant 6, Kerrigan 5, Walker 4, Duncan 3, Henderson 3, Sloan 3, Ferguson 2, McGuire 2, McMillan 2, Bilsland 1, Crawford 1, Howard 1, Hughes 1, McAulay 1, Reilly 1, Robertson 1, own goal 1.
Scottish Cup (0).
Coca-Cola Cup (0).
League Challenge Cup (0).

BELL'S SCOTTISH LEAGUE—PREMIER DIVISION RESULTS 1995–96

	Aberdeen	Celtic	Falkirk	Hearts	Hibernian	Kilmarnock	Motherwell	Partick T	Raith R	Rangers
Aberdeen	—	2-3	3-1	1-2	1-2	4-1	1-0	3-0	3-0	0-1
Celtic	2-0	—	2-1	1-1	2-1	3-0	2-1	1-0	0-0	0-1
Falkirk	5-0	—	—	3-1	2-2	4-2	1-1	2-0	4-1	0-2
Hearts	2-3	0-1	4-0	—	2-0	1-1	1-0	4-0	2-1	0-0
Hibernian	1-1	0-0	0-2	0-2	—	0-2	0-0	0-1	2-3	0-4
Kilmarnock	1-3	1-2	4-1	2-2	2-1	—	0-1	1-2	4-2	0-2
Motherwell	1-2	0-4	2-1	2-1	1-1	1-0	—	3-0	2-0	2-0
Partick T	1-2	1-2	2-1	3-1	—	1-0	4-0	—	1-2	1-4
Raith R	2-1	0-0	4-0	0-2	0-3	2-0	4-2	0-3	—	0-2
Rangers	1-1	3-3	2-0	4-1	7-0	3-0	3-2	5-0	4-0	—

BELL'S SCOTTISH LEAGUE—DIVISION ONE RESULTS 1995–96

	Airdrie	Clydebank	Dumbarton	Dundee	Dundee U	Dunfermline	Gr Morton	Hamilton Ac	St Johnstone	St Mirren
Airdrie	—	1-1	2-1	2-3	1-1	0-1	3-2	0-0	1-1	1-2
Clydebank	1-1	—	5-1	0-0	1-1	1-2	0-2	3-0	1-3	1-3
Dumbarton	2-1	1-2	—	0-1	1-0	0-4	0-1	1-3	2-0	1-1
Dundee	1-2	0-1	1-5	—	2-3	2-3	0-2	1-0	1-2	1-2
Dundee U	1-2	3-0	8-0	2-3	—	0-3	0-0	2-1	0-3	0-0
Dunfermline	2-0	2-1	6-1	2-0	3-0	—	4-0	4-0	2-1	3-1
Gr Morton	3-0	4-3	1-2	1-1	2-2	2-0	—	1-3	3-2	1-2
Hamilton Ac	4-1	1-1	3-0	0-2	0-0	1-0	0-2	—	2-1	1-0
St Johnstone	0-0	3-1	4-1	1-0	1-1	0-2	6-1	4-1	—	1-0
St Mirren	2-1	1-2	5-0	2-1	1-3	2-1	0-1	0-1	1-3	—

BELL'S SCOTTISH LEAGUE—DIVISION TWO RESULTS 1995-96

(home \ away)	Ayr U	Berwick R	Clyde	East Fife	Forfar Ath	Montrose	Queen o' South	Stenhousemuir	Stirling A	Stranraer
Ayr U	—	1-4, 5-0	1-1, 2-1	0-1, 1-0	1-3, 1-1	2-0, 2-0	2-0, 3-0	1-2, 2-1	1-2, 2-2	0-0, 0-0
Berwick R	2-2, 2-1	—	0-0, 2-1	0-1, 1-2	1-1, 1-0	2-2, 4-1	0-0, 4-1	3-1, 0-1	3-0, 0-3	4-0, 1-0
Clyde	1-2, 2-0	3-1, 2-1	—	0-1, 2-2	1-0, 1-2	3-0, 1-3	2-1, 0-0	1-0, 3-0	1-2, 1-3	1-1, 2-2
East Fife	1-0, 1-1	1-0, 0-0	1-0, 1-1	—	3-1, 1-0	3-0, 7-0	2-1, 3-0	0-2, 3-1	0-3, 0-1	3-3, 2-1
Forfar Ath	2-1, 1-0	1-4, 1-3	4-2, 0-0	0-2, 0-2	—	0-0, 2-1	1-2, 2-1	1-0, 3-1	0-6, 1-4	2-1, 0-0
Montrose	0-1, 1-3	0-1, 1-2	2-3, 0-3	1-2, 0-1	1-0, 3-1	—	0-3, 1-4	1-4, 1-3	2-2, 2-1	2-2, 4-2
Queen o' South	0-1, 1-4	0-0, 1-4	2-1, 1-0	0-2, 1-0	1-1, 4-1	1-4, 0-6	—	2-2, 3-3	1-5, 0-7	0-1, 0-3
Stenhousemuir	0-0, 2-2	4-1, 0-3	1-0, 1-1	2-2, 0-2	3-1, 0-2	3-1, 1-3	1-3, 2-2	—		3-0, 2-0
Stirling A	1-1, 2-0	2-0, 4-3	3-0, 0-0	2-2, 2-0	4-1, 1-0	4-2, 1-1	1-3, 2-2	2-1, 0-1	—	1-1, 2-0
Stranraer	2-0, 1-1	2-0, 0-3	0-0, 2-2	2-0, 0-0	1-1, 1-2	3-1, 1-2	4-1, 3-1	2-1, 0-0	0-0, 2-2	—

BELL'S SCOTTISH LEAGUE—DIVISION THREE RESULTS 1995–96

	Albion Rovers	Alloa	Arbroath	Brechin C	Caledonian T	Cowdenbeath	East Stirling	Livingston	Queen's Park	Ross Co
Albion Rovers	—	2-1	0-2	1-0	2-2	2-3	1-2	0-2	3-1	3-4
Alloa	3-2	—	1-1	1-0	0-2	2-0	2-2	0-1	0-2	0-3
Arbroath	3-1	1-0	—	0-3	0-1	2-1	1-3	0-2	0-0	1-0
Brechin C	2-0	1-1	0-1	—	1-2	0-0	3-0	1-0	1-1	1-2
Caledonian T	6-1	3-0	5-1	1-2	—	3-2	4-2	0-3	3-2	2-1
Cowdenbeath	1-1	1-0	1-1	0-0	2-0	—	1-4	1-2	1-2	0-0
East Stirling	5-1	3-0	1-0	3-0	0-5	3-1	—	0-3	2-0	1-1
Livingston	2-1	1-0	3-0	1-0	0-2	2-1	1-1	—	2-0	2-0
Queen's Park	4-1	0-0	0-2	0-0	3-1	2-2	1-0	1-2	—	1-2
Ross Co	1-1	0-0	1-2	0-0	2-1	4-1	1-3	2-2	0-1	—

SCOTTISH LEAGUE 1995–96

Premier Division

	P	W	D	L	F	A	W	D	L	F	A	Pt	GD
		Home			Goals		Away			Goals			
Rangers	36	13	3	2	47	16	14	3	1	38	9	87	+60
Celtic	36	12	5	1	40	12	12	6	0	34	13	83	+49
Aberdeen	36	11	1	6	31	17	5	6	7	21	28	55	+7
Hearts	36	10	2	6	33	26	5	5	7	22	27	55	+2
Hibernian	36	7	5	6	25	26	4	5	9	18	31	43	–14
Raith R	36	7	5	6	23	21	5	2	11	18	36	43	–16
Kilmarnock	36	8	4	6	25	21	3	4	11	14	33	41	–15
Motherwell	36	6	6	6	15	16	3	6	9	13	23	39	–11
Partick T	36	3	5	10	12	28	5	1	12	17	34	30	–33
Falkirk	36	4	4	10	17	26	2	2	14	14	34	24	–29

First Division

	P	W	D	L	F	A	W	D	L	F	A	Pt	GD
		Home			Goals		Away			Goals			
Dunfermline Ath	36	11	4	3	40	23	10	4	4	33	18	71	+32
Dundee U	36	11	3	4	47	18	8	7	3	26	19	67	+36
Greenock Morton	36	10	4	4	32	16	10	3	5	25	23	67	+18
St Johnstone	36	11	5	2	33	14	8	7	3	27	22	65	+24
Dundee	36	5	5	8	24	20	10	4	4	29	20	57	+13
St Mirren	36	6	2	10	23	30	7	6	5	23	21	47	–5
Clydebank	36	6	4	8	20	24	4	6	8	19	34	40	–19
Airdrieonians	36	4	7	7	24	25	5	4	9	19	29	38	–11
Hamilton A	36	5	3	10	22	26	5	3	10	18	31	36	–17
Dumbarton	36	2	1	15	10	36	1	1	16	13	58	11	–71

Second Division

	P	W	D	L	F	A	W	D	L	F	A	Pt	GD
		Home			Goals		Away			Goals			
Stirling Albion	36	12	4	2	36	15	12	5	1	47	15	81	+53
East Fife	36	8	6	4	27	17	11	4	3	23	12	67	+21
Berwick R	36	10	4	4	32	18	8	2	8	32	29	60	+17
Stenhousemuir	36	8	3	7	26	21	6	4	8	25	28	49	+2
Clyde	36	7	4	7	28	23	4	8	6	19	22	45	+2
Ayr U	36	7	6	5	26	18	4	6	8	14	22	45	0
Queen of the S	36	6	6	6	27	38	5	4	9	27	29	43	–13
Stranraer	36	6	10	2	21	14	2	8	8	17	29	42	–5
Forfar Ath	36	8	3	7	21	32	3	4	11	16	29	40	–24
Montrose	36	3	4	13	18	39	2	3	13	15	47	20	–53

Third Division

	P	W	D	L	F	A	W	D	L	F	A	Pt	GD
		Home			Goals		Away			Goals			
Livingston	36	8	5	5	21	14	13	4	1	30	10	72	+27
Brechin C	36	10	3	5	25	9	8	6	4	16	12	63	+20
Caledonian T	36	5	8	5	28	23	10	4	4	36	15	57	+26
Ross County	36	6	9	3	30	20	6	8	4	26	19	53	+17
Arbroath	36	6	7	5	22	21	7	6	5	19	20	52	0
Queen's Park	36	6	8	4	21	15	6	4	8	19	28	48	–3
East Stirling	36	6	3	9	26	32	5	8	5	32	30	44	–4
Cowdenbeath	36	7	5	6	26	23	3	2	12	19	36	38	–14
Alloa	36	5	3	10	18	37	1	8	9	8	21	29	–32
Albion R	36	4	4	9	20	28	2	4	12	17	46	29	–37

PLAY-OFF: Partick T (9th place, Premier Division) v Dundee U (runners-up, First Division)

SCOTTISH LEAGUE HONOURS

*On goal average/difference. †Held jointly after indecisive play-off.
‡Won on deciding match. ††Held jointly. ¶Two points deducted for
fielding ineligible player. Competition suspended 1940–45 during war.
‡‡Two points deducted for registration irregularities.

PREMIER DIVISION

Maximum points: 72

	First	Pts	Second	Pts	Third	Pts
1975–76	Rangers	54	Celtic	48	Hibernian	43
1976–77	Celtic	55	Rangers	46	Aberdeen	43
1977–78	Rangers	55	Aberdeen	53	Dundee U	40
1978–79	Celtic	48	Rangers	45	Dundee U	44
1979–80	Aberdeen	48	Celtic	47	St Mirren	42
1980–81	Celtic	56	Aberdeen	49	Rangers*	44
1981–82	Celtic	55	Aberdeen	53	Rangers	43
1982–83	Dundee U	56	Celtic*	55	Aberdeen	55
1983–84	Aberdeen	57	Celtic	50	Dundee U	47
1984–85	Aberdeen	59	Celtic	52	Dundee U	47
1985–86	Celtic*	50	Hearts	50	Dundee U	47

Maximum points: 88

	First	Pts	Second	Pts	Third	Pts
1986–87	Rangers	69	Celtic	63	Dundee U	60
1987–88	Celtic	72	Hearts	62	Rangers	60

Maximum points: 72

	First	Pts	Second	Pts	Third	Pts
1988–89	Rangers	56	Aberdeen	50	Celtic	46
1989–90	Rangers	51	Aberdeen*	44	Hearts	44
1990–91	Rangers	55	Aberdeen	53	Celtic*	41

Maximum points: 88

	First	Pts	Second	Pts	Third	Pts
1991–92	Rangers	72	Hearts	63	Celtic	62
1992–93	Rangers	73	Aberdeen	64	Celtic	60
1993–94	Rangers	58	Aberdeen	55	Motherwell	54

Maximum points: 108

	First	Pts	Second	Pts	Third	Pts
1994–95	Rangers	69	Motherwell	54	Hibernian	53
1995–96	Rangers	87	Celtic	83	Aberdeen*	55

DIVISION 1

Maximum points: 52

	First	Pts	Second	Pts	Third	Pts
1975–76	Partick T	41	Kilmarnock	35	Montrose	30

Maximum points: 78

	First	Pts	Second	Pts	Third	Pts
1976–77	St Mirren	62	Clydebank	58	Dundee	51
1977–78	Morton*	58	Hearts	58	Dundee	57
1978–79	Dundee	55	Kilmarnock*	54	Clydebank	54
1979–80	Hearts	53	Airdrieonians	51	Ayr U*	44
1980–81	Hibernian	57	Dundee	52	St Johnstone	51
1981–82	Motherwell	61	Kilmarnock	51	Hearts	50
1982–83	St Johnstone	55	Hearts	54	Clydebank	50
1983–84	Morton	54	Dumbarton	51	Partick T	46
1984–85	Motherwell	50	Clydebank	48	Falkirk	45
1985–86	Hamilton A	56	Falkirk	45	Kilmarnock	44

161

	First	Pts	Second	Pts	Third	Pts
1986–87	Morton	57	Dunfermline Ath	56	Dumbarton	53
1987–88	Hamilton A	56	Meadowbank T	52	Clydebank	49

Maximum points: 78

1988–89	Dunfermline Ath	54	Falkirk	52	Clydebank	48
1989–90	St Johnstone	58	Airdrieonians	54	Clydebank	44
1990–91	Falkirk	54	Airdrieonians	53	Dundee	52

Maximum points: 88

1991–92	Dundee	58	Partick T*	57	Hamilton A	57
1992–93	Raith R	65	Kilmarnock	54	Dunfermline Ath	52
1993–94	Falkirk	66	Dunfermline Ath	65	Airdrieonians	54

Maximum points: 108

1994–95	Raith R	69	Dunfermline Ath*	68	Dundee	68
1995–96	Dunfermline Ath	71	Dundee U*	67	Morton	67

DIVISION 2

Maximum points: 52

1975–76	Clydebank*	40	Raith R	40	Alloa	35

Maximum points: 78

1976–77	Stirling A	55	Alloa	51	Dunfermline Ath	50
1977–78	Clyde*	53	Raith R	53	Dunfermline Ath	48
1978–79	Berwick R	54	Dunfermline Ath	52	Falkirk	50
1979–80	Falkirk	50	East Stirling	49	Forfar Ath	46
1980–81	Queen's Park	50	Queen of the S	46	Cowdenbeath	45
1981–82	Clyde	59	Alloa*	50	Arbroath	50
1982–83	Brechin C	55	Meadowbank T	54	Arbroath	49
1983–84	Forfar Ath	63	East Fife	47	Berwick R	43
1984–85	Montrose	53	Alloa	50	Dunfermline Ath	49
1985–86	Dunfermline Ath	57	Queen of the S	55	Meadowbank T	49
1986–87	Meadowbank T	55	Raith R*	52	Stirling A*	52
1987–88	Ayr U	61	St Johnstone	59	Queen's Park	51
1988–89	Albion R	50	Alloa	45	Brechin C	43
1989–90	Brechin C	49	Kilmarnock	48	Stirling A	47
1990–91	Stirling A	54	Montrose	46	Cowdenbeath	45
1991–92	Dumbarton	52	Cowdenbeath	51	Alloa	50
1992–93	Clyde	54	Brechin C*	53	Stranraer	53
1993–94	Stranraer	56	Berwick R	48	Stenhousemuir*	47

Maximum points: 108

1994–95	Morton	64	Dumbarton	60	Stirling A	58
1995–96	Stirling A	81	East Fife	67	Berwick R	60

DIVISION 3

Maximum points: 108

1994–95	Forfar Ath	80	Montrose	67	Ross Co	60
1995–96	Livingston	72	Brechin C	63	Caledonian T	57

DIVISION 1 to 1974–75

Maximum points: a 36; b 44; c 40; d 52; e 60; f 68; g 76; h 84.

	First	Pts	Second	Pts	Third	Pts
1890–91a	Dumbarton††	29	Rangers††	29	Celtic	21
1891–92b	Dumbarton	37	Celtic	35	Hearts	34

Season	1st	Pts	2nd	Pts	3rd	Pts
1892–93a	Celtic	29	Rangers	28	St Mirren	20
1893–94a	Celtic	29	Hearts	26	St Bernard's	23
1894–95a	Hearts	31	Celtic	26	Rangers	22
1895–96a	Celtic	30	Rangers	26	Hibernian	24
1896–97a	Hearts	28	Hibernian	26	Rangers	25
1897–98a	Celtic	33	Rangers	29	Hibernian	22
1898–99a	Rangers	36	Hearts	26	Celtic	24
1899–						
1900a	Rangers	32	Celtic	25	Hibernian	24
1900–01c	Rangers	35	Celtic	29	Hibernian	25
1901–02a	Rangers	28	Celtic	26	Hearts	22
1902–03b	Hibernian	37	Dundee	31	Rangers	29
1903–04d	Third Lanark	43	Hearts	39	Celtic*	38
1904–05d	Celtic‡	41	Rangers	41	Third Lanark	35
1905–06e	Celtic	49	Hearts	43	Airdrieonians	38
1906–07f	Celtic	55	Dundee	48	Rangers	45
1907–08f	Celtic	55	Falkirk	51	Rangers	50
1908–09f	Celtic	51	Dundee	50	Clyde	48
1909–10f	Celtic	54	Falkirk	52	Rangers	46
1910–11f	Rangers	52	Aberdeen	48	Falkirk	44
1911–12f	Rangers	51	Celtic	45	Clyde	42
1912–13f	Rangers	53	Celtic	49	Hearts*	41
1913–14g	Celtic	65	Rangers	59	Hearts*	54
1914–15g	Celtic	65	Hearts	61	Rangers	50
1915–16g	Celtic	67	Rangers	56	Morton	51
1916–17g	Celtic	64	Morton	54	Rangers	53
1917–18f	Rangers	56	Celtic	55	Kilmarnock*	43
1918–19f	Celtic	58	Rangers	57	Morton	47
1919–20h	Rangers	71	Celtic	68	Motherwell	57
1920–21h	Rangers	76	Celtic	66	Hearts	50
1921–22h	Celtic	67	Rangers	66	Raith R	51
1922–23g	Rangers	55	Airdrieonians	50	Celtic	46
1923–24g	Rangers	59	Airdrieonians	50	Celtic	46
1924–25g	Rangers	60	Airdrieonians	57	Hibernian	52
1925–26g	Celtic	58	Airdrieonians*	50	Hearts	50
1926–27g	Rangers	56	Motherwell	51	Celtic	49
1927–28g	Rangers	60	Celtic*	55	Motherwell	55
1928–29g	Rangers	67	Celtic	51	Motherwell	50
1929–30g	Rangers	60	Motherwell	55	Aberdeen	53
1930–31g	Rangers	60	Celtic	58	Motherwell	56
1931–32g	Motherwell	66	Rangers	61	Celtic	48
1932–33g	Rangers	62	Motherwell	59	Hearts	50
1933–34g	Rangers	66	Motherwell	62	Celtic	47
1934–35g	Rangers	55	Celtic	52	Hearts	50
1935–36g	Celtic	66	Rangers*	61	Aberdeen	61
1936–37g	Rangers	61	Aberdeen	54	Celtic	52
1937–38g	Celtic	61	Hearts	58	Rangers	49
1938–39g	Rangers	59	Celtic	48	Aberdeen	46
1946–47e	Rangers	46	Hibernian	44	Aberdeen	39
1947–48e	Hibernian	48	Rangers	46	Partick T	36
1948–49e	Rangers	46	Dundee	45	Hibernian	39
1949–50e	Rangers	50	Hibernian	49	Hearts	43
1950–51e	Hibernian	48	Rangers*	38	Dundee	38

1951–52e Hibernian	45	Rangers	41	East Fife	37
1952–53e Rangers*	43	Hibernian	43	East Fife	39
1953–54e Celtic	43	Hearts	38	Partick T	35
1954–55e Aberdeen	49	Celtic	46	Rangers	41
1955–56f Rangers	52	Aberdeen	46	Hearts*	45
1956–57f Rangers	55	Hearts	53	Kilmarnock	42
1957–58f Hearts	62	Rangers	49	Celtic	46
1958–59f Rangers	50	Hearts	48	Motherwell	44
1959–60f Hearts	54	Kilmarnock	50	Rangers*	42
1960–61f Rangers	51	Kilmarnock	50	Third Lanark	42
1961–62f Dundee	54	Rangers	51	Celtic	46
1962–63f Rangers	57	Kilmarnock	48	Partick T	46
1963–64f Rangers	55	Kilmarnock	49	Celtic*	47
1964–65f Kilmarnock*	50	Hearts	50	Dunfermline Ath	49
1965–66f Celtic	57	Rangers	55	Kilmarnock	45
1966–67f Celtic	58	Rangers	55	Clyde	46
1967–68f Celtic	63	Rangers	61	Hibernian	45
1968–69f Celtic	54	Rangers	49	Dunfermline Ath	45
1969–70f Celtic	57	Rangers	45	Hibernian	44
1970–71f Celtic	56	Aberdeen	54	St Johnstone	44
1971–72f Celtic	60	Aberdeen	50	Rangers	44
1972–73f Celtic	57	Rangers	56	Hibernian	45
1973–74f Celtic	53	Hibernian	49	Rangers	48
1974–75f Rangers	56	Hibernian	49	Celtic	45

DIVISION 2 to 1974–75

Maximum points: a 76; b 72; c 68; d 52; e 60; f 36; g 44.

1893–94f Hibernian	29	Cowlairs	27	Clyde	24
1894–95f Hibernian	30	Motherwell	22	Port Glasgow	20
1895–96f Abercorn	27	Leith Ath	23	Renton	21
1896–97f Partick T	31	Leith Ath	27	Kilmarnock*	21
1897–98f Kilmarnock	29	Port Glasgow	25	Morton	22
1898–99f Kilmarnock	32	Leith Ath	27	Port Glasgow	25
1899–1900f Partick T	29	Morton	28	Port Glasgow	20
1900–01f St Bernard's	25	Airdrieonians	23	Abercorn	21
1901–02g Port Glasgow	32	Partick T	31	Motherwell	26
1902–03g Airdrieonians	35	Motherwell	28	Ayr U*	27
1903–04g Hamilton A	37	Clyde	29	Ayr U	28
1904–05g Clyde	32	Falkirk	28	Hamilton A	27
1905–06g Leith Ath	34	Clyde	28	Albion R	27
1906–07g St Bernard's	32	Vale of Leven*	27	Arthurlie	27
1907–08g Raith R	30	Dumbarton	‡‡27	Ayr U	27
1908–09g Abercorn	31	Raith R*	28	Vale of Leven	28
1909–10g Leith Ath‡	33	Raith R	33	St Bernard's	27
1910–11g Dumbarton	31	Ayr U	27	Albion R	25
1911–12g Ayr U	35	Abercorn	30	Dumbarton	27
1912–13d Ayr U	34	Dunfermline Ath	33	East Stirling	32
1913–14g Cowdenbeath	31	Albion R	27	Dunfermline Ath*	26

164

Season	Champions		Runners-up		Third	
1914–15d	Cowdenbeath*	37	St Bernard's*	37	Leith Ath	37
1921–22a	Alloa	60	Cowdenbeath	47	Armadale	45
1922–23a	Queen's Park	57	Clydebank ¶	50	St Johnstone ¶	45
1923–24a	St Johnstone	56	Cowdenbeath	55	Bathgate	44
1924–25a	Dundee U	50	Clydebank	48	Clyde	47
1925–26a	Dunfermline Ath	59	Clyde	53	Ayr U	52
1926–27a	Bo'ness	56	Raith R	49	Clydebank	45
1927–28a	Ayr U	54	Third Lanark	45	King's Park	44
1928–29b	Dundee U	51	Morton	50	Arbroath	47
1929–30a	Leith Ath*	57	East Fife	57	Albion R	54
1930–31a	Third Lanark	61	Dundee U	50	Dunfermline Ath	47
1931–32a	East Stirling*	55	St Johnstone	55	Raith R*	46
1932–33c	Hibernian	54	Queen of the S	49	Dunfermline Ath	47
1933–34c	Albion R	45	Dunfermline Ath*	44	Arbroath	44
1934–35c	Third Lanark	52	Arbroath	50	St Bernard's	47
1935–36c	Falkirk	59	St Mirren	52	Morton	48
1936–37c	Ayr U	54	Morton	51	St Bernard's	48
1937–38c	Raith R	59	Albion R	48	Airdrieonians	47
1938–39c	Cowdenbeath	60	Alloa*	48	East Fife	48
1946–47d	Dundee	45	Airdrieonians	42	East Fife	31
1947–48e	East Fife	53	Albion R	42	Hamilton A	40
1948–49e	Raith R*	42	Stirling A	42	Airdrieonians*	41
1949–50e	Morton	47	Airdrieonians	44	Dunfermline Ath*	36
1950–51e	Queen of the S*	45	Stirling A	45	Ayr U*	36
1951–52e	Clyde	44	Falkirk	43	Ayr U	39
1952–53e	Stirling A	44	Hamilton A	43	Queen's Park	37
1953–54e	Motherwell	45	Kilmarnock	42	Third Lanark*	36
1954–55e	Airdrieonians	46	Dunfermline Ath	42	Hamilton A	39
1955–56b	Queen's Park	54	Ayr U	51	St Johnstone	49
1956–57b	Clyde	64	Third Lanark	51	Cowdenbeath	45
1957–58b	Stirling A	55	Dunfermline Ath	53	Arbroath	47
1958–59b	Ayr U	60	Arbroath	51	Stenhousemuir	46
1959–60b	St Johnstone	53	Dundee U	50	Queen of the S	49
1960–61b	Stirling A	55	Falkirk	54	Stenhousemuir	50
1961–62b	Clyde	54	Queen of the S	53	Morton	44
1962–63b	St Johnstone	55	East Stirling	49	Morton	48
1963–64b	Morton	67	Clyde	53	Arbroath	46
1964–65b	Stirling A	59	Hamilton A	50	Queen of the S	45
1965–66b	Ayr U	53	Airdrieonians	50	Queen of the S	47
1966–67a	Morton	69	Raith R	58	Arbroath	57
1967–68b	St Mirren	62	Arbroath	53	East Fife	49
1968–69b	Motherwell	64	Ayr U	53	East Fife*	48
1969–70b	Falkirk	56	Cowdenbeath	55	Queen of the S	50
1970–71b	Partick T	56	East Fife	51	Arbroath	46
1971–72b	Dumbarton*	52	Arbroath	52	Stirling A	50
1972–73b	Clyde	56	Dunfermline Ath	52	Raith R*	47
1973–74b	Airdrieonians	60	Kilmarnock	58	Hamilton A	55
1974–75a	Falkirk	54	Queen of the S*	53	Montrose	53

Elected to Division 1: 1894 Clyde; 1895 Hibernian; 1896 Abercorn; 1897 Partick T;
1899 Kilmarnock; 1900 Morton and Partick T; 1902 Port Glasgow and Partick T;
1903 Airdrieonians and Motherwell; 1905 Falkirk and Aberdeen; 1906 Clyde and
Hamilton A; 1910 Raith R; 1913 Ayr U and Dumbarton.

RELEGATED CLUBS

From Premier Division	From Division 1
1974–75 *No relegation due to League reorganisation*	1974–75 *No relegation due to League reorganisation*
1975–76 Dundee, St Johnstone	1975–76 Dunfermline Ath, Clyde
1976–77 Hearts, Kilmarnock	1976–77 Raith R, Falkirk
1977–78 Ayr U, Clydebank	1977–78 Alloa Ath, East Fife
1978–79 Hearts, Motherwell	1978–79 Montrose, Queen of the S
1979–80 Dundee, Hibernian	1979–80 Arbroath, Clyde
1980–81 Kilmarnock, Hearts	1980–81 Stirling A, Berwick R
1981–82 Partick T, Airdrieonians	1981–82 East Stirling, Queen of the S
1982–83 Morton, Kilmarnock	1982–83 Dunfermline Ath, Queen's Park
1983–84 St Johnstone, Motherwell	1983–84 Raith R, Alloa
1984–85 Dumbarton, Morton	1984–85 Meadowbank T, St Johnstone
1985–86 *No relegation due to League reorganization*	1985–86 Ayr U, Alloa
1986–87 Clydebank, Hamilton A	1986–87 Brechin C, Montrose
1987–88 Falkirk, Dunfermline Ath, Morton	1987–88 East Fife, Dumbarton
1988–89 Hamilton A	1988–89 Kilmarnock, Queen of the S
1989–90 Dundee	1989–90 Albion R, Alloa
1990–91 None	1990–91 Clyde, Brechin C
1991–92 St Mirren, Dunfermline Ath	1991–92 Montrose, Forfar Ath
1992–93 Falkirk, Airdrieonians	1992–93 Meadowbank T, Cowdenbeath
1993–94 *See footnote*	1993–94 *See footnote*
1994–95 Dundee U	1994–95 Ayr U, Stranraer
1995–96 Partick T, Falkirk	1995–6 Hamilton A, Dumbarton

Relegated from Division 2

1994–95 Meadowbank T, Brechin C	1995–96 Forfar Ath, Montrose

Relegated from Division 1 1973–74

1921–22 *Queen's Park, Dumbarton, Clydebank	1931–32 Dundee U, Leith Ath
1922–23 Albion R, Alloa Ath	1932–33 Morton, East Stirling
1923–24 Clyde, Clydebank	1933–34 Third Lanark, Cowdenbeath
1924–25 Third Lanark, Ayr U	1934–35 St Mirren, Falkirk
1925–26 Raith R, Clydebank	1935–36 Airdrieonians, Ayr U
1926–27 Morton, Dundee U	1936–37 Dunfermline Ath, Albion R
1927–28 Dunfermline Ath, Bo'ness	1937–38 Dundee, Morton
1928–29 Third Lanark, Raith R	1938–39 Queen's Park, Raith R
1929–30 St Johnstone, Dundee U	1946–47 Kilmarnock, Hamilton A
1930–31 Hibernian, East Fife	1947–48 Airdrieonians, Queen's Park
	1948–49 Morton, Albion R

1949–50 Queen of the S, Stirling A
1950–51 Clyde, Falkirk
1951–52 Morton, Stirling A
1952–53 Motherwell, Third Lanark
1953–54 Airdrieonians, Hamilton A
1954–55 No clubs relegated
1955–56 Stirling A, Clyde
1956–57 Dunfermline Ath, Ayr U
1957–58 East Fife, Queen's Park
1958–59 Queen of the S, Falkirk
1959–60 Arbroath, Stirling A
1960–61 Ayr U, Clyde
1961–62 St Johnstone, Stirling A

1962–63 Clyde, Raith R
1963–64 Queen of the S, East Stirling
1964–65 Airdrieonians, Third Lanark
1965–66 Morton, Hamilton A
1966–67 St Mirren, Ayr U
1967–68 Motherwell, Stirling A
1968–69 Falkirk, Arbroath
1969–70 Raith R, Partick T
1970–71 St Mirren, Cowdenbeath
1971–72 Clyde, Dunfermline Ath
1972–73 Kilmarnock, Airdrieonians
1973–74 East Fife, Falkirk

*Season 1921–22 – only 1 club promoted, 3 clubs relegated.

Scottish League championship wins: Rangers 46, Celtic 35, Aberdeen 4, Hearts 4, Hibernian 4, Dumbarton 2, Dundee 1, Dundee U 1, Kilmarnock 1, Motherwell 1, Third Lanark 1.

The Scottish Football League was reconstructed into three divisions at the end of the 1974–75 season, so the usual relegation statistics do not apply. Further reorganization took place at the end of the 1985–86 season. From 1986–87, the Premier and First Division had 12 teams each. The Second Division remained at 14. From 1988–89, the Premier Division reverted to 10 teams, and the First Division to 14 teams but in 1991–92 the Premier and First Division reverted to 12.

PAST SCOTTISH LEAGUE CUP FINALS

1946–47	Rangers	4	Aberdeen	0	
1947–48	East Fife	0 4	Falkirk	0* 1	
1948–49	Rangers	2	Raith Rovers	0	
1949–50	East Fife	3	Dunfermline	0	
1950–51	Motherwell	3	Hibernian	0	
1951–52	Dundee	3	Rangers	2	
1952–53	Dundee	2	Kilmarnock	0	
1953–54	East Fife	3	Partick Thistle	2	
1954–55	Hearts	4	Motherwell	2	
1955–56	Aberdeen	2	St Mirren	1	
1956–57	Celtic	0 3	Partick Thistle	0 0	
1957–58	Celtic	7	Rangers	1	
1958–59	Hearts	5	Partick Thistle	1	
1959–60	Hearts	2	Third Lanark	1	
1960–61	Rangers	2	Kilmarnock	0	
1961–62	Rangers	1 3	Hearts	1 1	
1962–63	Hearts	1	Kilmarnock	0	
1963–64	Rangers	5	Morton	0	
1964–65	Rangers	2	Celtic	1	
1965–66	Celtic	2	Rangers	1	
1966–67	Celtic	1	Rangers	0	
1967–68	Celtic	5	Dundee	3	
1968–69	Celtic	6	Hibernian	2	
1969–70	Celtic	1	St Johnstone	0	
1970–71	Rangers	1	Celtic	0	
1971–72	Partick Thistle	4	Celtic	1	
1972–73	Hibernian	2	Celtic	1	
1973–74	Dundee	1	Celtic	0	
1974–75	Celtic	6	Hibernian	3	
1975–76	Rangers	1	Celtic	0	
1976–77	Aberdeen	2	Celtic	1	
1977–78	Rangers	2	Celtic	1*	
1978–79	Rangers	2	Aberdeen	1	
1979–80	Aberdeen	0 0	Dundee U	0* 3	
1980–81	Dundee	0	Dundee U	3	
1981–82	Rangers	2	Dundee U	1	
1982–83	Celtic	2	Rangers	1	
1983–84	Rangers	3	Celtic	2	
1984–85	Rangers	1	Dundee U	0	
1985–86	Aberdeen	3	Hibernian	0	
1986–87	Rangers	2	Celtic	1	
1987–88	Rangers†	3	Aberdeen	3*	
1988–89	Aberdeen	2	Rangers	3*	
1989–90	Aberdeen	2	Rangers	1	
1990–91	Rangers	2	Celtic	1	
1991–92	Rangers	2	Aberdeen	1	
1992–93	Rangers	2	Aberdeen	1*	
1993–94	Rangers	2	Hibernian	1	
1994–95	Raith R	2	Celtic	2†	

†Won on penalties   *After extra time

SCOTTISH COCA-COLA CUP 1995-96

FIRST ROUND

Albion R	(0) 0	Cowdenbeath	(1) 1
Alloa	(1) 2	Forfar Ath	(0) 1
Berwick R	(0) 1	Caledonian T	(0) 1

(aet; Berwick R won 5-3 on penalties)

Brechin C	(1) 2	East Fife	*(1) 3
Clyde	(1) 1	East Stirling	(2) 2
Montrose	(0) 0	Livingston	(1) 2
Queen of the S	(2) 3	Queen's Park	(0) 1
Ross Co	(0) 0	Arbroath	(0) 2

SECOND ROUND

Aberdeen	(2) 3	St Mirren	(1) 1
Ayr U	(0) 0	Celtic	(1) 3
Berwick R	(0) 0	Partick T	(2) 7
Clydebank	(1) 1	Motherwell	(0) 0
Cowdenbeath	(0) 0	Dundee U	(2) 4
Dunfermline Ath	(2) 3	Stranraer	(0) 0
East Fife	(1) 2	Airdrieonians	(0) 3
East Stirling	(0) 0	Dundee	(3) 6
Hearts	(1) 3	Alloa	(0) 0
Hibernian	(1) 3	Stenhousemuir	(0) 1
Kilmarnock	*(0) 1	Dumbarton	(0) 0
Queen of the S	(0) 0	Falkirk	(1) 2
Raith R	(1) 2	Arbroath	(1) 1
Rangers	(2) 3	Greenock Morton	(0) 0
St Johnstone	(1) 1	Livingston	(1) 1

(aet; Livingston won 4-2 on penalties)

Stirling Albion	(0) 2	Hamilton A	(0) 0

THIRD ROUND

Airdrieonians	(2) 2	Hibernian	(0) 0
Dundee U	(1) 1	Motherwell	(1) 2
Dundee	(0) 3	Kilmarnock	(1) 1
Falkirk	(1) 1	Aberdeen	(2) 4
Hearts	(1) 2	Dunfermline Ath	(1) 1
Livingston	(1) 1	Partick T	(0) 2
Rangers	(1) 3	Stirling Albion	(0) 2
Celtic	*(0) 2	Raith R	(0) 1

QUARTER-FINALS

Celtic	(0) 0	Rangers	(0) 1
Airdrieonians	(1) 1	Partick T	(1) 1

(aet; Airdrieonians won 3-2 on penalties)

Dundee	(2) 4	Hearts	(0) 4

(aet; Dundee won 5-4 on penalties)

Motherwell	(1) 1	Aberdeen	*(0) 2

SEMI-FINALS

Rangers	(0) 0	Aberdeen	(0) 2
Dundee	(1) 2	Airdrieonians	(0) 1

* after extra time

FINAL at Hampden Park
26 NOV

Aberdeen	(1) 2	Dundee	(0) 0

SCOTTISH LEAGUE CHALLENGE CUP
1995-96

FIRST ROUND

Albion R	(1) 2	Ross Co	(0) 2
(aet; Albion R won 3-2 on penalties)			
Ayr U	(1) 1	Dunfermline Ath	*(1) 2
Caledonian T	(1) 1	Alloa	(1) 2
Clyde	(0) 0	St Johnstone	(0) 2
Clydebank	(2) 2	Arbroath	(0) 0
Dumbarton	(0) 0	Brechin C	(1) 1
East Fife	(1) 2	Dundee	(2) 4
East Stirling	(0) 0	St Mirren	(2) 3
Hamilton A	(0) 2	Airdrieonians	(0) 2
(aet; Hamilton A won 4-3 on penalties)			
Montrose	(0) 2	Berwick R	(1) 1
Queen of the S	(0) 0	Forfar Ath	(1) 1
Stirling Albion	(2) 3	Queen's Park	(0) 0
Livingston	(1) 1	Greenock Morton	(0) 0
Stranraer	(0) 0	Dundee U	(1) 2
Dundee	(2) 3	Cowdenbeath	(0) 0
Albion R	(1) 1	Brechin C	(2) 3
Alloa	(1) 2	Stirling Albion	(1) 4
Clydebank	(0) 3	St Johnstone	(0) 0
Dundee U	(1) 3	Hamilton A	(0) 0
Dunfermline Ath	(0) 2	Forfar Ath	(0) 1
Stenhousemuir	(2) 3	Montrose	(0) 1
Livingston	(0) 2	St Mirren	(0) 0

2nd Rd

QUARTER-FINALS

Dundee	(0) 1	Stenhousemuir	(1) 3
Clydebank	(0) 0	Dundee U	(0) 1
Dunfermline Ath	(1) 2	Brechin C	(0) 0
Livingston	(0) 1	Stirling Albion	(0) 1
(aet; Stirling Albion won 4-2 on penalties)			

SEMI-FINALS

Dunfermline Ath	(0) 0	Dundee U	(3) 4
Stirling Albion	(0) 1	Stenhousemuir	(2) 2

* after extra time

FINAL at McDiarmid Park
5 NOV

Stenhousemuir	(0) 0	Dundee U	(0) 0
(aet; Stenhousemuir won 5-4 on penalties)			

TENNENT'S SCOTTISH CUP 1995-96

FIRST ROUND

Stranraer	(0) 0	Livingston	(2) 3
Stenhousemuir	(2) 2	Arbroath	(2) 2
Albion R	(0) 0	Deveronvale	(1) 2
Glasgow U	(0) 0	Spartans	(1) 1

FIRST ROUND REPLAY

Arbroath	(0) 0	Stenhousemuir	(0) 1
Ayr U	(0) 0	Ross Co	(0) 2
Berwick R	(2) 3	Annan Athletic	(1) 3
Caledonian T	(2) 3	Livingston	(0) 2
Clyde	(1) 2	Brechin C	(2) 2
Deveronvale	(0) 0	Keith	(0) 0
Forfar Ath	(2) 3	Lossiemouth	(0) 1
Montrose	(1) 2	Cowdenbeath	(1) 1
Queen of the S	(2) 2	Queen's Park	(1) 4
Spartans	(0) 0	East Fife	(0) 0
Stirling Albion	(0) 3	Alloa	(0) 0
Whitehill Welfare	(1) 2	Fraserburgh	(1) 2
East Stirling	(0) 0	Stenhousemuir	(1) 1

SECOND ROUND REPLAYS

Annan Athletic	(0) 1	Berwick R	(0) 2
Fraserburgh	(0) 1	Whitehill Welfare	(1) 2
Keith	(1) 2	Deveronvale	(0) 0
East Fife	(0) 2	Spartans	(0) 1
Brechin C	(0) 1	Clyde	*(0) 3

THIRD ROUND

Caledonian T	(1) 1	East Fife	(0) 1
Hibernian	(0) 0	Kilmarnock	(0) 2
Keith	(0) 1	Rangers	(6) 10
Raith R	(0) 3	Queen's Park	(0) 0
Ross Co	(0) 0	Forfar Ath	(1) 3
Whitehill Welfare	(0) 0	Celtic	(1) 3
Clydebank	(0) 0	Stirling Albion	(1) 1
Dumbarton	(0) 1	Airdrieonians	(0) 3
Falkirk	(0) 0	Stenhousemuir	(1) 2
Motherwell	(0) 0	Aberdeen	(1) 2
Clyde	(2) 3	Dundee	(1) 1
Hamilton A	(0) 0	St Johnstone	(1) 1
Hearts	(0) 1	Partick T	(0) 0
Dunfermline Ath	(1) 3	St Mirren	(0) 0
Greenock Morton	(1) 1	Montrose	(0) 1
Berwick R	(1) 1	Dundee U	(2) 2

THIRD ROUND REPLAYS

East Fife	(0) 1	Caledonian T	(0) 1
(aet; Caledonian T won 3-1 on penalties)			
Montrose	(2) 3	Greenock Morton	(2) 2

FOURTH ROUND

Clyde	(0) 1	Rangers	(0) 4
Airdrieonians	(2) 2	Forfar Ath	(1) 2
Celtic	(2) 2	Raith R	(0) 0

Dundee U	(0) 1	Dunfermline Ath	(0) 0
Kilmarnock	(0) 1	Hearts	(0) 2
St Johnstone	(1) 3	Montrose	(0) 0
Stenhousemuir	(0) 0	Caledonian T	(0) 1
Stirling Albion	(0) 0	Aberdeen	(1) 2

FOURTH ROUND REPLAY
| Forfar Ath | (0) 0 | Airdrieonians | (0) 0 |

(aet; Airdrieonians won 4-2 on penalties)

QUARTER-FINALS
St Johnstone	(0) 1	Hearts	(1) 2
Aberdeen	(1) 2	Airdrieonians	(1) 1
Caledonian T	(0) 0	Rangers	(2) 3
Celtic	(0) 2	Dundee U	(1) 1

SEMI-FINALS
| Aberdeen | (0) 1 | Hearts | (0) 2 |
| Celtic | (0) 1 | Rangers | (1) 2 |

FINAL at Hampden Park
18 MAY
| Rangers | (1) 5 | Hearts | (0) 1 |

PAST SCOTTISH CUP FINALS

1874	Queen's Park	2	Clydesdale	0
1875	Queen's Park	3	Renton	0
1876	Queen's Park	1 2	Third Lanark	1 0
1877	Vale of Leven	0 1 3	Rangers	0 1 2
1878	Vale of Leven	1	Third Lanark	0
1879	Vale of Leven	1	Rangers	1
	Vale of Leven awarded cup, Rangers did not appear for replay			
1880	Queen's Park	3	Thornliebank	0
1881	Queen's Park	2 3	Dumbarton	1 1
	Replayed because of protest			
1882	Queen's Park	2 4	Dumbarton	2 1
1883	Dumbarton	2 2	Vale of Leven	2 1
1884	*Queen's Park awarded cup when Vale of Leven did not appear for the final*			
1885	Renton	0 3	Vale of Leven	0 1
1886	Queen's Park	3	Renton	1
1887	Hibernian	2	Dumbarton	1
1888	Renton	6	Cambuslang	1
1889	Third Lanark	3 2	Celtic	0 1
	Replayed because of protest			
1890	Queen's Park	1 2	Vale of Leven	1 1
1891	Hearts	1	Dumbarton	0
1892	Celtic	1 5	Queen's Park	0 1
	Replayed because of protest			
1893	Queen's Park	2	Celtic	1
1894	Rangers	3	Celtic	1
1895	St Bernards	3	Renton	1
1896	Hearts	3	Hibernian	1
1897	Rangers	5	Dumbarton	1
1898	Rangers	2	Kilmarnock	0
1899	Celtic	2	Rangers	0
1900	Celtic	4	Queen's Park	3
1901	Hearts	4	Celtic	3
1902	Hibernian	1	Celtic	0
1903	Rangers	1 0 2	Hearts	1 0 0
1904	Celtic	3	Rangers	2
1905	Third Lanark	0 3	Rangers	0 1
1906	Hearts	1	Third Lanark	0
1907	Celtic	3	Hearts	0
1908	Celtic	5	St Mirren	1
1909	*After two drawn games between Celtic and Rangers, 2.2, 1.1, there was a riot and the cup was withheld*			
1910	Dundee	2 0 2	Clyde	2 0 1
1911	Celtic	0 2	Hamilton Acad	0 0
1912	Celtic	2	Clyde	0
1913	Falkirk	2	Raith R	0
1914	Celtic	0 4	Hibernian	0 1
1920	Kilmarnock	3	Albion R	2
1921	Partick Th	1	Rangers	0
1922	Morton	1	Rangers	0
1923	Celtic	1	Hibernian	0
1924	Airdrieonians	2	Hibernian	0
1925	Celtic	2	Dundee	1
1926	St Mirren	2	Celtic	0
1927	Celtic	3	East Fife	1
1928	Rangers	4	Celtic	0
1929	Kilmarnock	2	Rangers	0
1930	Rangers	0 2	Partick Th	0 1

1931	Celtic	2 4	Motherwell	2 2
1932	Rangers	1 3	Kilmarnock	1 0
1933	Celtic	1	Motherwell	0
1934	Rangers	5	St Mirren	0
1935	Rangers	2	Hamilton Acad	1
1936	Rangers	1	Third Lanark	0
1937	Celtic	2	Aberdeen	1
1938	East Fife	1 4	Kilmarnock	1 2
1939	Clyde	4	Motherwell	0
1947	Aberdeen	2	Hibernian	1
1948	Rangers	1 1	Morton	1 0
1949	Rangers	4	Clyde	1
1950	Rangers	3	East Fife	0
1951	Celtic	1	Motherwell	0
1952	Motherwell	4	Dundee	0
1953	Rangers	1 1	Aberdeen	1 0
1954	Celtic	2	Aberdeen	1
1955	Clyde	1 1	Celtic	1 0
1956	Hearts	3	Celtic	1
1957	Falkirk	1 2	Kilmarnock	1 1
1958	Clyde	1	Hibernian	0
1959	St Mirren	3	Aberdeen	1
1960	Rangers	2	Kilmarnock	0
1961	Dunfermline Ath	0 2	Celtic	0 0
1962	Rangers	2	St Mirren	0
1963	Rangers	1 3	Celtic	1 0
1964	Rangers	3	Dundee	1
1965	Celtic	3	Dunfermline Ath	2
1966	Rangers	0 1	Celtic	0 0
1967	Celtic	2	Aberdeen	0
1968	Dunfermline Ath	3	Hearts	1
1969	Celtic	4	Rangers	0
1970	Aberdeen	3	Celtic	1
1971	Celtic	1 2	Rangers	1 1
1972	Celtic	6	Hibernian	1
1973	Rangers	3	Celtic	2
1974	Celtic	3	Dundee U	0
1975	Celtic	3	Airdrieonians	1
1976	Rangers	3	Hearts	1
1977	Celtic	1	Rangers	0
1978	Rangers	2	Aberdeen	1
1979	Rangers	0 0 3	Hibernian	0 0 2
1980	Celtic	1	Rangers	0
1981	Rangers	0 4	Dundee U	0 1
1982	Aberdeen	4	Rangers	1 (aet)
1983	Aberdeen	1	Rangers	0 (aet)
1984	Aberdeen	2	Celtic	1 (aet)
1985	Celtic	2	Dundee U	1
1986	Aberdeen	3	Hearts	0
1987	St Mirren	1	Dundee U	0 (aet)
1988	Celtic	2	Dundee U	1
1989	Celtic	1	Rangers	0
1990	Aberdeen†	0	Celtic	0
1991	Motherwell	4	Dundee U	3 (aet)
1992	Rangers	2	Airdrieonians	1
1993	Rangers	2	Aberdeen	1
1994	Dundee U	1	Rangers	0
1995	Celtic	1	Airdrieonians	0

†won on penalties

WELSH FOOTBALL 1995–96

LEAGUE OF WALES

	P	Home W	D	L	Goals F	A	Away W	D	L	Goals F	A	GD	Pts
Barry Town	40	17	2	1	50	10	13	5	2	42	13	+69	97
Newtown	40	12	5	3	32	7	11	6	3	37	18	+44	80
Conwy United	40	11	7	2	53	23	10	6	4	48	35	+43	76
Bangor City	40	12	5	3	40	27	9	1	10	32	38	+7	69
Flint Town United	40	9	6	5	35	28	10	3	7	41	29	+19	66
Caernarfon Town	40	9	7	4	38	23	7	6	7	39	36	+18	61
Cwmbran Town	40	8	6	6	30	24	6	9	5	28	25	+9	57
Inter Cardiff	40	11	6	3	41	27	3	6	11	21	35	0	54
Caersws	40	10	3	7	46	46	5	6	9	35	51	−16	54
Connah's Quay Nomads	40	9	6	5	46	32	4	8	8	22	31	+5	53
Ebbw Vale	40	9	6	5	38	35	5	6	9	24	28	+3	53
Llansantffraid	40	9	3	8	36	29	5	7	7	30	28	+9	52
Porthmadog	40	7	7	6	34	28	6	4	10	22	34	−6	50
Aberystwyth Town	40	7	7	6	32	30	6	2	12	28	38	−8	48
Cemaes Bay	40	11	5	4	45	28	2	2	16	18	52	−17	46
Holywell Town	40	8	3	9	32	34	4	4	12	21	40	−21	43
Briton Ferry Athletic	40	8	5	7	38	35	3	4	13	26	56	−27	42
Rhyl	40	6	5	9	23	31	5	4	11	24	52	−36	42
Ton Pentre	40	4	8	8	25	29	4	8	8	21	36	−19	40
Afan Lido	40	7	2	11	21	33	2	7	11	12	38	−38	36
Llanelli	40	5	5	10	31	38	3	4	13	19	50	−38	33

NORTHERN IRISH FOOTBALL 1995–96

SMIRNOFF IRISH LEAGUE

Premier Division

	P	W	D	L	F	A	Pts
Portadown	28	16	8	4	61	40	56
Crusaders	28	15	7	6	45	32	52
Glentoran	28	13	7	8	56	38	46
Glenavon	28	13	5	10	47	32	44
Linfield	28	11	8	9	34	35	41
Cliftonville	28	6	11	11	27	48	29
Ards	28	6	7	15	29	43	25
Bangor	28	3	5	20	23	54	14

LEAGUE OF WALES—RESULTS 1994-95

	Aberystwyth	Afan Lido	Bangor City	Barry Town	Briton F A	Caernarfon T	Caersws	Cemaes Bay	Connah's Qvay	Conwy U	Cwmbran T	Ebbw Vale	Flint T U	Holywell T	Inter Cardiff	Llanelli	Llansant'rrd	Newtown	CPD Porth'dg	Rhyl	Ton Pentre
Ton Pentre	2-1	1-1	2-0	0-1	3-1	2-1	1-0	1-3	2-2	2-2	1-1	1-1	2-4	1-2	1-0	2-2	2-2	1-4	4-1	1-2	—
Rhyl	0-3	2-3	2-1	0-3	4-0	3-1	1-2	0-3	1-1	1-2	0-1	3-1	3-2	5-3	1-0	4-0	2-1	0-0	1-0	—	0-2
CPD Porth'dg	2-1	1-1	1-0	4-1	5-1	4-1	1-2	4-1	2-1	2-0	0-0	3-1	2-1	4-0	1-2	0-1	0-0	1-4	—	1-1	2-0
Newtown	1-4	0-0	1-0	2-1	0-1	3-3	1-0	0-4	2-4	0-2	1-1	1-3	0-2	0-1	1-3	0-7	0-0	—	0-3	1-0	2-2
Llansant'rrd	2-2	3-2	0-1	0-1	0-7	2-2	2-1	4-3	0-0	2-2	2-3	0-0	0-5	1-1	2-3	3-2	—	0-0	1-1	2-1	2-2
Llanelli	2-2	0-0	4-0	0-2	5-0	4-0	2-0	0-0	3-1	3-0	2-0	4-2	0-2	5-3	2-3	—	3-3	0-2	2-2	1-2	3-0
Inter Cardiff	1-0	2-0	2-1	0-1	3-1	2-1	1-4	1-2	1-2	3-0	1-0	2-0	2-1	1-1	—	1-1	0-0	2-4	2-1	2-1	1-0
Holywell T	1-2	0-1	2-1	1-4	2-4	5-3	2-2	4-1	4-1	1-4	0-3	4-1	1-0	—	1-2	2-3	0-3	1-1	2-1	2-3	2-0
Flint T U	2-4	0-1	3-2	2-1	1-0	0-2	0-5	2-3	0-3	4-2	1-3	4-2	—	3-5	1-0	3-1	1-0	1-1	1-1	2-3	2-0
Ebbw Vale	1-1	0-1	0-0	2-2	3-1	3-4	2-4	4-3	4-0	1-3	1-3	—	1-3	0-0	0-2	0-1	2-2	3-1	1-0	4-1	1-1
Cwmbran T	1-1	1-0	2-1	1-0	1-1	2-2	4-3	1-1	5-1	2-4	—	2-0	3-3	1-3	2-3	1-1	0-0	1-1	0-2	1-1	1-1
Conwy U	2-0	4-4	2-1	3-1	2-5	0-5	1-0	1-2	7-1	—	2-4	3-3	4-2	1-1	3-0	1-1	2-2	2-4	1-1	2-1	2-0
Connah's Qvay	1-0	2-1	2-1	1-1	0-1	1-4	2-2	4-3	—	1-1	1-1	1-1	2-1	1-3	1-1	7-1	0-0	2-4	2-1	2-1	3-0
Cemaes Bay	1-3	4-3	0-2	1-6	1-1	2-0	1-0	—	3-3	0-2	1-1	3-4	0-2	4-1	0-3	4-3	2-2	0-2	0-3	0-3	2-2
Caersws	1-1	1-0	1-2	0-2	1-1	2-0	—	1-0	2-2	0-1	3-3	3-1	0-2	3-2	1-3	5-2	2-1	3-1	3-1	4-0	3-0
Caernarfon T	3-3	3-1	1-0	1-0	1-1	—	2-0	4-3	4-1	2-4	1-2	3-1	0-2	5-3	2-1	0-0	3-2	1-2	4-1	3-1	2-0
Briton F A	3-1	0-4	4-1	1-6	—	1-1	1-1	3-3	8-3	2-1	2-1	3-1	0-2	2-4	0-1	4-0	2-1	5-1	5-1	4-0	1-2
Barry Town	0-1	0-3	0-3	—	1-6	1-0	2-0	1-0	0-0	4-0	5-1	2-1	0-2	2-1	2-1	5-0	2-1	4-2	0-4	1-6	0-0
Bangor City	2-0	2-0	—	0-3	0-4	1-0	1-2	0-2	0-2	4-1	1-2	2-1	3-2	2-1	2-1	4-0	0-0	0-0	1-1	2-0	0-0
Afan Lido	1-1	—	2-0	0-3	0-4	3-1	1-2	4-3	2-2	4-4	2-2	0-1	0-1	0-1	2-0	0-0	3-2	0-0	1-0	2-3	0-2
Aberystwyth	—	1-1	2-1	0-1	3-1	3-3	1-1	1-3	2-2	2-0	1-0	1-1	2-4	1-2	1-0	1-3	2-2	1-4	4-1	1-2	2-0

EUROPEAN REVIEW 1996

Juventus gained revenge for their 1-0 defeat at the hands of Ajax in 1973 to beat the European Cup holders 4-2 on penalties in the Olympic Stadium in Rome, after the match had finished 1-1 in extra time. The Italian club took the lead in the 13th minute through Fabrizio Ravanelli, but the Dutchmen replied through Finnish international Jari Litmanen four minutes before half-time.

In the penalty shoot-out, the Juventus goalkeeper Angelo Peruzzi was the hero, saving the first penalty from Edgar Davids and the fourth effort from Sonny Silooy, although neither attempts at goal had been convincing. Juventus had just about had the edge over the two hours of play, though deciding matches of this importance by the lottery of penalties is still far from satisfactory. This was the fifth such occasion in the history of the competition.

In the Cup-Winners' Cup final in Brussels, Paris St Germain created history by becoming the first French club to win a major trophy (Marseille having had their European Cup title stripped from them). When they defeated Rapid Vienna 1-0, the only goal of the game was scored after 29 minutes by Bruno N'Gotty.

In the UEFA Cup final, Bayern Munich achieved their first European success for 20 years when they beat Bordeaux over two legs. In Munich, they took a 2-0 lead with goals from Thomas Helmer in the 35th minute and Mehmet Scholl on the hour.

Any hopes that the French team had of fighting back in the return leg disappeared in the second half when Scholl put the Germans 3-0 up on aggregate in the 53rd minute. Emil Kostadinov, the Bulgarian international, added another goal for Bayern in the 66th minute and though Daniel Dutuel reduced the arrears for Bordeaux with 15 minutes remaining, Jurgen Klinsmann put the game beyond them with a third goal four minutes later to record a 5-1 aggregate success.

British involvement in the three major European competitions was disappointing. In the Champions Cup, Blackburn Rovers managed just one win and that in the last game against Rosenborg when they had already been eliminated from the group stage, while Rangers failed to win any of their matches.

In the Cup-Winners' Cup, there was possibly no disgrace for Celtic to be knocked out by the eventual winners Paris St Germain, though they were embarassingly beaten 3-0 at home in the second leg. Everton lost 1-0 on aggregate to Feyenoord, the only goal of the tie being scored by Regi Blinker before his move to Sheffield Wednesday.

Of the English representation, Nottingham Forest did at least reach the quarter-finals of the UEFA Cup. In the first round, they recovered from a 2-1 deficit in Malmo to go through on an away goal and in the second round, led by a single goal from their visit to Auxerre and held out for a goalless draw at the City ground.

In the third round, they again accounted for French opposition beating Lyon 1-0 at home when substitute Paul McGregor came on to score, while they kept a clean sheet in the return goalless draw.

However, they were well beaten in the quarter-finals by the eventual winners Bayern Munich. Having only lost 2-1 in Germany, hopes were high for the return leg but Forest were given a lesson in finishing as Bayern swept to a 5-1 win.

Bayern took the lead in the 29th minute through Christian Ziege and when Thomas Strunz added a second goal two minutes before half-time, Forest were facing a 4-1 deficit. Klinsmann then struck twice in the 64th and 79th minutes, sandwiching a goal from Jean-Pierre Papin in the 72nd minute and though Steve Stone replied with five minutes left, the tie was long over for Forest.

EUROPEAN CUP 1995-96

Preliminary Round, First Leg

Anderlecht	(0) 0	Ferencvaros		(0) 1
Dynamo Kiev	(0) 1	Aalborg		(0) 0
Grasshoppers	(0) 1	Maccabi Tel Aviv		(0) 0
Legia Warsaw	(0) 1	IFK Gothenburg		(0) 0
Panathinaikos	(0) 0	Hajduk Split		(0) 0
Rangers	(0) 1	Anorthosis		(0) 0
Rosenborg	(2) 3	Besiktas		(0) 0
Salzburg	(0) 0	Steaua		(0) 0

Preliminary Round Second Leg

Aalborg	(0) 1	Dynamo Kiev		(1) 3
Anorthosis	(0) 0	Rangers		(0) 0
Besiktas	(1) 3	Rosenborg		(0) 1
Ferencvaros	(0) 1	Anderlecht		(0) 1
IFK Gothenburg	(1) 1	Legia Warsaw		(0) 2
Hajduk Split	(1) 1	Panathinaikos		(0) 1
Maccabi Tel Aviv	(0) 0	Grasshoppers		(1) 1
Steaua	(1) 1	Salzburg		(0) 0

CHAMPIONS LEAGUE

Group A

Dynamo Kiev	(0) 1	Panathinaikos		(0) 0

(Dynamo Kiev banned from the competition for alleged bribery of a match official. Replaced by Aalborg)

Nantes	(0) 0	Porto		(0) 0
Panathinaikos	(2) 3	Nantes		(0) 1
Porto	(1) 2	Aalborg		(0) 0
Porto	(0) 0	Panathinaikos		(1) 1
Nantes	(1) 3	Aalborg		(0) 1
Aalborg	(0) 2	Panathinaikos		(1) 1
Panathinaikos	(0) 0	Porto		(0) 0
Aalborg	(0) 0	Nantes		(1) 2
Panathinaikos	(2) 2	Aalborg		(0) 0
Porto	(1) 2	Nantes		(2) 2
Aalborg	(1) 2	Porto		(0) 2
Nantes	(0) 0	Panathinaikos		(0) 0

Final table	P	W	D	L	F	A	Pts
Panathinaikos	6	3	2	1	7	3	11
Nantes	6	2	3	1	8	6	9
Porto	6	1	4	1	6	5	7
Aalborg	6	1	1	4	5	12	4

Group B

Blackburn R	(0) 0	Spartak Moscow		(1) 1
Legia Warsaw	(0) 3	Rosenborg		(0) 1
Rosenborg	(1) 2	Blackburn R		(0) 1
Spartak Moscow	(1) 2	Legia Warsaw		(0) 1
Legia Warsaw	(1) 1	Blackburn R		(0) 0
Rosenborg	(2) 2	Spartak Moscow		(0) 4
Spartak Moscow	(3) 4	Rosenborg		(0) 1
Blackburn R	(0) 0	Legia Warsaw		(0) 0
Spartak Moscow	(1) 3	Blackburn R		(0) 0
Rosenborg	(2) 4	Legia Warsaw		(0) 0
Blackburn R	(4) 4	Rosenborg		(1) 1
Legia Warsaw	(0) 0	Spartak Moscow		(1) 1

Final table	P	W	D	L	F	A	Pts
Spartak Moscow	6	6	0	0	15	4	18
Legia Warsaw	6	2	1	3	5	8	7
Rosenborg	6	2	0	4	11	16	6
Blackburn R	6	1	1	4	5	8	4

Group C

Steaua	(0) 1	Rangers		(0) 0
Borussia Dortmund	(1) 1	Juventus		(2) 3

Juventus	(2) 3	Steaua	(0) 0
Rangers	(0) 2	Borussia Dortmund	(1) 2
Juventus	(3) 4	Rangers	(0) 1
Borussia Dortmund	(0) 1	Steaua	(0) 0
Steaua	(0) 0	Borussia Dortmund	(0) 0
Rangers	(0) 0	Juventus	(1) 4
Rangers	(1) 1	Steaua	(0) 0
Juventus	(0) 1	Borussia Dortmund	(1) 2
Borussia Dortmund	(1) 2	Rangers	(1) 2
Steaua	(0) 0	Juventus	(0) 0

Final table	P	W	D	L	F	A	Pts
Juventus	6	4	1	1	15	4	13
Borussia Dortmund	6	2	3	1	8	8	9
Steaua	6	1	3	2	2	5	6
Rangers	6	0	3	3	6	14	3

Group D

Ajax	(1) 1	Real Madrid	(0) 0
Grasshoppers	(0) 0	Ferencvaros	(0) 3
Ferencvaros	(0) 1	Ajax	(0) 5
Real Madrid	(0) 2	Grasshoppers	(0) 1
Real Madrid	(3) 6	Ferencvaros	(0) 1
Ajax	(1) 3	Grasshoppers	(0) 0
Ferencvaros	(1) 1	Real Madrid	(0) 1
Grasshoppers	(0) 0	Ajax	(0) 2
Real Madrid	(0) 0	Ajax	(0) 2
Ferencvaros	(2) 3	Grasshoppers	(1) 3
Grasshoppers	(0) 0	Real Madrid	(0) 2
Ajax	(2) 4	Ferencvaros	(0) 0

Final table	P	W	D	L	F	A	Pts
Ajax	6	5	1	0	15	1	16
Real Madrid	6	3	1	2	11	5	10
Ferencvaros	6	1	2	3	9	19	5
Grasshoppers	6	0	2	4	3	13	2

Quarter-finals, First leg

Borussia Dortmund	(0) 0	Ajax	(1) 2
Legia Warsaw	(0) 0	Panathinaikos	(0) 0
Nantes	(1) 2	Spartak Moscow	(0) 0
Real Madrid	(1) 1	Juventus	(0) 0

Quarter-finals, Second leg

Ajax	(0) 1	Borussia Dortmund	(0) 0
Juventus	(1) 2	Real Madrid	(0) 0
Panathinaikos	(1) 3	Legia Warsaw	(0) 0
Spartak Moscow	(2) 2	Nantes	(0) 2

SEMI-FINALS, FIRST LEG

Ajax	(0) 0	Panathinaikos	(0) 1
Juventus	(0) 2	Nantes	(0) 0

Semi-finals, Second leg

Nantes	(1) 3	Juventus	(1) 2
Panathinaikos	(0) 0	Ajax	(1) 3

Final

Ajax (1) 1, Juventus (1) 1

(in Rome, 22 May 1996, 67,000)

Ajax: Van der Sar; Silooy, Blind, Frank de Boer (Scholton 69), Bogarde, Ronald de Boer (Wooter 90), Litmanen, Davids, George, Kanu, Musampa (Kluivert 46).
Scorer: Litmanen 41.
Juventus: Peruzzi; Torricelli, Ferrara, Vierchowod, Pessotto, Conte (Jugovic 43), Sousa (Di Livio 58), Deschamps, Ravanelli (Padovano 77), Vialli, Del Piero.
Scorer: Ravenelli 13.
(aet; Juventus won 4-2 on penalties).
Referee: Vega (Spain).

EUROPEAN CUP WINNERS CUP 1995-96

Preliminary Round, First Leg

Apoel	(2) 3	Neftchi Baku	(0) 0
DAG Liepaja	(1) 1	Lantana Tallinn	(1) 2

(Match awarded 3-0 to DAG Liepaja as Lantana fielded an ineligible player)

Derry City	(1) 1	Lokomotiv Sofia	(0) 0
Donetsk	(3) 4	Linfield	(0) 1
Dynamo 93 Minsk	(1) 1	Molde	(0) 1
Grevenmacher	(1) 3	KR Reykjavik	(0) 2
Katowice	(2) 2	Ararat Erevan	(0) 0
Maccabi Haifa	(2) 4	KI Klakksvik	(0) 0
Obilic	(0) 0	Dynamo Batumi	(0) 1
Tiligul	(0) 0	Sion	(0) 0
TPS Turku	(1) 1	Teuta	(0) 0
Vac	(0) 1	Sileks	(0) 1
Vaduz	(0) 0	Hradec Kralove	(3) 5
Valletta	(0) 0	Inter Bratislava	(0) 0
Wrexham	(0) 0	Petrolul	(0) 0
Zalgiris	(0) 2	Mura Murska	(0) 0

Preliminary Round, Second Leg

Ararat Erevan	(2) 2	Katowice	(0) 0

(aet; Ararat won 5-4 on penalties)

Dynamo Batumi	(0) 2	Obilic	(2) 2
Hradec Kralove	(5) 9	Vaduz	(1) 1
Inter Bratislava	(3) 5	Valletta	(0) 2
KI Klakksvik	(0) 3	Maccabi Haifa	(1) 2
KR Reykjavik	(1) 2	Grevenmacher	(0) 0
Lantana	(0) 0	DAG Liepaja	(0) 0
Linfield	(2) 2	Derry City	(0) 0
Lokomotiv Sofia	(2) 2	Dynamo 93 Minsk	(1) 1
Molde	(0) 2	Zalgiris	(0) 1
Mura Murska	(0) 2	Apoel	(0) 0
Neftchi Baku	(0) 0	Wrexham	(0) 0
Petrolul	(0) 1	Vac	(1) 1
Sileks	(2) 3	Vac	(0) 2
Sion	(3) 3	Tiligul	(0) 0
Teuta	(2) 3	TPS Turku	(0) 0

First Round, First Leg

AEK Athens	(1) 2	Sion	(0) 0
Apoel	(0) 0	La Coruna	(0) 0
FC Brugge	(0) 1	Donetsk	(0) 0
DAG Liepaja	(0) 0	Feyenoord	(1) 7
Dynamo Batumi	(1) 2	Celtic	(2) 3
Dynamo Moscow	(1) 3	Ararat Erevan	(0) 1
Hardec Cralove	(2) 5	FC Copenhagen	(0) 0
Inter Bratislava	(0) 0	Zaragoza	(1) 2
KR Reykjavik	(1) 2	Everton	(1) 3
Lokomotiv Sofia	(2) 3	Halmstad	(0) 1
Moenchengladbach	(2) 3	Sileks	(0) 0
Molde	(0) 2	Paris St Germain	(0) 3
Rapid	(1) 3	Petrolul	(0) 0
Sporting Lisbon	(2) 4	Maccabi Haifa	(0) 0
Teuta	(0) 0	Parma	(0) 2
Zalgiris	(1) 2	Trabzonspor	(1) 2

First Round, Second Leg

Ararat Erevan	(0) 0	Dynamo Moscow	(0) 1
Celtic	(2) 4	Dynamo Batumi	(2) 2
FC Copenhagen	(1) 2	Hradec Kralove	(2) 2
Donetsk	(0) 1	FC Brugge	(0) 1
Everton	(0) 3	KR Reykjavik	(1) 1

Feyenoord	(2) 6	DAG Liepaja	(0) 0
Halmstad	(1) 2	Lokomotiv Sofia	(0) 0
La Coruna	(5) 8	Apoel	(0) 0
Maccabi Haifa	(0) 0	Sporting Lisbon	(0) 0
Paris St Germain	(2) 3	Molde	(0) 0
Parma	(1) 2	Teuta	(0) 0
Petrolul	(0) 0	Rapid	(0) 0
Sileks	(0) 2	Moenchengladbach	(1) 3
Sion	(1) 2	AEK Athens	(0) 2
Trabzonspor	(0) 1	Zalgiris	(0) 0
Zaragoza	(1) 3	Inter Bratislava	(0) 1

Second Round, First Leg

Dynamo Moscow	(0) 1	Hradec Kralove	(0) 0
Everton	(0) 0	Feyenoord	(0) 0
Halmstad	(2) 3	Parma	(0) 0
Moenchengladbach	(0) 4	AEK Athens	(0) 1
Paris St Germain	(0) 1	Celtic	(0) 0
Sporting Lisbon	(2) 2	Rapid	(0) 0
Trabzonspor	(0) 0	La Coruna	(0) 0
Zaragoza	(2) 2	FC Brugge	(0) 1

Second Round, Second Leg

AEK Athens	(0) 0	Moenchengladbach	(0) 1
FC Brugge	(0) 0	Zaragoza	(0) 1
Celtic	(0) 0	Paris St Germain	(2) 3
Feyenoord	(1) 1	Everton	(0) 0
Hradec Kralove	(1) 1	Dynamo Moscow	(0) 0
(aet; Dynamo Moscow won 3-1 on penalties)			
La Coruna	(2) 3	Trabzonspor	(0) 0
Parma	(2) 4	Halmstad	(0) 0
Rapid	(1) 4	Sporting Lisbon	(0) 0

Quarter-finals, First Leg

Dynamo Moscow	(0) 0	Rapid	(1) 1
La Coruna	(0) 1	Zaragoza	(0) 0
Moenchengladbach	(2) 2	Feyenoord	(2) 2
Parma	(0) 1	Paris St Germain	(0) 0

Quarter-finals, Second Leg

Feyenoord	(0) 1	Moenchengladbach	(0) 0
Paris St Germain	(2) 3	Parma	(1) 1
Rapid	(0) 3	Dynamo Moscow	(0) 0
Zaragoza	(1) 1	La Coruna	(0) 1

Semi-finals, First Leg

Feyenoord	(0) 1	Rapid	(0) 1
La Coruna	(0) 0	Paris St Germain	(0) 1

Semi-finals, Second Leg

Paris St Germain	(0) 1	La Coruna	(0) 0
Rapid	(3) 3	Feyenoord	(0) 0

Final

Paris St Germain (1) 1, Rapid (0) 0

(in Brussels, 8 May 1996, 37,500)

Paris St Germain: Lama; Roche, Le Guen, N'Gotty, Fournier (Llacer 77), Bravo, Guerin, Colleter, Loko, Rai (Dely Valdes 11), Djorkaeff.
Scorer: N'Gotty 29.
Rapid: Konsel; Schottel, Ivanov, Hatz, Heraf, Kuhbauer, Stoger, Guggi, Marasek, Stumpf (Barisic 46), Jancker.
Referee: Pairetto (Italy).

UEFA CUP 1995-96

Preliminary Round, First Leg

Afan Lido	(1) 1	RAF Yelgava	(1) 2
Apollon	(1) 1	Olimpija	(0) 0
Bangor City	(0) 0	Widzew Lodz	(2) 4
Botev Plovdiv	(1) 1	Dynamo Tbilisi	(0) 0
Brondby	(2) 3	Inkaras	(0) 0
Crusaders	(0) 1	Silkeborg	(1) 2
Dinamo Bucharest	(0) 0	Levski	(1) 1
Dundalk	(0) 0	Malmo	(2) 2
Fenerbahce	(0) 2	Partizani	(0) 0
Glenavon	(1) 2	Hafnarfjordur	(0) 0
Hibernians	(0) 0	Odessa	(3) 5
Jeunesse Esch	(0) 0	Lugano	(0) 0
Kapaz	(0) 0	FK Austria	(2) 4
Karlsruhe	(0) 0	Bordeaux	(1) 2
Kosice	(0) 0	Ujpesti TE	(1) 1
Lillestrom	(1) 4	Flora Tallinn	(0) 0
Motherwell	(1) 1	MyPa	(2) 3
Omonia	(1) 3	Sliema Wanderers	(0) 0
Orebro	(0) 0	Avenir Beggen	(0) 0
Raith Rovers	(1) 4	GI Gotu	(0) 0
Red Star Belgrade	(0) 0	Neuchatel Xamax	(0) 1
Shelbourne	(0) 0	IA Akranes	(1) 3
Skonto Riga	(1) 1	Branik Maribor	(0) 0
Slavia Sofia	(0) 0	Olympiakos	(0) 2
Slovan Bratislava	(3) 4	Osijek	(0) 1
Sparta Prague	(2) 3	Galatasaray	(0) 1
Sturm Graz	(0) 0	Slavia Prague	(0) 1
Tampere	(0) 0	Viking	(0) 4
SK Tirana	(0) 0	Hapoel Beer Sheva	(1) 1
Tirol	(0) 1	Strasbourg	(1) 1
Uni Craiova	(0) 0	Dynamo Minsk	(0) 0
Vardar Skopje	(1) 1	Samtredia	(0) 0
Zaglebie Lubin	(0) 0	Shirak Gumri	(0) 0
Zimbru Chisinau	(1) 2	Hapoel Tel Aviv	(0) 0

Preliminary Round, Second Leg

IA Akranes	(1) 3	Shelbourne	(0) 0
Avenir Beggen	(1) 1	Orebro	(0) 1
FK Austria	(4) 5	Kapaz	(1) 2
Bordeaux	(2) 2	Karlsruhe	(1) 2
Branik Maribor	(2) 2	Skonto Riga	(0) 0
Dynamo Minsk	(0) 0	Uni Craiova	(0) 0
Dynamo Tbilisi	(0) 0	Botev Plovdiv	(1) 1
Flora Tallinn	(0) 1	Lillestrom	(0) 0
Galatasaray	(1) 1	Sparta Prague	(1) 1
GI Gotu	(0) 2	Raith Rovers	(1) 2
Hafnarfjordur	(0) 0	Glenavon	(0) 1
Hapoel Beer Sheva	(2) 2	SK Tirana	(0) 0
Hapoel Tel Aviv	(0) 0	Zimbru Chisinau	(0) 0
Inkaras	(0) 0	Brondby	(0) 3
Levski	(0) 1	Dinamo Bucharest	(0) 1
Lugano	(3) 4	Jeunesse Esch	(0) 0
Malmo	(1) 2	Dundalk	(0) 0
MyPa	(0) 0	Motherwell	(1) 2
Neuchatel Xamax	(0) 0	Red Star Belgrade	(0) 2
Odessa	(1) 2	Hibernians	(0) 0
Olimpija	(1) 3	Apollon	(1) 1

Olympiakos	(1) 1	Slavia Sofia	(0) 0
Osijek	(0) 0	Slovan Bratislava	(0) 2
Partizani	(0) 0	Fenerbahce	(2) 4
RAF Yelgava	(0) 0	Afan Lido	(0) 0
Samtredia	(0) 0	Vardar Skopje	(2) 2
Shirak Gumri	(0) 0	Zaglebie Lubin	(1) 1
Silkeborg	(1) 4	Crusaders	(0) 0
Slavia Prague	(1) 1	Sturm Graz	(0) 1
Sliema Wanderers	(1) 1	Omonia	(0) 2
Strasbourg	(1) 6	Tirol	(0) 1
Ujpest TE	(0) 2	Kosice	(0) 1
Viking	(2) 3	Tampere	(0) 1
Widzew Lodz	(0) 1	Bangor City	(0) 0

First Round, First Leg

FK Austria		Dynamo Minsk	(2) 2
Bayern Munich	(0) 0	Lokomotiv Moscow	(0) 1
Brondby	(1) 3	Lillestrom	(0) 0
Farense	(0) 0	Lyon	(1) 1
Fenerbahce	(0) 1	Betis	(1) 2
Freiburg	(0) 1	Slavia Prague	(1) 2
Glenavon	(0) 0	Werder Bremen	(0) 2
Guimaraes	(1) 3	Standard Liege	(1) 1
Hapoel Beer Sheva	(0) 0	Barcelona	(2) 7
Lazio	(2) 5	Omonia	(0) 0
Lens	(2) 6	Avenir Beggen	(0) 0
Levski	(0) 1	Aalst	(0) 2
Lierse	(1) 1	Benfica	(1) 3
Lugano	(0) 1	Internazionale	(1) 1
Malmo	(0) 2	Nottingham F	(1) 1
AC Milan	(1) 4	Zaglebie Lubin	(0) 0
Monaco	(0) 0	Leeds U	(1) 3
MyPa	(1) 1	PSV Eindhoven	(1) 1
Neuchatel Xamax	(1) 1	Roma	(1) 1
Odessa	(0) 1	Widzew Lodz	(0) 0
Olympiakos	(0) 2	Branik Maribor	(0) 0
Raith R	(1) 3	IA Akranes	(1) 1
Roda	(4) 5	Olimpija	(0) 0
Rota Volgograd	(0) 0	Manchester U	(0) 0
Sevilla	(2) 2	Botev Plovdiv	(0) 0
Slovan Bratislava	(1) 2	Kaiserslautern	(0) 1
Sparta Prague	(0) 0	Silkeborg	(1) 1
Spartak Vladikavkaz	(1) 1	Liverpool	(1) 2
Strasbourg	(1) 3	Ujpest TE	(0) 1
Vadar Skopje	(0) 0	Bordeaux	(1) 2
Viking	(0) 1	Auxerre	(1) 1
Zimbru Chisinau	(1) 1	RAF Yelgava	(0) 0

First Round, Second Leg

Aalst	(0) 1	Levski	(0) 0
IA Akranes	(0) 1	Raith R	(0) 0
Auxerre	(0) 1	Viking	(0) 0
Avenir Beggen	(0) 0	Lens	(3) 7
Barcelona	(2) 5	Hapoel Beer Sheva	(0) 0
Benfica	(1) 2	Lierse	(1) 1
Betis	(2) 2	Fenerbahce	(0) 1
Bordeaux	(0) 1	Vardar Skopje	(0) 1
Botev Plovdiv	(0) 1	Sevilla	(0) 0
Branik Maribor	(0) 1	Olympiakos	(1) 3
Dynamo Minsk	(0) 1	FK Austria	(0) 0
Internazionale	(0) 0	Lugano	(0) 1

Kaiserslautern	(2) 3	Slovan Bratislava	(0) 0
Leeds U	(0) 0	Monaco	(1) 1
Lillestrom	(0) 0	Brondby	(0) 0
Liverpool	(0) 0	Spartak Vladikavkaz	(0) 0
Lokomotiv Moscow	(0) 0	Bayern Munich	(4) 5
Lyon	(0) 1	Farense	(0) 0
Manchester U	(0) 2	Rotor Volgograd	(2) 2
Nottingham F	(0) 1	Malmo	(0) 0
Olimpija	(1) 2	Roda	(0) 0
Omonia	(0) 1	Lazio	(1) 2
PSV Eindhoven	(2) 7	MyPa	(1) 1
RAF Yelgava	(0) 1	Zimbru Chisinau	(2) 2
Roma	(3) 4	Neuchatel Xamax	(0) 0
Silkeborg	(0) 1	Sparta Prague	(1) 2
Slavia Prague	(0) 0	Freiburg	(0) 0
Standard Liege	(0) 0	Guimaraes	(0) 0
Ujpesti TE	(0) 0	Strasbourg	(1) 2
Werder Bremen	(4) 5	Glenavon	(0) 0
Widzew Lodz	(0) 1	Odessa	(0) 0
(aet; Odessa won 6-5 on penalties)			
Zaglebie Lubin	(0) 1	AC Milan	(0) 4

Second Round, First Leg

Auxerre	(0) 0	Nottingham F	(1) 1
Barcelona	(1) 3	Guimaraes	(0) 0
Benfica	(0) 1	Roda	(0) 0
Bordeaux	(0) 2	Rotor Volgograd	(1) 1
Brondby	(0) 0	Liverpool	(0) 0
Kaiserslautern	(0) 1	Betis	(1) 3
Leeds U	(1) 3	PSV Eindhoven	(3) 5
Lugano	(0) 1	Slavia Prague	(2) 2
Lyon	(1) 2	Lazio	(1) 1
Odessa	(0) 0	Lens	(0) 0
Raith R	(0) 0	Bayern Munich	(1) 2
Roma	(1) 4	Aalst	(0) 0
Sevilla	(0) 1	Olympiakos	(0) 0
Sparta Prague	(2) 4	Zimbru Chisinau	(0) 3
Strasbourg	(0) 0	AC Milan	(0) 1
Werder Bremen	(0) 5	Dynamo Minsk	(0) 0

Second Round, Second Leg

Aalst	(0) 0	Roma	(0) 0
Bayern Munich	(0) 2	Raith R	(1) 1
Betis	(0) 1	Kaiserslautern	(0) 0
Dynamo Minsk	(0) 2	Werder Bremen	(1) 1
Guimaraes	(0) 0	Barcelona	(1) 4
Lazio	(0) 0	Lyon	(1) 2
Lens	(3) 4	Odessa	(0) 0
Liverpool	(0) 0	Brondby	(0) 1
AC Milan	(2) 2	Strasbourg	(0) 1
Nottingham F	(0) 0	Auxerre	(0) 0
Olympiakos	(0) 2	Sevilla	(0) 1
PSV Eindhoven	(2) 3	Leeds U	(0) 1
Roda	(0) 2	Benfica	(0) 2
Rotor Volgograd	(0) 0	Bordeaux	(0) 1
Slavia Prague	(0) 1	Lugano	(0) 0
Zimbru Chisinau	(0) 0	Sparta Prague	(1) 2

Third Round, First Leg

Bayern Munich	(3) 4	Benfica	(1) 1
Bordeaux	(1) 2	Betis	(0) 0
Brondby	(1) 2	Roma	(1) 1

184

AC Milan	(1) 2	Sparta Prague	(0) 0
Nottingham F	(0) 1	Lyon	(0) 0
PSV Eindhoven	(1) 2	Werder Bremen	(0) 1
Sevilla	(1) 1	Barcelona	(0) 1
Slavia Prague	(0) 0	Lens	(0) 0

Third Round, Second Leg

Barcelona	(0) 3	Sevilla	(0) 1
Benfica	(1) 1	Bayern Munich	(1) 3
Betis	(2) 2	Bordeaux	(1) 1
Lens	(0) 0	Slavia Prague	(0) 1
Lyon	(0) 0	Nottingham F	(0) 0
Roma	(1) 3	Brondby	(0) 1
Sparta Prague	(0) 0	AC Milan	(0) 0
Werder Bremen	(0) 0	PSV Eindhoven	(0) 0

Quarter-finals, First Leg

Barcelona	(1) 2	PSV Eindhoven	(1) 2
Bayern Munich	(2) 2	Nottingham F	(1) 1
AC Milan	(1) 2	Bordeaux	(0) 0
Slavia Prague	(1) 2	Roma	(0) 0

Quarter-finals, Second Leg

Bordeaux	(1) 3	AC Milan	(0) 0
Nottingham F	(0) 1	Bayern Munich	(2) 5
PSV Eindhoven	(1) 2	Barcelona	(2) 3
Roma	(0) 3	Slavia Prague	(0) 1

Semi-finals, First Leg

Bayern Munich	(0) 2	Barcelona	(1) 2
Slavia Prague	(0) 0	Bordeaux	(1) 1

Semi-finals, Second Leg

Barcelona	(0) 1	Bayern Munich	(1) 2
Bordeaux	(0) 1	Slavia Prague	(0) 0

FINAL First Leg

Bayern Munich (1) 2, Bordeaux (0) 0

(in Munich, 1 May 1996, 62,000)

Bayern Munich: Kahn; Kruezer, Matthaus (Frey 54), Helmer, Hamann, Sforza, Babbel, Scholl, Ziege, Papin (Witeczek 68), Klinsmann.
Scorers: Helmer 35, Scholl 60.
Bordeaux: Huard; Grenet, Dogon, Friis-Hansen, Lizarazu, Bancarel, Croci, Dutuel, Lucas, Witschge, Tholot (Anselin 89).
Referee: Muhmenthaler (Switzerland).

FINAL Second Leg

Bordeaux (0) 1, Bayern Munich (0) 3

(in Bordeaux, 15 May 1996, 36,000)

Bordeaux: Huard; Bancarel, Dogon, Friis-Hansen, Lizarazu (Anselin 31), Zidane, Croci (Dutuel 57), Lucas (Grenet 80), Witschge, Tholot, Dugarry.
Scorer: Dutuel 76.
Bayern Munich: Kahn; Babbel, Matthaus, Helmer, Frey (Zickler 60), Strunz, Sforza, Ziege, Scholl, Kostadinov (Witeczek 75), Klinsmann.
Scorers: Scholl 53, Kostadinov 66, Klinsmann 78.
Referee: Zhuk (Belarus).

PAST EUROPEAN CUP FINALS

Year	Winner	Score	Runner-up	Score
1956	Real Madrid	4	Stade de Rheims	3
1957	Real Madrid	2	Fiorentina	0
1958	Real Madrid	3	AC Milan	2*
1959	Real Madrid	2	Stade de Rheims	0
1960	Real Madrid	7	Eintracht Frankfurt	3
1961	Benfica	3	Barcelona	2
1962	Benfica	5	Real Madrid	3
1963	AC Milan	2	Benfica	1
1964	Internazionale	3	Real Madrid	1
1965	Internazionale	1	SL Benfica	0
1966	Real Madrid	2	Partizan Belgrade	1
1967	Celtic	2	Internazionale	1
1968	Manchester U	4	Benfica	1*
1969	AC Milan	4	Ajax	1
1970	Feyenoord	2	Celtic	1*
1971	Ajax	2	Panathinaikos	0
1972	Ajax	2	Internazionale	0
1973	Ajax	1	Juventus	0
1974	Bayern Munich	1 4	Atletico Madrid	1 0
1975	Bayern Munich	2	Leeds U	0
1976	Bayern Munich	1	St Etienne	0
1977	Liverpool	3	Borussia Moenchengladbach	1
1978	Liverpool	1	FC Brugge	0
1979	Nottingham F	1	Malmö	0
1980	Nottingham F	1	Hamburg	0
1981	Liverpool	1	Real Madrid	0
1982	Aston Villa	1	Bayern Munich	0
1983	Hamburg	1	Juventus	0
1984	Liverpool†	1	Roma	1
1985	Juventus	1	Liverpool	0
1986	Steaua Bucharest†	0	Barcelona	0
1987	Porto	2	Bayern Munich	1
1988	PSV Eindhoven†	0	Benfica	0
1989	AC Milan	4	Steaua Bucharest	0
1990	AC Milan	1	Benfica	0
1991	Red Star Belgrade†	0	Marseille	0
1992	Barcelona	1	Sampdoria	0
1993	Marseille	1	AC Milan	0

(Marseille subsequently stripped of title)

Year	Winner	Score	Runner-up	Score
1994	AC Milan	4	Barcelona	0
1995	Ajax	1	AC Milan	0

PAST EUROPEAN CUP-WINNERS FINALS

Year	Winner	Score	Runner-up	Score
1961	Fiorentina	4	Rangers	1‡
1962	Atletico Madrid	1 3	Fiorentina	1 0
1963	Tottenham H	5	Atletico Madrid	1
1964	Sporting Lisbon	3 1	MTK Budapest	3* 0
1965	West Ham U	2	Munich 1860	0
1966	Borussia Dortmund	2	Liverpool	1*
1967	Bayern Munich	1	Rangers	0*
1968	AC Milan	2	Hamburg	0
1969	Slovan Bratislava	3	Barcelona	2
1970	Manchester C	2	Gornik Zabrze	1

1971	Chelsea	1 2	Real Madrid	1* 1*
1972	Rangers	3	Dynamo Moscow	2
1973	AC Milan	1	Leeds U	0
1974	Magdeburg	2	AC Milan	0
1975	Dynamo Kiev	3	Ferencvaros	0
1976	Anderlecht	4	West Ham U	2
1977	Hamburg	2	Anderlecht	0
1978	Anderlecht	4	Austria Vienna	0
1979	Barcelona	4	Fortuna Dusseldorf	3*
1980	Valencia†	0	Arsenal	0
1981	Dynamo Tbilisi	2	Carl Zeiss Jena	1
1982	Barcelona	2	Standard Liege	1
1983	Aberdeen	2	Real Madrid	1*
1984	Juventus	2	Porto	1
1985	Everton	3	Rapid Vienna	1
1986	Dynamo Kiev	3	Atletico Madrid	0
1987	Ajax	1	Lokomotiv Leipzig	0
1988	Mechelen	1	Ajax	0
1989	Barcelona	2	Sampdoria	0
1990	Sampdoria	2	Anderlecht	0
1991	Manchester U	2	Barcelona	1
1992	Werder Bremen	2	Monaco	0
1993	Parma	3	Antwerp	1
1994	Arsenal	1	Parma	0
1995	Real Zaragoza	2	Arsenal	1*

FAIRS CUP FINALS

1958	Barcelona	8	London	2‡
1960	Barcelona	4	Birmingham C	1‡
1961	Roma	4	Birmingham C	2‡
1962	Valencia	7	Barcelona	3‡
1963	Valencia	4	Dynamo Zagreb	1‡
1964	Real Zaragoza	2	Valencia	1
1965	Ferencvaros	1	Juventus	0
1966	Barcelona	4	Real Zaragoza	3‡
1967	Dynamo Zagreb	2	Leeds U	0‡
1968	Leeds U	1	Ferencvaros	0
1969	Newcastle U	6	Ujpest Dozsa	2‡
1970	Arsenal	4	Anderlecht	3‡
1971	Leeds U	3**	Juventus	3‡

PAST UEFA CUP FINALS

1972	Tottenham H	2 1	Wolverhampton W	1 1
1973	Liverpool	3 0	Borussia Moenchengladbach	0 2
1974	Feyenoord	2 2	Tottenham H	2 0
1975	Borussia Moenchengladbach	0 5	Twente Enschede	0 1
1976	Liverpool	3 1	FC Brugge	2 1
1977	Juventus**	1 1	Athletic Bilbao	0 2
1978	PSV Eindhoven	0 3	SEC Bastia	0 0
1979	Borussia Moenchengladbach	1 1	Red Star Belgrade	1 0
1980	Borussia Moenchengladbach	3 0	Eintracht Frankfurt**	2 1
1981	Ipswich T	3 2	AZ 67 Alkmaar	0 4
1982	IFK Gothenburg	1 3	SV Hamburg	0 0
1983	Anderlecht	1 1	Benfica	0 1

1984	Tottenham H†	1 1	RSC Anderlecht	1 1
1985	Real Madrid	3 0	Videoton	0 1
1986	Real Madrid	5 0	Cologne	1 2
1987	IFK Gothenburg	1 1	Dundee U	0 1
1988	Bayer Leverkusen†	0 3	Espanol	3 0
1989	Napoli	2 3	Stuttgart	1 3
1990	Juventus	3 0	Fiorentina	1 0
1991	Internazionale	2 0	AS Roma	0 1
1992	Ajax**	0 2	Torino	2 0
1993	Juventus	3 3	Borussia Dortmund	1 0
1994	Internazionale	1 1	Salzburg	0 0
1995	Parma	1 1	Juventus	0 1

*After extra time ** Won on away goals † Won on penalties ‡ Aggregate score*

EUROPEAN CUP DRAWS 1996–97

EUROPEAN CUP
Qualifying Round
Maccabi Tel Aviv (Israel) v Fenerbahce (Turkey), Rangers v Vladikavkaz (Russia), Panathinaikos (Greece) v Rosenborg (Norway), Gothenburg (Sweden) v Ferencvaros (Hungary), Widzew Lodz (Poland) v Bronby (Denmark), Grasshoppers (Switzerland) v Slavia Prague (Czech Republic), FC Brugge (Belgium) v Steaua (Romania), Rapid Vienna (Austria) v Dynamo Kiev (Ukraine).

EUROPEAN CUP-WINNERS' CUP
Qualifying Round
Humenne (Slovakia) v Flamurtari (Albania), Sion (Switzerland) v Kareda (Lithuania), Olimpija (Slovenia) v Levski Sofia (Bulgaria), Red Star Belgrade (Yugoslavia) v Hearts, Karabakh (Azerbaijan) v MyPa (Finland), Kotaik (Armenia) v AEK (Cyprus), Constructorul (Moldova) v Hapoel Ironi Rishon (Israel), Valletta (Malta) v Gloria (Romania), MPCC (Belarus) v FC Reykjavik (Iceland), Brann (Norway) v Shelbourne, Llansantffraid v Ruch Chorzow (Poland), Kispest Honved (Hungary) v Sloga (Macedonia), Varteks (Croatia) v Union (Luxembourg), Universitate (Latvia) v Vaduz (Liechtenstein), Glentoran v Sparta Prague (Czech Republic), Dynamo Batumi (Georgia) v HB (Faeroes), Sadam (Estonia) v vinnitsa (Ukraine).

UEFA CUP
Preliminary Round
Jeunesse Esch (Luxembourg) v Legia (Poland), Lantana (Estonia) v Vestmann (iceland), Becej (Yugoslavia) v Mura (Slovenia), Zalgiris (Lithuania) v Crusaders, Newtown v Skonto Riga (Latvia), Tiligul (Moldova) v Dynamo 93 Minsk (Belarus), Khazri (Azerbaijan) v Hutnik (Poland), Portadown v Vojvodina (Yugoslavia), GI (Faeroes) v Jazz Pori (Finland), Akranes (Iceland) v Sileks (Macedonia), Bohemians v Dynamo Minsk (Belarus), Haka (Finland) v Flora (Estonia), Barry Town v Dinaburg (Latvia), Dynamo Tbilisi (Georgia) v Grevenmacher (Luxembourg), Maccabi Haifa (Israel) v Partizan Belgrade (Yugoslavia), Gorika (Slovenia) v Vardar (Macedonia), Croatia Zagreb (Croatia) v SK Tirana (Albania), Beitar Jerusalem (Israel) v Floriana (Malta), Pyunic (Armenia) v HJK Helsinki (Finland), Sandoyar (Faeroes) v Apoel (Cyprus), Lokomotiv Sofia (Bulgaria) v Neftchi Baku (Azerbaijan), Zimbru (Moldovo) v Hajduk Split (Croatia), Slovan Bratislava (Slovakia) v St Patrick's Ath, Kosice (Slovakia) v Teuta (Albania), Anorthosis (Cyprus) v Shirak (Armenia), Margveti (Georgia) v Silema Wanderers (Malta), Slavia Sofia (Bulgaria) v Inkaras (Lithuania).

PAST EUROPEAN CHAMPIONSHIP FINALS

Paris, 10 July 1960 USSR 2, YUGOSLAVIA 1*
USSR: Yachin; Tchekeli, Kroutikov, Voinov, Maslenkin, Netto, Metreveli, Ivanov, Ponedelnik, Bubukin, Meshki. **Scorers:** Metreveli, Ponedelnik.
Yugoslavia: Vidinic; Durkovic, Jusufi, Zanetic, Miladinovic, Perusic, Sekularac, Jerkovic, Galic, Matus, Kostic. **Scorer:** Netto (og).

Madrid, 21 June 1964 SPAIN 2, USSR 1
Spain: Iribar, Rivilla, Calleja, Fuste, Olivella, Zoco, Amancio, Pereda, Marcellino, Suarez, Lapetra. **Scorers:** Pereda, Marcellino.
USSR: Yachin; Chustikov, Mudrik, Voronin, Shesternjev, Anitchkin, Chislenko, Ivanov, Ponedelnik, Kornaev, Khusainov. **Scorer:** Khusainov.

Rome, 8 June 1968 ITALY 1, YUGOSLAVIA 1
Italy: Zoff; Burgnich, Facchetti, Ferrini, Guarneri, Castano, Domenghini, Juliano, Anastasi, Lodetti, Prati. **Scorer:** Domenghini.
Yugoslavia: Pandelic; Fazlagic, Damjanovic, Pavlovic, Paunovic, Holcer, Petkovic, Acimovic, Musemic, Trivic, Dzajic. **Scorer:** Dzajic.

Replay: Rome, 10 June 1968 ITALY 2, YUGOSLAVIA 0
Italy: Zoff; Burgnich, Facchetti, Rosato, Guarneri, Salvadore, Domenghini, Mazzola, Anastasi, De Sista, Riva. **Scorers:** Riva, Anastasi.
Yugoslavia: Pantelic; Fazlagic, Damjanovic, Pavlovic, Paunovic, Holcer, Hosic, Acimovic, Musemic, Trivic, Dzajic.

Brussels, 18 June 1972 WEST GERMANY 3, USSR 0
West Germany: Maier; Hottges, Schwarzenbeck, Beckenbauer, Breitner, Hoeness, Wimmer, Netzer, Heynckes, Müller, Kremers. **Scorers:** Müller 2, Wimmer.
USSR: Rudakov; Dzodzuashvili, Khurtsilava, Kaplichny, Istomin, Troshkin, Kolotov, Baidachni, Konkov (Dolmatov), Banishevski (Konzinkievits), Onishenko.

Belgrade, 20 June 1976 CZECHOSLOVAKIA 2, WEST GERMANY 2*
Czechoslovakia: Viktor; Dobias (Vesely F), Pivarnik, Ondrus, Capkovic, Gogh, Moder, Panenka, Svehlik (Jurkemik), Masny, Nehoda. **Scorers:** Svehlik, Dobias.
West Germany: Maier; Vogts, Beckenbauer, Schwarzenbeck, Dietz, Bonhof, Wimmer (Flohe), Müller D, Beer (Bongartz), Hoeness, Holzenbein. **Scorers:** Müller, Holzenbein.
Czechoslovakia won 5-3 on penalties.

Rome, 22 June 1980 WEST GERMANY 2, BELGIUM 1
West Germany: Schumacher; Briegel, Forster K, Dietz, Schuster, Rummenigge, Hrubesch, Müller, Allofs, Stielike, Kalz. **Scorers:** Hrubesch 2.
Belgium: Pfaff; Gerets, Millecamps, Meeuws, Renquin, Cools, Van der Eycken, Van Moer, Mommens, Van der Elst, Ceulemans. **Scorer:** Van der Eycken.

Paris, 27 June 1984 FRANCE 2, SPAIN 0
France: Bats; Battiston (Amoros), Le Roux, Bossis, Domergue, Giresse, Platini, Tigana, Fernandez, Lacombe (Genghini), Bellone. **Scorers:** Platini, Bellone.
Spain: Arconada; Urquiaga, Salva (Roberto), Gallego, Camacho, Francisco, Julio Alberto (Sarabia), Senor, Victor, Carrasco, Santilana.

Munich, 25 June 1988 HOLLAND 2, USSR 0
Holland: Van Breukelen; Van Aerle, Van Tiggelen, Wouters, Koeman R, Rijkaard, Vanenburg, Gullit, Van Basten, Muhren, Koeman E. **Scorers:** Gullit, Van Basten.
USSR: Dassayev; Khidiatulin, Aleinikov, Mikhailichenko, Litovchenko, Demianenko, Belanov, Gotsmanov (Baltacha), Protasov (Pasulko), Zavarov, Rats.

Gothenburg, 26 June 1992 DENMARK 2, GERMANY 0
Denmark: Schmeichel; Sivebaek (Christiansen); Nielsen K, Olsen L, Christofte, Jensen, Povlsen, Laudrup, Piechnik, Larsen, Vilfort. **Scorers:** Jensen, Vilfort.
Germany: Illgner; Reuter, Brehme, Kohler, Buchwald, Hässler, Riedle, Helmer, Sammer (Doll), Effenberg (Thon), Klinsmann.

* *After extra time*

EUROPEAN CHAMPIONSHIP 1994-96

Qualifying tournament

Gronp 1

Tel Aviv, 4 September 1994, 3500

Israel (1) 2 *(Harazi R 43, 58)*
Poland (0) 1 *(Kosecki 80)*
Israel: Ginzburg; Harazi A, Klinger, Balbul, Glam, Hazan, Berkovitch (Levi 86), Banin, Revivo, Rosenthal (Atar 89), Harazi R.
Poland: Wandzik; Bak, Szewczyk, Waldoch, Maciejewski, Lapinski, Jalocha (Czerwiec 46), Mielcarski (Gesior 58), Brzeczek, Kosecki, Kowalczyk.
Referee: Van den Wijngaert (Belgium).

Bratislava, 7 September 1994, 14,238

Slovakia (0) 0
France (0) 0
Slovakia: Molnar; Glonek, Stupala, Zeman, Tittel, Kinder, Tomaschek, Kristofik, Zvara (Penksa 63), Rusnak (Weiss 80), Moravcik.
France: Lama; Angloma, Blanc, Roche, Di Meco, Deschamps, Le Guen, Ginola, Djorkaeff (Lizarazu 82), Cantona, Pedros (Dugarry 63).
Referee: Mikkelsen (Denmark).

Bucharest, 7 September 1994, 10,000

Romania (1) 3 *(Belodedici 43, Petrescu 58, Raducioiu 88)*
Azerbaijan (0) 0
Romania: Stelea (Stingaciu 85); Petrescu, Prodan, Belodedici, Selymes (Carstea 82), Lupescu (Timofte D 75), Popescu, Munteanu, Lacatus, Raducioiu, Dumitrescu.
Azerbaijan: Jidkov; Allahverdiev, Asadov, Ahmedov T, Drozdov, Abusov, Diniyev, Huseynov Y (Agayev 80), Alekberov, Suleymanov (Rzayev 59), Kasumov.
Referee: Sedlacek (Austria).

St Etienne, 8 October 1994, 31,744

France (0) 0
Romania (0) 0
France: Lama; Blanc, Angloma, Roche, Lizarazu, Karembeu, Desailly, Loko (Dugarry 83), Pedros, Cantona, Ouedec (Zidane 71).
Romania: Stelea; Belodedici, Prodan, Petrescu, Lupescu, Timofte D (Lacatus 71), Popescu, Hagi, Selymes, Dumitrescu, Raducioiu (Panduru 80).
Referee: Sundell (Sweden).

Tel Aviv, 12 October 1994, 10,000

Israel (2) 2 *(Harazi R 23, Banin 32 (pen))*
Slovakia (2) 2 *(Rusnak 5, Moravcik 14)*
Israel: Ginzburg; Balbul, Glam, Klinger (Shelach 67), Harazi A, Hazan, Berkovitch, Banin (Nimni 60), Revivo, Harazi R, Rosenthal.
Slovakia: Molnar; Stupala, Tittel, Glonek, Kinder, Zeman, Kristofik, Dubovsky, Weiss (Kozak 75), Moravcik, Rusnak (Zvara 76).
Referee: Blankenstein (Holland).

Mielec, 12 October 1994, 10,000

Poland (1) 1 *(Juskowiak 44)*
Azerbaijan (0) 0
Poland: Wandzik; Waldoch, Jaskulski, Lapinski (Maciejewski 79), Kozminski (Fedoruk 70), Swierczewski P, Czereszewski, Brzeczek, Kosecki, Warzycha, Juskowiak.
Azerbaijan: Jidkov; Allahverdiev, Karimov, Ahmedov T, Asadov, Abusov (Gurbanov M 89), Huseynov Y, Diniyev, Mardanov, Kasumov, Alekberov.
Referee: Koho (Finland).

Bucharest, 12 November 1994, 15,000
Romania (1) 3 *(Popescu 7, Hagi 46, Prodan 80)*
Slovakia (0) 2 *(Dubovsky 56, Chvila 78)*
Romania: Stelea; Petrescu, Belodedici, Prodan, Munteanu, Lacatus (Timofte D 75), Popescu, Lupescu, Hagi, Raducioiu (Vladoiu 83), Dumitrescu.
Slovakia: Molnar; Stupala, Chvila, Tittel, Glonek, Kinder, Tomaschek, Kristofik, Moravcik, Penksa (Timko 46), Dubovsky.
Referee: Zhuk (Russia).

Zabrze, 16 November 1994, 20,000
Poland (0) 0
France (0) 0
Poland: Wandzik; Jaskulski, Czereszewski, Swierczewski M, Waldoch, Swierczewski P, Baluszynski (Gesior 80), Kozminski (Bak 28), Juskowiak, Kosecki, Warzycha.
France: Lama; Angloma, Blanc, Roche, Di Meco, Karembeu, Desailly, Le Guen, Ouedec (Dugarry 76), Cantona, Pedros (Djorkaeff 25).
Referee: Amendolia (Italy).

Trabzon, 16 November 1994, 3000
Azerbaijan (0) 0
Israel (1) 2 *(Harazi R 30, Rosenthal 51)*
Azerbaijan: Jidkov; Allahverdiev, Ahmedov T, Mayorov (Agayev 46), Cabarov, Asadov, Huseynov Y (Rzayev 77), Diniyev, Kasumov, Suleymanov, Alekberov.
Israel: Ginzburg; Balbul, Harazi A, Klinger, Glam, Hazan, Banin, Berkovitch (Nimni 66), Revivo, Harazi R (Shelah 83), Rosenthal.
Referee: Vagner (Hungary).

Tel Aviv, 14 December 1994, 40,000
Israel (0) 1 *(Rosenthal 84)*
Romania (0) 1 *(Lacatus 70)*
Israel: Ginzburg; Balbul, Klinger, Harazi A, Glam, Hazan, Berkovitch, Levi (Zohar 75), Revivo, Harazi R (Shelach 90), Rosenthal.
Romania: Stelea; Petrescu, Belodedici, Prodan, Selymes, Hagi, Popescu, Lupescu, Munteanu (Vladoiu 52), Lacatus, Dumitrescu (Galca 74).
Referee: Navarrete (Spain).

Trabzon, 14 December 1994, 4000
Azerbaijan (0) 0
France (1) 2 *(Papin 25, Loko 56)*
Azerbaijan: Jidkov (Hasanov 41); Allahverdiev, Vahabzadze, Abusov, Agayev, Cabarov, Asadov (Gadirov 78), Kasumov, Diniyev (Rzayev 78), Huseynov Y, Alekberov.
France: Lama; Angloma, Roche, Blanc, Di Meco, Desailly (Ferri 71), Le Guen, Cantona, Loko, Papin, Pedros (Martins 76).
Referee: Pedersen (Norway).

Bucharest, 29 March 1995, 22,000
Romania (1) 2 *(Raducioiu 45, Wandzik 55 (og))*
Poland (1) 1 *(Juskowiak 43 (pen))*
Romania: Stelea; Petrescu, Prodan, Belodedici, Selymes, Hagi (Vladoiu 88), Dumitrescu, Popescu, Munteanu, Lacatus (Lupu 46), Raducioiu.
Poland: Wandzik; Jaskulski, Swierczewski M, Waldoch, Swierczewski P, Nowak (Wieszyczcki 58), Czereszewski (Sokolowski 73), Baluszynski, Warzycha, Juskowiak, Kosecki.
Referee: Rothlisberger (Switzerland).

Kosice, 29 March 1995, 12,400

Slovakia (3) 4 *(Tittel 35, Timko 40, 50, Dubovsky 45 (pen))*

Azerbaijan (0) 1 *(Suleymanov 80 (pen))*

Slovakia: Molnar; Stupala, Glonek, Zeman, Kinder, Kristofik, Tittel, Moravcik (Prazenica 73), Dubovsky, Timko, Penksa.

Azerbaijan: Hasanov; Aliyev (Gadirov 65), Vahabzadze, Abusov, Cabarov, Asadov, Huseynov Y, Agayev, Diniyev, Suleymanov, Kasumov (Alekberov 56).

Referee: Nikakis (Greece).

Tel Aviv, 29 March 1995, 45,000

Israel (0) 0

France (0) 0

Israel: Ginzburg; Halfon, Klinger, Harazi A, Glam, Hazan, Banin, Revivo, Berkovitch (Zohar 64), Rosenthal, Harazi R.

France: Lama; Angloma, Roche, Blanc, Di Meco, Desailly, Le Guen, Martins (Djorkaeff 78), Pedros, Loko, Ouedec (Ginola 66).

Referee: McCluskey (Scotland).

Zabrze, 25 April 1995, 5500

Poland (1) 4 *(Nowak 1, Juskowiak 50, Kowalczyk 55, Kosecki 62)*

Israel (2) 3 *(Rosenthal 37, Revivo 42, Zohar 77)*

Poland: Wandzik; Lapinski, Swierczewski M, Waldoch, Swierczewski P, Nowak (Bukalski 46), Kozminski, Baluszynski (Wieszczycki 46), Juskowiak, Kowalczyk, Kosecki.

Israel: Ginzburg; Halfon, Harazi A, Klinger, Glam, Hazan, Banin, Revivo, Berkovitch, Mizrahi (Zohar 73), Rosenthal.

Referee: Frisk (Sweden).

Trabzon, 26 April 1995, 500

Azerbaijan (1) 1 *(Suleymanov 4)*

Romania (2) 4 *(Raducioiu 1 (pen), 68, 76, Dumitrescu 38)*

Azerbaijan: Hasanov; Asadov, Getmam, Ahmedov T (Vahabzadze 21), Cabarov (Gadirov 75), Abusov, Huseynov Y, Diniyev, Lichkin, Suleymanov, Alekberov.

Romania: Stelea (Prunea 85); Petrescu, Prodan, Belodedici, Selymes, Popescu (Timofte D 81), Munteanu, Lupescu, Dumitrescu, Lacatus (Lupu 69), Raducioiu.

Referee: Momirov (Bulgaria).

Nantes, 26 April 1995, 26,000

France (2) 4 *(Kristofik 27 (og), Ginola 42, Blanc 57, Guerin 62)*

Slovakia (0) 0

France: Lama; Angloma, Blanc, Roche, Di Meco, Deschamps, Desailly, Guerin, Zidane (Djorkaeff 73), Loko, Ginola.

Slovakia: Molnar; Stupala, Zeman, Glonek, Kinder, Kristofik, Tittel, Tomaschek (Timko 46), Moravcik, Penksa (Maixner 73), Dubovsky.

Referee: Heynemann (Germany).

Zabrze, 7 June 1995, 20,000

Poland (1) 5 *(Juskowiak 10, 70, Wieszczycki 58, Kosecki 63, Nowak 70)*

Slovakia (0) 0

Poland: Szczesny; Jaskulski (Czereszewski 76), Zielinski, Bukalski, Waldoch, Kozminski, Swierczewski P, Nowak, Kosecki, Juskowiak, Kowalczyk, (Wieszczycki 46).

Slovakia: Vencel; Kozak (Penksa 60), Zeman, Glonek, Prazenica, Tomaschek, Solar, Kristofik (Weiss 71), Timko, Dubovsky, Moravcik.

Referee: Sedlacek (Austria).

Bucharest, 7 June 1995, 20,000
Romania (1) 2 *(Lacatus 16, Munteanu 65)*
Israel (0) 1 *(Berkovitch 50)*
Romania: Stelea; Petrescu, Prodan, Belodedici, Selymes, Munteanu, Lupescu, Lupu (Panduru 87), Dumitrescu (Vladoiu 63), Lacatus, Raducioiu.
Israel: Cohen; Halfon, Shelah (Balbul 65)(Zohar 74), Brumer, Amsalem, Hazan, Klinger, Mizrahi, Banin, Berkovitch, Driks.
Referee: Pedersen (Norway).

Trabzon, 16 August 1995, 50
Azerbaijan (0) 0
Slovakia (0) 1 *(Jancula 60)*
Azerbaijan: Sadygov; Getmam, Gadirov, Ahmedov T, Agayev (Asadov 71), Abusov, Huseynov Y, Diniyev (Mahmoud 46), Nosenko, Lichkin, Alekberov.
Slovakia: Molnar; Pecko, Tittel, Balis (Prazenica 89), Zeman, Kinder, Tomaschek, Simon, Moravcik (Faktor 75), Rusnak (Jancula 58), Dubovsky.
Referee: Hamer (Luxemburg).

Paris, 16 August 1995, 40,496
France (0) 1 *(Djorkaeff 85)*
Poland (1) 1 *(Juskowiak 35)*
France: Lama; Angloma (Karembeu 66), Thuram, Leboeuf (Djorkaeff 69), Lizarazu, Deschamps, Desailly, Guerin, Zidane, Dugarry, Ginola (Pedros 64).
Poland: Wozniak; Lapinski, Waldoch, Zielinski, Kozminski, Iwan, Swierczewski P, Nowak (Czerwiec 56), Kosecki (Wojtala 71), Juskowiak, Kowalczyk (Bukalski 60).
Referee: Diaz Vega (Spain).

Auxerre, 6 September 1995, 15,000
France (3) 10 *(Desailly 13, Djorkaeff 17, 78, Guerin 33, Pedros 49, Leboeuf 54, 74, Dugarry 65, Zidane 72, Cocard 90)*
Azerbaijan (0) 0
France: Lama; Angloma (Thuram 57), Desailly, Leboeuf, Lizarazu, Deschamps, Guerin, Djorkaeff, Zidane, Dugarry (Cocard 68), Pedros (Ginola 65).
Azerbaijan: Hasanov (Sadygov 38); Asadov, Getman, Ahmedov T, Agayev, Abusov, Gadirov (Huseynov M 75), Diniyev, Gurbanov M (Alekberov 46), Huseynov Y, Lichkin.
Referee: Micallef (Malta).

Zabrze, 6 September 1995, 18,000
Poland (0) 0
Romania (0) 0
Poland: Wozniak; Jaskulski, Zielinski, Waldoch, Kozminski, Bednarz (Bukalski 62), Swierczewski P, Iwan (Czerwiec 76), Kosecki, Juskowiak, Wieszczicki (Podbrozny 67).
Romania: Stelea; Petrescu, Prodan, Popescu, Mihali, Selymes, Lupescu, Munteanu (Galca 76), Lacatus (Timofte I 85), Sabau, Vladoiu (Panduru 66).
Referee: Gallagher (England).

Kosice, 6 September 1995, 7810
Slovakia (0) 1 *(Jancula 54)*
Israel (0) 0
Slovakia: Molnar; Tittel, Pecko, Karhan, Kinder, Balis (Kostka 89), Simon (Faktor 82), Juriga, Moravcik, Jancula (Rusnak 66), Dubovsky.
Israel: Cohen; Brumer, Glam, Harazi A, Shelah, Hazan, Klinger (Rosenthal 46), Banin, Revivo, Mizrahi, Berkovitch (Driks 65).
Referee: Piraux (Belgium).

Bucharest, 11 October 1995, 25,000
Romania (0) 1 *(Lacatus 51)*
France (2) 3 *(Karembeu 29, Djorkaeff 41, Zidane 72)*
Romania: Stelea; Petrescu, Mihali (Lupu 46), Popescu, Prodan, Selymes, Lupescu, Hagi (Panduru 62), Munteanu, Lacatus, Dumitrescu (Vladoiu 46).
France: Barthez; Angloma, Leboeuf, Desailly, Di Meco, Karembeu, Deschamps, Guerin, Djorkaeff (Lizarazu 73), Dugarry (Madar 62), Zidane (Thuram 84).
Referee: Pairetto (Italy).

Bratislava, 11 October 1995, 12,000
Slovakia (1) 4 *(Dubovsky 31 (pen), Jancula 68, Ujlaky 78, Simon 83)*
Poland (1) 1 *(Juskowiak 19)*
Slovakia: Molnar; Karhan, Tittel, Zeman, Kinder, Balis, Juriga (Ujlaky 71), Simon, Moravcik, Jancula (Bochnovic 87), Dubovsky.
Poland: Wozniak; Lapinski, Zielinski, Waldoch, Kozminski (Bednarz 58), Iwan, Swierczewski P, Bukalski, Baluszynski (Czereszewski 79), Juskowiak, Kosecki.
Referee: Coroado (Portugal).

Tel Aviv, 11 October 1995, 8000
Israel (1) 2 *(Harazi R 31, 50)*
Azerbaijan (0) 0
Israel: Ginzburg; Halfon, Brumer, Shelah, Amsalem, Hazan, Banin, Berkovitch (Zohar 71), Revivo (Klinger 87), Harazi R (Atar 79), Rosenthal.
Azerbaijan: Jidkov; Asadov, Vahabzadze, Mayorov (Agayev 52), Ahmedov T, Abusov, Lichkin (Mamedov 70), Gadirov, Rzayev (Gurbanov M 70), Suleymanov, Kasumov.
Referee: Detruche (Switzerland).

Caen, 15 November 1995, 21,500
France (0) 2 *(Djorkaeff 69, Lizarazu 89)*
Israel (0) 0
France: Lama; Angloma, Desailly, Leboeuf, Di Meco (Lizarazu 63), Karembeu (Keller 90), Deschamps, Guerin, Zidane, Djorkaeff, Madar (Loko 63).
Israel: Cohen; Halfon, Brumer, Shelah, Glam (Zohar 79), Hazan, Klinger, Banin, Berkovitch (Atar 70), Rosenthal, Harazi R (Mizrahi 85).
Referee: Grabner (Austria).

Kosice, 15 November 1995, 8000
Slovakia (0) 0
Romania (0) 2 *(Hagi 68, Munteanu 82)*
Slovakia: Molnar; Pecko (Juriga 46), Tittel, Karhan, Kinder, Simon (Semenik 77), Balis, Tomaschek, Moravcik, Jancula (Ujlaky 69), Dubovsky.
Romania: Stelea; Petrescu, Prodan, Dobos, Selymes, Hagi (Panduru 85), Lupescu, Popescu, Munteanu, Lacatus (Dumitrescu 73), Moldovan (Timofte I 89).
Referee: Uilenberg (Holland).

Trabzon, 15 November 1995, 1000
Azerbaijan (0) 0
Poland (0) 0
Azerbaijan: Jidkov; Getman, Gaishumov, Ahmedov T, Vahabzadze, Abusov, Agayev, Rzayev (Gurbanov K 69), Nosenko (Gurbanov M 66), Suleymanov (Lichkin 86), Kasumov.
Poland: Wozniak; Jaskulski, Sokolowski, Bukalski (Lenart 71), Waldoch, Czereszewski, Wojtala, Swierczewski P, Baluszynski (Kuzba 64), Czerwiec, Majak (Siadaczka 46).
Referee: Mottram (Scotland).

	P	W	D	L	F	A	Pts
Romania	10	6	3	1	18	9	21
France	10	5	5	0	22	2	20
Slovakia	10	4	2	4	14	18	14
Poland	10	3	4	3	14	12	13
Israel	10	3	3	4	13	13	12
Azerbaijan	10	0	1	9	2	29	1

Group 2
Brussels, 7 September 1994, 11,000
Belgium (1) 2 *(Oliveira 3, Degryse 73)*
Armenia (0) 0
Belgium: Preud'homme; Genaux, De Wolf, Albert, Smidts, Staelens (Emmers 75), Van der Elst F, Van der Heyden (Boffin 67), Degryse, Oliveira, Weber.
Armenia: Arm. Petrossian; Art. Petrossian, Kerpasian, Tonoian, Hovsepian, Khachatrian V, Soukiassian, Oganesian, Shakhgeldian (Avetissian A 46), Grigorian, Mikhitarian.
Referee: Ferry (Northern Ireland).

Limassol, 7 September 1994, 12,000
Cyprus (1) 1 *(Sotiriou 35)*
Spain (2) 2 *(Higuera 18, 26)*
Cyprus: Panayiotou; Costa, Constandinou C, Christophi E, Charalambous M, Pittas, Ioannou D, Phasouliotis (Malekos 62), Savvides (Andreou 77), Gogic, Sotiriou.
Spain: Zubizarreta; Voro, Nadal, Camarasa, Sergi, Goicoechea, Hierro, Guerrero, Guardiola (Caminero 63), Higuera, Amavisca (Ciganda 78).
Referee: Batta (France).

Skopje, 7 September 1994, 22,000
Macedonia (1) 1 *(Stojkovski 4)*
Denmark (0) 1 *(Povlsen 87)*
Macedonia: Trajcev; Stanojkovic, Najdoski, Markovski, Jovanovski, Stojkovski, Boskovski (Serafimovski 82), Djurovski B, Babunski (Kanatlarovski 65), Pancev, Micevski.
Denmark: Schmeichel; Helveg, Rieper, Olsen, Friis-Hansen, Steen-Nielsen, Jensen J (Larsen 65), Vilfort (Povlsen 50), Christensen B, Laudrup M, Laudrup B.
Referee: Van der Ende (Holland).

Erevan, 8 October 1994, 6000
Armenia (0) 0
Cyprus (0) 0
Armenia: Abramian; Soukiassian, Khachatrian V (Kerpasian 46), Tonoian, Oganesian, Vardanian, Art. Petrossian, Grigorian, Adamian, Avetissian A, Mikhitarian (Avetissian Y 79).
Cyprus: Christophi M; Kalotheou, Pittas, Ioannou D, Stephani, Zembashis, Charalambous, Sotiriou, Gogic, Phasouliotis (Malekos 70), Savvides.
Referee: Bremisla (Poland).

Copenhagen, 12 October 1994, 40,000
Denmark (1) 3 *(Vilfort 35, Jensen J 72, Strudal 86)*
Belgium (1) 1 *(Degryse 31)*
Denmark: Schmeichel; Helveg, Olsen, Rieper, Friis-Hansen, Risager (Kjeldbjerg 78), Vilfort (Jensen J 72), Laudrup M, Steen-Nielsen, Laudrup B, Strudal.
Belgium: Bodart; Genaux, Van Meir, Albert, Smidts, Borkelmans (Oliveira 77), Verheyen, Van der Elst F, Staelens, Degryse, Weber.
Referee: Pairetto (Italy).

Skopje, 12 October 1994, 30,000
Macedonia (0) 0
Spain (2) 2 *(Julio Salinas 16, 25)*
Macedonia: Trajcev (Celeski 50); Stanojkovic, Stojkovski, Djurovski B, Najdoski, Jovanovski, Boskovski, Savevski, Babunski (Markovski 39), Djurovski M (Serafimovski 70), Micevski.
Spain: Zubizarreta; Ferrer, Abelardo, Alkorta, Caminero, Nadal, Hierro (Amavisca 76), Sergi, Luis Enrique, Higuera, Julio Salinas (Pier 65).
Referee: Grabner (Austria).

Brussels, 16 November 1994, 17,000

Belgium (1) 1 *(Verheyen 31)*

Macedonia (0) 1 *(Boskovski 54)*

Belgium: Preud'homme; Genaux, Crasson, Smidts, Boffin, Staelens, Van der Elst F, Walem (De Bilde 72), Verheyen, Degryse, Nilis.
Macedonia: Celeski; Stanojkovic, Djurovski B, Najdoski, Janevski, Jovanovski, Boskovski (Kanatlarovski 87), Markovski, Djurovski M (Serafimovski 80), Stojkovski, Micevski.
Referee: Kusainov (Russia).

Limassol, 16 November 1994, 8000

Cyprus (1) 2 *(Sotiriou 7, Phasouliotis 87)*

Armenia (0) 0

Cyprus: Christophi M; Andreou A, Ioannou D, Christophi E, Stephani, Zembashis (Élia 89), Malekos (Phasouliotis 68), Savvides, Pittas, Gogic, Sotiriou.
Armenia: Abramian; Tonoian, Oganesian, Vardanian, Kerpasian, Art. Petrossian, Grigorian, Mikhitarian (Avetissian V 85), Hovsepian, Soukiassian, Gsepian (Avetissian A 69).
Referee: Ashby (England).

Seville, 16 November 1994, 38,000

Spain (1) 3 *(Nadal 41, Donato 57, Luis Enrique 87)*

Denmark (0) 0

Spain: Zubizarreta; Ferrer, Belsue, Alkorta, Abelardo, Nadal, Luis Enrique, Caminero (Bakero 72), Sergi, Donato, Julio Salinas (Higuera 57).
Denmark: Schmeichel; Helveg, Rieper, Olsen, Risager, Friis Hansen (Christensen B 65), Steen-Nielsen (Jensen J 46), Vilfort, Strudal, Laudrup B, Laudrup M.
Referee: McCluskey (Scotland).

Skopje, 17 December 1994, 12,000

Macedonia (2) 3 *(Djurovski B 15, 36, 89)*

Cyprus (0) 0

Macedonia: Celeski; Stanojkovic, Janevski, Najdoski, Stojkovski, Markovski, Babunski (Jovanovski 72), Djurovski B, Boskovski (Serafimovski 86), Djurovski M, Micevski.
Cyprus: Christophi M; Kalotheou, Charalambous M, Ioannou D, Christophi E, Stephani, Charalambous C, Phasouliotis, Savvides (Malekos 67), Gogic, Sotiriou (Andreou 78).
Referee: Strampe (Germany).

Brussels, 17 December 1994, 25,000

Belgium (1) 1 *(Degryse 6)*

Spain (1) 4 *(Hierro 28, Donato 55 (pen), Julio Salinas 68, Luis Enrique 89)*

Belgium: Preud'homme; Genaux, Crasson, Albert, Smidts, Bettagno (Verheyen 46), Van der Elst F, Staelens, Boffin, Degryse, De Bilde.
Spain: Zubizarreta; Belsue, Abelardo, Nadal, Alkorta, Hierro, Sergi, Donato, Guerrero (Voro 57), Luis Enrique, Julio Salinas (Goicoechea 70).
Referee: Cakar (Turkey).

Seville, 29 March 1995, 27,000

Spain (1) 1 *(Guerrero 24)*

Belgium (1) 1 *(Degryse 25)*

Spain: Zubizarreta; Belsue, Abelardo, Nadal, Sergi, Hierro, Luis Enrique, Guerrero (Higuera 37), Donato, Julio Salinas (Pizzi 63), Amavisca.
Belgium: Bodart; Genaux, Medved, Renier, Smidts, Walem (Verheyen 68), Karagiannis (Crasson 83), Staelens, Degryse, De Bilde, Schepens.
Referee: Harrel (France).

Limassol, 29 March 1995, 15,000

Cyprus (1) 1 *(Agathocleous 45)*

Denmark (1) 1 *(Schjonberg 2)*

Cyprus: Panayiotou; Costa, Pittas, Ioannou D,
Charalambous M, Christodolou G, Engomitis, Andreou A, Hadjilucas (Constandinou C 89), Gogic, Agathocleous.

Denmark: Schmeichel; Laursen, Rieper, Friis-Hansen (Helveg 46), Hogh, Schjonberg, Steen-Nielsen, Nielsen P, Laudrup M, Rasmussen, Laudrup B.

Referee: Shorte (Republic of Ireland).

Erevan, 26 April 1995, 40,000

Armenia (0) 0

Spain (0) 2 *(Amavisca 49, Goicoechea 63)*

Armenia: Abramian; Soukiassian, Hovsepian, Tonoian, Oganesian, Vardanian, Art. Petrossian, Grigorian (Takhmazian 65), Mikhitarian, Shakhgeldian, Adamian (Avetissian A 55).

Spain: Zubizarreta; Belsue, Alkorta, Karanka, Otero, Nadal, Donato (Camarasa 69), Luis Enrique, Goicoechea, Pizzi (Julio Salinas 58), Amavisca.

Referee: Porumboiu (Romania).

Copenhagen, 26 April 1995, 38,888

Denmark (0) 1 *(Nielsen P 70)*

Macedonia (0) 0

Denmark: Schmeichel; Laursen, Rieper, Hogh, Schjonberg, Thomsen, Steen-Nielsen, Rasmussen (Andersen 46), Laudrup M, Nielsen P (Helveg 78), Laudrup B.

Macedonia: Celeski; Stanojkovic, Stojkovski, Najdoski, Markovski (Memed 26), Jovanovski, Boskovski, Djurovski B, Micevski, Pancev, Serafimovski (Marjan Stojkovski 77).

Referee: Ihring (Slovakia).

Brussels, 26 April 1995, 13,000

Belgium (1) 2 *(Karagiannis 20, Schepens 47)*

Cyprus (0) 0

Belgium: Bodart; Renier, Medved, Grun, Smidts, Staelens, Karagiannis, Degryse, Schepens, Nilis, De Bilde (Goossens 81).

Cyprus: Panayiotou; Kalotheou, Charalambous M, Ioannou D, Pittas, Christodolou G, Gogic, Andreou A, Engomitis, Agathocleous (Larkou 62), Papavassiliou (Sotiriou 85).

Referee: Elleray (England).

Erevan, 10 May 1995, 12,500

Armenia (1) 2 *(Grigorian 21, 51)*

Macedonia (0) 2 *(Hristov 59, Markovski 70)*

Armenia: Abramian; Soukiassian, Hovsepian, Tonoian, Oganesian, Vardanian, Art. Petrossian, Grigorian, Mikhitarian (Gsepian 79), Shakhgeldian, Avetissian A (Tahmazian 69).

Macedonia: Celeski; Stanojkovic, Stojkovski, Najdoski, Markovski, Janevski (Kanatlarovski 69), Hristov, Babunski, Micevski (Memed 59), Pancev, Serafimovski.

Referee: Fajilstrom (Sweden).

Copenhagen, 7 June 1995, 40,199

Denmark (1) 4 *(Vilfort 45, 50, Laudrup B 58, Laudrup M 75)*

Cyprus (0) 0

Denmark: Schmeichel; Laursen, Rieper, Hogh, Schjonberg, Steen-Nielsen (Rasmussen 46), Jensen, Vilfort (Andersen 87), Beck, Laudrup M, Laudrup B.

Cyprus: Petrides; Costa, Pittas, Christodolou G, Charalambous M, Andreou A, Engomitis, Larkou, Hadjilucas (Phasouliotis 60), Gogic, Sotiriou (Andreou P 68).

Referee: Muller (Switzerland).

Seville, 7 June 1995, 20,000

Spain (0) 1 *(Hierro 64 (pen))*

Armenia (0) 0

Spain: Zubizarreta; Belsue, Aranzabal, Alkorta, Abelardo, Hierro, Goicoechea (Julio Salinas 46), Guerrero (Caminero 78), Nadal, Luis Enrique, Amavisca.

Armenia: Abramian; Soukiassian, Hovsepian, Tonoian, Nigoian (Ter-Petrossian 71), Vardanian, Art. Petrossian (Avetissian V 76), Tahmazian, Mikhitarian, Shakhgeldian, Avetissian A.

Referee: Philippi (Luxembourg).

Skopje, 7 June 1995, *

Macedonia (0) 0

Belgium (4) 5 *(Grun 15, Scifo 18, 60, Schepens 28, Versavel 43)*

Macedonia: Celeski; Stanojkovic, Najdovski, Stojkovski, Boskovski, Djurovski B (Hristov 61), Janevski, Babunski, Micevski, Pancev, Serafimovski (Memed 35).

Belgium: Bodart; Genaux, Renier, Grun, Smidts, Staelens, Karagiannis, Schepens (Leonard 83), Scifo, Versavel, De Bilde.

Referee: Wojciki (Poland).

*Match played behind closed doors as disciplinary punishment.

Erevan, 16 August 1995, 22,000

Armenia (0) 0

Denmark (1) 2 *(Laudrup M 34, Nielsen A 47)*

Armenia: Arm. Petrossian; Khachatrian V, Khachatrian A, Oganesian, Hovsepian, Tonoian, Art. Petrossian, Grigorian, Avetissian A (Avetissian V 80), Tahmazian (Ter-Petrossian 41), Shakhgeldian.

Denmark: Schmeichel; Laursen, Rieper, Hogh, Risager (Schjonberg 85), Thomsen, Jensen (Nielsen A 46), Steen-Nielsen, Beck, Laudrup M, Rasmussen.

Referee: Dardenne (Germany).

Brussels, 6 September 1995, 40,000

Belgium (1) 1 *(Grun 25)*

Denmark (2) 3 *(Laudrup M 19, Beck 21, Vilfort 70)*

Belgium: Bodart; Genaux, Medved, Grun, Smidts (Renier 76), Staelens (Nilis 12), Karagiannis, Scifo, Schepens (Foguenne 57), Degryse, De Bilde.

Denmark: Schmeichel; Risager, Rieper, Hogh, Laursen, Steen-Nielsen, Vilfort, Nielsen A, Laudrup M, Beck (Rasmussen 73), Laudrup B (Andersen 77).

Referee: Zhouk (Belarus).

Skopje, 6 September 1995 *

Macedonia (1) 1 *(Micevski 10)*

Armenia (0) 2 *(Grigorian 61, Shakhgeldian 78)*

Macedonia: Celeski; Nikolovski, Stojkovski, Jovanovski, Markovski, Babunski, Serafimovski, Memed, Savevski, Hristov, Micevski.

Armenia: Arm. Petrossian; Gsepian, Khachatrian V, Vardanian, Oganesian, Stepanian, Ter-Petrossian, Mikhitarian, Avetissian A, Grigorian, Shakhgeldian.

Referee: Pereira (Portugal).

*Match played behind closed doors as disciplinary punishment.

Grenada, 6 September 1995, 30,000

Spain (1) 6 *(Guerrero 45, Alfonso 51, Pizzi 74, 79, Hierro 78, Caminero 82)*

Cyprus (0) 0

Spain: Zubizarreta; Belsue, Aranzabal, Alkorta, Nadal, Hierro, Luis Enrique, Guerrero (Manjarin 77), Caminero, Amavisca (Fran 54), Alfonso (Pizzi 61).

Cyprus: Panayiotou; Charalambous M, Panayi, Pittas, Christodolou G, Ashiotis, Andoniou (Kalotheou 79), Ioannou Y, Malekos (Sotiriou 57), Gogic, Hadjilukas (Ioannou D 75).

Referee: Jol (Holland).

Erevan, 7 October 1995, 5000
Armenia (0) 0
Belgium (2) 2 *(Nilis 28, 39)*
Armenia: Abramian; Gsepian, Khachatrian V, Khachatrian A, Soukiassian, Hovsepian, Grigorian (Avetissian V 46), Mikhitarian (Margarian 71), Art. Petrossian, Shakhgeldian, Avetissian A.
Belgium: De Wilde; Genaux, Crasson, De Boeck, Smidts, Staelens, Karagiannis (Vermant 80), Scifo, Schepens, De Bilde (Goossens 64), Nilis.
Referee: Mitrev (Bulgaria).

Copenhagen, 11 October 1995, 40,262
Denmark (0) 1 *(Vilfort 47)*
Spain (1) 1 *(Hierro 17 (pen))*
Denmark: Schmeichel; Laursen, Piechnik, Hogh, Rieper, Risager, Vilfort, Steen-Nielsen (Wieghorst 67), Laudrup M, Beck, Rasmussen.
Spain: Zubizarreta; Belsue, Abelardo, Alkorta, Nadal, Sergi, Luis Enrique, Hierro, Caminero (Francisco 30), Manjarin (Donato 62), Pizzi (Alfonso 46).
Referee: Krondl (Czech Republic).

Limassol, 11 October 1995, 15,000
Cyprus (0) 1 *(Agathocleous 90)*
Macedonia (1) 1 *(Jovanovski B 31)*
Cyprus: Petrides; Costa, Pittas, Christodolou G, Charalambous M, Kalotheou (Agathocleous 64), Engomitis (Papavassiliou 46), Sotiriou (Larkou 80), Gogic, Savvides, Malekos.
Macedonia: Celeski; Jovanovski B, Karadzov, Markovski, Nikolovski, Jovanovski Z, Veselinovski (Christov 84), Ciric, Serafimovski (Karanfilovski 77), Memed, Savevski.
Referee: Irvine (Republic of Ireland).

Elche, 15 November 1995, 34,000
Spain (1) 3 *(Kiko 8, Manjarin 72, Caminero 79)*
Macedonia (0) 0
Spain: Zubizarreta; Sergi, Nadal, Alkorta, Belsue, Amavisca (Ferrer 46), Caminero, Donato, Manjarin, Kiko (Goicoechea 75), Pizzi (Alfonso 46).
Macedonia: Celeski; Jovanovski B, Stojkovski, Serafimovski (Pecelinovski 52) (Hristov 78), Babunski, Jovanovski Z (Nikolovski 72), Karadzov, Memed, Boskovski, Ciric, Nikovski.
Referee: Steinborn (Germany).

Copenhagen, 15 November 1995, 40,208
Denmark (2) 3 *(Schjonberg 19, Beck 35, Laudrup M 58)*
Armenia (0) 1 *(Art. Petrossian 47)*
Denmark: Schmeichel; Helveg, Rieper, Hogh, Risager, Schjonberg, Steen-Nielsen, Vilfort, Beck, Laudrup M, Rasmussen.
Armenia: Abramian; Artoian, Khachatrian V, Hovsepian, Vardanian, Gsepian (Kerpasian 80), Art. Petrossian, Avetissian V (Margarian 71), Mikhitarian, Nikolian, Avetissian A.
Referee: Veissiere (France).

Limassol, 15 November 1995, 10,000
Cyprus (1) 1 *(Agathocleous 18)*
Belgium (0) 1 *(De Bilde 66)*
Cyprus: Panayiotou; Costa, Pittas A, Christodolou G, Charalambous M, Engomitis, Gogic (Elia 86), Andreou A, Malekos (Larkou 49), Papavassiliou, Agathocleous (Zembashis 75).

Belgium: De Wilde; Genaux, Grun, De Boeck, Smidts (Schepens 77), Staelens, Karagiannis (Goossens 46), Boffin (Huysmans 58), Degryse, De Bilde, Nilis.
Referee: Cesari (Italy).

	P	W	D	L	F	A	Pts
Spain	10	8	2	0	25	4	26
Denmark	10	6	3	1	19	9	21
Belgium	10	4	3	3	17	13	15
Macedonia	10	1	4	5	9	18	7
Cyprus	10	1	4	5	6	20	7
Armenia	10	1	2	7	5	17	5

Group 3
Reykjavik, 7 September 1994, 15,000
Iceland (0) 0
Sweden (1) 1 *(Ingesson 37)*
Iceland: Kristinsson B; Kristinsson R, Jonsson K, Bergsson, Gislason, Gudjohnsen, Orlygsson (Gunnlaugsson B 60), Jonsson S, Stefansson, Gunnlaugsson A, Sverrisson.
Sweden: Ravelli; Nilsson R, Andersson P, Bjorklund, Ljung, Brolin, Mild, Schwarz, Ingesson, Dahlin (Larsson 67), Andersson K.
Referee: Mottram (Scotland).

Budapest, 7 September 1994, 10,000
Hungary (2) 2 *(Kiprich 4, Halmai 45)*
Turkey (0) 2 *(Hakan 66, Bulent K 70)*
Hungary: Petry; Telek, Meszoly, Lipcsei, Kozma, Halmai, Detari, Urban, Duro (Banfi 62), Kiprich (Wukovics 67), Kovacs K.
Turkey: Engin; Gokhan K (Arif 46), Recep, Bulent K, Ilker, Ogun, Oguz, Tugay, Orhan, Ertugrul (Abdullah 87), Hakan.
Referee: Pairetto (Italy).

Istanbul, 12 October 1994, 20,000
Turkey (3) 5 *(Saffet 11, 28, Hakan 30, 62, Sergen 65)*
Iceland (0) 0
Turkey: Engin (Rustu 87); Gokhan K, Recep, Bulent K, Orhan (Mutlu 3), Arif, Oguz, Ogun, Abdullah, Saffet, Hakan (Sergen 64).
Iceland: Kristinsson B (Finnbogason 5), Jonsson S, Kristinsson R, Bergsson, Gislason, Gudjohnsen, Orlygsson, Jonsson K, Stefansson (Gunnlaugsson B 85), Sverrisson, Gunnlaugsson A (Gretarsson 72).
Referee: Levnikov (Russia).

Berne, 12 October 1994, 24,000
Switzerland (1) 4 *(Ohrel 36, Blomqvist 64 (og), Sforza 79, Turkyilmaz 81)*
Sweden (1) 2 *(Andersson K 6, Dahlin 61)*
Switzerland: Pascolo; Hottiger, Herr, Geiger, Thuler, Ohrel, Yakin (Henchoz 83), Sforza, Sutter A, Grassi (Turkyilmaz 69), Chapuisat.
Sweden: Ravelli; Nilsson R, Andersson P, Bjorklund, Kamark, Brolin, Thern (Mild 49), Schwarz, Blomqvist (Larsson 82), Dahlin, Andersson K.
Referee: Elleray (England).

Stockholm, 16 November 1994, 27,571
Sweden (1) 2 *(Brolin 44, Dahlin 70)*
Hungary (0) 0
Sweden: Ravelli; Nilsson R, Andersson P, Bjorklund, Kamark, Brolin (Rehn 70), Schwarz, Thern, Andersson K, Dahlin, Larsson.
Hungary: Petry; Banfi, Meszoly, Lorincz, Kozma, Lipcsei (Halmai 58), Urban, Detari, Duro (Kovacs K 75), Kiprich, Klausz.
Referee: Van der Ende (Holland).

Lausanne, 16 November 1994, 15,800
Switzerland (1) 1 *(Bickel 45)*
Iceland (0) 0
Switzerland: Pascolo; Hottiger, Henchoz, Geiger, Thuler, Ohrel, Sforza, Bickel, Sutter A, Grassi (Turkyilmaz 68), Chapuisat.
Iceland: Kristinsson B; Kristinsson R, Bergsson, Gislason (Ingolfsson 84), Jonsson K, Dervic, Gretarsson (Gunnlaugsson B 64), Orlygsson, Stefansson, Sverrisson, Gunnlaugsson A.
Referee: Kelly (Republic of Ireland).

Istanbul, 14 December 1994, 25,000
Turkey (1) 1 *(Recep 39)*
Switzerland (2) 2 *(Koller 7, Bickel 16)*
Turkey: Rustu; Recep, Bulent K, Gokhan K, Abdullah, Ogun, Oguz, Cengiz (Ilker 46), Arif (Sergen 75), Hakan, Saffet.
Switzerland: Pascolo; Hottiger, Herr, Geiger, Thuler, Ohrel, Sforza, Koller, Sutter A, Bickel (Bonvin 65), Subiat (Grassi 80).
Referee: Craciunescu (Romania).

Budapest, 29 March 1995, 13,000
Hungary (0) 2 *(Kiprich 50, Illes 72)*
Switzerland (0) 2 *(Subiat 73, 85)*
Hungary: Petry; Mracsko, Lorincz, Meszoly, Kovacs E, Kozma, Halmai, Salloi, Illes, Kiprich (Marton 69), Vincze (Klausz 82).
Switzerland: Pascolo; Hottiger, Herr, Geiger, Fernandez, Koller, Ohrel, Sforza, Bickel (Grassi 65), Sutter A, Subiat (Henchoz 89).
Referee: Wieser (Austria).

Istanbul, 29 March 1995, 20,000
Turkey (0) 2 *(Emre 64, Sergen 75)*
Sweden (1) 1 *(Andersson K 23 (pen))*
Turkey: Engin; Recep, Bulent K, Emre, Alpay, Abdullah, Metin, Tolunay, Sergen (Mutlu 77), Hakan, Ertugrul (Oguz 46).
Sweden: Ravelli; Nilsson R, Andersson P, Bjorklund, Ljung, Schwarz, Zetterberg (Rehn 81), Thern, Larsson (Blomqvist 75), Dahlin, Andersson K.
Referee: Trentalange (Italy).

Budapest, 26 April 1995, 10,000
Hungary (1) 1 *(Halmai 2)*
Sweden (0) 0
Hungary: Vegh; Csabi, Meszoly, Mracsko, Kozma, Halmai, Lipcsei, Illes, Salloi, Csertoi (Szlezak 86), Vincze (Urban 68).
Sweden: Ravelli; Nilsson R, Andersson P, Kamark, Ljung, Schwarz, Zetterberg, Mild (Andersson R 62), Ingesson, Alexandersson (Gudmundsson 82), Andersson K.
Referee: Lopez Nieto (Spain).

Berne, 26 April 1995, 24,000
Switzerland (1) 1 *(Hottiger 38)*
Turkey (1) 2 *(Hakan 17, Ogun 56)*
Switzerland: Pascolo; Hottiger, Herr, Geiger, Fernandez (Walker 75), Ohrel, Sforza, Bickel, Sutter A, Grassi, Bonvin (Zuffi 70).
Turkey: Engin; Emre, Bulent K, Alpay, Recep, Ogun, Oguz (Ertugrul 83), Tolunay, Sergen (Suat 79), Abdullah, Hakan.
Referee: Van den Wijngaert (Belgium).

Stockholm, 1 June 1995, 25,676
Sweden (1) 1 *(Brolin 16 (pen))*
Iceland (1) 1 *(Gunnlaugsson A 2)*
Sweden: Ravelli; Sundgren, Andersson P, Mattsson, Kamark, Brolin, Schwarz, Thern, Limpar (Larsson 51), Dahlin, Andersson K.
Iceland: Kristinsson B; Orlygsson, Bergsson, Adolfsson, Jonsson K, Gudjohnsen (Thordarson 90), Stefansson, Jonsson S, Kristinsson R, Sverrisson, Gunnlaugsson A (Gunnlaugsson B 78).
Referee: Ouzounov (Bulgaria).

Reykjavik, 11 June 1995, 4500
Iceland (0) 2 *(Bergsson 63, Jonsson S 69)*
Hungary (1) 1 *(Vincze 20)*
Iceland: Kristinsson B; Bergsson, Adolfsson, Jonsson K, Jonsson S, Kristinsson R, Gretarsson, Gunnlaugsson A, Thordarson (Gunnlaugsson B 68), Gudjohnsen, Sverrisson.
Hungary: Petry; Csabi, Meszoly, Lipcsei, Mracsko, Halmai, Illes (Marton 68), Salloi, Kozma, Csertoi, Vincze (Hamar 70).
Referee: Sars (France).

Reykjavik, 16 August 1995, 12,000
Iceland (0) 0
Switzerland (2) 2 *(Knup 4, Turkyilmaz 17)*
Iceland: Kristinsson B; Adolfsson, Jonsson K (Dervic 89), Jonsson S, Bergsson, Kristinsson R, Orlygsson, Thorvaldsson, Gunnlaugsson A, Sverrisson (Ingolfsson 67), Gunnlaugsson B.
Switzerland: Pascolo; Hottiger, Geiger, Henchoz, Quentin, Ohrel, Fournier, Sforza, Sutter A (Bickel 81), Knup, Turkyilmaz (Bonvin 84).
Referee: Wojcik (Poland).

Gothenburg, 6 September 1995, 40,505
Sweden (0) 0
Switzerland (0) 0
Sweden: Andersson B; Kamark, Andersson P, Bjorklund, Nilsson M, Alexandersson, Thern, Schwarz (Erlingmark 89), Brolin (Larsson 77), Andersson K, Dahlin.
Switzerland: Pascolo; Hottiger, Henchoz, Geiger, Quentin, Ohrel, Sforza, Fournier, Sutter A (Herr 46), Knup, Turkyilmaz (Grassi 90).
Referee: Ceccarini (Italy).

Istanbul, 6 September 1995, 35,000
Turkey (2) 2 *(Hakan 9, 32)*
Hungary (0) 0
Turkey: Rustu; Recep, Alpay, Ogun, Osman, Oguz, Tugay, Sergen (Tolunay 46), Abdullah, Hakan (Bulent K 88), Hami (Bulent U 85).
Hungary: Petry; Lipcesi, Telek, Meszoly, Kozma, Farkashazy, Arany, Illes (Klausz 46), Halmai, Nagy (Salloi 46), Kiprich.
Referee: Krondl (Czech Republic).

Zurich, 11 October 1995, 21,000
Switzerland (1) 3 *(Turkyilmaz 23, Sforza 56, Ohrel 89)*
Hungary (0) 0
Switzerland: Pascolo; Hottiger, Henchoz, Geiger, Quentin, Ohrel, Yakin, Sforza, Fournier (Bickel 81), Knup (Bonvin 90), Turkyilmaz (Sutter A 85).
Hungary: Hajdu; Halmai, Telek, Lipcsei, Urban, Mracsko, Simon (Jagodics 21), Nyilas (Monos 62), Illes (Arany 62), Jovan, Vincze.
Referee: Agius (Malta).

Reykjavik, 11 October 1995, 2308
Iceland (0) 0
Turkey (0) 0
Iceland: Kristinsson B; Bergsson, Gislason, Ingolfsson, Adolfsson, Jonsson S, Kristinsson R, Orlygsson, Gudjohnsen, Sverrisson (Gunnlaugsson B 80), Gunnlaugsson A.
Turkey: Rustu; Recep, Ogun, Osman, Tugay, Alpay, Oguz, Sergen (Tolunay 75), Abdullah, Ertugrul, Hami.
Referee: Strampe (Germany).

Budapest, 11 November 1995, 3000
Hungary (0) 1 *(Illes 55)*
Iceland (0) 0
Hungary: Hajdu; Monos, Banfi, Csabi, Szlezak, Nyilas, Illes (Zombori 89), Duro, Bukszegi, Orosz (Farkashazy 75), Vincze (Nagy 88).
Iceland: Kristinsson B; Jonsson K, Bergsson, Adolfsson, Gislason, Orlygsson, Gretarsson (Stefansson 81), Kristinsson R (Danielsson 84), Gunnlaugsson A, Sverrisson, Gudjohnsen.
Referee: Bikas (Greece).

Stockholm, 15 November 1995, 11,700
Sweden (1) 2 *(Alexandersson 24, Pettersson 63)*
Turkey (0) 2 *(Hakan 62, Andersson P 72 (og))*
Sweden: Ravelli; Lucic, Bjorklund, Andersson P, Alexandersson, Mild, Fursth, Pettersson (Sahlin 81), Schwarz, Dahlin, Brolin (Zetterberg 75).
Turkey: Rustu; Alpay, Ogun, Osman, Tayfur, Oguz (Ertugrul 68), Tolunay, Tugay, Ibrahim (Kemalettin 46), Hakan, Oktay (Arif 46).
Referee: Wojcik (Poland).

	P	W	D	L	F	A	Pts
Switzerland	8	5	2	1	15	7	17
Turkey	8	4	3	1	16	8	15
Sweden	8	2	3	3	9	10	9
Hungary	8	2	2	4	7	13	8
Iceland	8	1	2	5	3	12	5

Group 4

Tallinn, 4 September 1994, 1500
Estonia (0) 0
Croatia (1) 2 *(Suker 45, 72)*
Estonia: Poom; Lemsalu, Prins, Kaljend, Kallaste T, Alonen, Olumets (Reim 46), Klavan, Kristal, Kirs (Krom 75), Linnumae.
Croatia: Ladic; Turkovic, Bilic, Stimac, Jarni, Jerkan, Asanovic (Cvitanovic 90), Prosinecki, Boban, Suker, Boksic.
Referee: Krondl (Czech Republic).

Maribor, 7 September 1994, 18,000
Slovenia (1) 1 *(Udovic 13)*
Italy (1) 1 *(Costacurta 15)*
Slovenia: Simeunovic; Jermanis, Novak, Milanic, Galic, Englaro, Katanec (Binkovski 58), Zidan (Krizan 90), Ceh, Udovic, Gliha.
Italy: Pagliuca; Mussi, Baresi, Costacurta, Panucci, Donadoni, Dino Baggio (Evani 55), Albertini, Signori, Casiraghi, Zola (Berti 55).
Referee: Heynemann (Germany).

203

Kiev, 7 September 1994, 25,000
Ukraine (0) 0
Lithuania (0) 2 *(Ivanauskas 55, Skarbalius 61)*
Ukraine: Tiapushkin; Skrypnik, Sak (Kovalets 8), Yevtushok, Popov, Petrov I, Pokhlebayev (Nagornyak 59), Maksimov, Finkel, Protasov, Konovalov.
Lithuania: Stauce; Ziukas, Sukristovas, Tereskinas, Vainoras, Vaineikis (Stonkus 81), Gudaitis, Stumbrys, Suika (Zuta 54), Ivanauskas, Skarbalius.
Referee: Karlsson (Sweden).

Tallinn, 8 October 1994, 4000
Estonia (0) 0
Italy (1) 2 *(Panucci 19, Casiraghi 77)*
Estonia: Poom; Lemsalu, Kallaste T, Alonen, Klavan (Kallaste R 75), Kaljend, Kristal, Reim, Krom (Olumets 67), Linnumae, Kirs.
Italy: Pagliuca; Panucci, Favalli (Apolloni 87), Evani (Albertini 83), Costacurta, Maldini, Rambaudi, Dino Baggio, Casiraghi, Zola, Signori.
Referee: Muller (Switzerland).

Zagreb, 9 October 1994, 12,000
Croatia (0) 2 *(Jerkan 56, Kozniku 61)*
Lithuania (0) 0
Croatia: Ladic; Mladenovic, Jarni, Bilic, Jerkan, Stimac (Brajkovic 88), Jurcevic, Asanovic, Suker, Boban, Boksic (Kozniku 78).
Lithuania: Stauce; Ziukas, Mazeikis, Gudaitis, Tereskinas, Vainoras, Sukristovas, Stumbrys, Zuta (Poderis 76), Skarbalius, Vaineikis (Korsakovas 59).
Referee: Wieser (Austria).

Kiev, 12 October 1994, 12,000
Ukraine (0) 0
Slovenia (0) 0
Ukraine: Tiapushkin; Luzhnyi, Diryavka, Kuznetsov O, Shmatovalenko, Lezhentsev, Mikhailichenko (Petrov I 70), Mikhailenko, Konovalov (Guseynov 61), Kovalets, Leonenko.
Slovenia: Boskovic, Galic, Krizan, Milanic, Jermanis, Ceh, Novak (Kokol 75), Zidan, Benedejcic, Udovic (Gliha 65), Florjancic.
Referee: Oezenov (Bulgaria).

Kiev, 13 November 1994, 500
Ukraine (2) 3 *(Konovalov 31, Kirs 45 (og), Guseynov 76)*
Estonia (0) 0
Ukraine: Shovkovski (Suslov 83); Luzhnyi, Kuznetsov O, Lezhentsev, Popov, Bezhenar, Kovalets (Petrov I 75), Litovchenko, Orbu, Skachenko (Guseynov 46), Konovalov.
Estonia: Vessenberg; Lemsalu, Kirs, Linnumae, Kallaste R, Alonen, Olumets, Lindmaa, Pari, Kristal, Zelinski.
Referee: Schellings (Belgium).

Palermo, 16 November 1994, 33,570
Italy (0) 1 *(Dino Baggio 90)*
Croatia (1) 2 *(Suker 32, 60)*
Italy: Pagliuca; Negro, Costacurta, Maldini, Panucci, Lombardo, Albertini (Di Matteo 65), Dino Baggio, Rambaudi (Donadoni 46), Casiraghi, Roberto Baggio.
Croatia: Ladic; Brajkovic, Jarni, Bilic, Stimac, Asanovic, Jerkan, Prosinecki (Mladenovic 57), Boban, Suker, Jurcevic (Kozniku 90).
Referee: Quiniou (France).

Maribor, 16 November 1994, 2500
Slovenia (0) 1 *(Zahovic 55)*
Lithuania (0) 2 *(Sukristovas 64, Zuta 87)*
Slovenia: Boskovic; Galic, Krizan, Englaro (Polisak 46), Jermanis, Ceh, Zidan, Benedejcic (Binkovski 46), Zahovic, Florjancic, Gliha.
Lithuania: Stauce; Suika (Zuta 76), Sukristovas, Mazeikis, Tereskinas, Vainoras, Gudaitis, Stumbrys, Narbekovas, Ivanauskas, Apanavicius.
Referee: Ihring (Slovakia).

Zagreb, 25 March 1995, 30,000
Croatia (2) 4 *(Boban 13, Suker 21, 79, Prosinecki 71)*
Ukraine (0) 0
Croatia: Ladic; Jerkan, Bilic, Pavlicic, Jarni, Prosinecki, Boban, Asanovic, Jurcevic (Vlaovic 79), Boksic (Turkovic 75), Suker.
Ukraine: Tiapushkin; Luzhnyi, Shmatovalenko, Mizin, Telesnenko, Martynov (Orbu 46), Bukel, Kalitvintsev, Shevchenko, Leonenko, Konovalov.
Referee: Weber (Germany).

Salerno, 25 March 1995, 35,000
Italy (1) 4 *(Zola 45, 65, Albertini 58, Ravanelli 82)*
Estonia (0) 1 *(Reim 74)*
Italy: Peruzzi; Negro, Maldini, Minotti, Carboni, Albertini, Eranio (Lombardo 57), Dino Baggio, Del Piero (Berti 69), Zola, Ravanelli.
Estonia: Poom; Lemsalu, Kallaste T, Kirs, Kallaste R, Olumets, Lindmaa, Linnumae, Kristal, Lell (Pari 76), Krom (Reim 72).
Referee: Philippi (Luxembourg).

Vilnus, 29 March 1995, 9500
Lithuania (0) 0
Croatia (0) 0
Lithuania: Stauce; Ziukas, Sukristovas, Stonkus, Vainoras, Suika, Gudaitis, Zdancius (Zuta 70), Narbekovas (Pocius 69), Ivanauskas, Skarbalius.
Croatia: Ladic; Pavlicic (Mladenovic 46), Stimac, Bilic, Jarni, Soldo, Prosinecki, Brajkovic, Asanovic, Suker, Boksic.
Referee: Burge (Wales).

Kiev, 29 March 1995, 10,000
Ukraine (0) 0
Italy (2) 2 *(Lombardo 11, Zola 37)*
Ukraine: Tiapushkin; Luzhnyi (Bukel 60), Telesnenko, Khomin, Yevtushok, Orbu, Mizin, Kalitvintsev, Leonenko, Shevchenko, Konovalov (Pokhlebayev 76).
Italy: Peruzzi; Benarrivo, Apolloni, Minotti, Maldini, Albertini, Di Matteo, Zola, Berti, Lombardo (Conte 73), Casiraghi (Ravanelli 65).
Referee: Puhl (Hungary).

Maribor, 29 March 1995, 6000
Slovenia (1) 3 *(Zahovic 40, Gliha 53, Kokol 90)*
Estonia (0) 0
Slovenia: Boskovic; Galic, Milanic, Jermanis (Skaper 70), Englaro, Ceh, Novak, Zahovic (Kokol 68), Zidan, Florjancic, Gliha.
Estonia: Poom; Kallaste R, Kallaste T, Olesk, Arbeiter (Lell 77), Olumets, Linnumae, Lindmaa, Lepik, Reim, Kirs.
Referee: Mendes (Portugal).

Tallinn, 26 April 1995, 500
Estonia (0) 0
Ukraine (1) 1 *(Guseynov 17)*
Estonia: Poom; Lemsalu, Kirs, Kallaste T, Kallaste R, Alonen, Olumets, Reim (Pari 68), Krom (Lepa 46), Lell, Kristal.
Ukraine: Suslov; Luzhnyi, Shmatovalenko, Diryavka, Holovko, Orbu, Zhabchenko, Maksimov, Naduda (Yevtushok 85), Nagornyak (Konovalov 46), Guseynov.
Referee: Hollung (Norway).

Vilnius, 26 April 1995, 15,000
Lithuania (0) 0
Italy (1) 1 *(Zola 12)*
Lithuania: Stauce; Ziukas, Sukristovas, Vainoras, Tereskinas, Suika, Gudaitis (Poderis 70), Skarbalius, Apanavicius (Preiksaitis 46), Ivanauskas, Slekys.
Italy: Pagliuca; Benarrivo, Costacurta, Minotti, Maldini, Conte (Dino Baggio 24), Di Matteo, Crippa (Berti 85), Lombardo, Casiraghi, Zola.
Referee: McCluskey (Scotland).

Zagreb, 26 April 1995, 25,000
Croatia (1) 2 *(Prosinecki 17, Suker 90)*
Slovenia (0) 0
Croatia: Ladic; Jerkan, Bilic, Stimac, Jarni, Prosinecki, Boban, Asanovic, Jurcevic (Gabric 13), Suker (Pavlicic 90), Boksic.
Slovenia: Boskovic; Galic, Englaro, Milanic (Skaper 89), Binkovski, Jermanis, Novak, Zidan, Zahovic (Kokol 71), Florjancic, Gliha.
Referee: Saravan (Turkey).

Vilnius, 7 June 1995, 6000
Lithuania (0) 2 *(Stonkus 47, Suika 69)*
Slovenia (0) 1 *(Gliha 82)*
Lithuania: Stauce; Ziukas, Sukristovas, Tereskinas, Vainoras, Stonkus, Maciulevicius (Baltusnikas 75), Preiksaitis (Suika 68), Skarbalius, Slekys, Ivanauskas.
Slovenia: Boskovic; Galic (Krizan 78), Englaro, Milanic, Jermanis, Ceh, Novak (Skaper 58), Kokol, Zahovic, Florjancic, Gliha.
Referee: Vagner (Hungary).

Tallinn, 11 June 1995, 2000
Estonia (1) 1 *(Reim 27)*
Slovenia (1) 3 *(Novak 37, 68, Zahovic 78)*
Estonia: Poom; Lepa (Klavan 46), Kirs, Kallaste T, Olumets, Alonen, Pari, Linnumae, Kristal, Reim, Arbeiter (Rajala 59).
Slovenia: Boskovic; Galic, Englaro, Milanic, Novak, Jermanis (Cvikl 64), Kokol (Krizan 46), Ceh, Zahovic, Florjancic, Gliha.
Referee: Durkin (England).

Kiev, 11 June 1995, 8500
Ukraine (1) 1 *(Kalitvintsev 13)*
Croatia (0) 0
Ukraine: Suslov; Zhabchenko, Skripnik, Holovko, Maksimov, Orbu, Pokhlebayev, Kalitvintsev, Palyanitsa (Nagornyak 77), Horilyi, Guseynov (Shkapenko 46).
Croatia: Gabric; Pavlicic (Mrmic 28), Jarni, Soldo, Jerkan, Bilic, Asanovic (Pralija 48), Mladenovic, Suker, Boban (Butorovic 38), Boksic.
Referee: Rothlisberger (Switzerland).

Tallinn, 16 August 1995, 1500
Estonia (0) 0
Lithuania (0) 1 *(Maciulevicius 48)*
Estonia: Poom; Kallaste R, Lell, Kiisman (Krom 46), Lepa, Kirs, O'Konnel-Bronin (Olesk 73), Lemsalu, Reim, Lindmaa, Kristal.
Lithuania: Stauce; Ziukas, Sukristovas, Suika, Stonkus, Tereskinas, Vainoras, Maciulevicius, Ivanauskas, Skarbalius (Kanchelskis 77), Slekys (Zuta 67).
Referee: Nilsson (Sweden).

Zagreb, 3 September 1995, 25,000
Croatia (4) 7 *(Mladenovic 3, Suker 19 (pen), 58, 89, Boksic 29, Boban 42, Stimac 82)*
Estonia (1) 1 *(Reim 17)*
Croatia: Ladic (Mrmic 30); Mladénovic, Stimac (Turkovic 83), Jerkan, Bilic (Pralija 75), Jarni, Stanič, Boban, Prosinecki, Suker, Boksic.
Estonia: Poom; Kallaste R, Lemsalu, Kallaste T, Kirs, Kiisman (Lell 42), Lepa, Lindmaa, Rajala, Kristal, Reim.
Referee: Huzu (Romania).

Udine, 6 September 1995, 30,000
Italy (1) 1 *(Ravanelli 12)*
Slovenia (0) 0
Italy: Peruzzi; Ferrara, Costacurta, Tacchinardi, Carboni, Di Matteo, Albertini, Di Livio, Del Piero (Signori 46), Ravanelli (Dino Baggio 81), Zola (Roberto Baggio 61).
Slovenia: Zupan; Galic, Milanic, Polisak, Jermanis, Ceh, Kokol (Binkovski 46), Cvikl (Valentincic 77), Zahovic, Udovic, Gliha (Becaj 58).
Referee: Gadosi (Slovakia).

Vilnius, 6 September 1995, 6000
Lithuania (1) 1 *(Maciulevicius 16)*
Ukraine (0) 3 *(Gusevyov 66, 71, Gussine 84)*
Lithuania: Stauce; Suika, Vainoras, Ziukas, Tereskinas (Preiksaitis 68), Stonkus, Sukristovas, Maciulevicius, Skarbalius (Zvingilas 77), Ivanauskas, Slekys.
Ukraine: Suslov; Luzhnyi, Holovko, Skripnik, Bezhenar, Zhabchenko (Pokhlebayev 66), Horilyi, Kalitvintsev, Orbu, Gussine, Guseynov (Yevtushok 87).
Referee: Shorte (Republic of Ireland).

Split, 8 October 1995, 40,000
Croatia (0) 1 *(Suker 48 (pen))*
Italy (1) 1 *(Albertini 29)*
Croatia: Ladic; Stimac, Jerkan, Pavlicic, Mladenovic, Boban, Asanovic, Stanic, Jurcevic (Kozniku 46), Boksic, Suker.
Italy: Bucci; Ferrara (Benarrivo 84), Apolloni, Costacurta, Maldini, Di Livio, Di Matteo, Albertini, Del Piero (Crippa 86), Zola (Toldo 9), Ravanelli.
Referee: Uilenberg (Holland).

Vilnius, 11 October 1995, 2000
Lithuania (4) 5 *(Maciulevicius 8, Suika 13, 19, Slekys 44, Ivanauskas 61)*
Estonia (0) 0
Lithuania: Stauce (Martinkenas 46); Suika (Zvingilas 74), Vainoras, Kanchelskis, Stonkus, Rimkus, Maciulevicius, Baltusnikas, Vencevicius, Slekys (Jankauskas 46), Ivanauskas.
Estonia: Poom; Lell (Reim 46) (Krom 80), Olesk, Kallaste T, Lindmaa, Zelinski, Lepa (Kristal 46), Kallaste R, Linnumae, Rajala, Oper.
Referee: Pauchard (France).

Ljubljana, 11 October 1995, 4000
Slovenia (0) 3 *(Udovic 50, 90, Zahovic 73)*
Ukraine (2) 2 *(Skripnik 23, Guseynov 45)*
Slovenia: Zupan; Galic, Englaro, Milanic, Rudonja, Ceh, Novak, Zahovic, Udovic, Florjancic (Cvikl 72), Gliha.
Ukraine: Suslov; Luzhnyi, Shmatovalenko (Polunin 88), Holovko, Zhabchenko, Skripnik, Orbu, Kalitvintsev, Bezhenar, Guseynov, Gussine (Nagornyak 51).
Referee: Coroado (Portugal).

Bari, 11 November 1995, 50,000
Italy (1) 3 *(Ravanelli 21, 48, Maldini 53)*
Ukraine (1) 1 *(Polunin 18)*
Italy: Peruzzi; Benarrivo, Costacurta, Ferrara, Maldini, Di Matteo, Albertini, Dino Baggio (Crippa 46), Del Piero (Carboni 87), Zola (Simone 65), Ravanelli.
Ukraine: Suslov; Luzhnyi, Skripnik, Bezhenar, Horilyi (Yevtushok 14), Polunin, Orbu, Kalitvintsev, Nagornyak (Pokhlebayev 71), Sharan (Popov 50), Guseynov.
Referee: Muhmenthaler (Switzerland).

Ljubljana, 15 November 1995, 15,000
Slovenia (1) 1 *(Gliha 36)*
Croatia (1) 2 *(Suker 40 (pen), Jurcevic 55)*
Slovenia: Zupan; Galic, Englaro, Krizan, Jermanis, Zulic (Cvikl 62), Novak, Udovic, Ceh, Florjancic (Rudonja 62), Gliha.
Croatia: Ladic; Jurcevic, Jarni, Soldo, Jerkan, Bilic, Pralija (Mladenovic 63), Prosinecki, Suker, Stanic, Mornar.
Referee: Goethals (Belgium).

Reggio-Emilia, 15 November 1995, 30,000
Italy (0) 4 *(Suika 52 (og), Zola 65, 81, Vainoras 82 (og))*
Lithuania (0) 0
Italy: Peruzzi; Mussi, Ferrara, Costacurta, Maldini (Carboni 72), Statuto (Zola 46), Albertini, Di Matteo, Del Piero, Casiraghi (Ravanelli 46), Simone.
Lithuania: Stauce; Stonkus, Rimkus, Vainoras, Ziukas, Tereskinas, Suika (Vencevicius 78), Preiksaitis, Skarbalius, Maciulevicius (Zvingilas 46), Ivanauskas (Zutautas 68).
Referee: Diaz Vega (Spain).

	P	W	D	L	F	A	Pts
Croatia	10	7	2	1	22	5	23
Italy	10	7	2	1	20	6	23
Lithuania	10	5	1	4	13	12	16
Ukraine	10	4	1	5	11	15	13
Slovenia	10	3	2	5	13	13	11
Estonia	10	0	0	10	3	31	0

Group 5

Prague, 6 September 1994, 10,226
Czech Republic (3) 6 *(Smejkal 6 (pen), Kubik 33, Siegl 35, 49, 81, Berger P 89)*
Malta (0) 1 *(Laferla 75)*
Czech Republic: Kouba; Suchoparek, Kubik, Novotny J, Latal (Vesely 87), Nemecek, Frydek (Berger P 83), Nemec, Smejkal, Kuka, Siegl.
Malta: Cluett; Vella S, Galea, Buttigieg, Buhagiar, Camilleri J, Gregory (Camilleri E 83), Brincat, Saliba, Laferla, Busuttil.
Referee: Loizou (Cyprus).

Luxembourg, 7 September 1994, 8200

Luxembourg (0) 0

Holland (1) 4 *(Roy 22, Ronald de Boer 62, 64, Jonk 90)*

Luxembourg: Koch; Ferron, Weis, Strasser, Birsens, Wolf, Holtz, Saibene, Groff, Cardoni (Morocutti 80), Langers (Theis 89).

Holland: De Goey; Valckx, Blind, Frank de Boer, Winter, Jonk, Rob Witschge, Overmars, Bosman, Ronald de Boer, Roy (Van Vossen 75).

Referee: Snoddy (Northern Ireland).

Oslo, 7 September 1994, 16,739

Norway (0) 1 *(Frigaard 88)*

Belarus (0) 0

Norway: Grodaas; Lydersen, Pedersen T, Berg H, Bjornebye, Flo (Frigaard 70), Mykland, Rekdal, Bohinen (Leonhardsen 46), Jakobsen, Fjortoft.

Belarus: Shantolosov; Gurenko, Sosnitski, Zygmantovich, Khatskevich, Yakhimovich, Gerasimets, Metlitsky, Kulanin (Kachuro 46), Antonovitch, Markhel.

Referee: Goethals (Belgium).

Valletta, 12 October 1994, 4000

Malta (0) 0

Czech Republic (0) 0

Malta: Cluett; Buttigieg, Galea, Vella S, Camilleri J, Saliba (Sant-Fournier 77), Brincat, Carabott (Camilleri E 90), Gregory, Busuttil, Laferla.

Czech Republic: Srnicek; Suchoparek, Kubik, Novotny J, Latal, Nemecek (Kadlec 44), Hasek, Nemec, Smejkal (Frydek 70), Skuhravy, Kuka.

Referee: Coroado (Portugal).

Oslo, 12 October 1994, 22,293

Norway (0) 1 *(Rekdal 52 (pen))*

Holland (1) 1 *(Roy 22)*

Norway: Thorstvedt; Lydersen, Berg, Pedersen, Bjornebye, Rushfeldt (Flo 63), Bohinen, Rekdal, Mykland, Leonhardsen, Fjortoft (Frigaard 77).

Holland: De Goey; Blind, Reiziger (Van Gobbel 77), Valckx, Frank de Boer, Winter, Jonk, Rob Witschge, Overmars, Bergkamp (Ronald de Boer 71), Roy.

Referee: McCluskey (Scotland).

Minsk, 12 October 1994, 5000

Belarus (0) 2 *(Romashchenko 67, Gerasimets 76)*

Luxembourg (0) 0

Belarus: Shantolosov; Gurenko, Rodnionok (Sosnitski 80), Yakhimovich, Zygmantovich, Gerasimets, Markhel (Antonovitch 65), Aleinikov, Romashchenko, Shukanov, Metlitsky.

Luxembourg: Koch; Ferron (Vanek 83), Strasser, Birsens, Wolf, Cardoni, Hellers, Weis, Holtz (Morocutti 58), Saibene, Fanelli.

Referee: O'Hanlon (Republic of Ireland).

Minsk, 16 November 1994, 8000

Belarus (0) 0

Norway (2) 4 *(Berg 34, Leonhardsen 39, Bohinen 52, Rekdal 83)*

Belarus: Shantolosov; Yaskovich, Zygmantovich, Rodnionok, Yakhimovich, Metlitsky, Markhel (Youssipets 82), Antonovitch, Romashchenko (Gurinovich 82), Gerasimets, Shukanov.

Norway: Grodaas; Halle, Berg, Johnsen R (Jakobsen 80), Bjornebye (Lydersen 42), Mykland, Leonhardsen, Bohinen, Rekdal, Rushfeldt, Fjortoft.

Referee: Spassov (Bulgaria).

Rotterdam, 16 November 1994, 40,000

Holland (0) 0

Czech Republic (0) 0

Holland: De Goey; Valckx, Blind, Frank de Boer, Rob Witschge (Numan 78), Winter, Roy, Jonk, Van Vossen, Mulder (Kluivert 70), Taument.

Czech Republic: Srnicek; Latal, Kadlec, Suchoparek, Hapal, Kubik, Nemec, Bilek, Kuka (Samec 90), Siegl, Poborsky (Berger 75).

Referee: Puhl (Hungary).

Rotterdam, 14 December 199 , 26,000

Holland (3) 5 *(Mulder 6, Roy 17, Jonk 40, Ronald de Boer 52, Seedorf 90)*

Luxembourg (0) 0

Holland: De Goey; Valckx, Blind, Frank de Boer, Winter (Van Hooydonk 75), Jonk, Numan, Overmars, Ronald de Boer, Mulder (Seedorf 46), Roy.

Luxembourg: Koch; Ferron, Weis, Wolf, Birsens, Strasser, Holtz, Hellers, Cardoni, Groff, Langers (Theis 61).

Referee: Roduit (Switzerland).

Ta Qali, 14 December 1994, 9000

Malta (0) 0

Norway (1) 1 *(Fjortoft 10)*

Malta: Cluett; Vella S, Woods, Buttigieg, Camilleri J, Brincat, Busuttil, Saliba (Scerri 82), Carabott (Buhagiar 60), Gregory, Laferla.

Norway: Grodaas; Halle, Berg, Johnsen R, Bjornebye, Mykland, Rekdal, Rushfeldt (Jakobsen 82), Flo, Bohinen (Solbakken 72), Fjortoft.

Referee: Beschin (Italy).

Valletta, 22 February 1995, 6000

Malta (0) 0

Luxembourg (0) 1 *(Cardoni 54)*

Malta: Cluett; Vella S, Brincat, Buttigieg, Buhagiar, Camilleri J, Busuttil, Suda (Sciberras 60), Carabott (Saliba 78), Gregory, Laferla.

Luxembourg: Koch; Vanek, Weis, Wolf, Deville, Saibene, Hellers, Birsens, Groff, Langers (Schneider 89), Cardoni (Holtz 87).

Referee: Berusan (Croatia).

Luxembourg, 29 March 1995, 3000

Luxembourg (0) 0

Norway (1) 2 *(Leonhardsen 35, Aase 80)*

Luxembourg: Rohmann; Ferron, Vanek, Birsens (Schneider 85), Strasser, Deville, Saibene (Feyder 78), Weis, Groff, Langers, Cardoni.

Norway: Thorstvedt; Haaland, Johnsen R, Berg, Bjornebye, Flo (Aase 46), Leonhardsen, Rekdal (Solbakken 84), Bohinen, Fjortoft, Jakobsen.

Referee: Levnikov (Russia).

Rotterdam, 29 March 1995, 34,000

Holland (1) 4 *(Seedorf 39, Bergkamp 77 (pen), Winter 80, Kluivert 85)*

Malta (0) 0

Holland: De Goey; Valckx, Blind, Frank de Boer, Jonk, Winter, Seedorf, Overmars, Ronald de Boer (Kluivert 76), Bergkamp, Roy (Van de Luer 58).

Malta: Cluett; Vella S (Gregory 90), Buhagiar, Galea, Woods, Camilleri J, Busuttil (Agius 88), Saliba, Sant-Fournier, Camilleri E, Laferla.

Referee: Orrason (Iceland).

Ostrava, 29 March 1995, 5549

Czech Republic (2) 4 *(Kadlec 5, Berger 18, 63, Kuka 69)*

Belarus (1) 2 *(Gerasimets 44 (pen), Gurinovich 88)*

Czech Republic: Srnicek; Repka, Kadlec, Latal, Frydek (Bilek 86), Nemecek, Berger, Hapal, Smejkal, Kuka, Siegl (Samec 89).
Belarus: Shantolosov; Yakhimovich (Rodnionok 77), Gurenko, Zygmantovich, Sosnitski, Juravel (Kachentsev 81), Taikov, Metlitsky, Youssipets, Gerasimets, Gurinovich.
Referee: Veissiere (France).

Minsk, 26 April 1995, 13,000

Belarus (0) 1 *(Taikov 53)*

Malta (0) 1 *(Carabott 72)*

Belarus: Marchoukel; Gurenko, Zygmantovich, Taikov, Juravel, Metlitsky (Rodnionok 70), Youssipets (Romashchenko 75), Shukanov, Gerasimets, Gurinovich, Antonovitch.
Malta: Cluett; Vella S, Buttigieg, Camilleri E, Woods, Saliba, Gregory (Agius 24), Laferla, Sant-Fournier, Carabott, Busuttil (Attard 88).
Referee: Gadosi (Slovakia).

Prague, 26 April 1995, 20,000

Czech Republic (0) 3 *(Skuhravy 49, Nemecek 57, Berger 62)*

Holland (1) 1 *(Jonk 7)*

Czech Republic: Kouba; Repka, Kadlec, Suchoparek, Berger, Hapal, Nemecek, Nemec, Frydek (Latal 46), Kuka (Siegl 89), Skuhravy.
Holland: De Goey; Valckx, Blind, Frank de Boer, Winter (Kluivert 65), Jonk, Seedorf, Numan, Overmars, Ronald de Boer, Van Vossen (Bosz 46).
Referee: Krug (Germany).

Oslo, 26 April 1995, 15,124

Norway (3) 5 *(Jakobsen 11, Fjortoft 12, Brattbakk 24, Berg 46, Rekdal 49)*

Luxembourg (0) 0

Norway: Grodaas; Berg (Haaland 76), Johnsen R, Nilsen, Halle, Bohinen (Solbakken 35), Rekdal, Leonhardsen, Jakobsen, Brattbakk, Fjortoft.
Luxembourg: Koch; Feyder, Vanek, Holtz (Theis 34), Strasser, Deville, Hellers, Saibene (Lamborelle 75), Langers, Cardoni, Groff.
Referee: Ferry (Northern Ireland).

Luxembourg, 7 June 1995, 1500

Luxembourg (0) 1 *(Hellers 90)*

Czech Republic (0) 0

Luxembourg: Koch; Vanek, Strasser, Weis, Birsens, Ganser (Cardoni 87), Hellers, Groff, Deville, Langers, Theis (Saibene 75).
Czech Republic: Kouba; Suchoparek, Repka (Frydek 69), Kadlec, Hapal, Latal, Nemec, Nemecek, Berger, Kuka, Skuhravy (Drulak 60).
Referee: Ashman (Wales).

Oslo, 7 June 1995, 15,000

Norway (1) 2 *(Fjortoft 43, Flo 88)*

Malta (0) 0

Norway: Thorstvedt; Haaland (Brattbakk 69), Johnsen R, Berg, Nilsen, Flo, Mykland, Solbakken, Rekdal (Ingebrigtsen 83), Fjortoft, Jakobsen.
Malta: Cluett; Vella S, Buhagiar (Saliba 76), Attard, Woods, Buttigieg (Camilleri E 28), Busuttil, Agius, Laferla, Sant-Fournier, Carabott.
Referee: Przesmycki (Poland).

Minsk, 7 June 1995, 12,000
Belarus (1) 1 *(Gerasimets 27)*
Holland (0) 0
Belarus: Shantolosov; Dovnar (Kachentsev 86), Taikov, Gurenko, Rodnionok, Zygmantovitch, Juravel, Youssipets, Romashchenko (Antonovitch 54), Kachuro, Gerasimets.
Holland: Van der Sar; De Kock, Blind (Winter 69), Valckx (Numan 64), Seedorf, Jonk, Van't Schip, Davids, Ronald de Boer, Kluivert, Overmars.
Referee: Porumboiu (Romania).

Oslo, 16 August 1995, 22,054
Norway (1) 1 *(Berg 27)*
Czech Republic (0) 1 *(Suchoparek 84)*
Norway: Thorstvedt; Haaland, Johnsen R, Berg, Loken, Flo, Bohinen, Leonhardsen, Fjortoft (Brattbakk 80), Solbakken, Jakobsen (Brandesather 69).
Czech Republic: Kouba; Latal (Poborsky 78), Kadlec, Suchoparek, Repka, Hapal, Nemec, Berger (Nedved 46), Frydek, Kuka, Drulak (Samec 78).
Referee: Koushainov (Russia).

Prague, 6 September 1995, 19,522
Czech Republic (1) 2 *(Skuhravy 6 (pen), Drulak 87)*
Norway (0) 0
Czech Republic: Kouba; Latal, Kadlec, Suchoparek, Repka, Nemecek, Frydek (Poborsky 71), Nemec, Nedved, Kuka (Drulak 19), Skuhravy (Lokvenc 81).
Norway: Thorstvedt; Loken, Johnsen R, Johnsen E, Berg, Flo, Bohinen (Rekdal 75), Solbakken, Leonhardsen, Jakobsen, Fjortoft (Brattbakk 70).
Referee: Rothlisberger (Switzerland).

Rotterdam, 6 September 1995, 22,000
Holland (0) 1 *(Mulder 83)*
Belarus (0) 0
Holland: Van der Sar; Reiziger, Blind, De Kock, Frank de Boer, Ronald de Boer, Winter, Richard Witschge (Numan 86), Eykelkamp (Mulder 64), Bergkamp, Overmars.
Belarus: Satsunkevich; Gurenko, Zygmantovitch, Dovnar, Rodnionok, Gerasimets, Taikov, Juravel (Vekhtev 89), Romashchenko (Vergeichik 85), Youssipets (Kachentsev 69), Kachuro.
Referee: Sedlacek (Austria).

Luxemburg, 6 September 1995, 4,700
Luxemburg (1) 1 *(Holtz 44)*
Malta (0) 0
Luxemburg: Koch; Vanek, Deville, Birsens, Strasser, Saibene, Hellers, Weis, Holtz (Cardoni 85), Langers, Groff (Theis 68).
Malta: Cluett; Delia (Agius 28) (Gregory 89), Buhagiar, Galea, Woods, Buttigieg, Busuttil, Saliba, Sant-Fournier, Laferla, Carabott.
Referee: Dubinskas (Lithuania).

Minsk, 7 October 1995, 9500
Belarus (0) 0
Czech Republic (1) 2 *(Frydek 25, Berger 84)*
Belarus: Shantolosov; Taikov, Gurenko, Dovnar, Rodnionok, Juravel, Gerasimets, Youssipets (Baranov 74), Belkevich, Kachuro, Kachentsev.
Czech Republic: Kouba; Kadlec, Repka, Nedved (Berger 73), Hapal, Latal, Nemecek (Hornak 15), Frydek (Poborsky 87), Nemec, Drulak, Kuka.
Referee: Frisk (Sweden).

212

Valletta, 11 October 1995, 8000

Malta (0) 0

Holland (0) 4 *(Overmars 52, 61, 65, Seedorf 80)*

Malta: Cluett; Attard (Galea 71), Buhagiar, Brincat, Woods, Zammit, Busuttil, Saliba, Laferla, Carabott, Agius (Sant Fournier 5).
Holland: Van der Sar; Reijziger, Blind (Trustfull 71), Frank de Boer, Ronald de Boer, Seedorf, Numan, Richard Witschge, Overmars, Kluivert, Mulder (Helder 64).
Referee: Nielsen (Denmark).

Luxemburg, 11 October 1995, 4500

Luxemburg (0) 0

Belarus (0) 0

Luxemburg: Koch; Vanek, Deville, Birsens, Strasser, Saibene, Hellers, Weis, Holtz (Lamborelle 90), Langers (Theis 81), Morocutti (Cardoni 72).
Belarus: Shantolosov; Gurenko, Dovnar, Rodnionok, Taikov, Youssipets, Juravel, Baranov, Belkevich, Kachentsev (Vergeichik 90), Kachuro.
Referee: Durkin (England).

Ta'Qali, 12 November 1995, 2500

Malta (0) 0

Belarus (0) 2 *(Gerasimets 79, 83)*

Malta: Cluett; Attard, Vella S, Woods, Saliba, Zammit, Busuttil, Buhagiar, Brincat (Sant-Fournier 48), Agius (Carabott 73), Laferla.
Belarus: Shantolosov; Gurenko, Zygmantovitch (Youssipets 51), Taikov, Dovnar, Khmelnitski (Belkevich 80), Baranov, Maleyev (Makovski 68), Melitski, Gerasimets, Kachuro.
Referee: Metin (Turkey).

Prague, 15 November 1995, 20,239

Czech Republic (1) 3 *(Drulak 37, 46, Berger 56)*

Luxemburg (0) 0

Czech Republic: Kouba; Hapal, Kadlec, Suchoparek, Latal, Nemecek (Poborsky 70), Frydek, Berger (Smicer 83), Nedved, Kuka (Lokvenc 86), Drulak.
Luxemburg: Koch; Ferron, Vanek, Weis, Strasser, Deville (Theis 58), Holtz (Ganser 75), Hellers, Saibene (Cardoni 89), Groff, Langers.
Referee: Vieser (Austria).

Rotterdam, 15 November 1995, 49,000

Holland (0) 3 *(Seedorf 48, Mulder 88, Overmars 89)*

Norway (0) 0

Holland: Van der Sar; Reijziger, Blind, Frank de Boer, Numan, Richard Witschge (Davids 56), Seedorf, Bergkamp (Mulder 78), Overmars, Ronald de Boer, Helder (De Kock 85).
Norway: Grodaas; Loken (Haaland 62), Johnsen E, Berg, Bjornebye, Flo, Mykland (Leonhardsen 58), Rekdal, Bohinen (Solbakken 82), Jakobsen, Fjortoft.
Referee: Gallagher (England).

	P	W	D	L	F	A	Pts
Czech Republic	10	6	3	1	21	6	21
Holland	10	6	2	2	23	5	20
Norway	10	6	2	2	17	7	20
Belarus	10	3	2	5	8	13	11
Luxembourg	10	3	1	6	3	21	10
Malta	10	0	2	8	2	22	2

Group 6

Windsor Park, 20 April 1994, 7000
Northern Ireland (3) 4 *(Quinn 5, 33, Lomas 25, Dowie 48)*
Liechtenstein (0) 1 *(Hasler 84)*
Northern Ireland: Wright; Fleming, Taggart, Donaghy, Worthington, Magilton (O'Neill 81), Wilson, Lomas, Hughes, Quinn, Dowie (Gray 78).
Liechtenstein: Oehry; Stocker, Frick C, Ospelt J, Moser, Quaderer, Ritter, Zech H, Telser, Matt (Hasler 70), Frick M.
Referee: Luinge (Holland).

Riga, 7 September 1994, 2200
Latvia (0) 0
Republic of Ireland (2) 3 *(Aldridge 16, 75 (pen), Sheridan 29)*
Latvia: Karavayev; Troicki, Sevliakovs, Lobanev, Zemlinsky, Astafyev, Mikutsky (Yeliseyev 62), Milevskis (Stepanov 46), Sharando, Bulders, Babichev.
Republic of Ireland: Kelly A; Kelly G, Babb, McGrath, Irwin, McAteer (McGoldrick 80), Sheridan, Townsend, Staunton, Aldridge, Quinn (Cascarino 70).
Referee: Frisk (Sweden).

Eschen, 7 September 1994, 5800
Liechtenstein (0) 0
Austria (3) 4 *(Polster 18, 45, 79, Aigner 22)*
Liechtenstein: Heeb; Moser, Hefti, Ospelt J, Quaderer, Telser, Zech H (Matt 68), Klaunzer, Ospelt W (Hanselmann 28), Frick M, Hasler.
Austria: Wohlfahrt; Schottel, Werner, Kogler J, Prosenik, Stoger, Pfeifenberger (Flogel 74), Feiersinger, Aigner, Ogris (Cerny 63), Polster.
Referee: Ziller (Germany).

Windsor Park, 7 September 1994, 6000
Northern Ireland (0) 1 *(Quinn 58 (pen))*
Portugal (1) 2 *(Rui Costa 8, Oliveira 81)*
Northern Ireland: Fettis; Fleming, Morrow (Taggart 81), McDonald, Worthington, Gillespie (O'Boyle 81), Magilton, Lomas, Hughes, Quinn, Gray.
Portugal: Vitor Baia; Joao Pinto I, Paulo Madeira, Paulinho Santos, Helder, Tavares, Paulo Sousa, Vitor Paneira (Folha 63), Figo, Rui Costa, Sa Pinto (Domingos 80).
Referee: Pedersen (Norway).

Riga, 9 October 1994, 2000
Latvia (0) 1 *(Monyak 88)*
Portugal (1) 3 *(Joao Pinto II 33, 72, Vigo 73)*
Latvia: Karavayev; Troicki, Astafyev, Zemlinsky, Sevliakovs, Sprogis (Monyak 69), Stepanov, Ivanov, Babichev, Glazov (Milevskis 46), Semenov.
Portugal: Vitor Baia; Joao Pinto I, Helder, Paulo Madeira, Nelo, Paulo Sousa, Vitor Paneira (Paulo Alves 60), Joao Pinto II, Figo (Tavares 81), Rui Costa, Domingos.
Referee: Blareau (Belgium).

Vienna, 12 October 1994, 20,000
Austria (1) 1 *(Polster 24 (pen))*
Northern Ireland (2) 2 *(Gillespie 3, Gray 36)*
Austria: Wohlfahrt; Kogler J, Schottel, Werner, Artner, Prosenik (Pfeifenberger 65), Stoger, Feiersinger, Hutter, Ogris (Hasenhuttl 45), Polster.
Northern Ireland: Kee; Fleming, Worthington, Taggart, McDonald, Lomas, Gillespie (O'Neill 66), Magilton, Dowie (Quinn 74), Gray, Hughes.
Referee: Lopez Nieto (Spain).

Dublin, 12 October 1994, 32,980

Republic of Ireland (3) 4 *(Coyne 2, 4, Quinn 30, 82)*

Liechtenstein (0) 0

Republic of Ireland: Bonner; Kelly G, Irwin (McLoughlin 46), McAteer, Kernaghan, Babb, McGoldrick, Coyne, Quinn, Sheridan, Staunton.
Liechtenstein: Heeb; Hefti, Telser, Ritter, Moser, Ospelt W, Hanselmann, Zech H, Haas (Klaunzer 77), Frick M, Heidegger (Matt 71).
Referee: Bergmann (Iceland).

Lisbon, 13 November 1994, 50,000

Portugal (1) 1 *(Figo 36)*

Austria (0) 0

Portugal: Vitor Baia; Joao Pinto I, Paulo Madeira, Helder, Paulinho Santos, Paulo Sousa, Figo, Oceano, Rui Costa (Domingos 84), Joao Pinto II, Sa Pinto (Vitor Paneira 70).
Austria: Konrad; Schottel, Furstaller, Kogler J, Feiersinger, Artner, Stoger, Winklhofer, Kuhbauer (Prosenik 46), Cerny (Hutter 70), Polster.
Referee: Mikkelsen (Denmark).

Eschen-Mauren, 15 November 1994, 1300

Liechtenstein (0) 0

Latvia (1) 1 *(Babichev 14)*

Liechtenstein: Heeb; Moser, Telser, Hefti, Ritter, Hilti, Zech H (Klaunzer 60), Ospelt W, Frick M, Heidegger (Oehri 59), Hasler.
Latvia: Karavayev; Troicki, Astafyev, Zemlinsky, Sevliakovs, Sprogis, Blagonadezhdin (Mikutsky 46), Ivanov, Semenov, Milevskis, Babichev (Sharando 71).
Referee: Werner (Poland).

Windsor Park, 16 November 1994, 10,336

Northern Ireland (0) 0

Republic of Ireland (3) 4 *(Aldridge 6, Keane 11, Sheridan 38, Townsend 54)*

Northern Ireland: Kee; Fleming, Worthington, Morrow, Taggart, O'Neill (Patterson 46), Gillespie (Wilson 62), Magilton, Dowie, Gray, Hughes.
Republic of Ireland: Kelly A; Kelly G, Irwin, Keane (McAteer 44), McGrath, Babb, Sheridan, Aldridge (Coyne 46), Quinn, Townsend, Staunton.
Referee: Muhmenthaler (Switzerland).

Lisbon, 18 December 1994, 30,000

Portugal (3) 8 *(Domingos 2, 11, Oceano 45, Joao Pinto II 56, Fernando Couto 72, Folha 74, Paulo Alves 75, 79)*

Liechtenstein (0) 0

Portugal: Vitor Baia; Joao Pinto I, Fernando Couto, Oceano, Paulinho Santos, Figo, Vitor Paneira (Paulo Alves 57), Rui Costa, Joao Pinto II (Secretario 70), Domingos, Folha.
Liechtenstein: Heeb; Telser, Hefti, Ospelt W (Oehri R 44), Moser, Hilti, Ritter, Zech H, Hasler (Matt 58), Frick M, Heidegger.
Referee: Pucek (Czech Republic).

Dublin, 29 March 1995, 32,200

Republic of Ireland (0) 1 *(Quinn 47)*

Northern Ireland (0) 1 *(Dowie 72)*

Republic of Ireland: Kelly A; Kelly G, Irwin, Keane, McGrath, Babb, Sheridan, Kelly D (McAteer 75), Quinn (Cascarino 82), Townsend, Staunton.
Northern Ireland: Fettis; Patterson, Worthington, Hill, Taggart, McDonald, Morrow, Magilton, Dowie, Hughes, Gillespie.
Referee: Van der Ende (Holland).

Salzburg, 29 March 1995, 5500

Austria (2) 5 *(Herzog 18, 58, Pfeifenberger 41, Polster 69 (pen), 90)*

Latvia (0) 0

Austria: Konrad; Furstaller, Kogler J, Feiersinger, Pfeifenberger, Marasek, Artner (Hutter 76), Kuhbauer, Herzog, Ogris (Ramusch 46), Polster.
Latvia: Laizan; Sevliakovs, Sprogis, Lobanov, Troicki, Astafyev, Zemlinsky (Mikutsky 66), Blagonadezhdin, Teplov, Monyak, Babichev (Shtolcers 74).
Referee: Agius (Malta).

Riga, 26 April 1995, 1560

Latvia (0) 0

Northern Ireland (0) 1 *(Dowie 69 (pen))*

Latvia: Laizan; Troicki, Astafyev, Zemlinsky, Sevliakovs, Sprogis, Stepanov, Blagonadezhdin (Butkus 30), Teplov, Babichev, Yeliseyev.
Northern Ireland: Fettis; Patterson, Worthington, Hunter, McDonald, Hill, Gillespie (O'Boyle 78), Wilson, Dowie (Quinn 80), Horlock, Hughes.
Referee: Lambek (Denmark).

Salzburg, 26 April 1995, 5700

Austria (3) 7 *(Kuhbauer 8, Polster 11, 53, Sabitzer 17, Purk 84, Hutter 87, 90)*

Liechtenstein (0) 0

Austria: Konrad; Feiersinger, Kogler J, Furstaller (Hutter A 71), Ramusch, Artner, Herzog, Kuhbauer, Marasek, Sabitzer (Purk 69), Polster.
Liechtenstein: Oehry; Moser, Stocker, Ospelt J, Ritter (Matt 66), Hilti, Telser, Zech H, Hasler, Oehri (Marxer 46), Burgmaier.
Referee: Melnitschuk (Ukraine).

Dublin, 26 April 1995, 33,000

Republic of Ireland (1) 1 *(Vitor Baia 45 (og))*

Portugal (0) 0

Republic of Ireland: Kelly A; Kelly G, Irwin, Townsend, McGrath, Babb, Sheridan, Houghton (Kenna 84), Aldridge (Cascarino 84), Quinn, Staunton.
Portugal: Vitor Baia; Joao Pinto I, Fernando Couto, Helder (Folha 64), Paulinho Santos, Jorge Costa, Paulo Sousa, Figo (Pedro Barbosa 76), Rui Costa, Joao Pinto II, Domingos.
Referee: Amendolia (Italy).

Porto, 3 June, 1995, 40,000

Portugal (3) 3 *(Figo 5, Secretario 19, Domingos 21)*

Latvia (0) 2 *(Rimkus 49, 83)*

Portugal: Vitor Baia; Nelson (Pedro Barbosa 79), Fernando Couto, Jorge Costa, Paulinho Santos, Figo, Secretario, Domingos, Folha, Paulo Sousa (Futre 46), Rui Costa.
Latvia: Laizan; Troicki, Sevliakovs, Teplov (Sprogis 59), Astafyev, Zemlinsky, Monyak, Valeriy, Zeiberlins, Rimkus, Bleidelis (Babichev 37).
Referee: Petrovic (Yugoslavia).

Eschen, 3 June 1995, 4500

Liechtenstein (0) 0

Republic of Ireland (0) 0

Liechtenstein: Heeb; Hasler, Hanselmann, Ospelt J (Zech J 32), Ritter, Zech H, Hilti, Telser, Ospelt W (Marxer 64), Burgmaier, Frick M.
Republic of Ireland: Kelly A; Kelly G, Irwin, McAteer (Kenna 73), McGrath, Babb, Sheridan, Aldridge, Quinn (Cascarino 60), Whelan, Staunton.
Referee: Agius (Malta).

Windsor Park, 7 June 1995, 6000
Northern Ireland (1) 1 *(Dowie 44)*
Latvia (0) 2 *(Zeiberlins 58, Astafyev 62)*
Northern Ireland: Fettis; McGibbon (Patterson 46), Worthington, Morrow, Taggart, McDonald, McMahon, Magilton, Dowie, Hughes, Rowland (Gillespie 64).
Latvia: Laizan; Monyak, Sprogis, Zakresevskis, Bleidelis, Troicki, Astafyev, Zeiberlins, Ivanov, Rimkus (Yeliseyev 69), Babichev (Teplov 82).
Referee: Roca (Spain).

Dublin, 11 June 1995, 33,000
Republic of Ireland (0) 1 *(Houghton 65)*
Austria (0) 3 *(Polster 69, 78, Ogris 72)*
Republic of Ireland: Kelly A; Kelly G, Irwin, Houghton, McGrath, Babb, Sheridan, Coyne, Quinn (Cascarino 57), Whelan, Staunton (Kenna 46).
Austria: Konsel; Pfeffer, Schottel, Furstaller, Kogler J, Prosenik, Kuhbauer, Pfeifenberger (Hutter 83), Masarek, Ramusch (Ogris 71), Polster.
Referee: Merk (Germany).

Eschen, 15 August 1995, 3500
Liechtenstein (0) 0
Portugal (3) 7 *(Domingos 25, Paulinho Santos 33, Rui Costa 41, 71 (pen), Paulo Alves 67, 73, 90)*
Liechtenstein: Heeb; Hasler, Hanselmann, Hilti, Zech J, Stocker (Frick C 46), Klaunzer (Marxer 46), Telser (Oehri 68), Moser, Zech H, Frick M.
Portugal: Alfredo (Rui Correa 82); Oceano (Sa Pinto 46), Fernando Couto, Jorge Costa, Dimas (Paulo Alves 55), Secretario, Paulinho Santos, Rui Costa, Rui Barros, Fohla, Domingos.
Referee: Poljak (Croatia).

Riga, 16 August 1995, 2600
Latvia (1) 3 *(Rimjus 11, 59, Zeiberlins 88)*
Austria (0) 2 *(Polster 68, Ramusch 78)*
Latvia: Laizan; Sevliakovs, Troicki, Zemlinsky, Zakresevskis (Monyak 82), Zeiberlins, Ivanov, Bleidelis, Babichev (Yeliseyev 75), Rimkus, Astafyev.
Austria: Konrad; Schottel, Kogler W, Pfeffer, Kogler J (Schopp 46), Prosenik (Stoger P 64), Feiersinger, Pfeifenberger, Marasek, Ogris (Ramusch 64), Polster.
Referee: Koho (Finland).

Oporto, 3 September 1995, 50,000
Portugal (0) 1 *(Domingos 47)*
Northern Ireland (0) 1 *(Hughes 66)*
Portugal: Vitor Baia; Secretario, Jorge Costa (Rui Barros 74), Fernando Couto, Paulinho Santos, Oceano, Paulo Sousa, Figo, Rui Costa (Paulo Alves 82), Domingos, Folha.
Northern Ireland: Fettis; Morrow, Worthington, Hunter, Hill, Lomas, Gillespie, Magilton (Rowland 79), Dowie (Gray 77), Lennon, Hughes.
Referee: Harrel (France).

Vienna, 6 September 1995, 24,000
Austria (1) 3 *(Stoger P 3, 64, 77)*
Republic of Ireland (0) 1 *(McGrath 74)*
Austria: Konsel; Furstaller, Schottel, Pfeffer, Schopp, Stoger P, Kuhbauer, Herzog, Marasek, Pfeifenberger, Polster (Cerny 78).
Republic of Ireland: Kelly A; Kelly G, Irwin, Keane, McGrath, Kernaghan, Houghton (Cascarino 67), Townsend, Quinn, Kennedy, Sheridan.
Referee: Cakar (Turkey).

Riga, 6 September 1995, 3800

Latvia (0) 1 *(Zeiberlins 83)*

Liechtenstein (0) 0

Latvia: Karavayev; Troicki, Zemlinsky, Sevliakovs, Astafyev, Bleidelis (Bulders 31), Ivanov, Zeiberlins, Babichev (Karachausks 74), Rimkus, Monyak.
Liechtenstein: Heeb; Frick C, Oehri R (Bicker 64), Hasler, Zech J, Telser, Stocker (Klaunzer 89), Hilti, Frick M, Schadler, Marxer (Frick D 74).
Referee: Henning (Norway).

Vienna, 11 October 1995, 44,000

Austria (1) 1 *(Stoger 21)*

Portugal (0) 1 *(Paulinho Santos 49)*

Austria: Konsel; Feiersinger, Schottel, Pfeffer, Schopp, Kuhbauer, Stoger, Herzog, Marasek, Pfeifenberger, Polster (Cerny 81).
Portugal: Vitor Baia; Nelson, Jorge Costa, Helder, Paulinho Santos, Secretario (Sa Pinto 59), Oceano, Paulo Sousa, Rui Costa, Joao Pinto II (Folha 46), Domingos (Jose Dominguez 72).
Referee: Levnikov (Russia).

Dublin, 11 October 1995, 33,000

Republic of Ireland (0) 2 *(Aldridge 61 (pen), 64)*

Latvia (0) 1 *(Rimkus 78)*

Republic of Ireland: Kelly A; Kelly G, Phelan, McAteer, McGrath, Babb, Staunton, Aldridge (Kelly D 79) (Kennedy 84), Quinn, Townsend, Kenna.
Latvia: Karavayev; Troicki, Astafyev, Sevliakovs, Stepanov, Zemlinsky, Babichev (Elisejev 75), Ivanov, Zakresevskis, Zieberlins, Rimkus.
Referee: Marin (Spain).

Eschen, 11 October 1995, 1100

Liechtenstein (0) 0

Northern Ireland (1) 4 *(O'Neill 36, McMahon 49, Quinn 55, Gray 72)*

Liechtenstein: Oehry; Telser, Hefti, Hasler, Frick C (Hanselmann 78), Hilti (Ospelt J 66), Klaunzer, Stocker (Sele 46), Zech H, Oehri, Schadler.
Northern Ireland: Fettis (Wood 75); Lomas, Worthington, McMahon (McGibbon 80), Hill, Hunter, O'Neill, Quinn, Gray, Lennon, Hughes (Rowland 89).
Referee: Lubos (Slovakia).

Lisbon, 15 November 1995, 80,000

Portugal (0) 3 *(Rui Costa 60, Helder 74, Cadete 89)*

Republic of Ireland (0) 0

Portugal: Vitor Baia (Neno 86); Secretario, Fernando Couto, Helder, Paulinho Santos, Oceano, Figo, Paulo Sousa, Rui Costa, Joao Pinto II (Folha 67), Domingos (Cadete 67).
Republic of Ireland: Kelly A; Kelly G, Irwin, McAteer, McGrath, Babb, Staunton (Kernaghan 78), Aldridge, Quinn, Kenna, Kennedy (Cascarino 75).
Referee: Ceccarini (Italy).

Belfast, 15 November 1995, 8400

Northern Ireland (2) 5 *(O'Neill 27, 78, Dowie 32 (pen), Hunter 53, Gray 64)*

Austria (0) 3 *(Schopp 56, Stumpf 70, Wetl 81)*

Northern Ireland: Fettis; Lomas, Worthington, Hunter, Hill, Gillespie, Hughes, Dowie (Quinn 81), Gray (McDonald 78), Lennon, O'Neill.
Austria: Konsel; Schopp, Kogler W, Feiersinger, Pfeiffer, Marasek, Pfeifenberger, Stoger, Kuhbauer (Stumpf 46), Herzog (Wetl 46), Polster.
Referee: Sundell (Sweden).

	P	W	D	L	F	A	Pts
Portugal	10	7	2	1	29	7	23
Republic of Ireland	10	5	2	3	17	11	17
Northern Ireland	10	5	2	3	20	15	17
Austria	10	5	1	4	29	14	16
Latvia	10	4	0	6	11	20	12
Liechtenstein	10	0	1	9	1	40	1

Group 7

Tbilisi, 7 September 1994, 40,000

Georgia (0) 0

Moldova (1) 1 *(Oprea 40)*

Georgia: Zoidze; Nemsadze, Tskhadadze, Shelia, Kavelashvili, Arveladze R (Revishvili 70), Arveladze A, Jamarauli, Arveladze S, Guruli (Inalishvili 46), Kinkladze.

Moldova: Coselev; Secu, Belous, Pogorelov, Stroenco A, Stroenco S (Rebeja 55), Curtianu, Nani, Clescenco, Oprea, Spiridon (Kosse 82).

Referee: Sakari (Turkey).

Cardiff Arms Park, 7 September 1994, 15,791

Wales (1) 2 *(Coleman 9, Giggs 67)*

Albania (0) 0

Wales: Southall; Williams, Melville, Coleman, Bodin, Goss (Pembridge 74), Phillips, Speed, Giggs, Rush, Blake (Roberts I 80).

Albania: Strakosha; Shulku, Xhumba, Vata, Kacaj, Kola A (Fortuzi 53), Bellai, Kola B, Demollari, Pano, Shehu (Dosti 81).

Referee: Beschin (Italy).

Kishinev, 12 October 1994, 12,000

Moldova (2) 3 *(Belous 9, Secu 29, Pogorelov 79)*

Wales (1) 2 *(Speed 6, Blake 70)*

Moldova: Coselev; Secu, Stroenco S, Nani, Pogorelov, Rebeja, Belous (Caras 86), Oprea, Curtianu, Spiridon, Miterev (Kosse 46).

Wales: Southall; Bowen M, Coleman, Symons, Williams, Horne, Phillips, Blake (Melville 87), Roberts, Pembridge, Speed.

Referee: Vad (Hungary).

Sofia, 12 October 1994, 45,000

Bulgaria (0) 2 *(Kostadinov 55, 62)*

Georgia (0) 0

Bulgaria: Popov; Kiriakov, Ivanov, Hubchev, Tsvetanov, Yankov, Borimirov (Kostadinov 55), Lechkov, Balakov, Sirakov (Penev 70), Stoichkov.

Georgia: Devadze; Revishvili, Tskhadadze, Shelia, Chikhradze, Kudinov, Nemsadze (Inalishvili 71), Gogichaishvili, Ketsbaia, Kinkladze, Arveladze S (Guruli 76).

Referee: Gadosi (Slovakia).

Tirana, 16 November 1994, 20,000

Albania (1) 1 *(Zmijani 32)*

Germany (1) 2 *(Klinsmann 18, Kirsten 46)*

Albania: Strakosha; Vata, Kacaj, Xhumba, Zmijani (Pano 65), Lekbello, Demollari (Kola B 55), Millo, Bellai, Kushta, Rraklli.

Germany: Kopke; Matthaus, Kohler, Berthold, Reuter, Eilts, Sammer (Strunz 46), Weber (Schuster 83), Moller, Kirsten, Klinsmann.

Referee: Melnitschuk (Ukraine).

Sofia, 16 November 1994, 50,000

Bulgaria (1) 4 *(Stoichkov 45, 85, Balakov 65, Kostadinov 88)*

Moldova (0) 1 *(Clescenco 60)*

Bulgaria: Mikhailov; Hubchev, Kiriakov, Ivanov, Tsvetanov, Penev (Sirakov 80), Yordanov, Lechkov (Stoilov 86), Balakov, Stoichkov, Kostadinov.
Moldova: Coselev; Stroenco S, Secu, Pogorelov, Nani, Rebeja, Belous, Curtianu (Kosse 86), Spiridon, Oprea, Clescenco.
Referee: McArdle (Republic of Ireland).

Tbilisi, 16 November 1994, 45,000

Georgia (2) 5 *(Ketsbaia 31, 49, Kinkladze 41, Gogrichiani 59, Arveladze S 67)*

Wales (0) 0

Georgia: Devadze; Gogichaishvili, Tskhadadze, Shelia, Chikhradze, Revishvili, Kinkladze, Nemsadze (Inalishvili 41), Ketsbaia (Kavelashvili 75), Gogrichiani, Arveladze S.
Wales: Southall; Neilson (Symons 46), Bowen M, Horne, Melville, Coleman, Phillips, Saunders, Rush, Hughes, Speed.
Referee: Sars (France).

Chisinau, 14 December 1994, 20,000

Moldova (0) 0

Germany (2) 3 *(Kirsten 7, Klinsmann 38, Matthaus 73)*

Moldova: Coselev; Secu, Stroenco S, Nani, Pogorelov, Rebeja (Testimitanu 81), Spiridon, Curtianu, Belous, Oprea (Gaidamasciuc 58), Clescenco.
Germany: Kopke; Berthold, Matthaus, Helmer, Reuter, Hassler, Sammer, Moller (Kuntz 79), Weber, Kirsten (Strunz 69), Klinsmann.
Referee: Van Vliet (Holland).

Cardiff, 14 December 1994, 20,000

Wales (0) 0

Bulgaria (2) 3 *(Ivanov 5, Kostadinov 15, Stoichkov 51)*

Wales: Southall; Phillips, Bowen M, Aizlewood, Coleman, Melville, Jones, Saunders, Rush, Hughes, Speed.
Bulgaria: Mikhailov; Kremenliev, Ivanov, Tsvetanov, Yankov, Yordanov, Lechkov, Balakov, Kostadinov (Sirakov 73), Penev (Kiriakov 73), Stoichkov.
Referee: Sundell (Sweden).

Tirana, 14 December 1994, 15,000

Albania (0) 0

Georgia (1) 1 *(Arveladze S 17)*

Albania: Strakosha; Dema, Vata (Shulku 30), Xhumba, Kacaj, Lekbello (Malko 46), Bellai, Rraklli, Demollari, Fortuzi, Kola B.
Georgia: Devadze; Revishvili, Shelia, Kudinov, Chikhradze, Gogichaishvili (Jishkariani 62), Inalishvili, Gogrichiani, Ketsbaia, Kinkladze, Arveladze S (Jamarauli 30).
Referee: Molnar (Hungary).

Kaiserslautern, 18 December 1994, 20,310

Germany (2) 2 *(Matthaus 8 (pen), Klinsmann 17)*

Albania (0) 1 *(Rraklli 58)*

Germany: Kopke; Matthaus, Berthold, Helmer, Weber, Reuter, Sammer, Hassler (Strunz 77), Moller, Kirsten (Kuntz 59), Klinsmann.
Albania: Strakosha; Xhumba, Dema, Kajac, Shulku, Zmijani, Demollari, Malko, Bellai, Rraklli, Kola B (Zalla 62).
Referee: Christensen (Denmark).

Tbilisi, 29 March 1995, 75,000

Georgia (0) 0

Germany (2) 2 *(Klinsmann 24, 45)*

Georgia: Devadze; Revishvili, Tskhadadze, Shelia, Chikhradze, Gogichaishvili, Kudinov, Kinkladze, Jamarauli (Gogrichiani 70), Arveladze R (Kavelashvili 75), Arveladze S.

Germany: Kopke; Reuter, Kohler, Helmer, Babbel, Weber (Freund 46), Eilts, Basler, Moller, Klinsmann, Herrlich.

Referee: Bodenham (England).

Sofia, 29 March 1995, 60,000

Bulgaria (1) 3 *(Balakov 37, Penev 70, 82)*

Wales (0) 1 *(Saunders 83)*

Bulgaria: Mikhailov; Ivanov, Hubchev, Tsvetanov (Kiriakov 85), Balakov, Yankov, Kremenliev, Lechkov, Stoichkov, Penev, Kostadinov.

Wales: Southall; Phillips, Bowen M, Jones (Cornforth 78), Symons, Coleman, Speed, Horne, Saunders, Hartson, Giggs.

Referee: Piraux (Belgium).

Tirana, 29 March 1995, 20,000

Albania (2) 3 *(Kushta 32, 78, Kacaj 73)*

Moldova (0) 0

Albania: Strakosha (Nallbani 80); Malko, Xhumba (Fortuzi 66), Vata, Shulku, Kacaj, Bellai, Rraklli, Abazi, Kushta (Dalipi 88), Demollari.

Moldova: Coselev; Secu, Pogorelov, Belous, Gaidamasciuc (Stroenco A 66), Stroenco S, Oprea, Curtianu (Caras 72), Spiridon, Nani, Clescenco.

Referee: Meier (Switzerland).

Tbilisi, 26 April 1995, 20,000

Georgia (2) 2 *(Arveladze S 3, Ketsbaia 43)*

Albania (0) 0

Georgia: Devadze; Chikhradze, Gudushauri, Kudinov, Shelia (Lobjanidze 70), Ketsbaia, Gogichaishvili, Jamarauli, Kizilashvili (Arveladze A 59), Arveladze S, Inalishvili.

Albania: Strakosha; Mema, Vata, Xhumba, Kacaj, Fortuzi (Prenga 46), Malko, Dalipi, Demollari, Rraklli, Kushta (Dosti 87).

Referee: Luinge (Holland).

Chisinau, 26 April 1995, 17,000

Moldova (0) 0

Bulgaria (1) 3 *(Balakov 29, Stoichkov 54, 68)*

Moldova: Coselev; Secu, Fistican, Nani, Pogorelov, Caras (Gaidamasciuc 65), Rebeja, Oprea (Cibotaru 72), Belous, Curtianu, Clescenco.

Bulgaria: Mikhailov; Kremenliev (Kiriakov 82), Hubchev, Ivanov, Tsvetanov, Yankov, Lechkov, Balakov, Yordanov, Penev, Stoichkov (Mikhtarski 79).

Referee: Ulrich (Czech Republic).

Dusseldorf, 26 April 1995, 45,000

Germany (1) 1 *(Herrlich 42)*

Wales (1) 1 *(Saunders 7)*

Germany: Kopke; Reuter, Freund, Babbel, Eilts, Basler (Scholl 76), Hassler, Weber (Kuntz 86), Ziege, Herrlich, Klinsmann.

Wales: Southall; Phillips, Bowen M, Jones, Symons, Coleman (Williams 45), Horne, Hughes (Hartson 90), Rush, Saunders, Speed.

Referee: Encinar (Spain).

Sofia, 7 June 1995, 50,000

Bulgaria (1) 3 *(Stoichkov 45 (pen), 66 (pen), Kostadinov 69)*

Germany (2) 2 *(Klinsmann 18, Strunz 44)*

Bulgaria: Mikhailov; Kremenliev, Hubchev, Ivanov, Tsvetanov, Yankov, Lechkov (Sirakov 80), Balakov, Yordanov (Kostadinov 65), Penev, Stoichkov.
Germany: Kopke; Helmer, Sammer, Babbel, Reuter, Eilts, Basler (Moller 80), Hassler, Strunz (Kirsten 89), Klinsmann, Herrlich.
Referee: Pairetto (Italy).

Cardiff, 7 June 1995, 6500

Wales (0) 0

Georgia (0) 1 *(Kinkladze 73)*

Wales: Southall; Phillips, Bowen M, Jones, Williams, Symons, Horne, Saunders (Pembridge 84), Rush, Cornforth, Hughes (Hartson 84).
Georgia: Devadze; Beradze, Tskhadadze, Shelia, Chikhradze, Inalishvili, Gogichashvili, Kinkladze, Ketsbaia, Kavelashvili (Tskitishvili 74), Arveladze S (Kilasonia 88).
Referee: Koho (Finland).

Chisinau, 7 June 1995, 7000

Moldova (2) 2 *(Curtianu 10, Clescenco 15)*

Albania (2) 3 *(Kushta 7, Bellai 25, Vata 71)*

Moldova: Ivanov; Secu, Fistican, Pogorelov, Rebeja (Kosse 74), Stroenko S, Stroenko A, Belous (Miterev 55), Nani, Curtianu, Clescenco.
Albania: Strakosha; Bano, Shulku, Malko, Vata, Kacaj, Kushta, Bellai, Kola B, Rraklli (Prenga 87), Demollari (Pano 79).
Referee: Schelings (Belgium).

Tirana, 6 September 1995, 10,000

Albania (1) 1 *(Rraklli 16)*

Bulgaria (1) 1 *(Stoichkov 8)*

Albania: Strakosha; Abazi, Vata, Xhumba, Shulku, Lekbello, Kushta, Bellai, Kola B (Shehu 65), Rraklli, Bozgo (Demollari 85).
Bulgaria: Mikhailov; Kremenliev, Ivanov, Hubchev, Tsvetanov, Lechkov (Chomakov 75), Balakov, Borimirov, Kostadinov, Penev (Sirakov 75), Stoichkov.
Referee: Agius (Malta).

Nuremburg, 6 September 1995, 40,000

Germany (1) 4 *(Moller 39, Ziege 57, Kirsten 62, Babbel 72)*

Georgia (1) 1 *(Ketsbaia 28)*

Germany: Kahn; Helmer, Kohler, Babbel, Freund, Hassler, Moller, Strunz, Ziege, Klinsmann, Kirsten.
Georgia: Devadze; Kudinov, Gujabidze, Shelia, Tskhadadze, Gogichaishvili (Arveladze A 67), Nemsadze, Kinkladze, Ketsbaia, Arveladze S, Kavelashvili (Kilasonia 46).
Referee: McCluskey (Scotland).

Cardiff, 6 September 1995, 5000

Wales (0) 1 *(Speed 55)*

Moldova (0) 0

Wales: Southall; Bowen M, Coleman, Williams, Symons, Pembridge, Horne, Speed, Nogan (Phillips 46), Rush (Hartson 69), Hughes.
Moldova: Ivanov; Fistican, Testimitanu, Culibaba, Rebeja, Stroenco S, Oprea, Belous, Nani (Soucharev 76), Cibotaru, Clescenco.
Referee: Orrason (Iceland).

Sofia, 7 October 1995, 25,000

Bulgaria (1) 3 *(Lechkov 14, Kostadinov 80, 82)*

Albania (0) 0

Bulgaria: Mikhailov; Kiriakov (Borimirov 87), Kremenliev, Ivanov, Tsvetanov, Lechkov, Yankov, Balakov, Kostadinov (Sirakov 86), Penev, Stoichkov.
Albania: Strakosha; Dema, Malko, Xhumba, Shulku, Zmijani, Bellai, Kola B, Abazi (Demollari 86), Kushta, Rraklli.
Referee: Hirvinemi (Finland).

Leverkusen, 8 October 1995, 18,300

Germany (3) 6 *(Stroenko S 16 (og), Helmer 18, Sammer 24, 71, Moller 47, 61)*

Moldova (0) 1 *(Rebeja 82)*

Germany: Kopke; Sammer (Worns 83), Babbel, Helmer, Eilts, Hassler, Freund, Moller (Scholl 78), Ziege, Klinsmann, Herrlich (Bobic 74).
Moldova: Ivanov; Culibaba, Seku, Stroenko S, Testimitanu, Rebeja, Belous, Nani (Chisinau 59) (Oprea 87), Curtianu, Gavriliuc, Clescenco.
Referee: Ziober (Poland).

Tbilisi, 11 October 1995, 45,000

Georgia (1) 2 *(Arveladze S 1, Kinkladze 46 (pen))*

Bulgaria (0) 1 *(Stoichkov 88)*

Georgia: Devadze; Kudinov, Shelia, Chikhradze, Nemsadze, Gudushauri (Beradze 46), Jamarauli, Kinkladze, Arveladze A (Kavelashvili 46), Arveladze S, Gogichaishvili.
Bulgaria: Mikhailov; Kiriakov, Ivanov, Tsvetanov, Balakov, Borimirov, Lechkov, Sirakov, Kostadinov, Penev, Stoichkov.
Referee: Meier (Switzerland).

Cardiff, 11 October 1995, 25,000

Wales (0) 1 *(Symons 78)*

Germany (0) 2 *(Kuntz 75, Klinsmann 80)*

Wales: Southall; Symons, Bowen M, Melville, Jenkins (Mardon 70), Blake (Williams G 82), Horne, Pembridge (Hodges 82), Saunders, Speed, Giggs.
Germany: Kopke; Babbel (Worns 46), Sammer, Helmer, Freund, Eilts, Moller, Ziege, Hassler, Klinsmann, Herrlich (Kuntz 73).
Referee: Craciunescu (Romania).

Berlin, 15 November 1995, 75,841

Germany (0) 3 *(Klinsmann 50, 76 (pen), Hassler 56)*

Bulgaria (0) 1 *(Stoichkov 47)*

Germany: Kopke; Babbel, Kohler (Strunz 46), Sammer, Freund, Helmer, Eilts, Basler, Hassler (Reuter 86), Klinsmann, Kuntz (Bobic 82).
Bulgaria: Popov; Kremenliev, Dartilov, Guentchev, Tsvetanov, Lechkov (Kiriakov 62), Yankov, Balakov (Borimirov 82), Kostadinov, Penev (Sirakov 79), Stoichkov.
Referee: Nikakis (Greece).

Tirana, 15 November 1995, 6000

Albania (1) 1 *(Kushta 4 (pen))*

Wales (1) 1 *(Pembridge 43)*

Albania: Strakosha; Zmijani, Shulku, Dema (Miloti 84), Vata, Lekbello, Kushta (Bushi 57), Malko, Bozgo (Zalla 80), Rraklli, Pano.
Wales: Southall; Young, Bowen M, Jenkins, Phillips, Melville, Taylor (Robinson 84), Pembridge, Saunders, Savage (Hughes C 63), Giggs.
Referee: Suheil (Israel).

Kichinev, 15 November 1995, 9000
Moldova (2) 3 *(Testimitanu 5, Miterev 17, 72)*
Georgia (0) 2 *(Dzhanashia 68, Culibaba 82 (og))*

Moldova: Coselev; Secu, Testimitanu, Culibaba, Nani, Oprea (Soukharev 54), Kirilov (Gavriliuc 80), Belous, Curtianu (Cibotaru 76), Clescenco, Miterev.
Georgia: Zoidze; Gudushauri (Dzhanashia 56), Kudinov, Beradze, Chikhradze, Gogichaishvili, Tsikarishvili, Jamarauli (Machavariani 62), Ketsbaia, Kinkladze, Arveladze S.
Referee: Van der Ende (Holland).

	P	W	D	L	F	A	Pts
Germany	10	8	1	1	27	10	25
Bulgaria	10	7	1	2	24	10	22
Georgia	10	5	0	5	14	13	15
Moldova	10	3	0	7	11	27	9
Wales	10	2	2	6	9	19	8
Albania	10	2	2	6	10	16	8

Group 8

Toftir, 7 September 1994, 2412
Faeroes (0) 1 *(Apostolakis (og) 89)*
Greece (2) 5 *(Saravakos 12, Tsalouhidis 18, 85, Alexandris 54, 60)*

Faeroes: Knudsen; Hansen T, Hansen A, Johannesen O, Jarnskor M, Hansen J, Morkore A (Rasmussen J E 85), Dam J, Muller, Jonsson, Hansen O (Jarnskor H 56).
Greece: Karkamanis; Apostolakis, Pavlopoulos, Kallitzakis, Karataidis, Hantzidis (Zagorakis 82), Tsalouhidis, Tsartas, Kostis (Markos 77), Alexandris, Saravakos.
Referee: Piraux (Belgium).

Helsinki, 7 September 1994, 12,845
Finland (0) 0
Scotland (1) 2 *(Shearer 29, Collins 66)*

Finland: Jakonen; Makela, Hyrylainen, Kanerva, Heinola (Holmgren 28), Suominen, Litmanen, Lindberg, Rantanen (Jarvinen 41), Paatelainen, Hjelm.
Scotland: Goram; McKimmie, Hendry, Levein (McCall 78), Boyd, McLaren, McStay, McAllister, Collins, Walker (Jess 65), Shearer.
Referee: Wocjik (Poland).

Hampden Park, 12 October 1994, 20,885
Scotland (3) 5 *(McGinlay 4, Booth 34, Collins 40, 72, McKinlay 61)*
Faeroes (0) 1 *(Muller 75)*

Scotland: Goram; McLaren, McKimmie, Levein, Hendry (McKinlay W 58), McStay, Boyd, Nevin, Booth (Walker 69), McGinlay, Collins.
Faeroes: Knudsen; Dam J (Joensen 53), Hansen T, Johannesen O, Hansen J, Hansen O (Rasmussen J 73), Jarnskor H, Morkore K, Jarnskor M, Muller, Jonsson.
Referee: Hauge (Norway).

Salonika, 12 October 1994, 30,000
Greece (1) 4 *(Markos 23, Batista 70, Mahlas 76, 90)*
Finland (0) 0

Greece: Atmatzidis; Apostolakis, Kassapis, Dabizas, Kallitzakis, Tsalouhidis, Zagorakis, Markos (Toursounidis 65), Mahlas, Tsartas, Vrizas (Batista 43).
Finland: Jakonen; Makela, Kanerva, Hyrylainen, Heinola (Holmgren 30), Suominen, Jarvinen (Sumiala 73), Lindberg, Hjelm, Litmanen, Paatelainen.
Referee: Leduc (France).

Moscow, 12 October 1994, 20,000

Russia (1) 4 *(Karpin 43, Kolyvanov 64, Nikiforov 65, Radchenko 67)*
San Marino (0) 0

Russia: Cherchesov; Kulkov (Tetradze 65), Nikiforov, Tsymbalar (Kolyvanov 55), Shalimov, Karpin, Onopko, Kanchelskis, Pyatnitski, Radchenko, Kiryakov.
San Marino: Benedettini; Gobbi, Gennari, Mazza M, Valentini M, Guerra (Della Valle 23), Manzaroli, Matteoni, Bacciocchi, Bonini, Francini (Canti 67).
Referee: Hamer (Luxembourg).

Helsinki, 16 November 1994, 2240

Finland (1) 5 *(Sumiala 37, Litmanen 51 (pen), 71, Paatelainen 75, 85)*
Faeroes (0) 0

Finland: Laukkanen; Makela, Kanerva, Eriksson, Helin, Litmanen, Ukkonen, Lindberg (Rajamaki 78), Sumiala (Ruhanen 90), Hjelm, Paatelainen.
Faeroes: Knudsen; Johannesen O, Rasmussen J, Hansen O (Rasmussen J E 80), Hansen T, Morkore K, Jarnskor M, Jarnskor H, Joensen D, Muller, Jonsson.
Referee: Orrason (Iceland).

Athens, 16 November 1994, 15,000

Greece (1) 2 *(Mahlas 21, Frantzeskos 84)*
San Marino (0) 0

Greece: Atmatzidis; Apostolakis, Dabizas, Kallitzakis, Kassapis, Maragos (Frantzeskos 46), Zagorakis, Toursounidis, Tsartas, Mahlas, Vrizas (Batista 70).
San Marino: Benedettini; Gobbi, Valentini M, Guerra, Gennari (Canti 46), Manzaroli, Della Valle (Gasperoni 75), Francini, Bonini, Bacciocchi, Gualtieri.
Referee: Lipkovitch (Israel).

Hampden Park, 16 November 1994, 31,254

Scotland (1) 1 *(Booth 19)*
Russia (1) 1 *(Radchenko 25)*

Scotland: Goram; McKimmie, Boyd, McCall, Levein, McLaren, McKinlay W (Nevin 83), McAllister, Booth, McGinlay (Spencer 63), Collins.
Russia: Cherchesov; Gorlukovich, Nikiforov, Kulkov, Shalimov, Kanchelskis, Karpin, Pyatniski (Tetradze 75), Onopko, Radimov, Radchenko.
Referee: Karlsson (Sweden).

Helsinki, 14 December 1994, 3140

Finland (2) 4 *(Paatelainen 24, 30, 85, 90)*
San Marino (1) 1 *(Della Valle 34)*

Finland: Laukkanen; Makela, Kanerva, Eriksson, Lindberg, Helin (Myyry 74), Ukkonen, Sumiala, Litmanen, Hjelm, Paatelainen.
San Marino: Benedettini; Canti, Gasperoni, Gobbi, Gennari, Bonini, Guerra, Manzaroli, Della Valle, Bacciocchi (Peverani 15), Mularoni (Gualtieri 60).
Referee: Albrecht (Germany).

Athens, 18 December 1994, 20,310

Greece (1) 1 *(Apostolakis 18 (pen))*
Scotland (0) 0

Greece: Atmatzidis; Apostolakis, Vlahos, Kallitzakis, Kassapis, Tsalouhidis, Zagorakis, Nioblias (Karassavidis 88), Toursounidis, Mahlas, Alexandris (Maragos 72).
Scotland: Goram (Leighton 78); McKimmie, Hendry, McLaren, Boyd, McCall, McAllister, Collins, McGinlay, McKinlay W (Spencer 46), Ferguson D.
Referee: Blankenstein (Holland).

Moscow, 29 March 1995, 25,000

Russia (0) 0

Scotland (0) 0

Russia: Kharine; Khlestov, Nikiforov, Kovtun, Karpin, Onopko, Dobrovolski, Shalimov (Radimov 69), Kanchelskis, Kiryakov, Radchenko (Pisarev 57).
Scotland: Leighton; McKimmie, Calderwood, Hendry, McLaren, McStay, Boyd, Collins, McAllister, McGinlay (McKinlay W 84), Jackson (Shearer 78).
Referee: Strampe (Germany).

San Marino, 29 March 1995, 1000

San Marino (0) 0

Finland (1) 2 *(Litmanen 45, Sumiala 65)*

San Marino: Benedettini; Gobbi, Valentini M, Guerra, Gennari, Mazza M (Matteoni 70), Manzaroli, Francini, Bonini, Montagna (Gualtieri 75), Mularoni.
Finland: Laukkanen; Makela (Hyypia 74), Ukkonen, Helin, Lindberg, Eriksson, Sumiala, Myyry, Litmanen, Hjelm, Jarvinen (Rajamaki 69).
Referee: Suheli (Israel).

Serrevalle, 26 April 1995, 2738

San Marino (0) 0

Scotland (1) 2 *(Collins 19, Calderwood 85)*

San Marino: Benedettini; Manzaroli, Canti, Guerra, Gobbi, Gennari, Mazza M, Della Valle, Bonini (Matteoni 46), Mularoni (Gualtieri 72), Bacciocchi.
Scotland: Leighton; McLaren, Boyd, Calderwood, Hendry, Jackson, Collins, McGinlay, Shearer (Spencer 67), McAllister, Nevin (McKinlay W 78).
Referee: Loizou (Cyprus).

Salonika, 26 April 1995, 30,000

Greece (0) 0

Russia (1) 3 *(Nikiforov 36, Zagorakis 78 (og), Bestchastnikh 79)*

Greece: Atmatzidis; Apostolakis, Kallitzakis, Dabizas, Zagorakis, Tsalouhidis, Kassapis, Nioblias (Tsartas 46), Toursounidis, Mahlas (Nikolaidis 60), Donis.
Russia: Kharine; Kovtun, Nikiforov, Kulkov, Khlestov, Karpin, Onopko, Dobrovolski, Pyatnitski (Kiryakov 46), Radchenko (Mostovoi 77), Bestchastnikh.
Referee: Stafoggia (Italy).

Toftir, 26 April 1995, 1000

Faeroes (0) 0

Finland (0) 4 *(Hjelm 55, Paatelainen 75, Lindberg 78, Helin 83)*

Faeroes: Knudsen; Morkore A, Rasmussen J, Johannesen O, Hansen J, Hansen O, Johnsson, Morkore K, Joensen D, Jarnskor M (Jarnskor H 80), Jonsson.
Finland: Laukkanen; Makela, Ukkonen, Eriksson, Helin, Hyypia, Litmanen, Lindberg (Suominen 82), Sumiala (Kolkka 61), Hjelm, Paatelainen.
Referee: Howells (Wales).

Moscow, 6 May 1995, 9500

Russia (0) 3 *(Ketschinov 52, Pisarev 73, Moukhamadiev 80)*

Faeroes (0) 0

Russia: Cherchesov; Khlestov, Nikiforov, Kovtun, Tetradze, Kechinov, Onopko, Cheryshev, Pyatnitski (Lebed 22), Pisarev, Mukhamadiev.
Faeroes: Knudsen; Johannesen O, Hansen J, Rasmussen J, Morkore K, Joensen A, Jarnskor M, Hansen E, Jarnskor H (Joensen D 69), Jonsson, Rasmussen J E.
Referee: Kvartskelia (Georgia).

Toftir, 25 May 1995, 3452

Faeroes (2) 3 *(Hansen J 7, Rasmussen J E 9, Johnsson 62)*

San Marino (0) 0

Faeroes: Knudsen; Jarnskor H, Hansen J, Johannesen O, Rasmussen J, Hansen O, Johnsson, Morkore K, Jarnskor M, Jonsson, Rasmussen J E.
San Marino: Benedettini; Gasperoni, Gobbi, Valentini M, Gennari, Canti, Manzaroli, Bonini (Ugolini 57), Francini, Bacciocchi, Mularoni.
Referee: Shorte (Republic of Ireland).

Serravalle, 7 June 1995, 1400

San Marino (0) 0

Russia (2) 7 *(Dobrovolski 30 (pen), Gobbi 35 (og), Kiryakov 49, Shalimov 50, Bestchastnikh 59, Kolyvanov 65, Tcherychev 88)*

San Marino: Benedettini; Gobbi, Gennari, Mazza M, Valentini M, Guerra, Manzaroli, Della Valle (Canti 64), Francini, Montagna (Bonini 78), Bacciocchi.
Russia: Cherchesov; Kulkov, Tetradze, Kovtun, Karpin, Onopko, Shalimov, Dobrovolski (Radchenko 60), Kiryakov, Kolyvanov, Bestchastnikh (Cheryshev 84).
Referee: Bohunek (Czech Republic).

Toftir, 7 June 1995, 3881

Faeroes (0) 0

Scotland (2) 2 *(McKinlay W 25, McGinlay 29)*

Faeroes: Knudsen; Jarnskor H, Hansen T, Johannesen O, Rasmussen J, Hansen J, Johnsson, Jarnskor M (Joensen A 56), Hansen O, Rasmussen J E (Muller 75), Jonsson.
Scotland: Leighton; McKimmie, McLaren, Burley, Calderwood, McKinnon, McKinlay W, Jackson, Shearer (Robertson 86), McGinlay (Gemmill 75), Collins.
Referee: Hrinak (Slovakia).

Helsinki, 11 June 1995, 7000

Finland (1) 2 *(Litmanen 45 (pen), Hjelm 55)*

Greece (1) 1 *(Nikolaidis 6)*

Finland: Laukkanen; Makela, Tuomela, Holmgren, Helin, Lindberg, Sumiala (Jarvinen 63), Myyry, Hjelm, Litmanen, Paatelainen (Tiainen 85).
Greece: Michopoulos; Apostolakis, Kassapis, Dabizas, Alexiou, Tsalouhidis, Nikolaidis, Markos (Batista 57), Zagorakis, Tsartas (Mahlas 70), Donis.
Referee: Krug (Germany).

Helsinki, 16 August 1995, 14,200

Finland (0) 0

Russia (3) 6 *(Kulkov 32, 49, Karpin 40, Radchenko 43, Kolyvanov 67, 69)*

Finland: Laukkanen; Makela, Kanerva, Holmgren, Nieminen, Lindberg, Sumiala, Rantanen (Gronlund 65), Tiainen, Hjelm, Paatelainen.
Russia: Kharine (Cherchesov 74); Khlestov, Kovtun, Nikiforov, Tsymbalar, Karpin (Kanchelskis 54), Onopko, Kulkov, Mostovoi, Radchenko (Kiryakov 68), Kolyvanov.
Referee: Puhl (Hungary).

Hampden Park, 16 August 1995, 34,910

Scotland (0) 1 *(McCoist 72)*

Greece (0) 0

Scotland: Leighton; Burley, McKinlay W, Calderwood, McKimmie, Boyd, McCall, Jackson (Robertson), Shearer (McCoist 71), McAllister, Collins.
Greece: Atmatzidis; Kallitzakis, Karataidis, Dabizas, Zagorakis (Georgiadis G), Apostolakis, Tsalouhidis, Kassapis, Tsartas, Batista (Alexandris), Vrizas (Mahlas 30).
Referee: Mikkelsen (Denmark).

Hampden Park, 6 September 1995, 35,505
Scotland (1) 1 *(Booth 10)*
Finland (0) 0
Scotland: Leighton; McKimmie (McKinlay W 89), Boyd, McLaren, Calderwood, Hendry, McKinlay T, Collins, Booth (Jackson 80), McAllister, Spencer (McCoist 75).
Finland: Laukkanen; Rissanen, Kanerva, Holmgren, Suominen, Lindberg, Nieminen (Gronlund 63), Myyry, Litmanen, Hjelm, Jarvinen.
Referee: Melnichuk (Ukraine).

Toftir, 6 September 1995, 1792
Faeroes (1) 2 *(Jarnskor H 12, Jonsson T 55)*
Russia (1) 5 *(Mostovoi 10, Kiryakov 60, Kolyvanov 65, Tsymbalar 84, Shalimov 87)*
Faeroes: Knudsen; Johannesen O, Hansen T (Joensen A 81), Rasmussen J, Hansen J, Hansen O, Morkore K, Johnsson, Muller (Rasmussen J E 15), Jonsson, Jarnskor H.
Russia: Cherchesov; Kulkov (Mamedov 64), Kovtun, Nikiforov, Tsymbalar, Shalimov, Kanchelskis (Bestchastnikh 57), Onopko, Mostovoi, Radchenko (Kiryakov 46), Kolyvanov.
Referee: Snoddy (Northern Ireland).

Serravalle, 6 September 1995, 1000
San Marino (0) 0
Greece (2) 4 *(Tsalouhidis 5, Georgiadis G H 31, Alexandris 61, Donis 81)*
San Marino: Muccioli; Gennari, Gobbi, Guerra, Mazza M, Matteoni, Manzaroli (Peverani 89), Della Valle, Francini (Canti 76), Bacciocchi, Mularoni (Montagna 79).
Greece: Atmatzidis; Apostolakis, Ouzounidis, Karataidis, Dabizas, Tsalouhidis, Zagorakis, Nikolaidis (Alexandris 46), Georgiadis G H (Georgatos 57), Mahlas (Batista 77), Donis.
Referee: Mitrovic (Slovenia).

Moscow, 11 October 1995, 40,000
Russia (1) 2 *(Ouzounidis 35 (og), Onopko 71)*
Greece (0) 1 *(Tsalouhidis 64)*
Russia: Kharine; Khlestov, Nikiforov, Kovtun, Karpin (Shalimov 76), Kulkov, Onopko, Mostovoi, Tsymbalar (Radchenko 69), Yuran (Kiryakov 46), Kolyvanov.
Greece: Mihopoulos; Apostolakis, Ouzounidis, Kallitzakis (Dabizas 46), Kassapis, Tsalouhidis, Tsartas (Georgatos 46), Zagorakis, Donis, Alexandris, Batista (Mahlas 71).
Referee: Graber (Austria).

San Marino, 11 October 1995, 1000
San Marino (0) 1 *(Valentini M 50)*
Faeroes (2) 3 *(Jonsson 40, 45, 62)*
San Marino: Muccioli; Valentini V, Gennari, Matteoni (Peverani 72), Valentini M, Guerra, Manzaroli, Mazza M (Mularoni 58), Bacciocchi, Francini, Montagna (Gasperoni 82).
Faeroes: Knudsen; Hansen A, Hansen J, Rasmussen J, Jarnskor H (Bertholdsen 89), Morkore A, Jarnskor M, Hansen O (Reynheim 82), Muller, Jonsson (Petersen 75), Dam J.
Referee: Beck (Liechtenstein).

Hampden Park, 15 November 1995, 30,306
Scotland (2) 5 *(Jess 30, Booth 45, McCoist 49, Nevin 71, Francini 90 (og))*
San Marino (0) 0
Scotland: Leighton; McLaren, Boyd, Calderwood, Hendry, Gemmill, Nevin, Jess, Booth (Jackson 66), McAllister (McCoist 48), Collins (McKinlay W 59).
San Marino: Muccioli; Manzaroli, Moroni, Guerra (Montagna 71), Valentini M, Gennari, Mazza M (Della Valle 82), Francini, Matteoni, Mularoni (Canti 52), Bacciocchi.
Referee: Bohunek (Czech Republic).

Moscow, 15 November 1995, 6000
Russia (1) 3 *(Radchenko 40, Kulkov 55, Kiryakov 70)*
Finland (1) 1 *(Suominen 45)*

Russia: Cherchesov; Khlestov, Nikiforov, Mamedov (Dobrovolski 46), Onopko, Tsymbalar, Kulkov, Karpin (Kanchelskis 75), Mostovoi, Yuran, Radchenko (Kiryakov 62).
Finland: Niemi; Rissanen, Nuorela, Hyrylainen, Nieminen, Lindberg, Sumiala (Kangaskorpi 76), Suominen (Yionen 88), Gronlund (Koskinen 70), Hjelm, Myyry.
Referee: Merk (Germany).

Iraklis, 15 November 1995, 12,000
Greece (0) 5 *(Alexandris 58, Nikolaidis 62, Mahlas 66, Donis 75, Tsartas 80)*
Faeroes (0) 0

Greece: Atmazidis; Apostolakis, Katzidis, Ouzounidis, Dabizas, Tsalouhidis (Nikolaidis 46), Zagorakis (Konstantinidis C 70), Alexandris (Georgatos 76), Mahlas, Tsartas, Donis.
Faeroes: Mikkelsen; Johannesen O, Hansen T, Hansen G, Hansen E (Bertoldsen 89), Morkore A, Jarnskor M, Jarnskor G, Muller (Petersen 84), Reynheim (Jonsson 55), Dam J.
Referee: Mitrev (Bulgaria).

	P	W	D	L	F	A	Pts
Russia	10	8	2	0	34	5	26
Scotland	10	7	2	1	19	3	23
Greece	10	6	0	4	23	9	18
Finland	10	5	0	5	18	18	15
Faeroes	10	2	0	8	10	35	6
San Marino	10	0	0	10	2	36	0

Play-off

Anfield, 13 December 1995, 40,000
Republic of Ireland (0) 0
Holland (1) 2 *(Kluivert 29, 89)*

Republic of Ireland: Kelly A; Kelly G, Irwin, Kenna, McGrath, Babb, Sheridan, Aldridge (Kernaghan 73), Cascarino, Townsend (McAteer 50), Phelan.
Holland: Van der Sar; Reiziger, Blind, Bogarde, Ronald de Boer, Seedorf, Bergkamp (De Kock 58), Davids, Overmars, Kluivert, Helder (Winter 79).
Referee: Zhuk (Belarus).

EUROPEAN CHAMPIONSHIP 1994-95

Finals

Group A

Wembley, 8 June 1996, 76,567
England (1) 1 *(Shearer 23)*
Switzerland (0) 1 *(Turkyilmaz 83 (pen))*

England: Seaman; Neville G, Pearce, Ince, Southgate, Adams, Anderton, Gascoigne (Platt 74), Shearer, Sheringham (Barmby 67), McManaman (Stone 67).
Switzerland: Pascolo; Jeanneret, Vega, Henchoz, Quentin, Vogel, Geiger (Kollo 67), Sforza, Bonvin (Chapuisat 67), Grassi, Turkyilmaz.
Referee: Diaz Vega (Spain).

Villa Park, 10 June 1996, 34,363

Holland (0) 0
Scotland (0) 0

Holland: Van der Sar; Reiziger, De Kock, Bogarde, Davids, Ronald de Boer (Winter 68), Seedorf, Witschge (Cocu 76), Taument (Kluivert 61), Bergkamp, Jordi Cruyff.
Scotland: Goram; McKimmie (Burley 83), Boyd, McCall, Hendry, Calderwood, Durie, Gallagher (McKinlay W 55), Booth (Spencer 46), McAllister, Collins.
Referee: Sundell (Sweden).

Villa Park, 13 June 1996, 36,800

Switzerland (0) 0
Holland (0) 2 *(Jordi Cruyff 65, Bergkamp 78)*

Switzerland: Pascolo; Henchoz, Jeanneret, Vega, Hottiger (Comisetti 68), Sforza, Vogel, Quentin, Turkyilmaz, Grassi, Chapuisat.
Holland: Van der Sar; Reiziger, Blind, Seedorf (De Kock 25), Bogarde, Jordi Cruyff (Kluivert 82), Witschge, Winter, Ronald de Boer (Davids 80), Hoekstra, Bergkamp.
Referee: Ouzounov (Bulgaria).

Wembley, 15 June 1996, 76,864

Scotland (0) 0
England (0) 2 *(Shearer 53, Gascoigne 79)*

Scotland: Goram; McKimmie, Boyd, McCall, Hendry, Calderwood, Durie (Jess 85), McKinlay T (Burley 81), Spencer (McCoist 66), McAllister, Collins.
England: Seaman; Neville G, Pearce (Redknapp 46) (Campbell 84), Ince (Stone 79), Southgate, Adams, Anderton, Gascoigne, Shearer, Sheringham, McManaman.
Referee: Pairetto (Italy).

Wembley, 18 June 1996, 76,798

Holland (0) 1 *(Kluivert 77)*
England (1) 4 *(Shearer 23 (pen), 57, Sheringham 51, 62)*

Holland: Van der Sar; Reiziger, Bogarde, Seedorf, Blind, Ronald de Boer (Kluivert 72), Jordi Cruyff, Witschge (De Kock 46), Winter, Hoekstra (Cocu 72), Bergkamp.
England: Seaman; Neville G, Pearce, Ince (Platt 67), Southgate, Adams, Anderton, Gascoigne, Shearer (Fowler 76), Sheringham (Barmby 76), McManaman.
Referee: Grabher (Austria).

Villa Park, 18 June 1996, 34,926

Scotland (1) 1 *(McCoist 37)*
Switzerland (0) 0

Scotland: Goram; Burley, Boyd, McCall, Hendry, Calderwood, Durie, McKinlay T (Booth 60), McCoist (Spencer 83), McAllister, Collins.
Switzerland: Pascolo; Hottiger, Vega, Henchoz, Quentin (Comisetti 80), Vogel, Sforza, Koller (Fournier 46), Bonvin, Turkyilmaz, Chapuisat (Wicky 46).
Referee: Krondl (Czech Republic).

Group A Final Table	P	W	D	L	F	A	Pts
England	3	2	1	0	7	2	7
Holland	3	1	1	1	3	4	4
Scotland	3	1	1	1	1	2	4
Switzerland	3	0	1	2	1	4	1

230

Group B

Elland Road, 9 June 1996, 26,006

Spain (0) 1 *(Munoz 73)*

Bulgaria (0) 1 *(Stoichkov 65 (pen))*

Spain: Zubizarreta; Belsue, Alkorta, Abelardo, Sergi, Caminero (Donato 82), Amor (Alfonso 72), Hierro, Luis Enrique, Guerrero (Amavisca 51), Pizzi.
Bulgaria: Mikhailov; Kischischev, Hubchev, Ivanov, Kiriakov (Tsvetanov 72), Lechkov, Iankov, Balakov, Kostadinov (Yordanov 72), Stoichkov, Penev (Borimirov 77).
Referee: Ceccarini (Italy).

St James' Park, 10 June 1996, 26,323

Romania (0) 0

France (1) 1 *(Dugarry 24)*

Romania: Stelea; Petrescu (Filipescu 77), Belodedici, Mihali, Selymes, Lupescu, Popescu, Munteanu, Lacatus (Ilie A 52), Raducioiu (Moldovan 46), Hagi.
France: Lama; Thuram, Blanc, Desailly, Di Meco (Lizarazu 68), Karembeu, Deschamps, Guerin, Zidane (Roche 79), Djorkaeff, Dugarry (Loko 68).
Referee: Krug (Germany).

St James' Park, 13 June 1996, 19,107

Bulgaria (1) 1 *(Stoichkov 3)*

Romania (0) 0

Bulgaria: Mikhailov; Kischischev, Iankov, Ivanov, Tsvetanov, Lechkov (Guentchev 89), Yordanov, Balakov, Kostadinov (Borimirov 31), Penev (Sirakov 71), Stoichkov.
Romania: Stelea; Petrescu, Belodedici, Prodan, Selymes, Lupescu (Galca 46), Popescu (Ilie A 76), Munteanu, Hagi, Lacatus (Moldovan 28), Raducioiu.
Referee: Mikkelsen (Denmark).

Elland Road, 15 June 1996, 35,626

France (0) 1 *(Djorkaeff 48)*

Spain (0) 1 *(Caminero 85)*

France: Lama; Angloma (Roche 65), Desailly, Blanc, Karembeu, Zidane, Deschamps, Guerin (Thuram 80), Lizarazu, Djorkaeff, Loko (Dugarry 73).
Spain: Zubizaretta; Otero (Kiko 58), Lopez, Abelardo, Sergi, Luis Enrique (Manjarin 55), Caminero, Hierro, Alkorta, Amavisca, Alfonso (Julio Salinas 82).
Referee: Zhuk (Belarus).

St James' Park, 18 June 1996, 26,976

France (1) 3 *(Blanc 20, Penev 63 (og), Loko 90)*

Bulgaria (0) 1 *(Stoichkov 69)*

France: Lama; Thuram, Blanc, Desailly, Lizarazu, Karembeu, Deschamps, Guerin, Zidane (Pedros 61), Djorkaeff, Dugarry (Loko 67).
Bulgaria: Mikhailov; Kremenliev, Ivanov, Hubchev, Tsvetanov, Lechkov, Yordanov, Iankov (Borimirov 77), Balakov (Donkov 77), Penev, Stoichkov.
Referee: Gallagher (England) Durkin (England 28).

Elland Road, 18 June 1996, 32,719

Romania (1) 1 *(Raducioiu 29)*

Spain (1) 2 *(Manjarin 11, Amor 85)*

Romania: Prunea; Dobos, Prodan (Lupescu 86), Galca, Petrescu, Stinga, Popescu, Hagi, Selymes, Raducioiu (Vladoiu 78), Ilie A (Munteanu 65).
Spain: Zubizarreta; Lopez, Alkorta, Abelardo (Amor 64), Sergi, Hierro, Nadal, Manjarin, Kiko, Amavisca (Guerrero 72), Pizzi (Alfonso 57).
Referee: Caker (Turkey).

Group B Final Table

	P	W	D	L	F	A	Pts
France	3	2	1	0	5	2	7
Spain	3	1	2	0	4	3	5
Bulgaria	3	1	1	1	3	4	4
Romania	3	0	0	3	1	4	0

Group C

Old Trafford, 9 June 1996, 37,300

Germany (2) 2 *(Ziege 25, Moller 31)*

Czech Republic (0) 0

Germany: Kopke; Reuter, Sammer, Kohler (Babbel 14), Helmer, Ziege, Hassler, Eilts, Moller, Bobic (Strunz 65), Kuntz (Bierhoff 82).
Czech Republic: Kouba; Kadlec, Hornak, Suchoparek, Latal, Frydek (Berger 46), Bejbl, Nemec, Nedved, Poborsky (Drulak 46), Kuka.
Referee: Elleray (England).

Anfield, 11 June 1996, 35,120

Italy (1) 2 *(Casiraghi 4, 52)*

Russia (1) 1 *(Tsymbalar 20)*

Italy: Peruzzi; Mussi, Costacurta, Apolloni, Maldini, Di Livio (Fuser 61), Albertini, Di Matteo, Del Piero (Donadoni 46), Casiraghi (Ravanelli 79), Zola.
Russia: Cherchesov; Tetradze, Bushmanov (Yanovski 46), Onopko, Kovtun, Mostovoi, Radimov, Karpin (Kiryakov 63), Tsymbalar (Dobrovolski 72), Kanchelskis, Kolyvanov.
Referee: Mottram (Scotland).

Anfield, 14 June 1996, 37,320

Czech Republic (2) 2 *(Nedved 4, Bejbl 35)*

Italy (1) 1 *(Chiesa 18)*

Czech Republic: Kouba; Hornak, Kadlec, Suchoparek, Latal (Nemecek 88), Nedved, Berger (Smicer 64), Bejbl, Nemec, Poborsky, Kuka.
Italy: Peruzzi; Mussi, Costacurta, Apolloni, Fuser, Albertini, Dino Baggio (Carboni 38), Donadoni, Ravanelli (Casiraghi 58), Chiesa (Zola 78).
Referee: Lopez Nieto (Spain).

Old Trafford, 16 June 1996, 50,760

Russia (0) 0

Germany (0)3 *(Sammer 56, Klinsmann 77, 90)*

Russia: Kharine; Nikiforov, Kovtun, Onopko, Kanchelskis, Khokhlov (Simutenkov 66), Radimov (Karpin 46), Tetradze, Tsymbalar, Mostovoi, Kolyvanov.
Germany: Kopke; Helmer, Babbel, Sammer, Reuter, Hassler (Freund 66), Eilts, Moller (Strunz 87), Ziege, Bierhoff (Kuntz 84), Klinsmann.
Referee: Nielsen (Denmark).

Anfield, 19 June 1996, 21,128

Russia (0) 3 *(Mostovoi 49, Tetradze 54, Beschastnykh 85)*

Czech Republic (2) 3 *(Suchoparek 6, Kuka 19, Smicer 89)*

Russia: Cherchesov; Tetradze, Gorlukovich, Nikiforov, Yanovski, Karpin, Radimov, Khokhlov, Tsymbalar (Shalimov 67), Simutenkov (Mostovoi 46), Kolyvanov (Beschastnykh 46).
Czech Republic: Kouba; Kubik, Hornak, Suchoparek, Latal, Bejbl, Nedved, Berger (Nemecek 90), Nemec, Poborsky, Kuka (Smicer 68).
Referee: Frisk (Sweden).

Old Trafford, 19 June 1996, 53,740

Italy (0) 0

Germany (0) 0

Italy: Peruzzi; Mussi, Maldini, Carboni (Torricelli 77), Costacurta, Albertini, Fuser (Di Livio 80), Di Matteo (Chiesa 71), Casiraghi, Zola, Donadoni.
Germany: Kopke; Strunz, Sammer, Helmer, Freund, Ziege, Hassler, Eilts, Moller (Bode 88), Bobic, Klinsmann.
Referee: Goethals (Belgium).

Group C Final Table	P	W	D	L	F	A	Pts
Germany	3	2	1	0	5	0	7
Czech Republic	3	1	1	1	5	6	4
Italy	3	1	1	1	3	3	4
Russia	3	0	1	2	4	8	1

Group D

Hillsborough, 9 June 1996, 34,993

Denmark (1) 1 *(Laudrup B 21)*

Portugal (0) 1 *(Sa Pinto 52)*

Denmark: Schmeichel; Helveg, Rieper, Hogh, Thomsen (Piechnik 83), Steen-Nielsen, Larsen (Vilfort 90), Risager, Laudrup B, Laudrup N, Beck.
Portugal: Vitor Baia; Paulinho Santos, Cristovao, Fernando Couto, Dimas, Oceano (Folha 37), Paulo Sousa (Tavares 77), Sa Pinto, Figo (Domingos 62), Rui Costa, Joao Pinto.
Referee: Van der Ende (Holland).

City Ground, 11 June 1996, 22,460

Turkey (0) 0

Croatia (0) 1 *(Vlaovic 86)*

Turkey: Rustu; Vedat, Rahim, Alpay, Ogun, Tolunay (Saffet 89), Abdullah, Tugay, Arif (Hami 82), Segen, Hakan.
Croatia: Ladic; Stimac, Jerkan, Bilic, Jarni, Asanovic, Boban (Soldo 57), Stanic, Prosinecki, Suker (Pavlicic 90), Boksic (Vlaovic 73).
Referee: Muhmenthaler (Switzerland).

City Ground, 14 June 1996, 22,670

Portugal (0) 1 *(Fernando Couto 66)*

Turkey (0) 0

Portugal: Vitor Baia; Paulinho Santos, Fernando Couto, Helder, Dimas, Sa Pinto (Cadete 65), Paulo Sousa, Figo, Rui Costa, Folha (Tavares 46), Joao Pinto (Porfirio 76).
Turkey: Rustu; Ogun (Rahim 46), Recep, Alpay, Vedat, Abdullah, Oguz (Arif 70), Tugay, Sergen, Hakan, Saffet (Tolunay 63).
Referee: Puhl (Hungary).

Hillsborough, 16 June 1996, 33,671

Croatia (0) 3 *(Suker 53 (pen), 90, Boban 81)*

Denmark (0) 0

Croatia: Ladic; Stanic, Asanovic, Bilic, Jerkan, Stimac, Prosinecki (Mladenovic 87), Boban (Soldo 83), Suker, Vlaovic (Jurcevic 82), Jarni.
Denmark: Schmeichel; Helveg (Laursen 46), Thomsen, Hogh, Rieper, Vilfort (Beck 58), Steen-Nielsen, Larsen (Tofting 68), Schjonberg, Laudrup B, Laudrup M.
Referee: Batta (France).

233

City Ground, 19 June 1996, 20,484

Croatia (0) 0

Portugal (2) 3 *(Vigo 4, Joao Pinto 33, Domingos 83)*

Croatia: Mrmic; Pavlicic, Bilic, Soldo, Jurcevic, Simic, Mladenovic (Asanovic 46), Pamic (Suker 46), Prosinecki (Boban 46), Vlaovic, Jarni.
Portugal: Vitor Baia; Secretario, Fernando Couto, Cristovao, Oceano, Rui Costa (Barbosa 61), Paulo Sousa (Tavares 70), Figo, Teixera, Joao Pinto, Sa Pinto (Domingos 46).
Referee: Heynemann (Germany).

Hillsborough, 19 June 1996, 28,951

Turkey (0) 0

Denmark (0) 3 *(Laudrup B 50, 84, Nielsen 70)*

Turkey: Rustu; Recep (Saffet 67), Alpay, Ogun, Vedat, Tayfun, Tugay, Abdullah, Orhan (Bulent 67), Hami, Hakan (Arif 46).
Denmark: Schmeichel; Helveg, Hogh, Thomsen, Rieper, Nielsen, Steen-Nielsen, Schjonberg (Larsen 46), Andersen E (Andersen S 88), Laudrup B, Laudrup M.
Referee: Levnikov (Russia).

Group D Final Table	P	W	D	L	F	A	Pts
Portugal	3	2	1	0	5	1	7
Croatia	3	2	0	1	4	3	6
Denmark	3	1	1	1	4	4	4
Turkey	3	0	0	3	0	5	0

QUARTER-FINALS

Wembley, 22 June 1996, 75,440

Spain (0) 0

England (0) 0

Spain: Zubizarreta; Belsue, Nadal, Alkorta (Lopez 73), Abelardo, Manjarin (Caminero 46), Hierro, Amor, Sergi, Kiko, Julio Salinas (Alfonso 46).
England: Seaman; Neville G, Pearce, Platt, Southgate, Adams, Anderton (Stone 109), Gascoigne, Shearer, Sheringham (Barmby 109), McManaman (Fowler 109).
aet; England 4-2 on penalties.
Referee: Batta (France).

Anfield, 22 June 1996, 37,465

France (0) 0

Holland (0) 0

France: Lama; Thuram, Blanc, Desailly, Lizarazu, Karembeu, Deschamps, Guerin, Zidane, Djorkaeff, Loko (Dugarry 61) (Pedros 80).
Holland: Van der Sar; Reiziger, Bogarde, Blind, De Kock, Ronald de Boer, Jordi Cruyff (Winter 68), Witschge (Mulder 80), Kluivert, Bergkamp (Seedorf 59), Cocu.
aet; France won 5-4 on penalties.
Referee: Nieto (Spain).

Old Trafford, 23 June 1996, 43,412

Germany (1) 2 *(Klinsmann 21 (pen), Sammer 58)*

Croatia (0) 1 *(Suker 51)*

Germany: Kopke; Reuter, Helmer, Sammer, Babbel, Moller, Scholl (Hassler 87), Eilts, Ziege, Bobic (Kuntz 46), Klinsmann (Freund 38).

Croatia: Ladic; Stanic, Bilic, Jerkan, Stimac, Jurcevic (Mladenovic 77), Asanovic, Boban, Suker, Vlaovic, Jarni.
Referee: Sundell (Sweden).

Villa Park, 23 June 1996, 26,832

Portugal (0) 0
Czech Republic (0) 1 *(Poborsky 53)*

Portugal: Vitor Baia; Secretario, Fernando Couto, Helder, Dimas, Oceano (Folha 65), Rui Costa, Paulo Sousa, Figo (Cadete 83), Joao Pinto, Sa Pinto (Domingos 46).
Czech Republic: Kouba; Kadlec, Hornak, Suchoparek, Latal, Bejbl, Nemecek (Berger 90), Nemec, Poborsky, Smicer (Kubik 85), Kuka.
Referee: Krug (Germany).

SEMI-FINALS

Wembley, 26 June 1996, 75,862

England (1) 1 *(Shearer 3)*
Germany (1) 1 *(Kuntz 16)*

England: Seaman; Southgate, Pearce, Platt, Ince, Adams, Anderton, Gascoigne, Shearer, Sheringham, McManaman.
Germany: Kopke; Babbel, Helmer (Bode 110), Sammer, Reuter, Freund (Strunz 119), Scholl (Hassler 76), Eilts, Ziege, Moller, Kuntz.
aet; Germany won 6-5 on penalties.
Referee: Puhl (Hungary).

Old Trafford, 26 June 1996, 43,877

France (0) 0
Czech Republic (0) 0

France: Lama; Thuram (Angloma 84), Blanc, Roche, Lizarazu, Lamouchi (Pedros 64), Desailly, Guerin, Zidane, Djorkaeff, Loko.
Czech Republic: Kouba; Kadlec, Hornak, Rada, Nedved, Nemecek, Nemec (Kubik 84), Novotny, Poborsky, Smicer (Berger 46), Drulak (Kotulek 70).
aet; Czech Republic won 6-5 on penalties.
Referee: Mottram (Scotland).

FINAL

WEMBLEY, 30 JUNE 1996, 73,611
Germany (0) 2 *(Bierhoff 73, 95)*
Czech Republic (0) 1 *(Berger 59 pen)*

Germany: Kopke; Helmer, Sammer, Scholl (Bierhoff 69), Hassler, Kuntz, Babbel, Ziege, Klinsmann, Strunz, Eilts (Bode 46).
Czech Republic: Kouba; Suchoparek, Nedved, Kadlec, Nemec, Poborsky (Smicer 88), Kuka, Bejbl, Berger, Hornak, Rada.
Score 1-1 after 90 minutes.
Germany won with first extra time (sudden death) goal.
Referee: Pairetto (Italy).

PAST WORLD CUP FINALS

Uruguay 1930
URUGUAY 4, ARGENTINA 2 (1-2) *Montevideo*
Uruguay: Ballesteros; Nasazzi (capt), Mascheroni, Andrade, Fernandez, Gestido, Dorado, Scarone, Castro, Cea, Iriarte. **Scorers:** Dorado, Cea, Iriarte, Castro.
Argentina: Botasso; Della, Torre, Paternoster, Evaristo, J., Monti, Suarez, Peucelle, Varallo, Stabile, Ferreira (capt), Evaristo, M. **Scorers:** Peucelle, Stabile.
Leading scorer: Stabile (Argentina) 8.

Italy 1934
ITALY 2, CZECHOSLOVAKIA 1 (0-0) (1-1)* *Rome*
Italy: Combi (capt); Monseglio, Allemandi, Ferraris IV, Monti, Bertolini, Guaita, Meazza, Schiavio, Ferrari, Orsi. **Scorer:** Orsi, Schiavio.
Czechoslovakia: Planicka (capt); Zenisek, Ctyroky, Kostalek, Cambal, Krcil, Junek, Svoboda, Sobotka, Nejedly, Puc. **Scorer:** Puc.
Leading scorers: Schiavio (Italy), Nejedly (Czechoslovakia), Conen (Germany) each 4.

France 1938
ITALY 4, HUNGARY 2 (3-1) *Paris*
Italy: Olivieri; Foni, Rava, Serantoni, Andreolo, Locatelli, Biaveti, Meazza (capt), Piola, Ferrari, Colaussi. **Scorer:** Colaussi 2, Piola 2.
Hungary: Szabo; Polgar, Biro, Szalay, Szucs, Lazar, Vincze, Sarosi (capt), Szengeller, Titkos. **Scorers:** Titkos, Sarosi.
Leading scorer: Leonidas (Brazil) 8.

Brazil 1950
Final pool (replaced knock-out system)

Uruguay 2, Spain 2	Brazil 6, Spain 1
Brazil 7, Sweden 1	Sweden 3, Spain 1
Uruguay 3, Sweden 2	Uruguay 2, Brazil 1

Final positions	P	W	D	L	F	A	Pts
Uruguay	3	2	1	0	7	5	5
Brazil	3	2	0	1	14	4	4
Sweden	3	1	0	2	6	11	2
Spain	3	0	1	2	4	11	1

Leading scorers: Ademir (Brazil) 7, Schiaffino (Uruguay), Basora (Spain) 5.

Switzerland 1954
WEST GERMANY 3, HUNGARY 2 (2-2) *Berne*
West Germany: Turek; Posipal, Kohlmeyer, Eckel, Liebrich, Rahn, Morlock, Walter, O., Walter, F. (capt), Schaefer. **Scorers:** Morlock, Rahn 2.
Hungary: Grosics; Buzansky, Lantos, Bozsik, Lorant, Zakarias, Czibor, Kocsis, Hidegkuti, Puskas (capt), Toth, J. **Scorers:** Puskas, Czibor.
Leading scorer: Kocsis (Hungary) 11.

Sweden 1958
BRAZIL 5, SWEDEN 2 (2-1) *Stockholm*
Brazil: Gilmar; Santos, D., Santos, N., Zito, Bellini, Orlando, Garrincha, Didi, Vavà, Pelé, Zagalo. **Scorers:** Vavà 2, Pelé 2, Zagalo.
Sweden: Svensson; Bergmark, Axbom, Boerjesson, Gustavsson, Parling, Hamrin, Gren, Simonsson, Liedholm, Skoglund. **Scorers:** Liedholm, Simonsson.
Leading scorer: Fontaine (France) 13 (present record total).

Chile 1962
BRAZIL 3, CZECHOSLOVAKIA 1 (1-1) *Santiago*
Brazil: Gilmar; Santos, D., Mauro, Zozimo, Santos, N., Zito, Didi, Garrincha, Vavà, Amarildo, Zagalo. **Scorers:** Amarildo, Zito, Vavà.
Czechoslovakia: Schroiff; Tichy, Novak, Pluskal, Popluhar, Masopust, Pospichal, Scherer, Kvasniak, Kadraba, Jelinek. **Scorer:** Masopust.
Leading scorer: Jerkovic (Yugoslavia) 5.

England 1966
ENGLAND 4, WEST GERMANY 2 (1-1) (2-2)* *Wembley*
England: Banks; Cohen, Wilson, Stiles, Charlton, J., Moore, Ball, Hurst, Hunt, Charlton, R., Peters. **Scorers:** Hurst 3, Peters.
West Germany: Tilkowski; Hottges, Schulz, Weber, Schnellinger, Haller, Beckenbauer, Overath, Seeler, Held, Emmerich. **Scorers:** Haller, Weber.
Leading scorer: Eusebio (Portugal) 9.

Mexico 1970
BRAZIL 4, ITALY 1 (1-1) *Mexico City*
Brazil: Felix; Carlos Alberto, Piazza, Everaldo, Gerson, Clodoaldo, Jairzinho, Pelé, Tostão, Rivelino. **Scorers:** Pelé, Gerson, Jairzinho, Carlos Alberto.
Italy: Albertosi; Burgnich, Cera, Rosato, Facchetti, Bertini (Juliano), Riva, Domenghini, Mazzola, De Sista, Boninsegna (Rivera). **Scorer:** Boninsegna.
Leading scorer: Müller (West Germany) 10.

West Germany 1974
WEST GERMANY 2, HOLLAND 1 (2-1) *Munich*
West Germany: Maier; Vogts, Schwarzenbeck, Beckenbauer, Breitner, Bonhof, Hoeness, Overath, Grabowski, Müller, Holzenbein. **Scorers** Breitner (pen), Müller.
Holland: Jongbloed; Suurbier, Rijsbergen (De Jong), Haan, Krol, Jansen, Van Hanegem, Neeskens, Rep (Nanninga), Cruyff, Rensenbrink (Van der Kerkhof, R.)
Scorer: Neeskens (pen).
Leading scorer: Lato (Poland) 7.

Argentina 1978
ARGENTINA 3, HOLLAND 1 (1-1)* *Buenos Aires*
Argentina: Fillol; Olguin, Passarella, Galvan, Tarantini, Ardiles (Larrosa), Gallego, Ortiz (Houseman), Bertoni, Luque, Kempes. **Scorers:** Kempes 2, Bertoni.
Holland: Jongbloed; Poortvliet, Brandts, Krol, Jansen (Suurbier), Neeskens, Van der Kerkhof, W., Van der Kerkhof, R., Haan, Rep (Nanninga), Rensenbrink.
Scorer: Nanninga.
Leading scorer: Kempes (Argentina) 6.

Spain 1982
ITALY 3, WEST GERMANY 1 (0-0) *Madrid*
Italy: Zoff; Bergomi, Cabrini, Collovati, Scirea, Gentile, Oriali, Tardelli, Conti, Graziani (Altobelli), Rossi (Causio). **Scorers:** Rossi, Tardelli, Altobelli.
West Germany: Schumacher; Kaltz, Forster, K.-H., Stielike, Forster, B., Breitner, Dremmler (Hrubesch), Littbarski, Briegel, Fischer, Rummenigge (Müller). **Scorer:** Breitner.
Leading scorer: Rossi (Italy) 6.

Mexico 1986
ARGENTINA 3, WEST GERMANY 2 (1-0) *Mexico City*
Argentina: Pumpido; Cuciuffo, Olarticoechea, Ruggeri, Brown, Giusti, Burruchaga (Trobbiani), Batista, Valdano, Maradona, Enrique. **Scorers:** Brown, Valdano, Burruchaga.
West Germany: Schumacher; Berthold, Briegel, Jacobs, Forster, Eder, Brehme, Matthäus, Allofs (Völler), Magath (Hoeness), Rummenigge. **Scorers:** Rummenigge, Völler.
Leading scorer: Lineker (England) 6.

Italy 1990
WEST GERMANY 1, ARGENTINA 0 (0-0) *Rome*
West Germany: Ilgner; Berthold (Reuter), Kohler, Augenthaler, Buchwald, Brehme, Littbaski, Hässler, Matthäus, Völler, Klinsmann. **Scorer:** Brehme (pen).
Argentina: Goycochea; Lorenzo, Serrizuela, Sensini, Ruggeri (Monzon), Simon, Basualdo, Burruchago (Calderon), Maradona, Troglio, Dezotti.
Referee: Codesal (Mexico). Monzon and Dezotti sent off.
Leading scorer: Schillaci (Italy) 6.

USA 1994
BRAZIL 0, ITALY 0* *Los Angeles*
Brazil: Taffarel; Jorginho (Cafu 21), Marcio Santos, Aldair, Branco, Mazinho, Mauro Silva, Dunga, Zinho (Viola 109), Bebeto, Romario.
Italy: Pagliuca; Mussi (Apolloni 34), Maldini, Baresi, Benarrivo, Donadoni, Albertini, Dino Baggio (Evani 101), Berti, Roberto Baggio, Massaro.
Brazil won 3-2 on penalties
Referee: Puhl (Hungary).
Penalty sequence: Baresi (shot over); Marcio Santos (saved); Albertini (scored); Romario (scored off upright); Evani (scored); Branco (scored); Massaro (saved); Dunga (scored); Roberto Baggio (shot over).
Leading scorers: Salenko (Russia) 6, Stoichkov (Bulgaria) 6.

* After extra time

1998 FIFA WORLD CUP

Qualifying draw for France 1998

EUROPE

Group 2
Italy, England, Poland, Georgia, Moldova.
01.09.96 Moldova v England
05.10.96 Moldova v Italy
09.10.96 England v Poland
09.10.96 Italy v Georgia
09.11.96 Georgia v England
10.11.96 Poland v Moldova
12.02.97 England v Italy
29.03.97 Italy v Moldova
02.04.97 Poland v Italy
30.04.97 England v Georgia
30.04.97 Italy v Poland
07.06.97 Georgia v Moldova
14.06.97 Poland v Georgia
10.09.97 England v Moldova
10.09.97 Georgia v Italy
24.09.97 Moldova v Georgia
07.10.97 Moldova v Poland
11.10.97 Italy v England
11.10.97 Georgia v Poland

Group 4
Sweden, Scotland, Austria, Latvia, Belarus, Estonia
01.06.96 Sweden v Belarus
31.08.96 Austria v Scotland
31.08.96 Belarus v Estonia
01.09.96 Latvia v Sweden
05.10.96 Estonia v Belarus

05.10.96 Latvia v Scotland
09.10.96 Sweden v Austria
09.10.96 Estonia v Scotland
09.10.96 Belarus v Latvia
09.11.96 Austria v Latvia
10.11.96 Scotland v Sweden
29.03.97 Scotland v Estonia
02.04.97 Scotland v Austria
30.04.97 Austria v Estonia
30.04.97 Sweden v Scotland
30.04.97 Latvia v Belarus
18.05.97 Estonia v Latvia
08.06.97 Estonia v Sweden
08.06.97 Latvia v Austria
08.06.97 Belarus v Scotland
20.08.97 Estonia v Austria
20.08.97 Belarus v Sweden
06.09.97 Austria v Sweden
06.09.97 Scotland v Belarus
06.09.97 Latvia v Estonia
10.09.97 Sweden v Latvia
10.09.97 Belarus v Austria
11.10.97 Austria v Belarus
11.10.97 Scotland v Latvia
11.10.97 Sweden v Estonia

Group 7
Holland, Belgium, Turkey, Wales, San Marino
02.06.96 San Marino v Wales
31.08.96 Belgium v Turkey
31.08.96 Wales v San Marino

05.10.96 Wales v Netherlands
09.10.96 San Marino v Belgium
09.11.96 Netherlands v Wales
10.11.96 Turkey v San Marino
14.12.96 Belgium v Netherlands
20.03.97 Netherlands v San Marino
29.03.97 Wales v Belgium
02.04.97 Turkey v Netherlands
30.04.97 Turkey v Belgium
30.04.97 San Marino v Netherlands
07.06.97 Belgium v San Marino
20.08.97 Turkey v Wales
06.09.97 Netherlands v Belgium
10.09.97 San Marino v Turkey
11.10.97 Belgium v Wales
11.10.97 Netherlands v Turkey

Group 8
Romania, Republic of Ireland, Lithuania, Iceland, Macedonia, Liechtenstein
24.04.96 Macedonia v Lichtenstein
01.06.96 Iceland v Macedonia
31.08.96 Liechtenstein v Republic of Ireland

238

31.08.96 Romania v Lithuania	02.04.97 Macedonia v Republic of Ireland	06.09.97 Iceland v Republic of Ireland
05.10.96 Lithuania v Iceland		06.09.97 Liechtenstein v Romania
09.10.96 Iceland v Romania	30.04.97 Liechtenstein v Lithuania	
09.10.96 Republic of Ireland v Macedonia	30.04.97 Romania v Republic of Ireland	06.09.97 Lithuania v Macedonia
09.10.96 Lithuania v Liechtenstein	07.06.97 Republic of Ireland v Liechtenstein	10.09.97 Romania v Iceland
09.11.96 Liechtenstein v Macedonia	07.06.97 Macedonia v Iceland	10.09.97 Lithuania v Republic of Ireland
10.11.96 Republic of Ireland v Iceland	11.06.97 Iceland v Lithuania	11.10.97 Iceland v Liechtenstein
14.12.96 Macedonia v Romania	19.08.97 Liechtenstein v Iceland	11.10.97 Republic of Ireland v Romania
29.03.97 Romania v Liechtenstein	20.08.97 Republic of Ireland v Lithuania	11.10.97 Macedonia v Lithuania
02.04.97 Lithuania v Romania	20.08.97 Romania v Macedonia	

1998 WORLD CUP – opening games

Athens, 24 April 1996, 9000
Greece (0) 2 (*Batista 56, Nikolaidis 66*)
Slovenia (0) 0
Greece: Atmatzidis; Apostolakis, Kassapis, Ouzounidis, Kalitzakis, Costantinidis (Alexandris 46), Zagorakis, Vrizas, Batista, Tsartas (Franzeskos 82), Donis (Nikolaidis 61).
Slovenia: Boskovic; Galic, Englaro, Milanic, Jermanis, Seh, Novak, Zidan (Gaiser 36), Udovic (Gliha 70), Gregor, Florjancic.
Referee: Pedersen (Denmark).

Skopje, 24 April 1996, 12,000
Macedonia (1) 3 (*Milosevski 5, Babunski 49 (pen), Zaharievski 80*)
Liechtenstein (0) 0
Macedonia: Celeski; Babunski, Markovski (Nikolovski 60), Jovanovski, Stojkovski, Milosevski, Milosavov, Gosev (Zaharievski 75), Ciric, Boskovski, Hristov (Naumovski 71).
Liechtenstein: Heeb; Hanselmann, Hasler, Stocker, Zech, Frick C, Frick D, Frick M, Hilti, Oehri, Telser (Sele 51).

Belgrade, 24 April 1996, 25,000
Yugoslavia (3) 3 (*Savicevic 3, 30, Milosevic 38*)
Faeroes (0) 1 (*Petersen 54*)
Yugoslavia: Kocic; Curcic (Mirkovic 75), Djorovic, Jokanovic, Braovic, Mihajlovic (Pantic 40), Jugovic, Savicevic, Mijatovic, Stojkovic, Milosevic (Nadj 87).
Faeroes: Knudsen; Johannsen O, Hansen J, Hansen A, Johnsson J, Morkore A, Jarnskor H, Dam, Muller, Petersen, Rasmussen J E (Jarnskor M 75).
Referee: Bec (Liechtenstein).

Buenos Aires, 24 April 1996, 60,000
Argentina (2) 3 (*Ortega 8, 18, Batistuta 49*)
Bolivia (1) 1 (*Baldivieso 42*)
Argentina: Passet; Zanetti, Ayala, Sensini, Chamot, Simeone, Almeyda, Ortega, Morales, Caniggia (Balbo 72), Batistuta (Lopez C 87).
Bolivia: Barrero; Rimba, Pena, Paraba, Sanchez, Ramos (Castillo I 80), Coimbra (Paniagua 77), Tufino, Baldivieso, Etcheverry (Suarez 78), Castillo R.
Referee: Sanchez (Chile).

Barranquilla, 24 April 1996, 60,000
Colombia (0) 1 (*Asprilla 55*)
Paraguay (0) 0
Colombia: Mondragon; Perez (Estrada 69), Bermudez, Mendoza, Moreno, Alvarez, Serna, Valderrama, Rincon, Valenciano (Valencia 75), Asprilla.
Paraguay: Chilavert; Arce, Gamarra, Celso, Ayala, Rivarola, Jara (Sarabia 80), Acuna, Sotelo, Struway, Ferreira (Benitez 64), Campos (Rojas 69).
Referee: Castrilli (Argentina).

Guyaquil, 24 April 1996, 65,000
Ecuador (0) 4 *(Hurtado E 54, 90, Tenorio 65, Gavica 77)*
Peru (0) 1 *(Palacios 62)*
Ecuador: Morales; Rivera, Montano, Hurtado I (Obregon 84), Capurro, De Souza, Tenorio, Carabali W (Carabali H 46), Aguinaga, Fernandez (Gavica 76), Hurtado E.
Peru: Miranda; Solano, Reynoso, Marengo, Ferrari (Magallanes 67), Carranza, Jayo, Del Solar, Palacios, Maestri, Guadalupe (Ramirez 68).
Referee: Matto (Uruguay).

Caracas, 24 April 1996, 12,000
Venezuela (0) 0
Uruguay (0) 2 *(Otero 54, Poyet 71)*
Venezuela: Angelucci; Filosa, Gonzalez W, Tortolero, Gonzalez L, Vallenilla, Valiente (McIntosh 74), Hernandez, Castellin, Diaz (Rivas 55), Guerra.
Uruguay: Arbiza; Olivera, Herrera, Moas, Montero, Saralegui, Gutierrez, Bengoechea (Abeijon 90), Poyet, Otero (Cedres 87).
Referee: Tejada (Peru).

Stockholm, 1 June 1996, 30,014
Sweden (2) 5 *(Andersson K 20 (pen), 62, Dahlin 30, Andersson P 77, Larsson 88)*
Belarus (0) 1 *(Belkevich 75)*
Sweden: Andersson B; Nilsson R, Andersson P, Bjorklund, Sundgren, Ingesson (Mild 85), Thern, Zetterberg, Limpar, Dahlin (Larsson 77), Andersson K.
Belarus: Satsunkhevich; Gurenko, Khatskevich, Staniouk, Kachentsev (Koulty 63), Vergeichik, Belkevich, Maleiev, Romashchenko (Kachuro 57), Makovski, Baranov.
Referee: Harrel (France).

Reykjavik, 1 June 1996, 5000
Iceland (0) 1 *(Gudjohnsen A 63)*
Macedonia (0) 1 *(Memedi 62)*
Iceland: Kristinsson B; Sigurdsson, Gretarsson, Jonsson S, Adolfsson, Kristinsson R, Bergsson, Gudjohnsen A, Thordarsson (Stefansson 68), Gudjonsson T (Benediktsson 81), Gunnlaugsson B (Gylfason 29).
Macedonia: Celeski; Milosavov, Markovski, Nikolovski, Stojkovski, Sedloski, Memedi, Gosev, Kiric (Sakiri 36), Hristov (Borov 84), Milosevski.
Referee: Luinge (Holland).

Oslo, 2 June 1996, 14,012
Norway (2) 5 *(Solbakken 8, 46, Solskjaer 37, 90, Strandli 60)*
Azerbaijan (0) 0
Norway: Grodaas; Haaland, Berg, Johnsen, Bjornebye, Rudi, Solbakken (Larsen 79), Rekdal, Leonhardsen (Flo 46), Solskjaer, Strandli.
Azerbaijan: Jidkov; Gasimov, Getman, Ahmedov, Agayev (Nossenko 40), Idigov, Abusev (Asadov 79), Ryzalev (Kurbanov 46), Guseynov, Lichin, Suleimanov.\
Referee: Snoddy (Northern Ireland).

Belgrade, 2 June 1996, 20,000
Yugoslavia (3) 6 *(Milosevic 2, 68, Mijatovic 39, Stojkovic 45, Savicevic 71, 73)*
Malta (0) 0
Yugoslavia: Kocic; Mirkovic, Djorovic (Saveljic 85), Jokanovic, Djukic, Mihajlovic, Jugovic (Nadj 50), Savicevic, Mijatovic, Stojkovic, Milosevic (Kovacevic 79).
Malta: Cluett; Attard (Woods 46), Buhagiar, Vella, Debono, Zammit (Camilleri 75), Busuttil, Turner, Brincat, Cetcutti, Agius.
Referee: Albrecht (Germany).

Serravalle, 2 June 1996, 1613
San Marino (0) 0
Wales (3) 5 *(Melville 20, Hughes M 32, 43, Giggs 50, Pembridge 85)*
San Marino: Muccioli S; Gasperoni, Valentini M, Guerra, Gobbi, Manzaroli, Pasolini (Muccioli R 69), Mazza, Casadei (Peverani 74), Mularoni (Valentini V 46), Montagna.
Wales: Southall; Bowen, Melville, Coleman, Pembridge, Browning (Goss 74), Horne (Savage 81), Robinson (Legg 80), Hughes M, Saunders, Giggs.
Referee: Lubos (Slovakia).

Montevideo, 2 June 1996, 60,000
Uruguay (0) 0
Paraguay (1) 2 *(Arce 10, Rojas 89)*
Uruguay: Arbiza; Mendez, Herrera, Moas, Montero, Saralegui (Romero 46), Gutierrez (Dorta 69), Poyet, Bengoechea, Otero, Martinez (Cedres 60).

Paraguay: Chilavert; Arce, Rivarola, Ayala, Gamarra, Struway, Enciso, Bourdier, Acuna (Suarez 90), Baez E (Gonzalez 60), Baez R (Rojas 70).
*Referee:*Rezende (Brazil).

Quito, 2 June 1996, 55,000
Ecuador (0) 2 *(Montano 52, Hurtado E 89)*
Argentina (0) 0
Ecuador: Morales; Rivera, Hurtado I (Obregon 84), Tenorio, Capurro, Montano, Gavica (Fernandez 46), Aguinaga, Carabali, De Souza, Hurtado E.
Argentina: Bossio; Zanetti, Caceres, Sensini, Chamot, Almeyda, Simeone, Morales (Lopez 76), Ortega (Cardoso 71), Batistuta (Crespo 76), Caniggia.
Referee: Perez (Colombia).

Barinas, 2 June 1996, 9850
Venezuela (1) 1 *(Guerra 7)*
Chile (0) 1 *(Margas 90)*
Venezuela: Dudamel; McIntosh, Tortolero, Gonzalez L, Diaz (Hezzel 67) (Urdanetta 85), Hernandez S, Valiente, Hernandez F, Rivas, Guerra, Castellin (Savarese 67).
*Chile:*Tapia; Mendoza, Ramirez, Fuentes, Margas, Vilches (Nunez 73), Estay, Vega (Rozental 46), Valencia (Musrri 46), Zamorano, Salas.
Referee: Gonzales (Paraguay).

Lima, 2 June 1996, 45,000
Peru (0) 1 *(Reynoso 48)*
Colombia (0) 1 *(Aristizabal 60)*
Peru: Balerio; Marengo, Reynoso, Olivares, Legario, Carranza (Guadalupe 75), Solano, Del Solar, Maestri, Palacios, Zegarra (Magallanes 79).
Colombia: Mondragon; Mendoza, Herrera, Bermudez, Valencia (Aristizabal 46), Estrada, Valderrama (Bolado 90), Asprilla, Rincon.
Referee: Rodas (Ecuador).

Santiago, 6 July 1996, 75,000
Chile (1) 4 *(Zamorano 21, 85, Salas 75, Estay 83)*
Ecuador (0) 1 *(Aguinaga 74)*
Chile: Tapia; Castaneda C, Gonzalez, Margas, Miranda, Musrri, Valencia (Estay 58), Vega (Sierra 76), Castaneda V (Mora 68), Salas, Zamorano.
Ecuador: Morales; Tenorio M (Gonzalez 78), Rivera, Montano (Tenorio B 46), Capurro, Hurtado I, Obregon (Fernandez 46), Carabali, Aguinaga, Gilson, Hurtado E.
Referee: Duran (Bolivia).

La Paz, 7 July 1996, 40,000
Bolivia (2) 6 *(Sandy 3, Etcheverry 27 (pen), Baldivieso 49, Coimbra 67, Suarez 77, Paniagua 80)*
Venezuela (0) 1 *(Tortolero 65 (pen))*
Bolivia: Trucco; Sanchez, Quinteros, Sandy, Rimba, Pena, Cristaldo, Castillo R (Suarez 75), Baldivieso, Etcheverry (Moreno 68), Coimbra (Paniagua 78).
Venezuela: Dudamel; Filosa, McIntosh, Tortolero, Hernandez S (Diaz 46), Vera, Gonzalez, Hernandez F, Rivas S (Urdaneta 46), Savarese (Miranda 46), Guerra.
Referee: Da Rosa (Uruguay).

Lima, 7 July 1996, 45,000
Peru (0) 0
Argentina (0) 0
Peru: Balerio; Solano, Reynoso, Soto, Olivares, Jayo, Zegarra (Magallanes 68), Carranza (Farfan 83), Palacios, Julinho, Maestri.
Argentina: Burgos; Zanetti, Ayala, Sensini, Chamot, Almeyda, Simeone, Morales (Bassedas 46), Ortega (Lopez 89), Caniggia (Paz 72).
Referee: Souza (Brazil).

Barranquilla, 7 July 1996, 40,000
Colombia (2) 3 *(Asprilla 10, Valderrama 22, De Avila 77)*
Uruguay (0) 1 *(Cedres 55)*
Colombia: Mondragon; Cabrera, Bermudez, Mendoza, Moreno, Alvarez, Serna, Rincon, Valderrama, Asprilla, Aristizabal (De Avila 64).
Uruguay: Arbiza; Oliveira (Bengoechea 36), Moas, Aguirregaray, Lima (Silva T 54), Pereyra, Dorta (Sosa H 71), Poyet, Saralegui, Cedres, Romero.
Referee: Ruscio (Argentina).

WORLD CLUB CHAMPIONSHIP

Played annually up to 1974 and intermittently since then between the winners of the European Cup and the winners of the South American Champions Cup—known as the Copa Libertadores. In 1980 the winners were decided by one match arranged in Tokyo in February 1981 and the venue has been the same since. AC Milan replaced Marseille who had been stripped of their European Cup title in 1993.

1960   Real Madrid beat Penarol 0-0, 5-1
1961   Penarol beat Benfica 0-1, 5-0, 2-1
1962   Santos beat Benfica 3-2, 5-2
1963   Santos beat AC Milan 2-4, 4-2, 1-0
1964   Inter-Milan beat Independiente 0-1, 2-0, 1-0
1965   Inter-Milan beat Independiente 3-0, 0-0
1966   Penarol beat Real Madrid 2-0, 2-0
1967   Racing Club beat Celtic 0-1, 2-1, 1-0
1968   Estudiantes beat Manchester United 1-0, 1-1
1969   AC Milan beat Estudiantes 3-0, 1-2
1970   Feyenoord beat Estudiantes 2-2, 1-0
1971   Nacional beat Panathinaikos* 1-1, 2-1
1972   Ajax beat Independiente 1-1, 3-0
1973   Independiente beat Juventus* 1-0
1974   Atletico Madrid* beat Independiente 0-1, 2-0
1975   Independiente and Bayern Munich could not agree dates; no matches.
1976   Bayern Munich beat Cruzeiro 2-0, 0-0
1977   Boca Juniors beat Borussia Moenchengladbach* 2-2, 3-0
1978   Not contested
1979   Olimpia beat Malmö* 1-0, 2-1
1980   Nacional beat Nottingham Forest 1-0
1981   Flamengo beat Liverpool 3-0
1982   Penarol beat Aston Villa 2-0
1983   Gremio Porto Alegre beat SV Hamburg 2-1
1984   Independiente beat Liverpool 1-0
1985   Juventus beat Argentinos Juniors 4-2 on penalties after a 2-2 draw
1986   River Plate beat Steaua Bucharest 1-0
1987   FC Porto beat Penarol 2-1 after extra time
1988   Nacional (Uru) beat PSV Eindhoven 7-6 on penalties after 1-1 draw
1989   AC Milan beat Atletico Nacional (Col) 1-0 after extra time
1990   AC Milan beat Olimpia 3-0
1991   Red Star Belgrade beat Colo Colo 3-0
1992   Sao Paulo beat Barcelona 2-1
1993   Sao Paulo beat AC Milan 3-2

*European Cup runners-up; winners declined to take part.

1994

1 December in Tokyo

Velez Sarsfield (0) 2 *(Trotta 50 (pen), Asad 57)*

AC Milan (0) 0 55,860

Velez Sarsfield: Chilavert; Trotta, Cardozo, Almandoz, Gomez, Sotomayor, Bassedas, Basualdo, Asad, Pompei, Flores.

AC Milan: Rossi; Tassotti, Maldini, Albertini, Costacurta, Baresi, Bonadoni, Desailly, Boban, Savicevic (Simone 60), Massaro (Panucci 86).
Referee: Torres (Colombia).

EUROPEAN SUPER CUP

Played annually between the winners of the European Champions' Cup and the European Cup-Winners' Cup. AC Milan replaced Marseille in 1993–94.

Previous Matches
1972   Ajax beat Rangers 3-1, 3-2
1973   Ajax beat AC Milan 0-1, 6-0
1974   Not contested
1975   Dynamo Kiev beat Bayern Munich 1-0, 2-0
1976   Anderlecht beat Bayern Munich 4-1, 1-2
1977   Liverpool beat Hamburg 1-1, 6-0
1978   Anderlecht beat Liverpool 3-1, 1-2
1979   Nottingham F beat Barcelona 1-0, 1-1
1980   Valencia beat Nottingham F 1-0, 1-2
1981   Not contested
1982   Aston Villa beat Barcelona 0-1, 3-0
1983   Aberdeen beat Hamburg 0-0, 2-0
1984   Juventus beat Liverpool 2-0
1985   Juventus v Everton not contested due to UEFA ban on English clubs
1986   Steaua Bucharest beat Dynamo Kiev 1-0
1987   FC Porto beat Ajax 1-0, 1-0
1988   KV Mechelen beat PSV Eindhoven 3-0, 0-1
1989   AC Milan beat Barcelona 1-1, 1-0
1990   AC Milan beat Sampdoria 1-1, 2-0
1991   Manchester U beat Red Star Belgrade 1-0
1992   Barcelona beat Werder Bremen 1-1, 2-1
1993   Parma beat AC Milan 0-1, 2-0

1994-95

First Leg, 1 February 1995, Highbury

Arsenal (0) 0

AC Milan (0) 0   38,044

Arsenal: Seaman; Dixon, Winterburn, Schwarz, Bould, Adams, Jensen (Hillier 85), Wright, Hartson, Selley, Campbell (Merson 74).
AC Milan: Rossi; Tassotti, Maldini, Albertini, Costacurta, Baresi, Donadoni, Desailly, Simone, Savicevic (Di Canio 89), Massaro.
Referee: Van der Ende (Holland).

Second Leg, 8 February 1995, Milan

AC Milan (1) 2 *(Boban 41, Massaro 67)*

Arsenal (0) 0   23,953

AC Milan: Rossi; Tassotti, Albertini, Costacurta, Baresi, Donadoni, Desailly, Savicevic (Eranio 89), Boban, Massaro (Di Canio 80).
Arsenal: Seaman; Dixon (Keown 66), Winterburn, Schwarz, Bould, Adams, Campbell (Parlour 76), Wright, Hartson, Merson, Selley.
Referee: Krug (Germany).

SOUTH AMERICAN CHAMPIONSHIP

(Copa America)

1916	Uruguay	1937	Argentina	1959	Uruguay
1917	Uruguay	1939	Peru	1963	Bolivia
1919	Brazil	1941	Argentina	1967	Uruguay
1920	Uruguay	1942	Uruguay	1975	Peru
1921	Argentina	1945	Argentina	1979	Paraguay
1922	Brazil	1946	Argentina	1983	Uruguay
1923	Uruguay	1947	Argentina	1987	Uruguay
1924	Uruguay	1949	Brazil	1989	Brazil
1925	Argentina	1953	Paraguay	1991	Argentina
1926	Uruguay	1955	Argentina	1993	Argentina
1927	Argentina	1956	Uruguay	1995	Uruguay
1929	Argentina	1957	Argentina		
1935	Uruguay	1959	Argentina		

SOUTH AMERICAN CUP

(Copa Libertadores)

1960	Penarol (Uruguay)	1979	Olimpia (Paraguay)
1961	Penarol	1980	Nacional
1962	Santos (Brazil)	1981	Flamengo (Brazil)
1963	Santos	1982	Penarol
1964	Independiente (Argentina)	1983	Gremio Porto Alegre (Brazil)
1965	Independiente	1984	Independiente
1966	Penarol	1985	Argentinos Juniors (Argentina)
1967	Racing Club (Argentina)	1986	River Plate (Argentina)
1968	Estudiantes (Argentina)	1987	Penarol
1969	Estudiantes	1988	Nacional (Uruguay)
1970	Estudiantes	1989	Nacional (Colombia)
1971	Nacional (Uruguay)	1990	Olimpia
1972	Independiente	1991	Colo Colo (Chile)
1973	Independiente	1992	São Paulo (Brazil)
1974	Independiente	1993	São Paulo
1975	Independiente	1994	Velez Sarsfield (Argentina)
1976	Cruzeiro (Brazil)	1995	Gremio Porto Alegre
1977	Boca Juniors (Argentina)	1996	River Plate
1978	Boca Juniors		

OTHER BRITISH AND IRISH INTERNATIONAL MATCHES 1995–96

Wembley, 6 September 1995, 20,038

England (0) 0

Colombia (0) 0

England: Seaman; Neville G, Le Saux, Redknapp (Barnes), Howey, Adams, Barmby, Gascoigne (Lee), Shearer (Sheringham), McManaman, Wise.
Colombia: Higuita; Santa, Bermudez, Mendoza, Perez, Lozano (Quinonez), Alvarez, Valderrama, Rincon, Asprilla, Valenciano.

Oslo, 11 October 1995, 21,006

Norway (0) 0

England (0) 0

Norway: Thorstvedt; Loken, Johnsen, Berg, Bjornebye, Bohinen, Leonhardsen (Solbakken), Rekdal, Jakobsen, Flo, Fjortoft (Brattbakk).
England: Seaman; Neville G, Pearce, Redknapp, Pallister, Adams, Lee, Barmby (Sheringham), Shearer, McManaman, Wise (Stone).

Stockholm, 11 October 1995, 19,121

Sweden (2) 2 *(Pettersson, Schwarz)*

Scotland (0) 0

Sweden: Andersson B; Lucic (Kamark), Andersson P, Bjorklund, Schwarz, Alexandersson, Brolin, Gudmundsson (Pringle), Nilsson, Andersson K (Erlingmark), Pettersson.
Scotland: Leighton (Goram); McKimmie, Burley (McKinlay W), McLaren, Hendry, Calderwood, Collins, Boyd, McGinlay (Jess), McAllister (Jackson), Robertson (Nevin).

Wembley, 15 November 1995, 29,874

England (1) 3 *(Quentin (og), Sheringham, Stone)*

Switzerland (1) 1 *(Knup)*

England: Seaman; Neville G, Pearce, Redknapp (Stone), Pallister, Adams, Lee, Gascoigne, Shearer, Sheringham, McManaman.
Switzerland: Pascolo; Hottiger, Geiger, Henchoz, Quentin (Vega), Ohrel, Sforza, Fournier (Wolf), Sutter A (Grassi), Knup, Turkyilmaz.

Wembley, 12 December 1995, 28,592

England (1) 1 *(Stone)*

Portugal (0) 1 *(Alves)*

England: Seaman; Neville G, Pearce (Le Saux), Stone, Howey, Adams, Barmby (McManaman), Gascoigne, Shearer, Ferdinand (Beardsley), Wise (Southgate).
Portugal: Neno; Secretario, Fernando Couto, Jorge Costa, Dimas, Paolo Sousa (Dominguez), Helder, Folha (Pedro), Figo (Alves), Joao Pinto (Dani), Sa Pinto.

Terni, 24 January 1996, 20,000

Italy (1) 3 *(Del Piero, Ravanelli, Casiraghi)*

Wales (0) 0

Italy: Peruzzi (Toldo); Ferrara (Torricelli), Apolloni, Costacurta, Carboni, Del Piero (Casiraghi), Albertini, Di Matteo (Conte), Di Livio (Crippa), Ravaneilli, Zola.
Wales: Southall; Phillips, Jenkins, Williams A, Symons, Coleman, Horne, Hodges (Browning), Rush (Taylor), Hughes M, Speed (Blake).

Wembley, 27 March 1996, 29,708

England (1) 1 *(Ferdinand)*

Bulgaria (0) 0

England: Seaman; Neville G, Pearce, Stone, Howey, Southgate, Ince, Gascoigne (Lee), Ferdinand (Platt), Sheringham (Fowler), McManaman.

Bulgaria: Mikhailov (Popov); Hubchev, Iankov, Ivanov, Kremenliev (Kishishev), Lechkov, Kiriakov, Guinchev (Guentchev), Yordanov (Borimirov), Penev (Sirakov), Kostadinov.

Belfast, 27 March 1996, 5343

Northern Ireland (0) 0

Norway (0) 2 *(Solskjaer, Ostenstad)*
Northern Ireland: Fettis; Lomas, Worthington (Rowland), Magilton (Patterson), Hill, McDonald, Gillespie, Lennon, Dowie, O'Neill (McMahon), Hughes.
Norway: Grodaas (Thorstvedt); Haaland, Johnsen, Berg, Bjornebye, Rudi, Rekdal, Solbakken (Lundekvam), Leonhardsen (Jakobsen), Fjortoft (Ostenstad), Solskjaer.

Dublin, 27 March 1996, 41,600

Republic of Ireland (0) 0

Russia (1) 2 *(Mostovoi, Kolyvanov)*
Republic of Ireland: Given; McAteer, Phelan, Kernaghan, McGrath, Staunton, Keane, Aldridge (Cascarino), Quinn (Coyne), Townsend (Kenna), Kennedy.
Russia: Cherchesov; Nikiforov, Onopko, Kovtun, Karpin, Kanchelskis, Mostovoi (Shalimov), Radimov (Radichenko), Tsymbalar (Tetradze), Kiryakov (Simutenkov), Kolyvanov.

Hampden Park, 27 March 1996, 20,608

Scotland (0) 1 *(McCoist)*

Australia (0) 0
Scotland: Leighton; Burley, Boyd, McStay (Gallacher), Hendry, O'Neil (Booth), Collins, McKinlay W (Jackson), McCoist (Nevin), McAllister, Spencer.
Australia: Bosnich; Tobin, Horvat, Popovic, Vidmar T, Slater, Vidmar A, Corica, Van Blerk, Arnold, Veart (Tiatto).

Wembley, 24 April 1996, 33,650

England (0) 0

Croatia (0) 0
England: Seaman; Neville G, Pearce, Stone, Wright, Ince, Platt, Gascoigne, Sheringham, Fowler, McManaman.
Croatia: Mrmic; Stimac (Soldo), Jerkan, Bilic, Pavlicic (Mladenovic), Asanovic, Boban (Stanic), Prosinecki, Jarni, Boksic (Panic), Suker.

Prague, 24 April 1996, 6118

Czech Republic (0) 2 *(Frydek, Kuka)*

Republic of Ireland (0) 0
Czech Republic: Kouba; Hornak (Rada), Kadlec (Kubik), Repka, Latal (Nedved), Frydek, Nemecek (Bejbl), Berger, Hapal, Drulak, Kuka (Kerbr).
Republic of Ireland: Given; Cunningham, Kenna, Babb (Daish), McGrath, Irwin (Fleming), Houghton, Townsend, Quinn, Kennedy, Moore.

Copenhagen, 24 April 1996, 23,031

Denmark (2) 2 *(Laudrup M, Laudrup B)*

Scotland (0) 0
Denmark: Schmeichel (Krogh); Helveg, Schjonberg, Rieper, Olsen, Risager, Thomsen, Laudrup M (Nielsen A), Steen-Nielsen, Laudrup B, Beck.
Scotland: Leighton (Goram); McKimmie, Boyd, Burley, Hendry (McKinlay W), McCall (Gemmill), Collins, McKinlay T, Spencer (McCoist), McAllister, Gallacher (Jackson).

Belfast, 24 April 1996, 5666

Northern Ireland (0) 1 *(McMahon)*

Sweden (1) 2 *(Dahlin, Ingesson)*
Northern Ireland: Davison; Patterson, Worthington (Quinn JS), Hill, Hunter, Morrow, McCarthy, Lomas, McMahon, O'Neill (O'Boyle), Rowland.

Sweden: Andersson B; Nilsson, Andersson P, Bjorklund, Sundgren, Schwarz, Wilbran (Zetterberg), Ingesson, Thern, Dahlin (Larsson), Andersson K (Pettersson).

Lugano, 24 April 1996, 8000

Switzerland (2) 2 *(Coleman (og), Turkyilmaz (pen))*

Wales (0) 0

Switzerland: Pascolo (Lehmann); Vogel (Hottiger), Vega, Henchoz, Quentin, Ohrel (Lombardo), Sforza, Wicky (Comisetti), Turkyilmaz (Koller), Grassi (Knup), Chapuisat (Sutter A).
Wales: Coyne (Marriott); Symons, Bowen, Coleman (Edwards), Robinson, Horne (Goss), Jones (Savage), Pembridge, Legg (Speed), Taylor (Davies), Hartson.

Wembley, 18 May 1996, 34,184

England (1) 3 *(Anderton 2, Platt)*

Hungary (0) 0

England: Seaman (Walker); Neville G, Pearce, Ince (Campbell), Wright (Southgate), Platt (Wise), Lee, Anderton, Ferdinand (Shearer), Sheringham, Wilcox.
Hungary: Petry; Hahn, Banfi, Plokai, Balog (Illes), Mracsko (Telek), Urban, Sebok, Nagy (Lisztes), Horvath (Aranyos), Vincze (Egressy).

Beijing, 23 May 1996, 65,000

China (0) 0

England (1) 3 *(Barmby 2, Gascoigne)*

China: Ou Quliang; Xu Hong, Wei Qun, Jiang Feng (Gao Zhangxun), Fan Ziyi, Xie Yuxing (Mi Ling), Li Bing (Peng Weiguo), Ma Mingyu, Li Hongjun, Gao Feng, Hao Haidong.
England: Flowers (Walker); Neville G, Neville P, Southgate, Adams (Ehiogu), Redknapp, Anderton, Gascoigne, Shearer (Fowler), Barmby (Beardsley), McManaman (Stone).

New Britain, 26 May 1996, 8526

USA (1) 2 *(Wynalda, Jones)*

Scotland (1) 1 *(Durie)*

USA: Sommer; Burns, Agoos, Lalas, Balboa, Jones, Harkes, Dooley (Kirovski), Reyna (McBride), Stewart, Wynalda.
Scotland: Leighton (Walker); Burley (McCall), Boyd, Calderwood, Hendry, Whyte, Jess, Gemmill (Collins), Durie (Spencer), Jackson (McAllister), Booth.

Hong Kong, 26 May 1996, 26,000

Hong Kong Golden Select (0) 0

England (1) 1 *(Ferdinand)*

Hong Kong Golden Select: Hesford; Grainger, Duxbury, Watson, Van der Sander (Leung Shing Kit), Lee Fook Wing, Bajkusa (Pang Kam Chuen), Grabo, Roberts, Fairweather, Bullen.
England: Seaman; Neville P, Pearce, Stone (Anderton), Howey (Campbell), Adams, Platt, Ince, Ferdinand (Shearer), Sheringham (Fowler), McManaman (Wilcox).

Belfast, 29 May 1996, 11,770

Northern Ireland (0) 1 *(O'Boyle)*

Germany (0) 1 *(Scholl)*

Northern Ireland: Fettis; Griffin, Worthington (Rowland), Magilton, Hunter, Hill, Gillespie (O'Boyle), Lomas, Dowie, McMahon, Hughes.
Germany: Kahn; Basler, Kohler, Helmer, Strunz, Eilts, Ziege (Bode), Scholl, Moller, Bierhoff (Bobic), Klinsmann (Kuntz).

Dublin, 29 May 1996, 26,576

Republic of Ireland (0) 0

Portugal (0) 1 *(Folha)*
Republic of Ireland: Given; Cunningham, Kenna, Kernaghan (Breen), Fleming, Phelan, McLoughlin, Farrelly (Savage), Cascarino (Quinn), Townsend, Connolly (O'Neill).
Portugal: Vitor Baia; Helder, Fernando Couto, Dimas, Paulinho Santos, Paneira (Sa Pinto), Oceano (Porfirio), Tavares, Cadete (Secretario), Joao Pinto, Folha.

Miami, 30 May 1996, 5000

Colombia (0) 1 *(Asprilla)*

Scotland (0) 0
Colombia: Mondragon; Ortiz (Herrera), Bermudez, Cassiani (Mendoza), Moreno, Mafla (Valderrama), Serna, Rincon, Estrada (Alvarez), Valenciano (Aristizabal), Valencia (Asprilla).
Scotland: Goram; Burley, Boyd, Calderwood, Hendry (McKimmie), McCall, Collins, McKinlay T, McCoist (Gallacher), McAllister, Spencer (Jess).

Dublin, 2 June 1996, 29,100

Republic of Ireland (1) 2 *(O'Neill, Quinn)*

Croatia (2) 2 *(Boban, Suker)*
Republic of Ireland: Given; Cunningham (Fleming), Phelan (Harte), Breen (Cascarino), Daish, Kenna (Kernaghan), McLoughlin (Savage), O'Neill (Moore), Quinn, Kennedy, O'Brien.
Croatia: Mrmic (Ladic); Stanic (Soldo), Bilic, Jerkan, Stimac, Asanovic, Vlaovic (Jurcevic), Suker, Boksic, Boban, Jarni.

Rotterdam, 4 June 1996, 15,002

Holland (1) 3 *(Bergkamp, Seedorf, Cocu)*

Republic of Ireland (1) 1 *(Breen)*
Holland: Van der Sar; Reiziger, Bogarde, Blind (De Kock), Ronald de Boer (Winter), Davids, Witschge, Jordi Cruyff (Cocu), Seedorf, Hoekstra (Taument), Bergkamp.
Republic of Ireland: Given; Kenna (Fleming), Phelan, Breen, Kernaghan, Harte, McLoughlin, O'Brien (Cunningham), Moore (Kennedy), Cascarino (O'Neill), Connolly (Quinn).

Boston, 9 June 1996, 25,332

USA (0) 2 *(Ramos, Rayna)*

Republic of Ireland (0) 1 *(Connolly)*
USA: Freidel; Burns, Dooley, Harkes, Ramos (Lassiter), Agoss, Jones, Balboa, Rayna (Kirovski), Lalas, Wynalda (Caliguiri).
Republic of Ireland: Given; Breen, Kernaghan, Cunningham, Kenna (Fleming), McLoughlin, O'Brien (Savage), Farrelly (Kennedy), Phelan, Quinn (O'Neill), Connolly.

New Jersey, 13 June 1996, 21,322

Mexico (1) 2 *(Garcia L 2 (1 pen))*

Republic of Ireland (1) 2 *(Connolly, Davino (og))*
Mexico: Sanchez; Suarez, Davino, De Olmo, Villa, Lara, Sol, Garcia R (Blanco), Alfaro, Garcia L, Palencia (Abundis).
Republic of Ireland: Bonner; Breen, Daish, Harte, Fleming, Savage, McLoughlin, Moore, Kennedy (Phelan), Connolly, O'Neill.

New Jersey, 15 June 1996, 14,624

Bolivia (0) 0

Republic of Ireland (3) 3 *(O'Neill 2, Harte)*
Bolivia: Sorio; Pena, Sanchez, Rimba, Castillo, Baldivieso, Etcheverry, Ramos (Cristalda), Cossio, Sandy, Moreno (Coimbra).
Republic of Ireland: Given (Bonner); Cunningham, Kernaghan (Breen), Harte, Fleming, Savage, O'Brien (McLoughlin), Phelan, Farrelly, O'Neill, Moore.

ENGLAND UNDER-21 TEAMS 1995–96

England Under-21 internationals

2 Sept

Portugal (2) 2 *(Dani 2)*

England (0) 0   10,000
England: Gerrard; Neville P, Gordon, Beckham, Scimerca, Elliott, Butt (Bart-Williams), Thompson, Fowler, Shipperley, Sinclair.

10 Oct

Norway (1) 2 *(Solskjaer, Lund)*

England (0) 2 *(Campbell, Booth)*   2640
England: Watson D; Watson S (Neville P), Gordon, Pearce, Campbell (Bowyer), Unsworth, Roberts, Pollock (Holland), Shipperley, Booth (Dichio), Joachim.

14 Nov

England (2) 2 *(Fowler, Shipperley)*

Austria (1) 1 *(Cerny)*   13,496
England: Oakes; Watson S, Elliott, Campbell, Roberts, Unsworth, Butt, Pollock (Beckham), Shipperley, Bart-Williams (Holland), Fowler.

23 Apr

England (0) 0

Croatia (1) 1 *(Vucko)*   4376
England: Day (Davis); Brown, Briscoe, O'Connor (Plummer), Rufus, Thatcher (Carbon), Cooke, Ford (Hendrie), Gallen (Moore), Dyer, Holland.

24 May

England (1) 1 *(Slade)*

Belgium (0) 0   5000
England: Day; Plummer, Rufus, Stuart, Beckham, Holland, Brown, Bowyer, Cooke, Slade (Briscoe), Thornley (Moore).

28 May

England (0) 0

Angola (1) 2 *(Muhongo (pen), Costa)*   1600
England: Marshall; O'Connor (Holland), Challis, Plummer (Cooke), Rufus, Stuart, Beckham, Brown, Briscoe, Moore (Branch), Slade.

30 May

England (0) 1 *(Slade)*

Portugal (1) 3 *(Nuno, Beto (pen), Dani)*   2500
England: Davis; Brown, Challis (Plummer), Stuart, Rufus, Beckham, Bowyer, Cooke, Thornley, Slade, Moore.

1 June

England (0) 1 *(Moore)*

Brazil (0) 2 *(Alex, Abailcon)*   8000
England: Day; Rufus, Plummer, Stuart, O'Connor, Briscoe, Bowyer, Holland, Thornley, Slade, Moore.

POST-WAR INTERNATIONAL APPEARANCES

As at July 1996

ENGLAND

A'Court, A. (5) (Liverpool) 1957/8, 1958/9.

Adams, T.A. (45) (Arsenal) 1986/7, 1987/8, 1988/9, 1990/91, 1992/93, 1993/94, 1994/95, 1995/96.

Allen, C. (5) (QPR) 1983/4, 1986/7 (Tottenham Hotspur) 1987/8.

Allen, R. (5) (West Bromwich Albion) 1951/2, 1953/4, 1954/5.

Allen, T. (3) (Stoke City) 1959/60.

Anderson, S. (2) (Sunderland) 1961/2.

Anderson, V. (30) (Nottingham Forest) 1978/9, 1979/80, 1980/1, 1981/2, 1983/84, (Arsenal) 1984/5, 1985/6, 1986/7, (Manchester United).

Anderton, D.R. (16) (Tottenham Hotspur) 1993/94, 1994/95, 1995/96.

Angus, J. (1) (Burnley) 1960/1.

Armfield, J. (43) (Blackpool) 1958/9, 1959/60, 1960/1, 1961/2, 1962/3, 1963/4, 1965/6.

Armstrong, D. (3) (Middlesbrough) 1979/80, (Southampton) 1982/3, 1983/4.

Armstrong, K. (1) (Chelsea) 1954/5.

Astall, G. (2) (Birmingham) 1955/6.

Astle, J. (5) (West Bromwich Albion) 1968/9, 1969/70.

Aston, J. (17) (Manchester United) 1948/9, 1949/50, 1950/1.

Atyeo, J. (6) (Bristol City) 1955/6, 1956/7.

Bailey, G.R. (2) Manchester United) 1984/5.

Bailey, M. (2) (Charlton) 1963/4, 1964/5.

Baily, E. (9) (Tottenham Hotspur) 1949/50, 1950/1, 1951/2, 1952/3.

Baker, J. (8) (Hibernian) 1959/60, 1965/6, (Arsenal).

Ball, A. (72) (Blackpool) 1964/5, 1965/6, 1966/7, (Everton) 1967/8, 1968/9, 1969/70, 1970/1, 1971/2 (Arsenal) 1972/3, 1973/4, 1974/5.

Banks, G. (73) (Leicester) 1962/3, 1963/4, 1964/5, 1965/6, 1966/7, 1967/8, (Stoke City) 1968/9, 1969/70, 1970/1, 1971/2.

Banks, T. (6) (Bolton Wanderers) 1957/8, 1958/9.

Bardsley, D. (2) (QPR) 1992/93.

Barham, M. (2) (Norwich City) 1982/3.

Barlow, R. (1) (West Bromwich Albion) 1954/5.

Barmby, N.J. (9) (Tottenham Hotspur) 1994/95, (Middlesbrough) 1995/96.

Barnes, J. (79) (Watford) 1982/3, 1983/4, 1984/5, 1985/6, 1986/7, (Liverpool) 1987/8, 1988/9, 1989/90, 1990/91, 1991/2, 1992/93, 1994/95, 1995/96.

Barnes, P. (22) (Manchester City) 1977/8, 1978/9, 1979/80 (West Bromwich Albion) 1980/1, 1981/2 (Leeds United).

Barrass, M. (3) (Bolton Wanderers) 1951/2, 1952/3.

Barrett, E.D. (3) (Oldham Athletic) 1990/91 (Aston Villa) 1992/93.

Barton, W.D. (3) (Wimbledon) (Blackburn Rovers) 1994/95.

Batty, D. (17) (Leeds United) 1990/91, 1991/2, 1992/93, (Blackburn Rovers) 1993/94, 1994/95.

Baynham, R. (3) (Luton Town) 1955/6.

Beardsley P.A. (59) (Newcastle United) 1985/6, 1986/7 (Liverpool) 1987/8, 1988/9, 1989/90, 1990/1, (Newcastle United) 1993/94, 1994/95, 1995/96.

Beasant, D.J. (2) (Chelsea), 1989/90.

Beattie, T.K. (9) (Ipswich Town) 1974/5, 1975/6, 1976/7, 1977/8.

Bell, C. (48) (Manchester City) 1967/8, 1968/9, 1969/70, 1971/2, 1972/3, 1973/4, 1974/5, 1975/6.

Bentley, R. (12) (Chelsea) 1948/9, 1949/50, 1952/3, 1954/5.

250

Berry, J. (4) (Manchester United) 1952/3, 1955/6.
Birtles, G. (3) (Nottingham Forest) 1979/80, 1980/1 (Manchester United).
Blissett, L. (14) (Watford) 1982/3, 1983/4 (AC Milan).
Blockley, J. (1) (Arsenal) 1972/3.
Blunstone, F. (5) (Chelsea) 1954/5, 1956/7.
Bonetti, P. (7) (Chelsea) 1965/6, 1966/7, 1967/8, 1969/70.
Bould, S.A. (2) (Arsenal) 1993/94.
Bowles, S. (5) (QPR) 1973/4, 1976/7.
Boyer, P. (1) (Norwich City) 1975/6.
Brabrook, P. (3) (Chelsea) 1957/8, 1959/60.
Bracewell, P.W. (3) (Everton) 1984/5, 1985/6.
Bradford, G. (1) (Bristol Rovers) 1955/6.
Bradley, W. (3) (Manchester United) 1958/9.
Bridges, B. (4) (Chelsea) 1964/5, 1965/6.
Broadbent, P. (7) (Wolverhampton Wanderers) 1957/8, 1958/9, 1959/60.
Broadis, I. (14) (Manchester City) 1951/2, 1952/3 (Newcastle United) 1953/4.
Brooking, T. (47) (West Ham United) 1973/4, 1974/5, 1975/6, 1976/7, 1977/8, 1978/9, 1979/80, 1980/1, 1981/2.
Brooks, J. (3) (Tottenham Hotspur) 1956/7.
Brown, A. (1) (West Bromwich Albion) 1970/1.
Brown, K. (1) (West Ham United) 1959/60.
Bull, S.G. (13) (Wolverhampton Wanderers) 1988/9, 1989/90, 1990/1
Butcher, T. (77) (Ipswich Town) 1979/80, 1980/1, 1981/2, 1982/3, 1983/4, 1984/5, 1985/6, 1986/7 (Rangers) 1987/8, 1988/9, 1989/90.
Byrne, G. (2) (Liverpool) 1962/3, 1965/6.
Byrne, J. (11) (Crystal Palace) 1961/2, 1962/3, (West Ham United) 1963/4, 1964/5.
Byrne, R. (33) (Manchester United) 1953/4, 1954/5, 1955/6, 1956/7, 1957/8.

Callaghan, I. (4) (Liverpool) 1965/6, 1977/8.
Campbell, S. (2) (Tottenham Hotspur) 1995/96.
Carter, H. (7) (Derby County) 1946/7.
Chamberlain, M. (8) (Stoke City) 1982/3, 1983/4, 1984/5.
Channon, M. (46) (Southampton) 1972/3, 1973/4, 1974/5, 1975/6, 1976/7, (Manchester City) 1977/8.
Charles, G.A. (2) (Nottingham Forest) 1990/1.
Charlton, J. (35) (Leeds United) 1964/5, 1965/6, 1966/7, 1967/8, 1968/9, 1969/70.
Charlton, R. (106) (Manchester United) 1957/8, 1958/9, 1959/60, 1960/1, 1961/2, 1962/3, 1963/4, 1964/5, 1965/6, 1966/7, 1967/8, 1968/9, 1969/70.
Charnley, R. (1) (Blackpool) 1961/2.
Cherry, T. (27) (Leeds United) 1975/6, 1976/7, 1977/8, 1978/9, 1979/80.
Chilton, A. (2) (Manchester United) 1950/1, 1951/2.
Chivers, M. (24) (Tottenham Hotspur) 1970/1, 1971/2, 1972/3, 1973/4.
Clamp, E. (4) (Wolverhampton Wanderers) 1957/8.
Clapton, D. (1) (Arsenal) 1958/9.
Clarke, A. (19) (Leeds United) 1969/70, 1970/1, 1972/3, 1973/4, 1974/5, 1975/6.
Clarke, H. (1) (Tottenham Hotspur) 1953/4.
Clayton, R. (35) (Blackburn Rovers) 1955/6, 1956/7, 1957/8, 1958/9, 1959/60.
Clemence, R (61) (Liverpool) 1972/3, 1973/4, 1974/5, 1975/6, 1976/7, 1977/8, 1978/9, 1979/80, 1980/1, 1981/2, (Tottenham Hotspur) 1982/3, 1983/4.
Clement, D. (5) (QPR) 1975/6, 1976/7.
Clough, B. (2) (Middlesbrough) 1959/60.
Clough, N.H. (14) (Nottingham Forest) 1988/9, 1990/91, 1991/2, 1992/93.
Coates, R. (4) (Burnley) 1969/70, 1970/1, (Tottenham Hotspur).
Cockburn, H. (13) (Manchester United) 1946/7, 1947/8, 1948/9, 1950/1, 1951/2.
Cohen, G. (37) (Fulham) 1963/4, 1964/5, 1965/6, 1966/7, 1967/8.
Cole, A. (1) (Manchester United) 1994/95.

251

Collymore, S. V. (2) (Nottingham Forest) 1994/95.
Compton, L. (2) (Arsenal) 1950/1.
Connelly J. (20) (Burnley) 1959/60, 1961/2, 1962/3, 1964/5 (Manchester United) 1965/6.
Cooper, C. T. (2) (Nottingham Forest) 1994/95.
Cooper, T. (20) (Leeds United) 1968/9, 1969/70, 1970/1, 1971/2, 1974/5.
Coppell, S. (42) (Manchester United) 1977/8, 1978/9, 1979/80, 1980/1, 1981/2, 1982/3.
Corrigan J. (9) (Manchester City) 1975/6, 1977/8, 1978/9, 1979/80, 1980/1, 1981/2.
Cottee, A.R. (7) (West Ham United) 1986/7, 1987/8, (Everton) 1988/9.
Cowans, G. (10) (Aston Villa) 1982/3, 1985/6 (Bari) 1990/1 (Aston Villa).
Crawford, R. (2) (Ipswich Town) 1961/2.
Crowe, C. (1) (Wolverhampton Wanderers) 1962/3.
Cunningham, L. (6) (West Bromwich Albion) 1978/9 (Real Madrid) 1979/80, 1980/1.
Curle, K. (3) (Manchester City) 1991/2.
Currie, A. (17) (Sheffield United) 1971/2, 1972/3, 1973/4, 1975/6 (Leeds United) 1977/8, 1978/9.

Daley, A.M. (7) (Aston Villa) 1991/2.
Davenport, P. (1) (Nottingham Forest) 1984/5.
Deane, B.C. (3) (Sheffield United) 1990/91, 1992/93.
Deeley, N. (2) (Wolverhampton Wanderers) 1958/9.
Devonshire, A. (8) (West Ham United) 1979/80, 1981/2, 1982/3, 1983/4
Dickinson, J. (48) (Portsmouth) 1948/9, 1949/50, 1950/1, 1951/2, 1952/3, 1953/4, 1954/5, 1955/6, 1956/7.
Ditchburn, E. (6) (Tottenham Hotspur) 1948/9, 1952/3, 1956/7.
Dixon, K.M. (8) (Chelsea) 1984/5, 1985/6, 1986/7.
Dixon, L.M. (21) (Arsenal) 1989/90, 1990/1, 1991/2, 1992/93, 1993/94.
Dobson, M. (5) (Burnley) 1973/4, 1974/5 (Everton).
Dorigo, A.R. (15) (Chelsea) 1989/90, 1990/1, (Leeds United) 1991/2, 1992/93, 1993/94.
Douglas, B. (36) (Blackburn Rovers) 1957/8, 1958/9, 1959/60, 1960/1, 1961/2, 1962/3.
Doyle, M. (5) (Manchester City) 1975/6, 1976/7
Duxbury, M. (10) (Manchester United) 1983/4, 1984/5.

Eastham, G. (19) (Arsenal) 1962/3, 1963/4, 1964/5, 1965/6.
Eckersley, W. (17) (Blackburn Rovers) 1949/50, 1950/1, 1951/2, 1952/3, 1953/4.
Edwards, D. (18) (Manchester United) 1954/5, 1955/6, 1956/7, 1957/8.
Ehiogu, U. (1) (Aston Villa) 1995/96.
Ellerington, W. (2) (Southampton) 1948/9.
Elliott, W. H. (5) (Burnley) 1951/2, 1952/3.

Fantham, J. (1) (Sheffield Wednesday) 1961/2.
Fashanu, J. (2) (Wimbledon) 1988/9.
Fenwick, T. (20) (QPR) 1983/4, 1984/5, 1985/6 (Tottenham Hotspur) 1987/8.
Ferdinand, L. (10) (QPR) 1992/93, 1993/94, 1994/95 (Newcastle United) 1995/96.
Finney, T. (76) (Preston North End) 1946/7, 1947/8, 1948/9, 1949/50, 1950/1, 1951/2, 1952/3, 1953/4, 1954/5, 1955/6, 1956/7, 1957/8, 1958/9.
Flowers R. (49) (Wolverhampton Wanderers) 1954/5, 1958/9, 1959/60, 1960/1, 1961/2, 1962/3, 1963/4, 1964/5, 1965/6.
Flowers T. (8) (Southampton) 1992/93, (Blackburn Rovers) 1993/94, 1994/95, 1995/96.
Foster, S. (3) (Brighton) 1981/2.
Foulkes, W. (1) (Manchester United) 1954/5.

252

Fowler, R. B. (5) (Liverpool) 1995/96.

Francis, G. (12) (QPR) 1974/5, 1975/6.

Francis, T. (52) (Birmingham City) 1976/7, 1977/8 (Nottingham Forest) 1978/9, 1979/80, 1980/1, 1981/2 (Manchester City) 1982/3, (Sampdoria) 1983/4, 1984/5, 1985/6.

Franklin, N. (27) (Stoke City) 1946/7, 1947/8, 1948/9, 1949/50.

Froggatt, J. (13) (Portsmouth) 1949/50, 1950/1, 1951/2, 1952/3.

Froggatt, R. (4) (Sheffield Wednesday) 1952/3.

Garrett, T. (3) (Blackpool) 1951/2, 1953/4.

Gascoigne, P.J. (43) (Tottenham Hotspur) 1988/9, 1989/90, 1990/1 (Lazio) 1992/93, 1993/94, 1994/95 (Rangers) 1995/96.

Gates, E. (2) (Ipswich Town) 1980/1.

George, F.C. (1) (Derby County) 1976/7.

Gidman, J. (1) (Aston Villa) 1976/7.

Gillard, I. (3) (QPR) 1974/5, 1975/6.

Goddard, P. (1) (West Ham United) 1981/2.

Grainger, C. (7) (Sheffield United) 1955/6, 1956/7 (Sunderland).

Gray, A.A. (1) (Crystal Palace) 1991/2.

Greaves, J. (57) (Chelsea) 1958/9, 1959/60, 1960/1, 1961/2 (Tottenham Hotspur) 1962/3, 1963/4, 1964/5, 1965/6, 1966/7.

Greenhoff, B. (18) (Manchester United) 1975/6, 1976/7, 1977/8, 1979/80.

Gregory, J. (6) (QPR) 1982/3, 1983/4.

Hagan, J. (1) (Sheffield United) 1948/9.

Haines, J. (1) (West Bromwich Albion) 1948/9.

Hall, J. (17) (Birmingham City) 1955/6, 1956/7.

Hancocks, J. (3) (Wolverhampton Wanderers) 1948/9, 1949/50, 1950/1.

Hardwick, G. (13) (Middlesbrough) 1946/7, 1947/8.

Harford, M.G. (2) (Luton Town) 1987/8, 1988/9.

Harris, G. (1) (Burnley) 1965/6.

Harris, P. (2) (Portsmouth) 1949/50, 1953/4.

Harvey, C. (1) (Everton) 1970/1.

Hassall, H. (5) (Huddersfield Town) 1950/1, 1951/2 (Bolton Wanderers) 1953/4.

Hateley, M. (32) (Portsmouth) 1983/4, 1984/5, (AC Milan) 1985/6, 1986/7, (Monaco) 1987/8, (Rangers) 1991/2.

Haynes, J. (56) (Fulham) 1954/5, 1955/6, 1956/7, 1957/8, 1958/9, 1959/60, 1960/1, 1961/2.

Hector, K. (2) (Derby County) 1973/4.

Hellawell, M. (2) (Birmingham City) 1962/3.

Henry, R. (1) (Tottenham Hotspur) 1962/3.

Hill, F. (2) (Bolton Wanderers) 1962/3.

Hill, G. (6) (Manchester United) 1975/6, 1976/7, 1977/8.

Hill, R. (3) (Luton Town) 1982/3, 1985/6.

Hinton A. (3) (Wolverhampton Wanderers) 1962/3, 1964/5 (Nottingham Forest).

Hirst, D.E. (3) (Sheffield Wednesday) 1990/91, 1991/2.

Hitchens, G. (7) (Aston Villa) 1960/1, (Inter Milan) 1961/2.

Hoddle, G. (53) (Tottenham Hotspur) 1979/80, 1980/1, 1981/2, 1982/3, 1983/4, 1984/5, 1985/6, 1986/7 (Monaco) 1987/8.

Hodge, S.B. (24) (Aston Villa) 1985/6, 1986/7, (Tottenham Hotspur), (Nottingham Forest) 1988/9, 1989/90, 1990/1.

Hodgkinson, A. (5) (Sheffield United) 1956/7, 1960/1.

Holden, D. (5) (Bolton Wanderers) 1958/9.

Holliday, E. (3) (Middlesbrough) 1959/60.

Hollins, J. (1) (Chelsea) 1966/7.

Hopkinson, E. (14) (Bolton Wanderers) 1957/8, 1958/9, 1959/60.
Howe, D. (23) (West Bromwich Albion) 1957/8, 1958/9, 1959/60.
Howe, J. (3) (Derby County) 1947/8, 1948/9.
Howey, S. N. (4) (Newcastle United) 1994/95, 1995/96.
Hudson, A. (2) (Stoke City) 1974/5.
Hughes, E. (62) (Liverpool) 1969/70, 1970/1, 1971/2, 1972/3, 1973/4, 1974/5, 1976/7, 1977/8, 1978/9 (Wolverhampton Wanderers) 1979/80.
Hughes, L. (3) (Liverpool) 1949/50.
Hunt, R. (34) (Liverpool) 1961/2, 1962/3, 1963/4, 1964/5, 1965/6, 1966/7, 1967/8, 1968/9.
Hunt, S. (2) (West Bromwich Albion) 1983/4.
Hunter, N. (28) (Leeds United) 1965/6, 1966/7, 1967/8, 1968/9, 1969/70, 1970/1, 1971/2, 1972/3, 1973/4, 1974/5.
Hurst, G. (49) (West Ham United) 1965/6, 1966/7, 1967/8, 1968/9, 1969/70, 1970/1, 1971/2.

Ince, P. (23) (Manchester United) 1992/93, 1993/94, 1994/95, (Internazionale) 1995/96.

Jezzard, B. (2) (Fulham) 1953/4, 1955/6.
Johnson, D. (8) (Ipswich Town) 1974/5, 1975/6, (Liverpool) 1979/80.
Johnston, H. (10) (Blackpool) 1946/7, 1950/1, 1952/3, 1953/4.
Jones, M. (3) (Sheffield United) 1964/5 (Leeds United) 1969/70.
Jones, R. (8) (Liverpool) 1991/2, 1993/94, 1994/95.
Jones, W.H. (2) (Liverpool) 1949/50.

Kay, A. (1) (Everton) 1962/3.
Keegan, K. (63) (Liverpool) 1972/3, 1973/4, 1974/5, 1975/6, 1976/7 (SV Hamburg) 1977/8, 1978/9, 1979/80 (Southampton) 1980/1, 1981/2.
Kennedy, A. (2) (Liverpool) 1983/4.
Kennedy, R. (17) (Liverpool) 1975/6, 1977/8, 1979/80.
Keown, M.R. (11) (Everton) 1991/2 (Arsenal) 1992/93.
Kevan, D. (14) (West Bromwich Albion) 1956/7, 1957/8, 1958/9, 1960/1.
Kidd, B. (2) (Manchester United) 1969/70.
Knowles, C. (4) (Tottenham Hotspur) 1967/8.

Labone, B. (26) (Everton) 1962/3, 1966/7, 1967/8, 1968/9, 1969/70.
Lampard, F. (2) (West Ham United) 1972/3, 1979/80.
Langley, J. (3) (Fulham) 1957/8.
Langton, R. (11) (Blackburn Rovers) 1946/7, 1947/8, 1948/9, (Preston North End) 1949/50, (Bolton Wanderers) 1950/1.
Latchford, R. (12) (Everton) 1977/8, 1978/9.
Lawler, C. (4) (Liverpool) 1970/1, 1971/2.
Lawton, T. (15) (Chelsea) 1946/7, 1947/8, (Notts County) 1948/9.
Lee, F. (27) (Manchester City) 1968/9, 1969/70, 1970/1, 1971/2.
Lee, J. (1) (Derby County) 1950/1.
Lee. R.M. (7) (Newcastle United) 1994/95, 1995/96.
Lee, S. (14) (Liverpool) 1982/3, 1983/4.
Le Saux, G.P. (12) (Blackburn Rovers) 1993/94, 1994/95, 1995/96.
Le Tissier, M.P. (6) (Southampton) 1993/94, 1994/95.
Lindsay, A. (4) (Liverpool) 1973/4.
Lineker, G. (80) (Leicester City) 1983/4, 1984/5 (Everton) 1985/6, 1986/7, (Barcelona) 1987/8, 1988/9 (Tottenham H) 1989/90, 1990/1, 1991/2.
Little, B. (1) (Aston Villa) 1974/5.
Lloyd, L. (4) (Liverpool) 1970/1, 1971/2, (Nottingham Forest) 1979/80.

254

Lofthouse, N. (33) (Bolton Wanderers) 1950/1, 1951/2, 1952/3, 1953/4, 1954/5, 1955/6, 1958/9.
Lowe, E. (3) (Aston Villa) 1946/7.

Mabbutt, G. (16) (Tottenham Hotspur) 1982/3, 1983/4, 1986/7, 1987/8, 1991/2.
Macdonald, M. (14) (Newcastle United) 1971/2, 1972/3, 1973/4, 1974/5, (Arsenal) 1975/6.
Madeley, P. (24) (Leeds United) 1970/1, 1971/2, 1972/3, 1973/4, 1974/5, 1975/6, 1976/7.
Mannion, W. (26) (Middlesbrough) 1946/7, 1947/8, 1948/9, 1949/50, 1950/1, 1951/2.
Mariner, P. (35) (Ipswich Town) 1976/7, 1977/8, 1979/80, 1980/1, 1981/2, 1982/3, 1983/4, 1984/5 (Arsenal)
Marsh, R. (9) (QPR) 1971/2 (Manchester City) 1972/3.
Martin, A. (17) (West Ham United) 1980/1, 1981/2, 1982/3, 1983/4, 1984/5, 1985/6, 1986/7.
Marwood, B. (1) (Arsenal) 1988/9.
Matthews, R. (5) (Coventry City) 1955/6, 1956/7.
Matthews, S. (37) (Stoke City) 1946/7, (Blackpool) 1947/8, 1948/9, 1949/50, 1950/1, 1953/4, 1954/5, 1955/6, 1956/7.
McDermott, T. (25) (Liverpool) 1977/8, 1978/9, 1979/80, 1980/1, 1981/2.
McDonald, C. (8) (Burnley) 1957/8, 1958/9.
McFarland, R. (28) (Derby County) 1970/1, 1971/2, 1972/3, 1973/4, 1975/6, 1976/7.
McGarry, W. (4) (Huddersfield Town) 1953/4, 1955/6.
McGuinness, W. (2) (Manchester United) 1958/9.
McMahon, S. (17) (Liverpool) 1987/8, 1988/9, 1989/90, 1990/1.
McManaman, S. (15) (Liverpool) 1994/95, 1995/96.
McNab, R. (4) (Arsenal) 1968/9.
McNeil, M. (9) (Middlesbrough) 1960/1, 1961/2.
Martyn, A.N. (3) (Crystal Palace) 1991/2, 1992/93.
Meadows, J. (1) (Manchester City) 1954/5.
Medley, L. (Tottenham Hotspur) 1950/1, 1951/2.
Melia, J. (2) (Liverpool) 1962/3.
Merrick, G. (23) (Birmingham City) 1951/2, 1952/3, 1953/4.
Merson, P.C. (14) (Arsenal) 1991/2, 1992/93, 1993/94.
Metcalfe, V. (2) (Huddersfield Town) 1950/1.
Milburn, J. (13) (Newcastle United) 1948/9, 1949/50, 1950/1, 1951/2, 1955/6.
Miller, B. (1) (Burnley) 1960/1.
Mills, M. (42) (Ipswich Town) 1972/3, 1975/6, 1976/7, 1977/8, 1978/9, 1979/80, 1980/1, 1981/2.
Milne, G. (14) (Liverpool) 1962/3, 1963/4, 1964/5.
Milton, C.A. (1) (Arsenal) 1951/2.
Moore, R. (108) (West Ham United) 1961/2, 1962/3, 1963/4, 1964/5, 1965/6, 1966/7, 1967/8, 1968/9, 1969/70, 1970/1, 1971/2, 1972/3, 1973/4.
Morley, A. (6) (Aston Villa) 1981/2, 1982/3.
Morris, J. (3) (Derby County) 1948/9, 1949/50.
Mortensen, S. (25) (Blackpool) 1946/7, 1947/8, 1948/9, 1949/50, 1950/1, 1953/4.
Mozley, B. (3) (Derby County) 1949/50.
Mullen, J. (12) (Wolverhampton Wanderers) 1946/7, 1948/9, 1949/50, 1953/4.
Mullery, A. (35) (Tottenham Hotspur) 1964/5, 1966/7, 1967/8, 1968/9, 1969/70, 1970/1, 1971/2.

Neal, P. (50) (Liverpool) 1975/6, 1976/7, 1977/8, 1978/9, 1979/80, 1980/1, 1981/2, 1982/3, 1983/4.
Neville, G. A. (14) (Manchester United) 1994/95, 1995/96.
Neville, P. J. (1) (Manchester United) 1995/96.

Newton, K. (27) (Blackburn Rovers) 1965/6, 1966/7, 1967/8, 1968/9, 1969/70, (Everton).

Nicholls, J. (2) (West Bromwich Albion) 1953/4.

Nicholson W. (1) (Tottenham Hotspur) 1950/1.

Nish, D. (5) (Derby County) 1972/3, 1973/4.

Norman, M. (23) (Tottenham Hotspur) 1961/2, 1962/3, 1963/4, 1964/5.

O'Grady, M. (2) (Huddersfield Town) 1962/3, 1968/9 (Leeds United).

Osgood, P. (4) (Chelsea) 1969/70, 1973/4.

Osman, R. (11) (Ipswich Town) 1979/80, 1980/1, 1981/2, 1982/3, 1983/4.

Owen, S. (3) (Luton Town) 1953/4.

Paine, T. (19) (Southampton) 1962/3, 1963/4, 1964/5, 1965/6.

Pallister, G. (20) (Middlesbrough) 1987/8, 1990/91 (Manchester United), 1991/2, 1992/93, 1993/94, 1994/95, 1995/96.

Palmer, C.L. (18) (Sheffield Wednesday) 1991/2, 1992/93, 1993/94.

Parker, P.A. (19) (QPR) 1988/9, 1989/90, 1990/1, (Manchester United) 1991/2, 1993/94.

Parkes, P. (1) (QPR) 1973/4.

Parry, R. (2) (Bolton Wanderers) 1959/60.

Peacock, A. (6) (Middlesbrough) 1961/2, 1962/3, 1965/6 (Leeds United).

Pearce, S. (70) (Nottingham Forest) 1986/7, 1987/8, 1988/9, 1989/90, 1990/1, 1991/2, 1992/93, 1993/94, 1994/95, 1995/96.

Person, Stan (8) (Manchester United) 1947/8, 1948/9, 1949/50, 1950/1, 1951/2.

Pearson, Stuart (15) (Manchester United) 1975/6, 1976/7, 1977/8.

Pegg, D. (1) (Manchester United) 1956/7.

Pejic, M. (4) (Stoke City) 1973/4.

Perry, W. (3) (Blackpool) 1955/6.

Perryman, S. (1) (Tottenham Hotspur) 1981/2.

Peters, M. (67) (West Ham United) 1965/6, 1966/7, 1967/8, 1968/9, 1969/70, (Tottenham Hotspur) 1970/1, 1971/2, 1972/3, 1973/4.

Phelan, M.C. (1) (Manchester United) 1989/90.

Phillips, L. (3) (Portsmouth) 1951/2, 1954/5.

Pickering, F. (3) (Everton) 1963/4, 1964/5.

Pickering, N. (1) (Sunderland) 1982/3.

Pilkington, B. (1) (Burnley) 1954/5.

Platt, D. (62) (Aston Villa) 1989/90, 1990/1, (Bari) 1991/2 (Juventus), 1992/93 (Sampdoria) 1993/94, 1994/95, (Arsenal) 1995/96.

Pointer, R. (3) (Burnley) 1961/2.

Pye, J. (1) (Wolverhampton Wanderers) 1949/50.

Quixall, A. (5) (Sheffield Wednesday) 1953/4, 1954/5.

Radford, J. (2) (Arsenal) 1968/9, 1971/2.

Ramsey, A. (32) (Southampton) 1948/9, 1949/50, (Tottenham Hotspur) 1950/1, 1951/2, 1952/3, 1953/4.

Reaney, P. (3) (Leeds United) 1968/9, 1969/70, 1970/1.

Redknapp, J. F. (5) (Liverpool) 1995/96.

Reeves, K. (2) (Norwich City) 1979/80.

Regis, C. (5) (West Bromwich Albion) 1981/2, 1982/3, (Coventry City).

Reid, P. (13) (Everton) 1984/5, 1985/6, 1986/7.

Revie, D. (6) (Manchester City) 1954/5, 1955/6, 1956/7.

Richards, J. (1) (Wolverhampton Wanderers) 1972/3.

Richardson, K. (1) (Aston Villa) 1993/94.

Rickaby, S. (1) (West Bromwich Albion) 1953/4.

Rimmer, J. (1) (Arsenal) 1975/6.

Ripley, S.E. (1) (Blackburn Rovers) 1993/94.\
Rix, G. (17) (Arsenal) 1980/1, 1981/2, 1982/3, 1983/4.
Robb, G. (1) (Tottenham Hotspur) 1953/4.
Roberts, G. (6) (Tottenham Hotspur) 1982/3, 1983/4.
Robson, B.(90) (West Bromwich Albion) 1979/80, 1980/1, 1981/2, (Manchester United) 1982/3, 1983/4, 1984/5, 1985/6, 1986/7, 1987/8, 1988/9, 1989/90, 1990/1, 1991/2.
Robson, R. (20) (West Bromwich Albion) 1957/8, 1959/60, 1960/1, 1961/2.
Rocastle, D. (14) (Arsenal) 1988/9, 1989/90, 1991/2.
Rowley, J. (6) (Manchester United) 1948/9, 1949/50, 1951/2.
Royle, J. (6) (Everton) 1970/1, 1972/3, (Manchester City) 1975/6, 1976/7.
Ruddock, N. (1) (Liverpool) 1994/95.

Sadler, D. (4) (Manchester United) 1967/8, 1969/70, 1970/1.
Salako, J.A. (5) (Crystal Palace) 1990/91, 1991/2.
Sansom, K. (86) (Crystal Palace) 1978/9, 1979/80, 1980/1, (Arsenal) 1981/2, 1982/3, 1983/4, 1984/5, 1985/6, 1986/7, 1987/8.
Scales, J.R. (3) (Liverpool) 1994/95.
Scott, L. (17) (Arsenal) 1946/7, 1947/8, 1948/9.
Seaman, D.A. (29) (QPR) 1988/9, 1989/90, 1990/1 (Arsenal), 1991/2, 1993/94, 1994/95, 1995/96.
Sewell, J. (6) (Sheffield Wednesday) 1951/2, 1952/3, 1953/4.
Shackleton, L. (5) (Sunderland) 1948/9, 1949/50, 1954/5.
Sharpe, L.S. (8) (Manchester United) 1990/1, 1992/93, 1993/94.
Shaw, G. (5) (Sheffield United) 1958/9, 1962/3.
Shearer, A. (28) (Southampton) 1991/2 (Blackburn Rovers), 1992/93, 1993/94, 1994/95, 1995/96.
Shellito, K. (1) (Chelsea) 1962/3.
Sheringham, E. (20) (Tottenham Hotspur) 1992/93, 1994/95, 1995/96.
Shilton, P. (125) (Leicester City) 1970/1, 1971/2, 1972/3, 1973/4, 1974/5, (Stoke City) 1976/7, (Nottingham Forest) 1977/8, 1978/9, 1979/80, 1980/1, 1981/2, (Southampton) 1982/3, 1983/4, 1984/5, 1985/6, 1986/7, (Derby County) 1987/8, 1988/9, 1989/90.
Shimwell, E. (1) (Blackpool) 1948/9.
Sillett, P. (3) (Chelsea) 1954/5.
Sinton, A. (12) (QPR) 1991/2, 1992/93 (Sheffield Wednesday) 1993/94.
Slater, W. (12) (Wolverhampton Wanderers) 1954/5, 1957/8, 1958/9, 1959/60.
Smith, A.M. (13) (Arsenal) 1988/9, 1990/1, 1991/2.
Smith, L (6) (Arsenal) 1950/1, 1951/2, 1952/3.
Smith, R. (15) (Tottenham Hotspur) 1960/1, 1961/2, 1962/3, 1963/4.
Smith, Tom (1) (Liverpool) 1970/1.
Smith, Trevor (2) (Birmingham City) 1959/60.
Southgate, G. (9) (Aston Villa) 1995/96.
Spink, N. (1) (Aston Villa) 1982/3.
Springett, R. (33) (Sheffield Wednesday) 1959/60, 1960/1, 1961/2, 1962/3, 1965/6.
Staniforth, R. (8) (Huddersfield Town) 1953/4, 1954/5.
Statham, D. (3) (West Bromwich Albion) 1982/3.
Stein, B. (1) (Luton Town) 1983/4.
Stepney, A. (1) (Manchester United) 1967/8.
Sterland, M. (1) (Sheffield Wednesday) 1988/9.
Steven, T.M. (36) (Everton) 1984/5, 1985/6, 1986/7, 1987/8, 1988/9 (Glasgow Rangers) 1989/90, 1990/1, (Marseille) 1991/2.
Stevens, G.A. (7) (Tottenham Hotspur) 1984/5, 1985/6.
Stevens, M.G. (46) (Everton) 1984/5, 1985/6, 1986/7, 1987/8 (Rangers) 1988/9, 1989/90, 1990/1, 1991/2.
Stewart, P.A. (3) (Tottenham Hotspur) 1991/2.

Stiles, N. (28) (Manchester United) 1964/5, 1965/6, 1966/7, 1967/8, 1968/9, 1969/70.
Stone, S.B. (9) (Nottingham Forest) 1995/96.
Storey-Moore, I. (1) (Nottingham Forest) 1969/70.
Storey, P. (19) (Arsenal) 1970/1, 1971/2, 1972/3.
Streten, B. (1) (Luton Town) 1949/50.
Summerbee, M. (8) (Manchester City) 1967/8, 1971/2, 1972/3.
Sunderland, A. (1) (Arsenal) 1979/80.
Swan, P. (19) (Sheffield Wednesday) 1959/60, 1960/1, 1961/2.
Swift, F. (19) (Manchester City) 1946/7, 1947/8, 1948/9.

Talbot, B. (6) (Ipswich Town) 1976/7, 1979/80.
Tambling, R. (3) (Chelsea) 1962/3, 1965/6.
Taylor, E. (1) (Blackpool) 1953/4.
Taylor, J. (2) (Fulham) 1950/1.
Taylor, P.H. (3) (Liverpool) 1947/8.
Taylor, P.J. (4) (Crystal Palace) 1975/6.
Taylor, T. (19) (Manchester United) 1952/3, 1953/4, 1955/6, 1956/7, 1958/9.
Temple, D. (1) (Everton) 1964/5.
Thomas, Danny (2) (Coventry City) 1982/3.
Thomas, Dave (8) (QPR) 1974/5, 1975/6.
Thomas, G.R. (9) (Crystal Palace) 1990/1, 1991/2.
Thomas, M.L. (2) (Arsenal) 1988/9, 1989/90.
Thompson, P. (16) (Liverpool) 1963/4, 1964/5, 1965/6, 1967/8, 1969/70.
Thompson, P.B. (42) (Liverpool) 1975/6, 1976/7, 1978/9, 1979/80, 1980/1, 1981/2, 1982/3.
Thompson, T. (2) (Aston Villa) 1951/2, (Preston North End) 1956/7.
Thomson, R. (8) (Wolverhampton Wanderers) 1963/4, 1964/5.
Todd, C. (27) (Derby County) 1971/2, 1973/4, 1974/5, 1975/6, 1976/7.
Towers, T. (3) (Sunderland) 1975/6.
Tueart, D. (6) (Manchester City) 1974/5, 1976/7.

Ufton, D. (1) (Charlton Athletic) 1953/4.
Unsworth, D.G. (1) (Everton) 1994/95.

Venables, T. (2) (Chelsea) 1964/5.
Venison, B. (2) (Newcastle United) 1994/95.
Viljoen, C. (2) (Ipswich Town) 1974/5.
Viollet, D. (2) (Manchester United) 1959/60, 1961/2.

Waddle, C.R. (62) (Newcastle United) 1984/5, (Tottenham Hotspur) 1985/6, 1986/7, 1987/8, 1988/9, (Marseille) 1989/90, 1990/1, 1991/2.
Waiters, A. (5) (Blackpool) 1963/4, 1964/5.
Walker, D.S. (59) (Nottingham Forest) 1988/9, 1989/90, 1990/1, 1991/2 (Sampdoria) 1992/93, (Sheffield Wednesday) 1993/94.
Walker, I.M. (2) (Tottenham Hotspur) 1995/96.
Wallace, D.L. (1) (Southampton) 1985/6.
Walsh, P. (5) (Luton Town) 1982/3, 1983/4.
Walters, K.M. (1) (Rangers) 1990/91.
Ward, P. (1) (Brighton) 1979/80.
Ward, T. (2) (Derby County) 1947/8, 1948/9.
Watson, D. (12) (Norwich City) 1983/4, 1984/5, 1985/6, 1986/7 (Everton) 1987/8.
Watson D.V. (65) (Sunderland) 1973/4, 1974/5, 1975/6 (Manchester City) 1976/7, 1977/8, (Southampton) 1978/9 (Werder Bremen), 1979/80, (Southampton) 1980/1 , 1981/2, (Stoke City).
Watson, W. (4) (Sunderland) 1949/50, 1950/1.

Webb, N. (26) (Nottingham Forest) 1987/8, 1988/9 (Manchester United) 1989/90, 1991/2.

Weller, K. (4) (Leicester City) 1973/4.

West, G. (3) (Everton) 1968/9.

Wheeler, J. (1) (Bolton Wanderers) 1954/5.

White, D. (1) (Manchester City) 1992/93.

Whitworth, S. (7) (Leicester City) 1974/5, 1975/6.

Whymark, T. (1) (Ipswich Town) 1977/8.

Wignall, F. (2) (Nottingham Forest) 1964/5.

Wilcox, J.M. (1) (Blackburn Rovers) 1995/96.

Wilkins, R. (84) (Chelsea) 1975/6, 1976/7, 1977/8, 1978/9, (Manchester United) 1979/80, 1980/1, 1981/2, 1982/3, 1983/4, 1984/5, (AC Milan) 1985/6, 1986/7.

Williams, B. (24) (Wolverhampton Wanderers) 1948/9, 1949/50, 1950/1, 1951/2, 1954/5, 1955/6.

Williams, S. (6) (Southampton) 1982/3, 1983/4, 1984/5.

Willis, A. (1) (Tottenham Hotspur) 1951/2.

Wilshaw, D. (12) (Wolverhampton Wanderers) 1953/4, 1954/5, 1955/6, 1956/7.

Wilson, R. (63) (Huddersfield Town) 1959/60, 1961/2, 1962/3, 1963/4, 1964/5, (Everton) 1965/6, 1966/7, 1967/8.

Winterburn, N. (2) (Arsenal) 1989/90, 1992/93.

Wise, D.F. (12) (Chelsea) 1990/91, 1993/94, 1994/95, 1995/96.

Withe, P. (11) (Aston Villa) 1980/1, 1981/2, 1982/3, 1983/4, 1984/5.

Wood, R. (3) (Manchester United) 1954/5, 1955/6.

Woodcock, A. (42) (Nottingham Forest) 1977/8, 1978/9, 1979/80 (FC Cologne) 1980/1, 1981/2, (Arsenal) 1982/3, 1983/4, 1984/5, 1985/6.

Woods, C.C.E. (43) (Norwich City) 1984/5, 1985/6, 1986/7, (Rangers) 1987/8, 1988/9, 1989/90, 1990/1, (Sheffield Wednesday) 1991/2. 1992/93.

Worthington, F. (8) (Leicester City) 1973/4, 1974/5.

Wright, I.E. (20) (Crystal Palace) 1990/1, 1991/2 (Arsenal) 1992/93, 1993/94, 1994/95.

Wright M. (45) (Southampton) 1983/4, 1984/5, 1985/6, 1986/7, (Derby County) 1987/8, 1988/9, 1989/90, 1990/1, (Liverpool) 1991/2, 1992/93, 1995/96.

Wright, T. (11) (Everton) 1967/8, 1968/9, 1969/70.

Wright, W. (105) (Wolverhampton Wanderers) 1946/7, 1947/8, 1948/9, 1949/50, 1950/1, 1951/2, 1952/3, 1953/4, 1954/5, 1955/6, 1956/7, 1957/8, 1958/9.

Young, G. (1) (Sheffield Wednesday) 1964/5.

NORTHERN IRELAND

Aherne, T. (4) (Belfast Celtic) 1946/7, 1947/8, 1948/9, 1949/50 (Luton Town).

Anderson, T. (22) (Manchester United) 1972/3, 1973/4, 1974/5, (Swindon Town) 1975/6, 1976/7, 1977/8, (Peterborough United) 1978/9.

Armstrong, G. (63) (Tottenham Hotspur) 1976/7, 1977/8, 1978/9, 1979/80, 1980/1, (Watford) 1981/2, 1982/3, (Real Mallorca) 1983/4, 1984/5, (West Bromwich Albion) 1985/6 (Chesterfield).

Barr, H. (3) (Linfield) 1961/2, 1962/3, (Coventry City).

Best, G. (37) (Manchester United) 1963/4, 1964/5, 1965/6, 1966/7, 1967/8, 1968/9, 1969/70, 1970/1, 1971/2, 1972/3, 1973/4 (Fulham) 1976/7, 1977/8.

Bingham, W. (56) (Sunderland) 1950/1, 1951/2, 1952/3, 1953/4, 1954/5, 1955/6, 1956/7, 1957/8, 1958/9 (Luton Town) 1959/60, 1960/1 (Everton) 1961/2, 1962/3, 1963/4 (Port Vale).

Black, K. (30) (Luton Town) 1987/8, 1988/9, 1989/90, 1990/1, (Nottingham Forest) 1991/2, 1992/93, 1993/94.

Blair, R. (5) (Oldham Athletic) 1974/5, 1975/6.

259

Blanchflower, D. (54) (Barnsley) 1949/50, 1950/1 (Aston Villa) 1951/2, 1952/3, 1953/4, 1954/5, (Tottenham Hotspur) 1955/6, 1956/7, 1957/8, 1958/9, 1959/60, 1960/1, 1961/2, 1962/3.
Blanchflower, J. (12) (Manchester United) 1953/4, 1954/5, 1955/6, 1956/7, 1957/8.
Bowler, G. (3) (Hull City) 1949/50.
Braithwaite, R. (10) (Linfield) 1961/2, 1962/3 (Middlesbrough) 1963/4, 1964/5.
Brennan, R. (5) (Luton Town) 1948/9, 1949/50 (Birmingham City) (Fulham), 1950/1.
Briggs, R. (2) (Manchester United) 1961/2, 1964/5 (Swansea).
Brotherston, N. (27) (Blackburn Rovers) 1979/80, 1980/1, 1981/2, 1982/3, 1983/4, 1984/5.
Bruce, W. (2) (Glentoran) 1960/1, 1966/7.

Campbell, A. (2) (Crusaders) 1962/3, 1964/5.
Campbell, D.A. (10) (Nottingham Forest) 1985/6, 1986/7, 1987/8 (Charlton Athletic).
Campbell, J. (2) (Fulham) 1950/1.
Campbell, R.M. (2) (Bradford City) 1981/2.
Campbell, W. (6) (Dundee) 1967/8, 1968/9, 1969/70.
Carey, J. (7) (Manchester United) 1946/7, 1947/8, 1948/9.
Casey, T. (12) (Newcastle United) 1954/5, 1955/6, 1956/7, 1957/8, 1958/9, (Portsmouth).
Caskey, A. (7) (Derby County) 1978/9, 1979/80, 1981/2 (Tulsa Roughnecks).
Cassidy, T. (24) (Newcastle United) 1970/1, 1971/2, 1973/4, 1974/5, 1975/6, 1976/7, 1979/80 (Burnley) 1980/1, 1981/2.
Caughey, M. (2) (Linfield) 1985/6.
Clarke, C.J. (38) (Bournemouth) 1985/6, 1986/7 (Southampton) 1987/8, 1988/9, 1989/90, 1990/1 (Portsmouth), 1991/2, 1992/93.
Cleary, J. (5) (Glentoran) 1981/2, 1982/3, 1983/4, 1984/5.
Clements, D. (48) (Coventry City) 1964/5, 1965/6, 1966/7, 1967/8, 1968/9, 1969/70, 1970/1, 1971/2 (Sheffield Wednesday) 1972/3 (Everton) 1973/4, 1974/5, 1975/6 (New York Cosmos).
Cochrane, D. (10) (Leeds United) 1946/7, 1947/8, 1948/9, 1949/50.
Cochrane, T. (26) (Coleraine) 1975/6, (Burnley) 1977/8, 1978/9, (Middlesbrough) 1979/80, 1980/1, 1981/2, (Gillingham) 1983/4.
Cowan, J. (1) (Newcastle United) 1969/70.
Coyle, F. (4) (Coleraine) 1955/6, 1956/7, 1957/8 (Nottingham Forest).
Coyle, L. (1) (Derry C) 1988/9.
Coyle, R. (5) (Sheffield Wednesday) 1972/3, 1973/4.
Craig, D. (25) (Newcastle United) 1966/7, 1967/8, 1968/9, 1969/70, 1970/1, 1971/2, 1972/3, 1973/4, 1974/5.
Crossan, E. (3) (Blackburn Rovers) 1949/50, 1950/1, 1954/5.
Crossan, J. (23) (Rotterdam Sparta) 1959/60, 1962/3 (Sunderland), 1963/4, 1964/5, (Manchester City) 1965/6, 1966/7, 1967/8 (Middlesbrough).
Cunningham, W. (30) (St Mirren) 1950/1, 1952/3, 1953/4, 1954/5, 1955/6, 1956/7, (Leicester City) 1957/8, 1958/9, 1959/60, 1960/1 (Dunfermline Athletic) 1961/2.
Cush, W. (26) (Glentoran) 1950/1, 1953/4, 1956/7, 1957/8 (Leeds United) 1958/9, 1959/60, 1960/1 (Portadown) 1961/2.

D'Arcy, S. (5) (Chelsea) 1951/2, 1952/3 (Brentford).
Davison, A.J. (1) (Bolton Wanderers) 1995/96.
Dennison, R. (17) (Wolverhampton Wanderers) 1987/8, 1988/9, 1989/90, 1990/1, 1991/2, 1992/93, 1993/94.
Devine, J. (1) (Glentoran) 1989/90.
Dickson, D. (4) (Coleraine) 1969/70, 1972/3.
Dickson, T. (1) (Linfield) 1956/7.

Dickson, W. (12) (Chelsea) 1950/1, 1951/2, 1952/3 (Arsenal) 1953/4, 1954/5.

Doherty, L. (2) (Linfield) 1984/5, 1987/8.

Doherty P. (6) (Derby County) 1946/7, (Huddersfield Town) 1947/8, 1948/9, (Doncaster Rovers) 1950/1.

Donaghy, M. (91) (Luton Town) 1979/80, 1980/1, 1981/2, 1982/3, 1983/4, 1984/5, 1985/6, 1986/7, 1987/8, (Manchester United) 1988/9, 1989/90, 1990/1, 1991/2 (Chelsea) 1992/93, 1993/94.

Dougan D. (43) (Portsmouth) 1957/8, 1959/60, (Blackburn Rovers), 1960/1, 1962/3 (Aston Villa) 1965/6 (Leicester City), 1966/7 (Wolverhampton Wanderers) 1967/8, 1968/9, 1969/70, 1970/1, 1971/2, 1972/3.

Douglas, J.P. (1) (Belfast Celtic) 1946/7.

Dowd, H. (3) (Glentoran) 1972/3, 1974/5 (Sheffield Wednesday).

Dowie, I. (36) (Luton Town) 1989/90, 1990/1, (Southampton) 1991/2, 1992/93, 1993/94, 1994/95 (Crystal Palace) 1995/96 (West Ham).

Dunlop, G. (4) (Linfield) 1984/5, 1986/7.

Eglington T. (6) (Everton) 1946/7, 1947/8, 1948/9.

Elder, A. (40) (Burnley) 1959/60, 1960/1, 1961/2, 1962/3, 1963/4, 1964/5, 1965/6, 1966/7, (Stoke City) 1967/8, 1968/9, 1969/70.

Farrell, P. (7) (Everton) 1946/7, 1947/8, 1948/9.

Feeney, J. (2) (Linfield) 1946/7 (Swansea City) 1949/50.

Feeney, W. (1) (Glentoran) 1975/6.

Ferguson, W. (2) (Linfield) 1965/6, 1966/7.

Ferris, R. (3) Birmingham City) 1949/50, 1950/1, 1951/2.

Fettis, A. (15) (Hull City) 1991/2, 1992/93, 1993/94, 1994/95, (Nottingham Forest) 1995/96.

Finney, T. (14) (Sunderland) 1974/5, 1975/6 (Cambridge United), 1979/80.

Fleming, J.G. (31) (Nottingham Forest) 1986/7, 1987/8, 1988/9 (Manchester City) 1989/90, 1990/1 (Barnsley), 1991/2, 1992/93, 1993/94, 1994/95.

Forde, T. (4) (Ards) 1958/9, 1960/1.

Gallogly, C. (2) (Huddersfield Town) 1950/1.

Garton, R. (1) (Oxford United) 1968/9.

Gillespie, K.R. (12) (Manchester United) 1994/95 (Newcastle United) 1995/96.

Gorman, W. (4) (Brentford) 1946/7, 1947/8.

Graham, W. (14) (Doncaster Rovers) 1950/1, 1951/2, 1952/3, 1953/4, 1954/5, 1955/6, 1958/9.

Gray, P. (17) (Luton Town) 1992/93, (Sunderland) 1993/94, 1994/95, 1995/96.

Gregg, H. (25) (Doncaster Rovers) 1953/4, 1956/7, 1957/8, (Manchester United) 1958/9, 1959/60, 1960/1, 1961/2, 1963/4.

Griffin, D.J. (1) (St Johnstone) 1995/96.

Hamilton, B. (50) (Linfield) 1968/9, 1970/1, 1971/2 (Ipswich Town), 1972/3, 1973/4, 1974/5, 1975/6 (Everton) 1976/7, 1977/8, (Millwall), 1978/9, (Swindon Town).

Hamilton, W. (41) (QPR) 1977/8, 1979/80 (Burnley) 1980/1, 1981/2, 1982/3, 1983/4, 1984/5, (Oxford United) 1985/6.

Harkin, T. (5) (Southport) 1967/8, 1968/9 (Shrewsbury Town), 1969/70, 1970/1.

Harvey, M. (34) (Sunderland) 1960/1, 1961/2, 1962/3, 1963/4, 1964/5, 1965/6, 1966/7, 1967/8, 1968/9, 1969/70, 1970/1.

Hatton, S. (2) (Linfield) 1962/3.

Healy, F. (4) (Coleraine) 1981/2 (Glentoran) 1982/3.

Hegan, D. (7) (West Bromwich Albion) 1969/70, 1971/2 (Wolverhampton Wanderers) 1972/3.

Hill, C.F. (14) (Sheffield United), 1989/90, 1990/1, 1991/2, 1994/95 (Leicester City) 1995/96.

Hill, J. (7) (Norwich City) 1958/9, 1959/60, 1960/1, (Everton) 1961/2, 1963/4.

Hinton, E. (7) (Fulham) 1946/7, 1947/8 (Millwall) 1950/1.

Horlock, K. (2) (Swindon Town), 1994/95.

Hughes, M.E. (31) (Manchester City) 1991/2 (Strasbourg) 1992/93, 1993/94, 1994/95, 1995/96.

Hughes, P. (3) (Bury) 1986/7.

Hughes, W. (1) (Bolton Wanderers) 1950/1.

Humphries, W. (14) (Ards) 1961/2 (Coventry City) 1962/3, 1963/4, 1964/5 (Swansea Town).

Hunter, A. (53) (Blackburn Rovers) 1969/70, 1970/1, 1971/2 (Ipswich Town) 1972/3, 1973/4, 1974/5, 1975/6, 1976/7, 1977/8, 1978/9, 1979/80.

Hunter, B.V. (6) (Wrexham) 1994/95, 1995/96.

Irvine, R. (8) (Linfield) 1961/2, 1962/3 (Stoke City) 1964/5.

Irvine, W. (23) (Burnley) 1962/3, 1964/5, 1965/6, 1966/7, 1967/8, 1968/9 (Preston North End) (Brighton & Hove Albion) 1971/2.

Jackson, T. (35) (Everton) 1968/9, 1969/70, 1970/1 (Nottingham Forest) 1971/2, 1972/3, 1973/4, 1974/5 (Manchester United) 1975/6, 1976/7.

Jamison, A. (1) (Glentoran) 1975/6.

Jennings, P. (119) (Watford) 1963/4, 1964/5, (Tottenham Hotspur) 1965/6, 1966/7, 1967/8, 1968/9, 1969/70, 1970/1, 1971/2, 1972/3, 1973/4, 1974/5, 1975/6, 1976/7, (Arsenal) 1977/8, 1978/9, 1979/80, 1980/1, 1981/2, 1982/3, 1983/4, 1984/5, (Tottenham Hotspur) 1985/6.

Johnston, W. (1) (Glentoran) 1961/2, (Oldham Athletic) 1965/6.

Jones, J. (3) (Glenavon) 1955/6, 1956/7.

Keane, T. (1) (Swansea Town) 1948/9.

Kee, P.V. (9) (Oxford United), 1989/90, 1990/91, (Ards) 1994/95.

Keith, R. (23) (Newcastle United) 1957/8, 1958/9, 1959/60, 1960/1, 1961/2.

Kelly, H. (4) (Fulham) 1949/50 (Southampton) 1950/1.

Kelly, P. (1) (Barnsley) 1949/50.

Lawther, I. (4) (Sunderland) 1959/60, 1960/1, 1961/2 (Blackburn Rovers).

Lockhart, N. (8) (Linfield) 1946/7, 1949/50, (Coventry City) 1950/1, 1951/2, 1953/4, (Aston Villa) 1954/5, 1955/6.

Lennon, N.F. (6) (Crewe Alexandra) 1993/94, 1994/95, (Leicester City) 1995/96.

Lomas, S.M. (12) (Manchester City) 1993/94, 1994/95, 1995/96.

Lutton, B. (6) (Wolverhampton Wanderers) 1969/70, 1972/3 (West Ham United) 1973/4.

Magill, E. (26) (Arsenal) 1961/2, 1962/3, 1963/4, 1964/5, 1965/6 (Brighton & Hove Albion).

Magilton, J. (32) (Oxford United) 1990/1, 1991/2, 1992/93, (Southampton) 1993/94, 1994/95, 1995/96.

Martin, C. (6) (Glentoran) 1946/7, 1947/8 (Leeds United) 1948/9 (Aston Villa) 1949/50.

McAdams, W. (15) (Manchester City) 1953/4, 1954/5, 1956/7, 1957/8, 1960/1 (Bolton Wanderers) 1961/2 (Leeds United).

McAlinden, J. (2) (Portsmouth) 1946/7, 1948/9, (Southend United).

McBride, S. (4) (Glenavon) 1990/1, 1991/2.

McCabe, J. (6) (Leeds United) 1948/9, 1949/50, 1950/1, 1952/3, 1953/4.

McCarthy, J.D. (1) (Port Vale) 1995/96.

McCavana, T. (3) (Coleraine) 1954/5, 1955/6.

McCleary, J.W. (1) (Cliftonville) 1954/5.

McClelland, J. (6) (Arsenal) 1960/1, 1965/6 (Fulham).

McClelland, J. (53) (Mansfield Town) 1979/80, 1980/1, 1981/2 (Rangers) 1982/3, 1983/4, 1984/5 (Watford) 1985/6, 1986/7, 1987/8, 1988/9 (Leeds U) 1989/90.

McCourt, F. (6) (Manchester City) 1951/2, 1952/3.

McCoy, R. (1) (Coleraine) 1986/7.

McCreery, D. (67) (Manchester United) 1975/6, 1976/7, 1977/8, 1978/9, 1979/80 (QPR) 1980/1 (Tulsa Roughnecks) 1981/2, 1982/3 (Newcastle United), 1983/4, 1984/5, 1985/6, 1986/7, 1987/8, 1988/9 (Hearts) 1989/90.

McCrory, S. (1) (Southend United) 1957/8.

McCullough, W. (10) (Arsenal) 1960/1, 1962/3, 1963/4, 1964/5, 1966/7, (Millwall).

McCurdy, C. (1) (Linfield) 1979/80.

McDonald, A. (52) (QPR) 1985/6, 1986/7, 1987/8, 1988/9, 1990/1, 1991/2, 1992/93, 1993/94, 1994/95, 1995/96.

McElhinney, G. (6) (Bolton Wanderers) 1983/4, 1984/5.

McFaul, I. (6) (Linfield) 1966/7, 1969/70 (Newcastle United) 1970/1, 1971/2, 1972/3, 1973/4.

McGarry, J.K. (3) (Cliftonville) 1950/1.

McGaughey, M. (1) (Linfield) 1984/5.

McGibbon, P.C.G. (4) (Manchester United) 1994/95, 1995/96.

McGrath, R. (21) (Tottenham Hotspur) 1973/4, 1974/5, 1975/6 (Manchester United) 1976/7, 1977/8, 1978/9.

McIlroy, J. (55) (Burnley) 1951/2, 1952/3, 1953/4, 1954/5, 1955/6, 1956/7, 1957/8, 1958/9, 1959/60, 1960/1, 1961/2, 1962/3, 1965/6 (Stoke City).

McIlroy, S.B. (88) (Manchester United) 1971/2, 1973/4, 1974/5, 1975/6, 1976/7, 1977/8, 1978/9, 1979/80, 1980/1, 1981/2, (Stoke City), 1982/3, 1983/4, 1984/5 (Manchester City) 1985/6, 1986/7.

McKeag, W. (2) (Glentoran) 1967/8.

McKenna, J. (7) (Huddersfield Town) 1949/50, 1950/1, 1951/2.

McKenzie, R. (1) (Airdrieonians) 1966/7.

McKinney, W. (1) (Falkirk) 1965/6.

McKnight, A. (10) (Celtic) 1987/8, (West Ham United) 1988/9.

McLaughlin, J. (12) (Shrewsbury Town) 1961/2, 1962/3 (Swansea City), 1963/4, 1964/5, 1965/6.

McMahon, G.J. (7) (Tottenham Hotspur) 1994/95, 1995/96.

McMichael, A. (39) (Newcastle United) 1949/50, 1950/1, 1951/2, 1952/3, 1953/4, 1954/5, 1955/6, 1956/7, 1957/8, 1958/9, 1959/60.

McMillan, S. (2) (Manchester United) 1962/3.

McMordie, E. (21) (Middlesbrough) 1968/9, 1969/70, 1970/1, 1971/2, 1972/3.

McMorran, E. (15) (Belfast Celtic) 1946/7 (Barnsley) 1950/1, 1951/2, 1952/3, (Doncaster Rovers) 1953/4, 1955/6, 1956/7.

McNally, B.A. (5) (Shrewsbury Town) 1985/6, 1986/7, 1987/8.

McParland, P. (34) (Aston Villa) 1953/4, 1954/5, 1955/6, 1956/7, 1957/8, 1958/9, 1959/60, 1960/1, 1961/2 (Wolverhampton Wanderers).

Montgomery, F.J. (1) (Coleraine) 1954/5.

Moore, C. (1) (Glentoran) 1948/9.

Moreland, V. (6) (Derby County) 1978/9, 1979/80.

Morgan, S. (18) (Port Vale) 1971/2, 1972/3, 1973/4 (Aston Villa), 1974/5, 1975/6 (Brighton & Hove Albion) (Sparta Rotterdam) 1978/9.

Morrow, S.J. (19) (Arsenal) 1989/90, 1990/1, 1991/2, 1992/93, 1993/94, 1994/95, 1995/96.

Mullan, G. (4) (Glentoran) 1982/3.

Napier, R. (1) (Bolton Wanderers) 1965/6.

Neill, T. (59) (Arsenal) 1960/1, 1961/2, 1962/3, 1963/4, 1964/5, 1965/6, 1966/7, 1967/8, 1968/9, 1969/70 (Hull City) 1970/1, 1971/2, 1972/3.

Nelson, S. (51) (Arsenal) 1969/70, 1970/1, 1971/2, 1972/3, 1973/4, 1974/5, 1975/6, 1976/7, 1977/8, 1978/9, 1979/80, 1980/1, 1981/2 (Brighton & Hove Albion).

Nicholl, C. (51) (Aston Villa) 1974/5, 1975/6, 1976/7 (Southampton), 1977/8, 1978/9, 1979/80, 1980/1, 1981/2, 1982/3 (Grimsby Town) 1983/4.

Nicholl, J.M. (73) (Manchester United) 1975/6, 1976/7, 1977/8, 1978/9, 1979/80, 1980/1, 1981/2 (Toronto Blizzard) 1982/3 (Sunderland) (Toronto Blizzard) (Rangers) 1983/4 (Toronto Blizzard) 1984/5 (West Bromwich Albion) 1985/6.

Nicholson, J. (41) (Manchester United) 1960/1, 1961/2, 1962/3, 1964/5 (Huddersfield Town) 1965/6, 1966/7, 1967/8, 1968/9, 1969/70, 1970/1, 1971/2.

O'Boyle, G. (8) (Dunfermline Athletic) 1993/94 (St Johnstone) 1994/95, 1995/96.

O'Doherty, A. (2) (Coleraine) 1969/70.

O'Driscoll, J. (3) (Swansea City) 1948/9.

O'Kane, L. (20) (Nottingham Forest) 1969/70, 1970/1, 1971/2, 1972/3, 1973/4, 1974/5.

O'Neill, C. (3) (Motherwell) 1988/9, 1989/90, 1990/91.

O'Neill, H.M. (64) (Distillery) 1971/2 (Nottingham Forest) 1972/3, 1973/4, 1974/5, 1975/6, 1976/7, 1977/8, 1978/9, 1979/80, 1980/1 (Norwich City) 1981/2 (Manchester City) (Norwich City) 1982/3 (Notts County) 1983/4, 1984/5.

O'Neill, J. (1) (Sunderland) 1961/2.

O'Neill, J. (39) (Leicester City) 1979/80, 1980/1, 1981/2, 1982/3, 1983/4, 1984/5, 1985/6.

O'Neill, M.A. (29) (Newcastle United) 1987/8, 1988/9 (Dundee United) 1989/90, 1990/1, 1991/2, 1992/93, (Hibernian) 1993/94, 1994/95, 1995/96.

Parke, J. (13) (Linfield) 1963/4 (Hibernian), 1964/5 (Sunderland), 1965/6, 1966/7, 1967/8.

Patterson, D.J. (10) (Crystal Palace) 1993/94, 1994/95, (Luton Town) 1995/96.

Peacock, R. (31) (Celtic) 1951/2, 1952/3, 1953/4, 1954/5, 1955/6, 1956/7, 1957/8, 1958/9, 1959/60, 1960/1 (Coleraine) 1961/2.

Penney, S. (17) (Brighton & Hove Albion) 1984/5, 1985/6, 1986/7, 1987/8, 1988/9.

Platt, J.A. (23) (Middlesbrough) 1975/6, 1977/8, 1979/80, 1980/1, 1981/2, 1982/3, (Ballymena United) 1983/4 (Coleraine) 1985/6.

Quinn, J.M. (46) (Blackburn Rovers) 1984/5, 1985/6, 1986/7, 1987/8 (Leicester) 1988/9 (Bradford City) 1989/90 (West Ham United), 1990/1, (Bournemouth) 1991/2 (Reading) 1992/93, 1993/94, 1994/95, 1995/96.

Quinn, S.J. (1) (Blackpool) 1995/96.

Rafferty, P. (1) (Linfield) 1979/80.

Ramsey, P. (14) (Leicester City) 1983/4, 1984/5, 1985/6, 1986/7, 1987/8, 1988/9.

Rice, P. (49) (Arsenal) 1968/9, 1969/70, 1970/1, 1971/2, 1972/3, 1973/4, 1974/5, 1975/6, 1976/7, 1977/8, 1978/9, 1979/80.

Rogan, A. (17) (Celtic) 1987/8, 1988/9, 1989/90, 1990/1, 1991/2.

Ross, E. (1) (Newcastle United) 1968/9.

Rowland, K. (8) (West Ham United) 1994/95, 1995/96.

Russell, A. (1) (Linfield) 1946/7.

Ryan, R. (1) (West Bromwich Albion) 1949/50.

Sanchez, L.P. (3) (Wimbledon) 1986/7, 1988/9.

Scott, J. (2) (Grimsby Town) 1957/8.

Scott, P. (10) (Everton) 1974/5, 1975/6, (York City) 1977/8, (Aldershot) 1978/9.

Sharkey, P. (1) (Ipswich Town) 1975/6.

Shields, J. (1) (Southampton) 1956/7.

Simpson, W. (12) (Rangers) 1950/1, 1953/4, 1954/5, 1956/7, 1957/8, 1958/9.

Sloan, D. (2) (Oxford) 1968/9, 1970/1.

Sloan, T. (3) (Manchester United) 1978/9.

Sloan, W. (1) (Arsenal) 1946/7.

Smyth, S. (9) (Wolverhampton Wanderers) 1947/8, 1948/9, 1949/50 (Stoke City) 1951/2.

Smyth, W. (4) (Distillery) 1948/9, 1953/4.

Spence, D. (29) (Bury) 1974/5, 1975/6, (Blackpool) 1976/7, 1978/9, 1979/80, (Southend United) 1980/1, 1981/2.

Stevenson, A. (3) (Everton) 1946/7, 1947/8.

Stewart, A. (7) (Glentoran) 1966/7, 1967/8 (Derby) 1968/9.

Stewart, D. (1) (Hull City) 1977/8.

Stewart, I. (31) (QPR) 1981/2, 1982/3, 1983/4, 1984/5, (Newcastle United) 1985/6, 1986/7.

Stewart, T. (1) (Linfield) 1960/1.

Taggart, G.P. (35) (Barnsley) 1989/90, 1990/1, 1991/2, 1992/93, 1993/94, 1994/95.

Todd, S. (11) (Burnley) 1965/6, 1966/7, 1967/8, 1968/9, 1969/70 (Sheffield Wednesday) 1970/1.

Trainor, D. (1) (Crusaders) 1966/7.

Tully, C. (10) (Celtic) 1948/9, 1949/50, 1951/2, 1952/3, 1953/4, 1955/6, 1958/9.

Uprichard, N. (18) (Swindon Town) 1951/2, 1952/3 (Portsmouth) 1954/5, 1955/6, 1957/8, 1958/9.

Vernon, J. (17) (Belfast Celtic) 1946/7 (West Bromwich Albion) 1947/8, 1948/9, 1949/50, 1950/1 , 1951/2.

Walker, J. (1) (Doncaster Rovers) 1954/5.

Walsh, D. (9) (West Bromwich Albion) 1946/7, 1947/8, 1948/9, 1949/50.

Walsh, W. (5) (Manchester City) 1947/8, 1948/9.

Watson, P. (1) (Distillery) 1970/1.

Welsh, S. (4) (Carlisle United) 1965/6, 1966/7.

Whiteside, N. (38) (Manchester United) 1981/2, 1982/3, 1983/4, 1984/5, 1985/6, 1986/7, 1987/8, (Everton) 1989/90.

Williams, P. (1) (WBA) 1990/1.

Wilson, D.J. (24) (Brighton & Hove Albion) 1986/7 (Luton) 1987/8, 1988/9, 1989/90, 1990/1, (Sheffield Wednesday) 1991/2.

Wilson, K.J. (42) (Ipswich Town) 1986/7 (Chelsea) 1987/8, 1988/9, 1989/90, 1990/1, 1991/2 (Notts County) 1992/93, 1993/94 (Walsall) 1994/95.

Wilson, S. (12) (Glenavon) 1961/2, 1963/4, (Falkirk) 1964/5 (Dundee), 1965/6, 1966/7, 1967/8.

Wood, T. J. (1) (Walsall) 1995/96.

Worthington, N. (64) (Sheffield Wednesday) 1983/4, 1984/5, 1985/6, 1986/7, 1987/8, 1988/9, 1989/90, 1990/1, 1991/2, 1992/93, 1993/94 (Leeds United) 1994/95, 1995/96.

Wright, T.J. (22) (Newcastle United) 1988/9, 1989/90, 1991/2, 1992/93, (Nottingham Forest) 1993/94.

SCOTLAND

Aird, J. (4) (Burnley) 1953/4.
Aitken, G.G. (8) (East Fife) 1948/9, 1949/50, 1952/3 (Sunderland) 1953/4.
Aitken, R. (57) (Celtic) 1979/80, 1982/3, 1983/4, 1984/5, 1985/6, 1986/7, 1987/8, (Newcastle United) 1989/90, (St Mirren) 1991/2.
Albiston, A. (14) (Manchester United) 1981/2, 1983/4, 1984/5, 1985/6.
Allan, T. (2) (Dundee) 1973/4.
Anderson, J. (1) (Leicester City) 1953/4.
Archibald, S. (27) (Aberdeen) 1979/80 (Tottenham Hotspur) 1980/1, 1981/2, 1982/3, 1983/4, 1984/5, (Barcelona) 1985/6.
Auld, B. (3) (Celtic) 1958/9, 1959/60.

Baird, H. (1) (Airdrieonians) 1955/6.
Baird, S. (7) (Rangers) 1956/7, 1957/8.
Bannon, E. (11) (Dundee United) 1979/80, 1982/3, 1983/4, 1985/6.
Bauld, W. (3) (Heart of Midlothian) 1949/50.
Baxter, J. (34) (Rangers) 1960/1, 1961/2, 1962/3, 1963/4, 1964/5 (Sunderland) 1965/6, 1966/7, 1967/8.
Bell, W. (2) (Leeds United) 1965/6.
Bernard, P.R.(2) (Oldham Athletic) 1994/95.
Bett, J. (25) (Rangers) 1981/2, 1982/3 (Lokeren) 1983/4, 1984/5 (Aberdeen) 1985/6, 1986/7, 1987/8, 1988/9, 1989/90.
Black, E. (2) (Metz) 1987/8.
Black, I. (1) (Southampton) 1947/8.
Blacklaw, A. (3) (Burnley) 1962/3, 1965/6.
Blackley, J. (7) (Hibernian) 1973/4, 1975/6, 1976/7.
Blair, J. (1) (Blackpool) 1946/7.
Blyth, J. (2) (Coventry City) 1977/8.
Bone, J. (2) (Norwich City) 1971/2, 1972/3.
Booth, S. (13) (Aberdeen) 1992/93, 1993/94, 1994/95, 1995/96.
Bowman, D. (6) (Dundee United) 1991/2, 1992/93, 1993/94.
Boyd, T. (38) (Motherwell) 1990/1 (Chelsea) 1991/2 (Celtic) 1992/93, 1993/94, 1994/95, 1995/96.
Brand, R. (8) (Rangers) 1960/1, 1961/2.
Brazil, A. (13) (Ipswich Town) 1979/80, 1981/2, 1982/3 (Tottenham Hotspur).
Bremner, D. (1) (Hibernian) 1975/6.
Bremner, W. (54) (Leeds United) 1964/5, 1965/6, 1966/7, 1967/8, 1968/9, 1969/70, 1970/1, 1971/2, 1972/3, 1973/4, 1974/5, 1975/6.
Brennan, F. (7) (Newcastle United) 1946/7, 1952/3, 1963/4.
Brogan, J. (4) (Celtic) 1970/1.
Brown, A. (14) (East Fife) 1949/50 (Blackpool) 1951/2, 1952/3, 1953/4.
Brown, H. (3) (Partick Thistle) 1946/7.
Brown, J. (1) (Sheffield United) 1974/5.
Brown, R. (3) (Rangers) 1946/7, 1948/9, 1951/2.
Brown, W. (28) (Dundee) 1957/8, 1958/9, 1959/60 (Tottenham Hotspur) 1961/2, 1962/3, 1963/4, 1964/5, 1965/6.
Brownlie, J. (7) (Hibernian) 1970/1, 1971/2, 1972/3, 1975/6.
Buchan, M. (34) (Aberdeen) 1971/2 (Manchester United), 1972/3, 1973/4, 1974/5, 1975/6, 1976/7, 1977/8, 1978/9.
Buckley, P. (3) (Aberdeen) 1953/4, 1954/5.
Burley, C.W. (12) (Chelsea) 1994/95, 1995/96.
Burley, G. (11) (Ipswich Town) 1978/9, 1979/80, 1981/2.
Burns, F. (1) (Manchester United) 1969/70.
Burns, K. (20) (Birmingham City) 1973/4, 1974/5, 1976/7 (Nottingham Forest) 1977/8, 1978/9, 1979/80, 1980/1.

Burns, T. (8) (Celtic) 1980/1, 1981/2, 1982/3, 1987/8.

Calderwood, C. (14) (Tottenham Hotspur) 1994/95, 1995/96.
Caldow, E. (40) (Rangers) 1956/7, 1957/8, 1958/9, 1959/60, 1960/1, 1961/2, 1962/3.
Callaghan, W. (2) (Dunfermline) 1969/70.
Campbell, R. (5) (Falkirk) 1946/7 (Chelsea) 1949/50.
Campbell, W. (5) (Morton) 1946/7, 1947/8.
Carr, W. (6) (Coventry City) 1969/70, 1970/1, 1971/2, 1972/3.
Chalmers, S. (5) (Celtic) 1964/5, 1965/6, 1966/7.
Clark, J. (4) (Celtic) 1965/6, 1966/7.
Clark, R. (17) (Aberdeen) 1967/8, 1969/70, 1970/1, 1971/2, 1972/3.
Clarke, S. (6) (Chelsea) 1987/8, 1993/94.
Collins, J. (36) (Hibernian) 1987/8, 1989/90, 1990/1 (Celtic) 1991/2, 1992/93, 1993/94, 1994/95, 1995/96.
Collins, R. (31) (Celtic) 1950/1, 1954/5, 1955/6, 1956/7, 1957/8, 1958/9, (Everton) 1964/5, (Leeds United).
Colquhoun, E. (9) (Sheffield United) 1971/2, 1972/3.
Colquhoun, J. (1) (Hearts) 1987/8.
Combe, R. (3) (Hibernian) 1947/8.
Conn, A. (1) (Heart of Midlothian) 1955/6.
Conn, A. (2) (Tottenham Hotspur) 1974/5.
Connachan, E. (2) (Dunfermline Athletic) 1961/2.
Connelly, G. (2) (Celtic) 1973/4.
Connolly, J. (1) (Everton) 1972/3.
Connor, R. (4) (Dundee) 1985/6 (Aberdeen) 1987/8, 1988/9, 1990/91.
Cooke, C. (16) (Dundee) 1965/6 (Chelsea) 1967/8, 1968/9, 1969/70, 1970/1, 1974/5.
Cooper, D. (22) (Rangers) 1979/80, 1983/4, 1984/5, 1985/6, 1986/7 (Motherwell) 1989/90.
Cormack, P. (9) (Hibernian) 1965/6, 1969/70 (Nottingham Forest) 1970/1, 1971/2.
Cowan, J. (25) (Morton) 1947/8, 1948/9, 1949/50, 1950/1, 1951/2 (Motherwell).
Cowie, D. (20) (Dundee) 1952/3, 1953/4, 1954/5, 1955/6, 1956/7, 1957/8.
Cox, C. (1) (Hearts) 1947/8.
Cox, S. (24) (Rangers) 1947/8, 1948/9, 1949/50, 1950/1, 1951/2, 1952/3, 1953/4.
Craig, J. (1) (Celtic) 1976/7.
Craig, J.P. (1) (Celtic) 1967/8.
Craig, T. (1) (Newcastle United) 1975/6.
Crawford, S. (1) (Raith Rovers) 1994/95.
Crerand, P. (16) (Celtic) 1960/1, 1961/2, 1962/3 (Manchester United) 1963/4, 1964/5, 1965/6.
Cropley, A. (2) (Hibernian) 1971/2.
Cruickshank, J. (6) (Heart of Midlothian) 1963/4, 1969/70, 1970/1, 1975/6.
Cullen, M. (1) (Luton Town) 1955/6.
Cumming, J. (9) (Heart of Midlothian) 1954/5, 1959/60.
Cunningham, W. (8) (Preston North End) 1953/4, 1954/5.
Curran, H. (5) (Wolverhampton Wanderers) 1969/70, 1970/1.

Dalglish, K. (102) (Celtic) 1971/2, 1972/3, 1973/4, 1974/5, 1975/6, 1976/7, (Liverpool) 1977/8, 1978/9, 1979/80, 1980/1, 1981/2, 1982/3, 1983/4, 1984/5, 1985/6, 1986/7.
Davidson, J. (8) (Partick Thistle) 1953/4, 1954/5.
Dawson, A. (5) (Rangers) 1979/80, 1982/3.
Deans, D. (2) (Celtic) 1974/5.
Delaney, J. (4) (Manchester United) 1946/7, 1947/8.
Dick, J. (1) (West Ham United) 1958/9.
Dickson, W. (5) (Kilmarnock) 1969/70, 1970/1.

Docherty, T. (25) (Preston North End) 1951/2, 1952/3, 1953/4, 1954/5, 1956/7, 1957/8, 1958/9 (Arsenal).

Dodds, D. (2) (Dundee United) 1983/4.

Donachie, W. (35) (Manchester City) 1971/2, 1972/3, 1973/4, 1975/6, 1976/7, 1977/8, 1978/9.

Dougall, C. (1) (Birmingham City) 1946/7.

Dougan, R. (1) (Heart of Midlothian) 1949/50.

Doyle, J. (1) (Ayr United) 1975/6.

Duncan, A. (6) (Hibernian) 1974/5, 1975/6.

Duncan, D. (3) (East Fife) 1947/8.

Duncanson, J. (1) (Rangers) 1946/7.

Durie, G.S. (31) (Chelsea) 1987/8, 1988/9, 1989/90, 1990/1, (Tottenham Hotspur) 1991/2, 1992/93, (Rangers) 1993/94, 1995/96.

Durrant, I. (11) (Rangers) 1987/8, 1988/9, 1992/93, 1993/94.

Evans, A. (4) (Aston Villa) 1981/2.

Evans, R. (48) (Celtic) 1948/9, 1949/50, 1950/1, 1951/2, 1952/3, 1953/4, 1954/5, 1955/6, 1956/7, 1957/8, 1958/9, 1959/60 (Chelsea).

Ewing, T. (2) (Partick Thistle) 1957/8.

Farm, G. (10) (Blackpool) 1952/3, 1953/4, 1958/9.

Ferguson, D. (2) (Rangers) 1987/8.

Ferguson, D. (5) (Dundee United) 1991/2, 1992/93 (Everton) 1994/95.

Ferguson, I. (8) (Rangers) 1988/9, 1992/93, 1993/94.

Ferguson, R. (7) (Kilmarnock) 1965/6, 1966/7.

Fernie, W. (12) (Celtic) 1953/4, 1954/5, 1956/7, 1957/8.

Flavell, R. (2) (Airdrieonians) 1946/7.

Fleck, R. (4) (Norwich City) 1989/90, 1990/1.

Fleming, C. (1) (East Fife) 1953/4.

Forbes, A. (14) (Sheffield United) 1946/7, 1947/8 (Arsenal) 1949/50, 1950/1, 1951/2.

Ford, D. (3) (Heart of Midlothian) 1973/4.

Forrest, J. (1) (Motherwell) 1957/8.

Forrest, J. (5) (Rangers) 1965/6 (Aberdeen) 1970/1.

Forsyth, A. (10) (Partick Thistle) 1971/2, 1972/3 (Manchester United) 1974/5, 1975/6.

Forsyth, C. (4) (Kilmarnock) 1963/4, 1964/5.

Forsyth, T. (22) (Motherwell) 1970/1 (Rangers) 1973/4, 1975/6, 1976/7, 1977/8.

Fraser, D. (2) (West Bromwich Albion) 1967/8, 1968/9.

Fraser, W. (2) (Sunderland) 1954/5.

Gabriel, J. (2) (Everton) 1960/1, 1961/2.

Gallacher, K.W. (23) (Dundee United) 1987/8, 1988/9, 1990/91 (Coventry City), 1991/2 (Blackburn Rovers) 1992/93, 1993/94, 1995/96.

Galloway, M. (1) (Celtic) 1991/2.

Gardiner, W. (1) (Motherwell) 1957/8.

Gemmell, T. (2) (St Mirren) 1954/5.

Gemmell, T. (18) (Celtic) 1965/6, 1966/7, 1967/8, 1968/9, 1969/70, 1970/1.

Gemmill, A. (43) (Derby County) 1970/1, 1971/2, 1975/6, 1976/7, 1977/8 (Nottingham Forest) 1978/9 (Birmingham City) 1979/80, 1980/1.

Gemmill, S. (6) (Nottingham Forest) 1994/95, 1995/96.

Gibson, D. (7) (Leicester City) 1962/3, 1963/4, 1964/5.

Gillespie, G.T. (13) (Liverpool) 1987/8, 1988/9, 1989/90, (Celtic) 1990/91.

Gilzean, A. (22) (Dundee) 1963/4, 1964/5 (Tottenham Hotspur) 1965/6, 1967/8, 1968/9, 1969/70, 1970/1.

Glavin, R. (1) (Celtic) 1976/7.

Glen, A. (2) (Aberdeen) 1955/6.

Goram, A.L. (39) (Oldham Athletic) 1985/6, 1986/7, (Hibernian) 1988/9, 1989/90, 1990/1, (Rangers) 1991/2, 1992/93, 1993/94, 1994/95, 1995/96.

Gough, C.R. (61) (Dundee United) 1982/3, 1983/4, 1984/5, 1985/6, 1986/7 (Tottenham Hotspur) 1987/8 (Rangers) 1988/9, 1989/90, 1990/1, 1991/2, 1992/93.

Govan, J. (6) (Hibernian) 1947/8, 1948/9.

Graham, A. (10) (Leeds United) 1977/8, 1978/9, 1979/80, 1980/1.

Graham, G. (12) (Arsenal) 1971/2, 1972/3 (Manchester United).

Grant, J. (2) (Hibernian) 1958/9.

Grant, P. (2) (Celtic) 1988/9.

Gray, A. (20) (Aston Villa) 1975/6, 1976/7, 1978/9 (Wolverhampton Wanderers) 1979/80, 1980/1, 1981/2, 1982/3, 1984/5 (Everton).

Gray, E. (12) (Leeds United) 1968/9, 1969/70, 1970/71, 1971/2, 1975/6, 1976/7.

Gray F. (32) (Leeds United) 1975/6, 1978/9, 1979/80 (Nottingham Forest) 1980/1, (Leeds United) 1981/2, 1982/3.

Green, A. (6) (Blackpool) 1970/1 (Newcastle United) 1971/2.

Greig, J. (44) (Rangers) 1963/4, 1964/5, 1965/6, 1966/7, 1967/8, 1968/9, 1969/70, 1970/1, 1975/6.

Gunn, B. (6) (Norwich C) 1989/90, 1992/93, 1993/94.

Haddock, H. (6) (Clyde) 1954/5, 1957/8.

Haffey, F. (2) (Celtic) 1959/60, 1960/1.

Hamilton, A. (24) (Dundee) 1961/2, 1962/3, 1963/4, 1964/5, 1965/6.

Hamilton, G. (5) (Aberdeen) 1946/7, 1950/1, 1953/4.

Hamilton, W. (1) (Hibernian) 1964/5.

Hansen, A. (26) (Liverpool) 1978/9, 1979/80, 1980/1, 1981/2, 1982/3, 1984/5, 1985/6, 1986/7.

Hansen J. (2) (Partick Thistle) 1971/2.

Harper, J. (4) (Aberdeen) 1972/3, 1975/6, 1978/9.

Hartford, A. (50) (West Bromwich Albion) 1971/2, 1975/6 (Manchester City) 1976/7, 1977/8, 1978/9, 1979/80 (Everton) 1980/1, 1981/2 (Manchester City).

Harvey, D. (16) (Leeds United) 1972/3, 1973/4, 1974/5, 1975/6, 1976/7.

Haughney, M. (1) (Celtic) 1953/4.

Hay, D. (27) (Celtic) 1969/70, 1970/1, 1971/2, 1972/3, 1973/4.

Hegarty, P. (8) (Dundee United) 1978/9, 1979/80, 1982/3.

Henderson, J. (7) (Portsmouth) 1952/3, 1953/4, 1955/6, 1958/9 (Arsenal).

Henderson, W. (29) (Rangers) 1962/3, 1963/4, 1964/5, 1965/6, 1966/7, 1967/8, 1968/9, 1969/70.

Hendry, E.C.J. (21) (Blackburn Rovers) 1992/93, 1993/94, 1994/95, 1995/96.

Herd, D. (5) (Arsenal) 1958/9, 1960/1.

Herd, G. (5) (Clyde) 1957/8, 1959/60, 1960/1.

Herriot, J. (8) (Birmingham City) 1968/9, 1969/70.

Hewie, J. (19) (Charlton Athletic) 1955/6, 1956/7, 1957/8, 1958/9, 1959/60.

Holt, D. (5) (Heart of Midlothian) 1962/3, 1963/4.

Holton, J. (15) (Manchester United) 1972/3, 1973/4, 1974/5.

Hope, R. (2) (West Bromwich Albion) 1967/8, 1968/9.

Houliston, W. (3) (Queen of the South) 1948/9.

Houston, S. (1) (Manchester United) 1975/6.

Howie, H. (1) (Hibernian) 1948/9.

Hughes, J. (8) (Celtic) 1964/5, 1965/6, 1967/8, 1968/9, 1969/70.

Hughes, W. (1) (Sunderland) 1974/5.

Humphries, W. (1) (Motherwell) 1951/2.

Hunter, A. (4) (Kilmarnock) 1971/2, 1972/3, (Celtic) 1973/4.

Hunter, W. (3) (Motherwell) 1959/60, 1960/1.

Husband, J. (1) (Partick Thistle) 1946/7.

Hutchison, T. (17) (Coventry City) 1973/4, 1974/5, 1975/6.

Imlach, S. (4) (Nottingham Forest) 1957/8.
Irvine, B. (9) (Aberdeen) 1990/1, 1992/93, 1993/94.

Jackson, C. (8) (Rangers) 1974/5, 1975/6.
Jackson, D. (12) (Hibernian) 1994/95, 1995/96.
Jardine, A. (38) (Rangers) 1970/1, 1971/2, 1972/3, 1973/4, 1974/5, 1976/7, 1977/8, 1978/9, 1979/80.
Jarvie, A. (3) (Airdrieonians) 1970/1.
Jess, E. (13) (Aberdeen) 1992/93, 1993/94, 1994/95, 1995/96.
Johnston, M. (38) (Watford) 1983/4, 1984/5 (Celtic) 1985/6, 1986/7, (Nantes) 1987/8, 1988/9 (Rangers) 1989/90, 1991/2.
Johnston, W. (22) (Rangers) 1965/6, 1967/8, 1968/9, 1969/70, 1970/1 (West Bromwich Albion) 1976/7, 1977/8.
Johnstone, D. (14) (Rangers) 1972/3, 1974/5, 1975/6, 1977/8, 1979/80.
Johnstone, J. (23) (Celtic) 1964/5, 1965/6, 1966/7, 1967/8, 1968/9, 1969/70, 1970/1, 1971/2, 1973/4, 1974/5.
Johnstone, L. (2) (Clyde) 1947/8.
Johnstone, R. (17) (Hibernian) 1950/1, 1951/2, 1952/3, 1953/4, 1954/5, (Manchester City) 1955/6.
Jordan, J. (52) (Leeds United) 1972/3, 1973/4, 1974/5, 1975/6, 1976/7, 1977/8, (Manchester United) 1978/9, 1979/80, 1980/1, 1981/2 (AC Milan).

Kelly, H. (1) (Blackpool) 1951/2.
Kelly, J. (2) (Barnsley) 1948/9.
Kennedy, J. (6) (Celtic) 1963/4, 1964/5.
Kennedy, S. (8) (Aberdeen) 1977/8, 1978/9, 1981/2.
Kennedy, S. (5) (Rangers) 1974/5.
Kerr, A. (2) (Partick Thistle) 1954/5.

Lambert, P. (2) (Motherwell) 1994/95.
Law, D. (55) (Huddersfield Town) 1958/9, 1959/60 (Manchester City) 1960/1, 1961/2 (Torino) 1962/3 (Manchester United) 1963/4, 1964/5, 1965/6, 1966/7, 1967/8, 1968/9, 1971/2, 1973/4 (Manchester City).
Lawrence, T. (3) (Liverpool) 1962/3, 1968/9.
Leggat, G. (18) (Aberdeen) 1955/6, 1956/7, 1957/8, 1958/9 (Fulham) 1959/60.
Leighton, J. (74) (Aberdeen) 1982/3, 1983/4, 1984/5, 1985/6, 1986/7, 1987/8, (Manchester United) 1988/9, 1989/90 (Hibernian) 1993/94, 1994/95, 1995/96.
Lennox, R. (10) (Celtic) 1966/7, 1967/8, 1968/9.
Leslie, L. (5) (Airdrieonians) 1960/1.
Levein, C. (16) (Hearts) 1989/90, 1991/2, 1992/93, 1993/94, 1994/95.
Liddell, W. (28) (Liverpool) 1946/7, 1947/8, 1949/50, 1950/1, 195/2, 1952/3, 1953/4, 1954/5, 1955/6.
Linwood, A. (1) (Clyde) 1949/50.
Little, A. (1) (Rangers) 1952/3.
Logie, J. (1) (Arsenal) 1952/3.
Long, H. (1) (Clyde) 1946/7.
Lorimer, P. (21) (Leeds United) 1969/70, 1970/1, 1971/2, 1972/3, 1973/4, 1974/5, 1975/6.

Macari, L. (24) (Celtic) 1971/2, 1972/3 (Manchester United) 1974/5, 1976/7, 1977/8, 1978/9.
Macaulay, A. (7) (Brentford) 1946/7 (Arsenal) 1947/8.
MacDougall, E. (7) (Norwich City) 1974/5, 1975/6.
Mackay, D. (22) (Heart of Midlothian) 1956/7, 1957/8, 1958/9 (Tottenham Hotspur) 1959/60, 1960/1, 1962/3, 1963/4, 1965/6.
Mackay, G. (4) (Heart of Midlothian) 1987/8.

Malpas, M. (55) (Dundee United) 1983/4, 1984/5, 1985/6, 1986/7, 1987/8, 1988/9, 1989/90, 1990/1, 1991/2, 1992/93.

Marshall, G. (1) (Celtic) 1991/2.

Martin, B. (2) (Motherwell) 1994/95.

Martin, F. (6) (Aberdeen) 1953/4, 1954/5.

Martin, N. (3) (Hibernian) 1964/5, 1965/6 (Sunderland).

Martis, J. (1) (Motherwell) 1960/1.

Mason, J. (7) (Third Lanark) 1948/9, 1949/50, 1950/1.

Masson, D. (17) (QPR) 1975/6, 1976/7, 1977/8 (Derby County) 1978/9.

Mathers, D. (1) (Partick Thistle) 1953/4.

McAllister, G. (44) (Leicester City) 1989/90, 1990/1 (Leeds United), 1991/2, 1992/93, 1993/94, 1994/95, 1995/96.

McAvennie, F. (5) (West Ham United) 1985/6 (Celtic) 1987/8.

McBride, J. (2) (Celtic) 1966/7.

McCall, S.M. (37) (Everton) 1989/90, 1990/1, (Rangers) 1991/2, 1992/93, 1993/94, 1994/95, 1995/96.

McCalliog, J. (5) (Sheffield Wednesday) 1966/7, 1967/8, 1968/9, 1970/1 (Wolverhampton Wanderers).

McCann, R. (5) (Motherwell) 1958/9, 1959/60, 1960/1.

McClair, B. (30) (Celtic) 1986/7 (Manchester United) 1987/8, 1988/9, 1989/90, 1990/1, 1991/2, 1992/93.

McCloy, P. (4) (Rangers) 1972/3.

McCoist, A. (54) (Rangers) 1985/6, 1986/7, 1987/8, 1988/9, 1989/90, 1990/1, 1991/2, 1992/93, 1995/96.

McColl, I. (14) (Rangers) 1949/50, 1950/1, 1956/7, 1957/8.

McCreadie, E. (23) (Chelsea) 1964/5, 1965/6, 1966/7, 1967/8, 1968/9.

MacDonald, A. (1) (Rangers) 1975/6.

MacDonald, J. (2) (Sunderland) 1955/6.

McFarlane, W. (1) (Heart of Midlothian) 1946/7.

McGarr, E. (2) (Aberdeen) 1969/70.

McGarvey, F. (7) (Liverpool) 1978/9 (Celtic) 1983/4.

McGhee, M. (4) (Aberdeen) 1982/3, 1983/4.

McGinlay, J. (9) (Bolton Wanderers) 1993/94, 1994/95, 1995/96.

McGrain, D. (62) (Celtic) 1972/3, 1973/4, 1974/5, 1975/6, 1976/7, 1977/8, 1979/80, 1980/1, 1981/2.

McGrory, J. (3) (Kilmarnock) 1964/5, 1965/6.

McInally, A. (8) (Aston Villa) 1988/9 (Bayern Munich) 1989/90.

McInally, J. (10) (Dundee United) 1986/7, 1987/8, 1990/1, 1991/2, 1992/93.

McKay, D. (14) (Celtic) 1958/9, 1959/60, 1960/1, 1961/2.

McKean, R. (1) (Rangers) 1975/6.

McKenzie, J. (9) (Partick Thistle) 1953/4, 1954/5, 1955/6.

McKimmie, S. (40) (Aberdeen) 1988/9, 1989/90, 1990/1, 1991/2, 1992/93, 1993/94, 1994/95, 1995/96.

McKinlay, T. (6) (Celtic) 1995/96.

McKinlay, W. (18) (Dundee United) 1993/94, 1994/95, 1995/96 (Blackburn Rovers).

McKinnon, R. (28) (Rangers) 1965/6, 1966/7, 1967/8, 1968/9, 1969/70, 1970/1.

McKinnon, R. (3) (Motherwell) 1993/94, 1994/95.

McLaren, A. (4) (Preston North End) 1946/7, 1947/8.

McLaren, A. (24) (Heart of Midlothian) 1991/2, 1992/93, 1993/94, 1994/95 (Rangers), 1995/96.

McLean, G. (1) (Dundee) 1967/8.

McLean, T. (6) (Kilmarnock) 1968/9, 1969/70, 1970/1.

McLeish, A. (77) (Aberdeen) 1979/80, 1980/1, 1981/2, 1982/3, 1983/4, 1984/5, 1985/6, 1986/7, 1987/8, 1988/9, 1989/90, 1990/1, 1992/93.

McLeod, J. (4) (Hibernian) 1960/1.

MacLeod, M. (20) (Celtic) 1984/5, 1986/7 (Borussia Dortmund) 1987/8, 1988/9, 1989/90, 1990/1 (Hibernian).

McLintock, F. (9) (Leicester City) 1962/3, 1964/5 (Arsenal) 1966/7, 1969/70, 1970/1.

McMillan, I. (6) (Airdrieonians) 1951/2, 1954/5, 1955/6 (Rangers) 1960/1.

McNaught, W. (5) (Raith Rovers) 1950/1, 1951/2, 1954/5.

McNeill, W. (29) (Celtic) 1960/1, 1961/2, 1962/3, 1963/4, 1964/5, 1965/6, 1966/7, 1967/8, 1968/9, 1969/70, 1971/2.

McPhail, J. (5) (Celtic) 1949/50, 1950/1, 1953/4.

McPherson, D. (27) (Hearts) 1988/9, 1989/90, 1990/1, 1991/2 (Rangers) 1992/93.

McQueen, G. (30) (Leeds United) 1973/4, 1974/5, 1975/6, 1976/7, 1977/8, (Manchester United) 1978/9, 1979/80, 1980/1.

McStay, P. (73) (Celtic) 1983/4, 1984/5, 1985/6, 1986/7, 1987/8, 1988/9, 1989/90, 1990/1, 1991/2, 1992/93, 1993/94, 1994/95, 1995/96.

Millar, J. (2) (Rangers) 1962/3.

Miller, W. (6) (Celtic) 1946/7, 1947/8.

Miller, W. (65) (Aberdeen) 1974/5, 1977/8, 1979/80, 1980/1, 1981/2, 1982/3, 1983/4, 1984/5, 1985/6, 1986/7, 1987/8, 1988/9, 1989/90.

Mitchell, R. (2) (Newcastle United) 1950/1.

Mochan, N. (3) (Celtic) 1953/4.

Moir, W. (1) (Bolton Wanderers) 1949/50.

Moncur, R. (16) (Newcastle United) 1967/8, 1969/70, 1970/1, 1971/2.

Morgan, W. (21) (Burnley) 1967/8 (Manchester United) 1971/2, 1972/3, 1973/4.

Morris, H. (1) (East Fife) 1949/50.

Mudie, J. (17) (Blackpool) 1956/7, 1957/8.

Mulhall, G. (3) (Aberdeen) 1959/60, 1962/3 (Sunderland) 1963/4.

Munro, F. (9) (Wolverhampton Wanderers) 1970/1, 1974/5.

Munro, I. (7) (St Mirren) 1978/9, 1979/80.

Murdoch, R. (12) (Celtic) 1965/6, 1966/7, 1967/8, 1968/9, 1969/70.

Murray, J. (5) (Heart of Midlothian) 1957/8.

Murray, S. (1) (Aberdeen) 1971/2.

Narey, D. (35) (Dundee United) 1976/7, 1978/9, 1979/80, 1980/1, 1981/2, 1982/3, 1985/6, 1986/7, 1988/9.

Nevin, P.K.F. (28) (Chelsea) 1985/6, 1986/7, 1987/8 (Everton) 1988/9, 1990/1, 1991/2 (Tranmere Rovers) 1992/93, 1993/94, 1994/95, 1995/96.

Nicholas, C. (20) (Celtic) 1982/3, (Arsenal) 1983/4, 1984/5, 1985/6, 1986/7, (Aberdeen) 1988/9.

Nicol, S. (27) (Liverpool) 1984/5, 1985/6, 1987/8, 1988/9, 1989/90, 1990/1, 1991/2.

O'Donnell, P. (1) (Motherwell) 1993/94.

O'Hare, J. (13) (Derby County) 1969/70, 1970/1, 1971/2.

O'Neil, B. (1) (Celtic) 1995/96.

Ormond, W. (6) (Hibernian) 1953/4, 1958/9.

Orr, T. (2) (Morton) 1951/2.

Parker, A. (15) (Falkirk) 1954/5, 1955/6, 1956/7, 1957/8.

Parlane, D. (12) (Rangers) 1972/3, 1974/5, 1975/6, 1976/7.

Paton, A. (2) (Motherwell) 1951/2.

Pearson, T. (2) (Newcastle United) 1946/7.

Penman, A. (1) (Dundee) 1965/6.

Pettigrew, W. (5) (Motherwell) 1975/6, 1976/7.

Plenderleith, J. (1) (Manchester City) 1960/1.

Provan, D. (5) (Rangers) 1963/4, 1965/6.

Provan, D. (10) (Celtic) 1979/80, 1980/1, 1981/2.

Quinn, P. (4) (Motherwell) 1960/1, 1961/2.

Redpath, W. (9) (Motherwell) 1948/9, 1950/1, 1951/2.
Reilly, L. (38) (Hibernian) 1948/9, 1949/50, 1950/1, 1951/2, 1952/3, 1953/4, 1954/5, 1955/6, 1956/7.
Ring, T. (12) (Clydebank) 1952/3, 1954/5, 1956/7, 1957/8.
Rioch, B. (24) (Derby County) 1974/5, 1975/6, 1976/7, (Everton) 1977/8, (Derby County) 1978/9.
Robb, D. (5) (Aberdeen) 1970/1.
Robertson, A. (5) (Clyde) 1954/5, 1957/8.
Robertson, D. (3) (Rangers) 1991/2, 1993/94.
Robertson, H. (1) (Dundee) 1961/2.
Robertson, J. (1) (Tottenham Hotspur) 1964/5.
Robertson, J. (16) (Heart of Midlothian) 1990/1, 1991/2, 1992/93, 1994/95, 1995/96.
Robertson, J.N. (28) (Nottingham Forest) 1977/8, 1978/9, 1979/80, 1980/1, 1981/2, 1982/3 (Derby County) 1983/4.
Robinson, B. (4) (Dundee) 1973/4, 1974/5.
Rough, A. (53) (Partick Thistle) 1975/6, 1976/7, 1977/8, 1978/9, 1979/80, 1980/1, 1981/2, (Hibernian) 1985/6.
Rougvie, D. (1) (Aberdeen) 1983/4.
Rutherford, E. (1) (Rangers) 1947/8.

St John, I. (21) (Motherwell) 1958/9, 1959/60, 1960/1, 1961/2 (Liverpool) 1962/3, 1963/4, 1964/5.
Schaedler, E. (1) (Hibernian) 1973/4.
Scott, A. (16) (Rangers) 1956/7, 1957/8, 1958/9, 1961/2 (Everton) 1963/4, 1964/5, 1965/6.
Scott, J. (1) (Hibernian) 1965/6.
Scott, J. (2) (Dundee) 1970/1.
Scoular, J. (9) (Portsmouth) 1950/1, 1951/2, 1952/3.
Sharp, G.M. (12) (Everton) 1984/5, 1985/6, 1986/7, 1987/8.
Shaw, D. (8) (Hibernian) 1946/7, 1947/8, 1948/9.
Shaw, J. (4) (Rangers) 1946/7, 1947/8.
Shearer, D. (7) (Aberdeen) 1993/94, 1994/95, 1995/96.
Shearer, R. (4) (Rangers) 1960/1.
Simpson, N. (4) (Aberdeen) 1982/3, 1983/4, 1986/7, 1987/8.
Simpson, R. (5) (Celtic) 1966/7, 1967/8, 1968/9.
Sinclair, J. (1) (Leicester City) 1965/6.
Smith, D. (2) (Aberdeen) 1965/6, 1967/8 (Rangers).
Smith, E. (2) (Celtic) 1958/9.
Smith, G. (18) (Hibernian) 1946/7, 1947/8, 1951/2, 1954/5, 1955/6, 1956/7.
Smith, H.G. (3) (Heart of Midlothian) 1987/8, 1991/2.
Smith, J. (4) (Aberdeen) 1967/8, 1973/4 (Newcastle United).
Souness, G. (54) (Middlesbrough) 1974/5 (Liverpool) 1977/8, 1978/9, 1979/80, 1980/1, 1981/2, 1982/3, 1983/4, (Sampdoria) 1984/5, 1985/6.
Speedie, D.R. (10) (Chelsea) 1984/5, 1985/6, (Coventry City) 1988/9
Spencer, J. (12) (Chelsea) 1994/95, 1995/96.
Stanton, P. (16) (Hibernian) 1965/6, 1968/9, 1969/70, 1970/1, 1971/2, 1972/3, 1973/4.
Steel, W. (30) (Morton) 1946/7, 1947/8 (Derby County) 1948/9, 1949/50, (Dundee) 1950/1, 1951/2, 1952/3.
Stein, C. (21) (Rangers) 1968/9, 1969/70, 1970/1, 1971/2 (Coventry City).
Stephen, J. (2) (Bradford City) 1946/7, 1947/8.
Stewart, D. (1) (Leeds United) 1977/8.
Stewart, J. (2) (Kilmarnock) 1976/7 (Middlesbrough) 1978/9.
Stewart, R. (10) (West Ham United) 1980/1, 1981/2, 1983/4, 1986/7.
Strachan, G. (50) (Aberdeen) 1979/80, 1980/1, 1981/2, 1982/3, 1983/4 (Manchester United) 1984/5, 1985/6, 1986/7, 1987/8, 1988/9 (Leeds United) 1989/90, 1990/1, 1991/2.

Sturrock, P. (20) (Dundee United) 1980/1, 1981/2, 1982/3, 1983/4, 1984/5, 1985/6, 1986/7.

Telfer, W. (1) (St Mirren) 1953/4.
Thomson, W. (7) (St Mirren) 1979/80, 1980/1, 1981/2, 1982/3, 1983/4.
Thornton, W. (7) (Rangers) 1946/7, 1947/8, 1948/9, 1951/2.
Toner, W. (2) (Kilmarnock) 1958/9.
Turnbull, E. (8) (Hibernian) 1947/8, 1950/1, 1957/8.

Ure, I. (11) (Dundee) 1961/2, 1962/3 (Arsenal) 1963/4, 1967/8.

Waddell, W. (17) (Rangers) 1946/7, 1948/9, 1949/50, 1950/1, 1951/2, 1953/4, 1954/5.
Walker, A. (3) (Celtic) 1987/8, 1994/95.
Walker, J.N. (2) (Heart of Midlothian) 1992/93 (Partick Thistle) 1995/96.
Wallace, I.A. (3) (Coventry City) 1977/8, 1978/9.
Wallace, W.S.B. (7) (Heart of Midlothian) 1964/5, 1965/6, 1966/7 (Celtic) 1967/8, 1968/9.
Wardhaugh, J. (2) (Heart of Midlothian) 1954/5, 1956/7.
Wark, J. (29) (Ipswich Town) 1978/9, 1979/80, 1980/1, 1981/2, 1982/3, 1983/4 (Liverpool) 1984/5.
Watson, J. (2) (Motherwell) 1947/8 (Huddersfield Town) 1953/4.
Watson, R. (1) (Motherwell) 1970/1.
Weir, A. (6) (Motherwell) 1958/9, 1959/60.
Weir, P. (6) (St Mirren) 1979/80, 1982/3, (Aberdeen) 1983/4.
White, J. (22) (Falkirk) 1958/9, 1959/60 (Tottenham Hotspur) 1960/1, 1961/2, 1962/3, 1963/4.
Whyte, D. (9) (Celtic) 1987/8, 1988/9, 1991/2 (Middlesbrough) 1992/93, 1994/95, 1995/96.
Wilson, A. (1) (Portsmouth) 1953/4.
Wilson, D. (22) (Rangers) 1960/1, 1961/2, 1962/3, 1963/4, 1964/5.
Wilson, I.A. (5) (Leicester City) 1986/7, (Everton) 1987/8.
Wilson, P. (1) (Celtic) 1974/5.
Wilson, R. (2) (Arsenal) 1971/2.
Wood, G. (4) (Everton) 1978/9, 1981/2 (Arsenal).
Woodburn, W. (24) (Rangers) 1946/7, 1947/8, 1948/9, 1949/50, 1950/1, 1951/2.
Wright, K. (1) (Hibernian) 1991/2.
Wright, S. (2) (Aberdeen) 1992/93.
Wright, T. (3) (Sunderland) 1952/3.

Yeats, R. (2) (Liverpool) 1964/5, 1965/6.
Yorston, H. (1) (Aberdeen) 1954/5.
Young, A. (9) (Heart of Midlothian) 1959/60. 1960/1 (Everton) 1965/6.
Young, G. (53) (Rangers) 1946/7, 1947/8, 1948/9, 1949/50, 1950/1, 1951/2, 1952/3, 1953/4, 1954/5, 1955/6, 1956/7.
Younger, T. (24) (Hibernian) 1954/5, 1955/6, 1956/7 (Liverpool) 1957/8.

WALES
Aizlewood, M. (39) (Charlton Athletic) 1985/6, 1986/7 (Leeds United) 1987/8, 1988/9 (Bradford City) 1989/90, 1990/1 (Bristol City), 1991/2, 1992/93, 1993/94 (Cardiff City) 1994/95.
Allchurch, I. (68) (Swansea Town) 1950/1, 1951/2, 1952/3, 1953/4, 1954/5, 1955/6, 1956/7, 1957/8, 1958/9 (Newcastle United) 1959/60, 1960/1, 1961/2, 1962/3 (Cardiff City) 1963/4, 1964/5, 1965/6 (Swansea Town).
Allchurch L. (11) (Swansea Town) 1954/5, 1955/6, 1957/8, 1958/9, 1961/2, (Sheffield United) 1963/4.

Allen, B. (2) (Coventry City) 1950/1.
Allen, M. (14) (Watford) 1985/6, (Norwich City) 1988/9 (Millwall) 1989/90, 1990/1, 1991/2, 1992/93 (Newcastle United) 1993/94.

Baker, C. (7) (Cardiff City) 1957/8, 1959/60. 1960/1, 1961/2.
Baker, W. (1) (Cardiff City) 1947/8.
Barnes, W. (22) (Arsenal) 1947/8, 1948/9, 1949/50, 1950/1, 1951/2, 1953/4, 1954/5.
Berry, G. (5) (Wolverhampton Wanderers) 1978/9, 1979/80, 1982/3 (Stoke City).
Blackmore, C.G. (38) (Manchester United) 1984/5, 1985/6, 1986/7, 1987/8, 1988/9, 1989/90, 1990/1, 1991/2, 1992/93, 1993/94.
Blake, N. (6) (Sheffield United) 1993/94, 1994/95, 1995/96 (Bolton Wanderers).
Bodin, P.J. (23) (Swindon Town) 1989/90, 1990/1 (Crystal Palace), 1991/2 (Swindon Town) 1992/93, 1993/94, 1994/95.
Bowen, D. (19) (Arsenal) 1954/5, 1956/7, 1957/8, 1958/9.
Bowen, J.P. (1) (Swansea City) 1993/94.
Bowen, M.R. (37) (Tottenham Hotspur) 1985/6 (Norwich City) 1987/8, 1988/9, 1989/90, 1991/2, 1992/93, 1993/94, 1994/95, 1995/96.
Boyle, T. (2) (Crystal Palace) 1980/1.
Browning, M.T. (2) (Bristol Rovers) 1995/96.
Burgess, R. (32) (Tottenham Hotspur) 1946/7, 1947/8, 1948/9, 1949/50, 1950/1, 1951/2, 1952/3, 1953/4.
Burton, O. (9) (Norwich City) 1962/3 (Newcastle United) 1963/4, 1968/9, 1971/2.

Cartwright, L. (7) (Coventry City) 1973/4, 1975/6, 1976/7 (Wrexham) 1977/8, 1978/9.
Charles, J. (38) (Leeds United) 1949/50, 1950/1, 1952/3, 1953/4, 1954/5, 1955/6, 1956/7 (Juventus) 1957/8, 1959/60, 1961/2, 1962/3, (Leeds United) (Cardiff City) 1963/4, 1964/5.
Charles, J.M. (19) (Swansea Town) 1980/1, 1981/2, 1982/3, 1983/4 (QPR), (Oxford United) 1984/5, 1985/6, 1986/7.
Charles, M. (31) (Swansea Town) 1954/5, 1955/6, 1956/7, 1957/8, 1958/9 (Arsenal) 1960/1, 1961/2 (Cardiff City) 1962/3.
Clarke, R. (22) (Manchester City) 1948/9, 1949/50, 1950/1, 1951/2, 952/3, 1953/4, 1954/5, 1955/6.
Coleman, C. (14) (Crystal Palace) 1991/2, 1992/93, 1993/94, 1994/95, 1995/96 (Blackburn Rovers).
Cornforth, J.M. (2) (Swansea City) 1994/95.
Coyne, D. (1) (Tranmere Rovers) 1995/96.
Crowe, V. (16) (Aston Villa) 1958/9, 1959/60, 1960/1, 1961/2, 1962/3.
Curtis, A. (35) (Swansea City) 1975/6, 1976/7, 1977/8, 1978/9, 1979/80, 1981/2, 1982/3, 1983/4 (Southampton) 1984/5, 1985/6, 1986/7 (Cardiff City).

Daniel, R. (21) (Arsenal) 1950/1, 1951/2, 1952/3, 1953/4 (Sunderland) 1954/5, 1956/7.
Davies, A. (13) (Manchester United) 1982/3, 1983/4, 1984/5, (Newcastle United) 1985/6 (Swansea City) 1987/8, 1988/9 (Bradford City) 1989/90.
Davies, D. (52) (Everton) 1974/5, 1975/6, 1976/7, 1977/8, (Wrexham) 1978/9, 1979/80, 1980/1 (Swansea City) 1981/2, 1982/3.
Davies, G. (16) (Fulham) 1979/80, 1981/2, 1982/3, 1983/4, 1984/5 (Chelsea), (Manchester City) 1985/6.
Davies, R. Wyn (34) (Bolton Wanderers) 1963/4, 1964/5, 1965/6, 1966/7 (Newcastle United) 1967/8, 1968/9, 1969/70, 1970/1, 1971/2 (Manchester City), (Blackpool) 1972/3 (Manchester United) 1973/4.
Davies, Reg (6) (Newcastle United) 1952/3, 1953/4, 1957/8.
Davies, Ron (29) (Norwich City) 1963/4, 1964/5, 1965/6, 1966/7, (Southampton) 1967/8, 1968/9, 1969/70, 1970/1, 1971/2, 1973/4 (Portsmouth).

Davies, S.I. (1) (Manchester United) 1995/96.
Davis, C. (1) (Charlton Athletic) 1971/2.
Davis, G. (4) (Wrexham) 1977/8.
Deacy, N. (11) (PSV Eindhoven) 1976/7, 1977/8 (Beringen) 1978/9.
Derrett, S. (4) (Cardiff City) 1968/9, 1969/70, 1970/1.
Dibble, A. (3) (Luton Town) 1985/6, (Manchester City) 1988/9.
Durban, A. (27) (Derby County) 1965/6, 1966/7, 1967/8, 1968/9, 1969/70, 1970/1, 1971/2.
Dwyer, P. (10) (Cardiff City) 1977/8, 1978/9, 1979/80.

Edwards. C.N.H. (1) (Swansea City) 1995/96.
Edwards, I. (4) (Chester) 1977/8, 1978/9, 1979/80.
Edwards, G. (12) (Birmingham City) 1946/7, 1947/8 (Cardiff City) 1948/9, 1949/50.
Edwards, T. (2) (Charlton Athletic) 1956/7.
Emanuel, J. (2) (Bristol City) 1972/3.
England, M. (44) (Blackburn Rovers) 1961/2, 1962/3, 1963/4, 1964/5, 1965/6, 1966/7 (Tottenham Hotspur) 1967/8, 1968/9, 1969/70, 1970/1, 1971/2, 1972/3, 1973/4, 1974/5.
Evans, B. (7) (Swansea City) 1971/2, 1972/3 (Hereford United) 1973/4.
Evans, I. (13) (Crystal Palace) 1975/6, 1976/7, 1977/8.
Evans, R. (1) (Swansea Town) 1963/4.

Felgate, D. (1) (Lincoln City) 1983/4.
Flynn, B. (66) (Burnley) 1974/5, 1975/6, 1976/7, 1977/8 (Leeds United) 1978/9, 1979/80, 1980/1, 1981/2, 1982/3 (Burnley) 1983/4.
Ford, T. (38) (Swansea City) 1946/7 (Aston Villa) 1947/8, 1948/9, 1949/50, 1950/1 (Sunderland) 1951/2, 1952/3 (Cardiff City) 1953/4, 1954/5, 1955/6, 1956/7.
Foulkes, W. (11) (Newcastle United) 1951/2, 1952/3, 1953/4.

Giggs, R.J. (16) (Manchester United) 1991/2, 1992/93, 1993/94, 1994/95, 1995/96.
Giles, D. (12) (Swansea City) 1979/80, 1980/1, 1981/2 (Crystal Palace) 1982/3.
Godfrey, B. (3) (Preston North End) 1963/4, 1964/5.
Goss, J. (9) (Norwich City) 1990/1, 1991/2, 1993/94, 1994/95, 1995/96.
Green, C. (15) (Birmingham City) 1964/5, 1965/6, 1966/7, 1967/8, 1968/9.
Griffiths, A. (17) (Wrexham) 1970/1, 1974/5, 1975/6, 1976/7.
Griffiths, H. (1) (Swansea Town) 1952/3.
Griffiths, M. (11) (Leicester City) 1946/7, 1948/9, 1949/50, 1950/1, 1953/4.

Hall, G.D. (9) (Chelsea) 1987/8, 1988/9, 1990/91, 1991/2.
Harrington, A. (11) (Cardiff City) 1955/6, 1956/7, 1957/8, 1960/1, 1961/2.
Harris, C. (24) (Leeds United) 1975/6, 1977/8, 1978/9, 1979/80, 1980/1, 1981/2.
Harris, W. (6) (Middlesbrough) 1953/4, 1956/7, 1957/8.
Hartson, J. (5) (Arsenal) 1994/95, 1995/96.
Hennessey, T. (39) (Birmingham City) 1961/2, 1962/3, 1963/4, 1964/5, 1965/6, (Nottingham Forest) 1966/7, 1967/8, 1968/9, 1969/70 (Derby County) 1971/2, 1972/3.
Hewitt, R. (5) (Cardiff City) 1957/8.
Hill, M. (2) (Ipswich Town) 1971/2.
Hockey, T. (9) (Sheffield United) 1971/2, 1972/3 (Norwich City) 1973/4, (Aston Villa).
Hodges, G. (18) (Wimbledon) 1983/4, 1986/7 (Newcastle United) 1987/8, (Watford) 1989/90, (Sheffield United) 1991/2, 1995/96.
Holden, A. (1) (Chester) 1983/4.
Hole, B. (30) (Cardiff City) 1962/3, 1963/4, 1964/5, 1965/6, 1966/7, (Blackburn Rovers) 1967/8, 1968/9 (Aston Villa) 1969/70 (Swansea Town) 1970/71.
Hollins, D. (11) (Newcastle United) 1961/2, 1962/3, 1963/4, 1964/5, 1965/6.
Hopkins, J. (16) (Fulham) 1982/3, 1983/4, 1984/5 (Crystal P) 1989/90.

Hopkins, M. (34) (Tottenham Hotspur) 1955/6, 1956/7, 1957/8, 1958/9, 1959/60, 1960/1, 1961/2, 1962/3.

Horne, B. (54) (Portsmouth) 1987/8, (Southampton) 1988/9, 1989/90, 1990/1, 1991/2 (Everton) 1992/93, 1993/94, 1994/95, 1995/96.

Howells, R. (2) (Cardiff City) 1953/4.

Hughes, C.M. (5) (Luton Town) 1991/2, 1993/94, 1995/96.

Hughes, I. (4) (Luton Town) 1950/1.

Hughes, L.M. (60) (Manchester United) 1983/4, 1984/5, 1985/6, 1986/7 (Barcelona) 1987/8, 1988/9 (Manchester United) 1989/90, 1990/1, 1991/2, 1992/93, 1993/94, 1994/95 (Chelsea) 1995/96.

Hughes, W. (3) (Birmingham City) 1946/7.

Hughes, W.A. (5) (Blackburn Rovers) 1948/9.

Humphreys, J. (1) (Everton) 1946/7.

Jackett, K. (31) (Watford) 1982/3, 1983/4, 1984/5, 1985/6, 1986/7, 1987/8.

James, G. (9) (Blackpool) 1965/6, 1966/7, 1967/8, 1970/1.

James, L. (54) (Burnley) 1971/2, 1972/3, 1973/4, 1974/5, 1975/6 (Derby County) 1976/7, 1977/8 (QPR) (Burnley) 1978/9, 1979/80 (Swansea City) 1980/1, 1981/2 (Sunderland) 1982/3.

James, R.M. (47) (Swansea City) 1978/9, 1979/80, 1981/2, 1982/3 (Stoke City) 1983/4, 1984/5 (QPR) 1985/6, 1986/7 (Leicester City) 1987/8 (Swansea City).

Jarvis, A. (3) (Hull City) 1966/7.

Jenkins, S.R. (3) (Swansea City) 1995/96 (Huddersfield Town).

Johnson, M. (1) (Swansea City) 1963/4.

Jones, A. (6) (Port Vale) 1986/7, 1987/8 (Charlton Athletic) 1989/90.

Jones, Barrie (15) (Swansea Town) 1962/3, 1963/4, 1964/5 (Plymouth Argyle) 1968/9 (Cardiff City).

Jones, Bryn. (4) (Arsenal) 1946/7, 1947/8, 1948/9.

Jones, C. (59) (Swansea Town) 1953/4, 1955/6, 1956/7, 1957/8 (Tottenham Hotspur) 1958/9, 1959/60, 1960/1, 1961/2, 1962/3, 1963/4, 1964/5, 1966/7, 1967/8, 1968/9 (Fulham) 1969/70.

Jones, D. (8) (Norwich City) 1975/6, 1977/8, 1979/80.

Jones, E. (4) (Swansea Town) 1947/8 (Tottenham Hotspur) 1948/9.

Jones, J. (72) (Liverpool) 1975/6, 1976/7, 1977/8 (Wrexham) 1978/9, 1979/80, 1980/1, 1981/2, 1982/3 (Chelsea) 1983/4, 1984/5 (Huddersfield Town) 1985/6.

Jones, K. (1) (Aston Villa) 1949/50.

Jones, R. (1) (Sheffield Wednesday) 1993/94.

Jones, T.G. (13) (Everton) 1946/7, 1947/8, 1948/9, 1949/50.

Jones, V.P. (5) (Wimbledon) 1994/95, 1995/96.

Jones, W. (1) (Bristol City) 1970/1.

Kelsey, J. (41) (Arsenal) 1953/4, 1954/5, 1955/6, 1956/7, 1957/8, 1958/9, 1959/60, 1960/1, 1961/2.

King, J. (1) (Swansea Town) 1954/5.

Kinsey, N. (7) (Norwich City) 1950/1, 1951/2, 1953/4 (Birmingham City) 1955/6.

Knill, A.R. (1) (Swansea City) 1988/9.

Krzywicki, R. (West Bromwich Albion) 1969/70 (Huddersfield Town) 1970/1, 1971/2.

Lambert, R. (5) (Liverpool) 1946/7, 1947/8, 1948/9.

Law, B.J. (1) (QPR), 1989/90.

Lea, C. (2) (Ipswich Town) 1964/5.

Leek, K. (13) (Leicester City) 1960/1, 1961/2 (Newcastle United) (Birmingham City) 1962/3, 1964/5.

Legg, A. (2) (Birmingham City) 1995/96.

Lever, A. (1) (Leicester City) 1952/3.

277

Lewis, D. (1) (Swansea City) 1982/3.
Lloyd, B. (3) (Wrexham) 1975/6.
Lovell, S. (6) (Crystal Palace) 1981/2 (Millwall) 1984/5, 1985/6.
Lowndes, S. (10) (Newport County) 1982/3 (Millwall) 1984/5, 1985/6, 1986/7, (Barnsley) 1987/8.
Lowrie, G. (4) (Coventry City) 1947/8, 1948/9 (Newcastle United).
Lucas, M. (4) (Leyton Orient) 1961/2, 1962/3.
Lucas, W. (7) (Swansea Town) 1948/9, 1949/50, 1950/1.

Maguire, G.T. (7) (Portsmouth) 1989/90, 1991/2.
Mahoney, J. (51) (Stoke City) 1967/8, 1968/9, 1970/1, 1972/3, 1973/4, 1974/5, 1975/6, 1976/7 (Middlesbrough) 1977/8, 1978/9 (Swansea City) 1979/80, 1981/2, 1982/3.
Mardon, P.J. (1) (West Bromwich Albion) 1995/96.
Marriott, A. (1) (Wrexham) 1995/96.
Marustik, C. (6) (Swansea City) 1981/2, 1982/3.
Medwin, T. (30) (Swansea Town) 1952/3, 1956/7 (Tottenham Hotspur) 1957/8, 1958/9, 1959/60, 1960/1, 1962/3.
Melville, A.K. (27) (Swansea C). 1989/90, 1990/1 (Oxford United), 1991/2, 1992/93 (Sunderland) 1993/94, 1994/95, 1995/96.
Mielczarek, R. (1) (Rotherham United) 1970/1.
Millington, A. (21) (West Bromwich Albion) 1962/3, 1964/5 (Crystal Palace) 1965/6 (Peterborough United) 1966/7, 1967/8, 1968/9, 1969/70 (Swansea City) 1970/1, 1971/2.
Moore, G. (21) (Cardiff City) 1959/60, 1960/1, 1961/2 (Chelsea) 1962/3, (Manchester United) 1963/4 (Northampton Town) 1965/6, 1968/9 (Charlton Athletic) 1969/70, 1970/1.
Morris, W. (5) (Burnley) 1946/7, 1948/9, 1951/2.

Nardiello, D. (2) (Coventry City) 1977/8.
Neilson, A.B. (4) (Newcastle United) 1991/2, 1993/94, 1994/95.
Nicholas, P. (73) (Crystal Palace) 1978/9, 1979/80, 1980/1 (Arsenal) 1981/2, 1982/3, 1983/4 (Crystal Palace) 1984/5 (Luton Town) 1985/6, 1986/7, 1987/8 (Aberdeen), (Chelsea) 1988/9, 1989/90, 1990/1 (Watford), 1991/2.
Niedzwiecki, E.A. (2) (Chelsea) 1984/5, 1987/8.
Nogan, L.M. (2) (Watford) 1991/2 (Reading) 1995/96.
Nurse, E.A. (2) (Chelsea) 1984/5, 1987/8.
Norman, A.J. (5) (Hull City) 1985/6, 1987/8.
Nurse, M. (12) (Swansea Town) 1959/60, 1960/1, 1962/3 (Middlesbrough) 1963/4.

O'Sullivan, P. (3) (Brighton & Hove Albion) 1972/3, 1975/6, 1978/9.

Page, M. (28) (Birmingham City) 1970/1, 1971/2, 1972/3, 1973/4, 1974/5, 1975/6, 1976/7, 1977/8, 1978/9.
Palmer, D. (3) (Swansea Town) 1956/7, 1957/8.
Parry, J. (1) (Swansea Town) 1950/1.
Pascoe, C. (10) (Swansea Town) 1983/4, (Sunderland) 1988/9, 1989/90 1990/91, 1991/2.
Paul, R. (33) (Swansea Town) 1948/9, 1949/50 (Manchester City) 1950/1, 1951/2, 1952/3, 1953/4, 1954/5, 1955/6.
Pembridge, M.A. (16) (Luton Town) 1991/2 (Derby County) 1992/93, 1993/94, 1994/95 (Sheffield Wednesday) 1995/96.
Perry, J. (1) (Cardiff City) 1993/94.
Phillips, D. (62) (Plymouth Argyle) 1983/4 (Manchester City) 1984/5, 1985/6, 1986/7 (Coventry City) 1987/8, 1988/9 (Norwich City) 1989/90, 1990/1, 1991/2, 1992/93 (Nottingham Forest) 1993/94, 1994/95, 1995/96.
Phillips, J. (4) (Chelsea) 1972/3, 1973/4, 1974/5, 1977/8.

Phillips, L. (58) (Cardiff City) 1970/1, 1971/2, 1972/3, 1973/4,H1974/5, (Aston Villa) 1975/6, 1976/7, 1977/8, 1978/9 (Swansea City) 1979/80, 1980/1, 1981/2 (Charlton Athletic).

Pontin, K. (2) (Cardiff City) 1979/80.

Powell, A. (8) (Leeds United) 1946/7, 1947/8, 1948/9 (Everton) 1949/50, 1950/1 (Birmingham City).

Powell, D. (11) (Wrexham) 1967/8, 1968/9 (Sheffield United) 1969/70, 1970/1.

Powell, I. (8) (QPR) 1946/7, 1947/8, 1948/9 (Aston Villa) 1949/50, 1950/1.

Price, P. (25) (Luton Town) 1979/80, 1980/1, 1981/2 (Tottenham Hotspur) 1982/3, 1983/4.

Pring, K. (3) (Rotherham United) 1965/6, 1966/7.

Pritchard, H.K. (1) (Bristol City) 1984/5.

Rankmore, F. (l (Peterborough United) 1965/6.

Ratcliffe, K. (59) (Everton) 1980/1, 1981/2, 1982/3, 1983/4, 1984/5, 1985/6, 1986/7, 1987/8, 1988/9, 1989/90, 1990/1, 1991/2 (Cardiff City) 1992/93.

Reece, G. (29) (Sheffield United) 1965/6, 1966/7, 1969/70, 1970/1, 1971/2, (Cardiff City) 1972/3, 1973/4, 1974/5.

Reed, W. (2) (Ipswich Town) 1954/5.

Rees, A. (1) (Birmingham City) 1983/4.

Rees, J.M. (1) (Luton Town) 1991/2.

Rees, R. (39) (Coventry City) 1964/5, 1965/6, 1966/7, 1967/8 (West Bromwich Albion) 1968/9 (Nottingham Forest) 1969/70, 1970/1, 1971/2.

Rees, W. (4) (Cardiff City) 1948/9 (Tottenham Hotspur) 1949/50.

Richards, S. (1) (Cardiff City) 1946/7.

Roberts, A. M. (1) (QPR) 1992/93.

Roberts, D. (17) (Oxford United) 1972/3, 1973/4, 1974/5 (Hull City) 1975/6, 1976/7, 1977/8.

Roberts, I.W. (7) (Watford) 1989/90, (Huddersfield Town) 1991/2, (Leicester City) 1993/94, 1994/95.

Roberts, J.G. (22) (Arsenal) 1970/1, 1971/2, 1972/3, (Birmingham City) 1973/4, 1974/5, 1975/6..

Roberts, J.H. (1) (Bolton Wanderers) 1948/9.

Roberts, P. (4) (Portsmouth) 1973/4, 1974/5.

Robinson, J. R. C. (3) (Charlton Athletic) 1995/96.

Rodrigues, P. (40) (Cardiff City) 1964/5, 1965/6 (Leicester City) 1966/7, 1967/8, 1968/9, 1969/70 (Sheffield Wednesday) 1970/1, 1971/2, 1972/3, 1973/4.

Rouse, V. (1) (Crystal Palace) 1958/9.

Rowley, T. (1) (Tranmere Rovers) 1958/9.

Rush, I. (73) (Liverpool) 1979/80, 1980/1, 1981/2, 1982/3, 1983/4, 1984/5, 1985/6, 1986/7 (Juventus) 1987/8, (Liverpool) 1988/9, 1989/90, 1990/1, 1991/2, 1992/93, 1993/94, 1994/95, 1995/96.

Saunders, D. (52) (Brighton & Hove Albion) 1985/6, 1986/7 (Oxford United) 1987/8, (Derby County) 1988/9, 1989/90, 1990/91, (Liverpool) 1991/2 (Aston Villa) 1992/93, 1993/94, 1994/95 (Galatasaray) 1995/96.

Savage, R. W. (3) (Crewe Alexandra) 1995/96.

Sayer, P. (7) (Cardiff City) 1976/7, 1977/8.

Scrine, F. (2) (Swansea Town) 1949/50.

Sear, C. (1) (Manchester City) 1962/3.

Sherwood, A. (41) (Cardiff City) 1946/7, 1947/8, 1948/9, 1949/50, 1950/1, 1951/2, 1952/3, 1953/4, 1954/5, 1955/6, 1956/7 (Newport County).

Shortt, W. (12) (Plymouth Argyle) 1946/7, 1949/50, 1951/2, 1952/3.

Showers, D. (2) (Cardiff City) 1974/5.

Sidlow, C. (7) (Liverpool) 1946/7, 1947/8, 1948/9, 1949/50.

Slatter, N. (22) (Bristol Rovers) 1982/3, 1983/4, 1984/5 (Oxford United) 1985/6, 1986/7, 1987/8, 1988/9.

Smallman, D. (7 (Wrexham) 1973/4 (Everton) 1974/5, 1975/6.

Southall, N. (86) (Everton) 1981/2, 1982/3, 1983/4, 1984/5, 1985/6, 1986/7, 1987/8, 1988/9, 1989/90, 1990/1, 1991/2, 1992/93, 1993/94, 1994/95, 1995/96.

Speed, G.A. (35) (Leeds United) 1989/90, 1990/91, 1991/2, 1992/93, 1993/94, 1994/95, 1995/96.

Sprake, G. (37) (Leeds United) 1963/4, 1964/5, 1965/6, 1966/7, 1967/8, 1968/9, 1969/70, 1970/1, 1971/2, 1972/3, 1973/4 (Birmingham City) 1974/5.

Stansfield, F. (1) (Cardiff City) 1948/9.

Stevenson, B. (15) (Leeds United) 1977/8, 1978/9, 1979/80, 1981/2 (Birmingham City).

Stevenson, N. (4) (Swansea City) 1981/2, 1982/3.

Stitfall, R. (2) (Cardiff City) 1952/3, 1956/7.

Sullivan, D. (17) (Cardiff City) 1952/3, 1953/4, 1954/5, 1956/7, 1957/8, 1958/9, 1959/60.

Symons, C.J. (22) (Portsmouth) 1991/2, 1992/93, 1993/94, 1994/95 (Manchester City) 1995/96.

Tapscott, D. (14) (Arsenal) 1953/4, 1954/5, 1955/6, 1956/7, 1958/9 (Cardiff City).

Taylor, G. K. (3) (Crystal Palace) 1995/96 (Sheffield United).

Thomas, D. (2) (Swansea Town) 1956/7, 1957/8.

Thomas, M. (51) (Wrexham) 1976/7, 1977/8, 1978/9 (Manchester United) 1979/80, 1980/1, 1981/2 (Everton) (Brighton) 1982/3 (Stoke City) 1983/4, (Chelsea) 1984/5, 1985/6 (West Bromwich Albion).

Thomas, M.R. (1) (Newcastle United) 1986/7.

Thomas, R. (50) (Swindon Town) 1966/7, 1967/8, 1968/9, 1969/70, 1970/1, 1971/2, 1972/3, 1973/4 (Derby County) 1974/5, 1975/6, 1976/7, 1977/8 (Cardiff City).

Thomas, S. (4) (Fulham) 1947/8, 1948/9.

Toshack, J. (40) (Cardiff City) 1968/9, 1969/70 (Liverpool) 1970/1, 1971/2, 1972/3, 1974/5, 1975/6, 1976/7, 1977/8 (Swansea City) 1978/9, 1979/80.

Van Den Hauwe, P.W.R. (13) (Everton) 1984/5, 1985/6, 1986/7, 1987/8, 1988/9.

Vaughan, N. (10) (Newport County) 1982/3, 1983/4 (Cardiff City) 1984/5.

Vearncombe, G. (2) (Cardiff City) 1957/8, 1960/1.

Vernon, R. (32) (Blackburn Rovers) 1956/7, 1957/8, 1958/9, 1959/60 (Everton) 1960/1, 1961/2, 1962/3, 1963/4, 1964/5 (Stoke City) 1965/6, 1966/7, 1967/8.

Villars, A. (3) (Cardiff City) 1973/4.

Walley, T. (1) (Watford) 1970/1.

Walsh, I. (18) (Crystal Palace) 1979/80, 1980/1, 1981/2 (Swansea City).

Ward, D. (2) (Bristol Rovers) 1958/9, 1961/2 (Cardiff City).

Webster, C. (4) (Manchester United) 1956/7, 1957/8.

Williams, A. (7) (Reading) 1993/94, 1994/95, 1995/96.

Williams, D.G. (13) 1987/8 (Derby County) 1988/9, 1989/90 (Ipswich Town) 1992/93, 1995/96.

Williams, D.M. (5) (Norwich City) 1985/6, 1986/7.

Williams, G. (1) (Cardiff City) 1950/1.

Williams, G.E. (26) (West Bromwich Albion) 1959/60, 1960/1, 1962/3, 1963/4, 1964/5, 1965/6, 1966/7, 1967/8, 1968/9.

Williams, G.G. (5) (Swansea Town) 1960/1, 1961/2.

Williams, H. (4) (Newport County) 1948/9 (Leeds United) 1949/50, 1950/1.

Williams, Herbert (3) (Swansea Town) 1954/5, 1970/1.

Williams, S. (43) (West Bromwich Albion) 1953/4, 1954/5, 1955/6, 1957/8, 1958/9, 1959/60, 1960/1, 1961/2, 1962/3 (Southampton) 1963/4, 1964/5, 1965/6.

Witcomb, D. (3) (West Bromwich Albion) 1946/7 (Sheffield Wednesday).

Woosnam, P. (17) (Leyton Orient) 1958/9 (West Ham United) 1959/60, 1960/1, 1961/2, 1962/3 (Aston Villa).

Yorath, T. (59) (Leeds United) 1969/70, 1970/1, 1971/2, 1972/3, 1973/4, 1974/5, 1975/6 (Coventry City) 1976/7, 1977/8, 1978/9 (Tottenham Hotspur) 1979/80, 1980/1.

Young, E. (21) (Wimbledon) 1989/90, 1990/1 (Crystal Palace), 1991/2, 1992/93, 1993/94, (Wolverhampton Wanderers) 1995/96.

EIRE

Aherne, T. (16) (Belfast Celtic) 1945/6 (Luton Town) 1949/50, 1950/1, 1951/2, 1952/3, 1953/4.

Aldridge, J.W. (68) (Oxford United) 1985/6, 1986/7 (Liverpool) 1987/8, 1988/9 (Real Sociedad) 1989/90, 1990/1, (Tranmere Rovers) 1991/2, 1992/93, 1993/94, 1994/95, 1995/96.

Ambrose, P. (5) (Shamrock Rovers) 1954/5, 1963/4.

Anderson, J. (16) (Preston North End) 1979/80, 1981/2 (Newcastle United) 1983/4, 1985/6, 1986/7, 1987/8, 1988/9.

Babb, P. (20) (Coventry City) 1993/94 (Liverpool) 1994/95, 1995/96.

Bailham, E. (1) (Shamrock Rovers) 1963/4.

Barber, E. (2) (Shelbourne) 1965/6 (Birmingham City) 1965/6.

Beglin, J. (15) (Liverpool) 1983/4, 1984/5, 1985/6, 1986/7.

Bonner, P. (80) (Celtic) 1980/1, 1981/2, 1983/4, 1984/5, 1985/6, 1986/7, 1987/8, 1988/9, 1989/90, 1990/1, 1991/2, 1992/93, 1993/94, 1994/95, 1995/96.

Braddish, S. (1) (Dundalk) 1977/8.

Brady T.R. (6) (QPR) 1963/4.

Brady, W. L. (72) (Arsenal) 1974/5, 1975/6, 1976/7, 1977/8, 1978/9, 1979/80 (Juventus) 1980/1, 1981/2 (Sampdoria) 1982/3, 1983/4 (Internazionale) 1984/5, 1985/6 (Ascoli) 1986/7 (West Ham United) 1987/8, 1988/9, 1989/90.

Breen, G. (6) (Birmingham City) 1995/96.

Breen, T. (3) (Shamrock Rovers) 1946/7.

Brennan, F. (1) (Drumcondra) 1964/5.

Brennan, S.A. (19) (Manchester United) 1964/5, 1965/6, 1966/7, 1968/9, 1969/70 (Waterford) 1970/1.

Browne, W. (3) (Bohemians) 1963/4.

Buckley, L. (2) (Shamrock Rovers) 1983/4 (Waregem) 1984/5.

Burke, F. (1) (Cork Athletic) 1951/2.

Byrne, A.B. (14) (Southampton) 1969/70, 1970/1, 1972/3, 1973/4.

Byrne, J. (23) (QPR) 1984/5, 1986/7, 1987/8 (Le Havre) 1989/90, 1990/1 (Brighton & Hove Albion), 1991/2 (Sunderland) 1992/93 (Millwall).

Byrne, P. (8) (Shamrock Rovers) 1983/4, 1984/5, 1985/6.

Campbell, A. (3) (Santander) 1984/5.

Campbell, N. (11) (St Patrick's Athletic) 1970/1 (Fortuna Cologne) 1971/2, 1972/3, 1974/5, 1975/6.

Cantwell, N. (36) (West Ham United) 1953/4, 1955/6, 1956/7, 1957/8, 1958/9, 1959/60, 1960/1 (Manchester United) 1960/1, 1961/2, 1962/3, 1963/4, 1964/5, 1965/6, 1966/7.

Carey, B.P. (3) (Manchester United) 1991/2, 1992/93 (Leicester City) 1993/94.

Carey, J.J. (21) (Manchester United) 1945/6, 1946/7, 1947/8, 1948/9, 1949/50, 1950/1, 1952/3.

Carolan, J. (2) (Manchester United) 1959/60.

Carroll, B. (2) (Shelbourne) 1948/9, 1949/50.

Carroll, T.R. (17) (Ipswich Town) 1967/8, 1968/9, 1969/70, 1970/1 (Birmingham City) 1971/2, 1972/3.

Cascarino, A.G. (63) (Gillingham) 1985/6 (Millwall) 1987/8, 1988/9, 1989/90 (Aston Villa), 1990/9 (Celtic) 1991/2 (Chelsea) 1992/93, 1993/94 (Marseille) 1994/95, 1995/96.

Chandler, J. (2) (Leeds United) 1979/80.

Clarke, J. (1) (Drogheda United) 1977/8.

Clarke, K. (2) (Drumcondra) 1947/8.

Clarke, M. (1) (Shamrock Rovers) 1949/50.

Clinton, T.J. (3) (Everton) 1950/1, 1953/4.

Coad, P. (11) (Shamrock Rovers) 1946/7, 1947/8, 1948/9, 1950/1, 1951/2.

Coffey, T. (1) (Drumcondra) 1949/50.

Colfer, M.D. (2) (Shelbourne) 1949/50, 1950/1.

Conmy, O.M. (5) (Peterborough United) 1964/5, 1966/7, 1967/8, 1969/70.

Connolly, D.J. (4) (Watford) 1995/96.

Conroy, G.A. (27) (Stoke City) 1969/70, 1970/1, 1972/3, 1973/4, 1974/5, 1975/6, 1976/7.

Conway, J.P. (20) (Fulham) 1966/7, 1967/8, 1968/9, 1969/70, 1970/1, 1973/4, 1974/5, 1975/6 (Manchester City) 1976/7.

Corr, P.J. (4) (Everton) 1948/9.

Courtney, E. (1) (Cork United) 1945/6.

Coyle, O. (1) (Bolton Wanderers) 1993/94.

Coyne, T. (21) (Celtic) 1991/2, (Tranmere Rovers) 1992/93, (Motherwell) 1993/94, 1994/95, 1995/96.

Cummins, G.P. (19) (Luton Town) 1953/4, 1954/5, 1955/6, 1957/8, 1958/9, 1959/60, 1960/1.

Cuneen, T. (1) (Limerick) 1950/1.

Cunningham, K. (6) (Wimbledon) 1995/96.

Curtis, D.P. (17) (Shelbourne) 1956/7 (Bristol City) 1956/7, 1957/8, (Ipswich Town) 1958/9, 1959/60, 1960/1, 1961/2, 1962/3 (Exeter City) 1963/4.

Cusack, S. (1) (Limerick) 1952/3.

Daish, L.S. (5) (Cambridge United) 1991/2, (Coventry City) 1995/96.

Daly, G.A. (48) (Manchester United) 1972/3, 1973/4, 1974/5, 1976/7 (Derby County) 1977/8, 1978/9, 1979/80 (Coventry City) 1980/1, 1981/2, 1982/3, 1983/4 (Birmingham City) 1984/5, 1985/6 (Shrewsbury Town) 1986/7.

Daly, M. (2) (Wolverhampton Wanderers) 1977/8.

Daly, P. (1) (Shamrock Rovers) 1949/50.

De Mange, K.J.P.P. (2) (Liverpool) 1986/7, (Hull City) 1988/9.

Deacy, E. (4) (Aston Villa) 1981/2.

Dempsey, J.T. (19) (Fulham) 1966/7, 1967/8, 1968/9 (Chelsea) 1968/9, 1969/70, 1970/1, 1971/2.

Dennehy, J. (11) (Cork Hibernian) 1971/2 (Nottingham Forest) 1972/3, 1973/4, 1974/5 (Walsall) 1975/6, 1976/7.

Desmond, P. (4) (Middlesbrough) 1949/50.

Devine, J. (12) (Arsenal) 1979/80, 1980/1, 1981/2, 1982/3 (Norwich City) 1983/4, 1984/5.

Donovan, D.C. (5) (Everton) 1954/5, 1956/7.

Donovan, T. (1) (Aston Villa) 1979/80.

Doyle, C. (1) (Shelbourne) 1958/9.

Duffy, B. (1) (Shamrock Rovers) 1949/50.

Dunne, A.P. (33) (Manchester United) 1961/2, 1962/3, 1963/4, 1964/5, 1965/6, 1966/7, 1968/9, 1969/70, 1970/1 (Bolton Wanderers) 1973/4, 1974/5, 1975/6.

Dunne, J.C. (1) (Fulham) 1970/1.

Dunne, P.A.J. (5) (Manchester United) 1964/5, 1965/6, 1966/7.

Dunne, S. (15) (Luton Town) 1952/3, 1953/4, 1955/6, 1956/7, 1957/8, 1958/9, 1959/60.
Dunne, T. (3) (St Patrick's Athletic) 1955/6, 1956/7.
Dunning, P. (2) (Shelbourne) 1970/1.
Dunphy, E.M. (23) (York City) 1965/6 (Millwall) 1965/6, 1966/7, 1967/8, 1968/9, 1969/70, 1970/1.
Dwyer, N.M. (14) (West Ham United) 1959/60 (Swansea Town) 1960/1, 1961/2, 1963/4, 1964/5.

Eccles, P. (1) (Shamrock Rovers) 1985/6.
Eglington, T.J. (24) (Shamrock Rovers) 1945/6 (Everton) 1946/7, 1947/8, 1948/9, 1950/1, 1951/2, 1952/3, 1953/4, 1954/5, 1955/6.

Fagan, E. (1) (Shamrock Rovers) 1972/3.
Fagan, F. (8) (Manchester City) 1954/5, 1959/60 (Derby County) 1959/60, 1960/1.
Fairclough, M. (2) (Dundalk) 1981/2.
Fallon, S. (8) (Celtic) 1950/1, 1951/2, 1952/3, 1954/5.
Farrell, P.D. (28) (Shamrock Rovers) 1945/6 (Everton) 1946/7, 1947/8, 1948/9, 1949/50, 1950/1, 1951/2, 1952/3, 1953/4, 1954/5, 1955/6, 1956/7.
Farrelly, G. (3) (Aston Villa) 1995/96.
Finucane, A. (11) (Limerick) 1966/7, 1968/9, 1969/70, 1970/1, 1971/2.
Fitzgerald, F.J. (2) (Waterford) 1954/5, 1955/6.
Fitzgerald, P.J. (5) (Leeds United) 1960/1 (Chester) 1961/2.
Fitzpatrick, K. (1) (Limerick) 1969/70.
Fitzsimons, A.G. (26) (Middlesbrough) 1949/50, 1951/2, 1952/3, 1953/4, 1954/5, 1955/6, 1956/7, 1957/8, 1958/9 (Lincoln City) 1958/9.
Fleming, C. (7) (Middlesbrough) 1995/96.
Fogarty, A. (11) (Sunderland) 1959/60, 1960/1, 1961/2, 1962/3, 1963/4, (Hartlepool United) 1963/4.
Foley, T.C. (9) (Northampton Town) 1963/4, 1964/5, 1965/6, 1966/7.
Fullam, J. (Preston North End) 1960/1 (Shamrock Rovers) 1963/4, 1965/6, 1967/8, 1968/9, 1969/70.

Gallagher, C. (2) (Celtic) 1966/7.
Gallagher, M. (1) (Hibernian) 1953/4.
Galvin, A. (29) (Tottenham Hotspur) 1982/3, 1983/4, 1984/5, 1985/6, 1986/7 (Sheffield Wednesday) 1987/8, 1988/9, 1989/90.
Gannon, E. (14) (Notts County) 1948/9 (Sheffield Wednesday) 1948/9, 1949/50, 1950/1, 1951/2, 1953/4, 1954/5 (Shelbourne K1954/5.
Gannon, M. (1) (Shelbourne) 1971/2.
Gavin, J.T. (7) (Norwich City) 1949/50, 1952/3, 1953/4 (Tottenham Hotspur) 1954/5 (Norwich City) 1956/7.
Gibbons, A. (4) (St Patrick's Athletic) 1951/2, 1953/4, 1955/6.
Gilbert, R. (1) (Shamrock Rovers) 1965/6.
Giles, C. (1) (Doncaster Rovers) 1950/1.
Giles, M.J. (59) (Manchester United) 1959/60, 1960/1, 1961/2, 1962/3 (Leeds United) 1963/4, 1964/5, 1965/6, 1966/7, 1968/9, 1969/70, 1970/1, 1972/3, 1973/4, 1974/5 (West Bromwich Albion) 1975/6, 1976/7 (Shamrock Rovers) 1977/8, 1978/9.
Given, S.J.J. (7) (Blackburn Rovers) 1995/96.
Givens, D.J. (56) (Manchester United) 1968/9, 1969/70 (Luton Town) 1969/70, 1970/1, 1971/2 (QPR) 1972/3, 1973/4, 1974/5, 1975/6, 1976/7, 1977/8 (Birmingham City) 1978/9, 1979/80, 1980/1 (Neuchatel Xamax) 1981/2.
Glynn, D. (2) (Drumcondra) 1951/2, 1954/5.
Godwin, T.F. (13) (Shamrock Rovers) 1948/9, 1949/50 (Leicester City) 1949/50, 1950/1 (Bournemouth) 1955/6, 1956/7, 1957/8.

Gorman, W.C. (2) (Brentford) 1946/7.

Grealish, A. (44) (Orient) 1975/6, 1978/9 (Luton Town) 1979/80, 1980/1, (Brighton & Hove Albion) 1981/2, 1982/3, 1983/4 (West Bromwich Albion) 1984/5, 1985/6.

Gregg, E. (8) (Bohemians) 1977/8, 1978/9, 1979/80.

Grimes, A.A. (17) (Manchester United) 1977/8, 1979/80, 1980/1, 1981/2, 1982/3 (Coventry City) 1983/4 (Luton Town) 1987/8.

Hale, A. (13) (Aston Villa) 1961/2 (Doncaster Rovers) 1962/3, 1963/4, (Waterford) 1966/7, 1967/8, 1968/9, 1969/70, 1970/1, 1971/2.

Hamilton, T. (2) (Shamrock Rovers) 1958/9.

Hand, E.K. (20) (Portsmouth) 1968/9, 1969/70, 1970/1, 1972/3, 1973/4, 1974/5, 1975/6.

Harte, I.P. (4) (Leeds United) 1995/96.

Hartnett, J.B. (2) (Middlesbrough) 1948/9, 1953/4.

Haverty, J. (32) (Arsenal) 1955/6, 1956/7, 1957/8, 1958/9, 1959/60, 1960/1, (Blackburn Rovers) 1961/2 (Millwall) 1962/3, 1963/4 (Celtic) 1964/5, (Bristol Rovers) 1964/5 (Shelbourne) 1965/6, 1966/7.

Hayes, A.W.P. (1) (Southampton) 1978/9.

Hayes, W.E. (2) (Huddersfield Town) 1946/7.

Hayes, W.J. (1) (Limerick) 1948/9.

Healey, R. (2) (Cardiff City) 1976/7, 1979/80.

Heighway, S.D. (34) (Liverpool) 1970/1, 1972/3, 1974/5, 1975/6, 1976/7, 1977/8, 1978/9, 1979/80, 1980/1 (Minnesota Kicks) 1981/2.

Henderson, B. (2) (Drumcondra) 1947/8.

Hennessy, J. (5) (Shelbourne) 1955/6, 1965/6 (St Patrick's Athletic) 1968/9.

Herrick, J. (3) (Cork Hibernians) 1971/2 (Shamrock Rovers) 1972/3.

Higgins, J. (1) (Birmingham City) 1950/1.

Holmes, J. (Coventry City) 1970/1, 1972/3, 1973/4, 1974/5, 1975/6, 1976/7 (Tottenham Hotspur) 1977/8, 1978/9, 1980/1 (Vancouver Whitecaps) 1980/1.

Houghton, R.J. (66) (Oxford United) 1985/6, 1986/7, 1987/8 (Liverpool) 1987/8, 1988/9, 1989/90, 1990/1, 1991/2 (Aston Villa) 1992/93, 1993/94 (Crystal Palace) 1994/95, 1995/96.

Howlett, G. (1) (Brighton & Hove Albion) 1983/4.

Hughton, C. (53) (Tottenham Hotspur) 1979/80, 1980/1, 1981/2, 1982/3, 1983/4, 1984/5, 1985/6, 1986/7, 1987/8, 1988/9, 1989/90, 1990/1 (West Ham United), 1991/2.

Hurley, C.J. (40) (Millwall) 1956/7, 1957/8 (Sunderland) 1958/9, 1959/60, 1960/1, 1961/2, 1962/3, 1963/4, 1964/5, 1965/6, 1966/7, 1967/8 (Bolton Wanderers) 1968/9.

Irwin, D.J. (40) (Manchester United) 1990/1, 1991/2, 1992/93, 1993/94, 1994/95, 1995/96.

Keane, R.M. (30) (Nottingham Forest) 1990/1, 1991/2, 1992/93, (Manchester United) 1993/94, 1994/95, 1995/96.

Keane, T.R. (4) (Swansea Town) 1948/9.

Kearin, M. (1) (Shamrock Rovers) 1971/2.

Kearns, F.T. (1) (West Ham United) 1953/4.

Kearns, M. (18) (Oxford United) 1969/70 (Walsall) 1973/4, 1975/6, 1976/7, 1977/8, 1978/9 (Wolverhampton Wanderers) 1979/80.

Kelly, A.T. (14) (Sheffield United) 1992/93, 1993/94, 1994/95, 1995/96.

Kelly, D.T. (20) (Walsall) 1987/8 (West Ham) 1988/9 (Leicester City) 1989/90, 1990/1 (Newcastle United) 1991/2, 1992/93 (Wolverhampton Wanderers) 1993/94, 1994/95 (Sunderland) 1995/96.

Kelly, G. (18) (Leeds United) 1993/94, 1994/95, 1995/96.

Kelly, J.A. (48) (Drumcondra) 1956/7 (Preston North End) 1961/2, 1962/3, 1963/4, 1964/5, 1965/6, 1966/7, 1967/8, 1969/70, 1970/1, 1971/2, 1972/3.

Kelly, J.P.V. (5) (Wolverhampton Wanderers) 1960/1, 1961/2.
Kelly, M.J. (4) (Portsmouth) 1987/8, 1988/9, 1990/1.
Kelly, N. (1) (Nottingham Forest) 1953/4.
Kenna, J.J. (12) (Blackburn Rovers) 1994/95, 1995/96.
Kennedy, M. (10) (Liverpool) 1995/96.
Kennedy, M.F. (2) (Portsmouth) 1985/6.
Keogh, J. (1) (Shamrock Rovers) 1965/6.
Keogh, S. (1) (Shamrock Rovers) 1958/9.
Kernaghan, A.N. (22) (Middlesbrough) 1992/93 (Manchester City) 1993/94, 1994/95, 1995/96.
Kiernan, F.W. (5) (Shamrock Rovers) 1950/1 (Southampton) 1951/2.
Kinnear, J.P. (26) (Tottenham Hotspur) 1966/7, 1967/8, 1968/9, 1969/70, 1970/1, 1971/2, 1972/3, 1973/4, 1974/5 (Brighton & Hove Albion) 1975/6.

Langan, D. (25) (Derby County) 1977/8, 1979/80 (Birmingham City) 1980/1, 1981/2 (Oxford United) 1984/5, 1985/6, 1986/7, 1987/8.
Lawler, J.F. (8) (Fulham) 1952/3, 1953/4, 1954/5, 1955/6.
Lawlor, J.C. (3) (Drumcondra) 1948/9 (Doncaster Rovers) 1950/1.
Lawlor, M. (5) (Shamrock Rovers) 1970/1, 1972/3.
Lawrenson, M. (38) (Preston North End) 1976/7 (Brighton & Hove Albion) 1977/8, 1978/9, 1979/80, 1980/1 (Liverpool) 1981/2, 1982/3, 1983/4, 1984/5, 1985/6, 1986/7, 1987/8.
Leech, M. (8) (Shamrock Rovers) 1968/9, 1971/2, 1972/3.
Lowry, D. (1) (St Patrick's Athletic) 1961/2.

McAlinden, J. (2) (Portsmouth) 1945/6.
McAteer, J.W. (18) (Bolton Wanderers) 1993/94, 1994/95 (Liverpool) 1995/96.
McCann, J. (1) (Shamrock Rovers) 1956/7.
McCarthy, M. (57) (Manchester City) 1983/4, 1984/5, 1985/6, 1986/7 (Celtic) 1987/8, 1988/9 (Lyon) 1989/90, 1990/1 (Millwall) 1991/2.
McConville, T. (6) (Dundalk) 1971/2 (Waterford) 1972/3.
McDonagh, A. (24) (Everton) 1980/1 (Bolton Wanderers) 1981/2, 1982/3, (Notts County) 1983/4, 1984/5, 1985/6.
McDonagh, Joe (3) (Shamrock Rovers) 1983/4, 1984/5.
McEvoy, M.A. (17) (Blackburn Rovers) 1960/1, 1962/3, 1963/4, 1964/5, 1965/6, 1966/7.
McGee, P. (15) (QPR) 1977/8, 1978/9, 1979/80 (Preston North End) 1980/1.
McGoldrick, E.J. (15) (Crystal Palace) 1991/2, 1992/93, (Arsenal) 1993/94, 1994/95.
McGowan, D. (3) (West Ham United) 1948/9.
McGowan, J. (1) (Cork United) 1946/7.
McGrath, M. (22) (Blackburn Rovers) 1957/8, 1958/9, 1959/60, 1960/1, 1961/2, 1962/3, 1963/4, 1964/5, 1965/6 (Bradford Park Avenue) 1965/6, 1966/7.
McGrath, P. (82) (Manchester United) 1984/5, 1985/6, 1986/7, 1987/8, 1988/9 (Aston Villa) 1989/90, 1990/1, 1991/2, 1992/93, 1993/94, 1994/95, 1995/96.
Macken, A. (1) (Derby County) 1976/7.
Mackey, G. (3) (Shamrock Rovers) 1956/7.
McLoughlin, A.F. (23) (Swindon T) 1989/90, 1990/1 (Southampton) 1991/2 (Portsmouth) 1992/93, 1993/94, 1994/95, 1995/96.
McMillan, W. (2) (Belfast Celtic) 1945/6.
McNally, J.B. (3) (Luton Town) 1958/9, 1960/1, 1962/3.
Malone, G. (1) (Shelbourne) 1948/9.
Mancini, T.J. (5) (QPR) 1973/4 (Arsenal) 1974/5.
Martin, C.J. (30) (Glentoran) 1945/6, 1946/7 (Leeds United) 1946/7, 1947/8, (Aston Villa) 1948/9, 1949/50 1950/1, 1951/2, K1953/4, 1954/5, 1955/6.

Martin, M.P. (51) (Bohemians) 1971/2, 1972/3 (Manchester United) 1972/3, 1973/4, 1974/5 (West Bromwich Albion) 1975/6, 1976/7 (Newcastle United) 1978/9, 1979/80, 1981/2, 1982/3.

Meagan, M.K. (17) (Everton) 1960/1, 1961/2, 1962/3, 1963/4 (Huddersfield Town) 1964/5, 1965/6, 1966/7, 1967/8 (Drogheda) 1969/70.

Milligan, M.J. (1) (Oldham Athletic) 1991/2.

Mooney, J. (2) (Shamrock Rovers) 1964/5.

Moore, A. (5) (Middlesbrough) 1995/96.

Moran, K. (70) (Manchester United) 1979/80, 1980/1, 1981/2, 1982/3, 1983/4, 1984/5, 1985/6, 1986/7, 1987/8 (Sporting Gijon) 1988/9 (Blackburn Rovers) 1989/90, 1990/1, 1991/2, 1992/93, 1993/94.

Moroney, T. (12) (West Ham United) 1947/8, 1948/9, 1949/50, 1950/1, 1951/2, 1953/4.

Morris, C.B. (35) (Celtic) 1987/8, 1988/9, 1989/90, 1990/1, 1991/2 (Middlesbrough) 1992/93.

Moulson, G.B. (3) (Lincoln City) 1947/8, 1948/9.

Mucklan, C. (1) (Drogheda) 1977/8.

Mulligan, P.M. (50) (Shamrock Rovers) 1968/9, 1969/70 (Chelsea) 1969/70, 1970/1, 1971/2 (Crystal Palace) 1972/3, 1973/4, 1974/5 (West Bromwich Albion) 1975/6, 1976/7, 1977/8, 1978/9 (Shamrock Rovers) 1979/80.

Munroe, L. (1) (Shamrock Rovers) 1953/4.

Murphy, A. (1) (Clyde) 1955/6.

Murphy, B. (1) (Bohemians) 1985/6.

Murphy, J. (1) (Crystal Palace) 1979/80.

Murray, T. (1) (Dundalk) 1949/50.

Newman, W. (1) (Shelbourne) 1968/9.

Nolan, R. (10) (Shamrock Rovers) 1956/7, 1957/8, 1959/60, 1961/2, 1962/3.

O'Brien, F. (4) (Philadelphia Fury) 1979/80.

O'Brien, L. (15) (Shamrock Rovers) 1985/6 (Manchester United) 1986/7, 1987/8 (Newcastle United) 1988/9, 1991/2, 1992/93 (Tranmere Rovers) 1993/94, 1995/96.

O'Brien R. (4) (Notts County) 1975/6, 1976/7.

O'Byrne, L.B. (1) (Shamrock Rovers) 1948/9.

O'Callaghan, B.R. (6) (Stoke City) 1978/9, 1979/80, 1980/1, 1981/2.

O'Callaghan, K. (20) (Ipswich Town) 1980/1, 1981/2, 1982/3, 1983/4, 1984/5, (Portsmouth) 1985/6, 1986/7.

O'Connnell, A. (2) (Dundalk) 1966/7 (Bohemians) 1970/1.

O'Connor, T. (4) (Shamrock Rovers) 1949/50.

O'Connor, T. (7) (Fulham) 1967/8 (Dundalk) 1971/2 (Bohemians) 1972/3.

O'Driscoll, J.F. (3) (Swansea Town) 1948/9.

O'Driscoll, S. (3) (Fulham) 1981/2.

O'Farrell, F. (9) (West Ham United) 1951/2, 1952/3, 1953/4, 1954/5, 1955/6 (Preston North End) 1957/8, 1958/9.

O'Flanagan, K.P. (3) (Arsenal) 1946/7.

O'Flanagan, M. (1) (Bohemians) 1946/7.

O'Hanlon, K.G. (1) (Rotherham United) 1987/8.

O'Keefe, E. (5) (Everton) 1980/1 (Port Vale) 1983/4.

O'Leary, D. (67) Arsenal 1976/7, 1977/8, 1978/9, 1979/80, 1980/1, 1981/2, 1982/3, 1983/4, 1984/5, 1985/6, 1988/9, 1989/90, 1990/1, 1991/2, 1992/93.

O'Leary, P. (7) (Shamrock Rovers) 1979/80, 1980/1.

O'Neill, F.S. (20) (Shamrock Rovers) 1961/2, 1964/5, 1965/6, 1966/7, 1968/9, 1971/2.

O'Neill, J. (17) (Everton) 1951/2, 1952/3, 1953/4, 1954/5, 1955/6, 1956/7, 1957/8, 1958/9.

O'Neill, J. (1) (Preston North End) 1960/1.

O'Neill, K.P. (6) (Norwich City) 1995/96.

O'Regan, K. (4) (Brighton & Hove Albion) 1983/4, 1984/5.
O'Reilly, J. (2) (Cork United) 1945/6.

Peyton, G. (33) (Fulham) 1976/7, 1977/8, 1978/9, 1979/80, 1980/1, 1981/2, 1984/5, 1985/6 (Bournemouth) 1987/8, 1988/9, 1989/90, 1990/1 (Everton) 1991/2.
Peyton, N. (6) (Shamrock Rovers) 1956/7 (Leeds United) 1959/60, 1960/1, 1962/3.
Phelan, T. (35) (Wimbledon) 1991/2 (Manchester City) 1992/93, 1993/94, 1994/95, 1995/96 (Chelsea).

Quinn, N.J. (60) (Arsenal) 1985/6, 1986/7, 1987/8, 1988/9 (Manchester City) 1989/90, 1990/1, 1991/2, 1992/93, 1993/94, 1994/95, 1995/96.

Richardson, D.J. (3) (Shamrock Rovers) 1971/2 (Gillingham) 1972/3, 1979/80.
Ringstead, A. (20) (Sheffield United) 1950/1, 1951/2, 1952/3, 1953/4, 1954/5, 1955/6, 1956/7, 1957/8, 1958/9.
Robinson, M. (23) (Brighton & Hove Albion) 1980/1, 1981/2, 1982/3, (Liverpool) 1983/4, 1984/5 (QPR) 1985/6.
Roche, P.J. (8) (Shelbourne) 1971/2 (Manchester United) 1974/5, 1975/6.
Rogers, E. (19) (Blackburn Rovers) 1967/8, 1968/9, 1969/70, 1970/1, (Charlton Athletic) 1971/2, 1972/3.
Ryan, G. (16) (Derby County) 1977/8 (Brighton & Hove Albion) 1978/9, 1979/80, 1980/1, 1981/2, 1983/4, 1984/5.
Ryan, R.A. (16) (West Bromwich Albion) 1949/50, 1950/1, 1951/2, 1952/3, 1953/4, 1954/5 (Derby County) 1955/6.

Savage, D.P.T. (5) (Millwall) 1995/96.
Saward, P. (18) (Millwall) 1953/4 (Aston Villa) 1956/7, 1957/8, 1958/9, 1959/60, 1960/1 (Huddersfield Town) 1960/1, 1961/2, 1962/3.
Scannell, T. (1) (Southend United) 1953/4.
Scully, P.J. (1) (Arsenal) 1988/9.
Sheedy, K. (45) (Everton) 1983/4, 1985/6, 1986/7, 1987/8, 1988/9, 1989/90, 1990/1 (Newcastle United) 1991/2, 1992/93.
Sheridan, J.J. (34) (Leeds United) 1987/8, 1988/9 (Sheffield Wednesday) 1989/90, 1990/1, 1991/2, 1992/93, 1993/94, 1994/95, 1995/96.
Slaven, B. (7) (Middlesbrough) 1989/90, 1990/91, 1992/93.
Sloan, J.W. (2) (Arsenal) 1945/6.
Smyth, M. (1) (Shamrock Rovers) 1968/9.
Stapleton, F. (70) (Arsenal) 1976/7, 1977/8, 1978/9, 1979/80, 1980/1 (Manchester United) 1981/2, 1982/3, 1983/4, 1984/5, 1985/6, 1986/7 (Ajax) 1987/8 (Derby County) 1987/8 (Le Havre) 1988/9 (Blackburn Rovers) 1989/90.
Staunton, S. (62) (Liverpool) 1988/9, 1989/90, 1990/1 (Aston Villa) 1991/2, 1992/93, 1993/94, 1994/95, 1995/96.

Stevenson, A.E. (6) (Everton) 1946/7, 1947/8, 1948/9.
Strahan, F. (5) (Shelbourne) 1963/4, 1964/5, 1965/6.
Swan, M.M.G. (1) (Drumcondra) 1959/60.
Synott, N. (3) (Shamrock Rovers) 1977/8, 1978/9.

Thomas, P. (2) (Waterford) 1973/4.
Townsend, A.D. (60) (Norwich City) 1988/9, 1989/90, 1990/1 (Chelsea) 1991/2, 1992/93 (Aston Villa) 1993/94, 1994/95, 1995/96.
Traynor, T.J. (8) (Southampton) 1953/4, 1961/2, 1962/3, 1963/4.
Treacy, R.C.P. (42) (West Bromwich Albion) 1965/6, 1966/7, 1967/8 (Charlton Athletic) 1967/8, 1968/9, 1969/70, 1970/1 (Swindon Town) 1971/2, 1972/3, 1973/4 (Preston North End) 1973/4, 1974/5, 1975/6 (West Bromwich Albion) 1976/7, 1977/8 (Shamrock Rovers) 1979/80.

Tuohy, L. (8) (Shamrock Rovers) 1955/6, 1958/9 (Newcastle United) 1961/2, 1962/3 (Shamrock Rovers) 1963/4, 1964/5.
Turner, P. (2) (Celtic) 1962/3, 1963/4.

Vernon, J. (2) (Belfast Celtic) 1945/6.

Waddock, G. (20) (QPR) 1979/80, 1980/1, 1981/2, 1982/3, 1983/4, 1984/5, 1985/6 (Millwall) 1989/90.
Walsh, D.J. (20) (West Bromwich Albion) 1945/6, 1946/7, 1947/8, 1948/9, 1949/50, 1950/1 (Aston Villa) 1951/2, 1952/3, 1953/4.
Walsh, J. (1) (Limerick) 1981/2.
Walsh, M. (21) (Blackpool) 1975/6, 1976/7 (Everton) 1978/9 (QPR) 1978/9 (Porto) 1980/1, 1981/2, 1982/3, 1983/4, 1984/5.
Walsh, M. (4) (Everton) 1981/2, 1982/3 (Norwich City) 1982/3.
Walsh, W. (9) (Manchester City) 1946/7, 1947/8, 1948/9, 1949/50.
Waters, J. (2) (Grimsby Town) 1976/7, 1979/80.
Whelan, R. (2) (St Patrick's Athletic) 1963/4.
Whelan, R. (53) (Liverpool) 1980/1, 1981/2, 1982/3, 1983/4, 1984/5, 1985/6, 1986/7, 1987/8, 1988/9, 1989/90, 1990/1, 1991/2, 1992/93, 1993/94 (Southend United) 1994/95.
Whelan, W. (4) (Manchester United) 1955/6, 1956/7.
Whittaker, R. (1) (Chelsea) 1958/9.

BRITISH ISLES INTERNATIONAL GOALSCORERS SINCE 1946

ENGLAND

A'Court, A.	1
Adams, T.A.	4
Allen, R.	2
Anderson, V.	2
Anderton, D.R.	5
Astall, G.	1
Atyeo, P.J.W.	5
Baily, E.F.	5
Baker, J.H.	3
Ball, A.J.	8
Barnes, J.	11
Barnes, P.S.	4
Barmby, N.J.	2
Beardsley, P.A.	9
Beattie, I.K.	1
Bell, C.	9
Bentley, R.T.F.	9
Blissett, L.	3
Bowles, S.	1
Bradford, G.R.W.	1
Bradley, W.	2
Bridges, B.J.	1
Broadbent, P.F.	2
Broadis, I.A.	8
Brooking, T.D.	5
Brooks, J.	2
Bull, S.G.	4
Butcher, T.	3
Byrne, J.J.	8
Carter, H.S.	7
(inc. 2 scored pre-war)	
Chamberlain, M.	1
Channon, M.R.	21
Charlton, J.	6
Charlton, R.	49
Chivers, M.	13
Clarke, A.J.	10
Connelly, J.M.	7
Coppell, S.J.	7
Cowans, G.	2
Crawford, R.	1
Currie, A.W.	3
Dixon, L.M.	1
Dixon, K.M.	4
Douglas, B.	11
Eastham, G.	2
Edwards, D.	5
Elliott, W.H.	3
Ferdinand, L.	4
Finney, T.	30
Flowers, R.	10
Francis, G.C.J.	3
Francis, T.	12
Froggatt, J.	2
Froggatt, R.	2
Gascoigne, P.J.	8
Goddard, P.	1
Grainger, C.	3
Greaves, J.	44
Haines, J.T.W.	2
Hancocks, J.	2
Hassall, H.W.	4
Hateley, M.	9
Haynes, J.N.	18
Hirst, D.E.	1
Hitchens, G.A.	5
Hoddle, G.	8
Hughes, E.W.	1
Hunt, R.	18
Hunter, N.	2
Hurst, G.C.	24
Johnson, D.E.	6
Kay, A.H.	1
Keegan, J.K.	21
Kennedy, R.	3
Keown, M.R.	1
Kevan, D.T.	8
Kidd, B.	1
Langton, R.	1
Latchford, R.D.	5
Lawler, C.	1
Lawton, T.	22
(inc. 6 scored pre-war)	
Lee, F.	10
Lee, J.	1
Lee, R.M.	1
Lee, S.	2
Le Saux, G.P.	1
Lineker, G.	48
Lofthouse, N.	30
Mabbutt, G.	1
McDermott, T.	3
Macdonald, M.	6
Mannion, W.J.	11
Mariner, P.	13
Marsh, R.W.	1
Matthews, S.	11
(inc. 8 scored pre-war)	
Medley, L.D.	1
Melia, J.	1
Merson, P.C.	1
Milburn, J.E.T.	10
Moore, R.F.	2
Morris, J.	3
Mortensen, S.H.	23
Mullen, J.	6
Mullery, A.P.	1
Neal, P.G.	5
Nicholls, J.	1
Nicholson, W.E.	1
O'Grady, M.	3
Own goals	23
Paine, T.L.	7
Palmer, C.L.	1
Parry, R.A.	1
Peacock, A.	3
Pearce, S.	4
Pearson, J.S.	5
Pearson, S.C.	5
Perry, W.	2
Peters, M.	20
Pickering, F.	5
Platt, D.	27
Pointer, R.	2
Ramsay, A.E.	3
Revie, D.G.	4
Robson, B.	26
Robson, R.	4
Rowley, J.F.	6
Royle, J.	2
Sansom, K.	1

Sewell, J.	3
Shackleton, L.F.	1
Shearer, A.	10
Sheringham, E.P.	4
Smith, A.M.	2
Smith, R.	13
Steven, T.M.	4
Stiles, N.P.	13
Stone, S.B.	2
Summerbee, M.G.	1
Tambling, R.V.	1
Taylor, P.J.	2
Taylor, T.	16
Thompson, P.B.	1
Tueart, D.	2
Viollet, D.S.	1
Waddle, C.R.	6
Wallace, D.L.	1
Walsh, P.	1
Watson, D.V.	4
Webb, N.	4
Weller, K.	1
Wignall, F.	2
Wilkins, R.G.	3
Wilshaw, D.J.	10
Wise, D.F.	1
Withe, P.	1
Woodcock, T.	16
Worthington, F.S.	2
Wright, I.E.	5
Wright, M.	1
Wright, W.A.	3

SCOTLAND

Aitken, R.	1
Archibald, S.	4
Baird, S.	2
Bannon, E.	1
Bauld, W.	2
Baxter, J.C.	3
Bett, J.	1
Bone, J.	1
Booth, S.	5
Brand, R.	8
Brazil, A.	1
Bremner, W.J.	3
Brown, A.D.	6
Buckley, P.	1
Burns, K.	1
Calderwood, C.	1
Caldow, E.	4
Campbell, R.	1
Chalmers, S.	3
Collins, J.	8
Collins, R.V.	10
Combe, J.R.	1
Conn, A.	1
Cooper, D.	6
Craig, J.	1
Crawford, S.	1
Curran, H.P.	1
Dalglish, K.	30
Davidson, J.A.	1
Docherty, T.H.	1
Dodds, D.	1
Duncan, D.M.	1
Durie, G.S.	5
Fernie, W.	1
Flavell, R.	2
Fleming, C.	2
Gallacher, K.W.	2
Gemmell, T.K (St Mirren)	1
Gemmell, T.K (Celtic)	1
Gemmill, A.	8
Gibson, D.W.	3
Gilzean, A.J.	12
Gough, C.R.	6
Graham, A.	2
Graham, G.	3
Gray, A.	7
Gray, E.	3
Gray, F.	1
Greig, J.	3
Hamilton, G.	4
Harper, J.M.	2
Hartford, R.A.	4
Henderson, J.G.	1
Henderson, W.	5
Hendry, E.C.J.	1
Herd, D.G.	4
Hewie, J.D.	2
Holton, J.A.	2
Houliston, W.	2
Howie, H.	1
Hughes, J.	1
Hunter, W.	1
Hutchison, T.	1
Jackson, C.	1
Jardine, A.	1
Jess, E.	1
Johnston, L.H.	1
Johnston, M.	14
Johnstone, D.	2
Johnstone, J.	4
Johnstone, R.	9
Jordan, J.	11
Law, D.	30
Leggat, G.	8
Lennox, R.	3
Liddell, W.	6
Linwood, A.B.	1
Lorimer, P.	4
Macari, L.	5
McAllister, G.	4
MacDougall, E.J.	3
MacKay, D.C.	4
Mackay, G.	1
MacKenzie, J.A.	1
MacLeod, M.	1
McAvennie, F.	1
McCall, S.M.	1
McCalliog, J.	1
McClair, B.	2
McCoist, A.	19
McGhee, M.	2
McGinlay, J.	3
McInally, A.	3
McKimmie, S.I.	1
McKinlay, W.	4
McKinnon, R.	1
McLaren, A.	4
McLean, T.	1
McLintock, F.	1
McMillan, I.L.	2
McNeill, W.	3
McPhail, J.	3
McQueen, G.	5
McStay, P.	9
Mason, J.	4
Masson, D.S.	5
Miller, W.	1
Mitchell, R.C.	1

Morgan, W.	1	**WALES**		Jones, Cliff	15
Morris, H.	3	Allchurch, I.J.	23	Jones, D.E.	1
Mudie, J.K.	9	Allen, M.	3	Jones, J.P.	1
Mulhall, G.	1				
Murdoch, R.	5	Barnes, W.	1	Kryzwicki, R.I.	1
Murray, J.	1	Blackmore, C.G.	1		
		Blake, N.A.	1	Leek, K.	5
Narey, D.	1	Bodin, P.J.	3	Lovell, S.	1
Nevin, P.K.F.	5	Bowen, D.I.	3	Lowrie, G.	2
Nicholas, C.	5	Bowen, M.	2		
		Boyle, T.	1	Mahoney, J.F.	1
O'Hare, J.	5	Burgess, W.A.R.	1	Medwin, T.C.	6
Ormond, W.E.	1			Melville, A.K.	1
Orr, T.	1	Charles, J.	1	Moore, G.	1
Own goals	7	Charles, M.	6		
		Charles, W.J.	15	Nicholas, P.	2
Parlane, D.	1	Clarke, R.J.	5		
Pettigrew, W.	2	Coleman, C.	3	O'Sullivan, P.A.	1
Provan, D.	1	Curtis, A.	6	Own goals	5
Quinn, J.	7	Davies, G.	2	Palmer, D.	1
Quinn, P.	1	Davies, R.T.	8	Paul, R.	1
		Davies, R.W	7	Pembridge, M.A.	3
Reilly, L.	22	Deacy, N.	4	Phillips, D.	2
Ring, T.	2	Durban, A.	2	Powell, A.	1
Rioch, B.D.	6	Dwyer, P.	2	Powell, D.	1
Robertson, A.	2			Price, P.	1
Robertson, J.	2	Edwards, G.	2		
Robertson, J.N.	9	Edwards, R.I.	4	Reece, G.I.	2
		England, H.M.	3	Rees, R.R.	3
St John, I.	9	Evans, I.	1	Roberts, P.S.	1
Scott, A.S.	5			Rush, I.	28
Sharp, G.	1	Flynn, B.	7		
Shearer, D.	2	Ford, T.	23	Saunders, D.	16
Smith, G.	4	Foulkes, W.J.	1	Slatter, N.	2
Souness, G.J.	3			Smallman, D.P.	1
Steel, W.	12	Giggs, R.J.	4	Speed, G.A.	2
Stein, C.	10	Giles, D.	2	Symons, C.J.	1
Stewart, R.	1	Godfrey, B.C.	2	Tapscott, D.R.	4
Strachan, G.	5	Griffiths, A.T.	6	Thomas, M.	4
Sturrock, P.	3	Griffiths, M.W	2	Toshack, J.B.	13
Thornton, W.	1	Harris, C.S.	1	Vernon, T.R.	8
		Hewitt, R.	1	Walsh, I.	7
Waddell, W.	6	Hockey, T.	1	Williams, G.E.	1
Wallace, I.A.	1	Hodges, G.	2	Williams, G.G.	1
Wark, J.	7	Horne, B.	2	Woosnam, A.P.	4
Weir, A.	1	Hughes, L.M.	14		
White, J.A.	3			Yorath, T.C.	2
Wilson, D.	9	James, L.	10	Young, E.	1
		James, R.	8		
Young, A.	2	Jones, A.	1		
		Jones, B.S.	2		

NORTHERN IRELAND

Anderson, T.	4
Armstrong, G.	12
Barr, H.H.	1
Best, G.	9
Bingham, W.L.	10
Black, K.	1
Blanchflower, D.	2
Blanchflower, J.	1
Brennan, R.A.	1
Brotherston, N.	3
Campbell, W.G.	1
Casey, T.	2
Caskey, W.	1
Cassidy, T.	1
Clarke, C.J.	13
Clements, D.	2
Cochrane, T.	1
Crossan, E.	1
Crossan, J.A.	10
Cush, W.W.	5
D'Arcy, S.D.	1
Doherty, I.	1
Doherty, P.D.	3
(inc. 1 scored pre-war)	
Dougan, A.D.	8
Dowie, I.	8
Elder, A.R.	1
Ferguson, W.	1
Ferris, R.O.	1
Finney, T.	2
Gillespie, K.R.	1
Gray, P.	5
Hamilton, B.	4
Hamilton, W.	5
Harkin, J.T.	2
Harvey, M.	3
Hill, C.F.	1
Humphries, W.	1
Hughes, M.E.	2
Hunter, A.	1
Hunter, B.V.	1
Irvine, W.J.	8

Johnston, W.C.	1
Jones, J.	1
Lockhart, N.	3
Lomas, S.M.	1
Magilton, J.	4
McAdams, W.J.	7
McClelland, J.	1
McCrory, S.	1
McCurdy, C.	1
McDonald, A.	3
McGarry, J.K.	1
McGrath, R.C.	4
McIlroy, J.	10
McIlroy, S.B.	5
McLaughlin, J.C.	6
McMahon, G.J.	2
McMordie, A.S.	3
McMorran, E.J.	4
McParland, P.J.	10
Moreland, V.	1
Morgan, S.	3
Morrow, S.J.	1
Neill, W.J.T.	2
Nelson, S.	1
Nicholl, C.J.	3
Nicholl, J.M.	2
Nicholson, J.J.	6
O'Boyle, G.	1
O'Kane, W.J.	1
O'Neill, J.	1
O'Neill, M.A.	4
O'Neill, M.H.	8
Own goals	4
Peacock, R.	2
Penney, S.	2
Quinn, J.M.	12
Simpson, W.J.	5
Smyth, S.	5
Spence, D.W.	3
Stewart, I.	2
Taggart, G.P.	5
Tully, C.P.	3
Walker, J.	1
Walsh, D.J.	5

Welsh, E.	1
Whiteside, N.	9
Wilson, D.J.	1
Wilson, K.J.	6
Wilson, S.J.	7

EIRE

Aldridge, J.	19
Ambrose, P.	1
Anderson, J.	1
Bermingham, P.	1
Bradshaw, P.	4
Brady, L.	9
Breen, G.	1
Brown, D.	1
Byrne, J. (Bray)	1
Byrne, J. (QPR)	4
Cantwell, J.	14
Carey, J.	3
Carroll, T.	1
Cascarino, A.	12
Coad, P.	3
Connolly, D.J.	2
Conroy, T.	2
Conway, J.	3
Coyne, T.	6
Cummings, G.	5
Curtis, D.	8
Daly, G.	13
Davis, T.	4
Dempsey, J.	1
Dennehy, M.	2
Donnelly, J.	3
Donnelly, T.	1
Duffy, B.	1
Duggan, H.	1
Dunne, J.	12
Dunne, L.	1
Eglinton, T.	2
Ellis, P.	1
Fagan, F.	5
Fallon, S.	2
Fallon, W.	2
Farrell, P.	3
Fitzgerald, J.	1
Fitzgerald, P.	2
Fitzsimons, A.	7

UEFA UNDER-21 CHAMPIONSHIP 1994–96

(Also used as qualification for Olympics)

Group 1
Israel 2, Poland 2
Romania 5, Azerbaijan 2
Slovakia 0, France 3
Israel 2, Slovakia 0
Poland 5, Azerbaijan 0
Romania 0, Slovakia 0
Poland 0, France 4
Azerbaijan 1, Israel 2
Israel 0, Romania 1
Azerbaijan 0, France 5
Israel 1, France 1
Romania 1, Poland 2
Slovakia 3, Azerbaijan 0
Poland 1, Israel 0
Azerbaijan 0, Romania 5
France 0, Slovakia 1
Poland 1, Slovakia 0
Romania 1, Israel 0

Group 2
Belgium 7, Armenia 0
Cyprus 0, Spain 6
Macedonia 5, Denmark 3
Armenia 1, Cyprus 2
Denmark 0, Belgium 1
Macedonia 0, Spain 1
Belgium 7, Macedonia 0
Spain 1, Denmark 0
Cyprus 2, Armenia 1
Belgium 3, Spain 3
Macedonia 1, Cyprus 0
Spain 1, Belgium 1
Cyprus 1, Denmark 5
Belgium 1, Cyprus 0
Denmark 5, Macedonia 2
Armenia 0, Spain 3
Armenia 2, Macedonia 0
Denmark 4, Cyprus 0
Spain 4, Armenia 0
Macedonia 3, Belgium 0

Group 3
Hungary 2, Turkey 1
Iceland 0, Sweden 1
Switzerland 0, Sweden 5
Turkey 3, Iceland 0
Sweden 0, Hungary 1
Switzerland 2, Iceland 1
Turkey 1, Switzerland 1
Hungary 1, Switzerland 0

Turkey 0, Sweden 0
Hungary 2, Sweden 1
Switzerland 0, Turkey 2
Sweden 1, Iceland 0
Iceland 1, Hungary 2

Group 4
Estonia 1, Croatia 2
Ukraine 3, Lithuania 2
Slovenia 1, Italy 1
Estonia 1, Italy 4
Croatia 2, Lithuania 0
Ukraine 1, Slovenia 0
Ukraine 3, Estonia 0
Slovenia 3, Lithuania 0
Italy 2, Croatia 1
Italy 7, Estonia 0
Croatia 1, Ukraine 0
Lithuania 0, Croatia 1
Slovenia 5, Estonia 0
Ukraine 2, Italy 1
Croatia 0, Slovenia 2
Estonia 2, Ukraine 5
Lithuania 0, Italy 2
Lithuania 1, Slovenia 2
Estonia 1, Slovenia 2
Ukraine 1, Croatia 1

Group 5
Czech Republic 1, Malta 0
Luxembourg 0, Holland 4
Norway 4, Belarus 0
Malta 0, Czech Republic 7
Norway 1, Holland 0
Belarus 3, Luxembourg 0
Holland 2, Czech Republic 2
Malta 2, Norway 3
Holland 3, Luxembourg 0
Malta 1, Luxembourg 0
Luxembourg 0, Norway 8
Holland 4, Malta 0
Czech Republic 2, Belarus 0
Norway 5, Luxembourg 0
Belarus 4, Malta 0
Czech Republic 2, Holland 2
Belarus 4, Norway 2
Luxembourg 0, Czech Republic 7
Norway 3, Malta 0
Belarus 3, Holland 1

Group 6

England 0, Portugal 0
Latvia 1, Republic of Ireland 1
Latvia 0, Portugal 1
Austria 1, England 3
Portugal 2, Austria 0
England 1, Republic of Ireland 0
Republic of Ireland 0, England 2
Austria 0, Latvia 0
Republic of Ireland 1, Portugal 1
Latvia 0, England 1
Portugal 4, Latvia 0
Republic of Ireland 3, Austria 0

Group 7
Georgia 3, Moldova 0
Bulgaria 1, Georgia 0
Moldova 1, Wales 0
Bulgaria 2, Moldova 0
Georgia 1, Wales 2
Wales 1, Bulgaria 1
Moldova 1, Germany 1

Bulgaria 3, Wales 1
Georgia 0, Germany 2
Germany 1, Wales 0
Moldova 0, Bulgaria 0
Bulgaria 2, Germany 0
Wales 5, Georgia 1

Group 8
Finland 1, Scotland 0
Greece 3, Finland 4
Russia 3, San Marino 0
Greece 4, San Marino 0
Scotland 2, Russia 1
Finland 4, San Marino 0
Greece 1, Scotland 2
San Marino 0, Finland 6
Russia 1, Scotland 2
Greece 0, Russia 1
San Marino 0, Scotland 1
San Marino 0, Russia 7
Finland 1, Greece 0

OLYMPIC FOOTBALL

Previous winners

1896	Athens*	1. Denmark	1956	Melbourne	1.	USSR
		2. Greece			2.	Yugoslavia
1900	Paris*	1. England			3.	Bulgaria
		2. France	1960	Rome	1.	Yugoslavia
1904	St Louis**	1. Canada			2.	Denmark
		2. USA			3.	Hungary
1908	London	1. England	1964	Tokyo	1.	Hungary
		2. Denmark			2.	Czechoslovakia
		3. Holland			3.	East Germany
1912	Stockholm	1. England	1968	Mexico City	1.	Hungary
		2. Denmark			2.	Bulgaria
		3. Holland			3.	Japan
1920	Antwerp	1. Belgium	1972	Munich	1.	Poland
		2. Spain			2.	Hungary
		3. Holland			3.	East Germany/ USSR joint bronze
1924	Paris	1. Uruguay				
		2. Switzerland	1976	Montreal	1.	East Germany
		3. Sweden			2.	Poland
1928	Amsterdam	1. Uruguay			3.	USSR
		2. Argentina	1980	Moscow	1.	Czechoslovakia
		3. Italy			2.	East Germany
1932	Los Angeles no competition				3.	USSR
1936	Berlin	1. Italy	1984	Los Angeles	1.	France
		2. Austria			2.	Brazil
		3. Norway			3.	Yugoslavia
1948	London	1. Sweden	1988	Seoul	1.	USSR
		2. Yugoslavia			2.	Brazil
		3. Denmark			3.	West Germany
1952	Helsinki	1. Hungary	1992	Barcelona	1.	Spain
		2. Yugoslavia			2.	Poland
		3. Sweden			3.	Ghana

*No official tournament
**No official tournament but gold medal later awarded by IOC

12TH EUROPEAN UNDER-18 YOUTH CHAMPIONSHIP

Group 1
Austria 0, Yugoslavia 3
Georgia 1, Austria 3
Yugoslavia 3, Georgia 0

Group 2
Luxembourg 0, Switzerland 3
Switzerland 1, Greece 5
Luxembourg 0, Greece 2
Switzerland 1, Luxembourg 0
Greece 1, Switzerland 1
Greece 3, Luxembourg 0

Group 3
Italy 2, Bulgaria 0
Bulgaria 3, Malta 0
Italy 5, Malta 0
Bulgaria 0, Italy 1
Malta 0, Italy 1
Malta 0, Bulgaria 1

Group 4
Czech Republic 2, Russia 1
Russia 4, Czech Republic 1
Russia 1, Turkey 1
Turkey 0, Czech Republic 0
Czech Republic 0, Turkey 1
Turkey 2, Russia 3

Group 5
Israel 2, Azerbaijan 1
Azerbaijan 0, Hungary 3
Hungary 1, Israel 1

Group 6
Romania 0, Germany 1
Croatia 1, Romania 0
Germany 4, Croatia 2

Group 7
Belgium 3, Slovenia 1
Slovenia 2, Moldova 1
Moldova 2, Belgium 3

Group 8
Macedonia 0, Denmark 2
Portugal 3, Macedonia 0
Denmark 0, Portugal 1

Group 9
Cyprus 2, Holland 5
Armenia 0, Cyprus 1
Holland 9, Armenia 2

Group 10
Spain 2, Ukraine 1
Slovakia 1, Ukraine 4
Spain 0, Slovakia 0

Group 11
Faeroes 0, Poland 4
Norway 7, Faeroes 0
Poland 2, Norway 4

Group 12
Estonia 1, Lithuania 4
Scotland 4, Estonia 1
Lithuania 0, Scotland 1

Group 13
Sweden 3, Latvia 1
Latvia 0, England 2
England 6, Sweden 2

Group 14
Finland 2, Republic of Ireland 5
Wales 3, Finland 2
Republic of Ireland 0, Wales 0
Finland 0, Wales 2
Republic of Ireland 3, Finland 0
Wales 0, Republic of Ireland 3

Group 15
Northern Ireland 2, Belarus 0
Belarus 0, Iceland 3
Iceland 3, Northern Ireland 2

SECOND STAGE

Group 1
Italy 4, Greece 0
Greece 1, Italy 3
Greece 1, Austria 0
Italy 2, Austria 0
Austria 0, Greece 1
Austria 0, Italy 0

Group 2
Russia 2, Hungary 4
Hungary 1, Russia 0

Group 3
Germany 0, Belgium 0
Belgium 2, Germany 1

Group 4
Portugal 4, Holland 1
Holland 2, Portugal 0

Group 5
Spain 3, Norway 1
Norway 4, Spain 0

Group 6
Scotland 0, England 3
England 3, Scotland 0

Group 7
Republic of Ireland 2, Iceland 1
Iceland 1, Republic of Ireland 1

297

WORLD UNDER-17 CHAMPIONSHIP

(in Ecuador, August 1995)

Group A
Ecuador 2, USA 0
Ghana 1, Japan 0
Ecuador 1, Ghana 2
USA 1, Japan 2
Ecuador 0, Japan 0
USA 0, Ghana 2

Group B
Argentina 3, Portugal 0
Costa Rica 2, Guinea 0
Argentina 2, Costa Rica 0
Portugal 2, Guinea 3
Argentina 2, Guinea 0
Portugal 3, Costa Rica 0

Group C
Nigeria 1, Qatar 1
Australia 2, Spain 2
Nigeria 2, Australia 0
Qatar 0, Spain 1
Nigeria 2, Spain 1
Qatar 0, Australia 3

Group D
Brazil 3, Germany 0
Oman 2, Canada 1
Brazil 0, Oman 0
Germany 3, Canada 0
Brazil 2, Canada 0
Germany 0, Oman 3

Quarter-finals
Ghana 2, Portugal 0
Nigeria 1, Oman 2
Brazil 3, Australia 1
Argentina 3, Ecuador 1

Semi-finals
Ghana 3, Oman 1
Argentina 0, Brazil 3

Third place
Oman 0, Argentina 2

Final
Ghana 3, Brazil 2

14th UEFA UNDER-16 CHAMPIONSHIP 1996

(in Austria)

Group A
Eire 1, Austria 0
Portugal 3, Poland 0
Austria 0, Poland 0
Eire 0, Portugal 2
Austria 2, Portugal 2
Poland 0, Eire 1

Group B
Greece 2, Germany 1
Romania 0, Ukraine 1
Romania 0, Greece 1
Ukraine 1, Germany 6
Romania 1, Germany 4
Ukraine 1, Greece 1

Group C
France 2, Croatia 0
Spain 4, Switzerland 1
France 3, Spain 0
Croatia 2, Switzerland 1
Switzerland 0, France 1
Croatia 1, Spain 0

Group D
England 2, Slovakia 0
Turkey 3, Israel 0
England 2, Turkey 1
Slovakia 0, Israel 2
Israel 2, England 1
Slovakia 2, Turkey 1

Quarter-finals
Portugal 5, Croatia 1
France 0, Eire 0 aet
France won 5-4 on penalties
Greece 1, England 0
Israel 3, Germany 2 aet

Semi-finals
Portugal 3, Greece 0
France 1, Israel 0

Third Place
Israel 3, Greece 2

Final (in Vienna)
Portugal 1, France 0

298

VAUXHALL CONFERENCE 1995–96

		Home			Goals		Away			Goals		
	P	W	D	L	F	A	W	D	L	F	A	Pts
Stevenage Borough	42	13	6	2	51	20	14	4	3	50	24	91
Woking	42	16	5	0	47	13	9	3	9	36	41	83
Hednesford Town	42	13	5	3	38	21	10	4	7	33	25	76
Macclesfield Town	42	12	5	4	32	16	10	4	7	34	33	75
Gateshead	42	9	7	5	32	24	9	6	6	26	22	67
Southport	42	10	7	4	42	25	8	5	8	35	39	66
Kidderminster Harriers	42	13	4	4	49	26	5	6	10	29	40	64
Northwich Victoria	42	9	3	9	38	35	7	9	5	34	29	60
Morecambe	42	12	2	7	51	33	5	6	10	27	39	59
Farnborough Town	42	8	6	7	29	23	7	8	6	34	35	59
Bromsgrove Rovers	42	11	6	4	33	20	4	8	9	26	37	59
Altrincham	42	9	6	6	33	29	6	7	8	26	35	58
Telford United	42	8	7	6	27	23	7	3	11	24	33	55
Stalybridge Celtic	42	9	3	9	29	37	7	4	10	30	31	55
Halifax Town	42	8	7	6	30	25	5	6	10	19	38	52
Kettering Town	42	9	5	7	38	32	4	4	13	30	52	48
Slough Town	42	4	6	11	35	44	9	2	10	28	32	47
Bath City	42	9	4	8	29	31	4	3	14	16	35	46
Welling United	42	6	8	7	21	23	4	7	10	21	30	45
Dover Athletic	42	8	1	12	29	38	3	6	12	22	36	40
Runcorn	42	4	5	12	25	43	5	3	13	23	44	35
Dagenham & Redbridge	42	5	7	9	31	34	2	5	14	12	39	33

Leading Goalscorers 1995–96

Conf.			FAC	SCC	FAT
29	Barry Hayles (*Stevenage Borough*)	+	—	—	5
23	Joe O'Connor (*Hednesford Town*)	+	1	2	—
22	Carl Alford (*ex-Kettering Town*)	+	2	—	1
21	Mark West (*Slough Town*)	+	—	4	3
	Chris Boothe (*Farnborough Town*)	+	5	5	1
20	David Leworthy (*Dover Athletic*)	+	1	3	1
19	Steve Harkus (*Gateshead*)	+	—	1	—
18	Clive Walker (*Woking*)	+	1	—	—
17	Carwyn Williams (*Northwich Victoria*)	+	3	—	—
16	Andy Whittaker (*Southport*)	+	—	3	1
15	Corey Browne (*Stevenage Borough*)	+	1	—	—
14	Mike Bignall (*Runcorn*)	+	2	—	—
	Brian Butler (*Northwich Victoria*)	+	2	—	4
	Kim Casey (*Kidderminster Harriers*)	+	1	2	—
	Paul Davies (*Kidderminster Harriers*)	+	—	—	—
	Darran Hay (*Woking*)	+	4	—	—
	Junior Hunter (*Woking*)	+	—	—	—

FAC: FA Cup; SCC: Spalding Challenge Cup; FAT: FA Trophy.

VAUXHALL CONFERENCE RESULTS 1995–96

	Altrincham	Bath City	Bromsgrove Rovers	Dagenham & Redbridge	Dover Athletic	Farnborough Town	Gateshead	Halifax Town	Hednesford Town	Kettering Town	Kidderminster Harriers	Macclesfield Town	Morecambe	Northwich Victoria	Runcorn	Slough Town	Southport	Stalybridge Celtic	Stevenage Borough	Telford United	Welling United	Woking
Altrincham		1-2	3-0		2-2	2-2	1-1	3-2	2-1		1-1	0-4	3-0	3-4	2-2	0-1	1-0	1-0	0-2	1-0	1-0	2-0
Bath City			0-1	0-2	2-1	1-0	1-1		2-1	3-1	2-1	0-3	3-2	0-3	2-0	0-1	4-0	0-4	1-2	0-3	1-0	0-3
Bromsgrove Rovers	0-0	4-1			3-0	1-2	3-1	0-1	1-4	3-2	4-2	1-0	2-2	1-0	3-0	0-0	4-1	4-1	1-2	0-2	1-1	2-1
Dagenham & Redbridge	1-4	0-1	2-2		3-0	1-2	0-4	0-1	1-1	1-2	0-1	2-3	2-2	1-2	2-3	1-3	1-2	4-1	1-1	0-2	1-1	0-0
Dover Athletic	1-1	1-0		3-2		1-3	2-3	3-0	2-1	1-3	0-1	2-3	2-2	0-1	3-1	0-0	1-0	1-1	0-3	2-1	2-1	4-3
Farnborough Town	1-1	0-0	2-0	1-2	1-3		0-0	3-0	1-3	2-1	1-1	0-1	3-1	1-1	1-0	1-0	1-0	2-1	2-2	2-1	0-1	0-2
Gateshead	2-3	3-1	3-0	3-0	1-0	1-1		3-0	0-3	1-1	3-1	0-1	3-0	2-0	1-0	1-0	1-0	2-3	2-1	2-2	0-1	1-2
Halifax Town	2-1	2-1	2-2	4-1	1-0	2-3	0-1		3-1	0-2	0-2	0-1	1-1	2-2	1-3	3-1	2-1	1-6	2-3	4-0	1-1	2-2
Hednesford Town	4-2	3-0	1-2	0-0	2-1	1-0	6-1	3-0		3-1	1-3	0-4	1-1	2-2	4-3	1-1	2-1	1-0	1-2	0-3	1-3	3-0
Kettering Town	1-3	2-2	2-2	5-1	1-2	0-1	1-0	7-0	2-2			0-1	0-0	0-2	1-1	4-3	2-3	2-3	2-3	2-0	2-0	3-2
Kidderminster Harriers	4-2	0-2	3-1	3-1	0-1	1-0	2-3	6-1	3-1	5-3		2-4	2-1	0-0	1-1	1-1	1-4	2-2	0-8	2-2	2-1	2-4
Macclesfield Town	7-0	2-2	4-1	1-0	0-1	1-0	3-3	1-0	0-1	6-2	5-2		4-2	2-0	2-0	3-1	1-2	5-3	2-6	1-2	2-1	3-0
Morecambe	2-1	2-2	0-0	1-2	1-2	0-1	0-2	2-0	2-2	4-2	5-4	1-2		3-1	2-0	0-2	2-5	2-1	1-0	2-2	1-0	2-3
Northwich Victoria	1-2	3-1	2-1	1-3	1-2	2-3	2-0	0-0	2-2	6-2	0-2	2-1	2-1		1-3	2-0	3-1	0-1	0-8	1-0	2-1	2-4
Runcorn	1-0	0-0	4-1	2-0	0-0	0-2	2-1	1-3	0-0	2-2	5-2	1-2	2-3	3-4		2-0	2-1	5-3	2-6	0-1	0-1	3-0
Slough Town	2-1	2-1	2-2	2-1	3-2	2-2	1-2	1-1	2-2	6-1	4-1	4-0	0-2	1-5	1-1		1-3	2-2	2-5	2-2	2-1	2-2
Southport	1-0	2-1	1-2	0-0	0-1	4-0	0-2	0-2	3-4	3-2	0-2	1-2	1-2	2-1	2-0	1-4		2-2	2-6	2-2	1-0	2-4
Stalybridge Celtic	1-0	3-1	0-0	0-0	1-2	0-0	1-1	2-3	2-1	3-4	0-2	4-0	2-1	2-2	4-1	2-0	1-3			0-1	0-0	1-2
Stevenage Borough	1-1	2-1	5-1	1-0	1-1	2-1	1-3	1-6	3-1	3-1	1-0	1-0	1-0	3-1	1-0	1-1	2-1	5-3		3-1	2-1	3-2
Telford United	1-0	3-1	2-1	2-1	1-0	2-1	1-2	1-0	2-0	5-1	2-1	1-2	1-0	2-2	3-0	2-0	2-1	2-2	0-1		4-0	5-1
Welling United	1-0	0-0	0-0	1-0	1-0	3-0	1-2	1-2	2-1	3-2	0-2	1-0	2-2	1-2	2-0	2-1	2-1	2-1	2-1	3-1		3-2
Woking	1-1	2-0	1-1	2-2	1-0	2-1	2-0	2-0	3-0	1-1	0-0	3-2	3-0	0-0	2-1	3-0	3-4	1-1	4-1	5-1	3-2	

BEAZER HOMES LEAGUE 1995-96

Premier Division

	P	W	D	L	F	A	Pts
Rusden & Diamonds	42	29	7	6	99	41	94
Halesowen Town	42	27	11	4	70	36	92
Cheltenham Town	42	21	11	10	76	57	74
Gloucester City	42	21	8	13	65	47	71
Gresley Rovers	42	20	10	12	70	58	70
Worcester City	42	19	12	11	61	43	69
Merthyr Tydfil	42	19	6	17	67	59	63
Hastings Town	42	16	13	13	68	55	61
Crawley Town	42	15	13	14	57	56	58
Sudbury Town	42	15	10	17	69	71	55
Gravesend & Northfleet	42	13	16	13	46	53	55
Chelmsford City	42	13	16	13	46	53	55
Dorchester Town	42	15	8	19	62	57	53
Newport AFC	42	13	13	16	53	59	52
Salisbury City	42	14	10	18	57	69	52
Burton Albion	42	13	12	17	55	56	51
Atherstone United	42	12	12	18	57	75	48
Baldock Town	42	11	14	17	51	56	47
Cambridge City	42	12	10	20	56	68	46
Ilkeston Town	42	11	10	21	53	87	43
Stafford Rangers	42	11	4	27	58	90	37
VS Rugby	42	5	10	27	37	92	25

**Leading Goalscorers 1995-96
(League and Cup)**

Premier Division

D. Collins (Rusden & Diamonds)	31
J. Smith (Cheltenham Town)	27
J. Eaton (Cheltenham Town)	24
I. Brown (Sudbury Town)	23
P. Evans (Merthyr Tydfil)	23
E. Wright (Halesowen Town)	23
S. Cuggy (Hastings Town)	21
M. Munday (Gravesend & Northfleet)	20
D. Taylor (Ilkeston Town)	18
D. Webley (Newport A.F.C.)	18
S. Norris (Worcester City)	17
O. Pickard (Dorchester Town)	17

BEAZER HOMES PREMIER DIVISION RESULTS 1995-96

Home \ Away	Atherstone United	Baldock Town	Burton Albion	Cambridge City	Chelmsford City	Cheltenham Town	Crawley Town	Dorchester Town	Gloucester City	Gravesend & Northfleet	Gresley Rovers	Halesowen Town	Hastings Town	Ilkeston Town	Merthyr Tydfil	Newport AFC	Rushden & Diamonds	Salisbury City	Stafford Rangers	Sudbury Town	VS Rugby	Worcester City
Atherstone United	—	1-1	1-0	0-3	2-2	1-2	1-2	2-1	3-4	2-1	2-0	1-2	0-1	1-0	3-3	1-3	0-0	1-3	3-1	2-2	0-0	4-1
Baldock Town	2-2	—	0-0	0-0	2-1	1-2	1-0	2-0	1-3	0-2	3-1	2-0	4-3	1-0	2-1	1-0	1-2	2-0	3-2	0-0	0-0	0-1
Burton Albion	2-2	1-0	—	0-0	1-0	3-2	1-0	4-1	5-0	3-1	2-1	2-2	1-2	0-1	1-3	1-2	3-2	2-0	5-1	1-3	0-0	2-0
Cambridge City	1-1	0-0	0-0	—	2-1	3-3	1-2	0-2	2-0	3-1	2-2	2-3	0-3	2-3	1-3	2-1	1-1	3-3	2-0	1-0	4-1	4-2
Chelmsford City	1-1	1-1	2-1	0-0	—	3-2	1-0	0-1	5-0	4-1	0-2	0-2	1-2	2-3	1-3	0-1	1-1	1-0	2-1	2-2	2-0	1-0
Cheltenham Town	3-1	3-2	1-2	3-3	4-1	—	1-1	0-3	0-3	0-4	2-1	2-2	3-2	4-0	3-1	4-0	1-4	3-3	4-2	1-1	4-0	1-3
Crawley Town	0-1	0-1	1-0	1-2	0-1	1-0	—	3-1	1-1	1-0	0-2	2-0	1-0	3-1	0-1	2-1	3-1	0-2	0-3	1-4	4-1	1-0
Dorchester Town	1-2	3-1	4-1	2-0	0-1	0-3	3-1	—	4-1	3-1	0-0	0-2	1-4	3-1	1-0	0-3	1-1	3-0	0-2	2-4	2-0	1-2
Gloucester City	2-1	1-2	5-0	2-0	5-0	0-3	1-1	4-1	—	3-1	0-1	1-2	0-1	2-2	3-1	4-0	1-4	1-0	0-2	3-0	4-0	2-1
Gravesend & Northfleet	2-1	2-0	3-1	3-1	4-1	0-4	1-0	3-1	3-1	—	0-1	2-1	2-1	2-1	2-1	6-1	2-2	0-1	0-3	5-3	1-3	0-1
Gresley Rovers	1-0	3-1	2-1	2-2	0-2	2-1	0-2	0-0	0-1	0-1	—	2-1	0-1	3-2	0-0	3-1	1-1	6-2	2-3	2-1	4-0	1-0
Halesowen Town	3-0	2-0	2-2	2-3	0-2	2-2	2-0	0-2	1-2	2-1	2-1	—	0-2	2-2	0-1	3-1	1-2	2-2	1-3	1-0	2-1	3-3
Hastings Town	5-0	4-3	1-2	0-3	1-2	3-2	1-0	1-4	0-1	2-1	0-1	0-2	—	1-0	0-1	0-3	3-4	0-1	5-1	4-2	5-2	0-0
Ilkeston Town	4-0	1-0	0-1	2-3	2-3	4-0	3-1	3-1	2-2	2-1	3-2	2-2	1-0	—	10-1	3-0	1-1	0-0	2-1	3-0	6-1	0-1
Merthyr Tydfil	1-2	2-1	1-3	1-3	1-3	3-1	0-1	1-0	3-1	2-1	0-0	0-1	0-1	0-0	—	0-0	0-2	2-1	0-1	1-2	1-2	0-1
Newport AFC	7-3	1-0	1-2	2-1	0-1	4-0	2-1	0-3	4-0	3-0	3-1	1-2	3-0	0-3	3-2	—	2-3	6-1	0-1	0-1	5-2	1-1
Rushden & Diamonds	2-0	1-2	3-2	1-1	1-1	1-4	3-1	1-1	1-4	2-2	1-1	2-1	4-3	1-1	0-2	3-2	—	3-1	2-1	5-1	3-0	0-1
Salisbury City	1-4	0-1	0-2	2-4	1-0	0-3	0-2	1-1	0-1	1-0	2-6	1-0	1-0	0-0	1-2	1-6	1-3	—	4-2	3-1	4-0	1-2
Stafford Rangers	2-0	2-1	1-5	0-2	1-2	2-4	3-0	2-0	2-0	3-0	3-2	2-1	1-5	1-2	2-1	1-0	0-1	2-1	—	2-2	0-3	0-0
Sudbury Town	2-1	1-3	0-1	0-1	0-0	1-1	0-3	4-2	1-3	3-5	2-1	5-2	1-1	0-3	1-0	1-0	1-1	4-0	3-1	—	2-3	0-2
VS Rugby	3-0	2-0	0-0	4-1	2-0	4-0	1-4	2-0	4-0	1-3	4-0	1-1	6-1	3-0	1-2	1-2	4-1	3-3	3-1	1-1	—	4-0
Worcester City	1-0	0-1	2-0	4-2	1-0	1-3	1-0	1-2	2-1	0-1	1-0	3-3	0-0	0-1	2-0	2-0	1-3	2-0	4-0	1-1	4-0	—

UNIBOND LEAGUE 1995–96

Premier Division

		Home			Goals		Away			Goals		
	P	W	D	L	F	A	W	D	L	F	A	Pts
Bamber Bridge	42	9	8	4	43	26	11	8	2	38	23	76
Boston United	42	10	4	7	40	31	13	2	6	46	28	75
Hyde United	42	12	5	4	57	24	9	6	6	29	27	74
Barrow	42	10	7	4	36	20	10	6	5	33	22	73
Gainsborough Trinity	42	10	6	5	30	21	10	7	4	30	20	73
Blyth Spartans	42	11	8	2	46	24	6	5	10	29	37	64
Accrington Stanley	42	8	6	7	29	25	9	8	4	33	29	62
Emley	42	11	3	7	34	26	6	7	8	23	27	61
Spennymoor United	42	7	10	4	36	30	7	8	6	31	31	60
Guiseley	42	9	5	7	36	29	6	9	6	26	28	59
Bishop Auckland	42	7	7	7	31	28	9	4	8	29	27	59
Marine	42	10	6	5	34	25	5	8	8	25	32	59
Witton Albion	42	12	4	5	37	26	5	4	12	23	36	59
Chorley	42	9	7	5	31	27	5	2	14	36	47	51
Knowsley United	42	10	3	8	34	30	4	3	14	27	39	48
Winsford United	42	7	5	9	30	42	3	11	7	26	37	46
Leek Town	42	7	8	6	33	24	3	7	11	19	31	45
Colwyn Bay	42	2	13	6	18	24	6	8	7	25	33	45
Frickley Athletic	42	6	7	8	35	40	5	7	9	28	47	44
Buxton	42	5	3	13	22	36	4	8	9	21	36	38
Droylsden	42	6	4	11	31	43	4	4	13	27	57	38
Matlock Town	42	6	7	8	42	35	2	4	15	29	51	35

Leading Goalscorers 1995–96

Lge	Cup	Tot	
23	9	32	Brian Ross (Chorley)
23	2	25	Nigel Evans (Droylsden)
21	14	35	Tony Carroll (Hyde United)
20	7	27	Jimmy Blackhurst (Marine)
19	3	22	Jock Russell (Winsford United)
17	6	23	Phil Brown (Boston United)
17	4	21	Mark Culley (Matlock Town)
17	3	20	Dave Leaver (Bamber Bridge)
16	15	31	Ged Kimmins (Hyde United)
16	11	27	Graham Roberts (Colwyn Bay)
16	4	20	Paddy Wilson (Knowsley United)
15	13	28	Liam Watson (Witton Albion)
15	6	21	Colin Little (Hyde United now Crewe Alex)
15	3	18	Chris Cook (Boston United)

Key to columns: 1 Accrington Stanley · 2 Bamber Bridge · 3 Barrow · 4 Bishop Auckland · 5 Blyth Spartans · 6 Boston United · 7 Buxton · 8 Chorley · 9 Colwyn Bay · 10 Droylsden · 11 Emley · 12 Frickley Athletic · 13 Gainsborough Trinity · 14 Guiseley · 15 Hyde United · 16 Knowsley United · 17 Leek Town · 18 Marine · 19 Matlock Town · 20 Spennymoor United · 21 Winsford United · 22 Witton Albion

Home \ Away	1	2	3	4	5	6	7	8	9	10	11	12	13	14	15	16	17	18	19	20	21	22
Accrington Stanley	—	1-2	2-1	0-2	2-1	4-0	0-1	0-1	0-0	1-2	1-3	4-1	1-3	0-0	1-0	1-0	2-2	2-3	2-0	3-4	2-1	0-2
Bamber Bridge	1-1	—	2-2	0-2	3-0	3-0	2-1	2-0	1-2	0-2	3-2	0-1	3-0	4-0	2-0	2-3	1-1	2-3	0-1	4-2	1-4	0-0
Barrow	0-3	0-2	—	0-0	1-0	1-3	1-1	3-1	0-1	3-3	1-0	1-3	0-1	1-3	2-0	2-0	2-2	2-2	3-3	0-1	4-3	1-2
Bishop Auckland	2-1	2-1	0-0	—	6-0	0-3	1-1	2-1	1-3	2-1	1-2	2-0	4-0	2-0	3-1	0-1	2-2	2-1	0-2	2-2	0-4	1-2
Blyth Spartans	2-1	1-2	3-0	6-0	—	0-1	2-1	1-1	0-4	0-1	1-2	0-3	1-0	3-1	2-1	0-1	1-0	1-1	3-3	2-1	2-4	1-0
Boston United	4-0	0-3	1-3	0-3	1-0	—	0-1	5-2	2-1	1-3	2-5	1-2	0-0	0-4	0-1	2-4	1-0	2-3	0-4	2-3	1-0	1-1
Buxton	0-1	1-1	2-1	0-1	2-1	9-3	—	1-1	1-3	2-1	1-0	3-0	0-2	0-0	2-1	7-0	2-0	2-0	0-1	0-2	0-1	1-3
Chorley	0-0	1-2	3-2	0-1	1-1	5-2	1-1	—	7-3	1-1	0-3	1-3	1-1	2-0	1-3	2-0	3-1	2-0	2-0	1-1	0-1	2-1
Colwyn Bay	1-2	0-1	0-1	1-3	0-4	2-1	1-3	0-3	—	6-0	1-1	4-1	1-2	1-0	2-0	5-1	1-1	2-0	1-3	3-2	0-0	2-3
Droylsden	1-1	1-2	0-4	1-4	1-3	1-3	0-0	0-1	1-1	—	4-0	4-5	3-0	0-1	7-2	3-0	2-4	6-1	2-2	2-0	3-2	2-1
Emley	1-3	1-1	1-1	1-2	2-3	2-5	3-0	1-2	1-0	0-0	—	3-0	0-6	0-0	1-3	3-0	1-0	4-0	1-4	2-0	0-2	3-1
Frickley Athletic	4-1	0-5	1-3	2-0	0-3	1-2	3-0	1-3	4-1	4-5	3-0	—	1-3	0-2	2-1	5-2	1-2	6-0	2-2	4-1	5-0	1-1
Gainsborough Trinity	1-3	3-0	0-1	4-0	1-0	0-0	0-2	1-1	1-2	3-0	0-6	1-3	—	3-0	2-1	3-0	1-3	1-0	2-1	1-1	1-2	0-2
Guiseley	0-0	4-0	1-3	2-0	3-1	0-4	0-0	2-0	1-0	0-1	0-0	0-2	3-0	—	1-1	3-2	0-1	0-1	1-4	0-2	1-0	3-2
Hyde United	1-0	2-0	2-0	3-1	2-1	0-1	2-1	1-3	2-0	7-2	1-3	2-1	2-1	1-1	—	2-1	4-0	0-1	4-2	1-4	1-4	1-1
Knowsley United	1-0	2-3	2-0	0-1	0-1	2-4	7-0	2-0	5-1	3-0	3-0	5-2	3-0	3-2	2-1	—	2-0	8-0	1-1	1-0	2-2	0-0
Leek Town	2-2	1-1	2-2	2-2	1-0	1-0	2-0	3-1	1-1	2-4	1-0	1-2	1-3	0-1	4-0	2-0	—	2-0	1-0	4-2	2-1	2-1
Marine	2-3	2-3	2-2	2-1	1-1	2-3	2-0	2-0	2-0	6-1	4-0	6-0	1-0	0-1	0-1	8-0	2-0	—	2-1	3-3	1-2	2-0
Matlock Town	2-0	0-1	3-3	0-2	3-3	0-4	0-1	2-0	1-3	2-2	1-4	2-2	2-1	1-4	4-2	1-1	1-0	2-1	—	1-1	3-2	2-1
Spennymoor United	3-4	4-2	0-1	2-2	2-1	2-3	0-2	1-1	3-2	2-0	2-0	4-1	1-1	0-2	1-4	1-0	4-2	3-3	1-1	—	2-2	2-2
Winsford United	2-1	1-4	4-3	0-4	2-4	1-0	0-1	0-1	0-0	3-2	0-2	5-0	1-2	1-0	1-4	2-2	2-1	1-2	3-2	2-2	—	2-0
Witton Albion	0-2	0-0	1-2	1-2	1-0	1-1	1-3	2-1	2-3	2-1	3-1	1-1	0-2	3-2	1-1	0-0	2-1	2-0	2-1	2-2	2-0	—

ICIS FOOTBALL LEAGUE 1995–96
Premier Division

		Home			Goals		Away			Goals			
	P	W	D	L	F	A	W	D	L	F	A	Pts	
Hayes	42	12	7	2	41	16	12	7	2	35	16	86	44
Enfield	42	14	4	3	47	14	12	4	5	31	21	86	43
Boreham Wood	42	10	6	5	34	20	14	5	2	35	9	83	40
Yeovil Town	42	13	5	3	41	23	10	6	5	42	28	80	32
Dulwich Hamlet	42	11	7	3	42	27	12	4	5	43	32	80	26
Carshalton Athletic	42	10	7	4	38	22	12	1	8	30	27	74	19
St Albans City	42	13	4	4	43	16	7	8	6	27	25	72	29
Kingstonian	42	8	6	7	23	21	12	5	4	39	17	71	24
Harrow Borough	42	7	8	6	35	27	12	2	7	35	29	67	14
Sutton United	42	9	5	7	35	29	8	9	4	36	27	65	15
Aylesbury United	42	8	7	6	28	24	9	5	7	43	34	63	13
Bishop's Stortford	42	7	5	9	36	35	9	4	8	25	27	57	−1
Yeading	42	7	6	8	30	30	4	8	9	18	30	47	−12
Hendon	42	5	6	10	24	30	7	4	10	28	35	46	−13
Chertsey Town	42	8	2	11	26	37	5	4	12	19	34	45	−26
Purfleet	42	7	4	10	24	30	5	5	12	24	37	44	−19
Grays Athletic	42	8	4	9	25	29	3	7	11	18	34	44	−20
Hitchin Town	42	6	4	11	20	35	4	6	11	21	39	40	−33
Bromley	42	5	3	13	26	43	5	4	12	26	48	37	−39
Molesey	42	5	4	12	25	40	4	5	12	21	41	36	−35
Walton & Hersham	42	5	3	13	20	34	4	4	13	22	45	34	−37
Worthing	42	4	3	14	27	51	0	4	17	15	55	19	−64

Leading Goalscorers 1995–96

Premier Division		Lge	GIC	CC/T
29	Mark Xavier (Harrow Borough)	29		
26	Paul Whitmarsh (Dulwich Hamlet)	25	1	
25	Warren Patmore (Yeovil Town)	24		1
24	Andy Salako (Carshalton Athletic)	21	3	
	Dominic Feltham (Sutton United)	21		3

ICIS FOOTBALL LEAGUE PREMIER DIVISION RESULTS 1995–96

	Aylesbury United	Bishop's Stortford	Boreham Wood	Bromley	Carshalton Athletic	Chertsey Town	Dulwich Hamlet	Enfield	Grays Athletic	Harrow Borough	Hayes	Hendon	Hitchin Town	Kingstonian	Molesey	Purfleet	St Albans City	Sutton United	Walton & Hersham	Worthing	Yeading	Yeovil Town
Aylesbury United	—	0-0	1-3	3-0	0-1	2-0	0-3	2-3	2-2	2-0	1-3	1-0	2-1	0-2	4-0	1-0	1-1	4-1	0-0	1-1	1-1	3-1
Bishop's Stortford	3-6	—	0-1	3-1	0-1	3-0	1-2	0-3	2-3	2-3	1-3	0-1	2-1	0-2	4-0	1-1	2-0	0-1	0-0	1-1	1-1	2-2
Boreham Wood	2-2	0-1	—	4-1	2-0	2-2	2-2	4-1	3-0	3-2	0-0	4-0	1-0	1-1	4-0	2-0	0-1	0-1	3-1	3-1	1-0	0-2
Bromley	0-3	0-0	1-2	—	1-2	3-3	2-2	0-3	3-5	3-0	0-2	1-4	3-3	1-1	1-3	1-2	3-0	0-1	5-2	1-0	3-0	4-3
Carshalton Athletic	3-1	1-2	2-4	1-2	—	3-1	0-1	0-3	3-1	3-2	0-3	1-0	1-1	0-3	3-0	1-1	3-1	1-2	5-2	2-0	0-3	1-3
Chertsey Town	0-3	3-0	3-3	3-3	3-1	—	0-1	3-0	3-0	0-2	3-3	1-1	3-3	0-3	3-0	2-4	0-0	1-2	5-2	2-2	2-0	3-1
Dulwich Hamlet	1-0	4-1	0-2	2-1	0-0	3-1	—	0-3	3-0	2-1	1-0	2-0	3-3	1-3	2-0	3-0	1-2	0-2	4-0	1-0	3-1	1-3
Enfield	1-0	0-2	4-1	1-0	4-0	0-0	1-0	—	3-0	3-0	2-0	1-2	1-2	1-1	2-0	2-2	2-2	0-2	4-0	3-0	1-0	2-1
Grays Athletic	2-0	0-2	3-0	2-1	1-0	2-1	1-4	0-3	—	2-2	3-3	1-0	1-1	1-1	3-1	2-0	0-3	1-3	3-1	4-1	1-2	0-1
Harrow Borough	3-3	3-1	3-0	5-1	1-2	4-0	2-2	3-1	3-0	—	3-3	3-1	1-2	0-3	3-1	2-4	2-1	1-2	2-1	6-0	4-1	0-1
Hayes	0-1	1-1	0-2	2-0	1-5	2-0	0-3	0-3	5-1	0-2	—	0-1	3-0	0-3	0-2	2-4	0-0	0-4	4-0	3-0	0-0	2-1
Hendon	4-2	0-1	1-1	3-2	0-1	0-2	1-2	3-1	3-0	0-1	1-2	—	1-0	1-0	1-1	1-2	1-1	1-4	0-2	2-2	1-0	2-3
Hitchin Town	0-3	1-2	1-2	1-2	0-1	1-3	1-2	2-0	2-1	0-2	3-0	1-0	—	2-1	1-0	1-0	0-0	2-2	2-1	0-3	2-3	2-1
Kingstonian	1-4	1-1	1-3	1-1	3-1	2-0	1-3	2-1	3-1	3-1	4-1	1-2	1-2	—	1-1	2-4	3-1	1-0	2-2	0-0	1-1	1-3
Molesey	1-4	2-1	2-1	3-2	2-0	0-1	3-0	0-2	5-1	1-2	0-0	1-2	2-1	0-3	—	1-1	4-1	2-2	2-2	2-2	1-2	0-1
Purfleet	1-2	1-2	0-1	0-1	0-1	1-3	1-2	0-1	0-0	1-2	0-3	2-3	2-1	2-1	1-0	—	0-4	0-3	0-2	0-3	2-0	1-1
St Albans City	2-3	0-2	3-0	1-2	3-0	3-0	1-2	1-0	1-4	1-1	4-0	4-1	5-1	1-2	1-0	0-4	—	1-2	2-1	0-0	0-1	2-2
Sutton United	2-1	1-1	3-1	1-3	1-1	4-1	2-0	2-2	1-0	1-2	2-2	1-0	4-0	1-5	3-3	2-2	1-2	—	2-1	4-1	5-2	2-1
Walton & Hersham	1-3	1-3	1-3	1-3	0-1	2-0	0-1	0-2	1-2	0-2	0-1	0-5	2-0	0-2	4-4	2-1	2-0	2-1	—	3-1	3-0	4-1
Worthing	0-0	2-4	3-0	2-0	2-2	2-0	5-3	1-1	1-2	3-1	1-2	0-5	2-0	0-5	3-3	1-1	1-5	5-2	2-3	—	1-0	2-0
Yeading	0-0	2-4	0-1	3-0	1-3	3-1	1-0	1-2	1-3	0-1	1-2	0-1	2-0	0-2	0-5	2-2	2-2	1-0	3-0	1-0	—	1-1
Yeovil Town	3-2	1-3	1-3	4-3	2-1	3-1	0-1	2-1	2-1	1-1	2-2	1-1	1-1	1-1	3-2	2-1	0-0	4-1	2-0	3-1	2-0	—

306

PONTIN'S CENTRAL LEAGUE

Division One	P	W	D	L	F	A	Pts
Manchester United	34	22	5	7	71	35	71
Derby County	34	17	10	7	59	43	61
Stoke City	34	17	8	9	57	42	59
Leeds United	34	17	8	9	40	32	59
Liverpool	34	16	8	10	57	42	56
Tranmere Rovers	34	17	4	13	70	62	55
Everton	34	14	10	10	50	41	52
Oldham Athletic	34	12	11	11	55	54	47
Newcastle United	34	13	6	15	55	59	45
Bolton Wanderers	34	12	9	13	51	52	45
Birmingham City	34	13	5	16	57	64	44
Nottingham Forest	34	12	8	14	46	55	44
Sheffield Wednesday	34	11	8	15	66	63	41
Blackburn Rovers	34	9	13	12	48	44	40
Sheffield United	34	8	13	13	40	61	37
Wolverhampton Wanderers	34	10	5	19	42	48	35
Notts County	34	9	7	18	48	64	34
West Bromwich	34	5	6	23	33	84	21

Division Two	P	W	D	L	F	A	Pts
Middlesbrough	34	23	5	6	80	31	74
Huddersfield Town	34	19	7	8	62	34	64
Sunderland	34	18	9	7	62	37	63
Preston North End	34	17	11	6	51	34	62
Coventry City	34	17	7	10	67	52	58
Blackpool	34	15	9	10	55	40	54
Port Vale	34	14	11	9	69	50	53
Aston Villa	34	14	11	9	62	46	53
Leicester City	34	13	13	8	64	42	52
Manchester City	34	13	11	10	40	39	50
Barnsley	34	14	6	14	61	59	48
Burnley	34	11	10	13	62	68	43
Grimsby Town	34	10	9	15	59	68	39
Rotherham United	34	9	7	18	35	57	34
Bradford City	34	10	3	21	47	75	33
York City	34	8	9	17	38	66	33
Hull City	34	5	4	25	19	68	19
Mansfield Town	34	2	6	26	35	102	12

Division Three	P	W	D	L	F	A	Pts
Wrexham	28	20	2	6	74	36	62
Carlisle United	28	18	7	3	53	15	61
Stockport County	28	18	5	5	69	36	59
Shrewsbury Town	28	12	9	7	58	39	45
Bury	28	13	5	10	46	37	44
Wigan Athletic	28	12	7	9	59	43	43
Chesterfield	28	12	6	10	49	43	42
Walsall	28	12	5	11	40	39	41
Rochdale	28	9	8	11	64	70	35
Doncaster Rovers	28	10	4	14	42	49	34
Lincoln City	28	9	6	13	33	45	33
Scarborough	28	9	5	14	27	51	32
Chester City	28	6	7	15	39	54	25
Darlington	28	5	5	18	28	55	20
Scunthorpe United	28	4	1	23	34	103	13

AVON INSURANCE LEAGUE

Division One

	P	W	D	L	F	A	Pts
Queens Park Rangers	38	27	3	8	77	43	84
Tottenham Hotspur	38	26	4	8	80	33	82
Arsenal	38	22	10	6	82	37	76
Wimbledon	38	21	5	12	82	57	68
Norwich City	38	20	7	11	72	48	67
Crystal Palace	38	16	12	10	50	41	60
Luton Town	38	17	7	14	56	48	58
West Ham United	38	15	9	14	60	63	54
Chelsea	38	14	11	13	50	47	53
Southampton	38	13	11	14	48	56	50
Charlton Athletic	38	14	8	16	52	65	50
Ipswich Town	38	13	10	15	62	62	49
Bristol City	38	13	8	17	41	52	47
Portsmouth	38	12	10	16	47	57	46
Millwall	38	11	10	17	53	68	43
Brighton & Hove Albion	38	10	8	20	48	76	38
Oxford United	38	8	12	18	50	86	36
Bristol Rovers	38	9	6	23	47	79	33
Swindon Town	38	6	13	19	35	66	31
Watford	38	8	6	24	46	74	30

Division Two

	P	W	D	L	F	A	Pts
AFC Bournemouth	16	10	3	3	36	17	33
Swansea City	16	9	4	3	32	21	31
Birmingham City	16	8	2	6	32	25	26
Plymouth Argyle	16	7	4	5	39	18	25
Cardiff City	16	5	8	3	24	22	23
Bath City	16	5	5	6	21	33	20
Torquay United	16	5	4	7	29	31	19
Newport County	16	4	4	8	16	33	16
Cheltenham Town	16	1	2	13	10	39	5

League Cup

Group A

	P	W	D	L	F	A	Pts
Plymouth Argyle	6	5	0	1	20	8	15
AFC Bournemouth	6	3	1	2	13	10	10
Torquay United	6	2	0	4	12	23	6
Bath City	6	1	1	4	9	13	4

Group B

	P	W	D	L	F	A	Pts
Birmingham City	8	5	1	2	21	8	16
Cheltenham Town	8	4	2	2	15	19	14
Newport County	8	3	1	4	12	16	10
Cardiff City	8	2	2	4	15	13	8
Swansea City	8	2	2	4	8	15	8

Cup Final

Plymouth Argyle 0, Birmingham City 1

SOUTH EAST COUNTIES LEAGUE

Division One

	P	W	D	L	F	A	Pts
West Ham United	30	22	4	4	79	37	48
Tottenham Hotspur	30	21	2	7	88	37	44
Watford	30	19	6	5	70	34	44
Arsenal	30	19	5	6	64	27	43
Norwich City	30	16	6	8	56	30	38
Millwall	30	14	3	13	44	46	31
Gillingham	30	10	9	11	49	59	29
Charlton Athletic	30	10	8	12	50	51	28
Leyton Orient	30	12	4	14	40	49	28
Chelsea	30	10	7	13	57	50	27
Ipswich Town	30	10	6	14	51	57	26
Queens Park Rangers	30	8	6	16	46	58	22
Southend United	30	6	9	15	36	60	21
Portsmouth	30	6	8	16	28	55	20
Cambridge United	30	5	6	19	42	96	16
Fulham	30	5	5	20	26	80	15

Division Two

	P	W	D	L	F	A	Pts
Crystal Palace	30	21	4	5	76	35	46
Luton Town	30	17	4	9	58	41	38
Wycombe Wanderers	30	17	4	9	54	39	38
Oxford United	30	17	3	10	64	38	37
Brighton & Hove Albion	30	14	5	11	40	37	33
Wimbledon	30	13	6	11	51	41	32
Southampton	30	13	5	12	51	28	31
Tottenham Hotspur	30	10	11	9	46	46	31
AFC Bournemouth	30	12	7	11	48	51	31
Barnet	30	9	9	12	38	41	27
Swindon Town	30	10	7	13	35	43	27
Brentford	30	10	7	13	37	51	27
Reading	30	8	7	15	33	69	23
Bristol City	30	7	8	15	39	50	22
Colchester United	30	6	8	16	37	67	20
Bristol Rovers	30	6	5	19	34	64	17

REPUBLIC OF IRELAND LEAGUE

	P	W	D	L	F	A	Pts
St Patrick's Ath	33	19	10	4	53	34	67
Bohemians	33	18	8	7	60	29	62
Sligo Rovers	33	16	7	10	45	38	55
Shelbourne	33	15	9	9	45	33	54
Shamrock Rovers	33	14	8	11	31	32	50
Derry City	33	11	13	9	50	38	46
Dundalk	33	11	9	13	38	39	42
UCD	33	12	6	15	38	39	42
Cork City	33	12	8	13	37	40	44
Athlone T*+	33	8	7	18	38	59	31
Drogheda U*	33	7	9	17	38	51	30
Galway U*	33	5	6	22	26	67	21

Cork City three points deducted.

HIGHLAND LEAGUE

	P	W	D	L	F	A	Pt	GD
Huntly	30	27	0	3	103	34	81	+69
Cove Rangers	30	20	5	5	74	35	65	+39
Lossiemouth	30	18	3	9	55	37	57	+18
Peterhead	30	16	7	7	74	51	55	+23
Fraserburgh	30	14	9	7	85	46	51	+39
Keith	30	14	6	10	59	40	48	+19
Elgin City	30	15	3	12	59	55	48	+4
Brora Rangers	30	12	5	13	40	50	41	−10
Wick Academy	30	12	4	14	43	63	40	−20
Deveronvale	30	12	3	15	47	53	39	−6
Clachnacuddin	30	9	7	14	45	51	34	−6
Buckie Thistle	30	8	8	14	45	61	32	−16
Forres Mechanics	30	6	8	16	38	51	26	−13
Fort William	30	8	2	20	27	72	26	−45
Rothes	30	4	7	19	39	75	19	−36
Nairn County	30	4	5	21	26	85	17	−59

FA UMBRO TROPHY 1995-96

First Qualifying Round

Harrogate Town v Grantham Town 1-4
Farsley Celtic v Bedworth United 3-1
Droylsden v Matlock Town 0-3
Atherstone United v Lincoln United
    2-1
Accrington Stanley v Bradford (Park
    Avenue) 2-2, 3-2
Atherton LR v Chorley 1-2
Sutton Coldfield Town v Bilston
    Town 1-1, 4-4, 1-2
Racing Club Warwick v Warrington
    Town 1-0
Bridgnorth Town v Leigh RMI 1-1, 0-7
Winsford United v Paget Rangers
    1-1, 2-0
Curzon Ashton v Worksop Town 4-3
Knowlsley United v Moor Green 3-2
Alfreton Town v Congleton Town 5-0
Workington v Leicester United 1-1, 0-5
Barrow v Hinckley Town 3-0
Stourbridge v Frickley Athletic 1-2
Lancaster City v Solihull Borough 3-0
Fleetwood v Whitley Bay 2-1
Tamworth w.o. v Caernarfon Town
    withdrew
Radcliffe Borough v Redditch United
    3-1
Erith & Belvedere v Basingstoke
    Town 0-6
Leyton Pennant v Fleet Town 0-1
Hastings Town v Havant Town 2-2, 0-1
Chertsey Town v Poole Town 9-0
Bury Town v Trowbridge Town 1-2
Buckingham Town v Braintree Town
    1-1, 0-1
Carshalton Athletic v Dulwich Hamlet
    1-1, 1-1, 2-1
Ruislip Manor v Cinderford Town 3-1
Barton Rovers v Crawley Town 1-3
Salisbury City v Fisher 2-0
Weston-Super-Mare v Bognor Regis
    Town 2-6
Yate Town v Witney Town 3-2
Ashford Town v Sudbury Town 0-2
Billericay Town v Wembley 0-4
Fareham Town v Maidenhead United
    2-4
Barking v Baldock Town 0-0, 2-3
Forest Green Rovers v Sittingbourne
    1-2
Abingdon Town v Bishops Stortford
    1-1, 1-5
Berkhamsted Town v Purfleet 1-2

Newport (IW) v Chesham United 1-3
Kings Lynn v Uxbridge 1-2
Staines Town v Wokingham Town 2-1
Weymouth v Tonbridge 4-0
Hendon v Waterlooville 2-2, 1-0
Whyteleafe v Tooting & Mitcham
    United 1-2
Harrow Borough v Marlow 1-1, 4-1
Worthing v Thame United 1-1, 0-2
Bashley v Margate 1-1, 2-1

Second Qualifying Round

Barrow v Winsford United 0-1
Tamworth v Netherfield 3-1
Bilston Town v Leicester United 5-2
Alfreton Town v Dudley Town 2-2, 0-2
Great Harwood Town v Frickley
    Athletic 3-2
Atherstone United v Accrington
    Stanley 1-3
Radcliffe Borough v Fleetwood 2-0
Eastwood Town v Chorley 0-1
Grantham Town v Farsley Celtic 1-3
Leigh RMI v Matlock Town 0-2
Emley v Racing Club Warwick 2-1
Curzon Ashton v Lancaster City 1-1, 0-3
Nuneaton Borough v Knowsley
    United 3-2
Carshalton Athletic v Weymouth 5-1
Braintree Town v Harrow Borough 4-0
Chertsey Town v Chesham United
    2-2, 3-2
Staines Town v Havant Town 3-1
Walton & Hersham v Oxford City
    0-0, 2-5
Trowbridge Town v Bishops Stortford
    1-0
Clevedon Town v Worcester City 0-4
Crawley Town v Bashley 0-2
Evesham United v Aldershot Town 0-2
Newport AFC v Fleet Town 2-1
Tooting & Mitcham United v Baldock
    Town 2-1
Basingstoke Town v Uxbridge 0-2
Purfleet v Corby Town 6-1
Wembley v Ruislip Manor 1-1, 2-1
Bognor Regis Town v Sittingbourne
    2-2, 2-1
Hendon v Gravesend & Northfleet 3-0
Salisbury City v Sudbury Town
    2-2, 2-2, 2-3
Yate Town v Heybridge Swifts 1-2
Maidenhead United v Thame United
    0-5

Third Qualifying Round

Spennymoor United v Nuneaton
  Borough   0-2
Halesowen Town v Bilston Town
                  0-0, 4-1
Burton Albion v Bamber Bridge
                  3-3, 3-2
Ashton United v Lancaster City
                  1-1, 2-0
Bishop Auckland v Witton Albion
          0-0, 0-0, 3-1
Radcliffe Borough v Farsley Celtic 3-1
Emley v Great Harwood Town   3-1
Chorley v Winsford United   3-1
Stafford Rangers v Tamworth 1-1, 3-0
Matlock Town v Buxton   1-0
Blyth Spartans v Gretna   3-2
Dudley Town v VS Rugby   4-3
Accrington Stanley v Gresley Rovers
                    2-3
Leek Town v Boston United 0-0, 0-2
Ilkeston Town v Gainsborough Trinity
                    0-5
Chelmsford City v Yeading   2-1
Gloucester City v Aldershot Town 1-0
Boreham Wood v Heybridge Swifts 3-0
Bromley v Oxford City   1-1, 2-3
Worcester City v Aylesbury United 3-0
Chertsey Town v Purfleet   0-1
Molesey v Staines Town   2-2, 0-5
Carshalton Athletic v Braintree Town
                1-1, 5-0
St Albans City v Thame United   4-2
Sutton United v Trowbridge Town 0-1
Wembley v Bashley   2-0
Rothwell Town v Uxbridge   3-2
Dorchester Town v Hayes   2-3
Hitchin Town v Bognor Regis Town
                    1-2
Newport AFC v Grays Athletic   1-0
Cambridge City v Hendon   2-0
Sudbury Town v Tooting & Mitcham
  United   2-0

First Round

Stalybridge Celtic v Gresley Rovers 1-
  1, 0-1
Stafford Rangers v Guiseley 1-1, 1-2
Colwyn Bay v Altrincham   3-3, 0-2
Halifax Town v Southport   2-1
Ashton United v Blyth Spartans   1-3
Dudley Town v Halesowen Town 4-2
Macclesfield Town v Runcorn   1-0
Burton Albion v Telford United   3-1
Gainsborough Trinity v Nuneaton
  Borough   4-1
Morecambe v Emley   2-2, 1-3

Hednesford Town v Northwich
  Victoria   1-1, 0-2
Kidderminster Harriers v Gateshead
                  0-0, 0-2
Marine v Hyde United 0-0, 0-0, 0-3
Boston United v Chorley   1-1, 1-2
Bromsgrove Rovers v Bishop
  Auckland   1-0
Radcliffe Borough v Matlock Town 3-2
Oxford City v Merthyr Tydfil   1-2
Rothwell Town v Welling United
                  2-2, 0-3
Bognor Regis Town v Worcester City
                    1-0
Dover Athletic v Cheltenham Town
Chelmsford City v Newport AFC 0-1
Bath City v Yeovil Town   1-1, 3-2
Gloucester City v Staines Town   5-0
Trowbridge Town v Sudbury Town
        2-2, 1-1, 1-1, 3-4
Carshalton Athletic v Woking   3-1
Farnborough Town v Slough Town
                  1-1, 3-4
Rushden & Diamonds v Purfleet 0-1
Kettering Town v St Albans City
                  1-1, 3-2
Cambridge City v Boreham Wood 1-2
Hayes v Enfield 0-0, 2-2, 2-2, 2-0
Stevenage Borough v Dagenham &
  Redbridge   3-2
Wembley v Kingstonian   2-1

Second Round

Hyde United v Welling United   4-1
Sudbury Town v Gloucester City 3-1
Guiseley v Altrincham   4-0
Emley v Gateshead   1-2
Dudley Town v Merthyr Tydfil   1-2
Bognor Regis Town v Radcliffe Bor-
  ough   1-3
Boreham Wood v Dover Athletic 2-1
Slough Town v Kettering Town   1-2
Chorley v Gainsborough Trinity   2-0
Bath City v Hayes   2-0
Macclesfield Town v Purfleet   2-1
Blyth Spartans v Gresley Rovers 1-2
Carshalton Athletic v Newport AFC
                    2-1
Stevenage Borough v Burton Albion
                    2-1
Wembley v Northwich Victoria   0-2
Halifax Town v Bromsgrove Rovers
                    0-1

Third Round

Guiseley v Gresley Rovers   1-2

Merthyr Tydfil v Northwich Victoria
1-1, 2-2, 0-3
Hyde United v Carshalton Athletic
3-2
Macclesfield Town v Sudbury Town
1-0
Boreham Wood v Chorley 1-3, 3-4
Radcliffe Borough v Gateshead 1-2
Stevenage Borough v Kettering Town
3-0
Bath City v Bromsgrove Rovers
1-1, 1-2

Fourth Round
Hyde United v Stevenage Borough 3-2
Gresley Rovers v Macclesfield Town
0-2
Bromsgrove Rovers v Northwich
Victoria 0-1
Chorley v Gateshead 3-1

Semi-finals (two legs)
Hyde United v Northwich Victoria
1-2, 0-1
Macclesfield Town v Chorley 3-1, 1-1

FINAL AT WEMBLEY

19 MAY

Macclesfield Town (2) 3 *(Payne, Burgess (og), Hemmings)*
Northwich Victoria (0) 1 *(Williams)* 8672

Macclesfield Town: Price; Edey, Howarth, Payne, Gardiner, Lyons, Sorvel, Wood (Hulme), Hemmings (Cavell), Coates, Power.
Northwich Victoria: Greygoose; Ward, Abel (Steele), Burgess (Simpson), Duffy, Williams, Butler, Walters, Vicary, Cooke, Humphreys.
Referee: M. Reed (Birmingham).

FA CARLSBERG VASE 1995-96

Second Round

Guisborough Town v Crook Town
1-1, 2-1

Yorkshire Amateur v West Auckland
Town 1-1, 1-2

Winterton Rangers v North Allerton
1994 1-0

Brigg Town v Tow Law Town 3-0

Selby Town v Billingham Synthonia
3-2

Shildon v Mossley 1-2

Hebburn v Ossett Albion 2-1

Chester Le Street Town v Whickham
5-1

North Ferriby United v Oldham Town
7-0

Durham City v Whitby Town 4-1

Clitheroe v RTM Newcastle 2-1

Seaham Red Star v Peterlee Newtown
2-1

Dunston FB v Cammell Laird 2-0

Prudhoe Town v Goole Town 2-0

Easington Colliery v Ossett Town 2-1

Murton v Consett 2-1

Thackley v Bedlington Terriers 0-1

Nettleham v Pershore Town 1-4

Anstey Nomads v Shepshed Dynamo
4-1

Armitage v Rushall Olympic 0-2

Nuthall v Boldmere St Michaels 1-3

Oakham United v Lye Town 1-4

Raunds Town v Hinckley Athletic
2-2, 3-0

Willenhall Town v Newcastle Town
3-1

Flixton v Hucknall Town 5-1

Belper Town v Bloxwich Town 3-1

Trafford v Darlaston 3-0

Maine Road v Eastwood Hanley 1-4

Pelsall Villa v Barwell 0-2

Northwood v Ely City 2-1

Hampton v Ware 5-2

Brackley Town v Aveley 2-3

Diss Town v Herne Bay 2-0

Burgess Hill Town v Wootton Blue
Cross 3-2

Collier Row v Woodbridge Town 5-4

Cheshunt v Bedford Town 2-3

Wisbech Town v Wivenhoe Town 2-3

Slade Green v Newmarket Town 2-0

Arlesey Town v Thamesmead Town
1-2

Metropolitan Police v Canvey Island
1-3

Furness v Sawbridgeworth Town
0-0, 1-1, 2-1

Harwich & Parkeston v Tilbury 2-3

Langford v Whitstable Town 0-1

Wroxham v Brentwood 1-2

Whitehawk v Corinthian 3-1

Burnham v Windsor & Eton 0-4

Gorleston v Fakenham Town 3-2

Peacehaven & Telscombe v Harlow
Town 2-0

Hadleigh United v Edgware Town 0-2

Leighton Town v Chalfont St Peter
1-1, 0-2

Keynsham Town v Chard Town 0-1

Lymington AFC v Warminster Town
2-0

Paulton Rovers v Bideford 2-0

Bridport v Bemerton Heath Harle-
quins 2-0

Horsham v Falmouth Town 0-2

Torpoint Athletic v Eastleigh 1-0

Shoreham v Chichester City 1-2

Dorking v Bishop Sutton 2-2, 0-2

Godalming & Guildford v
Mangotsfield United 2-5

Wimborne Town v Torrington 1-2

Cranleigh v Banstead Athletic 0-2

Wick v Chippenham Town 0-1

Taunton Town v Bracknell Town
3-3, 2-1

bye Hungerford Town

Third Round

Winterton Rangers v Flixton 0-4

Rushall Olympic v Bedlington Terriers
0-4

Brigg Town v Guisborough Town 2-0

Hebburn v Durham City 0-4

Seaham Red Star v Belper Town 1-2

Prudhoe Town v Dunston FB 1-2

North Ferriby United v Eastwood
Hanley 4-2

Chester Le Street Town v Lye Town
1-3

Easington Colliery v Anstey Nomads
2-3

Boldmere St Michaels v Trafford 0-2

Barwell v Mossley 3-1

Merton v Selby Town 3-5

Clitheroe v West Auckland Town 6-0

Thamesmead Town v Brentwood 3-1

Willenhall Town v Chalfont St Peter
2-1

314

Whitstable Town v Peacehaven &
Telscombe   0-1
Tilbury v Aveley   2-4
Slade Green v Diss Town   0-2
Northwood v Gorleston   0-1
Wivenhoe Town v Edgware Town   3-1
Raunds Town v Furness   1-1
  (abandoned after 105 minutes;
  frozen pitch) 1-1, 5-2
Canvey Island v Bedford Town   2-0
Hampton v Collier Row   0-1
Taunton Town v Chippenham Town
                                           4-0
Bridport v Windsor & Eton   2-4
Lymington v Bishop Sutton   4-0
Whitehawk v Banstead Athletic   0-2
Burgess Hill Town v Pershore Town
                                           1-1
Torpoint Athletic v Chard Town   4-2
Paulton Rovers v Falmouth Town   2-0
Torrington v Chichester City   1-2
Hungerford Town v Mangotsfield
United   0-0, 1-5

Fourth Round
North Ferriby United v Anstey
Nomads   2-3
Lye Town v Barwell   0-2
Clitheroe v Willenhall Town   3-0
Trafford v Selby Town   0-0, 1-1, 3-0
Flixton v Dunston FB   2-0
Durham City v Belper Town   2-3
Brigg Town v Bedlington Terriers   2-1
Burgess Hill Town v Collier Row   0-1
Windsor & Eton v Peacehaven &
Telscombe   0-1

Diss Town v Banstead Athletic   1-2
Chichester City v Thamesmead Town
                                           1-3
Wivenhoe Town v Aveley   4-0
Paulton Rovers v Mangotsfield United
                                           0-3
Canvey Island v Gorleston   1-0
Raunds Town v Taunton Town   4-1
Lymington v Torpoint Athletic   1-3

Fifth Round
Raunds Town v Torpoint Athletic   2-0
Wivenhoe Town v Mangotsfield
United   2-2, 0-3
Banstead Athletic v Peacehaven &
Telscombe   2-3
Collier Row v Anstey Nomads   6-0
Brigg Town v Trafford   1-0
Flixton v Barwell   3-1
Thamesmead Town v Canvey Island
                                           1-2
  (at Slade Green)
Belper Town v Clitheroe   0-3

Sixth Round
Brigg Town v Collier Row   2-0
Mangotsfield United v Raunds Town
                                      2-2, 1-0
Clitheroe v Peacehaven & Telscombe
                                           1-0
Flixton v Canvey Island   3-0

Semi-finals (two legs)
Brigg Town v Flixton   0-0, 1-0
Mangotsfield United v Clitheroe
                                      1-0, 0-2

FINAL AT WEMBLEY

12 MAY

Brigg Town (1) 3 *(Stead C 2 (1 pen), Lampkin (og))*

Clitheroe (0) 0   7340

Brigg Town: Gawthorpe; Thompson, Buckley (Mail), Greaves (Clay), Rogers,
Elston, McLean, Stead C, Stead N (McNally), Roach, Flounders.
Clitheroe: Nash; Rowbotham (Otley), Baron, Westwell, Lampkin, Grimshaw,
Butcher, Rouine, Hill (Dunn), Darbyshire, Taylor (Smith).
Referee: S. Lodge (Sheffield & Hallam).

FA YOUTH CHALLENGE CUP 1995-96

First Round

Rotherham United v Hartlepool United	1-0
Southport v Burnley	1-2
Tranmere Rovers v Wrexham	2-2, 3-1
Newcastle United v Blackpool	3-1
Grimsby Town v Oldham Athletic	3-4
Derby County v Scunthorpe United	3-1
Preston North End v Huddersfield Town	1-1, 1-2
Everton v Notts County	1-0
Blackburn Rovers v Sheffield Wednesday	2-0
Doncaster Rovers v Hull City	1-0
Leeds United v Barnsley	3-1
Basildon United v Chelsea	2-2, 1-0
Boreham Wood v Enfield	0-3
Wivenhoe Town v Northampton Town	0-1
Wycombe Wanderers v Watford	2-2, 1-3
Shrewsbury Town v Cambridge United	3-0
Wolverhampton Wanderers v Birmingham City	5-6
Leicester City v Nuneaton Borough	10-0
Walsall v Mansfield Town	1-1, 1-0
Barnet v Leighton Town	7-1
Boldmere St Michaels v Rushden & Diamonds	4-1
Cambridge City v Luton Town	1-9
Colchester United v Peterborough United	2-4
AFC Bournemouth v Swansea City	1-2
Torquay United v Welling United	2-0
Southampton v Oxford United	1-1, 2-1
Woking v Croydon Athletic	5-1
Sutton United v Eastleigh	1-2
Reading v Cardiff City	2-4
Slough Town v Hereford United	2-4
Gillingham v Fulham	1-0
Dulwich Hamlet v Exeter City	0-0, 2-3
Uxbridge v Banstead Athletic	1-2
Plymouth Argyle v Charlton Athletic	1-4

(Charlton Athletic removed for fielding an ineligible player; Plymouth Argyle awarded the tie)

Second Round

Manchester City v Huddersfield Town	3-0
Leeds United v Middlesbrough	0-1
Everton v Tranmere Rovers	1-3
Oldham Athletic v York City	3-2
Sheffield United v Newcastle United	2-1
Sunderland v Crewe Alexandra	4-0
Manchester United v Rotherham United	3-1
Derby County v Doncaster Rovers	3-5
Burnley v Stoke City	1-0
Liverpool v Bradford City	4-2
Blackburn Rovers v Nottingham Forest	5-1
Ipswich Town v Walsall	0-0, 1-0
Peterborough United v Norwich City	1-1, 1-2
Barnet v Watford	0-4
Birmingham City v Basildon United	5-0
Tottenham Hotspur v Shrewsbury Town	4-1
West Ham United v Aston Villa	3-0
Leyton Orient v Enfield	0-2
Leicester City v Luton Town	1-2
Northampton Town v West Bromwich Albion	0-1
Coventry City v Arsenal	1-2
Boldmere St Michaels v Southend United	2-1
Wimbledon v Brighton & Hove Albion	1-0
Gillingham v Woking	1-3
Brentford v Exeter City	4-0
Swindon Town v Crystal Palace	0-2
Plymouth Argyle v Eastleigh	1-1, 3-1
Torquay United v Hereford United	0-1
Swansea City v Portsmouth	0-0, 1-3
Millwall v Southampton	3-2
Queens Park Rangers v Cardiff City	1-0
Bristol City v Banstead Athletic	2-1

Third Round

Norwich City v Burnley	2-1
Liverpool v Luton Town	5-0
Boldmere St Michaels v Manchester City	0-3
West Bromwich Albion v Sheffield United	0-3
Blackburn Rovers v Tranmere Rovers	0-2
Doncaster Rovers v Oldham Athletic	0-5

Sunderland v Manchester United	1-4	Manchester United v Norwich City	1-0
Ipswich Town v Middlesbrough	2-0	Queens Park Rangers v West Ham	
Queens Park Rangers v Brentford	2-0	United	1-4
Crystal Palace v Bristol City	7-0	Wimbledon v Ipswich Town	2-2, 2-1
Portsmouth v Watford	1-2	Tranmere Rovers v Watford	1-1, 1-4
Hereford United v Enfield	1-1, 2-0		

Plymouth Argyle v Tottenham
Hotspur   2-1
Woking v West Ham United   0-3
Arsenal v Wimbledon   3-4
Millwall v Birmingham City   5-2

Fifth Round
Liverpool v Manchester United   3-2
Oldham Athletic v West Ham United
                                   1-2
Crystal Palace v Watford   2-0
Manchester City v Wimbledon   1-3

Fourth Round
Plymouth Argyle v Crystal Palace   0-2
Hereford United v Manchester City
                                   1-2
Oldham Athletic v Millwall   2-0
Liverpool v Sheffield United   3-2

Semi-finals (two legs)
Liverpool v Crystal Palace   4-2, 3-3
West Ham United v Wimbledon
                                2-1, 3-2

FINAL FIRST LEG

30 APR

West Ham U (0) 0

Liverpool (1) 2 *(Newby, Larmour)*   15,386

West Ham U: Finn; Coyne, Ferdinand, Partridge, Moore, Omoyinmi, Lampard, McFarlane, Keith, Boylan, Hodges.
Liverpool: Naylor; Prior, Brazier, Carragher, Roberts, Quinn S, Thutson, Quinn M, Cassidy, Newby (Larmour), Parkinson.
Referee: M. Reilly (West Riding).

FINAL SECOND LEG

17 MAY

Liverpool (1) 2 *(Owen, Quinn S)*
West Ham U (1) 1 *(Lampard)*   20,600

Liverpool: Naylor; Prior, Brazier, Carragher, Roberts, Quinn S, Quinn M, Thompson, Cassidy (Turkington), Owen, Newby (Parkinson).
West Ham U: Finn; Moore, Coyne, McFarlane, Partridge (Bowen), Keith, Ferdinand, Lampard, Boylan (O'Reilly), Hodges, Omoyinmi.
Referee: M. Reilly (West Riding)

BRITISH FOOTBALL RECORDS

Records during 1995–96

HIGHEST SCORES
Auto Windscreens Shield
Crewe Alex 8, Hartlepool U 0 17.10.95.

HIGHEST AGGREGATE
FA Cup
Walsall 8, Torquay U 4 12.12.95.

MOST GOALS IN A SEASON
Scottish League
85 in 36 games, Rangers, Premier Division.

FEWEST GOALS IN A SEASON
Scottish League
23 in 36 games, Dumbarton, New Division 1.

MOST GOALS AGAINST IN A SEASON
Scottish League
94 in 36 games, Dumbarton, New Division 1.

FEWEST GOALS AGAINST IN A SEASON
Football League
20 in 46 games, Gillingham, Division 3.

MOST POINTS IN A SEASON
Football League
92 in 46 games, Swindon T, Division 2.

FEWEST POINTS IN A SEASON
Scottish League
11 in 36 games, Dumbarton, New Division 1.

MOST WINS IN A SEASON
Scottish League
27 in 36 games, Rangers, Premier Division.

FEWEST WINS IN A SEASON
Scottish League
3 in 36 games, Dumbarton, New Division 1.

MOST DEFEATS IN A SEASON
Scottish League
31 in 36 games, Dumbarton, New Division 1.

FEWEST DEFEATS IN A SEASON
Scottish League
3 in 36 games, Rangers, Premier Division.

MOST DRAWS IN A SEASON
Football League
20 in 46 games, Charlton Ath, Division 1.
20 in 46 games, Mansfield T, Division 3.

MOST GOALS IN A SEASON
FA Premier League
Alan Shearer (Blackburn R) 31.

318

OTHER AWARDS 1995–96

FOOTBALLER OF THE YEAR

The Football Writers' Association Award for the Footballer of the Year went to Eric Cantona of Manchester United and France.

Past Winners
1947–48 Stanley Matthews (Blackpool), 1948–49 Johnny Carey (Manchester U), 1949–50 Joe Mercer (Arsenal), 1950–51 Harry Johnston (Blackpool), 1951–52 Billy Wright (Wolverhampton W), 1952–53 Nat Lofthouse (Bolton W), 1953–54 Tom Finney (Preston NE), 1954–55 Don Revie (Manchester C), 1955–56 Bert Trautmann (Manchester C), 1956–57 Tom Finney (Preston NE), 1957–58 Danny Blanchflower (Tottenham H), 1958–59 Syd Owen (Luton T), 1959–60 Bill Slater (Wolverhampton W), 1960–61 Danny Blanchflower (Tottenham H), 1961–62 Jimmy Adamson (Burnley), 1962–63 Stanley Matthews (Stoke C), 1963–64 Bobby Moore (West Ham U), 1964–65 Bobby Collins (Leeds U), 1965–66 Bobby Charlton (Manchester U), 1966–67 Jackie Charlton (Leeds U), 1967–68 George Best (Manchester U), 1968–69 Dave Mackay (Derby Co) shared with Tony Book (Manchester C), 1969–70 Billy Bremner (Leeds U), 1970–71 Frank McLintock (Arsenal), 1971–72 Gordon Banks (Stoke C), 1972–73 Pat Jennings (Tottenham H), 1973–74 Ian Callaghan (Liverpool), 1974–75 Alan Mullery (Fulham), 1975–76 Kevin Keegan (Liverpool), 1976–77 Emlyn Hughes (Liverpool), 1977–78 Kenny Burns (Nottingham F), 1978–79 Kenny Dalglish (Liverpool), 1979–80 Terry McDermott (Liverpool), 1980–81 Frans Thijssen (Ipswich T), 1981–82 Steve Perryman (Tottenham H), 1982–83 Kenny Dalglish (Liverpool), 1983–84 Ian Rush (Liverpool), 1984–85 Neville Southall (Everton), 1985–86 Gary Lineker (Everton), 1986–87 Clive Allen (Tottenham H), 1987–88 John Barnes (Liverpool), 1988–89 Steve Nicol (Liverpool), 1989–90 John Barnes (Liverpool), 1990–91 Gordon Strachan (Leeds U), 1991–92 Gary Lineker (Tottenham H), 1992–93 Chris Waddle (Sheffield W), 1993–94 Alan Shearer (Blackburn R), 1995 Jurgen Klinsmann (Tottenham H).

THE PFA AWARDS 1996

Player of the Year: Les Ferdinand (Newcastle U)
Previous Winners: 1974 Norman Hunter (Leeds U); 1975 Colin Todd (Derby Co); 1976 Pat Jennings (Tottenham H); 1977 Andy Gray (Aston Villa); 1978 Peter Shilton (Nottingham F); 1979 Liam Brady (Arsenal); 1980 Terry McDermott (Liverpool); 1981 John Wark (Ipswich T); 1982 Kevin Keegan (Southampton); 1983 Kenny Dalglish (Liverpool); 1984 Ian Rush (Liverpool); 1985 Peter Reid (Everton); 1986 Gary Lineker (Everton); 1987 Clive Allen (Tottenham H); 1988 John Barnes (Liverpool); 1989 Mark Hughes (Manchester U); 1990 David Platt (Aston Villa); 1991 Mark Hughes (Manchester U); 1992 Gary Pallister (Manchester U); 1993 Paul McGrath (Aston Villa); 1994 Eric Cantona (Manchester U); 1995 Alan Shearer (Blackburn R).

Young Player of the Year: Robbie Fowler (Liverpool).
Previous Winners: 1974 Kevin Beattie (Ipswich T); 1975 Mervyn Day (West Ham U); 1976 Peter Barnes (Manchester C); 1977 Andy Gray (Aston Villa); 1978 Tony Woodcock (Nottingham F); 1979 Cyrille Regis (WBA); 1980 Glenn Hoddle (Tottenham H); 1981 Gary Shaw (Aston Villa); 1982 Steve Moran (Southampton); 1983 Ian Rush (Liverpool); 1984 Paul Walsh (Luton T); 1985 Mark Hughes (Manchester U); 1986 Tony Cottee (West Ham U); 1987 Tony Adams (Arsenal); 1988 Paul Gascoigne (Tottenham H); 1989 Paul Merson (Arsenal); 1990 Matthew Le Tissier (Southampton); 1991 Lee

Sharpe (Manchester U); 1992 Ryan Giggs (Manchester U); 1993 Ryan Giggs (Manchester U); 1994 Andy Cole (Newcastle U); 1995 Robbie Fowler (Liverpool).

Merit Award: Pele.

Previous Winners: 1974 Bobby Charlton CBE, Cliff Lloyd OBE; 1975 Denis Law; 1976 George Eastham OBE; 1977 Jack Taylor OBE; 1978 Bill Shankly OBE; 1979 Tom Finney OBE; 1980 Sir Matt Busby CBE; 1981 John Trollope MBE; 1982 Joe Mercer OBE; 1983 Bob Paisley OBE; 1984 Bill Nicholson; 1985 Ron Greenwood; 1986 The 1966 England World Cup team, Sir Alf Ramsey, Harold Shepherdson; 1987 Sir Stanley Matthews; 1988 Billy Bonds MBE; 1989 Nat Lofthouse; 1990 Peter Shilton; 1991 Tommy Hutchison; 1992 Brian Clough; 1993 the 1968 Manchester United team; 1994 Billy Bingham; 1995 Gordon Strachan.

THE SCOTTISH PFA AWARDS 1996

Player of the Year: Paul Gascoigne (Rangers).

Previous Winners: 1978 Derek Johnstone (Rangers); 1979 Paul Hegarty (Dundee U); 1980 Davie Provan (Celtic); 1981 Sandy Clark (Airdrieonians); 1982 Mark McGhee (Aberdeen); 1983 Charlie Nicholas (Celtic); 1984 Willie Miller (Aberdeen); 1985 Jim Duffy (Morton); 1986 Richard Gough (Dundee U); 1987 Brian McClair (Celtic); 1988 Paul McStay (Celtic); 1989 Theo Snelders (Aberdeen); 1990 Jim Bett (Aberdeen); 1991 Paul Elliott (Celtic); 1993 Ally McCoist (Rangers); 1993 Andy Goram (Rangers); 1994 Mark Hateley (Rangers); 1995 Brian Laudrup (Rangers).

Young Player of the Year: Jackie McNamara (Celtic).

Previous Winners: 1978 Graeme Payne (Dundee U); 1979 Graham Stewart (Dundee U); 1980 John MacDonald (Rangers); 1981 Francis McAvennie (St Mirren); 1982 Charlie Nicholas (Celtic); 1983 Pat Nevin (Clyde); 1984 John Robertson (Hearts); 1985 Craig Levein (Hearts); 1986 Craig Levein (Hearts); 1987 Robert Fleck (Rangers); 1988 John Collins (Hibernian); 1989 Bill McKinlay (Dundee U); 1990 Scott Crabbe (Hearts); 1991 Eoin Jess (Aberdeen); 1992 Phil O'Donnell (Motherwell); 1993 Eoin Jess (Aberdeen); 1994 Phil O'Donnell (Motherwell); 1995 Charlie Miller (Rangers).

SCOTTISH FOOTBALL WRITERS' ASSOCIATION

Player of the Year 1996 – Paul Gascoigne (Rangers)

1965 Billy McNeill (Celtic)
1966 John Greig (Rangers)
1967 Ronnie Simpson (Celtic)
1968 Gordon Wallace (Raith R)
1969 Bobby Murdoch (Celtic)
1970 Pat Stanton (Hibernian)
1971 Martin Buchan (Aberdeen)
1972 Dave Smith (Rangers)
1973 George Connelly (Celtic)
1974 Scotland's World Cup Squad
1975 Sandy Jardine (Rangers)
1976 John Greig (Rangers)
1977 Danny McGrain (Celtic)
1978 Derek Johnstone (Rangers)
1979 Andy Ritchie (Morton)
1980 Gordon Strachan (Aberdeen)

1981 Alan Rough (Partick Th)
1982 Paul Sturrock (Dundee U)
1983 Charlie Nicholas (Celtic)
1984 Willie Miller (Aberdeen)
1985 Hamish McAlpine (Dundee U)
1986 Sandy Jardine (Hearts)
1987 Brian McClair (Celtic)
1988 Paul McStay (Celtic)
1989 Richard Gough (Rangers)
1990 Alex McLeish (Aberdeen)
1991 Maurice Malpas (Dundee U)
1992 Ally McCoist (Rangers)
1993 Andy Goram (Rangers)
1994 Mark Hateley (Rangers)
1995 Brian Laudrup (Rangers)

EUROPEAN FOOTBALLER OF THE YEAR 1995

George Weah (AC Milan) became the first non-European to win the award. Liberia born Weah was in his initial season with the Italian club and he was also voted FIFA's World Player of the Year.

Past winners

1956 **Stanley Matthews** (Blackpool)
1957 **Alfredo Di Stefano** (Real Madrid)
1958 **Raymond Kopa** (Real Madrid)
1959 **Alfredo Di Stefano** (Real Madrid)
1960 **Luis Suarez** (Barcelona)
1961 **Omar Sivori** (Juventus)
1962 **Josef Masopust** (Dukla Prague)
1963 **Lev Yashin** (Moscow Dynamo)
1964 **Denis Law** (Manchester United)
1965 **Eusebio** (Benfica)
1966 **Bobby Charlton** (Manchester United)
1967 **Florian Albert** (Ferencvaros)
1968 **George Best** (Manchester United)
1969 **Gianni Rivera** (AC Milan)
1970 **Gerd Muller** (Bayern Munich)
1971 **Johan Cruyff** (Ajax)
1972 **Franz Beckenbauer** (Bayern Munich)
1973 **Johan Cruyff** (Barcelona)
1974 **Johan Cruyff** (Barcelona)
1975 **Oleg Blokhin** (Dynamo Kiev)

1976 **Franz Beckenbauer** (Bayern Munich)
1977 **Allan Simonsen** (Borussia Moenchengladbach)
1978 **Kevin Keegan** (SV Hamburg)
1979 **Kevin Keegan** (SV Hamburg)
1980 **Karl-Heinz Rummenigge** (Bayern Munich)
1981 **Karl-Heinz Rummenigge** (Bayern Munich)
1982 **Paolo Rossi** (Juventus)
1983 **Michel Platini** (Juventus)
1984 **Michel Platini** (Juventus)
1985 **Michel Platini** (Juventus)
1986 **Igor Belanov** (Dynamo Kiev)
1987 **Ruud Gullit** (AC Milan)
1988 **Marco Van Basten** (AC Milan)
1989 **Marco Van Basten** (AC Milan)
1990 **Lothar Matthaus** (Inter-Milan)
1991 **Jean-Pierre Papin** (Marseille)
1992 **Marco Van Basten** (AC Milan)
1993 **Roberto Baggio** (Juventus)
1994 **Hristo Stoichkov** (Barcelona)

Carling Manager of the Month

August	Kevin Keegan	Newcastle United
September	Kevin Keegan	Newcastle United
October	Frank Clark	Nottingham Forest
November	Alan Ball	Manchester City
December	Roy Evans	Liverpool
January	Roy Evans	Liverpool
February	Alex Ferguson	Manchester United
March	Alex Ferguson	Manchester United
April	Dave Merrington	Southampton

Each winner receives a Carling Manager of the Month trophy, a cheque for £750 and a magnum of champagne.

Carling Manager of the Season	**Alex Ferguson**	**Manchester United**

Carling Player of the Month

August	David Ginola	Newcastle United
September	Tony Yeboah	Leeds United
October	Trevor Sinclair	QPR
November	Robert Lee	Newcastle United
December	Robbie Fowler	Liverpool
January	Stan Collymore	Liverpool
	Robbie Fowler	Liverpool
February	Dwight Yorke	Aston Villa
March	Eric Cantona	Manchester United

Carling Player of the Season	**Eric Cantona**	**Manchester United**

VAUXHALL CONFERENCE FIXTURES 1996–97

	Altrincham	Bath City	Bromsgrove Rovers	Dover Athletic	Farnborough Town	Gateshead	Halifax Town	Hayes	Hednesford Town	Kettering Town
Altrincham	—	15.3	28.12	12.4	23.11	31.3	10.9	25.1	4.1	26.4
Bath City	5.10	—	8.3	26.8	1.1	7.9	9.11	17.9	7.12	24.8
Bromsgrove Rovers	17.9	31.3	—	19.10	21.12	5.10	1.2	1.3	5.4	3.9
Dover Athletic	7.9	1.10	15.2	—	12.10	19.4	2.11	20.8	3.5	1.2
Farnborough Town	1.3	26.12	24.9	28.12	—	31.8	31.3	3.9	26.4	9.11
Gateshead	26.8	14.12	29.3	21.9	5.4	—	28.12	22.3	15.2	8.3
Halifax Town	20.8	15.2	4.1	15.3	22.2	3.9	—	19.4	25.1	30.11
Hayes	19.10	26.4	31.8	4.1	16.11	30.11	21.9	—	29.3	21.12
Hednesford Town	9.11	31.8	9.9	17.8	5.10	21.12	17.2	14.12	—	22.3
Kettering Town	29.3	25.1	23.11	10.9	1.10	2.11	31.8	7.9	12.10	—
Kidderminster H.	15.2	28.12	26.12	7.12	2.11	17.8	8.3	30.9	23.11	14.12
Macclesfield Town	1.1	21.9	26.4	31.8	12.4	1.3	1.10	23.11	19.11	17.8
Morecambe	21.12	2.11	25.1	22.3	15.3	18.9	1.3	7.12	7.9	19.10
Northwich Victoria	1.2	17.8	26.8	5.10	7.12	15.3	1.1	2.11	23.9	11.1
R'den & Diamonds	3.5	30.11	14.12	9.11	17.9	19.10	11.1	31.3	8.3	1.1
Slough Town	31.8	3.9	14.9	31.3	11.1	1.2	26.4	15.3	21.9	24.9
Southport	14.12	4.1	7.12	22.2	8.3	1.10	26.8	3.5	28.12	19.4
Stalybridge Celtic	8.3	5.4	2.11	25.1	1.2	1.1	7.12	24.8	26.8	5.10
Stevenage Borough	5.4	9.9	21.9	30.11	29.3	23.11	17.8	28.12	15.3	15.2
Telford United	28.9	12.10	1.10	26.4	17.8	24.8	12.4	15.2	26.12	17.9
Welling United	11.1	16.11	17.8	26.12	26.8	26.4	22.3	12.10	2.11	31.3
Woking	30.11	20.8	19.4	24.9	10.9	25.1	21.12	1.1	24.8	5.4

Kidderminster H	Macclesfield Town	Morecambe	Northwich Victoria	Rushden & Diamonds	Slough Town	Southport	Stalybridge Celtic	Stevenage Borough	Telford United	Welling United	Woking
21.9	26.12	3.9	12.10	17.8	2.11	24.9	1.10	7.12	22.2	24.8	14.9
24.9	22.2	11.1	3.5	12.4	29.3	1.2	19.10	21.12	22.3	19.4	23.11
1.1	7.9	30.11	22.3	15.3	28.9	24.8	11.1	9.11	20.8	3.5	22.2
24.8	8.3	5.4	14.12	29.3	17.9	11.1	21.12	1.3	23.11	1.1	3.9
20.8	24.8	21.9	26.10	25.1	14.12	30.11	15.2	19.10	3.5	25.3	4.1
3.5	25.9	12.10	21.8	22.2	4.1	11.9	26.12	12.4	11.1	9.11	7.12
5.10	25.3	14.12	26.12	7.9	24.8	29.3	17.9	3.5	24.9	23.11	19.10
10.9	1.2	8.3	5.4	26.8	22.2	17.8	9.11	11.1	5.10	24.9	26.12
11.1	31.3	22.2	2.9	30.9	19.4	19.10	30.11	19.8	1.1	12.4	1.2
22.2	3.5	4.1	12.4	26.12	7.12	21.9	1.3	25.3	15.3	20.8	26.8
—	14.9	29.3	4.1	12.10	26.8	26.4	2.9	16.9	1.2	7.9	12.4
10.12	—	10.9	29.3	15.2	25.1	15.3	12.10	26.8	21.12	19.10	11.1
19.4	21.8	—	2.10	23.11	16.11	1.1	26.4	31.3	26.8	15.2	17.8
19.10	28.9	28.12	—	9.9	23.11	21.12	31.3	31.8	14.9	22.2	26.4
21.12	3.9	1.2	24.8	—	22.3	5.4	31.8	24.9	19.4	5.10	1.3
9.11	30.11	5.10	15.2	20.8	—	12.4	17.8	1.1	19.10	21.12	1.10
31.8	9.11	26.12	17.9	2.11	7.9	—	20.8	8.2	31.3	25.1	22.3
22.3	14.12	24.9	21.9	28.12	3.5	23.11	—	22.2	10.9	29.3	7.9
25.1	4.1	24.8	8.3	26.4	26.12	5.10	19.4	—	14.12	2.9	2.11
30.11	2.11	9.11	25.1	7.12	8.3	3.9	4.1	7.9	—	28.12	29.3
15.3	5.4	31.8	30.11	4.1	10.9	1.3	8.2	1.10	21.9	—	14.12
31.3	5.10	3.5	9.11	21.9	28.12	15.2	1.3	12.10	31.8	8.3	—

FA CARLING PREMIERSHIP FIXTURES 1996–97

	Arsenal	Aston Villa	Blackburn R	Chelsea	Coventry C	Derby Co	Everton	Leeds U
Arsenal	—	28.12	19.4	4.9	19.10	7.12	18.1	26.10
Aston Villa	7.9	—	21.8	26.12	15.2	24.8	5.4	19.10
Blackburn R	12.10	22.3	—	16.11	11.1	9.9	21.9	4.9
Chelsea	5.4	15.9	5.3	—	24.8	18.1	7.12	3.5
Coventry C	23.4	23.11	28.9	12.4	—	3.5	22.2	14.9
Derby Co	11.5	12.4	28.12	1.3	30.11	—	14.12	17.8
Everton	1.3	4.9	1.1	11.5	4.11	15.3	—	21.12
Leeds U	1.2	22.4	5.4	1.12	26.12	29.3	8.3	—
Leicester C	24.8	5.3	7.12	12.10	21.12	22.2	23.11	28.9
Liverpool	19.8	18.1	22.2	21.9	5.4	27.10	20.10	5.3
Manchester U	16.11	1.1	25.8	2.11	1.3	5.4	21.8	28.12
Middlesbrough	21.9	3.5	8.3	22.3	7.9	5.3	26.12	7.12
Newcastle U	30.11	30.9	14.9	15.2	15.3	19.4	29.3	1.1
Nottingham F	21.12	22.2	23.11	11.1	29.3	19.10	28.10	19.4
Sheffield W	26.12	17.8	19.10	7.9	1.2	21.9	11.1	22.3
Southampton	15.3	7.12	3.5	18.8	19.4	21.12	5.3	23.11
Sunderland	11.1	26.10	18.1	15.12	21.9	26.12	3.5	22.2
Tottenham H	15.2	12.10	29.3	1.2	11.5	21.8	24.8	15.3
West Ham U	29.3	14.12	26.10	8.3	21.8	23.11	19.4	18.1
Wimbledon	2.11	8.3	14.12	22.4	16.11	11.1	7.9	12.4

Leicester C	Liverpool	Manchester U	Middlesbrough	Newcastle U	Nottingham F	Sheffield W	Southampton	Sunderland	Tottenham H	West Ham U	Wimbledon
12.4	22.3	4.3	1.1	3.5	8.3	16.9	14.12	28.9	24.11	17.8	22.2
16.11	1.3	21.9	30.11	11.1	2.11	29.3	11.5	1.2	19.4	15.3	22.12
11.5	3.11	12.4	21.12	26.12	15.2	22.4	30.11	1.3	17.8	1.2	15.3
19.4	1.1	22.2	21.8	23.11	28.9	28.12	29.3	15.3	26.10	21.12	19.10
8.3	4.9	18.1	28.12	14.12	17.8	26.10	13.10	1.1	7.12	22.3	5.3
2.11	1.2	4.9	17.11	12.10	23.4	1.1	8.3	14.9	22.3	15.2	28.9
15.2	23.4	22.3	14.9	17.8	1.2	28.9	16.11	30.11	12.4	12.10	28.12
11.1	16.11	7.9	11.5	21.9	12.10	20.8	15.2	2.11	14.12	1.3	26.8
—	15.9	3.5	15.3	26.10	28.12	5.4	21.8	29.3	1.1	23.4	18.1
26.12	—	19.4	29.3	8.3	14.12	7.12	7.9	24.8	3.5	11.1	23.11
30.11	12.10	—	15.2	23.4	14.9	15.3	1.2	21.12	29.9	11.5	29.3
14.12	17.8	23.11	—	22.2	12.4	18.1	11.1	19.4	19.10	4.9	26.10
1.2	23.12	20.10	3.11	—	11.5	24.8	1.3	5.4	28.12	16.11	21.8
7.9	15.3	26.12	24.8	9.12	—	5.3	5.4	21.8	18.1	21.9	3.5
2.9	11.5	14.12	1.3	12.4	18.11	—	2.11	15.2	8.3	30.11	19.4
22.3	28.12	26.10	28.9	18.1	4.9	22.2	—	19.10	14.9	12.4	1.1
17.8	12.4	8.3	14.10	4.9	22.3	23.11	22.4	—	4.3	8.9	7.12
22.9	2.12	11.1	23.4	7.9	1.3	21.12	26.12	16.11	—	2.11	5.4
19.10	29.9	8.12	5.4	5.3	1.1	3.5	24.8	28.12	22.2	—	14.9
1.3	15.2	17.8	1.2	22.3	30.11	12.10	23.9	11.5	3.9	26.12	—

NATIONWIDE FOOTBALL LEAGUE FIXTURES 1996–97

DIVISION ONE

	Barnsley	Birmingham C	Bolton W	Bradford C	Charlton Ath	Crystal Palace	Grimsby T	Huddersfield T	Ipswich T	Manchester C
Barnsley	—	5.4	25.10	26.4	12.4	12.10	28.9	25.8	18.1	28.12
Birmingham C	31.8	—	9.11	12.10	31.3	18.8	7.12	12.4	15.10	1.1
Bolton W	30.11	1.2	—	1.1	26.4	16.11	10.9	2.11	14.12	20.8
Bradford C	19.10	19.4	21.9	—	15.2	29.10	8.3	1.2	16.11	1.3
Charlton Ath	5.10	27.8	19.10	23.11	—	8.3	9.11	29.3	1.1	5.4
Crystal Palace	19.4	29.3	4.3	8.2	21.12	—	26.10	5.4	10.9	14.9
Grimsby T	28.1	1.3	26.12	21.12	1.2	30.11	—	15.2	31.3	15.3
Huddersfield T	22.3	5.10	22.2	8.11	17.8	31.8	23.11	—	28.12	18.1
Ipswich T	1.10	4.5	15.3	4.3	20.9	26.12	27.8	7.9	—	28.3
Manchester C	7.9	21.9	9.4	7.12	31.8	11.1	14.12	20.11	16.8	—
Norwich C	1.2	30.11	22.3	28.12	2.11	14.12	18.1	1.3	11.10	26.4
Oldham Ath	21.9	26.12	19.4	22.2	28.1	22.3	8.2	11.1	31.8	21.12
Oxford U	4.5	18.10	5.10	14.9	30.11	1.3	1.1	16.11	2.11	1.2
Port Vale	29.10	2.11	17.8	29.9	15.3	15.10	14.9	30.11	15.2	10.9
Portsmouth	15.2	29.10	11.1	29.3	12.10	1.10	5.4	14.12	26.4	16.11
QPR	11.1	29.1	1.9	16.10	16.11	1.2	12.4	8.3	30.10	12.10
Reading	31.3	1.10	8.2	15.3	11.1	21.9	12.10	28.1	22.3	15.10
Sheffield U	21.12	24.8	23.11	10.9	15.10	12.4	22.2	27.8	14.9	28.9
Southend U	1.3	21.12	7.9	12.4	26.12	28.1	15.10	26.4	1.2	29.10
Stoke C	26.12	11.1	29.1	28.8	1.10	7.9	5.3	22.9	8.3	24.8
Swindon T	16.11	15.2	21.12	18.1	1.3	26.4	28.12	16.10	12.4	2.11
Tranmere R	15.3	7.9	4.5	4.4	29.10	2.11	23.8	26.12	30.11	15.2
WBA	17.8	15.3	7.12	26.10	22.3	31.3	26.4	12.10	28.9	12.4
Wolverhampton W	2.11	16.11	2.10	24.8	6.9	15.2	29.3	30.10	1.3	30.11

DIVISION TWO

Norwich C	Oldham Ath	Oxford U	Port Vale	Portsmouth	QPR	Reading	Sheffield U	Southend U	Stoke C	Swindon T	Tranmere R	WBA	Wolverhampton W
9.11	1.1	15.10	8.2	23.11	14.9	28.8	8.3	7.12	10.9	4.3	14.12	29.3	22.2
26.10	10.9	26.4	22.2	8.2	28.9	18.1	22.3	8.3	14.9	23.11	28.12	14.12	4.3
24.8	12.10	12.4	29.3	14.9	5.4	29.10	15.2	28.12	28.9	8.3	15.10	1.3	18.1
7.9	2.11	11.1	28.1	17.8	4.5	14.12	26.12	5.10	31.3	1.10	31.8	30.11	22.3
22.2	28.9	26.10	14.12	19.4	4.3	14.9	4.5	10.9	18.1	7.12	8.2	24.8	28.12
15.3	24.8	7.12	4.5	18.1	10.11	1.1	6.10	28.9	28.12	19.10	22.2	27.8	23.11
1.10	29.10	21.9	11.1	31.8	5.10	19.4	3.11	4.5	16.11	7.9	22.3	19.10	17.8
7.12	13.9	4.3	26.10	15.3	21.12	28.9	31.3	19.10	1.1	4.5	10.9	19.4	8.2
19.4	5.4	22.2	23.11	19.10	8.2	24.8	11.1	9.11	21.12	5.10	26.10	28.1	7.12
19.10	8.3	9.11	26.12	5.3	19.4	4.5	29.1	8.2	22.3	22.2	23.11	5.10	27.10
—	16.10	31.3	8.3	1.1	11.9	16.11	30.10	14.9	12.4	17.8	28.9	15.2	31.8
4.5	—	23.11	5.10	9.11	7.12	19.10	7.9	26.10	17.8	31.3	4.3	1.10	15.3
27.8	15.2	—	5.4	28.9	29.3	28.12	14.12	24.8	29.10	19.4	18.1	8.3	10.9
21.12	12.4	31.8	—	28.12	18.1	1.3	16.11	1.1	12.10	22.3	31.3	1.2	26.4
21.9	1.2	28.1	7.9	—	23.8	8.3	1.3	27.8	30.11	26.12	12.4	2.11	15.10
26.12	1.3	17.8	2.10	22.3	—	15.2	30.11	14.12	2.11	21.9	26.4	7.9	31.3
4.3	26.4	8.9	7.12	21.12	23.11	—	17.8	22.2	31.8	26.10	9.11	26.12	12.4
8.2	28.12	15.3	4.3	7.12	26.10	29.3	—	18.1	26.4	9.11	12.10	5.4	1.1
11.1	30.11	22.3	21.9	31.3	15.3	2.11	1.10	—	15.2	31.8	17.8	16.11	13.10
4.10	29.3	8.2	19.4	26.10	22.2	5.4	19.10	23.11	—	14.12	7.12	4.5	9.11
29.3	28.8	12.10	24.8	11.9	1.1	30.11	1.2	5.4	15.3	—	14.9	30.10	27.9
28.1	15.11	1.10	27.8	5.10	20.10	1.2	19.4	29.3	28.2	10.1	—	21.9	21.12
23.11	18.1	21.12	9.11	22.2	28.12	10.9	30.8	4.3	16.10	8.2	1.1	—	15.9
5.4	14.12	26.12	19.10	4.5	28.8	5.10	21.9	19.4	1.2	29.1	8.3	11.1	—

NATIONWIDE FOOTBALL LEAGUE FIXTURES 1996–97

Copyright © The Football League Ltd 1996. Copyright Licence No. NCH 10796. Compiled in association with SEMA Group.

DIVISION TWO

	Blackpool	AFC Bournemouth	Brentford	Bristol C	Bristol R	Burnley	Bury	Chesterfield	Crewe Alex	Gillingham
Blackpool	—	9.11	4.1	22.3	26.4	26.12	12.4	17.8	18.1	12.10
AFC Bournemouth	1.2	—	19.11	29.10	26.12	15.2	2.11	8.3	7.9	12.4
Brentford	14.9	22.2	—	18.1	25.1	15.3	29.3	28.12	19.4	27.8
Bristol C	24.8	25.1	1.10	—	15.12	11.1	5.4	12.4	22.2	29.3
Bristol R	19.10	10.9	29.10	15.3	—	19.11	30.11	28.9	5.10	2.11
Burnley	10.9	23.11	14.12	28.9	22.2	—	18.1	1.1	9.11	28.12
Bury	5.10	8.2	17.8	31.8	26.10	1.10	—	22.3	26.12	15.3
Chesterfield	29.3	21.12	7.9	5.10	11.1	21.9	24.8	—	19.10	5.4
Crewe Alex	16.10	28.12	12.10	19.11	12.4	1.2	10.9	26.4	—	1.3
Gillingham	19.4	5.10	31.3	17.8	8.2	7.9	14.12	31.8	3.12	—
Luton T	28.9	26.10	22.3	1.4	23.11	17.8	1.1	14.9	14.12	10.9
Millwall	30.10	15.3	30.11	1.2	7.9	31.8	16.10	12.10	21.9	26.4
Notts Co	15.2	1.1	1.3	30.11	12.10	26.4	19.11	15.10	8.3	18.1
Peterborough U	2.11	5.4	15.10	15.2	29.3	20.12	12.10	1.3	24.8	19.11
Plymouth Arg	1.3	3.5	26.12	19.10	21.9	30.11	15.2	19.11	11.1	29.10
Preston N E	13.12	14.9	8.3	28.12	24.8	29.10	1.3	1.2	27.8	30.11
Rotherham U	27.8	28.9	11.4	14.9	15.10	12.10	28.12	10.9	25.1	1.1
Shrewsbury T	1.1	3.12	31.8	10.9	9.11	1.4	14.9	18.1	26.10	15.10
Stockport Co	19.11	27.8	1.2	2.11	5.4	12.4	8.3	29.10	29.3	28.9
Walsall	28.12	18.1	26.4	1.1	3.12	22.3	28.9	1.4	23.11	14.9
Watford	30.11	29.3	2.11	1.3	4.1	15.10	26.4	15.2	5.4	21.12
Wrexham	3.5	19.10	15.2	21.12	27.8	1.3	29.10	2.11	4.1	1.2
Wycombe W	5.4	19.4	21.9	3.5	8.3	4.1	27.8	14.12	8.2	24.8
York C	8.3	24.8	11.1	19.4	1.10	2.11	1.2	30.11	3.5	15.2

Luton T	Millwall	Notts Co	Peterborough U	Plymouth Arg	Preston N E	Rotherham U	Shrewsbury T	Stockport Co	Walsall	Watford	Wrexham	Wycombe W	York C
11.1	25.1	23.11	8.2	3.12	15.3	31.3	21.9	22.2	7.9	26.10	15.10	31.8	21.12
30.11	14.12	21.9	31.8	15.10	4.1	11.1	1.3	1.4	1.10	17.8	26.4	12.10	22.3
24.8	26.10	3.12	3.5	10.9	21.12	5.10	5.4	9.11	19.10	8.2	23.11	1.1	28.9
27.8	9.11	26.10	23.11	26.4	7.9	4.1	26.12	8.2	21.9	3.12	8.3	15.10	11.10
15.2	28.12	20.4	17.8	1.1	23.3	3.5	1.2	31.8	1.3	14.9	31.3	21.12	18.1
29.3	5.4	19.10	8.3	26.10	25.1	19.4	27.8	5.10	24.8	3.5	3.12	14.9	8.2
21.9	3.5	22.2	19.4	23.11	3.12	7.9	4.1	21.12	11.1	19.10	25.1	31.3	9.11
4.1	19.4	3.5	3.12	22.2	9.11	26.12	1.10	25.1	27.8	23.10	8.2	15.3	26.10
15.3	1.1	20.12	22.3	28.9	31.3	29.10	30.11	17.8	15.2	31.8	14.9	2.11	15.10
26.12	19.10	1.10	22.2	25.1	26.10	21.9	3.5	11.1	4.1	8.3	9.11	22.3	23.11
—	8.3	9.11	19.10	8.2	22.2	31.8	19.4	3.5	5.10	25.1	18.1	28.12	3.12
18.12	—	4.1	26.12	12.4	11.1	15.2	20.11	2.10	2.11	22.3	17.8	1.3	2.4
1.2	14.9	—	31.3	28.12	17.8	14.12	2.11	22.3	29.10	10.9	28.9	12.4	31.8
26.4	10.9	27.8	—	18.1	12.4	30.11	29.10	15.3	1.2	1.1	28.12	28.9	14.9
2.11	5.10	7.9	1.10	—	31.8	8.3	14.12	4.1	19.4	31.3	22.3	1.2	17.8
19.11	28.9	29.3	5.10	5.4	—	2.11	19.10	19.4	3.5	18.1	1.1	15.2	10.9
5.4	23.11	15.3	26.10	21.12	8.2	—	24.8	3.12	29.3	9.11	22.2	18.1	26.4
12.10	22.2	8.2	25.1	15.3	26.4	22.3	—	23.11	21.12	28.9	12.4	18.8	28.12
15.10	18.1	24.8	14.12	14.9	12.10	1.3	15.2	—	30.11	28.12	10.9	26.4	1.1
12.4	8.2	25.1	9.11	12.10	15.10	17.8	8.3	26.10	—	14.12	31.8	10.9	22.2
29.10	24.8	26.12	21.9	27.8	1.10	1.2	11.1	7.9	15.3	—	12.10	19.11	12.4
1.10	28.3	11.1	7.9	24.8	21.9	19.11	4.10	26.12	5.4	19.4	—	30.11	15.3
7.9	3.12	5.10	11.1	9.11	23.11	1.10	29.3	19.10	26.12	22.2	26.10	—	25.1
1.3	27.8	5.4	4.1	29.3	26.12	19.10	7.9	21.9	19.11	5.10	14.12	29.10	—

NATIONWIDE FOOTBALL LEAGUE FIXTURES 1996–97

Copyright © The Football League Ltd 1996. Copyright Licence No. NCH 10796. Compiled in association with SEMA Group.

DIVISION THREE

	Barnet	Brighton & H A	Cambridge U	Cardiff C	Carlisle U	Chester C	Colchester U	Darlington	Doncaster R	Exeter C
Barnet	—	27.8	29.3	19.4	26.10	21.12	3.5	25.1	23.11	21.9
Brighton & H A	31.3	—	12.10	22.3	23.11	17.8	26.12	3.12	26.4	4.1
Cambridge U	17.8	19.4	—	31.8	22.2	22.3	7.3	1.10	25.10	11.1
Cardiff C	12.10	24.8	5.4	—	26.4	12.4	8.2	15.10	14.3	7.9
Carlisle U	30.11	15.2	19.11	19.10	—	29.10	1.10	21.9	29.3	3.5
Chester C	8.3	29.3	24.8	5.10	25.1	—	22.11	14.12	8.2	19.10
Colchester U	15.10	10.9	20.12	2.11	18.1	14.2	—	31.3	28.9	29.10
Darlington	29.10	1.3	18.1	3.5	1.1	15.3	27.8	—	5.4	19.11
Doncaster R	15.2	19.10	30.11	13.12	17.8	2.11	11.1	31.8	—	31.3
Exeter C	1.1	14.9	28.9	28.12	15.10	26.4	25.1	22.2	27.8	—
Fulham	19.11	30.11	15.10	1.2	31.8	1.3	7.9	11.1	12.10	26.12
Hartlepool U	26.4	2.11	12.4	19.11	10.9	28.9	29.3	12.10	18.1	30.11
Hereford U	2.11	3.5	29.10	15.2	14.12	30.11	5.4	4.1	24.8	1.3
Hull C	31.8	15.3	2.11	29.10	22.3	1.2	4.1	17.8	21.12	15.2
Leyton O	1.3	22.12	15.2	30.11	31.3	15.10	21.9	7.9	12.4	1.2
Lincoln C	14.9	18.1	27.8	28.9	3.12	28.12	26.10	9.11	25.1	5.10
Mansfield T	10.9	1.2	1.3	8.3	12.4	19.11	14.12	26.4	28.12	17.8
Northampton T	28.12	28.9	14.9	1	9.11	18.1	19.10	26.10	22.12	19.4
Rochdale	1.2	29.10	26.4	18.1	12.10	10.9	24.8	12.4	14.9	2.11
Scarborough	18.1	28.12	1.1	17.8	14.9	12.10	3.12	8.2	10.9	22.3
Scunthorpe U	28.9	5.4	10.9	14.9	8.3	1.1	22.2	23.11	9.11	14.12
Swansea C	13.12	19.11	31.1	1.3	28.12	31.3	4.10	22.3	1.1	8.3
Torquay U	12.4	1.1	28.12	10.9	28.9	14.9	9.11	8.3	15.10	31.8
Wigan Ath	22.3	5.10	15.3	31.3	8.2	31.8	19.4	26.12	3.12	1.10

Fulham	Hartlepool U	Hereford U	Hull C	Leyton O	Lincoln C	Mansfield T	Northampton T	Rochdale	Scarborough	Scunthorpe U	Swansea C	Torquay U	Wigan Ath
22.2	19.10	8.2	5.4	3.12	4.1	26.12	7.9	9.11	1.10	11.1	15.3	5.10	24.8
26.10	8.2	15.10	14.12	8.3	1.10	9.11	11.1	25.1	7.9	31.8	22.2	21.9	12.4
3.5	5.10	25.1	8.2	23.11	31.3	3.12	4.1	19.10	21.9	26.12	9.11	7.9	14.12
9.11	22.2	23.11	25.1	26.10	11.1	21.12	21.9	1.10	28.3	4.1	3.12	26.12	27.8
5.4	26.12	15.3	24.8	27.8	1.3	5.10	1.4	19.4	4.1	21.12	7.9	11.1	2.11
3.12	11.1	26.10	9.11	3.5	7.9	22.2	1.10	26.12	19.4	21.9	27.8	4.1	5.4
28.12	17.8	31.8	14.9	1.1	30.11	14.3	26.4	21.3	28.2	19.11	11.4	31.1	12.10
28.9	19.4	14.9	29.3	28.12	1.2	19.10	30.11	5.10	2.11	15.2	24.8	21.12	10.9
19.4	1.10	21.3	8.3	5.10	29.10	7.9	19.11	4.1	26.12	1.2	21.9	3.5	28.2
10.9	26.10	3.12	23.11	9.11	12.4	29.3	12.10	8.2	24.8	15.3	21.12	5.4	18.1
—	22.3	17.8	26.4	14.12	2.11	21.9	12.4	31.3	8.3	29.10	4.1	1.10	15.2
24.8	—	28.12	1.1	5.4	21.12	27.8	29.10	15.3	1.2	1.3	15.10	15.2	14.9
29.3	7.9	—	27.8	19.10	19.11	11.1	8.3	21.9	5.10	1.10	26.12	19.4	1.2
19.10	21.9	31.3	—	19.4	26.12	1.10	1.3	7.9	3.5	5.10	11.1	19.11	30.11
16.3	31.8	26.4	12.10	—	22.3	4.1	26.12	11.1	29.10	17.8	1.10	2.11	19.11
8.2	8.3	22.2	10.9	24.8	—	23.11	14.12	3.5	19.10	19.4	5.4	29.3	1.1
1.1	31.3	28.9	18.1	14.9	15.2	—	22.3	31.8	30.11	2.11	12.10	29.10	15.10
5.10	25.1	20.12	3.12	10.9	15.3	24.8	—	23.11	5.4	3.5	8.2	27.8	29.3
27.8	14.12	1.1	28.12	28.9	15.10	5.4	15.2	—	19.11	30.11	29.3	1.3	8.3
21.12	9.11	12.4	15.10	25.1	26.4	26.10	31.8	22.2	—	31.3	23.11	15.3	28.9
25.1	3.12	18.1	12.4	29.3	12.10	8.2	15.10	26.10	27.8	—	26.4	24.8	28.12
14.9	3.5	10.9	28.9	18.1	30.8	19.4	2.11	17.8	15.2	19.10	—	30.11	29.10
18.1	23.11	12.10	22.2	8.2	17.8	25.1	31.3	3.12	14.12	22.3	26.10	—	26.4
23.11	4.1	9.11	26.10	22.2	21.9	3.5	17.8	21.12	11.1	7.9	25.1	19.10	—

OTHER FIXTURES – SEASON 1996–97

August
7 Wed Euro Comps Prelim Rd (1)
10 Sat Official Start of Season
11 Sun Littlewoods FA Charity Shield
17 Sat Commencement of FA Premier
League and Football League
21 Wed Euro Comps Prelim (2)
FL Coca-Cola Cup 1st Rd (1)
26 Mon Bank Holiday
28 Wed FI Coca-Cola Cup 1st Rd (2)
31 Sat FA Cup Sponsored by Littlewoods
Prel Rd
Austria v Scotland (WC)
Wales v San Marino (WC)
Liechtenstein v Republic of Ireland
(WC)
Northern Ireland v Ukraine (WC)

September
1 Sun Moldova v England (WC)
4 Wed International
7 Sat FA Carlsberg Vase 1st Rd Qual
FA Youth Cup Extra Prel Rd*
8 Sun UK Living Women's FA Cup Preliminary Round
11 Wed Euro Comps 1st Round (1)
14 Sat FA Cup Sponsored by Littlewoods
1st Rd Qual
18 Wed FA Coca-Cola Cup 2nd Rd (1)
21 Sat FA Youth Cup Prel Rd*
25 Wed Euro Comps 1st Round (2)
28 Sat FA Cup Sponsored by Littlewoods
2nd Rd Qual
29 Sun UK Living Women's FA Cup 1st
Round

October
2 Wed FL Coca-Cola Cup 2nd Rd (2)
5 Sat FA Carlsberg Vase 2nd Rd Qual
Latvia v Scotland (WC)
Wales v Holland (WC)
Northern Ireland v Armenia (WC)
9 Wed England v Poland (WC)
Estonia v Scotland (WC)
Republic of Ireland v Macedonia
(WC)
12 Sat FA Cup Sponsored by Littlewoods
3rd Rd Qual
FA Youth Cup 1st Rd Qual Rd*
FA County Youth Cup 1st Rd*
16 Wed Euro Comps 2nd Round (1)
19 Sat FA Umbro Trophy 1st Rd Qual
23 Wed FL Coca-Cola Cup 3rd Rd
26 Sat FA Cup Sponsored by Littlewoods
4th Rd Qual
27 Sun FA Sunday Cup 1st Round
30 Wed Euro Comps 2nd Round (2)

November
2 Sat FA Carlsberg Vase 1st Rd Proper
FA Youth Cup 2nd Rd Qual*
3 Sun UK Living Women's FA Cup 2nd
Round

6 Wed FL Coca-Cola Cup 3rd Rd replays
9 Sat FA Umbro Trophy 2nd Rd Qual
Georgia v England (WC)
Holland v Wales (WC)
Germany v Northern Ireland (WC)
10 Sun Scotland v Sweden (WC)
Republic of Ireland v Iceland (WC)
16 Sat FA Cup Sponsored by Littlewoods
1st Rd Proper
20 Wed Euro Comps 3rd Round (1)
23 Sat FA Carlsberg Vase 2nd Rd Proper
FA Youth Cup 1st Rd Proper*
FA County Youth Cup 2nd Rd*
24 Sun FA Sunday Cup 2nd Round
27 Wed FA Cup Sponsored by Littlewoods
1st Proper Replays
FL Coca-Cola Cup 4th Rd
30 Sat FA Umbro Trophy 3rd Rd Qual

December
1 Sun UK Living Women's FA Cup 3rd
Round
4 Wed Euro Comps 3rd Round (2)
7 Sat FA Cup Sponsored by Littlewoods
2nd Rd Proper
14 Sat FA Carlsberg Vase 3rd Proper
Wales v Turkey (WC) (prov)
Northern Ireland v Albania (WC)
FA Youth Cup 2nd Rd Proper*
15 Sun FA Sunday Cup 3rd Round
Wales v Turkey (WC) (prov)
18 Wed FA Cup Sponsored by Littlewoods
2nd Rd Proper replays
FL Coca-Cola Cup 4th Rd replays
21 Sat
26 Thu Boxing Day
28 Sat

January 1997
1 Wed New Years Day
4 Sat FA Cup Sponsored by Littlewoods
3rd Rd Proper
5 Sun UK Living Women's FA Cup 4th
Round
8 Wed FL Coca-Cola Cup 5th Rd
11 Sat FA Carlsberg Vase 4th Rd Proper
FA Youth Cup 3rd Rd Proper*
FA County Youth Cup 3rd Rd*
12 Sun FA Sunday Cup 4th Round
15 Wed FA Cup Sponsored by Littlewoods
3rd Rd Proper replays
18 Sat FA Umbro Trophy 1st Rd Proper
22 Wed FL Coca-Cola Cup 5th Rd replays
25 Sat FA Cup sponsored by Littlewoods
4th Rd Proper

February
1 Sat FA Carlsberg Vase 5th Rd Proper
2 Sun UK Living Women's FA Cup 5th
Round
5 Wed FA Cup Sponsored by Littlewoods
4th Rd Proper replays
8 Sat FA Umbro Trophy 2nd Rd Proper

9	Sun	FA Sunday Cup 5th Round
12	Wed	England v Italy (WC)
15	Sat	FA Cup Sponsored by Littlewoods 5th Rd Proper
		FA Youth Cup 4th Rd Proper*
		FA County Youth Cup 4th Rd*
19	Wed	FL Coca-Cola Cup Semi-Finals (1)
22	Sat	FA Carlsberg Vase 6th Rd Proper
23	Sun	FL Coca-Cola Cup Semi-Finals (1)
26	Wed	FA Cup Sponsored by Littlewoods 5th Rd Proper replays

March

1	Sat	FA Umbro Trophy 3rd Rd Proper
2	Sun	UK Living Women's FA Cup 6th Round
5	Wed	Euro Comps QF (1)
8	Sat	FA Cup Sponsored by Littlewoods 6th Rd Proper
		FA Youth Cup 5th Rd Proper*
12	Wed	FL Coca-Cola Cup Semi-Finals (2)
15	Sat	FA Carlsberg Vase Semi-Final (1)
		FA County Youth Cup Semi-Finals*
16	Sun	FL Coca-Cola Cup Semi-Finals (2)
		FA Sunday Cup Semi-Final
19	Wed	Euro Comps QF (2)
		FA Cup Sponsored by Littlewoods 6th Rd Proper replays
22	Sat	FA Umbro Trophy 4th Rd Proper
		FA Carlsberg Vase Semi-Finals (2)
28	Fri	Good Friday
29	Sat	Scotland v Estonia (WC)
		Wales v Belgium (WC)
		Northern Ireland v Portugal (WC)
30	Sun	UK Living Women's FA Cup Semi-Finals
31	Mon	Easter Monday

April

2	Wed	Scotland v Austria (WC)
		Macedonia v Republic of Ireland (WC)
		Ukraine v Northern Ireland (WC)
5	Sat	FA Umbro Trophy Semi-Finals (1)
		FA Youth Cup Semi-Finals*
6	Sun	FL Coca-Cola Cup Final
9	Wed	Euro Comps SF (1)
12	Sat	FA Umbro Trophy Semi-Final (2)
13	Sun	FA Cup Sponsored by Littlewoods Semi-Finals

16	Wed	FA Cup Sponsored by Littlewoods Semi-Finals replays (prov)
19	Sat	
23	Wed	Euro Comps SF (2)
		FA Cup Sponsored by Littlewoods Semi-Finals replays (prov)
26	Sat	FA County Youth Final (fixed date)
27	Sun	FA Sunday Cup Final
30	Wed	England v Georgia (WC)
		Sweden v Scotland (WC)
		Romania v Republic of Ireland (WC)
		Armenia v Northern Ireland (WC)

May

3	Sat	Final matches in Football League
4	Sun	UK Living Women's FA Cup Final
5	Mon	Bank Holiday
7	Wed	UEFA Cup Final 1st Leg
10	Sat	Final matches in FA Premier League
		FA Carlsberg Vase Final – Wembley Stadium
		FA Youth Cup Final*
11	Sun	FL Play off Semi-Finals (1)
14	Wed	European Cup Winners Cup Final
		FL Play off Semi-finals (2)
17	Sat	FA Cup Sponsored by Littlewoods Final – Wembley Stadium
18	Sun	FA Umbro Trophy Final – Wembley Stadium
21	Wed	UEFA Cup Final 2nd Leg
22	Thu	FA Cup Sponsored by Littlewoods Final replay – Wembley Stadium
24	Sat	FL Play off Final Division 3
25	Sun	FL Play off Final Division 2
26	Mon	FL Play off Final Division 1
		Bank Holiday
28	Wed	European Champions Cup Final
31	Sat	Poland v England (WC)

June

7	Sat	Republic of Ireland v Liechtenstein (WC)
8	Sun	Belarus v Scotland (WC)
16	Mon	Commencement of Close Season

* closing date of rounds

NATIONAL LIST OF REFEREES FOR SEASON 1996–97

* Alcock, P.E. (Redhill, Surrey)
  Allison, D.B. (Lancaster)
* Ashby, G.R. (Worcester)
  Bailey, M.C. (Impington, Cambridge)
  Baines, S.J. (Chesterfield)
* Barber, G.P. (Warwick)
  Barry, N.S. (Scunthorpe)
  Bates, A. (Stoke-on-Trent)
  Bennett, S.G. (Dartford)
* Bodenham, M.J. (East Looe, Cornwall)
  Brandwood, M.J. (Lichfield, Staffs)
* Burge, K.W. (Tonypandy)
  Burns W.C. (Scarborough)
  Butler, A.N. (Sutton-in-Ashfield)
  Cain, G. (Bootle)
  Coddington, B. (Sheffield)
  Cruikshanks, I.G. (Hartlepool)
* Danson, P.S. (Leicester)
* Dilkes, L.R. (Mossley, Lancs)
* Dunn, S.W. (Bristol)
* Durkin, P.A. (Portland, Dorset)
  D'Urso, A.P. (Billericay, Essex)
* Elleray, D.R. (Harrow-on-the-Hill)
  Finch, C.T. (Bury St Edmunds)
  Fletcher, M. (Warley, West Midlands)
  Foy, C.J. (St Helens)
  Frankland, G.B. (Middlesbrough)
  Furnandiz, R.D. (Doncaster)
* Gallagher, D.J. (Banbury, Oxon)
  Halsay, M.R. (Welwyn Garden City, Herts)
  Harris, R.J. (Oxford)
  Heilbron, T. (Newton Aycliffe)
* Jones, P. (Loughborough)
  Jones, T. (Barrow-in-Furness)
  Kirkby, J.A. (Sheffield)

  Knight, B. (Orpington)
  Laws, D. (Whitley Bay)
  Laws, G. (Whitley Bay)
  Leach, K.A. (Wolverhampton)
  Leake, A.R. (Darwen, Lancashire)
* Lodge, S.J. (Barnsley)
  Lomas, E. (Manchester)
  Lunt, T. (Ashton-in-Makerfield, Lancs)
  Lynch, K.M. (Knaresborough)
  Mathieson, S.W. (Stockport)
  Orr, D. (Iver, Bucks)
  Pearson, R. (Peterlee, Durham)
  Pierce, M.E. (Portsmouth)
* Poll, G. (Tring, Hertfordshire)
  Pooley, G.R. (Bishop's Stortford)
  Poulain, R. (Huddersfield)
  Pugh, D. (Wirral)
* Reed, M.D. (Birmingham)
  Rejer, P. (Tipton, West Midlands)
  Rennie, U.D. (Sheffield)
  Richards, P.R. (Preston)
* Riley, M.A. (Leeds)
  Robinson, J.P. (Hull)
  Singh, G. (Wolverhampton)
  Stretton, F.G. (Nottingham)
  Styles, R. (Waterlooville, Hants)
  Taylor, P. (Cheshunt, Hertfordshire)
  West, T.E. (Hull)
  Wiley, A.G. (Burntwood, Staffs)
  Wilkes, C.R. (Gloucester)
* Wilkie, A.B. (Chester-le-Street)
* Willard, G.S. (Worthing, W. Sussex)
* Winter, J.T. (Stockton-on-Tees)
  Wolstenholme, E.K. (Blackburn)

* *Denotes Premier League Referee*

Assistant Referees

Adcock, D.J. (Long Eaton, Notts), Armstrong, P. (Thatcham, Berks), Ashman, J.J. (Swansea), Atkins, G. (Bradford), Babski, D.S. (Scunthorpe), Baker, B.L. (Warminster, Wilts), Baker, L. (Dulverton, Somerset), Barnes, P.W. (Peterborough), Bassindale, C. (Doncaster), Beale, G.A. (Taunton), Beeby, R.J. (Northampton), Bello, B. (Manchester), Binsley, D.E. (Sunderland), Bishop, B.P. (Bath), Blanchard, I. (Hull), Bone, R. (Orpington, Kent), Booth, D.A. (Barnsley), Boulton, J.T. (Birmingham), Boyeson, C. (Hull), Brammer, D.S. (Weston-s-Mare), Brand, S.R. (Wirral), Breakspear, C.N. (Weybridge), Breckell, A.S. (Accrington), Brown, A.R. (Chorley), Bryan, D.S. (Stamford), Buller, K.R. (Bridgwater), Burton, R. (Burton-upon-Trent), Butler, A.N. (Wigan), Cable, L.E. (Woking), Cairns, M.J. (Burton-upon-Trent), Canadine, P. (Rotherham), Carrington, M. (Loughborough), Castle, S. (Wolverhampton), Charlton, D. (Huddersfield), Clingo, S.G. (Wisbech, Cambs), Clyde, A.L. (Doncaster), Cockwill, N.R. (Barnstaple, N. Devon), Cooper, M.A. (Walsall), Cooper, R.J. (Tynemouth), Copeland, J.F. (Wirral), Cowburn, M.G. (Blackpool), Coxhead, R. (Huntingdon, Cambs), Crick, D.R. (Worcester Park, Surrey), Cullen, P. (Dukinfield, Cheshire), Curson, B. (Burbage,

Leics), Dean, M.L. (Wirral), Dearing, M.D. (Northolt, Middlesex), Devine, J.P. (Middlesbrough), Dexter, M.C. (Thurmaston, Leics), Douglas, M.J. (Blyth, Northumberland), Dowd, P. (Stoke-on-Trent), Downs, D.G. (Basingstoke), Drysdale, D. (Waddington, Lincs), Dyce, O. (Manchester), Eastwood, P. (Manchester), Edgeley, G. (Northwich), Edwards, C.D. (Oldham), Ellicott, B.P. (Redditch), Elwick, P.A. (Boston), Evans, E.M. (Manchester), Evans, R.J. (Beckenham, Kent), Francis, C.J. (Ely, Cambs), Fraser, G.R. (Barrow-in-Furness), French, S.J. (Wolverhampton), Gagen, S.L. (New Malden, Surrey), Gould, R. (Swadlincote, Derbyshire), Gowers, W.G. (Shipston-on-Stour, Warks), Green, A.J. (Hinckley, Leics), Green, E.W. (Henley-on-Thames), Green, N.E. (Stourport-on-Severn, Worcs), Griffin, P.J. (Hornchurch, Essex), Griffiths, J.H. (Chippenham), Griffiths, S.J. (Macclesfield), Griggs, P.J. (Dursley, Glos), Habgood, S. (Swindon), Hall, A.R. (Birmingham), Hall, G.A. (Hixon, Nr Stafford), Hall, M. (Whitley Bay), Hancox, N. (Aldridge, W. Midlands), Harding, P.D. (Crewe), Harris, P.I. (Warrington), Harteveld, A.C (York), Harvey, A.C. (Croxley Green, Herts), Hawkes, K.J. (Quedgeley, Glos), Haxby, M.D. (New Brighton, Wirral), Head, S. (Stokenchurch, Bucks), Hegley, G.K. (Bishop's Stortford), Hill, K.D. (Royston, Herts), Hine, D.J. (Worcester), Hogg, A.S. (Dronfield, Derbyshire), Holbrook, J.H. (Telford), Horlick, D.M. (Liverpool), Horton, A.J. (Wolverhampton), Howells, A.C. (Port Talbot), Howes, T.P. (Norwich), Hubbard, J.R. (Leicester), Ingram, B. (Bath), Ingram, K.R. (Kingswinford), Johnson, A.T. (Grantham), Jones, C. (Pontypridd), Jones, L.C. (Bournemouth), Jones, M.J. (Chester), Jordan, W.M. (Pinner, Middlesex), Joslin, P.J. (Newark), Joy, M.J. (Bristol), Kaye, A. (Bradford), Kellett, D.G. (Bradford), Lee, G.M. (Corby, Northants), Leech, J. (Wigan), Legg, A.R. (East Grinstead, W. Sussex), Lilley, S.J. (Bury St Edmunds), Lockhart, R. (Newcastle-u-Tyne), Lowe, B. (Doncaster), McGee, A. (Liverpool), McGregor, R.E. (Grimsby), March, P. (Ramsgate), Martin, A.J. (Stafford), Martin, E.A.C. (Williton, Somerset), Mellor, G.S. (Doncaster), Messias, M.D. (York), Millership, B.T. (Atherstone, Warks), Mills, A.D. (Bristol), Monk, G.C. (Grays, Essex), Moore, J.F. (Norwich), Morrall, D.A. (Sheffield), Morrison, D.P. (Littleover, Derbys), Mountain, M.J. (Mansfield), Nind, K.J. (Bromsgrove), Norbury, W.J. (Harlow), Norman, P.V. (Bath), North, M.J. (Wimborne), Oldham, A.B. (Poulton-le-Fylde, Lancs), Oliver, D.S. (Darlington), Olivier, R.J. (Sutton Coldfield, W. Mids), Oxley, P. (Rotherham), Parish, G.B. (Harlow), Parkes, T.A. (Birmingham), Pashley, R.A. (Chesterfield), Pawson, P.M. (Sheffield), Payne, R.G. (Fitwick, Beds), Peacock, D. (Redcar, Cleveland), Pearce, J.E. (Dagenham), Peeke, S. (Northfleet, Kent), Penn, A.M. (Kinswinford), Perkin, N.F. (Gravesend), Perlejewski, A.J. (Yeovil), Perry, M.J. (Wimborne, Dorset), Pettitt, J.W. (Welling, Kent), Phillips, D.C. (Bracknell, Berks), Pike, K. (Gillingham, Dorset), Pike, M.S. (Barrow-in-Furness), Polkey, B.L. (Nottingham), Pollard, T.J. (Bury St Edmunds), Pollock, R.M. (Liverpool), Postles, M.D. (Coneyhurst Common, W. Sussex), Powell, K. (Hartlepool), Priest, B.D. (Halesowen), Prosser, P.J. (Albrighton, W. Mids), Race, S. (Oldham), Rawson, R.R. (Sheffield), Reynolds, K.S. (East Barnet), Rice, B.M. (Pershore, Worcs), Richards, D.C. (Llanelli, Dyfed), Roberts, P.A. (Belper), Roberts, P.M. (Northampton), Robinson, M.G. (Darlington), Rogers, C.J. (Swindon), Ross, J.J. (London), Ryan, M. (Preston), Saunders, R.L. (East Bergholt, Essex), Sharp, P.R. (St Albans), Shaw, G. (Oldham), Shaw, I.D. (Crewe), Sheffield, J.A. (Burntwood, Staffs), Short, M.L. (Grantham, Lincs), Sims, M.R. (Bristol), Singh, M. (Coseley), Smith, A.N. (Castleford, W. Yorks), Smith, J.P. (Hyde, Cheshire), Smith, R.A. (Loughborough), Smith, S.J. (Ware, Herts), Spicer, D.R. (Totten, Hampshire), Spooner, G. (Sheffield), Stobbart, M. (Guildford), Stoddart, M.J. (Leeds), Stones, G.A. (Swadlincote, Derbys), Sutton, R. (Macclesfield), Swift, M. (Sheffield), Tarry, E.J. (Manchester), Taylor, F. (Preston), Thiarra, S.S. (Bedford), Thornewill, C. (Chaddesden, Derby), Thorpe, M. (Woodbridge, Suffolk), Tiffin, R. (Houghton-le-Spring), Tingey, M. (Lane End, Bucks), Tomlin, S.G. (Lewes, E. Sussex), Toms, W. [Mrs] (Poole), Torrance, K.R. (Camberley, Surrey), Unsworth, D. (Bolton), Vosper, P.A. (London), Walsh, E.J. (Rubery, Worcs), Walton, P. (West Haddon, Northants), Ward, J. (Ferryhill, Co Durham), Ward, R.B. (Milton Keynes), Wardle, K. (Houghton-le-Spring), Warren, M.R. (Walsall), Webb, A.J. (Winnersh, Berks), Webb, H.M. (Rotherham), Webster, C.H. (Chester-le-Street), Wedgwood, S. (Burscough, Lancs), Wesson, J.D. (Loughborough), Whitehouse, I. (Calne, Wiltshire), Williams, M.A. (Hereford), Wing, P.B. (Peterborough), Wood, A.R. (Birkenhead), Wood, D. (Harrogate), Wood, D.R. (Liverpool), Woodhall, D.J. (Shipley), Woolmer, K.A. (Kettering), Zipfel, R.J. (Thetford, Norfolk).

USEFUL ADDRESSES

The Football Association: R. H. G. Kelly, F.C.I.S., 16 Lancaster Gate, London W2 3LW *0171-262 4542*

Scotland: J. Farry, 6 Park Gardens, Glasgow G3 7YE. *0141-332 6372*

Northern Ireland (Irish FA): D. I. Bowen, 20 Windsor Avenue, Belfast BT9 6EG. *01232-669458*

Wales: A. Evans, 3 Westgate Street, Cardiff, South Glamorgan CF1 1JF. *01222-372325*

Republic of Ireland (FA of Ireland): S. Connolly, 80 Merrion Square South, Dublin 2. *01001-766864*

International Federation (FIFA): S. Blatter, FIFA House, Hitzigweg 11, CH-8032 Zurich, Switzerland. *0041-384-9595. Fax: 0041-384-9696*

Union of European Football Associations: G. Aigner, Chemin de la Redoute 54, Case Postale 303 CH-1260 Nyon, Switzerland. *0041 22 994 4444. Fax: 0041 22 994 4488.*

The Premier League: R.N. Parry, 16 Lancaster Gate, London W2 3LW. *0171 262 4542,*

The Football League: J. D. Dent, F.C.I.S., The Football League, Lytham St Annes, Lancs FY8 1JG. *01253-729421. Telex 67675*

The Scottish League: P. Donald, 188 West Regent Street, Glasgow G2 4RY. *0141-248 384415*

The Irish League: H. Wallace, 87 University Street, Belfast BT7 1HP. *01232-242888*

Football League of Ireland: E. Morris, 80 Merrion Square South, Dublin 2. *01001-765120*

Vauxhall Conference: J. A. Moules, Collingwood House, Schooner Court, Cross-ways, Dartford DA2 6QQ.

Northern Premier: R. D. Bayley, 22 Woburn Drive, Hale, Altrincham, Cheshire. *0161-980 7007*

Isthmian League: N. Robinson, 226 Rye Lane, Peckham, SE15 4NL. *0181-653 3903.*

English Schools FA: M. R. Berry, 1/2 Eastgate Street, Stafford ST16 2NN. *01785-51142*

Southern League: D.J. Studwick, 11 Welland Close, Durrington, Worthing, W. Sussex BN13 3NR. *01903-267788.*

National Federation of Football Supporters' Clubs: Chairman: Tony Kershaw, 87 Brookfield Avenue, Loughborough, Leicestershire LE11 3LN. *01509 267643 (and fax).* National Secretary: Mark Agate, "The Stadium", 14 Coombe Close, Lordswood, Chatham, Kent ME5 8NU. *01634 863520 (and fax)*

Professional Footballers' Association: G. Taylor, 2 Oxford Court, Bishopsgate, Off Lower Mosley Street, Manchester M2 3W2. *0161-236 0575*

Referees' Association: W. J. Taylor, Cross Offices, Summerhill, Kingswinford, West Midlands DY6 9JE. *01384-288386*

Women's Football Alliance: Miss H. Jeavons, 9 Wyllyotts Place, Potters Bar, Herts EN6 2JB. *01707 651840*

The Association of Football Statisticians: R. J. Spiller, 22 Bretons, Basildon, Essex SS15 5BY. *01268-416020*

The Football Programme Directory: David Stacey, 'The Beeches', 66 Southend Road, Wickford, Essex SS11 8EN. *01268 732041.*

England Football Supporters Association: Publicity Officer, David Stacey, 66 Southend Road, Wickford, Essex SS11 8EN.

The Football Trust: Second Floor, Walkden House, 10 Melton Street, London NW1 2EJ. *0171-388 4504*

The Football Supporters Association: PO Box 11, Liverpool L26 1XP. *0151-709-2594.*